Benefits for M
Handbook

14th edition

Rebecca Walker, Emma Terenius, Ravi Low-Beer, Henri Krishna and Ruth Mercer

Child Poverty Action Group

Child Poverty Action Group works on behalf of the more than one in four children in the UK growing up in poverty. It does not have to be like this. We use our understanding of what causes poverty and the impact it has on children's lives to campaign for policies that will prevent and solve poverty – for good. We provide training, advice and information to make sure hard-up families get the financial support they need. We also carry out high-profile legal work to establish and protect families' rights. If you are not already supporting us, please consider making a donation, or ask for details of our membership schemes, training courses and publications.

Published by Child Poverty Action Group
30 Micawber Street
London N1 7TB
Tel: 020 7837 7979
staff@cpag.org.uk
cpag.org.uk

A CIP record for this book is available from the British Library.

ISBN: 978 1 910715 91 8

Child Poverty Action Group is a charity registered in England and Wales (registration number 294841) and in Scotland (registration number SC039339), and is a company limited by guarantee, registered in England (registration number 1993854). VAT number: 690 808117.

Cover design by Colorido Studios
Internal design by Devious Designs
Content management system by Konnect Soft
Typeset by DLxml, a division of RefineCatch Limited, Bungay, Suffolk
Printed by CPI Group (UK) Ltd, Croydon CR0 4YY

The authors

Rebecca Walker is an advice worker at Sheffield Citizens Advice and Law Centre and a freelance trainer and writer on welfare rights.

Emma Terenius is a solicitor at Wilson Solicitors LLP.

Ravi Low-Beer is a legal advisor at the Asylum Support Appeals Project.

Henri Krishna is a welfare rights worker at CPAG in Scotland.

Ruth Mercer is an immigration and housing solicitor at Southwark Law Centre.

Acknowledgements

The authors would like to thank everyone who has contributed to this book and all the authors of previous editions.

Thanks are particularly due this year to Suzanne Abdulhadi, Dan Manville and Nick Turnill.

We would also like to thank Pauline Phillips for editing and managing the production of the book, Katherine Dawson for compiling the index and Kathleen Armstrong for proofreading the text.

The law covered in this book was correct on 1 February 2023. It includes regulations laid and judgments delivered up to this date.

Contents

Abbreviations

AA	attendance allowance
ACRS	Afghan Citizens Resettlement Scheme
ADP	adult disability payment
AIU	Asylum Intake Unit
ARAP	Afghan Relocations and Assistance Policy
ARC	application registration card
ASAP	Asylum Support Appeals Project
BIA	Border and Immigration Agency
BRC	biometric residence card
BRP	biometric residence permit
CA	carer's allowance
CDP	child disability payment
CJEU	Court of Justice of the European Union
CTC	child tax credit
CVP	cloud video platform
DLA	disability living allowance
DWP	Department for Work and Pensions
EC	European Community
ECAA	Turkish EC Association Agreement
ECHR	European Convention on Human Rights
ECtHR	European Court of Human Rights
EEA	European Economic Area
EFTA	European Free Trade Association
EHIC	European health insurance card
ESA	employment and support allowance
EU	European Union
EUSS	European Union Settlement Scheme
FNO	foreign national offender
FSU	Further Submissions Unit
HB	housing benefit
HMCTS	HM Courts and Tribunals Service
HMG	HM Government
HMRC	HM Revenue and Customs
IB	incapacity benefit
IS	income support
ISA	individual savings account
JSA	jobseeker's allowance
LES	locally employed staff
MA	maternity allowance
NASS	National Asylum Support Service
NRM	National Referral Mechanism
NI	national insurance
OISC	Office of the Immigration Services Commissioner
PC	pension credit
PIP	personal independence payment
REA	reduced earnings allowance
SAL	standard acknowledgement letter
SAP	statutory adoption pay
SDA	severe disablement allowance
SIAC	Special Immigration Appeals Commission
SMP	statutory maternity pay
SPBP	statutory parental bereavement pay
SPP	statutory paternity pay
SSP	statutory sick pay
SSPP	statutory shared parental pay
SSS	Social Security Scotland
TFEU	Treaty on the Functioning of the European Union
UC	universal credit
UK	United Kingdom
UKBA	UK Border Agency
UKVI	UK Visas and Immigration
UN	United Nations
WTC	working tax credit

Part 1

Introduction

Chapter 1

How to use this book

This chapter covers:

1. About this *Handbook*

This *Handbook* is for migrants and their advisers wanting information on how entitlements to social security benefits are affected by the country in which someone lives, how long someone has lived in Great Britain, absences abroad, nationality and immigration status. It also provides an overview of the main types of immigration status and covers the support available for people who have applied for asylum in the UK. By 'migrants' we mean people, including British citizens, who have come or returned to Great Britain from abroad and people who have left Great Britain either temporarily or to live abroad.

The law on benefit entitlement for migrants is complex and frequently changing. As a result, migrants are often refused benefits to which they are entitled, or are not paid for family members when they should be.

This *Handbook* explains the different requirements that must be satisfied in order to be entitled to benefits, so that you can understand whether or not you satisfy them and effectively challenge incorrect decisions.

This *Handbook* covers the rules that are most likely to affect migrant claimants and their families, and the practical problems that can arise. It is not a complete guide to the benefit rules and should be used together with general guides on social security benefits, such as CPAG's *Welfare Benefits and Tax Credits Handbook*.

How this book is organised

The book is split into parts, and related chapters are grouped under these parts. For a description of the information covered in each part, see below. For the chapters included in each part, see the table of contents on p5.

Part 1 is an introduction to this *Handbook*.

Part 2 gives an overview of immigration law to help you identify your immigration status and understand the immigration terms that appear in the rest of this *Handbook*.

Part 3 covers the way your, and your partner's and child's, immigration status affects your entitlement to benefits. If you and all the people included in your claim are British or Irish citizens, the rules in this part do not apply to you.

Part 4 covers the residence and presence requirements for all benefits and how you satisfy them, including details on how you satisfy the 'right to reside' requirement.

Part 5 explains the way your entitlement to benefits is affected if you, or your partner or child who is included in your claim, go abroad.

Part 6 describes the way in which the European Union social security co-ordination rules and international agreements on social security can assist you to satisfy entitlement conditions in the UK, or to be paid UK benefits abroad, or, in limited circumstances, can prevent you being entitled to UK benefits.

Part 7 covers some issues that can be particularly problematic for migrants – delays, satisfying the national insurance number requirement and providing evidence to show you meet the immigration status, residence and presence rules.

Part 8 covers the rules on asylum support for people who have made an application for asylum in the UK.

Part 9 gives an overview of other possible sources of help that may be available to migrants.

Finding information

The two most efficient ways of finding information in this *Handbook* are to use the contents and the index.

The contents shows the structure of the book and lists the parts, the chapters and the sections within each chapter.

The index contains entries in bold type, directing you to the general information on the subject or to the page(s) where the subject is covered more fully. Sub-entries under the bold headings are listed alphabetically and direct you to specific aspects of the subject.

Throughout this *Handbook* the text is referenced with the source of information, given in endnotes at the end of each chapter. For more information on finding the relevant law, see p6.

2. Checking the rules that affect you

As the rules are complicated, it is helpful to approach them systematically.

If you are *not* a British or Irish citizen, or if a partner or child who you could include in your claim is not a British or Irish citizen, work through the following steps.

- **Step one:** be clear about your immigration status and that of any partner you could make a joint claim with, or any partner or child you could include in your claim. See Chapter 6 for how to check the status you have in the UK. If you are unsure about your immigration status, get specialist immigration advice (see p7).
- **Step two:** check whether you are defined as a 'person subject to immigration control' (see Chapter 7). If you are not, your immigration status does not exclude you from benefit entitlement, but you must still satisfy the residence and presence requirements. If you have a partner who you could make a joint claim with, or a partner or child who could be included in your claim, check whether they are defined as a person subject to immigration control, and, if so, check the rules on partners and children for how your benefit is affected (see p119).
- **Step three:** if you are defined as a person subject to immigration control, check whether the rules on the particular benefit exclude people subject to immigration control (see p93). If not, your immigration status does not exclude you from entitlement to that benefit, but you must still satisfy the residence and presence requirements.
- **Step four:** if you are defined as a person subject to immigration control and the benefit you want to claim is one from which people subject to immigration control are generally excluded, check whether you come into an exempt group. These groups vary between the different benefits (see p113). If you do come within an exempt group you will not be excluded from benefit on the basis of being a person subject to immigration control, but you must still satisfy the residence and presence requirements.
- **Step five:** if you cannot claim the benefit you want because you are defined as a person subject to immigration control, but you have a partner who may be able to claim, check the rules on partners (see p119).
- **Step six:** if you or your partner or child have leave to enter or remain in the UK that is subject to a 'no recourse to public funds' condition, check whether any claim for benefits could breach this condition because this could put your (or their) current or future immigration status at risk (see p101).
- **Step seven:** if you are an asylum seeker or are dependent on an asylum seeker, check whether you are entitled to asylum support (see Chapter 21).

If you are a British or Irish citizen, or your immigration status does not exclude you from benefit entitlement, work through the following steps.

- **Step one**: check the residence and presence requirements for the benefit you want to claim (see Chapter 13).
- **Step two**: if the benefit you are claiming requires you to be 'habitually resident', check whether you are exempt from, or satisfy, this requirement (see Chapter 11).

- **Step three:** if the benefit you are claiming requires you have a right to reside, check whether you have a right to reside (see Chapter 12), and note that some residence rights are excluded for particular benefits (p168).
- **Step four:** if you are claiming universal credit and you have a partner, check whether they are exempt from, or satisfy, the habitual residence test, including having a right to reside, and check how this affects your award (see p158).
- **Step five:** if you are claiming a disability or carers' benefit, check whether you are covered by the European Union (EU) social security co-ordination rules (see p379). If so, check whether the UK is the 'competent state' to pay these benefits (see p399).
- **Step six:** if you are entitled to benefit and want to know whether you can continue to be paid when you, or someone who is included in your claim, go abroad, see Chapter 14 for an overview of the rules and Chapter 15 for the specific rules for individual benefits.
- **Step seven:** if you do not satisfy the residence and presence rules, check whether the EU co-ordination rules can assist you (but note also the competent state requirement for some disability and carers' benefits: Step five above). The ways these rules can assist you to be entitled to benefits in the UK is explained for specific benefits in Chapter 13, and to continue to be entitled when you move to a European country is explained for specific benefits in Chapter 15. An overview of the different rules and who each applies to is covered in Chapter 16.

Note: the rules for European Economic Area (EEA) nationals changed significantly at the end of 2020, and, in most cases, entitlements were reduced. However, if you are an EEA national already living in the UK before the end of 2020, or you are a family member of such an EEA national, you may be in a protected group able to claim benefits under the rules that applied previously. Similarly, if you were an EEA national living in the UK, or a British citizen living in an EEA country, before the end of 2020, you may be covered by protections that mean the main EU co-ordination rules continue to apply to you. For an overview of changes due to the UK leaving the EU, which apply after the end of 2020, see p183 and p374.

3. Finding the relevant law

The complexity of the rules that specifically affect migrants means that it can be useful to refer to the relevant law not only when you are challenging a decision, but also when you make your claim. In order to ensure that the decision maker makes the correct decision on your claim, it is advisable to provide a letter setting out the legal requirements that you must satisfy for the particular benefit (eg, the immigration status, residence or presence requirements) and the ways in which you satisfy them. You may need to set out additional law (eg, the legislation and caselaw on when you have a right to reside) and provide evidence to show how this applies to you.

However, this does not guarantee that the correct decision will be made. If you are refused benefit when you believe you are entitled to it, you should challenge the decision. In any challenge, wherever possible, try to set out the relevant legal requirements and explain clearly how you meet them, citing the relevant law as appropriate and providing as much evidence as you can to show you meet the requirements.

This *Handbook* provides references to the law (both legislation and caselaw) and to guidance, so you can locate the source of the information given in the text.

- Find the information in the book relevant to the legal requirement you must satisfy and the text on how you satisfy it that applies to you.
- Find the endnote number for that information and check the endnote text at the end of the chapter for the legal reference.
- Check Appendix 7 for an explanation of the abbreviations used in the references.
- See Appendices 2 and 4 for where to find the law and guidance online and for other useful sources of information.
- See Chapter 20 for information about providing evidence to show you satisfy legal requirements.

For a useful introduction to using legal sources, see CPAG's *Welfare Benefits and Tax Credits Handbook.*

Note: the law referred to in this *Handbook* applies in Great Britain. The equivalent law in Northern Ireland is often very similar and, in most cases, has the same effect. Many of the differences are due to the fact that the legislation and the administrative and adjudicating bodies in Northern Ireland are named differently. However, sometimes the law in Northern Ireland on a particular rule is different.

4. **Immigration advice**

If you are unsure about your immigration status, or that of anyone you could include in your claim, or you need to know what the immigration options are for you and your family, get specialist advice from your local law centre, Citizens Advice or other advice agency that gives immigration advice (see Appendix 2).

Anyone who gives immigration advice must be:

- a solicitor, barrister or legal executive, or supervised by such a person; *or*
- registered by the Office of the Immigration Services Commissioner (OISC); *or*
- an adviser with an organisation that is exempt from registration. For example, Citizens Advice offices are exempt, but only to give basic immigration advice.

It is a criminal offence for someone not covered by one of the above groups to give immigration advice.

Every OISC-registered or exempt advice agency should display a certificate issued by the OISC to show it meets the OISC standards.

A list of all OISC-registered and exempt advisers and advice organisations is on the OISC website, which also includes details of how to make a complaint about an immigration adviser.

Part 2

Immigration law

Chapter 2

Immigration and nationality law: overview

This chapter covers:

1. Immigration and nationality law

The right to live, work and settle in the UK is regulated and controlled by a complex system of laws. These are amended frequently. If you are unsure about your immigration status, or about the immigration status of anyone you could include in your benefit claim, get immigration advice from a regulated provider of immigration services. Citizens Advice can signpost or refer you (see p7).

Sources of law

The main UK Acts of Parliament that deal with immigration and nationality law are the:

- Immigration Act 1971;
- British Nationality Act 1981;
- Immigration Act 1988;
- Asylum and Immigration Appeals Act 1993;
- Asylum and Immigration Act 1996;
- Human Rights Act 1998;
- Immigration and Asylum Act 1999;
- Nationality, Immigration and Asylum Act 2002;
- Asylum and Immigration (Treatment of Claimants, etc.) Act 2004;
- Immigration, Asylum and Nationality Act 2006;
- UK Borders Act 2007;

- Borders, Citizenship and Immigration Act 2009;
- Immigration Act 2014;
- Immigration Act 2016;
- Nationality and Borders Act 2022.

These Acts are supplemented by:
- statutory instruments (regulations);
- the Immigration Rules;
- government policies.

You can find the original (as enacted) and revised versions of Acts of Parliament and statutory instruments at legislation.gov.uk, although more recent revisions may not be included.

The Immigration Rules and most government policies concerning immigration can be found at gov.uk/guidance/immigration-rules and gov.uk/topic/immigration-operational-guidance.

The UK has also signed various international treaties and conventions, which guarantee certain rights. These include the:
- European Convention for the Protection of Human Rights and Fundamental Freedoms 1950 (the 'European Convention on Human Rights'), incorporated, in part, into UK law by the Human Rights Act 1998;
- 1951 United Nations (UN) Convention Relating to the Status of Refugees and its 1967 Protocol, commonly referred to as 'the Refugee Convention';
- 1954 UN Convention Relating to the Status of Stateless Persons and the 1961 Convention on the Reduction of Statelessness.

The UK left the European Union (EU) at 11pm on 31 January 2020. This was followed by a transition period (also referred to as the implementation period) (see p183), which ended at 11pm on 31 December 2020. At the end of the transition period, existing EU law was incorporated into domestic law and is known as 'retained law'. As for all UK law, retained law can be amended or revoked. See p192 for details of European free movement rights that can apply for 'protected groups' after the end of the transition period, and Chapter 5 for immigration options for European Economic Area (EEA) nationals and their family members.

Caselaw of the tribunals and higher courts in the UK and Europe is also important in immigration and nationality law. Much of this can be accessed free of charge on the British and Irish Legal Information Institute website at bailii.org. See p195 for the status of decisions of the Court of Justice of the EU after the transition period.

Relevant institutions

The **Home Secretary** (Secretary of State for the Home Department) is responsible for the **Home Office.** The department within the Home Office that deals with immigration control is called **UK Visas and Immigration (UKVI)**. The term 'Home Office' is used throughout this *Handbook*.

Immigration officers are generally responsible for granting permission to enter the UK to people who arrive at the various ports of entry, and for arresting, detaining and enforcing the removal of people from the UK. They have powers of search, entry, seizure and arrest of those suspected of having committed a criminal offence under immigration law, and may arrest and detain people who can be lawfully removed to enforce their departure from the UK under immigration law.

Entry clearance officers stationed overseas are responsible for immigration control prior to entry to the UK. They process applications made outside of the UK and decide whether to give **entry clearance** or **visas** to applicants under the Immigration Rules and on human rights or on other grounds (see Chapter 3).

Civil servants in the Home Office are mainly responsible for deciding immigration and nationality applications made in the UK. Some applications made from outside the UK are referred to civil servants in the UK by entry clearance officers stationed overseas.

HM Passport Office is responsible for issuing UK passports. The General Register Office is the part of HM Passport Office that administers the civil registration process in England and Wales – eg, births, deaths, marriages and civil partnerships.

Police officers may arrest people suspected of having committed a criminal offence under immigration law, and arrest and detain people in order to enforce their departure from the UK under immigration law.

Judges of the **Immigration and Asylum Chambers of the First-tier Tribunal and the Upper Tribunal** are responsible for hearing and determining appeals against decisions made by entry clearance officers, immigration officers and the Home Office, applications for bail and most immigration-related judicial review applications.

Judges of the **Social Entitlement Chamber of the First-tier Tribunal** are responsible for determining appeals against decisions refusing asylum support.

Judges of the **Court of Appeal (in England and Wales), the Court of Session (in Scotland) and the UK Supreme Court** hear appeals from the Upper Tribunal, and judges of the **High Court** (in England and Wales) and the Court of Session (in Scotland) continue to decide applications for judicial review of certain types of decisions by the Home Office and the Upper Tribunal.

Cases may also be brought in the **European Court of Human Rights** if the matter concerns the European Convention on Human Rights.

2. **The main types of immigration status**

There are five main types of immigration status in the UK.

- British citizens and people with the right of abode. These people are not subject to immigration control (see p15).
- People who have indefinite leave to remain or enter (see Chapter 3), including if granted settled status under the European Union Settlement Scheme (EUSS) (see Chapter 5).
- People who have limited leave to remain or enter (see Chapter 3), including if granted pre-settled status under the EUSS (see Chapter 5).
- People who do not have an immigration status:
  - people who have entered the UK without leave to enter or remain, including those who have made an in-country immigration application or an asylum claim (see Chapter 4);
  - 'overstayers', who are people who had leave to remain and who stayed in the UK after the expiry date of their leave and did not make an in-time extension application.

  If you do not have immigration status, you are liable to be detained, but you may be granted immigration bail (previously called temporary admission, temporary release or bail – see below) as an alternative to detention.

Note: the term 'person subject to immigration control' is important for establishing someone's entitlement to benefits. It has a specific meaning that is explained on p93.

Immigration bail

The Home Office has the power to detain you if you require, but do not have, leave (permission) to remain in the UK. As an alternative to detention, the Home Office may grant you immigration bail. **Note**: immigration bail replaced all forms of bail, temporary admission and temporary release from 15 January 2018. Immigration bail is retrospective, so all types of bail granted before 15 January 2018 are known as immigration bail.

If you apply for leave to enter or remain (including an asylum or a human rights claim) at a port of entry or while in the UK when you do not have leave, you may be given immigration bail until your application is decided. You do not have to have been detained in order to be granted immigration bail. If you are in immigration detention, you may be released on immigration bail. Immigration bail may also be given if:

- you remain in the UK after your application for leave to remain has been refused; *or*
- you remain in the UK after your limited leave to enter or remain has expired; *or*
- you are discovered in the UK without leave to remain.

Immigration bail is an alternative to detention and may continue after the refusal of asylum or any other type of application. Immigration bail may also continue during Home Office consideration of further submissions or a new application (see p51).

If you were granted immigration bail (or temporary admission before 15 January 2018) at a port of entry, you will be considered to have been 'lawfully resident in the UK', if you are later granted leave to enter or remain. This can be significant if you must meet the requirement to have resided lawfully in the UK for a specified period of time to become eligible for citizenship or for leave to remain on the grounds of a period of lawful residence. It can also be relevant to your eligibility to claim benefits.

Immigration bail includes at least one condition, such as a requirement to live at a specified address, to report to an immigration officer at a specified time and place, or not to engage in paid or unpaid employment. There can be criminal penalties if you do not adhere to these conditions, and failing to do so will be taken into account in any decision on whether to place you into immigration detention.

If you are on immigration bail, you should have been issued with a notice (Form BAIL 201) informing you of your status and any conditions that apply.

Note: in certain circumstances, the Home Office must provide accommodation to people with, or applying for, immigration bail (see p551).

3. British nationality

You can acquire British nationality:

- at birth, depending on the date and place of your birth, and on the nationality/citizenship and immigration and/or marital status of your parents; *or*
- on adoption; *or*
- by applying to the Home Office for naturalisation or registration; *or*
- as the result of legislative change.

Note: the examples given in this *Handbook* of how British citizenship may be acquired are basic. British nationality law is complex and there are many other routes that are not covered here.

There are six different forms of British nationality, only one of which (British citizenship) gives the right of abode in the UK (see below). A British national may be a:

- British citizen;
- British overseas territories citizen;
- British subject;
- British protected person;
- British national (overseas);
- British overseas citizen.

Some of the above forms of British nationality are rare and can no longer be acquired. In time, only British citizenship and British overseas territories citizenship will exist.

Multiple nationalities

Although some countries do not allow dual or multiple nationality or citizenship, UK law permits you to be a British national and a national of any number of other countries.

British nationals and the right of abode

The **'right of abode'** gives you the freedom to enter, live in and leave the UK at any time.

All full British citizens have the right of abode, but most people who hold other forms of British nationality do not have this right. Some Commonwealth citizens also have the right of abode, including people who are British nationals and not British citizens. However, it has not been possible to gain the right of abode since 1983 without also being a British citizen.

A British national who does not have the right of abode generally requires leave to enter or remain in the UK but may be able to apply to register as a British citizen.

Acquiring British citizenship at birth

Most people, except children of diplomats and 'enemy aliens', born in the UK before 1 January 1983 automatically acquired British citizenship on that date.[1]

If you were born in the UK on or after 1 January 1983, you only acquired British citizenship if, at the time of your birth:

- your mother was a British citizen or was 'settled' in the UK – eg, she had indefinite leave or permanent residence;[2] *or*
- your father was a British citizen or was 'settled' in the UK. If you were born before 1 July 2006, you could only gain citizenship from your father in this way if your parents were married, either at the time or subsequently. Since 1 July 2006, this restriction has no longer applied. If you are affected by the restriction, you may be able to apply to register as a British citizen.

From 1 January 1983, if you were born overseas, you would have acquired British citizenship at birth if either parent was a British citizen, unless that parent was themself a British citizen 'by descent' – ie, because they were also born overseas.[3] The same provisions as above apply to unmarried British fathers of children born abroad.

Registering as a British citizen after 10 years

If you were born in the UK, you may be able to apply to register as a British citizen if, when you were born, neither of your parents were British citizens or settled in the UK. You can apply if you are aged 10 years or over and if you have spent no more than 90 days outside the UK in each of the first 10 years of your life. You must also meet the good character requirement.

Registering due to unfairness or exceptional circumstances

Since 28 June 2022, you can register as a British citizen if you would have been, or would have been able to become, a British citizen but for historic legislative unfairness, an act or omission of a public authority, or exceptional circumstances. This type of application is likely to be very complex. You may have to meet the good character requirement. You must be an adult at the time you make the application.[4]

4. Immigration and nationality applications

Applying from outside the UK

If you do not have the right of abode, you must obtain entry clearance before travelling to the UK to seek entry for most purposes.

Nationals of countries or territories listed in Appendix V of the Immigration Rules are known as **'visa nationals'**. See gov.uk/guidance/immigration-rules/immigration-rules-appendix-v-visitor. If you are a visa national, you must obtain a visa before travelling to the UK for any purpose (unless you are a refugee – see Chapter 4).

Nationals of all other countries (**'non-visa nationals'**) may apply to an immigration officer at the port of arrival for entry for certain purposes, mainly for short-term visits. If you are a non-visa national and you intend to stay for a longer period, you must usually obtain entry clearance before travelling.

Note: from 1 January 2021, if you are a non-European Economic Area (EEA) national family member of an EEA national, you must obtain an European Union Settlement Scheme (EUSS) family permit (see p68), or another form of entry clearance, before you travel to the UK.

An exempt vignette is issued to people, such as diplomats, who are exempt from the requirements of the Immigration Act 1971.

In most countries, you can apply for entry clearance online. All applicants must attend a visa application centre in person. There is not a visa application centre in every country in the world, so you may have to travel to a different country to apply. Most applicants must have their fingerprints and photograph (known as 'biometric information') taken at the visa application centre.

To apply for British nationality from outside the UK, you must either make an online application or send your application to the Home Office in the UK.

Applying from within the UK

The Home Office is responsible for processing applications made by people in the UK:

- for leave to remain in the UK, including for asylum;
- to extend their leave to remain;
- to vary their leave to remain – ie, to change the type of leave;
- for indefinite leave to remain;
- for settled status or pre-settled status under the EUSS;
- for British nationality.

Application procedure

Most applications must be made online. That includes human rights applications in which the applicant is not making a protection claim. Protection claims, which include asylum, humanitarian protection and some human rights claims, must normally be made in person at the Home Office (see Chapter 4). Applications made under Article 3 of the European Convention on Human Rights (ECHR) solely for health reasons can be made online or, in exceptional circumstances, by post.

Other types of application may also be made in person. A 'premium service' is available, with a shorter processing time (applications are sometimes dealt with on the same day), at an increased cost.

Home Office application fees

A fee is charged for most applications and for biometric enrolment. Some types of application are exempt from the fee, including:[5]

- an application for leave to remain on protection grounds, including asylum, humanitarian protection and human rights claims based on the Article 3 right not to be subjected to torture or inhuman or degrading treatment;
- an application made under Article 3 of the ECHR on medical grounds;
- an application for leave to remain by a child who is being looked after by a local authority;
- a 'Windrush' application for citizenship, a document confirming the right of abode, a no time limit/settlement permit, or indefinite leave to remain by a Commonwealth citizen who was either settled in the UK before 1 January 1973 or has the right of abode, or by their child, or by someone of any nationality who arrived in the UK before 31 December 1988 and is settled in the UK;
- an application for limited leave to enter or remain by a victim of trafficking (in limited circumstances only);
- an application for settled status or pre-settled status by an EEA national or the family member of an EEA national under the EUSS.

Home Office fee waiver policy

A fee waiver is an application to avoid paying the Home Office application fee and immigration health surcharge, on the basis that the person cannot afford to pay. Fee waivers are only possible for certain types of immigration application:

- an application for limited leave to enter or remain for certain purposes if the Home Office accepts that the applicant is destitute or that other exceptional circumstances apply. In these circumstances, you must provide evidence and complete an application form for a fee waiver (available at gov.uk/government/publications/applications-for-a-fee-waiver-and-refunds);
- applications for leave to remain under the five-year partner route from applicants who are not required to meet the minimum income threshold because their sponsor is in receipt of one or more specified benefits and who instead must demonstrate that their sponsor can provide adequate maintenance;
- applications for leave to remain under the five-year parent route;
- applications for leave to remain under the 10-year partner, parent or private life route in which the applicant claims that refusal of that application for leave to remain would breach their rights (or the rights of other specified persons) under Article 8 of the ECHR (the right to respect for private and family life);
- applications for leave to remain under the five-year private life route;
- applications for leave to remain on the basis of other ECHR rights except Article 3 claims, which are fee exempt;
- applications for further leave to remain from applicants granted discretionary leave following refusal of asylum or humanitarian protection in which the applicant claims that refusal to grant further leave to remain would breach their ECHR right (except Article 3 claims, which are fee exempt);
- applications for further discretionary leave made by victims of trafficking or slavery who have had a positive conclusive grounds decision from a competent authority of the National Referral Mechanism, have already accrued 30 months' discretionary leave and are seeking to extend it for reasons related to trafficking or slavery.

To benefit from the fee waiver policy, you must show that any one or more of the following apply:

- you cannot afford to pay the fee because you do not have sufficient funds at your disposal after meeting essential living needs, including housing, food, toiletries, non-prescription medication, household cleaning items and necessary travel and communication costs to maintain interpersonal relationships; *or*
- you are destitute, meaning that you cannot meet your essential living needs or that you are unable to obtain adequate accommodation; *or*
- you are at risk of imminent destitution; *or*

- your income is not sufficient to meet a child's particular and additional needs; *or*
- you are faced with exceptional financial circumstances.

Fee waivers for overseas applications

In 2022, the Home Office published guidance on fee waivers for overseas applications.[6] This confirms that fee waivers are only possible for certain types of overseas applications, including:

- applications made under Appendix FM (family members);
- applications made under Part 8 of the Immigration Rules where the sponsor has refugee or humanitarian protection in the UK, or in certain circumstances where the sponsor is present and settled in the UK;
- applications made by a partner or child of a member of the armed forces.

To benefit from this policy, you must demonstrate that:

- you cannot afford the fee because you do not have sufficient funds at your disposal after meeting essential living needs, including housing, food, toiletries, non-prescription medication, household cleaning items and necessary travel and communication costs to maintain interpersonal relationships; *or*
- your income is not sufficient to meet your child's needs.

Immigration health surcharge

An additional charge, described as an 'immigration health surcharge', is charged by the Home Office in applications for limited leave to enter or remain. Exceptions include applications for:[7]

- indefinite leave to enter or remain;
- entry clearance for leave to enter for six months or less – eg, for visitors, fiancé(e)s and some prospective students;
- leave to remain by a child under 18 who is being looked after by a local authority;
- leave to remain based on protection grounds, including asylum, humanitarian protection and some human rights claims (not including stand-alone Article 8 claims);
- leave to remain on medical grounds/for health reasons under Article 3 of the ECHR;
- leave to remain that relates to someone being identified as a victim of human trafficking;
- leave to remain outside the Immigration Rules with access to public funds under the Home Office policy known as the 'destitution domestic violence concession' (see p38).

The fee waiver application is an application for the waiver of the application fee, biometric enrolment fee and the immigration health surcharge. If you are making a free of charge application, or if you are granted a fee waiver, you will not be required to pay the immigration health surcharge.

The standard immigration health surcharge is £470 per person for each year of leave applied for by applicants aged under 18, students, applicants for leave to remain under the Youth Mobility Scheme (Tier 5) and each of their dependants. The standard immigration health surcharge is £624 a year per person for each year of leave applied for by everyone else. It is payable with the application fee at the time of making the application.

For information on NHS healthcare, including charges and who is exempt from them, see p639.

Fee waivers for children's citizenship applications

From 16 June 2022, if you are under the age of 18, you can apply for a fee waiver to apply for registration as a British citizen. You have to demonstrate that:

- you, and your parents, cannot afford the fee, because you do not have sufficient funds at your disposal after meeting essential living needs, including housing, food, toiletries, non-prescription medication, household cleaning items and necessary travel and communication costs to maintain interpersonal relationships.

If you are looked after by a local authority, the fee will be waived. Looked after children do not have to demonstrate that they meet the affordability test.

Section 3C extension of leave to remain

Section 3C of the Immigration Act 1971 operates to extend your leave to remain if the three conditions below are met. The exact section of section 3C that applies is important because it can affect your entitlement to benefits.

Your leave to remain is automatically extended, on the same conditions as before, while you wait for the Home Office to make a decision, if the following three conditions are met:[8]

- you have limited leave to remain and you apply to the Home Office to extend or vary your leave (section 3C(1)(a)); *and*
- your application is made 'in time' – ie, before your current leave expires (section 3C(1)(b)); *and*
- your current leave expires before a decision on the extension or variation application has been made (section 3C(1)(c)).

If the above conditions are satisfied and the Home Office refuses your application for leave to remain, your leave is further extended on the same conditions as before, if you have a right of appeal or administrative review (see below):

- section 3C(2)(b) extends your leave, during the period in which an appeal can be brought; *or*

- section 3(2)(c) extends your leave from the date that an in-time appeal is made, until it is concluded, and you have exhausted your appeal rights; *or*
- section 3(2)(ca) extends your leave from the date of a refusal of European Union (EU) pre-settled or settled status during the period in which an appeal can be brought; *or*
- section 3(2)(cb) extends your leave from the time that an in-time appeal against a refusal of EU pre-settled status or settled status is made, until it is concluded, and you have exhausted your appeal rights; *or*
- section 3C(2)(d)(i) extends your leave during the period in which an application for administrative review can be sought; *or*
- section 3C(2)(d)(ii) extends your leave from the date that an in-time application for administrative review is made, until it is decided.

For the way this can affect your entitlement to benefits, see p100 and p106.

5. **Appeals and other remedies**

Appeals to the First-tier Tribunal

The First-tier Tribunal (Immigration and Asylum Chamber) is a judicial authority that is independent of the UK government.

Rights of appeal

Rights of appeal to the tribunal against immigration decisions are provided by statute. If you lodge an appeal, you are known as an 'appellant' and the Home Office is known as the 'respondent'. There are a limited number of Home Office decisions that can be appealed, including:

- refusal of a protection claim – ie, a claim for asylum or humanitarian protection;[9]
- refusal of a human rights claim, including applications within the Immigration Rules made on private and family life grounds;[10]
- revocation of protection (ie, refugee or humanitarian protection) status;[11]
- deprivation of British citizenship;[12]
- refusal of pre-settled or settled status under the European Union Settlement Scheme (EUSS), provided the application was made on or after 11pm on 31 January 2020;[13]
- refusal of an application for an EUSS family or travel permit, provided the application was made on or after 11pm on 31 January 2020;
- curtailment, cancellation or revocation of pre-settled or settled status under the EUSS, if the decision was taken on or after 11pm on 31 January 2020;
- a decision to make a deportation order in respect of a person who has pre-settled or settled status under the EUSS.

To get the appeal started, you must 'give notice of appeal' by submitting the correct form to the tribunal or by lodging the appeal online.

Appeal time limits

If you are outside the UK when entry clearance is refused, you must file your notice of appeal with the tribunal in the UK within 28 calendar days of receiving the decision.[14] Most decisions are given to you in person and the 28 days runs from the date the decision is handed to you. If you receive the decision by post, there are another 28 days for 'service', making a total of 56 calendar days.

If you are in the UK when you receive a decision, you must give notice within 14 days of the date that the decision is 'sent'. Generally, the date that a notice is sent must be taken from the covering letter, but if there is a postmark on the envelope or a later date on any of the paperwork, that could be evidence of a later sending date.

Depending on the Home Office decision, if you are in the UK when you receive a decision, you may have to leave the UK before you can give notice of appeal. You then have 28 days after the date of departure to give notice of appeal.

In-country and out-of-country appeals

If you apply for entry clearance from outside the UK and you do not have leave to enter or remain in the UK, you will normally remain outside the UK to file a notice of appeal with the tribunal and until the appeal is finally determined.

If you arrive at a UK port or are in the UK when you receive the decision, you will normally be able to submit your notice of appeal while still in the UK and will remain in the UK until the appeal is fully determined.

Certification

In certain circumstances, the Home Office has powers to 'certify' a case so that you cannot appeal the decision at all or until after you have you have left the UK.[15] Claims that may be certified include:

- a human rights claim in which it is shown that you can appeal from outside the UK without your human rights being breached;
- an asylum claim that is not arguable or is bound to fail;
- a claim that raises a reason to remain in the UK that could have been raised in an earlier appeal.

The Home Office decision to certify the case may itself be suitable for a challenge by judicial review (see p25).

Tribunal fees

For most appeals, a tribunal appeal fee is payable. This fee does not currently apply:

- if you are receiving asylum support; *or*

- if you are receiving legal aid; *or*
- if the Home Office waived the fees for the application that has been refused; *or*
- if you are a child being supported by a local authority; *or*
- if you are the parent of a child being supported by the local authority under social work powers to safeguard and promote the care of children in the area; *or*
- if you are appealing against the deprivation of your British citizenship; *or*
- if you are appealing against the revocation of your protection status; *or*
- if you are a European Economic Area (EEA), or the family member of an EEA, citizen and you are appealing against removal; *or*
- in asylum appeals in which the appellant is detained and the decision has been served by the detained asylum casework team.

Alternatively, you can apply to have the fee reduced if you receive certain benefits or have limited savings and are on a low income.

If your appeal is allowed or dismissed in the First-tier Tribunal, you or the Home Office can appeal to the Upper Tribunal if there is an error of law that could have made a difference to the outcome. Appeals can progress from the Upper Tribunal to the Court of Appeal in England and Wales, the Court of Session in Scotland and, if it is a human rights appeal, to the European Court of Human Rights.

If your appeal is allowed in the First-tier Tribunal and the Home Office does not make an onward appeal, the Home Office must then decide whether to grant leave and, if so, what type of leave should be granted.

Administrative review

When a Home Office decision cannot be appealed, you may be able to apply to the Home Office for an 'administrative review'.[16] The Immigration Rules specify which decisions can be subject to administrative review. Administrative review is carried out by a different member of staff at the Home Office and not by an independent body. Decisions that can be subject to administrative review include:

- some entry clearance decisions; *and*
- some in-country decisions, including decisions on applications under the domestic violence rule; *and*
- some decisions to refuse or cancel leave to remain when a person arrives at the UK border.

There is a fee of £80.

Administrative review time limits

Time limits run from the date on which you receive the 'notice of decision' (ie, the cover letter) that accompanies the written reasons.[17]

Time limits to apply for administrative review of decisions made under Appendix EU[18] are:

- if you are in the UK and not detained, no more than 28 calendar days after you received the notice of decision; *or*
- if you are in UK immigration detention, no more than seven calendar days after you received the notice of decision; *or*
- if you are outside the UK, no more than 28 calendar days after you received the decision.

Time limits for other eligible decisions are:

- if you are in the UK, no later than 14 calendar days after you received the decision; *or*
- if you are in immigration detention in the UK, no later than seven calendar days after you received the decision; *or*
- if you are outside of the UK, no later than 28 calendar days after you received the decision; *or*
- if the decision is a grant of leave to remain, and you want to have the length and/or conditions reviewed, no later than 14 calendar days after you received the biometric information document which sets out the length and conditions of leave granted.

Judicial review

Some Home Office and tribunal decisions can be challenged by judicial review, including:

- a decision that does not carry a right of appeal; *and*
- a decision to certify a case; *and*
- a decision that carries a right of administrative review; *and*
- an administrative review decision.

In England and Wales, judicial review applications in immigration matters are made to the Upper Tribunal and in some cases to the Administrative Court – eg, unlawful detention, refusal of British citizenship and trafficking decisions. In Scotland, judicial review claims are made to the Court of Session. Applications for judicial review are legally and procedurally complex, and you are strongly advised to seek professional immigration advice before beginning proceedings.

The Administrative Court and the Court of Session hear applications for immigration bail if they are also considering a judicial review claim of unlawful detention.

6. Deportation and administrative removal

'Deportation' is a procedure under which a person is removed from the UK and is excluded for at least 10 years, or for as long as the deportation order remains in force.

Automatic deportation

If you are not a British citizen and are convicted as an adult in the UK of an offence and are sentenced to 12 months or more in prison, the Home Office must make a deportation order unless an exception applies.[19]

Public good deportation

If you do not have the right of abode (see p16), the Home Office can decide to deport you for any reason if it considers your presence to be 'not conducive to the public good'.[20] The reasons are usually associated with a person's criminality. Examples could include serious convictions (in the UK or elsewhere), persistent offending, police intelligence on criminal behaviour or threats to national security.

Family members of people facing deportation

The Home Office also has the power to deport your spouse or civil partner and children under 18,[21] but will not normally do so if they have indefinite leave in their own right or are separated from you.[22]

Challenging deportation decisions

You will only have a right of appeal against a deportation decision if you raise an exception on asylum or human rights grounds. Otherwise, the decision may be suitable for a judicial review challenge.

Administrative removal

Administrative removal is the procedure for removing someone who does not have leave to remain in the UK[23] – eg, because they entered without immigration leave or are an overstayer. If you are removed, you may be banned from returning to the UK for a number of months or years, depending on whether you left the UK voluntarily or not and whether you left at the expense of the Home Office.

Notes

3. **British nationality**
   1 s11 BNA 1981
   2 s1 BNA 1981
   3 s2 BNA 1981
   4 s4L BNA 1981

4. **Immigration and nationality applications**
   5 The Immigration and Nationality (Fees) Regulations 2016 No.226
   6 gov.uk/government/publications/affordability-fee-waiver-overseas-human-rights-based-applications-article-8
   7 The Immigration (Health Charge) (Amendment) Order 2020 No.1086
   8 s3C IA 1971

5. **Appeals and other remedies**
   9 s82(1) NIAA 2002
   10 s82(1) NIAA 2002
   11 s82(1) NIAA 2002
   12 s40 BNA 1981
   13 The Immigration (Citizens' Rights Appeals) (EU Exit) Regulations 2020 No.61
   14 The Tribunal Procedure (First-tier Tribunal) (Immigration and Asylum Chamber) Rules 2014 No.2604 (as amended)
   15 ss94-99 NIAA 2002
   16 Appendix AR and Appendix AR (EU) IR
   17 para 34R(1) IR
   18 para 34R(1A) IR

6. **Deportation and administrative removal**
   19 ss32-39 UK Borders Act 2007
   20 s3(5) and (6) IA 1971
   21 s5 IA 1971
   22 para 365 IR
   23 s10 IAA 1999

Chapter 3

Leave to enter or remain

This chapter covers:

1. Leave to enter or remain

If you do not have the right of abode (see p16), you may be subject to immigration control and require 'permission' to enter or remain in the UK. This permission is known as 'leave'. You may have 'leave to enter', 'leave to remain', which are both time limited, 'indefinite leave to remain' or 'indefinite leave to enter'.

The Immigration Rules set out the circumstances in which leave to enter or remain can be granted for various purposes, including for study, employment and business, family connections, private life, long residence, human rights and asylum. The Immigration Rules also stipulate the duration of the leave and any conditions attached, the circumstances in which leave will be refused, curtailed or revoked, and the criteria for deporting people whose presence in the UK is considered to be against the public interest – eg, if someone has committed a serious criminal offence.

Changes to the Immigration Rules must be notified to parliament, but there does not need to be any debate before the changes take effect. The rules are currently extremely lengthy, complicated and difficult to navigate. That was recognised by the judiciary and the Law Commission and, in response, the Home Office is now redeveloping the rules. The Immigration Rules are available at gov.uk/guidance/immigration-rules. The website also contains policy guidance that explains the Immigration Rules. The explanation given in the guidance is not always followed by tribunals and courts, but the guidance must usually be followed by the Home Office.

Note: leave may also be granted outside the Immigration Rules (see p48).

Conditions of leave

Limited leave to enter or remain in the UK may be granted with a limited number of conditions attached. If you breach the conditions attached to your leave, you may commit a criminal offence, your leave could be curtailed or revoked, and future applications for leave could be refused. You could also be detained and removed from the UK.

The conditions that may be attached to limited leave to remain include:

- a condition about where you live;
- a requirement to register with the police and/or report to the Home Office;
- restrictions on working or studying (see p31); *and/or*
- a 'no recourse to public funds' condition (see p32).

Who is exempt from the usual conditions

Some people are exempt from some of the usual conditions attached to leave to enter and remain in the UK. The main categories of people who are exempt are seamen and women, aircrew, diplomats and members of the UK or visiting armed forces.[1]

Turkish nationals

The Turkish EC Association Agreement (ECAA) ceased to have effect in the UK on 31 December 2020. Under the ECAA, Turkish nationals could establish themselves in the UK for economic purposes, relying on the more favourable Immigration Rules in place on 1 January 1973, the date that the UK joined the European Community (EC).

The Home Office introduced a five-year route to settlement (indefinite leave to remain) for these Turkish nationals and family members, under Appendix ECAA of the Immigration Rules.

The scheme is open to Turkish nationals who applied for leave to remain under the ECAA before 11pm on 31 December 2020 and were granted it. Turkish business persons, workers and their family members are eligible to apply for an extension of leave or for indefinite leave to remain. Partners who did not previously have leave in this category cannot apply and must consider an application under Appendix FM of the Immigration Rules. Dependent children younger than 21 years old can apply for entry clearance, leave to remain or indefinite leave to remain in this category. Children aged older than 21 cannot apply for entry clearance but can apply for an extension of leave or for indefinite leave to remain in this category only if they previously had leave in this category.

2. Time-limited leave

Leave may be granted for a limited period of time. Depending on the requirements in the Immigration Rules, you may be able to extend your leave to remain or 'switch' into another category. Not all types of leave can be extended or varied.

If you make a valid application to extend or vary your leave before it expires (an 'in-time' application), you will not then become an overstayer if your existing leave to remain expires before a decision is made on the extension or variation application. The law operates to extend your existing leave to remain, on the same conditions, until you have received a decision on the extension or variation application and, if refused, until you have exhausted your right to an administrative review or an appeal. See Chapter 2 for details of leave to remain under section 3C of the Immigration Act 1971.

The Home Office published turnaround time for a decision on an application is six months. The most straightforward applications are often decided within the six-month period, but for some types of application decisions may take many months or even years.

If the application is refused, you may be able to challenge it with a right of appeal or administrative review (see Chapter 2). The Home Office has the power to 'certify' some asylum and human rights claims with the effect that there is either no appeal right or the appeal right cannot be exercised until after the person has left the UK.

3. Indefinite leave

Indefinite leave to enter or remain in the UK is leave without a time restriction. Indefinite leave is also known as 'settlement'.

There are no conditions (eg, on employment and claiming 'public funds' – see p32) attached to indefinite leave.[2] However, if you have been granted leave as a result of a sponsor providing a written maintenance undertaking (see p37), this has the effect of defining you as a 'person subject to immigration control' (see p93), which means you are excluded from many social security benefits. For a list of the benefits you are excluded from and details of the exempt groups that can claim specific benefits, see Chapter 8. In limited circumstances, if you do receive specific benefits, the person who provided the undertaking may be liable to repay these benefits and could face criminal proceedings (see p529). If your leave has been granted as the result of an undertaking, this is not endorsed on your notice of decision or biometric residence permit. You may know if a sponsorship undertaking was given but, if not, you may have to make enquiries with the Home Office.

Indefinite leave can lapse if you are absent from the UK for too long.

With indefinite leave, you can leave the UK and return without your leave lapsing, if:

- you wish to return to settle in the UK; *and*
- you have indefinite leave to remain under the European Union Settlement Scheme, you have not been away from the UK for more than five years; *or*
- you have not been away from the UK for more than two years; *and*
- you did not receive any assistance from public funds towards the cost of leaving the UK. **Note:** 'public funds' in this context is the scheme that allows people to be reimbursed the costs of resettling in their country of origin. It does *not* refer to the fact that you may have claimed benefits or other assistance defined as public funds while in the UK (see p32).[3]

Indefinite leave may also be revoked, including if:

- you become liable to deportation (see p26); *or*
- the leave was obtained by deception.

Note: if you are outside the UK and are granted indefinite leave to enter, your visa shows an 'expiry' or 'valid until' date. This is the date by which you must enter the UK. Upon entry, you automatically have indefinite leave to remain and this date becomes irrelevant.[4]

4. Employment

Certain types of leave are granted with a condition prohibiting employment. For example, visitors are usually prohibited from working in the UK. Other types of leave have conditions that limit the number of hours that you can work (eg, as a condition of leave to remain as a student), or for a specific period of employment or business activity. That may be described as 'authorised' work. The details of what is authorised can be found in the relevant government policy published on the Home Office website.

If you have leave for specific employment (eg, under the points-based system), you can only work in the employment or undertake the activity for which you were granted leave. You must apply to the Home Office for permission to change employment.

Employers must check that all new employees have the right to work in the UK and can be prosecuted for employing anyone who cannot lawfully work. You can also be individually prosecuted for working illegally, and you may also lose your leave to remain. The law on the employment of migrant workers has changed several times since this requirement was introduced (in 1997), and the checks an employer must make (or should have made) depend on the date the worker was first employed by the employer. Applying such checks can raise race discrimination issues. If you believe that you have been treated unfavourably by an employer or potential employer, you should seek advice from an employment and discrimination specialist.

Note: in England since 1 December 2014, some landlords must check whether you have the right to live in the UK before letting a property to you. This includes landlords who take in lodgers or sublet property.

5. Recourse to public funds

In most categories within the Immigration Rules, when you apply for limited leave to enter or remain you have to show that you can maintain and accommodate yourself and your dependants without recourse to 'public funds'. In most categories within the Immigration Rules, a grant of limited leave to enter or remain has a condition that prohibits you from having recourse to public funds.

This condition now affects most grants of limited leave to enter or remain for family or private life reasons granted under Article 8 of the European Convention on Human Rights (see p45). The condition is notified in the decision and endorsed on the biometric residence permit as 'no public funds'. If you breach this condition, you may commit a criminal offence, your current leave could be curtailed or revoked, and future applications for leave could be refused. You could also be detained and removed from the UK and/or refused citizenship on character grounds.

What are public funds

'**Public funds**' for the purposes of the Immigration Rules are:[5]

- attendance allowance;
- carer's allowance;
- child benefit;
- child tax credit;
- council tax benefit (now abolished);
- council tax reduction;
- disability living allowance;
- housing benefit;
- income-based jobseeker's allowance;
- income-related employment and support allowance;
- income support;
- pension credit;
- personal independence payment;
- severe disablement allowance;
- social fund payments;
- universal credit;

- working tax credit;
- homelessness assistance and housing provided under specific provisions;
- local authority discretionary payments under section 1 of the Localism Act 2011, except payments under the Energy BIlls Support Scheme 2022 (see p103);
- welfare assistance payments by local authorities in Northern Ireland;
- Scottish Welfare Fund payments.

The restriction on public funds only applies to the benefits and other assistance listed in the Immigration Rules (listed above). Any other state support that is not in the list above is not restricted. This means that you may be able to access other forms of public funding, including legal aid, education, assistance from local authority social services departments (social work departments in Scotland) and social security benefits not listed above. NHS services are also not public funds under this definition, but they are restricted (see p639).

Note: in certain cases, you can still claim benefits defined as public funds without breaching the condition not to have recourse to public funds (see p113).

Applications to have 'no recourse to public funds' condition removed

If you have been granted leave to remain, which is subject to a 'no recourse to public funds' condition, and your circumstances change (eg, you have a baby, are unable to continue working or you have become unable to support yourself), you may be able to make a 'change of conditions' application. It is also possible to make this application if you were unable to support yourself at the time you applied for leave, but the Home Office was not made aware of this. Home Office guidance states that you can apply to have the no recourse to public funds condition removed, if:

- your financial circumstances have changed since being given permission to stay in the UK and you are no longer able to provide food or housing for yourself or your family; *or*
- your child's welfare is impacted as a result of your very low income; *or*
- you had financial problems when you first applied but you did not provide evidence of this and you now want to provide this evidence.

You can only make this application if you have been granted leave to remain:

- as a partner or parent or on private life grounds on the five-year or the 10-year route to settlement; *or*
- on human rights grounds; *or*
- on the Hong Kong British National (Overseas) route (see p50).

Home Office policy is to remove the no recourse to public funds condition if:

- you are destitute; *or*

- there are reasons relating to the welfare of your child which outweigh the considerations for maintaining the no recourse to public funds condition (treating the best interests of your child as a primary consideration); *or*
- there are exceptional circumstances in your case relating to your financial circumstances; *or*
- you are at risk of becoming destitute.

You are considered destitute if:
- you do not have adequate accommodation or any means of obtaining it (whether or not your other essential living needs are met); *or*
- you have adequate accommodation or the means of obtaining it, but cannot meet your other essential living needs; *or*
- you are at risk of destitution if either or both of the above are imminent.

Note: if you are on a five-year route to settlement and you apply to lift a no recourse to public funds condition, Home Office policy has been to automatically transfer you to a 10-year route to settlement. On 10 February 2022, migration minister Kevin Foster stated that this policy is currently being reviewed and that, pending this review, the Home Office has suspended the process of automatically requiring an applicant to complete 10 years on the family route following the lifting of no recourse to public funds conditions. Instead, it will review the situation in line with immigration rules at the next application for leave to remain. The online guidance has not been updated to reflect the migration minister's statement.[6]

The High Court has on several occasions found the no recourse to public funds scheme to be unlawful. In one case, the High Court found that the scheme did not adequately reflect Home Office obligations under section 55 of the Borders, Citizenship and Immigration Act 2009 to treat the best interests of children as a primary consideration.[7] The relevant rule, GEN.1.11A, was eventually amended on 20 June 2022 to take account of this judgment.

In a further case, the High Court found a section of the policy guidance to be unlawful as, again, it did not adequately reflect the duty to treat the best interests of children as a primary consideration.[8] The policy is yet to be amended to reflect this more recent judgment. It is therefore worth including a reference to this case when making an application to lift a no recourse to public funds condition.

6. Leave as a family member

Who is a sponsor

A sponsor can be a British citizen, a person with the right of abode, a person with indefinite leave, a European Economic Area (EEA) national with limited or indefinite leave under Appendix EU (the European Union Settlement Scheme – EUSS) or a person with refugee status or humanitarian protection. A sponsor supports another person (an applicant) to come to join them or remain with them in the UK. The Immigration Rules define a sponsor as the person in relation to whom you are seeking leave to enter or remain as a spouse, fiancé/e, civil partner, proposed civil partner, unmarried partner (including same-sex partner) or dependent relative.

A sponsor must usually demonstrate that they can maintain and support you in the UK without recourse to public funds. Parents must fulfil a similar role in the case of child applicants.[9]

Financial requirements

For most family applications, the sponsor must have a minimum specified annual income.[10] The amount increases depending on the number of applicants a person wishes to sponsor, including children and other dependants. A sponsor who is getting attendance allowance (AA), disability living allowance (DLA), personal independence payment (PIP), carer's allowance, industrial injuries disablement benefit, police injury pension and certain military and veteran payments does not have to have the specified minimum income. Note that this list of benefits has not been updated with more recent benefits such as adult disability payment and child disability payment, but arguably receipt of these should be treated the same.

If the sponsor has more than a certain amount of savings, these can be used to make up any shortfall in their annual income.

The applicant's income can be taken into account if the applicant is already in the UK with permission to work. If the applicant is outside the UK, their income and (in most cases) prospective income are disregarded. Support from a third party will only be taken into consideration in limited circumstances.

Adequate maintenance

For leave to be granted under other parts of the Immigration Rules, including some family cases, you must show that you can, and will, be maintained adequately without recourse to public funds. Whether or not there is adequate maintenance depends on the number of applicants and dependants and the nature of the income. The benchmark is still expressed in terms of income support (IS) levels, despite the introduction of universal credit. To be adequate, the income of the family as a whole must be equal to or greater than the amount an equivalent family would receive from IS if all the family members were entitled to have recourse to public funds. The use of this benchmark has been justified as necessary to prevent immigrant families or communities having a lower standard of living in the UK than the poorest British citizens.[11] However, the minimum income requirement used in most other cases is significantly higher than that.

AA, DLA and PIP claimed by a sponsor can be included when establishing whether a family's income is the same or higher than the IS amount.[12] It is arguable that the same approach should be applied to all current disability and incapacity benefits. Applicants and sponsors should obtain specialist advice if that might be an issue.

Adequate accommodation

In most cases, to be granted leave to enter or remain as a family member, a certain standard and/or type of accommodation must be available to you.

There must be adequate accommodation for you, your dependants and your sponsor, without you having recourse to public funds and which you and your family own or occupy exclusively.

The accommodation must not be overcrowded. The Housing Act 1985 contains statutory definitions of overcrowding. Accommodation is considered overcrowded if two people aged 10 years or older of the opposite sex (other than husband and wife or unmarried partners) have to sleep in the same room, or if the number of people sleeping in the accommodation exceeds that permitted in the Act, which specifies the number of people for a given number of rooms or given floor area.

The Immigration Rules often require that the accommodation must be owned or occupied 'exclusively' by the family unit concerned. This means that you, your sponsor and your dependants must have exclusive use of bedrooms but you can share other rooms, such as the kitchen, bathroom and living room, with other people.[13]

If your circumstances change

If you had to satisfy maintenance or accommodation requirements under the Immigration Rules before your leave was granted, your leave may be curtailed and/or a further application refused if you or your sponsor do not continue to meet these requirements throughout the period of leave granted.[14] **Note:** this does not apply to a grant of indefinite leave. The Home Office might discover that your circumstances have changed if, for example, you or your sponsor make a claim for social security benefits.

If you have been issued with a biometric residence permit (BRP), you are required to inform the Home Office, as soon as possible, if you know or suspect that a change in circumstances means that you no longer meet the requirements for leave to remain.

If you think that a change of circumstances may affect your entitlement to leave to remain, you should get specialist advice urgently.

See p38 if a qualifying relationship has ended because of domestic abuse or domestic violence.

Maintenance undertakings

A sponsor may be asked to give a written undertaking to be responsible for your maintenance and accommodation, or your care, for the period of leave applied for and any further period of leave to remain.[15] Undertakings are often requested for:

- dependent relatives, although not for children under 16 years coming for settlement;
- students relying on a private individual in the UK.

The benefit authorities sometimes mistakenly assume that every person referred to as a 'sponsor' will have given such an undertaking, but this is not the case. The definition of 'sponsor' is wider than that and not all sponsors are required to give a written undertaking.

If you have been granted leave to enter or remain as a result of a maintenance undertaking, you are defined as a 'person subject to immigration control' (see p93) and therefore excluded on this basis from the benefits listed on p111 unless you are in an exempt group (see Chapter 8). If you subsequently claim benefit while in the UK, your sponsor may be required to pay back the value of the benefit claimed.[16]

For further details if your leave has been granted as a result of a maintenance undertaking, see p105.

Unlike the condition not to have recourse to public funds, a maintenance undertaking is not stated on papers that notify a grant of leave or on the BRP.

Leave to remain as a partner on the five-year route to settlement

If you meet all the requirements of the Immigration Rules, you can be granted entry clearance for 33 months or leave to enter or remain for 30 months as the spouse, civil partner or unmarried partner of a:

- British citizen; *or*
- person with indefinite leave; *or*
- member of the armed forces with four years' service; *or*
- Turkish worker or business person with limited leave (under Appendix ECAA Extension of Stay); *or*
- an EEA citizen in the UK with limited leave under the EUSS (separate provisions apply to family relationships that started before 31 December 2020 – see Chapter 5); *or*
- holder of refugee status or humanitarian protection. This route is not the 'family reunion' route available to those partners and children who were in the sponsor's family before the sponsor left their country to claim asylum. See Chapter 4 for family reunion.

This leave is granted with a condition prohibiting recourse to public funds. When you have completed five years in this category, you can apply for indefinite leave to remain.

7. Private life routes

You may be granted leave if, at the date of the application:[17]

- you have lived in the UK continuously for at least 20 years; *or*
- you are under the age of 18, have lived continuously in the UK for at least seven years, and you cannot reasonably be expected to leave the UK (a 'seven-year child'); *or*
- you are aged 18 years or older and younger than 25 years, and have spent at least half of your life in the UK (a 'young adult'); *or*
- you are aged 18 years or older, have lived continuously in the UK for less than 20 years, but there would be very significant obstacles to your integration into the country where you would have to go if you had to leave the UK.

A valid passport is mandatory for private life applications. Seek immigration advice if you are not able to obtain a passport but otherwise meet the criteria for leave to remain on private life grounds. Periods of imprisonment are discounted. The 'suitability requirements' in the rules must be met.[18]

If you apply on the basis of more than 20 years' residency in the UK, or on the basis that you are over the age of 18 and would face very significant obstacles to integration in your country of return, you will, if you meet the requirements, be granted a period of 30 months' leave to remain, with a condition prohibiting recourse to public funds. You are able to apply for indefinite leave to remain after 10 years of leave to remain in this category.

If you are a 'seven-year child' or a 'young adult', you are able to apply for 60 months' leave to remain. If you meet the requirements, a period of 60 months of leave to remain will be granted, with a condition prohibiting recourse to public funds. You will be able to apply for indefinite leave to remain after 60 months of leave to remain in this category.

If you are a child who was born in the UK, you can apply for indefinite leave to remain immediately after spending the first seven years of your life here, even if you have never held leave to remain. You must demonstrate that it would not be reasonable to expect you to to leave the UK.[19]

8. Domestic violence and bereavement

If you have been granted limited leave, subject to a 'no recourse to public funds' condition, as the partner of a British person, a person with indefinite leave, a person with refugee leave or a person with pre-settled status (eg, if you are not eligible for leave under the European Union Settlement Scheme because your relationship only began after 31 December 2020), *and* if your relationship to that person breaks down because of **domestic violence or abuse**, you may be able to apply for indefinite leave to remain even though you have not completed five years in this category.[20]

The domestic violence application can be made after leave to remain has expired as long as your relationship broke down before your leave expired.

If you need to claim public funds while you prepare your application for indefinite leave as a victim of domestic violence, you can make an application under the destitution domestic violence concession.[21]

The application is made on a form that can be emailed to the Home Office. The Home Office makes a very quick decision, often on the same day. If successful, you will be granted discretionary leave to remain for three months. This leave is granted without any public funds restriction, so you can access benefits (see p104).

The Home Office then expects you to make the full application for indefinite leave to remain as a victim of domestic violence within those three months. If you submit this application before the discretionary leave expires, the discretionary leave is extended while that application is pending (see p21).

If you have been granted limited leave, subject to a no recourse to public funds condition, as the partner of a British person, a person with indefinite leave, or a person with pre-settled status, you may be able to apply for indefinite leave if your partner **dies**. Your relationship with your partner must have been genuine and subsisting at the time of death, and you must both have intended to live permanently with each other in the UK.[22] The application can be made even if your leave to remain has expired.

9. The points-based system

Since 2 December 2020, the Home Office has been operating a points-based system for people who wish to work or study in the UK. The categories of leave, all of which are granted subject to a 'no recourse to public funds' condition, are:
- student visa;
- skilled worker route;
- global talent route;
- graduate route;
- intra-company transfer;
- high potential individual visa;
- global business mobility visa;
- other:
  - start-up and innovators;

- health and care visa;
- creative route;
- international sportsperson;
- seasonal workers;
- Youth Mobility Scheme.

Notes

1. **Leave to enter or remain**
   1 s8 IA 1971

3. **Indefinite leave**
   2 s3(3)(a) IA 1971
   3 paras 18-19 IR
   4 See UKVI policy guidance ECB9.4 at gov.uk/government/publications/entry-clearance-vignettes-ecb09

5. **Recourse to public funds**
   5 para 6 IR
   6 questions-statements.parliament.uk/written-questions/detail/2022-02-07/119396
   7 *ST v SSHD* [2021] EWHC 1085 (Admin)
   8 *AB v SSHD* [2022] EWHC 1524 (Admin)

6. **Leave as a family member**
   9 para 297 and Appendix FM IR
   10 Appendix FM IR
   11 *KA (Pakistan)* [2006] UKAIT 00065; approved in *AM (Ethiopia) and Others and Another v Entry Clearance Officer* [2008] EWCA Civ 1082
   12 *MK (Somalia) v Entry Clearance Officer* [2007] EWCA Civ 1521
   13 Appendix FM IR s1.7A – 'Adequate maintenance and accommodation'
   14 paras 322(4)-23 IR
   15 para 35 IR
   16 para 35 IR; ss78, 105 and 106 SSAA 1992

7. **Private life routes**
   17 gov.uk/guidance/immigration-rules/immigration-rules-appendix-private-life
   18 See the suitability section of Appendix FM IR: gov.uk/guidance/immigration-rules/immigration-rules-appendix-fm-family-members
   19 gov.uk/guidance/immigration-rules/immigration-rules-appendix-private-life

8. **Domestic violence and bereavement**
   20 gov.uk/indefinite-leave-to-remain-domestic-violence-abuse
   21 gov.uk/government/publications/application-for-benefits-for-visa-holder-domestic-violence
   22 Section BPILR Appendix FM IR

Chapter 4

Asylum and human rights

This chapter covers:

1. **Asylum seekers**

Applying for asylum

If you apply for recognition as a refugee or as a person requiring protection from return to the country of your nationality or former habitual residence, you will be known as an 'asylum seeker'.[1]

Protection claims to the Home Office can be made on one or more of the following grounds:

- under the Refugee Convention (see p12); *or*
- under Article 3 of the European Convention on Human Rights (ECHR – see p12). This prescribes that no one shall be subjected to torture or to inhuman or degrading treatment or punishment; *or*
- under provisions in the Immigration Rules dealing with humanitarian protection.

A claim for humanitarian protection will be treated first as an application for asylum even if you do not expressly claim to be a refugee under the Refugee Convention. If you do not qualify for refugee status, the Home Office will go on to consider whether it is appropriate to grant humanitarian protection.

The other ECHR Article most commonly raised in immigration cases is Article 8, which protects a person's right to enjoy private and family life without unnecessary or disproportionate interference (see p45).

The definition of an asylum seeker for the purpose of support and accommodation (see p522) is limited to people who have applied under the Refugee Convention and/or Article 3 of the Human Rights Convention, so an application based only on Article 8 does not make someone an asylum seeker for asylum support purposes.[2] However, in certain situations, the Home Office can provide accommodation to people who are subject to immigration control who are not asylum seekers (see p551).

An asylum seeker may have applied for asylum at a port of entry before passing through passport control, or from inside the UK, having entered illegally or with leave for a different purpose under the Immigration Rules.

Note: if you delay making an in-country asylum application, your entitlement to asylum support may be affected (see p522).

If your asylum application is refused or withdrawn, and you have no further appeal rights, you may be able to make a fresh application (see p51).

Detention and removal

If you have leave to remain in another category when you claim asylum, you may be permitted to retain that leave or the Home Office may curtail your leave. If you do not have leave to remain when you claim asylum, you have entered the UK without immigration leave or are an overstayer and you are, therefore, liable to be detained.

Many asylum seekers are given immigration bail, but a significant number are detained while their application is considered, in the expectation that their application will be considered quickly and they can then be quickly removed from the UK if refused.

A refused asylum seeker can be detained without time limit if the purpose of the detention is removal from the UK and there is some prospect that this will be imminent. People in immigration detention can seek advice or assistance from specialist immigration providers and the organisation Bail for Immigration Detainees (biduk.org), which specialises in immigration detention.

Permission to work

If you have not received a decision on your asylum claim after one year, and the delay is not your fault, you can apply to the Home Office for permission to work.[3]

If granted permission, the jobs that you can do are usually restricted to those on a 'shortage occupation list' that comprises, with some exceptions, mainly high-skilled occupations. This list can change depending on the demands of the UK labour market. In some circumstances, the Home Office may exercise discretion and grant an asylum seeker unrestricted permission to work. **Note:** if you start work, you may no longer be eligible for asylum support (see p529).

2. Refugee leave and humanitarian protection

If you are an asylum seeker who is recognised by the Home Office as a refugee or as being in need of humanitarian protection, you are granted refugee leave or humanitarian protection leave respectively.

Refugees and humanitarian protection

A **'refugee'** is someone who, owing to a well-founded fear of being persecuted because of race, religion, nationality, membership of a particular social group or political opinion, is outside the country of their nationality, and is unable to or, owing to such fear, is unwilling to avail themself of the protection of that country.

A person in need of **'humanitarian protection'** is someone who does not qualify as a refugee, but there are substantial grounds for believing that if they were returned to their country of origin, they would face a real risk of suffering serious harm. A person could, for example, face a risk of serious harm for reasons other than race, religion, nationality, membership of a particular social group or political opinion – eg, due to serious violent conflict in their country.

If you claimed asylum before 28 June 2022 and you are granted refugee status or humanitarian protection, the Home Office usually grants five years' leave to remain, with the option of applying for indefinite leave shortly before this leave expires. This application is free of charge.

If you claimed asylum on or after 28 June 2022, you did so 'without delay' and you came directly from the country where your life or freedom was threatened, and you are granted refugee status, you will usually be granted five years' leave to remain with the option of applying for indefinite leave before this expires, as above. However, if you do not meet these additional requirements and you are granted refugee leave, you will usually be granted an initial period of 30 months' leave to remain and you will only be able to apply for indefinite leave after having leave to remain for 10 years.

If you claimed asylum on or after 28 June 2022 and are granted humanitarian protection, you will usually be granted an initial period of 30 months' leave to remain, which you will need to extend three times before you are able to apply for indefinite leave. You can apply for indefinite leave after having held leave to remain for 10 years.

Refugee leave and humanitarian protection leave can be reviewed and revoked, or not extended, if:

- your actions bring you within the scope of the 1951 Refugee Convention 'cessation clauses' – eg, if you travel back to your home country without a reasonable explanation;[4] *or*

- there is a 'significant or non-temporary' change in the conditions in your country of origin (or part of the country), making it safe to return, and a formal declaration of the change is made by the responsible state authority; *or*
- you commit a serious criminal offence.

Family reunion

If you have refugee status or humanitarian protection, you can sponsor your spouse, civil partner, unmarried and/or same-sex partner and dependent children aged under 18 to come to the UK. The family member making the application must have been part of your family unit before you left the country to claim asylum. That is known as 'family reunion'. There are no minimum income or maintenance and accommodation requirements that must be met, and their leave is granted without any conditions restricting public funds. If you claimed asylum on or after 28 June 2022 and you are granted either humanitarian protection or refugee leave for 30 months, you can only be joined by your family members if you can show there would otherwise be 'insurmountable obstacles' to your family life continuing.

Successful family reunion applicants are granted leave to remain in line with your leave, but that is not recognition of the applicants as refugees or holders of humanitarian protection. The leave granted will expire at the same time as yours and, therefore, may be limited leave of up to 30 months or up to five years, or indefinite leave.[5]

Family members who became part of your family unit after you fled your country must meet the usual immigration rules, including the minimum income and/or maintenance and accommodation requirements. Their leave will generally be subject to a condition prohibiting recourse to public funds (see p34).

Exclusions

You can be excluded from refugee status or humanitarian protection status if:

- you have committed a crime against peace, a war crime, a crime against humanity or a serious non-political crime outside the UK before being admitted; *or*
- you are guilty of acts that are contrary to the purposes and principles of the United Nations. That could include being involved in terrorism or encouraging others to commit terrorist acts.

You may be excluded from refugee status or humanitarian protection if you have committed a serious criminal offence.

Article 3 of the European Convention on Human Rights protects people from torture, inhuman and degrading treatment and cruel and unusual punishment. If you are excluded from refugee status or humanitarian protection but would face Article 3-type treatment in your home country, the Home Office cannot return you and may grant you a form of leave outside the rules, known as restricted leave (see p47).

3. Stateless people

A **'stateless person'** is defined by international law as someone who is 'not considered a national by any state under the operation of its law'.[6] On 6 April 2013, the UK introduced a provision in the Immigration Rules to recognise and grant leave to remain to certain stateless people.[7] Before this date, stateless people could obtain travel documents but could not obtain leave. If you are recognised as stateless in the UK, you can obtain a stateless person's travel document.

4. Leave for human rights and compassionate reasons

Leave granted under Article 8 of the European Convention on Human Rights grounds

Article 8 of the European Convention on Human Rights (ECHR) sets out the right to respect for your private and family life. That is not an absolute right and, in certain circumstances, the Home Office can interfere with this right. You may be able to rely on Article 8 to resist removal and gain leave to remain if you have family in the UK and/or have lived in the UK for some time and developed ties here. Some examples of Article 8 rights include the right to live with your British or settled partner or children, or to live in the UK after having built up a long residence here (typically seven years or longer for children, or 20 years or longer for adults). Article 8 rights can also be acquired by young people aged 18 to 24 who have lived in the UK for half their life or more, and by adults who would face very significant obstacles to integration on return to the country they would have to go back to (see p38).

Before 9 July 2012, leave to remain given for Article 8 reasons was granted outside the Immigration Rules and was called **'discretionary leave'** (see p46).

Since 9 July 2012, the Immigration Rules have set out the circumstances in which the Home Office will grant leave to remain for private and family life reasons. This includes leave to remain for parents and partners who do not meet the requirements of minimum income, immigration status or English language.

If you have private and family life grounds but do not meet the requirements of the Immigration Rules, you can seek specialist advice on applying outside the Immigration Rules on human rights grounds.

From 9 July 2012, leave is given for periods of no longer than 30 months, potentially leading to indefinite leave after 10 continuous years. Young people who have been granted leave to remain on Article 8 grounds due to having spent half their lives in the UK can potentially apply for indefinite leave after five years of continuous leave (see p38). That is twice the length of time in which a family member can become eligible for settlement under other parts of the Immigration Rules. Home Office policy is to grant leave subject to a 'no recourse to public funds' condition, unless you raise exceptional circumstances in your application. It is possible to apply for this condition to be lifted if there has been a change in your circumstances, or if the circumstances were not known to the Home Office at the time the leave was granted.[8] Home Office policy is that 'exceptional circumstances' apply when a person is destitute or is a parent on a low income and there are particularly compelling reasons relating to the welfare of their child.[9]

Note: if you are a carer or a sibling of a British citizen child, you may be able to apply for leave to remain on Article 8 grounds.

Unaccompanied children

In the case of an unaccompanied child whose claim for asylum has been refused, limited leave may be granted within the Immigration Rules for up to 30 months or until the child is 17 and a half, whichever is the shorter period.[10] It is important to recognise that a grant of limited leave under this rule operates as a refusal of the asylum claim, and the child should be assisted to access specialist legal advice on whether or not to appeal this refusal, at the time of the decision. At the expiry of this limited leave, if the child wishes to remain in the UK, they must make an application for further leave to remain and this application could be granted or refused. This form of leave is not subject to a no recourse to public funds condition.

Section 67 of the Immigration Act 2016 requires the UK government to support a specified number of unaccompanied refugee children living in other European countries in relocating to the UK. A number of children transferred under section 67 will be granted five years' leave under this provision. This grant of leave is not subject to a no recourse to public funds condition. An application for indefinite leave to remain can be made after completing five years of continuous residence. No new grants of leave will be issued in this category. The government confirmed in February 2022 that it has met its one-off commitment to transfer 480 unaccompanied asylum-seeking children from Europe to the UK under section 67.[11]

Leave outside the rules

Discretionary leave

Discretionary leave is granted:

- in medical cases. The threshold for leave on this basis is high: you must be seriously ill and face a real risk of being exposed to a serious, rapid and irreversible decline in your health, which would result in 'intense suffering', due to the absence of appropriate treatment were you to be removed from the UK;[12] *or*

- if returning you would breach the ECHR – eg, if the government of the country to which you would be returned would flagrantly deny your rights to a fair trial under Article 6 of the convention; *or*
- in other exceptional circumstances specified in Home Office enforcement policies; *or*
- to a victim of trafficking or modern slavery within the meaning of Article 4 of the Council of Europe Convention on Action Against Trafficking in Human Beings when leave is necessary owing to personal circumstances (such as ongoing treatment or therapy), or to pursue compensation, or when the victim is helping the police with their enquiries; *or*
- under transitional arrangements, if you have previously been granted discretionary leave.

People granted discretionary leave are able to work. Discretionary leave should not be granted with a condition prohibiting recourse to public funds. If this condition has been added in error, that should be challenged or an application should be made to remove the prohibition.

Discretionary leave is normally granted for a period of 30 months, with the possibility of further extension periods of 30 months. When you have had discretionary leave for 10 continuous years, you can apply for indefinite leave to remain, unless you do not satisfy the indefinite leave rules – eg, because of a criminal conviction or a recent out-of-court settlement such as a caution or for a county court debt.

The previous policy, applicable to those granted discretionary leave before 9 July 2012, was normally to grant discretionary leave for three years, with the possibility of being able to apply to extend this leave, and to grant indefinite leave to remain after six continuous years.

When you apply for an extension of discretionary leave or for indefinite leave to remain, the Home Office 'actively reviews' your case and will only grant leave if there have been no significant changes or criminality.

Restricted leave

If you are excluded from refugee status or humanitarian protection (see p43) for the reasons outlined on p44, but you cannot be removed from the UK for human rights reasons (eg, because you face a risk of torture on return), you may be granted restricted leave.

Restricted leave is usually only granted for a maximum of six months at a time, with restrictions:

- on your employment or occupation in the UK;
- on where you can live;

- requiring you to report to the Home Office or the police at regular intervals;
- prohibiting your studying at an educational institution; *and*
- prohibiting your doing voluntary work with children and/or vulnerable adults.

If you knowingly fail to comply with any restrictions imposed, you may commit a criminal offence.

If you have restricted leave and you depart from the UK and common travel area (the UK, Ireland, Channel Islands and the Isle of Man), your leave will lapse; if you want to return to the UK, you will need to make a fresh application. This leave will be subject to a no recourse to public funds condition, unless you have demonstrated that you are destitute and in need of public funds.

Exceptional leave

Exceptional leave was replaced by humanitarian protection and discretionary leave in 2003. It was granted for similar reasons but also under blanket policies to applicants from countries experiencing civil or military upheaval.

Leave outside the Immigration Rules for other reasons

You may be given leave outside the Immigration Rules in special or unusual situations that would not otherwise be covered, including in Article 8 cases (see p45).

The Home Office has a discretion to grant leave to remain outside the Immigration Rules for compassionate reasons. This leave will be subject to a no recourse to public funds condition, unless there are exceptional circumstances described on p45.

Afghan resettlement and relocation schemes

Afghan Relocations and Assistance Policy

Afghan nationals formerly employed by HM Government (HMG) can apply to relocate to the UK. The Afghan Relocations and Assistance Policy (ARAP) scheme launched in April 2021 and is open to former locally employed staff. People may be eligible for relocation if they fall into one of three categories:

- a person at high and imminent risk of threat to life (only for people employed directly by HMG);
- former employees eligible for relocation (for both directly employed staff and for those who provided linguistic services to the UK's armed forces under a contract to a UK government department) – additional criteria such as a risk to safety also need to be satisfied; *and*
- special cases (for applicants who worked in Afghanistan for, or alongside/in partnership with, HMG). Applicants must:
  - demonstrate that they have made a substantive and positive contribution towards the achievement of the UK government's military or national security objectives in Afghanistan; *and*

- have been left at increased risk due to the current situation in Afghanistan; *or*
- hold information which, if disclosed, could threaten UK government interests.

To be eligible for relocation, applicants need to have worked in Afghanistan for HMG in so-called 'exposed meaningful enabling roles' that have left them at risk due to the changing situation in Afghanistan – eg, interpreters, cultural advisors and counter-terrorism jobs. The application is made online and is free of charge. It is possible to apply from any country. Those who qualify can bring one partner and their minor dependent children with them to the UK. ARAP was incorporated into the Immigration Rules on 6 October 2021. Amendments to the rules introduced on 14 December 2021 made the ARAP scheme more restrictive.[13]

Those eligible under ARAP were previously granted five years' leave to enter, without a no recourse to public funds condition. In September 2021, the Home Office announced that all locally employed staff who meet the requirements for entry clearance will instead be issued with indefinite leave to enter. Those who were previously granted five years' limited leave to enter under this route can now apply to have their leave converted to indefinite leave to remain. The application is free of charge.[14]

Ex-gratia scheme

The ex-gratia scheme was another scheme for eligible locally employed staff in Afghanistan, which began in 2013 and ended on 30 November 2022. Eligible locally employed staff in Afghanistan must now apply through ARAP (see above).

Afghan Citizens Resettlement Scheme

The Afghan Citizens Resettlement Scheme (ACRS) was announced on 18 August 2021 and opened on 6 January 2022. The UK government has stated that it aims to resettle up to 20,000 people at risk. The Home Office has stated that those resettled under the ACRS will receive indefinite leave to enter or remain in the UK. Partners and minor dependent children are also eligible for the scheme.[15]

Appendix Ukraine Scheme

In response to Russia's invasion of Ukraine at the beginning of 2022, the UK government put in place three visa schemes for Ukrainian nationals fleeing Ukraine. The rules are in the Immigration Rules, Appendix Ukraine Scheme. The schemes all include access to work, study and public funds for 36 months. At present, there is no path to settlement.

Ukraine Family Scheme

The Ukraine Family Scheme allows people living in the UK to sponsor Ukrainian relatives for a family visa. Immediate or extended family members may apply, including aunts, uncles, parents, children, siblings and in-laws. Applications are free of charge and made online. The sponsor has to be a British citizen or have indefinite leave to remain, European Union settled or pre-settled status, refugee status or humanitarian protection. Successful applicants are granted permission to stay for 36 months, without a no recourse to public funds condition.

This scheme can also be used by people who are already in the UK if they have permission to stay, or if they had permission to stay immediately before 1 January 2022 which has since expired.

Ukraine Sponsorship Scheme (Homes for Ukraine)

This scheme allows Ukrainians to come to the UK if they have a sponsor who can provide them with accommodation for at least six months. It is open to applicants who lived in Ukraine immediately before 1 January 2022, including those who have since left Ukraine. Applications are free of charge and made online. Those arriving under this scheme can stay for up to 36 months, without a no recourse to public funds condition.

Ukraine Extension Scheme

This scheme is for Ukrainians who are already in the UK. Applicants must have had permission to enter or stay in the UK on 18 March 2022 or between 18 March 2022 and 16 May 2023, unless they had permission to stay in the UK immediately before 1 January 2022 and that permission has since expired. Children born in the UK to a parent who qualifies under the Ukraine Extension Scheme are also eligible. The application is free of charge and made online. Leave will be granted for 36 months, without a no recourse to public funds condition.

Hong Kong British National (Overseas) route

This route is for British National (Overseas) (BN(O)) citizens. Applicants must either be a BN(O) status holder or the eligible family member of a BN(O) status holder. They must be ordinarily resident in Hong Kong or the UK, and be able to demonstrate that they can maintain and accommodate themselves in the UK without recourse to public funds for at least six months. Applicants have the option of applying for either a 30-month visa (which costs £180) or a five-year visa (£250). In addition to the application fee, applicants must pay the health surcharge. Applicants will be eligible to apply for indefinite leave to remain after spending five years in the UK in this category. This visa is issued with a no recourse to public funds restriction. It is possible to apply to have this lifted in certain circumstances (see p33).[16]

5. Fresh applications

If you are a refused asylum seeker, you can be removed from the UK if you have used up all your appeal rights and are without leave to remain, or you have abandoned or withdrawn your asylum claim. Under the Immigration Rules, you may make 'further submissions' if there are new facts, fresh evidence, a change in the country of return or a change in the law.

The Home Office will decide whether the application should be granted or refused. If it is refused, the Home Office will then decide whether the further submissions amount to a 'fresh claim' – ie, a claim that includes significantly different material from the previous one, that is arguable and could succeed in front of a tribunal judge. If the Home Office accepts that it amounts to a fresh claim, a refusal will carry a right of appeal. If not, the only remedy is judicial review.

If you are a refused asylum seeker and you have made further submissions, you are entitled to claim asylum support while the submissions are being considered (see Chapter 21).

Notes

1. **Asylum seekers**

1 s94(1) IAA 1999
2 s94(1) IAA 1999
3 Art 11 EU Dir 2003/9; paras 360-61 IR

2. **Refugee leave and humanitarian protection**

4 Art 1C(1)-(6) 1951 UN Convention Relating to the Status of Refugees
5 Part 11, paras 352A-FJ IR and policy instructions

3. **Stateless people**

6 1954 UN Convention Relating to the Status of Stateless Persons
7 Part 14 IR

4. **Leave for human rights and compassionate reasons**

8 See UKVI, *Application for change of conditions of leave to allow access to public funds if your circumstances change*, April 2022, available at gov.uk/government/publications/application-for-change-of-conditions-of-leave-to-allow-access-to-public-funds-if-your-circumstances-change
9 The policy is contained in the IDI, 'Family Life (as a Partner or Parent)' FM 1.0a, and 'Partner and ECHR Article 8 Guidance', FM 8.0, which has been amended on several occasions
10 para 352ZC IR
11 gov.uk/government/publications/nationality-and-borders-bill-children-factsheet/nationality-and-borders-bill-children-factsheet

12 *Paposhvili v Belgium* (Application No.41738/10) [2016] ECHR 1113, 13 December 2016
13 gov.uk/guidance/immigration-rules/immigration-rules-part-7-other-categories
14 gov.uk/government/publications/afghan-locally-engaged-staff
15 gov.uk/guidance/afghan-citizens-resettlement-scheme
16 gov.uk/government/publications/hong-kong-british-national-overseas-route/hong-kong-british-national-overseas-route-accessible

Chapter 5

European Economic Area nationals and their families

This chapter covers:

This chapter provides an overview of the main immigration rules that apply to European Economic Area nationals and their family members. The information in this chapter is not a substitute for specialist legal immigration advice for individual cases. Further detail on free movement rights, including who can still use these for the purpose of claiming benefits, is set out in Chapter 12.

1. The European Economic Area member states

The '**European Economic Area**' (EEA) comprises the 27 member states of the European Union (EU) plus the European Free Trade Association (EFTA) countries.

The current member states of the EU are: Austria, Belgium, Bulgaria, Croatia, Cyprus, Czech Republic, Denmark, Estonia, Finland, France, Germany, Greece, Hungary, Ireland, Italy, Latvia, Lithuania, Luxembourg, Malta, Netherlands, Poland, Portugal, Romania, Slovenia, Slovakia, Spain and Sweden.

The EFTA countries are: Norway, Liechtenstein, Switzerland and Iceland.

Switzerland has bilateral agreements with the EU and UK, which provide for Swiss nationals to have similar rights to EEA nationals within the EEA and UK. References to EEA nationals in this *Handbook* therefore include Swiss nationals.

The UK ceased to be an EEA member state on leaving the EU on 31 January 2020.

2. **Changes due to the UK leaving the European Union**

The UK leaving the European Union (EU) has led to major changes in immigration law relating to European Economic Area (EEA) nationals and their family members.

Before the UK left the EU, the rights of EEA nationals and their families came from EU law and, though these rights were qualified, they were automatic. This meant that as long as EEA nationals were exercising free movement rights (see Chapter 12), they had the right to live in the UK without making immigration applications or holding residency documents.

In general, free movement rights were ended within UK law from 31 December 2020. Although these rights can still be used for the purpose of claiming benefits if you are in a 'protected group' (see p188), since the end of 2020, EEA nationals and their family members are required to actively apply for and hold leave under the Immigration Rules. The type of leave you are required to hold depends on when you came to the UK, and if you are joining particular family members. EEA nationals and their family members who were resident in the UK on or before 31 December 2020 are required to hold leave under the European Union Settlement Scheme (EUSS), whereas those arriving after this date cannot access the EUSS unless they are a pre-existing family member of a person with leave under the EUSS (see p67).

Overview of the Brexit process

Following a referendum on 23 June 2016, the UK began proceedings to leave the EU. On 29 March 2017, the UK invoked Article 50 of the Treaty on European Union, which began the country's withdrawal from the EU.

The UK formally left the EU on 31 January 2020, but a 'transition period' until 31 December 2020 meant that the majority of laws and immigration requirements remained the same during this period.

From 1 January 2021, free movement rights in general were ended (though they continue for the purpose of claiming benefits for those in a 'protected group' – see p188). EU nationals and their family members already resident in the UK on or before 31 December 2020 were given a 'grace period' until 30 June 2021 to submit EUSS applications to continue living lawfully in the UK.

EEA nationals arriving from 1 January 2021 cannot gain leave under the EUSS, unless they come to the UK to join an EEA family member who was already resident here before 31 December 2020. Instead, they will need to enter the UK under one of the other various categories of the Immigration Rules just as non-EEA nationals would (see Chapter 3).

Overview of immigration categories for European Economic Area nationals and their family members

EEA nationals and their family members will now effectively be in one of the following groups:

- those who have already obtained leave under the EUSS – ie:
  - those with settled status (indefinite leave to enter or remain); *or*
  - those with pre-settled status (limited leave to enter or remain); *or*
- those already resident in the UK before 31 December 2020 who have not yet obtained leave under the EUSS – ie:
  - those who have applied and are waiting for a decision or appeal;
  - those who have not yet applied and need to make a late application;
- those arriving from 1 January 2021 who are unable to apply to the EUSS and must use general immigration provisions, unless they are joining an EEA family member who was already resident prior to 31 December 2020 (see p67).

The documentation issued to EEA nationals and their family members has changed due to Brexit; many types of immigration leave are now electronic (see p71).

The rules on deporting EEA nationals have also changed due to Brexit (see p71).

3. The European Union Settlement Scheme

The European Union Settlement Scheme (EUSS) is the system of immigration control for European Economic Area (EEA) nationals who were already resident in the UK by 31 December 2020, and their family members who wish to reside in the UK. It is set out in Appendix EU of the Immigration Rules, and clarified in supporting Home Office caseworker guidance. Applications are mandatory, and the deadline to apply was 30 June 2021 (though late applications can be made – see p64).

Who is required to hold leave under the EUSS

Generally, EEA nationals and their family members who lived in the UK prior to 31 December 2020, and who continue to live in the UK, need to hold leave under the EUSS.

EEA nationals and their family members who previously held 'permanent residence' under the EEA Regulations are required to apply to the EUSS.

British nationals, including EEA nationals with dual British citizenship, do not need to hold leave under the EUSS.

Settled status may be helpful for those who already hold indefinite leave to remain, as it allows additional protection from loss of leave due to absence. Regular indefinite leave to remain allows you to be outside the UK for two years without losing your leave, while settled status allows you to be outside the UK for five years without losing your leave.

Irish nationals do not need to apply, though they can do if they wish. However, family members of Irish nationals do need to apply.

Some European Union (EU) nationals may already hold indefinite leave to remain – eg, if they entered the UK before 1973 or if they became settled in the UK before their country joined the EU. These people do not need to apply to the EUSS, though they can if they want to and it may be helpful for evidencing their leave.

Definition of family members under the EUSS

Direct family members of EEA nationals are defined in much the same way as under the EEA Regulations (see p240). Direct family members include spouses, civil partners, children and grandchildren under the age of 21, and dependent parents and grandparents.

Extended family members, including dependent adult relatives and durable partners (those who can show that their relationship is durable – eg, because they have cohabited for two years), can be treated as a family member only in certain circumstances (see p243). Note that the EUSS combines direct and recognised extended family members into a single category of 'family members', but to assist with considering eligibility for benefits we continue to address these two groups separately in this *Handbook*.

Dependent adult relatives can only access leave under the EUSS if their relationship existed before 31 December 2020 and they already held a residence document as a dependent adult relative issued under the EEA Regulations. For a detailed explanation of who is a dependent adult relative, see p242.

Durable partners can only access leave under the EUSS if their relationship with the EU national was durable before 31 December 2020 and either:

- the durable partner was resident in the UK before 31 December 2020 and held a residence document under the EEA Regulations; or
- the durable partner was not resident under the EEA Regulations before 31 December 2020 (though they may have been lawfully resident in another way – eg, as a student), or they were resident but have broken this continuity of residence (eg, through absence from the UK) and they are applying as a joining family member.

Note that the legal position for extended family members is complex. Seek specialist legal advice if this may apply to you.

The family members of Northern Irish citizens may also apply to the EUSS, provided that the Northern Irish person is either a British or Irish citizen or both, that they were born in Northern Ireland, and that at the time of their birth at least one of their parents was either a British or Irish citizen or both, or was otherwise entitled to reside in Northern Ireland without any residence restrictions.[1]

People who did not apply to the EUSS before the deadline

The deadline to apply for settled or pre-settled status was 30 June 2021.

Those who did not apply to the EUSS before the deadline of 30 June 2021 and did not obtain any other type of leave effectively became overstayers in the UK. If you missed the deadline to apply, you must apply as soon as possible and you must give a reason for your late application. See p64 on late EUSS applications.

For EEA nationals arriving after the end of the transition period, and family relationships formed after this date, see p67.

4. Leave under the European Union Settlement Scheme

There are two types of leave available under the European Union Settlement Scheme (EUSS):

- settled status, which is indefinite leave to enter or remain; *and*
- pre-settled status, which is limited leave to enter or remain, valid for five years.

Settled status and pre-settled status are based on your length of residence in the UK. Unlike under the European Economic Area (EEA) Regulations, it is not necessary for you to have held a free movement right to reside (eg, as a worker); you simply need to have been physically present in the UK.

Under the EUSS, progression from pre-settled status to settled status is not automatic. Pre-settled status holders are required to make a new application to progress to settled status or they will become overstayers. The requirement to make a second application to the EUSS, and the loss of rights if this is not done before pre-settled status expires, has recently been found to be unlawful by the High Court.[2] Although the Home Offce had been granted permission to appeal, it announced in February 2023 that it would not appeal. Changes need to be made to the EUSS to take account of the High Court judgment. You should ensure you apply for settled status before your pre-settled status expires.

Settled status

Settled status is a form of leave available to EEA nationals and their family members under the EUSS. It is indefinite leave, and gives the holder the right to live, work, study, access benefits and access NHS treatment in the UK.

Settled status is available to EEA nationals and their family members who have lived in the UK for five or more consecutive years. For pre-settled status holders approaching five years of residency, see p63. For EEA nationals and their family members who have lived in the UK for more than five years but not yet made an EUSS application, see p64.

Once granted, settled status can be lost if you remain outside the UK for more than five consecutive years. This is more generous that the usual two-year absence allowed for indefinite leave to enter or remain. Settled status can also be lost due to serious offending (see p72), or if it was obtained based on false representations or fraudulent documents.

Holders of settled status may be able to apply for British citizenship after holding settled status for one year.

For your residence to be considered continuous, you must not have been outside the UK for more than six months within any given 12-month period, though you maybe absent for up to one year for 'important reasons' – eg, pregnancy, childbirth, serious illness, study, vocational training, an overseas posting or because of Covid.[3] Absences of any length for compulsory military service are disregarded and do not break the continuity of residence.[4]

In addition, further flexibility has been introduced to the rules with regards to Covid-related absences. Absences of up to 12 months for Covid-related reasons will not break your continuity of residence. This has a wide meaning, including absences due to you being ill with Covid, caring for family affected by Covid, travel disruption or Covid restrictions, or due to seeking support or working remotely overseas during Covid.

If you were absent from the UK for more than 12 months because the Covid pandemic meant you were prevented from or advised against returning earlier, that will not break your continuity of residence. However, the period of absence exceeding 12 months will not count towards your five-year period of residence – the clock will be paused.

You can rely on any consecutive five-year period of residence, not just the most recent five years.[5] However, you are prevented from relying on a past period of residence if you have been absent from the UK for more than five years since the period of residence you wish to rely upon.[6] In addition, you must not have been excluded or deported since the period of residence you wish to rely upon.

Some applicants can be granted settled status with less than five years' residence, including EEA nationals who have stopped work in certain circumstances and their family members, and the family members of certain EEA nationals who have died.[7] In these cases, the same requirements apply as for those who can obtain permanent residence with less than five years' residence under the EEA Regulations. See p275 for details.

When a parent is granted settled status, their child can also be granted settled status even if the child has not yet lived in the UK for five years (though the child will need to make a separate application).[8]

If a person living in the UK holds settled status and then has a baby inside the UK, the baby will be born British and will not need to make an EUSS application (see p16).

Note that the deadline to apply for settled status has now passed, though holders of pre-settled status can continue to apply for settled status on reaching five years' residence. If you do not yet hold leave under the EUSS and you are applying for settled status, see p64 for late applications.

Applications for settled status are subject to suitability criteria (see below).

Pre-settled status

Pre-settled status is the other form of leave available under the EUSS. It is limited leave, valid for five years.

Pre-settled status is available to EEA nationals and their family members who were resident in the UK on or before 11pm on 31 December 2020 but who have not yet lived in the UK for five continuous years.[9]

Pre-settled status holders are granted five years of limited leave, valid from the date of their decision. They will be eligible for settled status when they have been resident in the UK for five continuous years. They do not need to wait until they have held pre-settled status for five years. **Note:** you must make a new EUSS application to progress from pre-settled to settled status (see p63); this will not happen automatically.

Pre-settled status can be lost if you are outside of the UK for two years or more (see p63).[10] In addition, pre-settled status may be curtailed in cases of deception or on the basis of serious offending (see below). It may also be curtailed if you no longer meet the requirements, though the Home Office has discretion in such cases.[11] Also note that if you hold pre-settled status and intend to progress to settled status, you must not be absent from the UK for more than six months in most circumstances (see p63).

If you do not yet hold pre-settled status and need to make a late application for it, see p64.

Applications for pre-settled status are subject to suitability criteria (see below).

Suitability for settled and pre-settled status

The EUSS contains suitability criteria that restrict who can be granted leave on the basis of criminality, deception and exclusion.

An application must be refused on grounds of suitability when there is a current deportation decision or order, or whether there is a current exclusion decision or order.[12]

An application may be refused on grounds of suitability if there is a live removal decision under the EEA Regulations, or if false evidence or information has been submitted.[13]

Certain criminal convictions may trigger suitability concerns. These include:

- any length of imprisonment within the last five years;
- imprisonment for a period of 12 months or more for a single offence at any time;
- for those who have lived in the UK less than five years, three or more convictions (whether or not imprisoned) within the last three years;
- previous involvement in serious deception.[14]

If your application triggers suitability concerns for any of the above reasons, your application will be referred from the Home Office's EUSS team to Immigration Enforcement. Immigration Enforcement will then consider whether the matter is serious enough to trigger deportation proceedings. If the suitability concern is not of such severity as to warrant deportation (see p71), then leave should be granted.

Applicants over the age of 18 are required to disclose previous criminal convictions, although spent convictions do not need to be disclosed. In addition, the Home Office will run a criminal record check on all applicants over the age of 10. If you fail to disclose criminal convictions, there is a risk this may trigger suitability concerns on the basis of deception.

If you have a pending prosecution (ie, you have been charged with a criminal offence but not yet been tried), the Home Office will normally put your application on hold until the matter has been concluded. In deciding whether to put an application on hold, the Home Office should consider proportionality and whether the offence is serious enough to trigger suitability concerns.[15]

A **'pending prosecution'** is defined as when a person either:

- has been arrested or summoned in respect of one or more criminal offences and one or more of these offences has not been disposed of either by the police or the courts; *or*
- is the subject of a live investigation by the police for a suspected criminal offence.[16]

If you are concerned that suitability issues may affect your application, you should seek specialist immigration advice.

Retained rights and the EUSS

The EUSS allows people who have a 'retained right of residence' under the EEA Regulations to make an application for settled or pre-settled status under the scheme. There are specific requirements for retained rights of residence, including for the family member of an EEA national when the EEA national has died or ended the marriage or civil partnership through divorce. These are broadly the same under the EUSS as under the EEA Regulations – see p249 for details.

The EUSS has a slightly broader definition of retained residence rights and allows applications for cases in which a variety of family relationships have broken down to due to **domestic abuse** (rather than just the breakdown of marriage or civil partnership). The EUSS requires that the relationship has broken down permanently as a result of domestic violence or abuse, and the couple need not have actually divorced or terminated a civil partnership.[17] In contrast, the EEA Regulations required that divorce proceedings had been initiated for retained rights to be engaged (see p249).

These applications can be complex, so if you think you are eligible to make an application because you hold a retained right, seek specialist advice before applying.

Derivative rights and the EUSS

The EUSS also allows people who have a 'derivative right of residence' under the EEA Regulations to make an application for settled or pre-settled status under the scheme. The deadline for these applications has now passed, but late applications are possible.

Derivative rights include the rights to reside as the carer of certain EEA national children, known as 'Chen' or 'Ibrahim/Texeira' rights after the cases that established them, and as the carer of certain British children, known as 'Zambrano' rights (see p261). These applications are complex, particularly as the EUSS deadline has now passed and because paper application forms are required. If you are considering a Zambrano application, you should seek specialist immigration advice.

A key change under the EUSS for carers with derivative rights is that they can access settled status after five years of residence, whereas they could not have progressed to permanent residence under the EEA Regulations.

For Zambrano carers (primary carers of British citizens – children or dependent adults), there is an additional barrier to gaining leave under the EUSS in that applicants must not already hold leave to remain under another part of the Immigration Rules. This was the subject of a recent court challenge and the Court of Appeal ordered the Home Office to redraft the EUSS rules for Zambrano carers. The Home Office has since redrafted the rules, but it has maintained the position that only people who do not hold another form of leave to remain under the Immigration Rules can receive pre-settled or settled status as a Zambrano carer.[18] This issue is likely to be the subject of ongoing litigation; see CPAG's *Welfare Rights Bulletin* and the online version of this *Handbook* on AskCPAG for updates. For those who meet the requirements as a Zambrano carer (see p261) and who do not hold leave to remain under another part of the Immigration Rules, the deadline for an EUSS application was 25 July 2022. Applications after this date are possible only where there are reasonable grounds for the lateness and an application is made within a reasonable time (see p64).

Family members of British citizens under the EUSS ('Surinder Singh' cases)

Certain family members of British citizens can gain leave under the EUSS. This is based on the EEA right to reside of non-EEA citizen family members of British citizens, returning to the UK after exercising treaty rights in an EEA member state. This is known as the 'Surinder Singh' route and can apply when, for example, a British citizen has lived and worked in another European Union (EU) country with a non-EEA family member and then seeks to return to the UK with them.[19] See p244 for a full explanation of the requirements.

Specific deadlines to return to the UK currently apply to EUSS applications from the family members of British citizens, which vary from the normal deadlines set out above.

- If the British citizen was already in a relationship with a spouse, civil partner or durable partner before 31 January 2020, they can return to the UK under the EUSS until 29 March 2022 (or later in cases which the Secretary of State is satisfied that there are reasonable grounds for the person's failure to meet that deadline).[20]
- If the relationship began after 31 January 2020 and before 31 December 2020, however, they must have returned to the UK before 31 December 2020 to be eligible for leave under the EUSS.[21]

It is possible to make a late Surinder Singh application, but you will need to justify reasonable grounds beyond your control. These applications are complex. Seek specialist advice if you are making an application.

Note: the family members of Northern Irish citizens can apply to the EUSS using the main route for family members (see p57).

How to apply to the EUSS

Most applications to the EUSS are made online, via the Home Office website.[22] However, people applying based on derivative rights (see p61) or without a valid passport or EEA identity card need to telephone the Home Office's EU Settlement Resolution Centre to request a paper application form which must be posted back to the Home Office.[23]

Those who can make an online application need to download an app (the EU Exit: ID Document Check app) onto a smartphone. This app will scan the biometric chip in your passport and take your photograph. The app is designed to be used by individuals without legal assistance, but if you need help there are a number of support organisations that have funding to assist. These are listed on the Home Office's website.[24] You may wish to contact a support organisation to help either if you have difficulty with managing the online application or if you have a more complicated case – eg, if you are making a late application (see p64) or an application without ID, or if you are relying on retained or derivative rights (see p60 and p61), or if you have any concerns about triggering the suitability criteria (see p59).

When you apply to the EUSS, you are asked whether you wish to apply for settled status or pre-settled status. If you have lived in the UK for five years or more, it is important that you request settled status, because settled status provides greater rights.

During the application you will have the option to enter your national insurance number, which will allow the Home Office to run an automated check with HM Revenue and Customs and the DWP for evidence that you have been living in the UK. Alternatively, you can upload your own residency evidence.

5. Progressing from pre-settled status to settled status

It is crucial for people with pre-settled status to apply for settled status when they reach five years of continuous residence. Pre-settled status does not automatically convert to settled status, and those who fail to apply risk becoming overstayers when their pre-settled status expires. The requirement for those with pre-settled status to make a second application to the European Union Settlement Scheme (EUSS) for settled status, and the loss of rights if this is not done before pre-settled status expires, has recently been found to be unlawful by the High Court.[25] At the time of writing, although the Home Office had been granted permission to appeal, it announced in February 2023 that it would not appeal. Changes need to be made to the EUSS to take account of the High Court judgment. You should ensure you apply for settled status as soon as you are eligible and before your pre-settled status expires.

If you hold pre-settled status and wish to progress in due course to settled status, you must be careful not to break the continuity of your residence through being outside the UK for more than six months at a time, except for important reasons (see p58). This is because settled status requires five years of continuous residence.

You can apply for settled status as soon as you have five years of continuous residence in the UK. You do not need to wait until you have held pre-settled status for five years.

Example

Lenka is a Polish national. She arrived in the UK in January 2017 and received pre-settled status in January 2020, which is valid for five years. She can apply for settled status in January 2022 and does not need to wait for her pre-settled status to expire. She must, however, be careful not to be outside the UK for longer than a six-month consecutive period, or up to a year for specified reasons, or she will break her continuity of residence and be unable to progress to settled status.

In addition, Appendix EU requires that for people with pre-settled status to progress to settled status they must continue to meet the eligibility criteria – ie, you must continue to be either a European Economic Area (EEA) national or the family member of an EEA national.[26]

This means that if you were granted pre-settled status as the family member of an EEA national, but the relationship then ends or the EEA national leaves the UK before obtaining five years of residence, you are not expected to be able to progress to settled status unless you can meet the requirements for a 'retained right of residence' – eg, through divorce (see p249).[27] If you are a family member of an EEA national and the relationship breaks down due to domestic violence, see p60.

Those granted pre-settled status on the basis of dependency as a child, parent or other relative will not need to evidence that they remain dependent to progress to settled status.[28]

6. Late applications to the European Union Settlement Scheme

The deadline to apply to the European Union Settlement Scheme (EUSS) for European Economic Area (EEA) nationals (and those family members who were already resident in the UK by 31 December 2020) was 30 June 2021. After this date, if you have not applied you will not be lawfully present in the UK. You will lose the right to work, to rent, to hold bank accounts and other rights, and you may be removed from the UK.

If you have missed the application deadline of 30 June 2021 and do not yet have leave granted under the EUSS, you should seek urgent immigration advice from a specialist adviser.

It is possible to make a late application to the EUSS after 30 June 2021. For a late application to be accepted, you must have 'reasonable grounds' for your late application and you must apply within a 'reasonable' time period.

As long as you can show reasonable grounds for your late application and you have applied within a reasonable time, you can still obtain leave under the EUSS. So, there is presently no absolute cut-off point for new applications.

Home Office guidance advises that the reason for failing to meet the 30 June 2021 deadline must be provided with the application.[29] Home Office caseworkers are instructed to look for reasons to grant leave and to treat each case on an individual basis. Examples of reasons for missing the deadline that are more likely to be accepted as reasonable are given in the Home Office guidance:[30]

- if the applicant is a child, or was a child, at the time of the deadline;
- physical or mental capacity;
- care or support needs;
- serious medical condition or serious medical treatment;
- victim of trafficking/modern slavery;
- abusive or controlling relationship or situation;
- other compelling practical or compassionate reasons;
- applicant was exempt from immigration control;
- applicant had existing leave;
- applicant had a valid document or leave under the Immigration (European Economic Area) Regulations.

To demonstrate that you have applied within a reasonable time, you will also need to explain when you became aware that you needed to make an EUSS explanation and set out what you have done since then to progress your application.

Example

Gabor is a Hungarian national. He came to the UK in 2012. He has addiction issues and has been sofa surfing and sleeping rough. He was not aware of the EUSS and has not made an application. Gabor recently received support from an addiction service. Its staff have explained to him that he needs to apply for settled status so that he can access public funds. Gabor makes an application, with evidence of his addiction issues and homelessness to show that he has reasonable grounds for his late application and that he has applied within a reasonable time. He is granted settled status.

If you are waiting for an application to be decided

If you applied to the EUSS before 30 June 2021 but have not yet received a decision, and if you had a right to reside under the EEA Regulations on 31 December 2020, you can continue to have the same or a different right to reside under the EEA Regulations until your application to the Home Office (including any appeals against a refusal) is determined. This means that you will continue to be lawfully resident while you wait for your application to be decided.

If you did not have a right to reside on 31 December 2020, or if you applied after the deadline on 30 June 2021, if you then make a valid EUSS application you will be lawfully present in the UK while you wait for your decision.

If you need the Home Office to make a decision more quickly on your case (eg, so that you can access public funds), you can try telephoning the EU Settlement Resolution Centre to explain your circumstances and request that your case be prioritised. Cases are more likely to be prioritised if you can provide evidence that the delay is causing you hardship – eg, if you are homeless or unable to access support that you require.

Deadlines for EUSS applications

The general deadline to apply to the EUSS was, in most circumstances, 30 June 2021. However, applications can continue to be made since that date (see p64).

In specific circumstances other deadlines applied or continue to apply:[31]

- you are the family member of an EEA national, who was living in the UK by 31 December 2020, and you join them in the UK on or after 1 April 2021 with a family permit, though you will need to apply to the EUSS within three months of your arrival;[32] *or*
- you are applying for your child, who was born or adopted in the UK on or after 1 April 2021;[33] *or*
- you are the family member of an eligible person of Northern Ireland, but they could not move back to the UK by 31 December 2020 without you (you must be from outside the European Union (EU), Switzerland, Norway, Iceland or Liechtenstein); *or*
- you are exempt from immigration control, or you stopped being exempt from immigration control after 30 June 2021; *or*
- you have another type of limited leave (eg, if you are here on a work or study visa) that expires after 30 June 2021;[34] *or*
- Surinder Singh cases – ie, the family members of British citizens who have lived together with the British citizen in the EU (see p62).

7. Challenging European Union Settlement Scheme decisions

If you have been refused leave under the European Union Settlement Scheme (EUSS), or if you have been granted pre-settled status when you think you should have received settled status, you can either make a new application or challenge the decision by administrative review and/or (depending on the date of application) by appeal. If you are in this position, seek specialist advice.

The decision letter you receive should explain your options for challenging the decision.

Making a **new application** might assist if you already have pre-settled status and you have been refused settled status due to a lack of evidence. You could consider gathering additional evidence and then making a new free of charge application as soon as possible.

Administrative review is asking the Home Office to look again at its decision on the basis that an error has been made, or that the decision is not in line with guidance, or where new information/evidence has become available. A fee is charged for this. Reviews are carried out by the Home Office, but by a different member of staff. Administrative review is available when an eligible decision[35] has been made.[36] This means that there is a right to an administrative review against a decision to:

- refuse an application under paragraph EU6 of Appendix EU because the applicant does not meet the eligibility requirements for indefinite leave to enter or remain under paragraphs EU11, EU11A or EU12 or for limited leave to enter or remain under paragraphs EU14 or EU14A;
- grant limited leave to enter or remain under paragraph EU3 of Appendix EU and not indefinite leave to enter or remain under paragraph EU2;
- grant limited leave to enter or remain under paragraph EU3A of Appendix EU and not indefinite leave to enter or remain under paragraph EU2A;
- cancel leave granted under Appendix EU on the grounds that the person ceases to meet the requirements of that appendix for that leave.

Appeals to the First-tier Tribunal are also possible for anyone who makes a valid application under Appendix EU on or after 11pm on 31 January 2020. They will have a right of appeal against a decision to:

- refuse their application on eligibility or suitability grounds; *or*
- grant pre-settled status when they believe they qualify for settled status; *or*
- when they have settled status or pre-settled status and a relevant decision is made on or after 11pm on 31 January 2020 to cancel, curtail or revoke that leave or make a deportation order in relation to them.[37]

8. **Arriving from 1 January 2021 onwards**

European Economic Area nationals newly arriving, *not* joining family already resident in the UK

European Economic Area (EEA) nationals coming to live in the UK for the first time from 1 January 2021 onwards will not be able to apply to the European Union Settlement Scheme (EUSS) unless they are joining family already resident in the UK.

If EEA nationals want to visit the UK, they can obtain six months' limited leave as a visitor on arrival. This leave will be automatically generated when you enter the UK through airport passport e-gates and you will not be provided with any documentation. Like any other person granted leave to enter as a visitor, you will not have the right to work and will be subject to a 'no recourse to public funds' restriction.

EEA nationals who want to live in the UK from 1 January 2021 will need to apply for leave to remain using one of the existing immigration routes open to non-EEA nationals. See Chapter 3.

Family members arriving to join European Economic Area nationals already resident in the UK

If you were already the family member of an EEA national on or before 31 December 2020 and continue to be so, and the EEA national was already resident in the UK before 31 December 2020, you have a right to join that person in the UK. That applies to both family members who are EEA nationals and family members who are non-EEA nationals. There are two potential options for family members to come to the UK in this way: EUSS family permits and EUSS travel permits.

EUSS family permits

The EUSS family permit is a type of entry clearance. It enables an eligible family member of an EEA national, or of a qualifying British citizen, to travel to and enter the UK.[38]

A family member of an EEA national may be eligible for an EUSS family permit if the EEA national:

- was resident in the UK before 31 December 2020; *and*
- holds leave under EUSS.

To be eligible as a family member, you must not have been resident in the UK before 31 December 2020 (unless you have broken your continuity of residence since), and your family relationship with the EEA national must have been established before this date.[39] These provisions apply to direct family members and also to durable partners. For durable partners, the relationship must have been durable before 31 December 2020 and the partner either must not have yet moved to the UK or have ended a previous period of residence in the UK – eg, through absence.

Entry clearance in the form of an EUSS family permit will be granted for a period of six months from the date of the decision.[40]

After your arrival, you will need to make an application to the EUSS. Those who arrived before 31 March 2021 must have applied to the EUSS by 30 June 2021, and family members arriving after that date must apply to the EUSS within three months of their arrival date.[41]

For information on EUSS travel permits, see below.

Applying to the EUSS from outside the UK

A family member of an EEA national may also apply to the EUSS from outside the UK, if they have the required proof of entitlement to apply from outside the UK.

- For EEA nationals, this means a valid passport or a valid national identity card with a biometric chip.
- For non-EEA nationals, this means a biometric residence card issued under the EEA Regulations or a biometric residence card issued under the EUSS – ie, if the person already has pre-settled status and wants to apply for settled status from outside the UK.

EUSS travel permits

Some non-EEA nationals will be issued with a biometric residence card under the EUSS. Other non-EEA citizens will have used a biometric residence card issued under the EEA Regulations as their evidence of identity when they applied to the EUSS, and so their leave under the EUSS will be linked to that old card. If these people lose their biometric residence card while they are outside the UK, they may have problems proving their right to return to the UK.

The EUSS travel permit provides those non-EEA citizens who hold valid leave under the EUSS, and who have reported to the Home Office that their biometric residence card has been lost or stolen or has expired while they are outside the UK, with an entry clearance which, together with a valid passport, will allow them to travel to the UK. Once granted, they will need to travel to the UK within six months. Once in the UK, they can apply for a replacement biometric residence card.[42]

9. **Frontier workers**

Frontier workers are European Economic Area (EEA) nationals who live in one country and work in another.

Before 31 December 2020, it was straightforward for an EEA national to work in the UK while living in another country, because this was permitted under European Union free movement law. EEA nationals could cross the border into the UK simply by showing their passport or national identity card.

EEA nationals who were cross-border working in the UK before 31 December 2020 may be able to access frontier worker rights through a frontier worker permit.[43] There is currently no deadline to apply for a frontier worker permit, though frontier workers have needed to hold permits since 1 July 2021 in order to work cross-border.

Frontier worker permits are valid for five years, with the exception of those granted on the basis of retained residence rights, which are valid for two years.

Frontier worker permits do not provide a route to settlement in the UK.

A frontier worker permit gives a right of admission to the UK rather than leave to enter: it is a right to be admitted, rather than a permission. A person who has a right of admission to the UK as a frontier worker, and from 30 June 2021 who holds a frontier worker permit, does not require leave to enter or remain the UK for the duration of their permit.

Who is eligible for a frontier worker permit

A person will be eligible for a frontier worker permit if they meet certain conditions, which must have been met:

- immediately before 11pm on 31 December 2020; *and*
- continuously since then.

The conditions are that the person is:

- an EEA national; *and*
- not primarily resident in the UK, which means:
  - they have been present in the UK for less than 180 days in the previous 12 months; *or*
  - they have returned to their country of residence at least once in the previous six months; *or*
  - they have returned to their country of residence at least twice in the previous 12 months; *and*
- a worker or self-employed person in the UK, or a person with retained worker or self-employed status. A person retains worker or self-employed status in certain situations, such as being temporarily unable to work due to illness or an accident.[44]

If you meet these conditions (both before 31 December 2020 and continuously since), you are entitled to apply for and be issued a frontier worker permit. You will then have a right of admission to the UK when you produce a valid identity document and a valid frontier worker permit.[45]

How to apply for a frontier worker permit

Applications are made online at gov.uk/frontier-worker-permit/apply and, similarly to the European Union Settlement Scheme (EUSS), can be made via a smartphone app. Applications are free of charge, and can be made both inside and outside the UK. Note that although there is no deadline to apply, on 1 July 2021 these permits became compulsory for cross-border work, so as time goes on it is less and less likely that you will be able to evidence that you have met the conditions specified above.

Family members of frontier workers

Family members of frontier workers cannot obtain frontier worker permits. They can apply to the EUSS instead.

If the frontier worker's family member is already resident in the UK, then the family member can apply to the EUSS on the basis of their relationship with the frontier worker. The deadline for EUSS applications was 30 June 2021, so family members applying late will need to provide an explanation and apply as soon as possible. **Note:** the frontier worker themself does not need to be eligible under the EUSS for a family member to use this route; it is sufficient that the worker meets the requirements for a frontier worker permit.

Alternatively, if the frontier worker's family member is outside the UK, the family member can apply for an EUSS family permit to come to the UK to join the frontier worker (see p67).

10. Documentation under the European Union Settlement Scheme

Most European Economic Area (EEA) nationals who are granted settled or pre-settled leave are not given any physical evidence of their status. Instead, you will receive an email confirming your grant of status and containing a 16-digit reference number. The leave holder can login to the government's status-checking website (gov.uk/view-prove-immigration-status), using the email address and the details of the passport or ID card connected to their status. This website allows you to generate a share code to provide to employers, landlords and others to prove your leave.

Non-EEA family members of EEA nationals will usually receive biometric residence permits (BRPs) confirming their leave under the European Settlement Scheme (EUSS). However, if the family member already held a BRP under the EEA Regulations, they will normally keep this permit and will not be issued with a new permit under the EUSS until their EEA Regulations permit expires.

As many people have only digital evidence of their leave under EUSS, it is vital to update the Home Office if you change your name, renew your passport/ID card or if you change the phone number or email address that is connected to your leave.

Anyone experiencing difficulty with evidencing their leave digitally is advised to seek legal advice – eg, if you are unable to claim benefits or receive housing assistance that you would otherwise be entitled to, you should seek advice.[46]

For the status of residence documents issued under the EEA Regulations, see p503.

11. Deportation

The rules for deporting European Economic Area (EEA) nationals and their family members changed on 1 January 2021. For any offences committed before 11pm on 31 December 2020, the more generous rights provided by the EEA Regulations continue to apply.[47] For offences committed after this time, the new stricter deportation rules apply.

Deportation rules for offences committed before 31 December 2020

EEA nationals and their family members who committed criminal offences prior to 31 December 2020 can only be deported from the UK for public policy, public security or public health reasons.[48] This applies even if the prosecution and conviction takes place on or after 1 January 2021; it is the date of the offence that matters. The pre-31 December 2020 domestic and Court of Justice of the European Union caselaw on deportation will, therefore, remain relevant.

A decision made on public policy, public security or public health grounds must:

- not be taken for the economic benefit of the UK; *and*
- be 'proportionate'; *and*
- be based exclusively on the conduct of the individual concerned, which must represent a genuine, present and sufficiently serious threat, affecting one of the fundamental interests of society; *and*
- be for reasons that relate to your case in particular, rather than being intended to deter others; *and*
- not be justified by a person's previous criminal convictions alone; *and*
- only be made after taking into account the person's age, state of health, family and economic situation, their length of residence in the UK, their social and cultural integration in the UK, and the extent of their links with their country of origin.

EEA nationals and family members with five years' continuous lawful residence cannot be deported unless there are 'serious' grounds of public policy or public security. An EEA national who has resided in the UK for 10 years cannot be excluded or removed except on imperative grounds of public security.[49] Similarly, an EEA national aged under 18 cannot be excluded or removed unless it is in their best interests or their removal is imperative on grounds of public security.[50]

Both settled and pre-settled grants of leave can be lost if they were obtained fraudulently. Pre-settled status can also be lost if a person ceases to meet the requirements and removal of the leave is considered to be proportionate.

Deportation rules for offences committed after 31 December 2020

If you commit a criminal offence after 31 December 2020, any deportation proceedings will be decided by national law. This allows EEA nationals and family members to be deported if it is considered to be 'conducive to the public good' (see p26).

This is a much harsher threshold. It is the same deportation test that applies to other non-EEA immigration routes in the UK. See Chapter 2 for further details of specific deportation criteria based on the conducive to the public good test.

Notes

3. The European Union Settlement Scheme

1 Home Office caseworker guidance, *EU Settlement Scheme: EU, other EEA and Swiss citizens and their family members*, version 18.0, 9 November 2022, p25

4. Leave under the European Union Settlement Scheme

2 *Independent Monitoring Authority v Secretary of State for the Home Department* [2022] EWHC 3274 (Admin)
3 Appendix EU Annex 1, definition of 'continuous qualifying period', IR
4 Appendix EU Annex 1, definition of 'continuous qualifying period', IR
5 Home Office caseworker guidance, *EU Settlement Scheme: EU, other EEA and Swiss citizens and their family members*, version 18.0, 9 November 2022, p159
6 Home Office caseworker guidance, *EU Settlement Scheme: EU, other EEA and Swiss citizens and their family members*, version 18.0, 9 November 2022, p159
7 Appendix EU EU11(4), (5) and (6), IR
8 Appendix EU EU11(7), IR
9 Appendix EU Annex 1, definition of 'continuous qualifying period', IR
10 Home Office caseworker guidance, *EU Settlement Scheme: EU, other EEA and Swiss citizens and their family members*, version 18.0, 9 November 2022, p232
11 Appendix EU Annex 3, IR
12 Appendix EU EU15(1), IR
13 Appendix EU EU16, IR
14 Home Office caseworker guidance, *EU Settlement Scheme: suitability requirements*, version 8.0, 24 January 2023, p14
15 Home Office caseworker guidance, *EU Settlement Scheme: suitability requirements*, version 8.0, 24 January 2023, p28
16 Home Office caseworker guidance, *EU Settlement Scheme: suitability requirements*, version 8.0, 24 January 2023, p28
17 Home Office caseworker guidance, *EU Settlement Scheme: EU, other EEA and Swiss citizens and their family members*, version 18.0, 9 November 2022, p206
18 gov.uk/government/publications/eu-settlement-scheme-zambrano-primary-carers
19 Home Office caseworker guidance, *EU Settlement Scheme: family member of a qualifying British citizen*, version 5.0, 9 November 2022, p7
20 Appendix EU Annex 1, definitions of 'qualifying British citizen' and 'family member of a qualifying British citizen', IR
21 Appendix EU Annex 1, definitions of 'family member of a qualifying British citizen' and 'qualifying British citizen', IR

22 gov.uk/settled-status-eu-citizens-families/applying-for-settled-status
23 gov.uk/contact-ukvi-inside-outside-uk/y/inside-the-uk/applying-to-continue-living-in-the-uk-including-settled-and-pre-settled-status/using-the-eu-exit-id-document-check-app
24 gov.uk/government/publications/eu-settlement-scheme-community-support-for-vulnerable-citizens/list-of-organisations

5. **Progressing from pre-settled status to settled status**

25 *Independent Monitoring Authority v Secretary of State for the Home Department* [2022] EWHC 3274 (Admin)
26 Appendix EU EU4, IR
27 Appendix EU Annex 1, definition of 'family member who has retained the right of residence', IR
28 Appendix EU EU4, IR

6. **Late applications to the European Union Settlement Scheme**

29 Home Office caseworker guidance, *EU Settlement Scheme: EU, other EEA and Swiss citizens and their family members*, version 18.0, 9 November 2022, p32
30 Home Office caseworker guidance, *EU Settlement Scheme: EU, other EEA and Swiss citizens and their family members*, version 18.0, 9 November 2022, pp37-50
31 gov.uk/settled-status-eu-citizens-families/eligibility
32 In this scenario, you need to apply to the EUSS within three months of arrival in the UK
33 In this scenario, you need to apply to the EUSS within three months of the date your child was born or adopted
34 In such scenarios, you need to apply before your leave expires: Appendix EU Annex 1, definition of 'required date', IR

7. **Challenging European Union Settlement Scheme decisions**

35 As set out in para AR(EU)1.1. Appendix EU, IR
36 See also Home Office caseworker guidance, *Administrative Review: EU Settlement Scheme*, version 7.0, 27 September 2022, p5
37 Home Office caseworker guidance, *EU Settlement Scheme: EU, other EEA and Swiss citizens and their family members*, version 18.0, 9 November 2022, p235

8. **Arriving from 1 January 2021 onwards**

38 Home Office caseworker guidance, *EU Settlement Scheme Family Permit and Travel Permit*, version 14.0, 9 November 2022, p9
39 Appendix EU (Family Permit) Annex 1, definition of 'joining family member of a relevant sponsor', IR
40 Home Office caseworker guidance, *EU Settlement Scheme Family Permit and Travel Permit*, version 14.0, 9 November 2022, p11
41 Home Office caseworker guidance, *EU Settlement Scheme Family Permit and Travel Permit*, version 14.0, 9 November 2022, pp11-12
42 Home Office caseworker guidance, *EU Settlement Scheme Family Permit and Travel Permit*, version 14.0, 9 November 2022, p13

9. **Frontier workers**

43 CR(FW) Regs
44 Reg 4 CR(FW) Regs
45 Reg 6 CR(FW) Regs

10. **Documentation under the European Union Settlement Scheme**

46 A judicial review challenging the potentially discriminatory impact of a 'digital-only' status was refused permission, principally on the basis of being prematurely brought (the hearing was in April 2021): *The 3million Ltd, R (on the Application of) v Secretary of State for the Home Department* [2021] EWHC 1159 (Admin)

11. **Deportation**

47 Reg 2 Citizens' Rights (Restrictions of Rights of Entry and Residence) (EU Exit) Regulations 2020 No.1210; Regs 3 and 7 CR(ADTP) Regs
48 s10 EU(W)A 2020
49 Reg 21(4)(b) I(EEA) Regs
50 Reg 21 I(EEA) Regs

Chapter 6

Checking your immigration status

This chapter covers:

1. Introduction

This chapter explains how to check your immigration status to establish your entitlement to social security benefits.

You can usually identify your immigration status in the UK from your biometric residence permit, your passport and any endorsements in it by the UK immigration authorities (eg, stamps, stickers or vignettes), from a grant of status letter from the Home Office, or through an online status checker.

Note: your status (or nationality) may have changed since your passport, endorsement or card was issued, or you may not hold any of these, including if the item has been lost or stolen.

If your immigration status is uncertain, you should contact a specialist adviser. A list of advisers and organisations is included in Appendix 2.

Note: anyone who gives immigration advice must be professionally regulated. For further details, see p7.

2. British nationals and people with the right of abode

If you are a British national, you can apply to HM Passport Office for a **UK passport** (see Appendix 6, Figure 1). However, not all British nationals have been issued with a passport and your British nationality does not depend on your being a passport holder.

All British nationals, not just British citizens, can apply for a UK passport and it is important to distinguish between the different types of British nationality when checking your immigration status (see p15). Your passport specifies the type of British nationality you have. Holders of UK passports who have the right of abode in the UK are described as: 'British citizens or British subjects with the right of abode in the UK'.

Note: UK passports may also be issued to people whose right of abode is awaiting verification. The passport contains the endorsement: 'The holder's status under the Immigration Act 1971 has not yet been determined.'

If you have been granted British citizenship after applying to register or naturalise as a British citizen, you will have been issued with a certificate confirming this (see Appendix 6, Figure 2).

If you have the right of abode in the UK and are also a national of another Commonwealth country, you may have a **certificate of entitlement** endorsed in a passport issued by that country (see Appendix 6, Figure 3).

Although rare, a **certificate of patriality** issued under the Immigration Act 1971, and which was valid immediately before 1 January 1983, is regarded as a certificate of entitlement unless the holder no longer has the right of abode – eg, if you have renounced this, or if there has been independence legislation.[1]

Some people with the right of abode in the UK may hold a **confirmation of 'right of abode' document**. This was a non-statutory document issued for a brief period before the commencement of the Immigration Act 1988 to dual nationals with the right of abode who had opted to travel on non-British passports.

If you do not hold a passport or certificate confirming your British citizenship or right of abode, you may be able to prove that you have this status in some other way – eg, by producing a birth certificate showing that you were born in the UK before 1983 or after this date if, when you were born, one of your parents was British or had indefinite leave. If your claim to British citizenship or the right of abode is complicated, you may need to prove descent from your parents and/or grandparents, and/or marriage to a person and that person's place of birth, ancestry and/or nationality status at specific times. If this applies to you, it may be helpful to get specialist immigration advice to check your citizenship and/or right of abode.

3. People with leave to enter or remain

Entry clearance confirming leave to enter

Entry clearance is endorsed by a sticker (known as a '**vignette**') placed in your passport or travel document, or by data stored digitally in an identity card and government database (see p79).

The vignette endorsement may be designated as a visa, entry clearance, European Union Settlement Scheme (EUSS) family permit or a European Economic Area (EEA) family permit. Applications for an EEA family permit under the EEA Regulations 2016 had to be made by 30 June 2021. See p503 for more information about these types of documents.

Two types of vignette are now issued. The type of vignette depends on the type of entry clearance you are given. Both include a photograph of the holder (see Appendix 6, Figure 9). Older versions look similar, but without a photograph (see Appendix 6, Figure 8). Even older ones comprise a smaller sticker, signed and date-stamped by an official (similar to the leave to remain endorsement vignette shown in Appendix 6, Figure 8).

Accompanying dependants whose details were included in the main applicant's passport might have received their own vignettes, fixed in the main applicant's passport.

Entry clearance granting you leave to enter allows you to enter the UK at a port without having to demonstrate that you satisfy the requirements of the Immigration Rules (unless you commit an act of fraud or there is a material change in circumstances). The vignette endorsement is usually date-stamped on entry (see Appendix 6, Figure 10) and confirms that you have been granted leave to enter the UK, often for the remaining period of validity stated on the vignette.

In some circumstances, an immigration officer can vary or extend your leave on your arrival in the UK.

The date the entry clearance first becomes valid is usually the same as the date of authorisation. As the holder, you may present yourself for initial entry under the entry clearance at any time during its validity. However, entry clearance officers have the discretion to defer the date the entry clearance first becomes valid for up to three months after authorisation if, for example, you wish to delay travelling to the UK.

If you are granted entry clearance, you may travel to, and remain in, the UK for the purpose for which it was granted. You may be able to travel in and out of the UK repeatedly, provided your entry clearance remains valid. However, if entry clearance has been authorised for multiple journeys to the UK of a fixed duration (eg, under the visitor category of the Immigration Rules), the duration of each visit is limited to a maximum of six months. This limitation is stated on the vignette under the heading 'duration of stay'.

If you are granted entry clearance with a vignette for leave to enter on certain conditions (eg, as a student on condition that you do not work except in authorised employment and do not have recourse to public funds), these should be stated on the endorsement (see Appendix 6, Figure 9). However, if you have been granted entry clearance for leave to enter on the basis of a maintenance undertaking (see p37), the reference on the vignette may be the name of the family member whom you are joining and there may be no indication that a maintenance undertaking has been given.

Entry clearance vignettes for employment, study and settlement are now usually valid for 30 or 90 days to enable the holder to travel to the UK and collect their **biometric residence permit** (BRP) card (see p79).You must usually collect this card before the vignette sticker in your travel document expires or within 10 days of arriving in the UK, whichever is later.[2] For those granted leave to enter for less than six months (eg, because they have been granted leave in line with their sponsor and their sponsor's leave is about to expire), a BRP may only be obtained once an in-country application for an extension of leave has been granted.

EUSS family permit vignettes issued to non-EEA national family members of EEA nationals with status under the EUSS are valid for four or six months. If you have entered the UK on an EUSS family permit, you are required to make an application under the EUSS within 90 days of your arrival in the UK. If you are a non-EEA national you will get a BRP if your application under the EUSS is granted.[3] See p85 and Chapter 5 for more information.

Leave to enter without entry clearance

Nationals of some countries cannot enter the UK for any purpose without first obtaining entry clearance (visa nationals). Others can apply at the port of entry for leave to enter for some of the purposes provided for under the Immigration Rules.

It is sometimes difficult to identify the purpose for which an endorsement of leave to enter has been given if someone made an application at the port of entry. If limited leave has been granted, the endorsement may be an **ink stamp**, stating the duration of the leave period for which leave is granted and the conditions (if any) attached to the leave (see Appendix 6, Figure 8). Each stamped endorsement by an immigration officer granting leave to someone without entry clearance should be accompanied by a rectangular date stamp, showing when the leave was granted.

Since 1 January 2020, European Union and non-visa nationals may have entered the UK through a passport eGate, in which case their status may be held electronically as an eVisa. That is also referred to as digital-only status.

The example shown in Appendix 6, Figure 8 is the endorsement usually made in the passport of someone given leave to enter at a port of entry as a visitor or student on a short course (of six months or less). The endorsement shows that leave has been granted on condition that the holder does not engage in any employment or have recourse to public funds.

If you are returning to the UK and already have indefinite leave to enter or remain, you may simply be given a date stamp on being readmitted.

If you leave the UK and return during a period of leave that has been given for more than six months, an immigration officer may endorse a grant of leave to enter with the same conditions, using an ink stamp stating this.[4]

If you are, or were, a Commonwealth citizen and you entered the UK before the Immigration Act 1971 came into force, you may have received an ink stamp on entry with no conditions attached. You are known as 'freely landed'. You may have been treated as having been given indefinite leave to enter or remain when the 1971 Act came into force and might have retained this status by remaining resident in the UK (see p30).

Leave to remain granted in the UK

The UK **residence permit** replaced all former stamp and ink endorsements for permission to stay in the UK for longer than six months. The permit was previously a vignette, without biometric data and similar in appearance to that used to endorse entry clearance (see p77), and included a photograph of the holder (see Appendix 6, Figure 8). The vignette has been replaced by BRPs (see below).

Previously, leave may have been endorsed using a smaller vignette sticker or by a rectangular stamp accompanied by a pentagonal date stamp (see Appendix 6, Figure 8).

If you were granted leave to remain on certain conditions (eg, as a student on condition that you do not work except in authorised employment and do not have recourse to public funds), these should be stated on the permit (see Appendix 6, Figure 9). However, if you were granted leave to remain on the basis of a maintenance undertaking (see p37), this is not stated on the permit.

Biometric residence permits

Biometric residence permit (BRP) cards for foreign nationals have replaced the vignette (sticker) endorsements and other UK immigration status documents (see Appendix 6, Figure 5). If your leave to remain has been granted in the UK, you are issued with a BRP as an alternative to having a sticker or ink stamp endorsement placed in your passport, which is not endorsed with your immigration status at all. If you have been granted leave to enter the UK, you will collect your BRP after you have arrived in the UK (see p78).

A BRP is a plastic card, the same size as a debit or credit card, which bears the holder's photograph, name, date of birth, nationality and immigration status. An electronic chip attached to the card holds digitised biometric details, including fingerprints, a facial image and biographical information (including name, and date and place of birth).

The card also shows details of your immigration status and entitlements in the UK, including what kind of leave you have and whether you can work. A database holds a record of the biometrics of every person to whom a card has been issued, so these can be cross-checked.

If you have the new BRP, you may need to inform the Home Office of specified changes in your circumstances. If you fail to do so, you may face prosecution or other sanctions (see p36). You must also notify the Home Office if your BRP is lost or stolen, within three months of the loss or theft.

BRPs are currently issued with a validity date of no later than 31 December 2024, regardless of the length of leave granted. Many people will, therefore, be issued with BRPs that expire sooner than their leave expires. Often, you will have received separate paperwork from the Home Office which states the actual expiry date of your leave. You can also enter your BRP reference number and your date of birth on a Home Office website and create a share code. In this way, you can prove that you have the right to rent or the right to work until a certain date.[5] You will not need a BRP to prove your status from 1 January 2025. The Home Office website states that you will be able to prove your immigration status online, without a BRP. Details of how to prove your immigration status online will be published in early 2024.[6]

Leave extended for an application, appeal or administrative review

Limited leave is automatically extended beyond the date it is due to expire if you make a valid application to extend or vary your leave before this date.[7] Leave extended in this way (called section 3C leave) continues on the same conditions as before, until a decision is made by the Home Office. If the Home Office refuses your application, and you make an in-time appeal, your leave continues until any in-country appeal rights or rights to administrative review are exhausted (unless the Home Office makes a separate decision to cancel your section 3C leave, which can happen in cases of deception or when you have breached the conditions of your leave). The same conditions attached to your original leave continue to apply during the extension (apart from the time limit).

The Home Office can take a long time to decide applications, and appeals against refusals to vary or to extend leave can take longer still, so you may have your leave extended in this way for many months, or even years. Also, if the result of the administrative review is significantly different or additional reasons are given for upholding the decision, you may apply for a further review that, if done in time, extends your leave even further. Your passport or BRP, if you had one when you applied, may be retained during this time. For these reasons, it can be difficult to show that your leave is ongoing. The Home Office may acknowledge a valid application for leave with a letter but does not always do so. However, the Home Office offers to confirm specifically that you have ongoing leave if you request that. There is a UK Visas and Immigration helpline for employers and landlords: see gov.uk/contact-ukvi-inside-outside-uk for details.

Travel and status documents issued to non-UK nationals

Where necessary, leave to enter or leave to remain may in the past have been endorsed on an **immigration status document** (which is simply an A4-sized piece of paper – see Appendix 6, Figure 4). Immigration status documents have been replaced by BRPs.

Refugees are entitled to a **Refugee Convention travel document** (coloured blue), which is similar in format to a passport (see Appendix 6, Figure 11).

A dependant of a refugee or person with humanitarian protection may be granted entry clearance on the basis of refugee family reunion on a standard **'uniform format form'** (UFF), if the dependant has no passport or cannot obtain one. The previous version, **a GV3 document**, had an endorsement stating: 'visa family reunion – sponsor'. The sponsor referred to is the relative with refugee status who the dependant is joining in the UK. This endorsement can confuse benefit decision makers who wrongly assume that a maintenance undertaking has been given (see p130). As with settlement vignette stickers endorsed in passports (see p77), if you hold a UFF document you will usually need to collect your BRP card before your vignette expires or within 10 days of arriving in the UK, whichever is later.

If you are recognised as stateless under the terms of the 1954 United Nations Convention Relating to the Status of Stateless Persons, you are entitled to a **stateless person's document** (coloured red).

If you have indefinite leave but were not recognised as a refugee, or you were granted exceptional leave, discretionary leave or humanitarian protection, you can apply for a **certificate of travel** (coloured black). However, to qualify for such a document, usually you must have applied to your national authorities (if they have a presence in the UK) for a passport or travel document and been formally and unreasonably refused one in writing.

4. People without leave

If you have entered the UK without permission or remained in the UK after your limited leave to enter or remain has expired, you may have committed a criminal offence and could be arrested and detained for removal from the UK. This also applies if you have remained in the UK after you have been refused further leave or had your leave revoked or curtailed and any appeal rights have been exhausted. Any conditions attached to the limited leave that has expired or been revoked or curtailed cease to apply.

If you are in the UK without leave and come to the attention of the Home Office, you are likely to be served with a **notice** informing you that you are liable to be removed from the UK, and explaining why (see Appendix 6, Figure 12). You may also be detained or given immigration bail (see p14). If so, you should have been issued with a notice informing you of this and of any conditions attached.

If further leave has been refused, a line may be drawn through the previous endorsement of leave in your passport. A decision refusing leave to enter at a port may be endorsed by a crossed-through ink date stamp.

You must be notified of any immigration decision in writing. Sending a notice to your last known address or the address of a representative (eg, a solicitor or other regulated person) might be sufficient, so you may not necessarily be aware of a decision concerning you. Get specialist advice if you are in any doubt.

5. Long-term residents and the 'Windrush generation'

Significant restrictive changes to immigration law in the UK came into force on 1 January 1973, under the Immigration Act 1971. Most people who were settled in the UK at that time without any time restriction on their leave retained their right to remain indefinitely, but many of these people do not hold a current passport or other document to show that they have this right.

If you are a Commonwealth citizen settled in the UK before 1 January 1973 (known as the 'Windrush generation') and were still in the UK on this date, you can be assumed to have had no time restriction on your right to be in the UK.

If you are a Commonwealth citizen who arrived in the UK on or after 1 January 1973 and you have been given leave to enter or remain in the UK (including indefinite leave), you have a right to stay in the UK for as long as your leave remains valid.

Spouses and children of Commonwealth citizens who were settled in the UK on 1 January 1973 were admitted to the UK with indefinite leave if they arrived at any time between 1 January 1973 and 1 August 1988, or after 1 August 1988 on a visa that was applied for before 1 August 1988.

Note: indefinite leave can be lost if:

- you are absent from the UK for over two years (for Commonwealth citizens, this only applies after 1 August 1988 – absences of any duration between 1 January 1973 and 1 August 1988 do not matter); *or*

- a deportation order (see p26) has been made against you. However, if you are a Commonwealth citizen, you may be exempt from deportation if you were living in the UK on 1 January 1973 and you have lived in the UK for at least the last five years immediately before deportation is considered (excluding any period of imprisonment of six months or more).

The Windrush Scheme

The Windrush Scheme is designed to assist people of any nationality who have lived in the UK for a long time, but who do not have the documents to prove this. The following people can apply for nationality or immigration documents under the scheme:

- a Commonwealth citizen who settled in the UK before 1 January 1973 or has right of abode;
- a child of a Commonwealth citizen who settled before 1 January 1973, where the child was in the UK or arrived in the UK before the age of 18;
- a person of any nationality who settled in the UK before 31 December 1988 and is still settled in the UK.

The Windrush Compensation Scheme exists to compensate those who have suffered losses because they could not produce documentation to establish immigration status. This might be because they lost a job or were refused employment or have been denied housing, benefits or NHS care free of charge.

The 'Windrush scandal' concerned people of the 'Windrush generation' who were wrongly denied their legal rights, detained, threatened with deportation, removed from the UK or denied re-entry to the UK. After the scandal broke in 2018, the Home Office announced that it would:

- waive the citizenship fee and some of the usual requirements for anyone of the 'Windrush generation' who wishes to apply for citizenship;
- ensure that those who made their lives here but who have now retired to their country of origin are able to return to the UK – the cost of any fees associated with this process will be waived;
- set up a new independent scheme to compensate people who have suffered loss;
- establish a new customer contact centre for anyone affected to get appropriate advice;
- ensure that people who arrived after 1973 but before 1 August 1988 can also access the dedicated Windrush team so they can access the support and assistance needed to establish their right to be in the UK;
- assist those who contact the dedicated Windrush team to obtain evidence of their residence in the UK, including employment and health records.

Note:

- The law in this area is complicated and the Home Office has, for many years, been unreasonable and hostile in its approach to long-term residents without documentation, including applying an unreasonably high standard of proof in cases and only backing down when challenged through the courts.
- A criminal offending history can lead to deportation action being taken, even if someone has been lawfully resident in the UK for many years.
- If the Home Office decides that someone does not have a right to be in the UK, they are at risk of arrest, indefinite detention and enforced removal from the UK.
- If possible, obtain legal advice and assistance before contacting the Home Office.
- Government cuts and high demand mean that legal aid may not be available, even if you are eligible.

6. Asylum seekers

People who have applied for refugee or humanitarian protection leave or other forms of international protection are commonly called 'asylum seekers' (see p41).

Since 2002, the Home Office has issued asylum seekers with an **application registration card** (ARC) (see Appendix 6, Figure 8). The ARC may state whether you have any dependants or permission to work (see p42).

If you claim asylum at a port of entry or if you do not have leave to remain and you claim asylum in-country, you may be given immigration bail (temporary admission before 15 January 2018) as an alternative to immigration detention until your application is decided. If you have been detained, you might have subsequently been granted immigration bail. If you have any of these types of status, you should have been issued with a notice informing you of this and of any conditions (see Appendix 6, Figure 13). See p14 for further information.

If you apply for asylum when you have leave to enter or remain for another purpose, you can apply for your leave to be extended until a decision is made by the Home Office and, if the application is refused, any appeal rights are exhausted.

7. European Economic Area nationals

European Economic Area (EEA) nationals and their family members, who were exercising European free movement rights in the UK, were previously able to obtain certain residence documents issued under the EEA Regulations, although in most cases the rights existed whether or not you held one of these documents. For details, see p503.

Now, if you are an EEA national or family member of an EEA national, you may have been granted leave under the European Union Settlement Scheme (EUSS) or under other parts of the Immigration Rules (see Chapter 5).

Under the European Union Settlement Scheme

If you are an EEA national or the family member of an EEA national, you may have been granted leave to remain, known as 'pre-settled status', or indefinite leave, known as 'settled status', under the EUSS. See Chapter 5 for further details.

For EEA nationals, these forms of status are currently granted electronically. Usually, you will receive an email confirming your grant of leave and containing a 16-digit reference number. This reference number acts as an electronic token, which can be used on the Home Office's website to view and confirm the grant of leave.[8] You will be given a 'share code', which proves your status to others.

The correspondence confirming a grant of 'settled status' or 'pre-settled status' under the EUSS makes it clear that the grant email (or letter, in the case of paper applications) itself is not valid proof of leave to remain under the scheme. To view or prove your immigration status and to obtain a share code, you will need to go to the website and input details of the identity document you used when you applied (your passport, national identity card, or biometric residence card or biometric residence permit (BRP)) and your date of birth. You will also need access to the mobile number or email address you used when you applied, as you will be sent a code for logging in.

For non-EEA family members of EEA nationals, if you already hold a BRP under the EEA Regulations, that will not be replaced until it expires and you will need to confirm your grant of leave under the EUSS online in the same way as EEA nationals. However, if you do not yet hold a BRP under the EEA Regulations, you will receive a new BRP confirming your leave under the EUSS.

Note: EEA nationals and their family members who lived in the UK before 11pm on 31 December 2020 had until the deadline of 30 June 2021 to apply to the EUSS.

If an EEA national or their non-EEA family member fails to apply to the EUSS, the EEA national loses their right to work in the UK. They are not able to pass a landlord immigration check and are vulnerable to detention and removal from the UK. If you have missed the deadline, you can make a late application to the scheme and you should do so as soon as possible. You need to demonstrate that there are 'reasonable grounds' for the failure to meet the deadline. Seek specialised immigration advice if this applies to you. See Chapter 5 for more information.

Under the Immigration Rules

EEA nationals and their family members who arrived in the UK from 1 January 2021 are generally required to apply for, and hold, leave to remain under the Immigration Rules (see Chapter 5).

8. Passport issues

Leaving the UK

Embarkation from (leaving) the UK is endorsed by a triangular ink stamp in the embarking person's passport (see Appendix 6, Figure 14). This practice was suspended in March 1998, but then reintroduced in 2015.

New or lost passports

If you have been granted leave to enter or remain that has been endorsed in a passport that has expired or been lost before your leave is due to expire, the expiry or loss of the passport does not affect your leave. This is most common for people granted indefinite leave – eg, if you had your leave endorsed in your passport, but this has now expired and your new passport is not endorsed.

In this situation, you can apply for confirmation of your status. This now takes the form of a biometric residence permit card (see p79).

Illegible passport stamps

Problems may arise if an endorsement on a passport is either unclear or illegible, or if you required leave and your passport was not endorsed on your last entry.

If your passport has been endorsed illegibly, you may be deemed to have been granted leave to enter for six months with a condition prohibiting employment,[9] or, if you arrived in the UK before 10 July 1998, to have been given indefinite leave to enter the UK.[10] If you required leave to enter the UK, but your passport was not endorsed on entry, you may be considered an illegal entrant.[11] You should obtain specialist advice. See also p82.

Note: certain documents, such as a passport that indicates that you have indefinite leave, must be current in order to demonstrate that you have a right to work in the UK. Other documents, such as a UK passport, can demonstrate a right to work if they are either current or if they have expired.[12]

Notes

2. **British nationals and people with the right of abode**
   1 s39(8) BNA 1981

3. **People with leave to enter or remain**
   2 gov.uk/biometric-residence-permits/getting-your-brp-if-you-applied-from-outside-the-uk
   3 gov.uk/family-permit/after-family-permit
   4 s3(3)(b) IA 1971
   5 gov.uk/prove-right-to-work and gov.uk/prove-right-to-rent
   6 gov.uk/biometric-residence-permits/report-problem
   7 s3C IA 1971

7. **European Economic Area nationals**
   8 gov.uk/view-prove-immigration-status

8. **Passport issues**
   9 Sch 2 para 6(1) IA 1971, as amended
   10 Sch 2 para 6(1) IA 1971, prior to amendment and as interpreted by the courts
   11 *Rehal v SSHD* [1989] Imm AR 576
   12 The Immigration (Restrictions on Employment) (Codes of Practice and Amendment) Order 2014 No.1183, and Home Office guidance, *An Employer's Guide to Right to Work Checks*, at gov.uk/government/publications/right-to-work-checks-employers-guide

Part 3

Benefits and immigration status

Chapter 7

People subject to immigration control

This chapter covers:

You should consult this chapter, together with Chapter 8, if you, your partner and children are *not* all British or Irish citizens.

If you, your partner, your parent or your child have applied for asylum in the UK, you should also check Chapter 9.

1. Introduction

Entitlement to most benefits and tax credits depends on your immigration status. The immigration status of your partner can also affect how much you are paid as a couple. In addition, it is important to know the immigration status of any partner or child included in your claim, because if they have leave that is subject to a 'no recourse to public funds' condition, their right to remain in the UK could be at risk if you are paid an additional amount for them. This chapter provides an overview of how immigration status affects your benefit and tax credit entitlement and how a benefit claim can affect your partner's or child's right to remain in the UK.

If you are defined as a 'person subject to immigration control', the general rule is that you are excluded from most benefits and tax credits. However, there are limited exceptions. This chapter explains who is defined as a person subject to immigration control. The relevant benefits, the exempt groups and the rules on how your benefits are affected if your partner or child is a person subject to immigration control are covered in Chapter 8.

If you applied for asylum in the UK and have been granted leave to remain in the UK, including refugee leave, humanitarian protection or leave granted outside the immigration rules such as discretionary leave, more generous benefit rules can apply (see Chapter 9).

In addition to immigration status restrictions, most benefits also have presence and residence conditions, which you must satisfy. See Part 4 for more details.

If your immigration status excludes you from benefits and consequently you do not have any, or enough, income to live on, you may be entitled to other forms of state support – eg, asylum support (see Chapter 21), or support from your local authority if you have care needs (see p637) or you are a child, or you have a child (see p638). See also Chapter 25.

2. How and why to check the effect of immigration status on benefits

It is important to know your immigration status, and that of anyone included in your claim, before making a claim for a benefit because:

- your immigration status may mean that you come within the definition of a 'person subject to immigration control'. In most cases, this means that you are excluded from many benefits, but there are limited exceptions;
- your immigration status can mean that you satisfy, or are exempt from, the residence or presence requirements for the benefit you want to claim;
- your partner's immigration status may affect whether or not you can be paid benefit for them;
- if your benefit includes an increased amount for a partner or child included in your claim, this can affect their right to remain in the UK if their leave is subject to a 'no recourse to public funds' condition.

If you are not a British or Irish citizen, or if anyone you could include in your claim is not a British or Irish citizen, work through the following steps.

- **Step one:** be clear about your immigration status and that of anyone you could include in your claim. See Chapter 6 for an overview of how to check your immigration status. However, if you are unsure about your immigration status, get specialist immigration advice before making any benefit claims (see p7).
- **Step two:** check whether you are defined as a person subject to immigration control (see p93). If you are not, your immigration status does not exclude you from benefit entitlement, but you must still satisfy any residence and presence requirements. If you have a partner or child who is subject to immigration control, see p119 for how your benefit, and in some circumstances their right to remain in the UK, can be affected.
- **Step three:** if you are defined as a person subject to immigration control, check whether the benefit you want to claim is one that excludes people subject to immigration control (see p111). If not, your immigration status does not

exclude you from entitlement to that benefit, but you must still satisfy any residence and presence requirements.

- **Step four:** if the benefit you want to claim is one from which people subject to immigration control are generally excluded, check whether you come into an exempt group. These vary between the different benefits (see p113). If you are in an exempt group, you must still satisfy all the other conditions of entitlement, including the residence and presence requirements.
- **Step five:** if you cannot claim the benefit you want, but you have a partner who may be able to include you in their claim, see p119.
- **Step six:** if you, or a member of your family, have leave to enter or remain in the UK that is subject to a no recourse to public funds condition, check whether any benefits claim could breach this condition because that could put your (or their) current or future immigration status at risk (see p101).
- **Step seven:** if you are not entitled to any, or enough, benefits, check whether you can obtain other state support – eg, asylum support (see Chapter 21), or support from your local authority if you have care needs (see p637) or you are a child, or you have a child (see p638). See also Chapter 25.

3. Who is a 'person subject to immigration control'

Most people, apart from British citizens, are subject to immigration control. However, for benefit and tax credit purposes, the term 'person subject to immigration control' has a specific meaning, given below. It is this meaning that is referred to when the phrase 'person subject to immigration control' is used in this *Handbook*.

For benefit and tax credit purposes, you are defined as a **'person subject to immigration control'** if you:[1]

- require leave to enter or remain in the UK but do not have it (see p98); *or*
- have leave to enter or remain in the UK that is subject to a condition that you do not have recourse to 'public funds' (see p101); *or*
- have leave to enter or remain in the UK, given as a result of a maintenance undertaking (see p105); *or*
- have leave to remain in the UK solely because you are appealing against a refusal to vary your previous leave (see p106).

Examples of circumstances in which you are *not* a person subject to immigration control include:

- if you are a **British or Irish citizen**. British and Irish citizens do not require leave to enter or remain in the UK;

- if you have **refugee leave or humanitarian protection.** For the duration of your leave you are not defined as a person subject to immigration control (for details of the duration of this leave, see p43). If you apply for a further period of refugee leave or humanitarian protection, or for indefinite leave to remain, *before* your current refugee leave or humanitarian protection expires, your leave is extended until your application is decided (see p100). However, if while your previous leave is extended, your application for further leave is refused and you request an appeal or administrative review, the benefit authorities may decide you are then a person subject to immigration control because the last bullet point of the above definition applies (see p106);
- if you have **indefinite leave to enter or remain in the UK** *unless* it has been given as a result of a maintenance undertaking (in which case, the third bullet point of the above definition applies). If you have settled status (indefinite leave to enter or remain in the UK granted under the European Union Settlement Scheme EUSS see p55), note that this is never given as a result of a maintenance undertaking;
- if you have **pre-settled status** (limited leave to enter or remain granted under the EUSS), you are *not* defined as a person subject to immigration control for the duration of that leave, because you have leave, it is not subject to a no recourse to public funds condition and it was not given as a result of a maintenance undertaking. If you apply for settled status before your pre-settled status expires, but this application is not decided by the date your pre-settled status would have expired, your pre-settled status is extended until your application is decided and you therefore continue to *not* be a person subject to immigration control (see p100). However if, while your pre-settled status is extended, your application for settled status is refused and you submit an appeal or administrative review, the benefit authority may decide that you are then a person subject to immigration control because the last bullet point of the above definition applies. (For details including why this cannot apply before August 2023 and an argument that it does not apply, see p106). **Note:** pre-settled status does not, *by itself,* satisfy the requirement to have a right to reside for those benefits that have that requirement (see p168), but it does mean you are in a protected group that can potentially have a free movement right to reside. You therefore need to check whether you have a free movement right to reside that satisfies that requirement for the benefit you need to claim. For the steps to follow, including potential arguments that may apply if you do *not* have a qualifying free movement right to reside, for means-tested benefits see p170 and for child benefit and child tax credit see p176;
- if you have leave to enter as the holder of an **EUSS family permit**, you are are *not* defined as a person subject to immigration control for the duration of that leave, because you have leave, it is not subject to a no recourse to public funds condition and it was not given as a result of a maintenance undertaking. If you apply for settled or pre-settled status before your leave to enter expires, but this

application is not decided by the date your leave would have expired, your leave is extended until your application is decided and you therefore continue to *not* be a person subject to immigration control (see p100). However if, while your leave is extended, your application for settled or pre-settled status is refused and you submit an appeal or administrative review, the benefit authority may decide that you are then a person subject to immigration control because the last bullet point of the above definition applies. (For details including an argument that it does not apply, see p106.) **Note:** leave to enter as the holder of an EUSS family permit does not, *by itself*, satisfy the requirement to have a right to reside for those benefits that have that requirement (see p168). Furthermore, you are not in a protected group that can use free movement rights *until* you apply to the EUSS for settled or pre-settled status (see below);

- if you have a pending EUSS application for settled or pre-settled status, and you are therefore in a protected group that can have a free movement right to reside, *and* you are either a European Economic Area (EEA) national or, if you are a non-EEA national, you currently have such a free movement right to reside. For further details of these protected groups, see below.

Note: if you are an **EEA national**, you could not be defined as a person subject to immigration control before the end of the transition period (11pm, 31 December 2020), because until then the definition only applied to non-EEA nationals. Since 31 December 2020, if you are an EEA national, you need to check whether you are defined as a person subject to immigration control – but you will *not* be if you have settled or pre-settled status (as noted in the third and fourth bullet points above), or if you have made a valid application for either status and that application has not been finally determined (see below), or if you are a frontier worker (see p69) and hold a valid frontier worker permit (see p70), because you do not require leave to enter or remain in the UK.

Even if *you* are not defined as a person subject to immigration control, you still need to check whether this definition applies to your partner or child.

Protected groups that can have free movement residence rights

If you are in one of the protected groups that can have a European free movement right to reside in the UK, this can mean you are not defined as a 'person subject to immigration control'.

For periods since 30 June 2021, you are in a protected group while you:

- have pre-settled status;[2] *or*
- have made a valid application to the EUSS for settled or pre-settled status and that application (or appeal against, or administrative review of, a refusal) has not been finally determined, withdrawn or abandoned.

While you have **pre-settled status**, whether you are an EEA or non-EEA national, you are *not* a person subject to immigration control for the reasons set out in the fourth bullet point of the examples listed above. For information on how to prove you have pre-settled status, see p186.

While you have a **pending valid EUSS application for settled or pre-settled status (or appeal against, or administrative review of, a refusal)**, provided the benefit authorities are satisfied this is your situation they will, in practice, generally accept that you are *not* defined as a person subject to immigration control, whether you are an EEA or non-EEA national. However, if this is not accepted, or if you need to set out the basis of your rights (eg, at an appeal tribunal), you may need to refer to specific legislation and guidance, and this will vary depending on the details of your circumstances – see box below.

If you have a pending EUSS application (or appeal or administrative review)

If you need to check, or explain, that your pending EUSS application for settled or pre-settled status means you are not defined as a person subject to immigration control, note the following.

1. All references to having a 'pending EUSS application' in this box refer to your having made a valid EUSS application for settled or pre-settled status (or an appeal against, or administrative review of, a refusal) which has not been finally determined, withdrawn or abandoned.
2. For details of how to prove that you have a pending EUSS application, see p186.
3. While you have a pending EUSS application, you have rights provided directly under the Withdrawal Agreements, which apply whether you made your EUSS application for settled or pre-settled status by, or after, the deadline of 30 June 2021.[3] This is confirmed in guidance.[4]
4. If your pending EUSS application was submitted on or before 30 June 2021, you may *also* have rights under UK regulations. However, these regulations require that you had, or were *treated as* having (see point 5 in the box on p191), a free movement right to reside in the UK on 31 December 2020.[5] If you are refused benefit because you did not satisfy this additional requirement, and therefore the benefit authority decided you are a person subject to immigration control, challenge this decision. The basis of your challenge is that this additional requirement goes beyond what is required by the Withdrawal Agreements, which is that you had a free movement to reside *at any time before the end of 2020*.[6] See also the box on p190.
5. If you are an **EEA national**, and you have a pending EUSS application that was submitted by 30 June 2021, showing that the UK regulations referred to in the point above apply to you can make it easier to show that you are not defined as a person subject to immigration control, because while these regulations apply, that definition is limited to only non-EEA nationals.[7]
6. If you are a **non-EEA national**, you have a pending EUSS application and you do not currently have any leave, you should always provide evidence of any free movement right

to reside you have – eg, as the family member of an EEA worker; other examples are listed beneath this box. Your pending EUSS application means you are in a protected group that can potentially have a free movement right to reside (see p188). If you are claiming a benefit that requires a right to reside, you need a free movement right to reside which satisfies that requirement for the benefit you are claiming (see p169 for means-tested benefits and p176 for child benefit and child tax credit (CTC)). If you are claiming a benefit that does *not* require a right to reside (eg, carer's allowance (CA)), *any* free movement right to reside should be accepted as meaning that you do not require leave and are therefore not a person subject to immigration control. If your claim for a benefit that does *not* require a right to reside is refused because you do not have *any* free movement right to reside or any immigration leave, and the benefit authority decides this makes you a person subject to immigration control, challenge the refusal and ask your adviser to contact CPAG. It may be arguable that having a pending EUSS application is sufficient by itself to mean that you do not *require* leave, due to the rights you have under the Withdrawal Agreements, and therefore you are not a person subject to immigration control.[8] The DWP's acceptance of this is suggested by DWP guidance, which describes rights that apply to non-EEA nationals with pending valid EUSS applications, as well as to EEA nationals.[9]

7. If you currently have leave to enter or remain that is subject to a condition that you do not have recourse to public funds, and you *also* have a pending EUSS application, this condition (together with any other conditions attached to your leave) does not have any effect while you have a free movement right to reside under the EEA Regulations.[10]

8. For an overview of who can have a European free movement right to reside, see p192.

9. If you had leave to enter as the holder of a **EUSS family permit** and, before that expired you applied to the EUSS for settled or pre-settled status and that application is still pending, your previous leave will be extended beyond the date it would have expired and this leave means you continue to not be defined as a person subject to immigration control (see p100). However, if your application is then refused and you challenge this with an appeal or administrative review, although your leave is then further extended pending the outcome of this challenge, the benefit authorities may decide you are then a person subject to immigration control. For details and an argument against this, see p106.

If you are a non-EEA national, the free movement rights to reside you are most likely to have are:

- as the 'family member' of an EEA national who has a relevant free movement right to reside – eg, as a worker (see p239);
- in limited circumstances, you may have retained a right to reside as a former family member (see p249);
- a permanent right to reside (see p265);
- a deriative right to reside – eg, as the primary carer of an EEA worker's child who is in education (see p253). **Note:** if you have a derivative right to reside as the primary carer of a British citizen (often referred to as a 'Zambrano carer' –

see p261), although while in a protected group with this derivative right to reside you are not defined as a person subject to immigration control, you are still excluded from benefits that require a right to reside (other than a very limited exception for child benefit and CTC – see p169), because this particular right to reside does not satisfy the right to reside requirement (see p168). However, you are not excluded from other benefits that do not require a right to reside, such as personal independence payment (PIP) and carer's allowance.[11] If the British citizen is a child, you may also be able to get support under the Children Act 1989 (or Children (Scotland) Act 1995) from your local authority (see p638). If you are a primary carer of a dependent British citizen, get specialist immigration advice about your options, as the law in this area can be complex (see p61).

Between 31 December 2020 and 30 June 2021, you were in a protected group if:

- you were covered by either of the two protected groups that continue to apply since 30 June 2021 (listed on p95); *or*
- on 31 December 2020 you either had a permanent right to reside or were resident in the UK with another free movement right to reside (or you were treated as having this – see point 5 in the box on p191);[12] *or*
- you were defined as the 'relevant family member' (see p192) of a person covered by the group in the bullet point immediately above and, on 31 December 2020, neither they nor you had leave under the EUSS.[13]

If you are an EEA national covered by either the second or third bullet point above, UK regulations limited the definition of 'person subject to immigration control' to only non-EEA nationals during that period.[14]

You require but do not have leave to enter or remain

If you require leave to enter or remain in the UK but do not have leave, you are a 'person subject to immigration control'[15] *unless* you are an EEA national and in one of the protected groups listed on p95.

You require leave to enter or remain in the UK *unless* you are:

- a British or Irish citizen; *or*
- a person with the right of abode (see p16); *or*
- an EEA national in the UK as a frontier worker (from 1 July 2021, you will need to hold a valid frontier worker permit – see p69);[16] *or*
- in one of the protected groups listed above that can have a free movement right to reside *and,* if you are a non-EEA national, you have such a right to reside.

Unless you are in one of the groups above, you require leave to enter or remain in the UK. For more information on when leave to enter or remain is granted, see Chapter 3.

Examples of when you require leave to enter or remain but do not have leave include if:

- you are an asylum seeker on immigration bail (before 15 January 2018, you would have had 'temporary admission' – see p14); *or*
- you have overstayed your limited leave to remain – ie, you did not apply for further leave before your period of leave expired. **Note:** if you apply for further leave on the same or a different basis before your current leave expires, your leave is extended from the date it would have expired until your application is decided, and, therefore, you are *not* someone who requires leave but does not have it (see 'Extension of leave' on p100). See also the first note below; *or*
- you entered the UK without leave to enter, and since then you have not obtained any leave to remain and you do not have a pending application (or appeal, or administrative review, against a refusal) to the EUSS; *or*
- you are subject to a deportation order.

Note:

- If you have pre-settled status (limited leave granted under the EUSS) you are not defined as a person subject to immigration control, but you need to apply for settled status *before* your pre-settled status expires. If you do not do so, as someone who requires leave but does not have it, you are then defined as a person subject to immigration control and excluded from benefits on that basis. If you *do* apply for settled status before your pre-settled status expires, your previous leave is extended, and you therefore continue *not* to be defined as a person subject to immigration control (see 'Extension of leave' below). At the time of writing, the High Court had just held that the UK government's position that a person with pre-settled status must make a further application for settled status, and that all rights (including to benefits) are lost if the application for settled status is not made before their pre-settled status expires, is unlawful under the Withdrawal Agreements.[17] The Home Office obtained permission to appeal, but announced in February 2023 that it would not appeal. Changes now need to be made to the EUSS to take account of the High Court judgment. The advice remains that you should ensure you apply for settled status before your pre-settled status expires. See CPAG's *Welfare Rights Bulletin* and the online version of this *Handbook* on AskCPAG for updates.
- If you came to live in the UK before 1 January 1973, and you are, or were, a Commonwealth citizen, or you came before 1 August 1988 and are now British or have a right of abode or indefinite leave, you may be entitled to compensation from the Home Office Windrush Compensation Scheme[18] if you, or your relative, experienced losses, including loss of benefits, due to lack of documentary evidence of your status (see also p82). Payments under this scheme are disregarded as income or capital for all the means-tested benefits, since 1 January 2022.[19] For earlier periods, DWP guidance states that payments

under this scheme, or the previous Windrush Exceptional Payments Scheme, should be disregarded for all means-tested benefits 'on an extra-statutory basis'.[20] The council tax reduction regulations also disregard these payments as income and capital. Also, interest on payments made under the compensation scheme are ignored as income for tax credits for 52 weeks.[21] If you have previously had a claim for benefits refused or terminated due to your lack of documents, you may still be able to challenge that decision.[22]

- There are close links between the benefit authorities and the Home Office. Making a claim for benefit could alert the Home Office to your presence and status in the UK. If you need immigration leave but do not have any, or you are unsure of your immigration status, get specialist immigration advice before making a claim or being included in someone else's claim (see Appendix 2).

Extension of leave

If you have time-limited leave to enter or remain in the UK and you make a valid application for a further period of leave, on the same or a different basis, *before* your current leave expires, your current leave is extended beyond the date it was due to expire, and until your application is decided or withdrawn (but it may be cancelled in certain circumstances, such as if you breach a condition attached to the leave).[23] If your leave has been extended, you continue to have the same benefit entitlements as you had previously (see examples below). If the extension of your leave means that you continue to be entitled to benefits, you *must* notify the relevant benefit authority. You should provide evidence that you made your application for leave before your previous leave expired, and explain that your leave has been extended under section 3C of the Immigration Act 1971 and therefore your benefit entitlements continue. It can also be helpful to refer the decision maker to the relevant part of the decision makers' guidance that confirms this.[24] **Note:** if you have an award of a disability or carer's benefit that is due to end on the date your original grant of leave expires, you will need to request a supersession of that decision on the basis that your leave has been extended and you continue to satisfy all the other conditions of entitlement. Alternatively, submit a renewal claim before your current award ends (see CPAG's *Welfare Benefits and Tax Credits Handbook* for further details).

Examples

Olabisi had been receiving universal credit (UC) for several months. She had discretionary leave (with no conditions attached) that was due to expire on 30 November 2022. On 15 November 2022, she submitted a valid application for a further period of discretionary leave, and she is still waiting for a decision from the Home Office. Her leave is extended, and Olabisi continues not to be defined as a person subject to immigration control and continues to be entitled to UC until the Home Office decides her application. However, because the DWP already had on record that Olabisi's discretionary leave was due to expire on 30 November 2022, it terminated her UC and notified her of its decision that she was not entitled to UC from 1 December 2022 because she had become a person subject to immigration control. Olabisi requested a mandatory reconsideration of this decision, provided a copy of the Home Office email confirming the date she applied for further leave, explained that her leave had, therefore, been automatically extended under section 3C of the Immigration Act 1971, and referred to the relevant UC guidance confirming this extension.[25] The DWP revised its decision and Olabisi's UC was put back into payment.

Azeez had leave to remain in the UK as the spouse of a British woman. His leave was subject to a 'no recourse to public funds' condition (see below) and was due to expire on 30 November 2021. On 15 November 2021, he submitted a valid application for indefinite leave to remain, and he is still waiting for a decision from the Home Office. His leave is extended and continues to be subject to the 'no recourse to public funds' condition. Consequently, Azeez continues to be defined as a person subject to immigration control and continues to be excluded from the benefits listed on p111 (unless he is in a relevant exempt group – see p113).

Note:

- If you have a biometric residence permit (often referred to as a BRP card) it may have a 'valid until' date of 31 December 2024, despite your having either indefinite leave in the UK or leave which expires after 2024. While you are still within the original period of your leave, you do not need to rely on your leave being extended in the way described above, but you should check that the benefit authority understands that the 'valid until' date relates to the card and not your leave. For more details, including how to prove the duration of your leave, see p79.
- If your application for further leave is refused, you may have a right to appeal (or seek an administrative review) against the refusal from within the UK. The time limits are very short, so get immigration advice immediately. If your leave had already been extended while your application to the Home Office was pending, your leave is further extended while an appeal (or administrative review) can be brought, and extended further while any such appeal (or administrative review) is pending. For information on whether you then become a person subject to immigration control, see p106.

Your leave has a 'no recourse to public funds' condition

You are a 'person subject to immigration control' if you have leave to enter or remain in the UK that is subject to the condition that you do not have recourse to public funds.[26]

Most people admitted to the UK with time-limited leave given for a particular purpose, such as spouses/civil partners, students or visitors, are given leave to stay on condition that they do not have recourse to public funds. Increasingly, this condition is also being added to those given time-limited leave to remain for other reasons, such as family ties, so you should always check whether your leave is subject to this condition.

People granted refugee leave, humanitarian protection (see p43), leave under family reunion provisions (see p44), leave granted under the EUSS (see p55) or leave under the destitution domestic violence concession (see p38) do not have a 'no recourse to public funds' condition attached to their leave. If you have leave granted outside the immigration rules, such as discretionary leave (see p46), you need to check whether your leave is subject to a no recourse to public funds condition.

Indefinite leave (see p30) is never given with this condition attached.[27] However, note that if you have been granted indefinite leave as a result of someone providing an undertaking to maintain and accommodate you, this means you are defined as a person subject to immigration control (see p105).

Public funds

'Public funds' are defined in the Immigration Rules as:[28]

- attendance allowance;
- CA;
- child benefit;
- CTC;
- council tax benefit (now abolished);
- council tax reduction;
- disability living allowance;
- income-related employment and support allowance (ESA);
- homelessness assistance and housing provided under specific provisions;
- housing benefit (HB);
- income support (IS);
- income-based jobseeker's allowance (JSA);
- local authority discretionary payments under section 1 of the Localism Act 2011, except payments under the Energy Bills Support Scheme 2022 (see below);
- welfare assistance payments by local authorities in Northern Ireland;
- pension credit;
- PIP;
- Scottish Welfare Fund payments;
- severe disablement allowance;
- social fund payments;
- UC;
- working tax credit.

It is understood that the inclusion of local authority discretionary payments under section 1 of the Localism Act 2011 in the definition of public funds, was intended to include welfare assistance scheme payments made by local authorities in England, and the Home Office does consider these payments to be public funds.[29] However, due to the breadth of the powers given to local authorities under this section, it is unclear which, if any, *other* discretionary payments may also be covered by this heading – with the exception of payments made under the Energy Bills Support Scheme 2022, which are specified as *not* being public funds. At the time of writing, confirmation as to whether Household Support Fund payments are classed as public funds was being sought. See CPAG's *Welfare Rights Bulletin* and the online version of this *Handbook* on AskCPAG for updates, and get specialist advice before applying for a Household Support Fund payment if you, or someone included in your application, has leave subject to a no recourse to public funds condition.

Only the benefits, tax credits and other assistance listed in the Immigration Rules (listed above) are public funds. If you receive any *other* benefit or assistance, you do not breach any no recourse to public funds condition attached to your leave.

If you have recourse to public funds when your leave prohibits that, you have breached a condition of your leave. This breach may affect your right to remain in the UK. You could have your leave curtailed, be liable to be deported, have further leave refused and/or be prosecuted for committing a criminal offence.[30]

If your leave is subject to a no recourse to public funds condition, you are defined as a person subject to immigration control and the benefit rules exclude you from entitlement to the above benefits.

However, if you are within an exempt group (which vary according to benefit – see Chapter 8), the rules for that benefit do not then exclude you and you can claim that benefit. If you receive one of the above benefits (except council tax reduction) because you come within a relevant exempt group, you are *not* regarded as having recourse to public funds under the Immigration Rules and so have not breached that condition of your leave.[31] If you receive council tax reduction as a result of being exempt, you still count as having recourse to public funds under the Immigration Rules. That is because the council tax reduction regulations are not referred to by the part of the Immigration Rules that disregards entitlements due to being in an exempt group.[32] Get specialist immigration advice before claiming council tax reduction (see Appendix 2). **Note:** although council tax reduction under a council tax reduction scheme is a public fund, council tax discounts or discretionary council tax reductions are not public funds, since neither are made under a council tax reduction scheme.[33]

If your leave is subject to a no recourse to public funds condition, you are regarded as having recourse to public funds if someone else's benefit is increased because of your presence.[34] For example, if the amount of your partner's HB is greater because you are included in their claim, that counts as recourse to public funds and means you will have breached the no recourse to public funds condition attached to your leave, which could put your current or future immigration status at risk (see p32). Get specialist immigration advice before someone makes a claim that includes extra benefit because of your presence (see Appendix 2). For details on how partners or children subject to immigration control affect benefit entitlement, see p119.

Note: if your leave is subject to a no recourse to public funds condition and you are, or are likely to become, destitute, seek immigration advice about applying to the Home Office to have that condition removed (see p33).

Domestic violence

If you were granted leave to enter or remain in the UK, subject to a no recourse to public funds condition, as a spouse, civil partner or partner, but that relationship has broken down due to domestic abuse or domestic violence, you may be able to apply for leave to remain under the destitution domestic violence concession (see p38). This leave lasts for three months and is *not* subject to a no recourse to public funds condition. During this period of leave, you are not defined as a 'person subject to immigration control' and can, therefore, claim all benefits, subject to the normal conditions of entitlement.[35] **Note:** having this type of leave means you are exempt from the habitual residence test for means-tested benefits (see p159) and exempt from the requirement to have been living in the UK for the past three months for child benefit and CTC (see p144). During your period of leave, you have a right to reside that satisfies this requirement for all benefits that have it (see p168).

If you apply for indefinite leave under what is commonly known as the 'domestic violence rule',[36] before the three-month period of concessionary leave expires, your leave is extended while the Home Office decides your application.[37] You continue not to be a person subject to immigration control and continue to be entitled to benefits.[38] You need to notify the relevant benefit authority that you have applied for indefinite leave before your previous leave expired, and provide evidence of this (see p100).

If you do not apply for indefinite leave by the end of the three months, you become someone who requires leave but does not have it and, therefore, once again you become a person subject to immigration control. If you are claiming any of the benefits listed on p111, your entitlement ceases unless you are in one of the exempt groups listed on p113.

Note: at the time of writing some support was available under the Support for Migrant Victims (SMV) pilot scheme, which was due to run until March 2023. The SMV scheme may provide accommodation and cash support for up to 12 weeks (in exceptional circumstances, this may be extended by four weeks) if you are not eligible for destitution domestic violence concession leave, have experienced domestic abuse or domestic violence, are at risk of destitution, and due to your immigration status you are excluded from means-tested benefits.

Referrals must be made through named organisations.[39] For details beyond March 2023, see CPAG's *Welfare Rights Bulletin* and the online version of this *Handbook* on AskCPAG.

Your leave is given as a result of a maintenance undertaking

If you have leave to enter or remain in the UK given as a result of a maintenance undertaking, you are a 'person subject to immigration control'.[40]

Maintenance undertaking

A **'maintenance undertaking'** is a written undertaking given by another person, under the Immigration Rules, to be responsible for your maintenance and accommodation.[41]

There are specific Home Office forms on which an undertaking can be given. However, no official form needs to be used, provided the undertaking is sufficiently formal and definite.[42] The document must contain a promise or agreement that the other person will maintain and accommodate you in the future. If it merely contains a statement about their present abilities and intentions, that does not amount to an undertaking.[43]

Your leave is considered to be 'as a result of a maintenance undertaking' if this was a factor in granting leave. It does not need to have been the only, or even a major, factor.[44] However, if the maintenance undertaking was not relevant to your being granted leave, the fact that the undertaking exists does not make you a person subject to immigration control.

If it is unclear whether or not your leave was granted as a result of a maintenance undertaking, the onus is on the benefit authority to prove that leave was granted on that basis.[45] If your leave has been granted outside the Immigration Rules, the causal connection between the leave and the undertaking cannot be inferred.[46]

If you are in doubt about whether you have leave given as a result of an undertaking, get specialist immigration advice (see Appendix 2).

Consequences for your sponsor if you claim benefits

If you have leave to enter or remain as a result of a maintenance undertaking and you claim benefits, the person/s who signed the undertaking to maintain and accommodate you could be asked to repay any UC, IS, income-based JSA or income-related ESA paid to you. However, in practice, this rarely happens because the rules for these benefits exclude people with this form of leave from entitlement for the first five years (unless the person/s who gave the undertaking has/have died – see p113).

The DWP can only recover UC or IS paid to you from the person who gave the undertaking in certain circumstances.[47] Recovery is through the family court (in Scotland, the sheriff court).

The DWP can also prosecute someone for failure to maintain you if that results in UC, IS, income-based JSA or income-related ESA being paid.[48]

As the DWP can take court action to recover benefit, if the DWP asks you about an undertaking, get independent advice (see Appendix 2).

Sponsors

People who have been given leave to enter or remain as the result of a maintenance undertaking are often referred to as **'sponsored people'**, and those giving the undertakings as **'sponsors'**. This terminology is used by the benefit authorities, including in their guidance to decision makers. However, the term 'sponsor' is also used in connection with other types of leave, and that can lead to confusion and errors in decision making. For example, the word occurs in the Immigration Rules in relation to those seeking leave to enter or remain on the basis of their relationship to their partner (see p34),[49] and people commonly describe themselves as having been 'sponsored' by their partner when they are granted such leave. The Upper Tribunal has provided a helpful discussion of this confusion.[50]

Another common area of confusion is when a family member of someone with refugee leave or humanitarian protection is given leave to enter or remain under the family reunion provisions (see p130). Although the person with refugee leave or humanitarian protection is not required to provide a maintenance undertaking, the confusion arises because the Home Office policy on family reunion, older entry clearance documentation given to the family member, and some benefit guidance still use the word 'sponsor'.

You only come within this definition of a person subject to immigration control if you have been given leave to enter or remain *as a result* of an undertaking. However, if you have been given time-limited leave to enter or remain because, for example, you were 'sponsored' by your spouse/civil partner, your leave is subject to a 'no recourse to public funds' condition and you come within the second group of people subject to immigration control (see p101).

If you only have leave to remain because you are appealing

You are a 'person subject to immigration control' if you have leave to enter or remain only because your leave has been extended while you appeal against a decision to vary, or refuse to vary, your leave (see p80).[51]

If you have time-limited leave (see p77), and you apply for a further period of leave, on the same or a different basis, *before* your existing leave expires, your current leave is extended beyond the date it was due to expire and until your application is decided by the Home Office (see p100).[52]

If your leave had been extended in this way and your application is then refused, you may be entitled to appeal (or seek an administrative review) against the refusal from within the UK. If so, your current leave is further extended during the short time period in which an appeal (or review) can be brought.[53]

If you then submit an appeal (or seek a review) within the time limit, your leave is further extended until the appeal or review is dealt with.[54] You continue to have the same type of leave, subject to the same conditions, while your appeal (or review) is pending.

However, during the time when your leave is extended, initially because you are within the short time period when you can appeal and subsequently, once you have appealed, because your appeal is pending, you are defined as a person subject to immigration control. Although this part of the definition of a person subject to immigration control refers to legislation which was repealed, the Upper Tribunal held that the reference must be read as if it is a reference to that legislation re-enacted in new legislation introduced at the same time.[55]

If your leave has been extended, initially because you are within the short time period when you can request an *administrative review* and subsequently because your administrative review is pending, it is strongly arguable that you are *not* a person subject to immigration control. This is because the specific part of the legislation which provides for your leave to be extended was only inserted several years after the re-enacting legislation referred to above was introduced, and therefore the argument of the Upper Tribunal summarised above does not apply.[56]

Most of the DWP guidance does not include this category of people within its summary of the definition of a person subject to immigration control (**note:** at the time of writing, most DWP guidance had still not been updated to include EEA nationals as potentially falling within the definition)[57] and nor does the Scottish guidance on adult and child disability payments.[58] However, HM Revenue and Customs (HMRC) does include this category as part of the definition in its tax credit and child benefit guidance.[59]

In practice, your entitlement to benefit is only affected by your being a person subject to immigration control while your appeal against a decision on varying your leave is pending, if your original leave was *not* subject to a 'no recourse to public funds' condition. If your original leave *was* subject to a no recourse to public funds condition, you were already a person subject to immigration control and an extension of your leave simply means that you carry on being so.

Example

Banu is an Iranian national who was granted 30 months' discretionary leave in the UK without any public funds condition attached. She is not a person subject to immigration control and so has full access to benefits during the period of her leave. Just before her discretionary leave expires, she applies for a further period of discretionary leave. Her original leave is extended while her application is pending. The Home Office refuses her application and, because she has a right to appeal against this decision from within the UK, Banu appeals immediately. Her discretionary leave is further extended while the appeal is pending. She is now a person subject to immigration control since she has leave only because she is appealing and, therefore, her entitlement to benefits ends.

Leave granted under the European Union Settlement Scheme

If you have pre-settled status (limited leave granted under the European Union Settlement Scheme – EUSS), your leave is granted for five years and you need to apply for settled status before your pre-settled status expires. The earliest date pre-settled status can expire is August 2023, because this leave only began to be granted in August 2018 and pre-settled status is always granted for five years.

If you apply for settled status before your pre-settled status expires, but your application is still pending when your pre-settled status was due to expire, your pre-settled status is extended. If your application for settled status is then refused, your pre-settled status is *further* extended during the short time period in which you can appeal (or seek an administrative review). If you appeal (or seek a review) within that time limit, your pre-settled status is *further* extended while the appeal (or review) is pending. The benefit authorities may decide that while your pre-settled status is further extended during the appeal (or review) time limit and during the period while an appeal (or review) is pending, you are defined as a 'person subject to immigration control'. If your benefit is refused or terminated for this reason, you should challenge that decision on the basis that you are *not* a person subject to immigration control, because the specific parts of the legislation which provide for your leave to be extended were only inserted recently and therefore the argument of the Upper Tribunal summarised above does not apply.[60] Furthermore, it is arguable that excluding you from benefits while you are appealing a refusal of settled status in these circumstances unlawfully restricts the rights you have under the Withdrawal Agreements.

These arguments also apply if you had leave to enter as the holder of an EUSS family permit, applied for settled or pre-settled status before your leave to enter expired, this was refused, you submitted an in-time appeal or administrative review and, during the further extention of your leave, the benefit authority refuses or terminates your benefit on the basis that you are not a person subject to immigration control.

Example

Huong is a Vietnamese national who came to the UK to join her Polish husband, Jakub, who has lived in the UK since 2019 and has pre-settled status. Huong obtained leave to enter the UK as the holder of an EUSS family permit and one month before it expired she applied for pre-settled status. After three months her application was refused and she immediately appealed. Her leave was extended while she was waiting for a decision on her application for pre-settled status and then *further* extended while she awaits a decision on her appeal. Since Huong submitted her appeal, Jakub's hours at work were reduced and so the couple made a joint application for UC. If the DWP decides that Huong is a person subject to immigration control because she only has leave while she is appealing the decision to vary her leave, and therefore only awards UC to Jakub (see p119), Huong should submit a mandatory reconsideration request and argue that she is *not* a person subject to immigration control as the definition does not apply to her circumstances.

Note: Huong also satisfies the requirement to have a right to reside as she is in a protected group, due to her pending appeal against the refusal of an application for pre-settled status (see p188), and is the family member (see p239) of an EEA worker (see p211).

Note: if your pre-settled status expires *before* you apply for settled status, you are then someone who is defined as a person subject to immigration control as you require leave but do not have it, and you are excluded from benefits on this basis. For details, including a recent High Court case on the loss of rights when pre-settled status ends, see p98. If your pre-settled status has already expired, you should apply to the EUSS for settled status as soon as possible, and from the date of your EUSS application, you are then in a protected group that can potentially have a free movement right to reside (see p95).

Notes

3. **Who is a 'person subject to immigration control'**

1 s115(9) IAA 1999
2 reg 83 and Sch 4 paras 1-4 ISSC Regs
3 Arts 4, 10 and 18(3) WA 2019; Arts 4, 9 and 17(3) UK-EFTA, Arts 4, 10 and 16(3) UK-Swiss Agreement; ss 7A-7C EU(W)A 2018
4 DMG Memo 14/21; ADM Memo 19/21; HB Circular A10/2021; Home Office caseworker guidance, *Public Funds: migrant access to public funds, including social housing, homelessness assistance and social care,* version 18, 20 August 2021, pp27-30
5 Regs 3(4)-(6), 4(2) and (5)-(8) CR(ADTP) Regs
6 Arts 10 and 18(3) WA 2019; Arts 9 and 17(3) UK-EFTA, Arts 10 and 16(3) UK-Swiss Agreement
7 Regs 3(4)-(6), 4(2) and (5)-(8) and 12(1)(i) CR(ADTP) Regs; DMG Memo 26/20, paras 36, 37 and 41; ADM 30/20, paras 36, 37 and 41; DMG Memos 6/21 and 7/21; ADM Memos 7/21 and 8/21
8 Art 18(3) WA 2019; Art 17(3) UK-EFTA, Art 16(3) UK-Swiss Agreement
9 DMG Memo 14/21, paras 1 and 5-9; ADM Memo 19/21, paras 1 and 5-9; HB Circular A10/2021, paras 1 and 7-12
10 Reg 43 and Sch 3 para 1 I(EEA) Regs; paras C1050 and C2012 ADM; Vol 2 Ch 7 Part 1 para 070838 DMG
11 See, for example, *DM v SSWP (PIP)* [2019] UKUT 26 (AAC)
12 Reg 3 CR(ADTP) Regs; ADM Memo 30/20, paras 9 and 11; DMG Memo 26/20, paras 9 and 11
13 Reg 3 CR(ADTP) Regs; ADM Memo 30/20, paras 9 and 11; DMG Memo 26/20, paras 9 and 11
14 Regs 3(4)-(6) and 12(1)(i) CR(ADTP) Regs; DMG Memo 26/20, paras 36, 37 and 41; ADM 30/20, paras 36, 37 and 41; DMG Memos 6/21 and 7/21; ADM Memos 7/21 and 8/21
15 s115(9)(a) IAA 1999
16 Regs 1(2)(b) and (4), 5 and 6 CR(FW) Regs; DMG Memo 29/20, paras 45 and 49; ADM Memo 33/20, paras 45 and 49
17 *R (on the application of the IMA) v SSHD* [2022] EWHC 3274 (Admin)
18 gov.uk/apply-windrush-compensation-scheme

19 The Social Security (Income and Capital Disregards) (Amendment) Regulations 2021 No.1405; DMG Memo 15/21; ADM Memo 21/21
20 **HB** Adjudication Circular A8/2019
21 Regs 10(2)(f) and 19 (table 6, para 24) TC(DCI) Regs
22 See, for example, HB Circular A8/2019 on the process for revising housing benefit decisions
23 s3C IA 1971
24 Vol 2 Part 3 para 073192 DMG; paras C1385, C1679 and C2017 ADM; TCM 0290150 (Step 8)
25 para C1679 ADM
26 s115(9)(b) IAA 1999
27 s3(1) IA 1971
28 para 6.2 IR
29 Home Office, *Public Funds: migrant access to public funds, including social housing, homelessness assistance and social care,* version 18, 20 August 2021 pp11-12 and p39
30 s24(1)(b)(ii) IA 1971
31 para 6.2, notes under 'public funds' definition, IR
32 para 6.2, notes under 'public funds' definition, IR
33 Confirmed in Valuation Tribunal for England appeal no.M219600, 1 March 2018
34 para 6.2, notes under 'public funds' definition, IR
35 Confirmed in Vol 2 Part 3 paras 073181-84 DMG and paras C1674-77 ADM
36 paras 289A-C IR
37 s3C IA 1971
38 Confirmed in Vol 2 Part 3 para 073183 DMG and para C1676 ADM; HB/CTB U4/2012; TCM 0290150, Step 9
39 Listed with contact details: southallblacksisters.org.uk/support-for-migrant-victims-scheme-smv-scheme
40 s115(9)(c) IAA 1999
41 s115(10) IAA 1999
42 *R (Begum) v Social Security Commissioner* [2003] EWHC 3380 (Admin); CIS/2474/1999; CIS/2816/2002 and CIS/47/2002
43 *Ahmed v SSWP* [2005] EWCA Civ 535; CIS/426/2003
44 CIS/3508/2001
45 R(PC) 1/09
46 R(PC) 1/09; *SJ v SSWP (SPC)* [2015] UKUT 505 (AAC), reported as [2016] AACR 17
47 s106 SSAA 1992
48 s105 SSAA 1992
49 For example, see para 6.2, notes under 'public funds' definition, IR
50 *OO v SSWP (SPC)* [2013] UKUT 335 (AAC)
51 s115(9)(d) IAA 1999; s3C(1) and (2)(b) and (c) IA 1971; *EE v City of Cardiff (HB)* [2018] UKUT 418 (AAC)
52 s3C(1) and (2)(a) IA 1971
53 s3C(1) and (2)(b), (ca) and (d) IA 1971
54 s3C(1) and (2) (c), (cb) and (d) IA 1971
55 s115(9)(d) IAA 1999 refers to leave continuing while you appeal because of the rule in Sch 4 para 17. Sch 4 para 17 was repealed by NIAA 2002, which also inserted s3C into IA 1971. In *EE v City of Cardiff (HB)* [2018] UKUT 418 (AAC) it was held that s17(2) IA 1978 requires that the reference in s115(9)(d) must be read as a reference to Sch 4 para 17 re-enacted as 3C(1) and (2)(b) and (c) IA 1971. See also *GO v HMRC (CHB)* [2018] UKUT 328 (AAC).
56 The argument in *EE v City of Cardiff (HB)* [2018] UKUT 418 (AAC) (where it was held that s17(2) IA 1978 requires that the reference in s115(9)(d) must be read as a reference to Sch 4 para 17 re-enacted as 3C(1) and (2)(b) and (c) IA 1971) arguably does not apply, as s3C(2)(d) does not re-enact Sch 4 para 17 IAA 1999 and was not inserted until 20 October 2014
57 See, for example, Vol 2 para 070833 DMG and paras C1041 and C2006 ADM
58 para 41 SSS DMG ADP(R and P); para 38 SSS DMG ADP(R and P)
59 See, for example, TCTM 02102 and para 10120 CBTM
60 As s3C(2)(ca), (cb) and (d) do not re-enact Sch 4 para 17 IAA 1999 and were not inserted until 31 January 2020, for (ca) and (cb), and 20 October 2014, for (d)

Chapter 8

People subject to immigration control and benefits

This chapter covers:

This chapter covers the benefit rules if you, your partner or child are defined as a 'person subject to immigration control'. To check whether this definition applies, see Chapter 7.

1. Benefits and tax credits affected by immigration status

The general rule is that if you are defined as a 'person subject to immigration control' (see p93), you are excluded from council tax reduction[1] (see p623) and the following benefits and tax credits:[2]

- adult disability payment (ADP) (in Scotland);[3]
- attendance allowance;
- carer's allowance;
- child benefit;
- child disability payment (CDP) (in Scotland);[4]
- child tax credit;
- contributory employment and support allowance (ESA) in youth;[5]
- disability living allowance;
- funeral support payment (in Scotland);[6]
- housing benefit;
- incapacity benefit in youth;[7]
- income-based jobseeker's allowance (JSA);
- income-related ESA:
- income support;
- pension credit;

- personal independence payment;
- severe disablement allowance;
- social fund payments;
- universal credit;
- working tax credit.

However, there are limited exceptions which mean that some people who are subject to immigration control can claim means-tested benefits (see below), disability, carers' and child benefits (see p115), tax credits (see p117) and social fund and other payments (see p119).

Even if you cannot claim yourself, a family member may be able to claim a benefit that includes an amount for you, or you might be able to make a joint claim (see p119).

Claiming other benefits

If you are a 'person subject to immigration control', you are only excluded from the benefits and tax credits listed above; you are not excluded from claiming other benefits.

For example, if you have paid sufficient national insurance contributions, you can claim any of the contributory benefits – eg, retirement pension, contribution-based JSA and contributory ESA. **Note:** if you have worked and paid contributions in a European Economic Area country and you are covered by the European Union co-ordination rules (see p379), or in a country with which the UK has a relevant reciprocal agreement (see p433), these contributions may be taken into account when working out your UK benefit entitlement.

You are also not excluded from benefits that depend on current or previous employment – eg, maternity allowance or industrial injuries benefits, or statutory payments such as statutory sick pay or statutory maternity pay.

You are also not excluded from the Scottish benefits, *other than* ADP, CDP and funeral support payment – eg, you are not excluded from young carer grant, Scottish child payment or a Best Start grant.

You may also be able to get help from your local welfare assistance scheme (see p628). However, if you have leave that is subject to a 'no recourse to public funds' restriction, receiving a payment under one of these schemes will breach that condition and put your current or future immigration status at risk (although, at the time of writing, it was unclear if the Home Office considers the Discretionary Assistance Fund in Wales to be a 'public fund') (see p101).

2. People subject to immigration control who can be entitled

Some people who are defined as a 'person subject to immigration control' are not excluded from claiming the benefits and tax credits on p111 because they are in an exempt group. These exempt groups vary between the different categories of benefits and tax credits, so being exempt for one category does not necessarily mean you can receive a benefit in a different category.

Note: if your leave prohibits you from having recourse to public funds (see p32), you can still claim any benefit (but not council tax reduction) to which you are entitled on the basis of being in an exempt group, even though these benefits (except adult disability payment (ADP), child disability payment (CDP), funeral support payment, employment and support allowance (ESA) in youth and incapacity benefit (IB) in youth) are defined as 'public funds'. This is because the Immigration Rules do not regard you as having recourse to public funds if you are entitled by virtue of being in an exempt group (see p101).[8]

Means-tested benefits

Being defined as a 'person subject to immigration control' does not exclude you from being entitled to universal credit (UC), income support (IS), income-based jobseeker's allowance (JSA), income-related ESA, pension credit (PC) and housing benefit (HB) if:[9]

- your leave was given as a result of a maintenance undertaking (see p105) and the person who gave the undertaking (often referred to as your 'sponsor') has died. If the undertaking was given by more than one person, they must all have died;[10]
- your leave was given as a result of a maintenance undertaking and you have been resident in the UK for five years (see below);
- (for existing claims only) you are a national of Turkey or North Macedonia or a European Economic Area (EEA) country (*except* Bulgaria, Liechtenstein, Lithuania, Romania or Slovenia), and lawfully present in the UK (see p114).

Note: these exempt groups can also mean that being a person subject to immigration control does not exclude you from social fund payments (see p119).

Your leave is on the basis of a maintenance undertaking and you have been resident for five years

You are not excluded from the above means-tested benefits on the basis of being a person subject to immigration control if you have:[11]

- leave to enter or remain given as a result of a maintenance undertaking (see p105); *and*

- been resident in the UK for at least five years since either the date the undertaking was given or the date when you came to the UK, whichever is later.

If you go abroad during the five years, you may still count as resident in the UK during your absence. This depends on the duration and circumstances of your absence (see p146).[12] If your absence abroad is such that you cease to be resident in the UK, you can add together periods of residence either side of the gaps in order to meet the five-year rule.[13]

Nationals of Turkey, North Macedonia and most European countries

This exempt group only enables you to *continue* receiving one of the means-tested benefits listed on p113 – it does not enable you to make a new claim (except for council tax reduction – see below).

You are not excluded, on the basis of being defined as a person subject to immigration control, if you are:[14]

- a national of a country that has ratified either the European Convention on Social and Medical Assistance or the European Social Charter (1961). This applies to all the EEA countries (*except* Bulgaria, Liechtenstein, Lithuania, Romania or Slovenia), as well as the non-EEA countries of Turkey and North Macedonia; *and*
- lawfully present in the UK. You satisfy this if you currently have leave to enter or remain in the UK.

You must have already claimed:

- UC before 1 January 2021;[15]
- HB or PC before 3 May 2022;[16]
- IS, income-related ESA or income-based JSA. There is no date by which you need to have claimed because it is no longer possible for anyone to make a new claim for these benefits.

If you made you claim before the relevant date, the exempt group continues to apply and therefore your entitlement to that benefit continues, despite your being defined as a person subject to immigration control.

Note:

- It may be arguable that excluding **UC, HB and PC** from this exempt group is unlawful on the basis that these means-tested benefits should be defined as 'social assistance' under these agreements and therefore lawfully present nationals of the countries that have ratified these agreements should not be excluded due to being a person subject to immigration control from UC, PC or HB, in addition to not being excluded from the other, legacy, means-tested benefits.[17]

- You are not excluded from **council tax reduction** by your immigration status if this exempt group applies and, if you are claiming in England, your claim relates to financial years before 1 April 2023.[18] However, if your leave is subject to a no recourse to public funds condition and you receive council tax reduction as a result of being in this category, this counts as having recourse to public funds under the Immigration Rules and so breaches the condition of your leave. That is because the council tax reduction regulations are not referred to by the part of the Immigration Rules that disregards entitlements due to being in an exempt group (see p101).[19] Get immigration advice before claiming council tax reduction if you fall into this category.
- You must satisfy all the other conditions of entitlement, including having a right to reside (see p168). **Note:** if you are an asylum seeker and have been given immigration bail, although you are 'lawfully present' in the UK, the courts have held you not to have a right to reside.[20]

Disability, carers' and child benefits

If you are in any of the exempt groups below, being defined as a 'person subject to immigration control' does not exclude you from being entitled to the following non-means-tested, non-contributory benefits:[21]

- ADP;
- attendance allowance (AA);
- carer's allowance;
- child benefit;
- CDP;
- disability living allowance (DLA);
- ESA in youth;
- IB for incapacity in youth;
- personal independence payment (PIP);
- severe disablement allowance;
- social fund payments (see p119).

You are not excluded if:

- your leave is as a result of a maintenance undertaking (see p105);[22]
- you are a national of Albania (child benefit only), Algeria, Morocco, San Marino, Tunisia or Turkey, and specific circumstances apply (see below); *or*
- (AA, DLA, PIP and child benefit only) you are covered by a reciprocal agreement (see p117).

Note: your entitlement to benefit still depends on your satisfying all the other conditions of entitlement, including those on presence and residence (see Part 4).

Nationals of Albania, Algeria, Morocco, San Marino, Tunisia and Turkey

You are not excluded from being entitled to one of the disability, carers' and child benefits listed above on the basis of being defined as a person subject to immigration control, if you are:[23]

- a national of Albania (for child benefit only – see below), Morocco, San Marino, Tunisia or Turkey (or Algeria if you made your claim before 1 January 2021 – see below) *and* you are either currently lawfully working (see below) in Great Britain, or you have ceased lawfully working for a reason such as pregnancy, childcare, illness or accident, or because you have reached retirement age;[24] *or*
- living with a member of your family (see p390) who is a national of Morocco, San Marino, Tunisia or Turkey (or Algeria if you made your claim before 1 January 2021) covered by the above bullet point.

If your claim began before 1 January 2021 (other than for Albania – see below), this protection was due to your being covered by European Union (EU) association and co-operation agreements (see p445). However, after the transition period ended at 11pm on 31 December 2020, these agreements ceased to have direct effect in the UK, but transitional rules mean, provided you claimed before 1 January 2021, you continue to be entitled as if the agreements were still in force.[25]

If your claim began on or after 1 January 2021, this protection is due to new trade and continuity agreements, which took effect from that date between the UK and each of the countries listed *except* Albania (see next paragraph) and *except*, at the time of writing, **Algeria**. If you, or the family member you are living with, are a national of Algeria wanting to claim one of these benefits, check whether a new agreement has been concluded.

If you are a national of **Albania**, HM Revenue and Customs (HMRC) guidance on child benefit states that you are not excluded from child benefit on the basis of being a person subject to immigration control, if you are lawfully working in the UK or ceased such work as described in the first bullet point above.[26] HMRC added Albania to the list of relevant countries after an agreement came into force between the UK and Albania in 2021.[27] This agreement incorporates, and continues with modifications, provisions of a previous agreement between the EU and Albania.[28] For further details on the agreements, see p447.

Lawfully working

'Lawfully working' was interpreted in relation to the EU association and co-operation agreements as being an 'insured person' under the EU co-ordination rules (see p379).[29] In broad terms, this means that you must have been insured by having paid (or been credited with) national insurance (NI) contributions.[30] However, this does not necessarily apply to the trade and continuity agreements. In practice, it is likely that you will only be accepted as lawfully working if your work does not breach any work restrictions attached to your leave or, if you are an asylum seeker, you have permission to work from the Home Office.

You are covered by a reciprocal agreement

You are not excluded from claiming AA, DLA, PIP or child benefit (but none of the other disability, carers' and child benefits listed on p115) on the basis of being a person subject to immigration control if you are covered by a reciprocal agreement the UK has with another country.[31] At the time of writing, only Denmark and Germany (and for claims made before 1 January 2021 only, Norway) had agreements in relation to AA and DLA, and the necessary amendments to include PIP had not been made to individual agreements. However, you may be able to claim child benefit if you are covered by the relevant agreement with Austria, Barbados, Belgium, Canada, Denmark, Finland, France, Germany, Israel, Mauritius, New Zealand, Portugal, Spain and Sweden, former Yugoslavia (Bosnia-Herzegovina, Croatia, Kosovo, North Macedonia, Montenegro, Serbia and Slovenia[32]) or (for claims made before 1 January 2021 only) Norway or (for claims made before 1 November 2021 only) Switzerland (see p437).

Note: at the time of writing, the main DWP and HMRC guidance on exempt groups had still not been updated to include the EEA countries that have reciprocal agreements.[33]

See Appendix 5 for a list of the countries that have reciprocal agreements and p433 for more information on them.

Tax credits

Being a 'person subject to immigration control' does not exclude you from getting child tax credit (CTC) or working tax credit (WTC) if:[34]

- your leave was given as a result of a maintenance undertaking (see p105) and the person who gave the undertaking (often referred to as your 'sponsor') has died. If the undertaking was given by more than one person, they must all have died;[35]
- your leave was given as a result of a maintenance undertaking and you have been resident in the UK for five years (see below);
- (for WTC) you are a national of an EEA state (*except* Bulgaria, Liechtenstein, Lithuania, Romania or Slovenia) or Turkey or North Macedonia and lawfully present in the UK (see p118);
- (for CTC) you are a national of Algeria, Morocco, San Marino, Tunisia or Turkey and lawfully working in the UK (see p118).

Note: if you are a person subject to immigration control, but your partner is not (or they are in one of the above exempt groups), you can receive tax credits on the basis of a joint claim (see p123).

Your leave is on the basis of a maintenance undertaking and you have been resident for five years

You are not excluded from CTC or WTC on the basis of being a person subject to immigration control if you have:[36]

- leave to enter or remain given as a result of a maintenance undertaking (see p105); *and*
- been resident in the UK for at least five years since either the date the undertaking was given or the date when you came to the UK, whichever is later.

If you go abroad during the five years, you may still count as resident in the UK during your absence. This depends on the duration and circumstances of your absence (see p146).[37] If your absence abroad is such that you cease to be resident in the UK, you can add together periods of residence either side of the gaps in order to meet the five-year rule.[38]

Nationals of Turkey, North Macedonia and most European countries

You are not excluded from WTC on the basis of being a person subject to immigration control, if you are:[39]

- a national of a country that has ratified either the European Convention on Social and Medical Assistance or the European Social Charter (1961). This applies to all the EEA countries (*except* Bulgaria, Liechtenstein, Lithuania, Romania or Slovenia), as well as the non-EEA countries of Turkey and North Macedonia; *and*
- lawfully present. You satisfy this if you currently have leave to enter or remain in the UK.

Note: you must still satisfy all the other conditions of entitlement, including working a sufficient number of hours to count as working 'full time', under the WTC rules.

Asylum seekers with temporary admission in the UK (see p14) have been accepted as 'lawfully present',[40] and this should also be accepted if you are an asylum seeker with immigration bail. However, to be entitled to WTC, you must work sufficient hours and so you will only benefit from this provision if you have obtained, and work in accordance with, permission from the Home Office (see p42).

Nationals of Albania, Algeria, Morocco, San Marino, Tunisia and Turkey

You are not excluded from CTC on the basis of being a person subject to immigration control if you are a national of Morocco, San Marino, Tunisia or Turkey (or Algeria, if you made your claim before 1 January 2021[41]), and you are either currently lawfully working in the UK (see p116) *or* you ceased lawfully working in the UK for a reason such as pregnancy, childcare, illness or accident, or because you have reached retirement age.[42]

Note: HMRC guidance also states you are not excluded from CTC on the basis of being a person subject to immigration control if you are a national of Albania and the circumstances of the first bullet point above apply.[43] For further details on the agreements with Albania, see p447, and with the other countries, see p445.

Social fund and other payments

You are not excluded from social fund payments on the basis of being a person subject to immigration control if you are in one of the exempt groups for either means-tested benefits (see p113) or non-means-tested benefits (see p115).[44]

In Scotland, you are not excluded from a **funeral support payment** on the basis of being a person subject to immigration control if you are in one of the exempt groups for disability, carers' and child benefits (see p115).[45] There are no immigration status requirements for **Best Start grants, child winter heating assistance** or **winter heating payment.**[46]

For all these payments, you must meet the other conditions of entitlement, including (except for winter fuel payments) either you or (except for a budgeting loan) your partner being in receipt of a qualifying benefit. What counts as a qualifying benefit varies for the different payments but is broadly a means-tested benefit or, in some circumstances, tax credits. **Note:** you may not need to receive a qualifying benefit for a Best Start grant if you are under 20. See CPAG's *Welfare Benefits and Tax Credits Handbook* for details.

Note:

- In England, if you are responsible for the costs of a funeral of a child aged under 18 or a stillborn baby, you may be entitled to a **children's funeral fund payment.** The burial or cremation must take place in England, but there are no immigration status (or residence) requirements.[47]
- In Wales, if you are responsible for the costs of a funeral of a child aged under 18 or a stillborn baby, you may be entitled to a **child funeral fund payment.** The child's family home must be in Wales. There are no immigration status (or other residence) requirements.[48]

3. Partners and children who are subject to immigration control

Some benefits and tax credits have special rules that apply if your partner or child who lives with you is a 'person subject to immigration control'. These rules vary, so check the rules for the benefit or tax credit you want to claim.

Means-tested benefits

Universal credit

If you live with your **partner** and claim universal credit (UC), you are generally required to make a joint claim. If your partner is a 'person subject to immigration control' and is not in one of the exempt groups who can get UC listed on p113, your joint claim is *treated as* a claim by you for UC as a single person and:[49]

- your award is based on the maximum amount for a single person;[50]
- your partner's income and capital are taken into account;[51]
- your partner does not need to accept a claimant commitment or comply with any work-related requirements because they are not a UC claimant;[52]
- your partner is not classed as a non-dependant and therefore no deduction (ie, 'housing costs contribution') is made from your UC;[53]
- if you are under 35, your partner does not prevent your rent being restricted to the one-bedroom shared accommodation rate;[54]
- if you have a child, your partner does not affect your being 'responsible' for the child (so you are entitled to a child element, and if you are receiving education, that does not exclude you from UC) nor being the child's 'responsible carer', when determining your work-related requirements;[55]
- the couple rate of the earnings threshold applies for determining when no work-related requirements apply to you, and in calculating any self-employed 'minimum income floor' that may apply if you are self-employed. (**Note**: the 'minimum income floor' does not apply to your partner if they are self-employed.)[56]

Other than in the two potential exceptions below, the claims described above do not include additional amounts for your partner. Therefore, if their leave is subject to a 'no recourse to public funds' condition, your claim for UC does not breach this condition because it does not result in your receiving increased public funds as a result of their presence (see p101). If your UC claim as a single person includes a housing costs element, other than in the first potential exception below, this will not be higher as a result of your partner's presence because they are not a claimant and therefore are ignored in the housing costs calculation.[57]

The first potential exception is if you and your partner are joint tenants *and* the housing costs calculation results in an additional amount of housing costs being paid as a result of your partner's presence. This potential arises because, if you are joint tenants, their share of the rent is used to calculate your housing costs element.[58] However, the only scenario that CPAG is aware of in which this can arise is if you and your partner are joint tenants with one or more other joint tenants, because then the share of the rent used to calculate your housing costs is greater due to the presence of your partner.

The second potential exception is if you are entitled to the childcare element due to both you and your partner working (or being treated as working), and the amount of the childcare element is greater due to the amount of work done by your partner *and* not fully offset by the amount of earned income from your partner's work taken into account.[59]

If you have concerns about breaching any condition attached to your partner's leave, get specialist immigration advice before making a claim (see Appendix 2) if either of the above exceptions risks breaching the no recourse to public funds condition attached to your partner's leave.

Note:

- If you have reached pension age and your partner is under pension age, but you cannot make a joint claim for UC because they are excluded as a person subject to immigration control, your claim is *not* treated as a single claim for UC. Instead, you can claim pension credit (PC) and housing benefit (HB) and you are treated as a single person for these claims.[60] If your partner subsequently ceases to be a person subject to immigration control before reaching pension age, provided they also satisfy the residence and presence rules for UC (see p293), your entitlement to PC and HB ends and you can make a joint claim for UC.
- If you are living in temporary or supported accommodation, you cannot claim the UC housing costs element, but you can claim HB to help with your rent alongside claiming the other elements of UC. The rules for HB in this situation are the same as for other HB claims: any partner or child is included in your HB claim and award, regardless of their immigration status. If this results in more HB being paid as a result of their presence, your HB claim will breach any no recourse to public funds condition attached to their leave (see below).

You can include any **child** for whom you are responsible in your UC claim, regardless of the child's immigration status (subject to the 'two-child limit'). However, if your child's leave is subject to a no recourse to public funds condition, receipt of UC elements for them breaches this condition and could affect their current or future right to remain in the UK. Get specialist immigration advice before making a claim (see Appendix 2).

Housing benefit

If your partner is a person subject to immigration control, they are included in your HB claim and your applicable amount includes the couple rate of the personal allowance and any premiums to which either of you are entitled. Your partner will need to satisfy the national insurance (NI) number requirement (see p482) unless they do not have leave to enter or remain in the UK and are therefore exempt from the NI number requirement (see p483).

However, the exception, when your HB claim is treated as a single claim, is if you have reached pension age and your partner is under pension age, but you cannot make a joint claim for UC because they are excluded as a person subject to immigration control (and not in one of the exempt groups on p113).[61] If that applies, your partner's income and capital do not affect your HB claim. **Note:** if your partner subsequently ceases to be a person subject to immigration control before reaching pension age, provided they also satisfy the residence and presence rules (see p293), your entitlement to HB ends and you can make a joint claim for UC.

If a child for whom you are responsible is a person subject to immigration control, they are included in your claim and (subject to the 'two-child limit') your applicable amount includes a personal allowance for them, together with any premiums for which they qualify.

If your partner's and/or child's leave is subject to a no recourse to public funds condition and your claim for HB could result in additional public funds being paid as a result of their presence, this breaches that condition of their leave and could put their current or future immigration status at risk (see p101). Obtain specialist immigration advice before making a claim (see Appendix 2).

Council tax reduction (see p623) is also defined as public funds, so if your council tax reduction is greater (eg, because you lose a single person's discount) as a result of the presence of someone whose leave is subject to a no recourse to public funds condition, this breaches that condition of their leave and could affect their current or future right to remain in the UK. Get specialist immigration advice before making a claim (see Appendix 2).

Income support, income-based jobseeker's allowance and income-related employment and support allowance

If your **partner** is a person subject to immigration control (see p93), they are included in your claim for income support (IS), income-based jobseeker's allowance (JSA), including if you are a joint-claim couple, or income-related employment and support allowance (ESA). However, you are only paid a personal allowance at the single person's rate, unless they come into one of the exempt groups that can get the means-tested benefits on p113, in which case you are paid at the couple rate.[62]

In all cases, your partner is still treated as part of your household and part of your claim. Therefore, their work, income and capital can all affect your benefit entitlement. Their presence also means you cannot be entitled to IS as a lone parent. Similarly, unless your partner receives a qualifying benefit or is severely sight impaired or blind, their presence might mean that you are not entitled to a severe disability premium.

Premiums are payable if either you or your partner satisfy the qualifying conditions and should be paid at the couple rate.

If your partner's leave to enter or remain in the UK is subject to the condition that they do not have recourse to public funds, be aware that receiving the couple rate of a premium breaches this condition and could affect their right to remain in the UK (see p101). Obtain specialist immigration advice before claiming the benefit that would result in the premium being paid.

Pension credit

If your **partner** is a person subject to immigration control (irrespective of whether or not they are in one of the exempt groups listed on p113), they are treated as not being part of your household for PC.[63] This means that you are paid as a single person and your partner's income and capital do not affect your claim. It also means that if they are under pension age, you can claim PC and HB (rather than UC) and you are treated as a single person for both PC and HB.[64] However, if your partner subsequently ceases to be a person subject to immigration control before reaching pension age, provided they also satisfy the residence and presence rules for UC (see p293), your entitlement to PC and HB ends and you can make a joint claim for UC.

If you would otherwise be entitled to the additional amount for severe disability, your partner's presence may mean that you are not entitled to it, as the DWP regards them as 'normally residing with' you for this purpose (unless they are disregarded under separate rules – eg, if they are blind or receive a qualifying benefit).[65]

You can include any **child** for whom you are responsible in your PC claim, regardless of their immigration status. However, if the child's leave is subject to a no recourse to public funds condition, receipt of PC amounts for them will breach that condition and could affect their right to remain in the UK (see p101). Get specialist immigration advice before making a claim.

Non-means-tested benefits

Non-means-tested benefits that are either contributory or based on employment are not affected by your or your partner's or child's immigration status.

If your own immigration status does not exclude you from **child benefit**, you can claim for any child for whom you are responsible, regardless of the child's immigration status. However, if you claim child benefit for a child who has leave which is subject to a 'no recourse to public funds' condition, your claim will result in additional public funds being paid as a result of their presence and this will breach that condition. This could put their current or future immigration status at risk (see p101). Get specialist immigration advice before making a claim.

If your child is not a 'person subject to immigration control', or they are but they come into one of the exempt groups on p115, they can claim **disability living allowance**, or **child disability payment** in Scotland, even if *you* are a person subject to immigration control.

They must still satisfy all the other conditions of entitlement, including the residence and presence rules (see Part 4).

Tax credits

If your **partner** is a 'person subject to immigration control' and you are not (or you are, but you are in one of the exempt groups on p117), your joint claim for tax credits is treated as if your partner were not subject to immigration control. You are therefore entitled to working tax credit (WTC) and child tax credit (CTC).[66] However, unless you or your partner are responsible for a child, or your partner is a national of a European Economic Area (EEA) country (except Bulgaria,

Liechtenstein, Lithuania, Romania or Slovenia), North Macedonia or Turkey and is lawfully present in the UK, your WTC does not include the couple element.[67]

There are no immigration status conditions for **children**. Any child for whom you are responsible is included in your claim and your WTC and/or (subject to the 'two-child limit') CTC includes amounts for them, provided you meet all the conditions of entitlement, including, for example, that the child normally lives with you.

If you are not a person subject to immigration control, but your partner is because their leave is subject to a 'no recourse to public funds' condition, they are not regarded as having such recourse by making a joint tax credits claim with you. This means that you and your partner can make the joint claim without it affecting their right to remain in the UK. If such a joint claim includes a child whose leave is subject to a no recourse to public funds condition, any tax credits awarded in respect of the child are also not regarded as recourse to public funds.[68]

However, if your claim for CTC or WTC is *not* a joint claim as described above (ie, it is a single claim or a joint claim but neither you nor your partner are a person subject to immigration control) and it includes an amount for a child whose leave is subject to a no recourse to public funds condition, this breaches that condition and could affect their right to remain in the UK (see p101). Get specialist immigration advice before including such a child in your claim (see Appendix 2).

Note: it is only possible to make a new claim for tax credits if you have been granted refugee leave and you are making a backdated claim (see p131). See the 2018/19 edition of this *Handbook* for how your partner's immigration status affects a new claim.

Notes

1. **Benefits and tax credits affected by immigration status**
   1 **E** Reg 13 CTRS(PR)E Regs
   W Reg 29 CTRSPR(W) Regs; Sch para 20 CTRS(DS)W Regs
   S Reg 19 CTR(SPC)S Regs; reg 19 CTR(S) Regs
   2 s115(1) IAA 1999; s42 TCA 2002; reg 3(1) TC(Imm) Regs
   3 Reg 15(1)(c) DAWAP(S) Regs
   4 Reg 5(1)(c) DACYP(S) Regs
   5 Reg 11(1)(b) ESA Regs; reg 12(1)(b) ESA Regs 2013
   6 Reg 9(5) FEA(S) Regs
   7 Reg 16(1)(b) SS(IB) Regs

2. **People subject to immigration control who can be entitled**
   8 para 6.2, notes under 'public funds' definition, IR
   9 Reg 2(1)-(1A) and Sch Part 1 SS(IA)CA Regs; Vol 2 Ch 7 para 070835 DMG; para C1060 ADM

10 Reg 2(1)-(1A) and Sch Part 1 para 3 SS(IA)CA Regs
11 Reg 2(1)-(1A) and Sch Part 1 para 3 SS(IA)CA Regs
12 CPC/1035/2005
13 R(IS) 2/02
14 Reg 2(1)-(1A) and Sch Part 1 para 4 SS(IA)CA Regs, confirmed in *OD v SSWP (JSA)* [2015] UKUT 438 (AAC); ADM Memo 29/20, paras 36-41; DMG Memo 25/20, paras 41-46
15 Reg 1(2) and 2(2)(a) SSCBCTC(A) Regs
16 Regs 1(1) and (3) and 2 The Social Security and Council Tax Reduction Schemes (Amendment) Regulations 2022 No.449
17 See justification for exclusion in Explanatory Memo to SSCBCTC(A) Regs, para 7.8 and in Explanatory Memo to The Social Security and Council Tax Reduction Schemes (Amendment) Regulations 2022, para 7.6
18 Reg 13(1A) CTRS(PR)E Regs; reg 19(2) CTR(S) Regs; reg 19(2) CTR(SPC)S Regs; reg 29(2) CTRSPR(W) Regs; Sch para 20(2) CTRS(DS)W Regs; regs 1(4) and 3 The Social Security and Council Tax Reduction Schemes (Amendment) Regulations 2022 No.449
19 para 6.2, notes under 'public funds' definition, IR
20 *Szoma v SSWP* [2005] UKHL 64, reported as R(IS) 2/06; *Yesiloz v London Borough of Camden* [2009] EWCA Civ 415. The case concerned an asylum seeker with temporary admission, which was replaced by immigration bail on 15 January 2018, but the same arguments are likely to apply.
21 **All** Reg 2(2), (3) and (4)(b) and Sch Part II SS(IA)CA Regs; Vol 2 Ch 7 para 070836-37 DMG; para 10140 CBTM
AA Reg 2(1)(a)(ib) SS(AA) Regs
ADP Reg 15(5) DAWAP(S) Regs
CA Reg 9(1)(ia) SS(ICA) Regs
CDP Reg 5(5A) DACYP(S) Regs
DLA Reg 2(1)(a)(ib) SS(DLA) Regs
ESA Reg 11(1)(b) and (3) ESA Regs; reg 12(1)(b) and (3) ESA Regs 2013
IB Reg 16(1)(b) and (5) SS(IB) Regs
PIP Reg 16(d)(ii) SS(PIP) Regs
SDA Reg 3(a)(ib) SS(SDA) Regs
22 Reg 2 and Sch Part 2 para 4 SS(IA)CA Regs
23 Reg 2 and Sch Part II para 2 SS(IA)CA Regs; reg 15 Reg 15(5) DAWAP(S) Regs; Reg 5(5A) DACYP(S) Regs; Vol 2 para 070836 DMG; para 10140 CBTM; DMG Memo 25/20, para 46(2) and (3); ADM Memo 29/20, para 41(2) and (3)
24 *Krid v Caisse Nationale d'Assurance Vieillesse des Travailleurs Salariés (CNAVTS)*, C-103/94 [1995], para 26; para 10140 CBTM
25 Reg 1(3) SSCBCTC(A) Regs
26 para 10140 CBTM
27 Partnership, Trade and Cooperation Agreement between UK and Albania (5 February 2021)
28 Stabilisation and Association Agreement between the European Communities and their Member States, 28 April 2009
29 *Sürül v Bundesanstalt für Arbeit*, C-262/96 [1999]
30 *Sürül v Bundesanstalt für Arbeit*, C-262/96 [1999], in particular paras 85-86 and 93
31 Reg 2(3) SS(IA)CA Regs; para 10140 CBTM
32 FANIII(Y)O
33 para 10140 CBTM; Vol 2 Ch 7 Part paras 070833-7 DMG; C2008 ADM
34 Reg 3(1) TC(Imm) Regs
35 Reg 3(1) TC(Imm) Regs, case 2
36 Reg 3(1) TC(Imm) Regs, case 1
37 CPC/1035/2005
38 R(IS) 2/02
39 Reg 3(1) TC(Imm) Regs, case 4
40 *Szoma v SSWP* [2005] UKHL 64, reported as R(IS) 2/06, and see *Yesiloz v LB Camden* [2009] EWCA Civ 415
41 Reg 3(1) TC(Imm) Regs, case 5 para (a)
42 Reg 3(1) TC(Imm) Regs, case 5; *Krid v Caisse Nationale d'Assurance Vieillesse des Travailleurs Salariés (CNAVTS)*, C-103/94 [1995], para 26; TCTM para 02108
43 TCTM para 02108
44 Reg 2 and Sch Parts I and II SS(IA)CA Regs
45 Reg 9(5) FEA(S) Regs
46 EYA(BSG)(S) Regs
47 The Social Fund (Children's Funeral Fund for England) Regulations 2019 No.1064; The Children's Funeral Fund for England – Technical Guidance, paras 1.7 and 1.8
48 gov.wales/child-funeral-and-other-related-costs-information

3. **Partners and children who are subject to immigration control**

49 ss3 and 4(1)(c) and (2) WRA 2012; Reg 3(3) UC Regs; reg 9 UC,PIP,JSA&ESA(C&P) Regs
50 Regs 3(3) and 36(3) UC Regs and, for housing costs, see Schs 4 and 5 UC Regs
51 Regs 18(2) and 22(3) UC Regs
52 ss3 and 4(1)(e) WRA 2012; reg 3(3) UC Regs; reg 9(1) UC,PIP,JSA&ESA(C&P) Regs
53 Sch 4 para 9(2)(b) UC Regs
54 Sch 4 paras 27 and 28 UC Regs
55 ss4(1)(d) and 19(6) WRA 2012; regs 4, 14(1)(c), 24 and 86 UC Regs
56 s39 WRA 2012; regs 62(1), (3) and (4) and 90(3) UC Regs; para H4077 ADM
57 They must be a claimant to be defined as a joint renter or joint owner-occupier: Schs 4 para 1 and 5 para 1 UC Regs
58 Sch 4 paras 6, 24 and 35 UC Regs
59 Regs 32(1)(b) and 34 UC Regs
60 Art 7(1),(2)(a) and (b) and (3)(b) WRA(No.31)O; HB Circular A9/2019, paras 15-17; Vol 13 ch 77 paras 77035 note 2, 77150-1 and 77160 DMG
61 Art 7(1),(2)(a) and (b) and (3)(b) WRA(No.31)O; HB Circular A9/2019, paras 15-17; Vol 13 ch 77 paras 77035 note 2, 77150-1 and 77160 DMG
62 **IS** Reg 21(3) and Sch 7 para 16A IS Regs
JSA Reg 85(4) and Sch 5 para 13A JSA Regs
ESA Reg 69 and Sch 5 para 10 ESA Regs
63 Reg 5(1)(h) SPC Regs
64 Confirmed in HB Circular A9/2019, paras 15-17, and Vol 13 Ch 77 paras 77035 note 2, 77150-1 and 77160 DMG
65 Sch 1 paras 1(1)(a)(ii) and 2 SPC Regs; Vol 13, para 78946 DMG
66 Reg 3(2) TC(Imm) Regs
67 Reg 11(4) and (5) WTC(EMR) Regs
68 para 6.2, notes under 'public funds' definition, IR. The TC(Imm) Regs are made under s42 TCA 2002.

Chapter 9

Asylum seekers and refugees

This chapter covers:

This chapter explains some of the specific benefit and tax credit rules that apply to asylum seekers and to people granted leave, such as refugee leave, humanitarian protection or discretionary leave, as a result of an asylum application. It also covers the rules on integration loans available to people granted refugee leave or humanitarian protection and their dependants. For more information about these categories of leave, see Chapter 4.

1. Asylum seekers

You are referred to as an **'asylum seeker'** while you are waiting for a Home Office decision on your application for refugee status (see p41).

If you are seeking asylum in the UK, you will generally be a 'person subject to immigration control' (as someone who requires, but does not have, leave – see p98). You are, therefore, excluded from the social security benefits listed on p111, unless you are in one of the exempt groups (see p113).

However, you are not a person subject to immigration control if you already have leave on some other basis (provided that leave is not subject to a 'no recourse to public funds' condition and was not given as the result of a maintenance undertaking) or you have a pending application for settled or pre-settled status under the European Union Settlement Scheme (or pending appeal or administrative review of a refusal), or for periods before 1 July 2021 you were covered by another protected group that can have a free movement right to reside *and* either you are a European Economic Area (EEA) national, or you *have* such a free movement right to reside (see p95).

If benefit can be paid for you, either because you are not excluded from making a claim or because your partner can include you in their claim, that does not affect your asylum application. You can receive any benefit defined as a 'public fund' (see p102) because asylum seekers are *not* subject to a no recourse to public funds condition, and if you receive public funds, this does not affect the outcome of your asylum application.

You are exempt from the national insurance (NI) number requirement (see p483) if (as is generally the case for asylum seekers) you require leave but do not have it and you are included in your partner's benefit claim or you make a joint tax credit claim with them, and you do not already have an NI number.

If you are excluded from claiming social security benefits because you are a person subject to immigration control, you may be entitled to alternative forms of state support, including asylum support from the Home Office if you are destitute.

If you are not eligible for asylum support or benefits, ask your local authority for help. If you have children, you may be eligible for support under the Children Act 1989 or Children (Scotland) Act 1995 (see p555). You may be able to get assistance from your local authority under one or more of the community care provisions, particularly if you have additional needs as a result of your age, health or disability (see p553). You may also be entitled to help from your local welfare assistance scheme (see p628).

See Chapter 21 for details of the support available for asylum seekers.

Note: asylum support is not taken into account for universal credit (UC).[1] Asylum support for essential living needs is only disregarded for income support (IS), income-based jobseeker's allowance (JSA) and income-related employment and support allowance (ESA) if it counts as 'income in kind'. If you claim asylum support and your partner claims housing benefit (HB), your asylum support for essential living needs is taken into account as income for HB *unless* your partner also receives UC, IS, income-based JSA, income-related ESA or pension credit, as these benefits 'passport' your partner onto maximum HB so all of your and your partner's other income is ignored.[2]

However, any social security benefit your partner receives *is* taken into account as income when calculating *your* asylum support, unless you can show that benefit cannot reasonably be expected to be available to you – eg, a disability benefit paid to your partner (see p565).

2. Benefits and tax credits for people granted leave following an asylum application

If, following your asylum application, you are granted leave that is not subject to a 'no recourse to public funds' condition, you are no longer a 'person subject to immigration control'. For example, if you are granted refugee leave or humanitarian protection (for details, including the duration of these types of leave, see p43), you are not a person subject to immigration control during that period of leave. You are no longer excluded from the benefits listed on p111 and can claim all benefits and tax credits, provided you meet the usual conditions of entitlement.

However, if you are granted leave outside the immigration rules, such as discretionary leave, you need to check whether your leave is subject to a no recourse to public funds condition. If it is subject to this condition, you are defined as a person subject to immigration control (see p101) and you are excluded from the benefits listed on p111, unless you are exempt (see p113). If this applies, get immigration advice as it may be possible for this condition to be removed (see p46).

Guidance summarising how to claim benefits once you are granted leave is available online and includes a list of the information you should take to your first interview with Jobcentre Plus.[3]

Note:

- If you are granted refugee leave, humanitarian protection or (provided it is not subject to a no recourse to public funds condition) leave outside the immigration rules (eg, discretionary leave), or you have leave and have come from Afghanistan or Ukraine and you satisfy other conditions, you are exempt from the habitual residence test for means-tested benefits (see p159). If you have been granted refugee leave in the last eight weeks or under the 'gateway protection scheme', DWP policy is to fast-track your claim (see p156).
- If you are granted refugee leave or humanitarian protection, you can be joined by certain family members under the family reunion provisions (see p44).
- If you, or the family member who you have joined under the family reunion provisions, have been granted refugee leave or humanitarian protection, or you have leave and have come from Afghanistan or Ukraine and you satisfy other conditions, you are exempt from the 'past presence test' and requirement to be habitually resident for personal independence payment, adult disability payment, disability living allowance, child disability payment, attendance allowance and carer's allowance (see p304).
- If you are granted refugee leave, you may be able to claim child benefit, guardian's allowance and, in limited circumstances, child tax credit (CTC) and working tax credit (WTC), backdated to the date of your asylum application (see p131).
- If you are granted refugee leave or humanitarian protection or if you have come from Ukraine or Afghanistan and satisfy additional conditions (see the second or third bullet points on p304), you are *not* excluded from a Sure Start maternity grant and you do *not* receive the lower amount of the Best Start grant pregnancy and baby payment on the basis that you already have a child under 16, if that child was a member of your family before you came to the UK – eg, if you arrived in the UK with your first child and then give birth to your second child in the UK.[4]

- If you are attending a part-time course to learn English and claim universal credit (UC), the course must be compatible with your work-related requirements.[5] Therefore, if you are subject to all work-related requirements, you must show that you meet these despite being on a part-time course, including that you are able and willing to immediately attend an interview and take up paid work. If your work coach agrees that studying English is part of your 'voluntary work preparation', the hours spent attending your course can be deducted from your work search requirements.[6]
- If you are granted refugee leave or humanitarian protection, you may be eligible for an integration loan (see p133).
- If you have been receiving asylum support, this stops (and if you were provided with accommodation, you are required to leave) 28 days after you are granted leave (see p525). You should claim benefits as soon as you can – you do not need to wait until the asylum support stops. **Note:** asylum support is not taken into account as income for UC.[7] It is also not taken into account as income for housing benefit (HB) if you are also claiming UC or pension credit, as these benefits 'passport' you onto maximum HB so all your, and any partner's, income is ignored.[8] If you do not receive a passporting benefit, your asylum support *does* count as income for HB. You do not need to wait to claim benefits until you have a national insurance (NI) number (see p485).[9]

Family reunion

If you have been granted refugee leave or humanitarian protection, certain family members may join you under the family reunion rules. For details, including the duration of leave granted, see p44.

A family member who comes to the UK and is given leave under these provisions is not a 'person subject to immigration control' for the duration of that leave and can claim all benefits, provided they meet the usual conditions of entitlement.

However, sometimes the benefit authorities wrongly decide that your family member is a person subject to immigration control. One reason for these wrong decisions is that older Home Office documents described you as your family member's 'sponsor', and this language is still used in some DWP guidance.[10] From this, the benefit authority may wrongly conclude that your family member has been given leave as a result of a maintenance undertaking (see p105).

This is incorrect. No undertaking is required for your family member to join you in the UK and DWP guidance states this clearly[11] (but note that both guidance paragraphs incorrectly state the family member has indefinite leave).

If you are a family member with leave in the UK under the family reunion provisions and you are refused benefits or tax credits because the decision maker decides you are a person subject to immigration control, challenge the decision and refer the decision maker to the DWP guidance.

In Scotland, you can claim a Scottish Welfare Fund family reunion crisis grant from your local authority if your family member(s) have been granted leave to enter the UK to join you under the family reunion provisions. You can apply before they arrive (see p628).

Note: if you are joining a family member in the UK but not under the family reunion provisions, you may be a person subject to immigration control (see p93) – eg, if you previously applied for asylum in a European Economic Area country and were transferred to the UK before the end of 2020 under the 'Dublin III Regulation'[12] to have your application considered by the Home Office, and you are in the UK as someone who requires leave but does not have it.

Backdating child benefit and tax credits

If you have been granted refugee leave or 'section 67 leave' as a relocated child (see p46) (not humanitarian protection or other types of leave), you can claim child benefit, guardian's allowance and, in the limited circumstances described below, tax credits, backdated to the date of your asylum application.[13] If you made more than one asylum application, these benefits can be backdated to the date of the first application, if the basis of the asylum applications remained the same. If refugee leave was granted as a result of events that only occurred after the first asylum application, then these benefits would only be backdated to the date of the asylum application made after these new events.[14]

Note: there is no provision to pay backdated UC.

You must claim backdated child benefit (and any guardian's allowance) within three months, and tax credits within one month, of being notified by the Home Office that you have been granted leave as a refugee (or section 67 leave as a relocated child).[15] If the Home Office letter is sent to a solicitor acting for you, the three- or one-month period starts from the date your solicitor receives the letter.[16] The Upper Tribunal recently held that a refugee was entitled to have her child benefit backdated to the date of her asylum application when she had claimed within three months of receiving her biometric residence permit (BRP), but *not* within three months of receiving the Home Office letter notifying her of having been granted refugee leave. This was because the latter was not a valid notification since it incorrectly stated that child benefit could not be claimed until receipt of the BRP.[17] The reasoning of the Upper Tribunal was based on the specific wording of the Home Office correspondence and may not apply to other cases. You should *always* ensure your claim for child benefit (and tax credits) is made within three months (one month for tax credits) of you (or a solicitor acting for you) first being notified that you have been granted refugee leave.

The wording of these backdating rules applies to a person who has *both* claimed asylum and been granted refugee leave (or section 67 leave). That is most significant for child benefit, because only one person makes the claim. Consequently, if you were a dependant on your partner's asylum application, and they have now been granted refugee leave, your partner should be the child benefit claimant to ensure the claim will be backdated. However, if you were a dependant on your partner's asylum application, you were also granted refugee leave, you made the child benefit claim and HM Revenue and Customs (HMRC) refused the claim on the basis that you were not the asylum applicant, you should challenge that decision on the basis that the words 'person who has claimed asylum' are not defined and must be interpreted as including a dependant on the asylum claim, to be consistent with the policy intention. This argument was recently accepted by the Upper Tribunal.[18]

The amount of tax credits paid is reduced by the amount of asylum support you received for your essential living needs over the period (see below).

The amount of child benefit and guardian's allowance paid is not reduced by any asylum support you may have received.

Backdating tax credits

In practice, it is hard to claim backdated tax credits. You can only claim if you applied for asylum on or before 31 January 2019, because that was the final day that a claim for tax credits could be made before UC was introduced. That is because your tax credits claim is *treated as* having been made on the date of your asylum application,[19] and if a claim for tax credits has been made by the above date, the legislation that abolishes tax credits is treated as not having come into force.[20] That was recently confirmed by both the Inner House of the Court of Session and the Court of Appeal.[21] Under the special backdating rules for refugees, your claim is then treated as having been renewed each April.[22] If successful, your claim can continue until you claim UC. If your claim for backdated tax credits is refused because you claimed asylum before 31 January 2019, but not before the date on which UC was introduced in the area that you lived, challenge this decision and ask your adviser to contact CPAG.

A further barrier is that the amount of tax credits paid is reduced by the amount of asylum support you received for your essential living needs over the period.[23] In many cases, the total amount of asylum support paid for essential living needs is more than the amount of tax credits and, therefore, cancels out any entitlement over the backdated period. However, if you did not receive asylum support or your tax credit entitlement exceeds the amount of asylum support paid (eg, if you worked sufficient hours to qualify for WTC), you can be entitled to an amount of backdated tax credits. Note that an argument that the reduction should only be for the amounts of asylum support paid in respect of children was rejected by the Upper Tribunal,[24] but it may be possible to challenge this again in a separate case.

Note: it can be extremely difficult to get HMRC to accept your claim for backdated tax credits. You should, therefore, telephone HMRC as soon as possible after receiving the Home Office letter granting you refugee leave and always within the one-month time limit. Be clear that you are making a claim and ask HMRC to take all the information required for your claim to be accepted.[25] On the same day as you make the call, send a completed claim form (see next paragraph) and covering letter detailing the time and date you made your claim over the telephone, including the HMRC number you rang and the telephone number that you rang from, and the name of the person with whom you spoke. HMRC can accept a claim by telephone or letter, but your claim must contain all the information required and must satisfy the NI number requirement (see p484).[26] If your claim is refused, challenge this decision and ask your adviser to contact CPAG.

For a copy of the claim form, a template mandatory reconsideration request if the claim is refused, links to recent caselaw and further information, see cpag.org.uk/welfare-rights/resources/test-case/retrospective-child-tax-credits-newly-recognised-refugees.

3. Integration loans

Integration loans are interest-free loans for people who have recently been granted either refugee leave or humanitarian protection, to assist with integration into UK society. For details of refugee leave and humanitarian protection, including the duration of leave, see p43.

The minimum amount of a loan is £100 and the maximum is £500, or £780 for a couple.[27]

Note: before applying for an integration loan, which has to be repaid, you may want to get advice from local refugee services on charitable and other assistance. You may also be entitled to help from your local welfare assistance scheme (see p628). Depending on your local scheme, you may be able to apply for grants or items such as furniture, but be aware that many local authorities do not give cash and some require the assistance to be repaid.

Applications

You must be eligible to apply for an integration loan and must make a valid application. Whether or not you are awarded a loan is at the discretion of the decision maker.

You are eligible to apply for an integration loan if you:[28]

- have been granted refugee leave, humanitarian protection (see p43) or leave to enter or remain as a dependant of someone with either refugee leave or humanitarian protection after 11 June 2007;
- are aged 18 or older;
- have not previously had an integration loan; *and*
- are capable of repaying the loan.

Applications are now made online.[29]

When deciding whether to give you a loan, the decision maker must take into account:[30]

- the length of time since your leave was granted;
- your financial position – ie, your income, assets, liabilities and outgoings;
- your likely ability to repay the loan;
- what you intend to use the loan for; *and*
- the total available budget for loans.

Although the legislation does not specify which intended uses of a loan are more likely to be accepted, the guidance to decision makers lists examples of 'integration needs' that can be accepted (if they cannot be met through assistance available from Jobcentre Plus):[31]

- help with housing, including:
  - deposits for rented accommodation;
  - rent payments;
  - house-moving expenses;
  - essential items;
- help with finding work, including:
  - travel expenses to attend interviews;
  - work clothing/equipment;
  - initial childcare costs;
  - subsistence while training;
- help with education, including:
  - the cost of a training programme;
  - requalification/professional qualification.

The guidance also states that a loan should normally be refused for:[32]

- non-essential items;
- domestic assistance and respite care;
- mobility items;
- general living expenses (including utility bills);
- council tax payments;
- medical items;
- cars, including driving lessons and a licence, unless this is essential for your employment;
- repayment of debts;
- airfares for dependants to join you in the UK.

It is helpful to read the guidance before making your application, as it covers examples of factors that can be relevant. For example, in addition to how long you have been in the UK, your financial independence can also be relevant. Your application may be considered weaker if you have been working and living independently in the UK for some time before you apply than if you were not working or living independently – eg, if you have been receiving asylum support. The guidance also states that decision makers can take your 'character' into account – eg, a loan will usually be refused if you have been convicted of an offence.

Decisions, payment and repayments

After you have applied for a loan, you should be sent a written decision by letter or email, within four weeks, stating:[33]

- whether the application was valid;
- if so, whether a loan will be made;
- if so, the amount, conditions and terms of repayment; *and*
- the deadline for responding to say whether you wish to take the loan.

If you are entitled to a loan, a loan agreement should be attached to the decision letter or email, asking you to accept the loan. If you are unhappy with the decision, either because you were refused a loan or offered a smaller amount than you need, you can ask for a reconsideration, which is carried out by a different decision maker. Your request for a reconsideration must be received within 14 days of the date on the decision letter or email.[34] There is no right to an independent appeal.

If the Home Office decides that you are entitled to an integration loan, it passes your details to the DWP, which then pays the loan, normally directly into your bank account, and manages your repayments.

Integration loans are recovered through direct deductions from benefits in the same way as for other third-party debts.[35] The rate of recovery and the start date of deductions should be notified to you. See CPAG's *Welfare Benefits and Tax Credits Handbook* for further details about deductions from benefit.

If direct deductions from your benefit are not possible (eg, because you do not receive a relevant benefit), you should be notified when repayments will begin, and the method, amount and frequency of these.

If your circumstances change, you can ask the DWP to revise the terms of recovery. These should be notified to you in writing.[36]

Notes

1. Asylum seekers

1 Reg 66 UC Regs
2 **IS** Sch 9 para 21 IS Regs
JSA Sch 7 para 22 JSA Regs
ESA Sch 8 para 22 ESA Regs
HB Sch 5 paras 4 and 23 HB Regs; regs 25 and 26 HB(SPC) Regs

2. Benefits and tax credits for people granted leave following an asylum application

3 gov.uk/government/publications/claiming-universal-credit-and-other-benefits-if-you-are-a-refugee
4 *SK and LL v SSWP* [2020] UKUT 145 (AAC); paras L2070 and L2076 ADM (due to be amended to include Afghan and Ukraine exemptions, but internal guidance has already been issued); Sch 2 para 6 EYA(BSG)(S) Regs
5 Reg 12(4) UC Regs
6 Reg 95(4) UC Regs
7 Reg 66 UC Regs
8 Sch 5 paras 4 and 23 HB Regs; regs 25 and 26 HB(SPC) Regs
9 gov.uk/government/publications/claiming-universal-credit-and-other-benefits-if-you-are-a-refugee
10 For example Vol 2 Ch 7 Part 1 para 070707 DMG
11 Vol 2 Ch 7 Part 1 para 070709 DMG
12 EU Reg 604/2013 – **note:** this ceased to apply after 31 December 2020
13 **CB/GA** Reg 6(2)(d) and (e) CB&GA(Admin) Regs
TC Regs 3(4)-(10) and 4 TC(Imm) Regs
14 *FK v HMRC* [2009] UKUT 134 (AAC); para 10140 CBTM
15 **CB/GA** Reg 6(2)(d) CB&GA(Admin) Regs
TC Reg 3(5) TC(Imm) Regs
16 *Tkachuk v SSWP* [2007] EWCA Civ 515; CIS/3797/2003
17 *HMRC v BZ* [2022] UKUT 264 (AAC)
18 CSF/33/2020
19 Reg 3(6)(a) TC(Imm) Regs
20 Art 3 WRA(No.32)O; Art 7 WRA(No.23)O
21 *HMRC v Adnan and Adnan* [2022] CSIH 2; *R (on the application of) DK v HMRC and SSWP* [2022] EWCA Civ 120
22 Reg 3(6)(b) TC(Imm) Regs
23 Reg 3(9) TC(Imm) Regs
24 **CTC**/3692/2008
25 Reg 5(2)(b) TC(CN) Regs; see also *MR v HMRC (TC)* [2018] UKUT 238 (AAC)
26 Reg 5 TC(CN) Regs; gov.uk/claim-tax-credits/backdate-a-claim

3. Integration loans

27 gov.uk/refugee-integration-loan/what-youll-get; **note**: older guidance states there is no maximum: UKVI, *Integration Loans Policy Guidance*, para 6.2, March 2015, available at gov.uk/government/publications/integration-loans-policy-guidance-process
28 Reg 4 ILRFO Regs
29 gov.uk/apply-refugee-integration-loan
30 Reg 6 ILRFO Regs
31 UKVI, *Integration Loans Policy Guidance*, para 9, March 2015; gov.uk/refugee-integration-loan
32 UKVI, *Integration Loans Policy Guidance*, para 9.3, March 2015
33 Reg 8(1) ILRFO Regs; gov.uk/refugee-integration-loan/how-to-apply
34 UKVI, *Integration Loans Policy Guidance*, Part 12, March 2015, available at gov.uk/government/publications/integration-loans-policy-guidance-process
35 Reg 9(1) and (3) ILRFO Regs; Sch 9 para 1 SS(C&P) Regs; Sch 6 para 12 UC,PIP,JSA&ESA(C&P) Regs
36 Reg 10 ILRFO Regs

Part 4

Benefits and residence rules

Chapter 10

Residence and presence rules: overview

This chapter covers:

This chapter describes the different residence and presence conditions that apply when you make a claim for benefits and tax credits in the UK. The two most well known conditions are the habitual residence test and the right to reside requirement, which are covered in more detail in Chapter 11. The groups of people who have a right to reside are covered in Chapter 12. The residence and presence requirements for individual benefits and tax credits are covered in Chapter 13.

If you are not a British or Irish citizen, first check Part 3 to see whether your immigration status means you are excluded from benefits as a 'person subject to immigration control'. If you are not excluded, you must still satisfy the residence and presence conditions described in this chapter.

If you live with a partner or child who is not British or Irish, check whether their immigration status affects your benefits. If their immigration leave is subject to a 'no recourse to public funds' condition, check whether any claim you make could affect their right to stay in the UK (see p119).

If you, or a member of your family included in your claim, go abroad (either temporarily or to stay), see Part 5 for the ways this affects your benefits and tax credits.

1. Introduction

There are residence and presence conditions for the following benefits and tax credits:
- adult disability payment (in Scotland);
- attendance allowance;
- bereavement support payment;
- Best Start grant (in Scotland);
- carer's allowance;
- category D retirement pension;
- child benefit;
- child disability payment (in Scotland);
- child tax credit;
- child winter heating allowance (in Scotland);
- contributory employment and support allowance (ESA) in youth;
- disability living allowance;
- funeral support payments (in Scotland);
- guardian's allowance;
- housing benefit (residence conditions only, except during an absence from your home);
- incapacity benefit for incapacity in youth;
- income support;
- income-based jobseeker's allowance (JSA);
- income-related ESA;
- pension credit;
- personal independence payment;
- Scottish child payment (in Scotland);
- severe disablement allowance;
- social fund payments;
- universal credit;
- winter fuel payment;
- winter heating payment (in Scotland);
- working tax credit;
- young carer grant (in Scotland).

There are presence conditions for the following benefits:
- contribution-based JSA;
- contributory ESA;
- incapacity benefit;
- industrial injuries benefit;
- maternity allowance;
- retirement pensions;
- severe disablement allowance.

Council tax reduction also has residence conditions (see p623).

There are no residence or presence requirements for widowed parent's allowance or for statutory sick pay, statutory maternity pay, statutory adoption pay, statutory paternity pay or statutory shared parental pay paid by your employer.

The residence and presence conditions vary between the different benefits and tax credits. If you satisfy the rules for one, you do not necessarily satisfy the rules for another.

The way in which the different residence and presence conditions affect your entitlement to benefit is set out in the UK benefits and tax credits legislation. Depending on the benefit or tax credit, you may be required to satisfy tests for:

- presence;
- past presence;
- 'living in' for three months;
- residence;
- ordinary residence;
- habitual residence;
- the right to reside.

However, these can be modified by the following.

- **European Union (EU) co-ordination rules.** If you are covered by particular co-ordination rules (see p379), they can help you get benefits in the UK – eg, by exempting you from certain past presence requirements or by enabling you to count certain periods of residence (or employment, or insurance) in (depending on which rules apply) a European Economic Area (EEA), or EU, country, or Ireland (under the principle of 'aggregation' – see p416). However, in limited circumstances, being covered by these rules can also exclude you from entitlement if the UK is not the 'competent state' to pay that benefit (see p399). These rules can also allow certain benefits to be paid when you go to an EEA country (or the EU or Ireland) (known as the benefit being 'exported'). The rules for each benefit are covered in Chapter 15. **Note:** the EU co-ordination rules are different from EU free movement residence rights, which can enable you to satisfy the right to reside requirement. In general, you do not need to know whether you are covered by the co-ordination rules to know whether you have a free movement right to reside, but you may need to know if you have a right to reside to know whether you are covered by the main co-ordination rules (see p380). The details of the EU co-ordination rules, including when and how they apply and how this has been affected by the UK leaving the EU, are covered in Chapter 16; the main ways they can assist with the residence and presence tests, or affect your entitlement in other ways, are noted for each benefit in Chapter 13.
- **International agreements**, including reciprocal agreements. There are reciprocal agreements between Great Britain and Northern Ireland, and

between the UK and some EEA and non-EEA countries. If these apply, they can help you to qualify for benefits and tax credits if you have recently moved between Great Britain and Northern Ireland, or if you have come to the UK or gone abroad. They operate in similar ways to the EU co-ordination rules and, in general, apply only when the EU co-ordination rules cannot assist you. There are also international agreements between EU and non-EU countries, which can continue to apply to existing claimants, and the replacement agreements between the UK and those non-EU countries all have similar effects (see Chapter 17).

Note: you must also check *where* you are required to satisfy a particular residence or presence test. This varies for different benefits and tax credits, and can be Scotland, England and Wales, Great Britain, the UK, the common travel area (ie, the UK, Ireland, Channel Islands and the Isle of Man) or the EEA. In this *Handbook*, all references to the EEA are to be read as including Switzerland. The EEA states are listed on p53.

2. **Presence**

Most benefits and tax credits have rules about presence and absence. You must usually be present in Great Britain (the UK for tax credits) at the time you make your claim and then continue to be present. There are specific rules that allow you to be treated as present during some temporary absences (see p332) and the European Union (EU) co-ordination rules can also mean that the requirement to be present in Great Britain does not apply if you are staying or living in a European Economic Area or EU state, or Ireland (depending on which co-ordination rules apply – see p379). These exceptions vary between the different benefits and tax credits, and are covered in Chapters 14 and 15.

To satisfy the presence requirement, you must show that you are physically present in Great Britain. For a benefit authority to disqualify you from benefit on the basis that you were absent from Great Britain, it must show you were absent throughout that day.[1] For further details on the meaning of presence and absence, see p331.

Other than adult disability payment and child disability payment (which require presence in the common travel area – see p302), Scottish benefits require residence, or ordinary residence, rather than presence.

3. **Past presence**

The following benefits have a past presence requirement:
- adult disability payment (ADP) (in Scotland);
- attendance allowance;
- carer's allowance;
- child disability payment (CDP) (in Scotland);
- disability living allowance (DLA);
- personal independence payment.

In addition to being present at the time you make your claim for the above benefits, you must also have been present (or treated as present – see p354) in Great Britain (the common travel area for ADP and CDP) for 104 weeks out of the past 156 weeks (26 out of the last 52 weeks for ADP, DLA and CDP) before you become entitled. However, there are exceptions when either no past presence, or a shorter period, is required.

If you are covered by the main European Union co-ordination rules or the UK–Ireland Convention (see p379), depending on the benefit, you may be exempt from the past presence requirement or you may be able to add certain periods of residence in a European Economic Area country (Ireland, if relying on the UK–Ireland Convention) to your period of presence in Great Britain (under the 'aggregation principle' – see p416).

For more details of the past presence test, including exceptions, see p302.

4. **Living in the UK for three months**

To be treated as present in Great Britain for **child benefit**, and present in the UK for **child tax credit (CTC)**, you must have been living in the UK for the three months before your first day of entitlement, or be covered by one of the exempt groups below.

While it was possible to make a new claim for **income-based jobseeker's allowance (JSA)**, it was a requirement that you had to be living in the common travel area (the UK, Ireland, Channel Islands and the Isle of Man) for the past three months in order to satisfy the habitual residence test for this benefit. However, as it is no longer possible to make a new claim for income-based JSA, this requirement is not covered in this *Handbook*. For details of how this requirement was applied, see p134 of the 13th edition of this *Handbook*.

The phrase 'living in' is not defined in the regulations and should therefore be given its ordinary, everyday meaning. It does not have the same meaning as 'presence' and you may satisfy this condition despite having been temporarily absent. 'Living in' also does not have the same meaning as habitual residence.[2] The Upper Tribunal held that a man continued to be 'living in' the UK despite a 15-month temporary absence while he was abroad travelling.[3]

When deciding whether your absence means that you stopped 'living in' the UK/common travel area, the following factors are relevant:[4]

- the reasons for your absence; *and*
- the intended, and actual, length of your absence; *and*
- the duration and connectedness (including your family ties, work, education, bank account and GP) of your previous residence in the UK/common travel area and whether any of these connections were maintained while you were abroad; *and*
- whether you maintained your accommodation in the UK/common travel area while you were abroad; *and*
- the nature of your accommodation abroad.

Note: if you return to the UK after a specific temporary absence, you are exempt from this requirement (see below). See p332 for the meaning of the phrase 'temporary absence'.

If you are covered by the European Union (EU) co-ordination rules (see p371) and have moved to the UK from a European Economic Area (EEA) country, you may be able to use periods of residence there to satisfy this condition (under the 'aggregation principle' – see p416). **Note:** although this is confirmed in guidance to child benefit and CTC decision makers,[5] it is arguable that the guidance is overly restrictive as it suggests that this only applies if your residence would satisfy an entitlement condition to a 'family benefit' in the other country, which would only be the case in Croatia, Cyprus, Denmark and Hungary.

Child benefit and child tax credit

To be treated as present in Great Britain for child benefit, and present in the UK for CTC, you must have been living in the UK for three months, ending on the first day of your entitlement.[6] This requirement does not apply if you:[7]

- are an EEA national who is a 'worker' in the UK (see p211), including if you have retained that status (see p222); *or*
- are an EEA national who is a 'self-employed person' in the UK (see p218), including if you have retained that status (see p222); *or*
- are an EEA national and would be in either of the above two groups *if* you had pre-settled status (and were therefore in a protected group – see p188); *or*
- are a non-EEA national who would be classed as a worker or self-employed person *if* you were an EEA national with pre-settled status; *or*
- are a family member of someone in any of the above four groups; *or*
- are a refugee (for details, including the duration of refugee leave, see p43, and if you are a family member of a refugee, see below); *or*

- have been granted humanitarian protection (for details, including the duration of this leave, see p43, and if you are a family member of a person granted humanitarian protection, see below); *or*
- you have been granted 'section 67 leave' as a relocated unaccompanied child (see p46); *or*
- have leave granted outside the Immigration Rules with no restriction on accessing public funds; *or*
- (from 15 September 2021, child benefit only) have leave granted by virtue of the Afghan Relocations and Assistance Policy, or the scheme for locally employed staff in Afghanistan, or the Afghan Citizens Resettlement Scheme, or you left Afghanistan in connection with the collapse of the Afghan government on 15 August 2021; *or*
- (from 22 March 2022, child benefit only) were living in Ukraine immediately before 1 January 2022 and you left in connection with the Russian invasion of 24 February 2022; *or*
- have been granted leave to remain in the UK under the destitution domestic violence concession, pending an application for indefinite leave to remain under the domestic violence rule (see p104); *or*
- have been deported or otherwise legally removed from another country to the UK;[8] *or*
- are returning to the UK after a period working abroad and, other than for last three months of your absence, you were paying UK class 1 or class 2 NI contributions; *or*
- are returning to the UK after an absence of less than 52 weeks and either:
  - before departing the UK you were ordinarily resident for three months; *or*
  - you were covered by the rules that treat you as present during a temporary absence for eight or 12 weeks during the payment of child benefit (see p351) or CTC (see p366).

If you are not covered by one of the above exemptions, you must satisfy the requirement to have been living in the UK for three months. However, see p143 for ways that you may be able to include time spent outside the UK.

Note: in most circumstances, it is no longer possible to make a new claim for CTC (see p318).

Family members of a refugee or person with humanitarian protection

If you are the family member of a refugee or a person with humanitarian protection and have leave on the basis that you joined them under the family reunion provisions (see p44), your leave does not mean you are exempt from the requirement to have been living in the UK for three months. You are therefore not entitled to child benefit (and CTC if you can claim that) until you have been living in the UK for three months.

In practice, HM Revenue and Customs does not always require such claimants to have been living in the UK for three months. However, if your claim is refused on this basis, you may be able to argue that this is unlawful discrimination. In a case involving the past presence test for disability living allowance, the Upper Tribunal held that the requirement was unlawful, not only for a claimant with leave as a refugee, but also for a claimant with leave as a family member of a refugee (and the subsequent guidance and amending regulations also cover dependent family members of someone with humanitarian protection – see p304).[9] To challenge a refusal of benefit on this basis, get advice and ask your adviser to contact CPAG, and also submit new claims for child benefit (and, if you are in one of the limited groups that can claim, CTC) as soon as you have been living in the UK for three months.

5. **Residence**

The requirement to be simply 'resident', rather than 'ordinarily resident' or 'habitually resident', is only a condition for:

- category D retirement pension – resident in Great Britain (see p314); *and*
- carer's allowance supplement – resident in Scotland (see p302); *and*
- winter heating payment and child winter heating assistance – resident in Scotland (see p317).

However, it is a necessary part of being ordinarily resident (see p147) or habitually resident (see p151).

Residence is more than a physical presence in a country and you can be resident without being present – eg, if you are abroad on holiday. Similarly, you can be present without being resident.

To be resident in a country, you must be seen to be making your home there for the time being; it need not be your only home, nor a permanent one.[10] You can remain resident during a temporary absence, depending on the duration and circumstances of your absence.[11] Your intentions to return, your accommodation, and where your family and your personal belongings are can all be relevant. It is possible to be resident in two countries at once.[12]

Note:

- You must 'reside in Scotland' to use the universal credit payment options that only apply in Scotland. In general, this applies if your address has a postcode in Scotland.[13]
- You are required to be 'living in' England or Wales for a funeral expenses payment (see p316) and a Sure Start maternity grant (see p318). The phrase 'living in' is not defined and therefore should have its ordinary, everyday meaning (see p143), which is arguably similar to 'resident'.

Children

The only benefits that can be claimed by a child under 16 which have residence requirements are disability living allowance (DLA), child disability payment (CDP), housing benefit (HB) and child benefit. For DLA and HB, the claimant must be habitually resident. For CDP, the child must be ordinarily resident and habitually resident. For child benefit, the claimant must be ordinarily resident and have a right to reside.

The residence rules apply to children in the same way as for adults. In practice, however, to decide whether or not a child satisfies the residence requirement,[14] ordinary or habitual residence is usually decided by looking at the residence of the child's parent(s), or person(s) with parental responsibility (in Scotland, parental rights and responsibilities) for them. A child who lives with that person usually has the same ordinary or habitual residence as them, so a child who joins a parent (or person with parental responsibility) may become ordinarily and habitually resident almost immediately.[15] If there is only one person with parental responsibility, the child usually has the same ordinary and habitual residence as them.[16]

Whether or not a child has a right to reside is determined in the same way as it is for an adult. So a child under 16 who is claiming child benefit (but not the child they are responsible for) must have a right to reside. A child under 16 who is claiming HB must have a right to reside in order to satisfy the habitual residence test. See Chapter 12 for who has a right to reside.

6. Ordinary residence

The following benefits and tax credits have a requirement to be ordinarily resident in Great Britain (or in the UK for child benefit, tax credits and social fund funeral payments, or Scotland for Scottish benefits):

- adult disability payment (in Scotland);
- bereavement support payment;
- Best Start grant (in Scotland);
- child benefit;
- child disability payment (in Scotland);
- child tax credit (CTC);
- employment and support allowance in youth;
- funeral support payments (in Scotland);
- incapacity benefit in youth;
- category D retirement pension;
- Scottish child payment (in Scotland);
- severe disablement allowance;
- social fund funeral payments and winter fuel payments;

- working tax credit (WTC);
- young carer grant (in Scotland).

There are some limited exceptions to the requirement to be ordinarily resident; also, the European Union (EU) co-ordination rules may assist you in satisfying it. The exceptions and assistance provided by the co-ordination rules vary between the different benefits and are covered in Chapter 13.

In practice, claims are rarely refused on the basis of ordinary residence.

You cannot be ordinarily resident without being resident (see p146).

The term 'ordinary residence' is not defined in the legislation, but caselaw has confirmed:

- the words should have their natural and ordinary meaning;[17]
- you are ordinarily resident in a country if you have a home there that you have adopted for a settled purpose and where you live for the time being (whether for a short or long duration);[18]
- subsequent events can be taken into account if they cast light on whether you were ordinarily resident on the date of your benefit claim;[19]
- ordinary residence can start on arrival (see below);
- a person in the country for a temporary purpose can be ordinarily resident in that country (see p149);
- in general, your residence must be voluntary for you to be ordinarily resident (see p149);
- ordinary residence can continue during absences abroad, but leaving to settle abroad usually ends ordinary residence (see p150);
- it is possible for a person to be ordinarily resident in more than one place or country;[20]
- a person who lives in the country but has no fixed abode can be ordinarily resident;[21]
- ordinary residence is different from the concept of 'domicile'.[22]

Ordinary residence on arrival

Ordinary residence can begin immediately on arrival in Great Britain (or the UK, or Scotland, for the relevant benefits).[23] In a family law case, a man who separated from his wife in one country (where he had lived and worked for three years) and went to live at his parents' house in another was found to become immediately ordinarily resident there. The Court of Appeal held that, where there is evidence that a person intends to make a place their home for an indefinite period, they are ordinarily resident when they arrive there.[24] In another case, a court decided that a woman returning from Australia after some months there had never lost her ordinary residence in England. However, if she had, she would have become ordinarily resident again when the boat embarked from Australia.[25] In a case involving students, they had to show that they were ordinarily resident within a few weeks of first arriving in the UK, and it was not argued that they could not be ordinarily resident because they had only just come to Great Britain.[26]

Ordinary residence while here for a temporary purpose

To be ordinarily resident in Great Britain (or the UK or Scotland), you do not have to intend, or be able, to live here permanently.

You should be ordinarily resident if you are living here 'for settled purposes as part of the regular order of [your] life for the time being whether of short or long duration'. The purpose can be for a limited period – eg, 'education, business or profession, employment, health, family, or merely love of the place'.[27]

If you are in the UK solely for business purposes, you can still be ordinarily resident here.[28] You may have several different reasons for a single stay – eg, to visit relatives, get medical advice, attend religious ceremonies and sort out personal affairs.[29]

The reason must be a settled one. This does not mean that the reason has to be long-standing,[30] but there must be evidence of it. The benefit authorities should consider how long you are likely to reside in the UK. If you intend to live here for the time being, they should accept your intention as sufficient, unless it is clearly unlikely that you are going to be able to stay. The benefit authorities should not make a deep examination of your long-term intentions.[31] The type of accommodation you occupy may be relevant.[32] If you have made regular visits to the UK, this may also be relevant.[33]

Involuntary residence

Ordinary residence generally requires that you have '*voluntarily* adopted' to live somewhere with a settled purpose.[34] Therefore, a person who is held in a place against their will is not usually ordinarily resident there. It can be arguable that if you were taken out of the country against your will (eg, as a child or for a forced marriage), you should be ordinarily resident on your return. However, if you are in the country because of circumstances that limit or remove your choice, this does not necessarily prevent you from being ordinarily resident here.

In practice, the question of determining ordinary residence if you lack the capacity to 'voluntarily adopt' your place of residence rarely arises when determining entitlement to benefits and tax credits. However, it is more common when trying to determine local authority responsibility for providing support, and so the principles established in that caselaw can be relevant. Depending on the facts, if you lack capacity you can be held to be ordinarily resident where the person who makes decisions on your behalf resides, if that is where you are based, or alternatively, where your residence is sufficiently settled (omitting the criteria for it to be 'voluntarily adopted').[35]

Deportation to the UK does not prevent you from becoming ordinarily resident here.[36] The issue is whether your residence is part of your settled purpose. If you have decided to live in the UK, it does not matter if the reason for your decision is because you were deported here. For the purposes of tax credits and child benefit, you are treated as ordinarily resident if you are in the UK as a result of deportation or having been otherwise legally removed from another country.[37]

Absence abroad

You may cease to be ordinarily resident if you go abroad. This depends on all the facts of your situation, including:

- your stated intentions when you go abroad and whether these are followed by your subsequent actions;
- why you go abroad;
- how long you stay abroad;
- what connections you keep with the country – eg, accommodation, furniture and other possessions, and visits back.[38]

If you decide to move abroad for the foreseeable future, you usually stop being ordinarily resident in Great Britain (or the UK, or Scotland) on the day you leave.[39] There can be exceptions, which depend on your circumstances, including if your plans are clearly impractical and you return to the UK very quickly.

If your absence abroad is part of your normal pattern of life, your ordinary residence may not be affected.[40] This can apply if you are out of the UK for half, or even most, of the year – eg, if you spend each summer in the UK and the winter abroad, you may still be ordinarily resident in the UK.[41]

If your absence abroad is extraordinary or temporary and you intend to return to Great Britain (or the UK or Scotland), your ordinary residence may not be affected.[42] Your subsequent actions can strengthen the relevance of your intentions – eg, if you intended to return to the UK and by the time of the decision you have, in fact, returned.[43]

However, if despite intending to return, you are away from the UK for a long time and do not keep strong connections with the UK, you may lose your ordinary residence. In one case, a citizen of the UK and colonies lived in the UK for over four years and then returned to Kenya for two years and five months because her business here failed and there was a business opportunity in Kenya. She intended to make enough money to support herself on her return to the UK. Her parents and parents-in-law remained in the UK. It was decided that she had lost her ordinary residence during her absence.[44]

In deciding whether an absence affects your ordinary residence, the decision maker must consider all your circumstances. Every absence is unique, and you should provide full details of all your circumstances including:

- why you wish to go abroad; *and*
- how long you intend to be abroad; *and*
- what you intend to do while you are abroad.

Each of these considerations must be taken into account, and it is your responsibility to demonstrate that your absence will be temporary.[45]

Note: in addition to affecting your ordinary residence, an absence may also affect your benefit entitlement if it means you cease to satisfy other residence or presence requirements for the benefit or tax credit you are claiming (see p331), or if it means you cease to be treated as a couple (see p334).

Legal residence

It may be arguable that whether or not residence must be lawful to count as ordinary residence, depends on the context. However, caselaw suggests that if this entails entitlement to a state benefit, the residence must be lawful.[46] This approach was applied recently to exclude from disability living allowance (DLA) a non-European Economic Area (EEA) national child who had overstayed his immigration leave in the UK, on the basis that he was not ordinarily resident.[47] (**Note:** ordinary residence ceased to be a requirement for DLA, attendance allowance and carer's allowance, for claims made on or after 8 April 2013.)

You may be affected by this if you are a non-EEA national defined as a 'person subject to immigration control' because you require leave and do not have it (see p98), but you are not excluded from benefits on this basis because you are in an exempt group. See p117 for the exempt groups for tax credits, p115 for child benefit and p119 for social fund payments. The requirement for residence to be lawful could also affect your entitlement to category D retirement pension (see p314).

Note: if you require leave but do not have it, but are entitled to tax credits because you are making a joint claim with a partner who is not excluded by their immigration status, HM Revenue and Customs sometimes appears to treat the provision that allows the immigration status of one partner to be ignored in a joint claim as overriding the requirement for that partner to be ordinarily resident (if interpreted as requiring the residence to be lawful) and as overriding the right to reside requirement for CTC (see p123).

7. Habitual residence

The following benefits and tax credits have a habitual residence requirement:
- adult disability benefit (in Scotland);
- attendance allowance;
- Best Start grant (in Scotland, only in limited circumstances – see p318);
- carer's allowance;
- child disability payment (in Scotland);
- disability living allowance;
- income-related employment and support allowance;

- housing benefit;
- income support;
- income-based jobseeker's allowance;
- pension credit;
- personal independence payment;
- universal credit;
- young carer grant (in Scotland).

You must satisfy (or be exempt from) the habitual residence test to get the above benefits. See Chapter 11 for details.

Note:

- You are also excluded from council tax reduction if you do not satisfy (and are not exempt from) the habitual residence requirement (see p625).[48]
- You may be entitled to a winter fuel payment from the social fund if, instead of being ordinarily resident in Great Britain, you are habitually resident in one of the listed European Economic Area (EEA) countries (see p317).
- You may be entitled to child winter heating assistance if, instead of being resident in Scotland, you are habitually resident in one of the listed EEA countries (see p317).

8. The right to reside

The following benefits and tax credits have a right to reside requirement:

- child benefit;
- child tax credit (CTC);
- income-related employment and support allowance;
- housing benefit;
- income support;
- income-based jobseeker's allowance;
- pension credit;
- universal credit.

The right to reside requirement for all the above benefits, other than child benefit and CTC, is part of the habitual residence test. To be entitled to the above benefits, you must satisfy the right to reside requirement, unless, for the means-tested benefits only, you are exempt from the habitual residence test (see p159).

You are also excluded from council tax reduction if you do not satisfy the right to reside requirement (see p625).[49]

See Chapter 11 for details of the habitual residence test and the right to reside requirement, Chapter 12 for who has a right to reside, and Chapter 13 for the residence and presence requirements for each benefit.

Notes

2. **Presence**
1 R(S) 1/66

4. **Living in the UK for three months**
2 *CL v SSWP* [2020] UKUT 146 (AAC), paras 34-39
3 *TC v SSWP (JSA)* [2017] UKUT 222 (AAC)
4 *AEKM v Department for Communities (JSA)* [2016] NICom 80, paras 21, 46-48 and 61; *TC v SSWP (JSA)* [2017] UKUT 222 (AAC), paras 21, 27 (which adopts this case into British caselaw) and 32-38
5 TCTM para 02035; para 10025 CBTM
6 **CB** Reg 23(5) CB Regs
CTC Reg 3(6) TC(R) Regs
7 **CB** Reg 23(6) CB Regs; see also para 10025 CBTM
CTC Reg 3(7) TC(R) Regs
8 **CB** Reg 23(3) CB Regs
CTC Reg 3(3) TC(R) Regs
9 *MM and IS v SSWP (DLA)* [2016] UKUT 149 (AAC); Vol 2 Ch 7 para 071716 DMG; Ch C2 para C2027 ADM; regs 2, 6, 7 and 14 The Social Security (Miscellaneous Amendments No.4) Regulations 2017 No.1015

5. **Residence**
10 R(IS) 6/96, para 19; R(P) 2/67
11 CPC/1035/2005; see also *TC v SSWP (JSA)* [2017] UKUT 222 (AAC)
12 R(IS) 9/99, para 10
13 The Universal Credit (Claims and Payments) (Scotland) Regulations 2017 No.227
14 *Re A (A Minor) (Abduction: Child's Objections)* [1994] 2 FLR 126: on habitual residence, but also applies to ordinary residence
15 *Re M (Minors) (Residence Order: Jurisdiction)* [1993] 1 FLR 495
16 *Re J (A Minor) (Abduction: Custody Rights)* [1990] 2 AC 562, p578

6. **Ordinary residence**
17 *Levene v Inland Revenue Commissioners* [1928] AC 217; R(M) 1/85
18 *R v Barnet LBC ex parte Shah* [1983] 2 AC 309
19 *Arthur v HMRC* [2017] EWCA Civ 1756
20 *IRC v Lysaght* [1928] AC 234; *Britto v SSHD* [1984] Imm AR 93; R(P) 1/01; CIS/1691/2004; *GC v HMRC (TC)* [2014] UKUT 251 (AAC)
21 *Levene v Inland Revenue Commissioners* [1928] AC 217
22 *R v Barnet LBC ex parte Shah* [1983] 2 AC 309
23 R(F) 1/62
24 *Macrae v Macrae* [1949] 2 All ER 34. The countries were Scotland and England, which are separate for family law purposes. In R(IS) 6/96, para 27, the commissioner doubted the correctness of *Macrae* because he considered it used a test very close to the 'real home' test rejected in *Shah*. He does not seem to have heard any argument about this; *Macrae* was cited in *Shah* and was not one of the cases mentioned there as wrong: pp342-43.
25 *Lewis v Lewis* [1956] 1 All ER 375
26 *R v Barnet LBC ex parte Shah* [1982] QB 688, p717E
27 *R v Barnet LBC ex parte Shah* [1983] 2 AC 309, p344; see also *Arthur v HMRC* [2017] EWCA Civ 1756, in particular paras 16 and 32
28 *Inland Revenue Commissioners v Lysaght* [1928] AC 234; *AA v SSWP (IS)* [2013] UKUT 406 (AAC)
29 *Levene v Inland Revenue Commissioners* [1928] AC 217, HL; *GC v HMRC (TC)* [2014] UKUT 251 (AAC)
30 *Macrae v Macrae* [1949] 2 All ER 34
31 *R v Barnet LBC ex parte Shah* [1983] 2 AC 309
32 R(F) 1/82; R(F) 1/62; R(P) 1/62; R(P) 4/54
33 *GC v HMRC (TC)* [2014] UKUT 251 (AAC)
34 *R v Barnet LBC ex parte Shah* [1983] 2 AC 309
35 *R Waltham Forest LBC ex parte Vale*, unreported, 11 February 1985; but see also *R (Cornwall Council) SSH and another* [2015] UKSC 46
36 *Gout v Cimitian* [1922] 1 AC 105
37 **TC** Reg 3(3) TC(R) Regs
CB Reg 23(3) CB Regs

38 R(F) 1/62; R(M) 1/85; *Britto v SSHD* [1984] Imm AR 93
39 *Hopkins v Hopkins* [1951]; *R v Hussain* [1971] 56 Crim App R 165; *R v IAT ex parte Ng* [1986] Imm AR 23 (QBD); *Al Habtoor v Fotheringham* [2001] EWCA Civ 186
40 *R v Barnet LBC ex parte Shah* [1983] 2 AC 309
41 *Levene v Inland Revenue Commissioners* [1928] AC 217; *Inland Revenue Commissioners v Lysaght* [1928] AC 234; *AA v SSWP (IS)* [2013] UKUT 406 (AAC)
42 *R v Barnet LBC ex parte Shah* [1983] 2 AC 309, p342D
43 *R v IAT Ex parte Siggins* [1985] Imm AR 14
44 *SSHD v Haria* [1986] Imm AR 165
45 *Chief Adjudication Officer v Ahmed and Others*, 16 March 1994 (CA), reported as R(S) 1/96
46 *R v Barnet LBC ex parte Shah* [1983] 2 AC 309, Lord Scarman – comments obiter; *Mark v Mark* [2005] UKHL 42, para 36 ; *MS v SSWP (DLA)* [2016] UKUT 42 (AAC)
47 *MS v SSWP (DLA)* [2016] UKUT 42 (AAC)

7. **Habitual residence**
48 Reg 12 CTRS(PR)E Regs; reg 16 CTR(SPC)S Regs; reg 16 CTR(S) Regs; reg 28 CTRSPR(W) Regs; Sch para 19 CTRS(DS)W Regs

8. **The right to reside**
49 Reg 12 CTRS(PR)E Regs; reg 16 CTR(SPC)S Regs; reg 16 CTR(S) Regs; reg 28 CTRSPR(W) Regs; Sch para 19 CTRS(DS)W Regs

Chapter 11

Habitual residence and the right to reside

This chapter covers:

This chapter explains how the habitual residence test and the right to reside requirement apply to the various benefits and tax credits, and how you can show habitual residence. For information on who has a right to reside, see Chapter 12.

1. The habitual residence test

The habitual residence test applies to the following benefits:

- adult disability payment (ADP) (in Scotland);
- attendance allowance (AA);
- Best Start grant (in Scotland, in limited circumstances – see p318);
- carer's allowance (CA);
- child disability payment (CDP) (in Scotland);
- disability living allowance (DLA);
- housing benefit (HB);
- income support (IS);
- income-based jobseeker's allowance (JSA);
- income-related employment and support allowance (ESA);
- pension credit (PC);
- personal independence payment (PIP);
- universal credit (UC);
- young carer grant (in Scotland).

To be entitled to one of these benefits, you must satisfy, or be exempt from, the habitual residence test for that benefit. The habitual residence test and the groups of people exempt from the test vary depending on the benefit you are claiming (see below).

Note:

- In this *Handbook* all references to the European Economic Area (EEA) are to be read as including Switzerland. The EEA countries are listed on p53.
- The habitual residence test only applies to the claimant(s). For further details on what this means for different benefits, see p157.
- Whether or not you satisfy, or are exempt from, the habitual residence test is a decision that must be made on the 'balance of probabilities' (see p496).
- You are also excluded from council tax reduction (see p623) if you do not satisfy (and are not exempt from) the habitual residence test.[1]
- You may be entitled to a winter fuel payment from the social fund if, instead of being ordinarily resident in Great Britain, you are habitually resident in one of the listed EEA countries (see p317).
- You may be entitled to child winter heating assistance if, instead of being resident in Scotland, you are habitually resident in one of the listed EEA countries (see p302).

Satisfying the habitual residence test for each benefit

To satisfy the habitual residence test for **means-tested benefits** you must:

- be 'habitually resident in fact' in the common travel area (the UK, Ireland, Channel Islands and the Isle of Man) (see p163); *and*
- have a right to reside in the common travel area that is not excluded for the benefit you want to claim (see p168).

However, if you are exempt from the habitual residence test for means-tested benefits (see p159), you are treated as satisfying both parts of the test.

To satisfy the habitual residence test for **AA, DLA, PIP, ADP, CA** and **CDP**, you must be 'habitually resident in fact' (see p163) in the common travel area, *unless*:

- you are exempt from this requirement (see p159); *or*
- your entitlement relies on you disapplying the 'past presence test' (on the basis that you are covered by the main European Union (EU) co-ordination rules and, other than for ADP or CDP, have a genuine and sufficient link to the UK), for which you must be 'habitually resident in fact' in Great Britain (or, for ADP or CDP, the UK and also be 'ordinarily resident' in Scotland) (see p306); *or*
- (other than for the mobility components of PIP, ADP, DLA or CDP) you are covered by the main EU co-ordination rules (or, for ADP or CDP, the UK–Ireland Convention or the agreement between the UK and Gibraltar) (see p379), and you are 'habitually resident in fact' in an EEA country (Ireland, if relying on the convention, or Gibraltar, if relying on that agreement). If this applies, you may be entitled to make a new claim (see p308), or continue to be paid an exisiting award (see p356).

To satisfy the habitual residence test for a **young carer grant**, unless you are exempt (see p159), you must be 'habitually resident in fact' (see p163) in the UK, Channel Islands, Isle of Man or the EEA (see p302).

You only need to satisfy the habitual residence test for a **Best Start grant** if you are aged under 20 and neither you nor your partner receive a 'qualifying benefit' (a means-tested benefit or tax credit). Unless you are exempt, you must be 'habitually resident in fact' in the UK, Channel Islands, Isle of Man, or, if you have pre-settled status or settled status granted under the EU Settlement Scheme or a specified free movement residence right, the EEA (see p318).

If you are exempt from the habitual residence test for the benefit you want to claim, your residence should not be examined further. Provided you meet the other conditions of entitlement, you are eligible for benefit. However, in practice, the decision maker may not consider whether you are exempt, so make this clear, particularly if you might not otherwise be accepted as satisfying the test – eg, because you have only recently arrived in the common travel area.

The DWP sometimes develops policies varying the usual procedures for specific groups. For example, internal guidance states that if, when you make your new claim, you can provide evidence that you have come to the UK under the 'gateway protection programme' or 'vulnerable person relocation scheme', or you have been granted leave as a refugee in the last eight weeks, a shorter habitual residence test applies (because you are clearly exempt) and your claim is fast-tracked.[2]

Who does the habitual residence test apply to

The habitual residence test applies to the benefit claimant.

If you have a partner living with you and you claim **UC**, you must make a joint claim and both of you must satisfy, or be exempt from, the habitual residence test. If your partner fails the test, see below.

For **other means-tested benefits** (except income-based JSA claimed as a joint-claim couple – see p158), only one partner in a couple claims the benefit. If that partner satisfies, or is exempt from, the habitual residence test, you are paid as a couple. You and your partner should therefore consider which one of you should make the claim.

However, if you have reached pension age and your partner is under pension age but is not entitled to UC because they fail the habitual residence test (and therefore you cannot make a joint claim for UC with your partner), you are treated as a single person for any claim you make for PC and/or HB.[3] If your partner subsequently satisfies the habitual residence test before reaching pension age, provided they are not defined as a 'person subject to immigration control' (see p119), your entitlement to PC and HB ends and you can make a joint claim for UC.

For **AA, DLA, PIP, ADP, CA, CDP, young carer grant** and (if you are under 20 and not getting a qualifying benefit) **Best Start grants**, the habitual residence test applies to the claimant.

The habitual residence test does not apply to any child included in your claim.

Couples claiming universal credit

If you live with your partner and claim UC, you are generally required to make a joint claim, and you and your partner must both satisfy, or be exempt from, the habitual residence test.

If you satisfy or are exempt from the habitual residence test, but your partner fails it, your joint claim is *treated as* a claim by you for UC as a single person and:[4]

- the maximum amount of UC is that for a single person;[5]
- your partner does not have to accept a claimant commitment or comply with any work-related requirements because your partner is not a claimant;[6]
- your partner's income and capital are taken into account in calculating your UC award;[7]
- your partner is not classed as a 'non-dependant' and therefore no deduction (ie, 'housing costs contribution') is made from your UC;[8]
- if you are under 35, your partner does not prevent your rent being restricted to the one-bedroom shared accommodation rate;[9]
- if you have a child, your partner does not affect your being 'responsible' for the child (so you are entitled to a child element, and, if you are receiving education, that does not exclude you from UC) nor being the child's 'responsible carer' – eg, when determining your work-related requirements;[10]
- the couple rate of the earnings threshold applies for determining when no work-related requirements apply to you, and for any self-employed 'minimum income floor'.[11]

Note: if you have reached pension age and your partner is under pension age but is not entitled to UC because they fail the habitual residence test, your claim is *not* treated as a single claim for UC. Instead, you must claim PC and HB and you are treated as a single person for each of these claims.[12] If your partner subsequently satisfies the habitual residence test before reaching pension age, provided they are not defined as a 'person subject to immigration control' (see p119), your entitlement to PC and HB ends and you can make a joint claim for UC.

Joint-claim jobseeker's allowance

If you are a member of a 'joint-claim couple' for income-based JSA (see CPAG's *Welfare Benefits and Tax Credits Handbook* for what this means) and either you or your partner do not satisfy, or you are not exempt from, the habitual residence test, you do not need to make a joint claim. The partner who is habitually resident receives income-based JSA for both of you.[13] You are paid as a couple.

Who is exempt from the habitual residence test

You are exempt from the habitual residence test for **means-tested benefits,** if you:[14]

- are a refugee (for details, including the duration of refugee leave, see p43). If you are a family member of a refugee, see p160;
- have humanitarian protection (for details, including the duration of this leave, see p43). If you are a family member of someone with humanitarian protection, see p160;
- have leave granted outside the Immigration Rules, including discretionary leave, or destitution domestic violence concession leave (see p38);
- (from 15 September 2021) have leave granted by virtue of the Afghan Relocations and Assistance Policy (ARAP), or the scheme for locally employed staff in Afghanistan ('LES Scheme'), or (for Best Start grant and young carer grant only) you have discretionary leave granted as a dependant of a person with either of the previous two types of leave, or the Afghan Citizens Resettlement Scheme or (other than for Best Start grant and young carer grant) you left Afghanistan in connection with the collapse of the Afghan government on 15 August 2021;[15]
- (from 22 March 2022) were living in Ukraine immediately before 1 January 2022 and you left in connection with the Russian invasion of 24 February 2022, *and* you have leave, or a right of abode (see p16), in the UK (including if you are British), or you are Irish;[16]
- have been deported, expelled or legally removed from another country to the UK and you are not a 'person subject to immigration control' (see p93);
- are an EEA national and are a 'worker' (see p211), including if you retain this status (see p222);
- are an EEA national and are a 'self-employed person' (see p218), including if you retain this status (see p222);
- are the family member (see p239), other than an extended family member, of someone in either of the above two bullet points;
- are an EEA national and a 'frontier worker' (see p278);
- have pre-settled status and you are a family member (see p240), other than an extended family member, of someone in the above bullet point;
- have pre-settled status, and you are a family member, other than an extended family member, of a 'relevant person of Northern Ireland' (see p169) and they would be a worker or self-employed person if they were an EEA national;[17]
- are an EEA national with a permanent right to reside acquired in less than five years – eg, certain former workers or self-employed people who have retired or are permanently incapacitated, and their family members (see p275);
- (for income-related ESA only) are being transferred from an award of IS which was transitionally protected from the requirement to have a right to reside (see p174);

- (for HB only) receive IS, income-related ESA or PC;[18]
- (for HB only) receive income-based JSA and either:
  - you have a right to reside other than one that is excluded for HB (see p169); *or*
  - you have been receiving both HB and income-based JSA since 31 March 2014. Your exemption on this basis ends when either you cease to be entitled to that income-based JSA or you make a new claim for HB.[19]

You are exempt from the requirement to be habitually resident for a **young carer grant** if you are in one of the first six bullet points listed above.[20]

You are exempt from the requirement to be habitually resident for a **Best Start grant** if you or your partner are receiving a 'qualifying benefit' (a means-tested benefit or tax credit) or you are in one of the first six bullet points listed above.[21]

For **AA, CA, DLA, CDP, PIP** and **ADP**, you are exempt from the requirement to be 'habitually resident in fact' in the common travel area, if you:[22]

- have leave in the UK granted under the Afghan Citizens Resettlement Scheme, or granted by virtue of ARAP or the LES Scheme or discretionary leave as the dependant of a person with leave under either of the last two schemes. **Note:** you are also exempt from the past presence requirement;[23] *or*
- left Ukraine and are in the fifth bullet point listed above. **Note:** you are also exempt from the past presence requirement;[24]
- have refugee status or humanitarian protection or have leave as the dependent family member of either. **Note:** you are also exempt from the past presence requirement;
- are abroad in your capacity as a serving member of the armed forces (or, for CDP or ADP, a civil servant, and immediately prior to the start of either employment you satisfied the residence and presence conditions), or are living with someone who is abroad as a serving member of the armed forces (or civil servant) and you are the spouse, civil partner, (or for CDP or ADP, living together as if married/civil partners), son, stepson, daughter, stepdaughter (or, for CDP or ADP, a child in the care of) or (except for CDP) father, stepfather, mother, stepmother, mother-in-law or father-in-law of that person. **Note**: you are also treated as present for the purpose of the presence and past presence requirements (and, for CDP and ADP, treated as ordinarily resident and exempt from the past presence test).

Family members of refugees or people with humanitarian protection

If you are the family member of a refugee or someone with humanitarian protection and you have leave on the basis that you joined them under the family reunion provisions (see p44), your leave does not mean you are exempt from the habitual residence test. You are therefore not entitled to means-tested benefits until you have established your habitual residence.

This exclusion from benefits is arguably unlawful discrimination. In a case involving the past presence test for DLA, the Upper Tribunal held that the requirement was unlawful, not only for a claimant with leave as a refugee but also for a claimant with leave as a family member of a refugee. When the regulations were amended, equivalent rights were also extended to dependent family members of someone with humanitarian protection (see p304). If you have leave on this basis and are refused a means-tested benefit for failing the habitual residence test, challenge the decision and get specialist advice to argue that this is unlawful discrimination.

Note: if you live with your partner and claim UC, both of you must satisfy, or be exempt from, the habitual residence test. If only your partner does so, your joint claim is *treated as* a claim made by your partner as a single person (see p158).[25]

If you fail the habitual residence test

If you do not satisfy, and are not exempt from, the habitual residence test, you are not entitled to UC, IS, income-based JSA, income-related ESA, PC, HB, AA, DLA, PIP, ADP, CA, CDP, young carer grant or (if the test applies to you) a Best Start grant.

- For UC and PC , you are treated as not present in Great Britain.[26]
- For IS, income-based JSA, income-related ESA and HB, you are classed as a 'person from abroad'. This means for IS, income-based JSA and income-related ESA, you have an applicable amount of nil,[27] and for HB you are treated as not liable for rent.[28]
- For AA, DLA, PIP, ADP, CA, CDP, young carer grant and a Best Start grant, you have failed to meet the prescribed residence requirements.[29]

Have you been refused benefit?

1. If you are refused benefit because you have failed the habitual residence test, consider challenging this decision. See CPAG's *Welfare Benefits and Tax Credits Handbook* for information on how to do so. You may want to contact an advice agency for help with this.
2. While you are challenging the decision, make another claim. If this is refused, also challenge this decision and make another claim, and so on. That is because when the decision refusing your initial claim is looked at again, the decision maker (or First-tier Tribunal) cannot take into account circumstances that did not exist at the time the original decision was made.[30] So, if the decision maker (or tribunal) considers that you were not habitually resident at the time benefit was originally refused, but you are now (eg, because you have now been resident for an 'appreciable period' of time), they cannot take this into account when looking again at the original decision. However, if by the date of the decision on your second or subsequent claim, you had, for example, completed an appreciable period of residence or now have evidence of your 'settled intention' (see p164), this can be taken this into account. The benefit authority may say that you cannot make another claim while your appeal (or reconsideration request) is pending. That is not

the case.[31] It may help to refer to the fact that when amending regulations were introduced, the Secretary of State in 2007 said in his report that 'it needs to be emphasised that neither the fact that a person's claim for benefit has been disallowed on the grounds that the habitual residence test has not been satisfied, nor the fact that there is an outstanding appeal against that decision, prevents that individual from making a fresh claim for benefit.'[32]

3. The decision maker must consider whether you satisfied, or were exempt from, the habitual residence test on your date of claim and, if not, on each day from then until the date of their decision.[33]

4. Check whether you are exempt from the habitual residence test for the benefit you are claiming (see p159).

5. Establish which part of the test the decision maker says you have failed (if you are exempt, you do not have to satisfy *any* part).

6. If you are claiming a means-tested benefit and the decision maker considers you do not have a right to reside, check Chapter 12 for the ways in which you can have a right to reside.

7. If the decision maker considers you not to be 'habitually resident in fact', see p163.

8. The local authority must make its own decision on HB and not just follow a DWP decision that you are not habitually resident. See p159 for who is exempt and p498 for the relevance of decisions on other benefit claims.[34]

9. If you made a joint claim for UC and your partner has satisfied, or is exempt from, the habitual residence test but you have been found not to be habitually resident, your joint claim is treated as a claim by your partner as a single person. Your partner is not paid benefit for you, but your income and capital are taken into account (see p158). Your partner can continue to be paid UC while you challenge the decision on your entitlement.

10. Although the onus of proof is on the benefit authority to establish that you are *not* habitually resident, produce as much evidence as possible to show that you *are*. All decisions should be made on the balance of probabilities. See Chapter 20 for more information on evidence.

11. If you claimed UC before 25 July 2022, and it was refused on the basis that you failed the habitual residence test, it had been arguable that this did not terminate an exisiting award of HB, IS, child tax credit (CTC) and/or working tax credit (WTC). This is because until that date regulations stated that an existing award of one of these four benefits is only ended if you had claimed UC *and* the DWP was satisfied that you met the first four of the basic conditions for UC.[35] One of these conditions is that you be in Great Britain, and if you fail the habitual residence test, separate regulations *treat* you as not in Great Britain. Therefore, a decision that you failed the habitual residence test meant the DWP was *not* satisfied that you met the condition of being in Great Britain, and so your previous award of benefit should arguably have continued while you challenged the refusal of UC. However, the requirement that the DWP be satisfied that you met the conditions was removed from the regulations from 25 July 2022.[36] Furthermore, it was held in an Upper Tribunal decision that this condition should be understood *without* reference to the regulations that treat you as not 'in Great Britain' if you fail the habitual residence test.[37] A

subsequent three-judge panel of the Upper Tribunal held that these comments on the meaning of the condition were not binding (although the panel agreed with them), as the question is simply whether the DWP was in fact satisfied that the claimant was in Great Britain, as evidenced by the DWP issuing of a 'stop notice' to HMRC.[38]

2. 'Habitual residence in fact'

There is no definition of 'habitual residence' in the regulations. However, there is a considerable amount of caselaw on its meaning and certain principles have emerged from this. To count as 'habitually resident in fact' in the required area for the benefit you are claiming (see note below):

- you must be resident (see below);
- your residence must be voluntary (see below);
- you must have a settled intention to make that area your home for the time being (see p164);
- in most cases, you must have resided in that area for an 'appreciable period of time' (see p165). **Note:** this is not a fixed period and there are some exceptions.

Most disputes about whether someone is 'habitually resident in fact' concern the last two bullet points.

The decision about whether or not you are habitually resident is a factual question and must be made on the 'balance of probabilities'. You should always provide as much evidence as you can about all your circumstances that are relevant to your habitual residence. Ultimately, the burden of proof lies with the benefit authority to show that you are *not* habitually resident, but you should always provide information and evidence to show that you are habitually resident, rather than rely on this 'burden of proof'.[39] See Chapter 20 for more information about providing evidence.

Note: the area in which you need to be 'habitually resident in fact' depends on the benefit you are claiming (see p156).

Residence

You cannot be habitually resident in the required area (see p156) unless you are actually resident there. It is not enough to intend to reside there in the future.[40] For information on residence, see p146.

Voluntary residence

You cannot be 'habitually resident in fact' unless your residence is voluntary.[41] In practice, this is rarely a barrier to your being found habitually resident in fact. However, it could be relevant if you are returning to live in the required area (see p156) after having been taken or kept away against your will (see p166). **Note:** if you have been deported, expelled or otherwise legally removed from another country to the UK and you are not a 'person subject to immigration control' (see p93), you are exempt from the habitual residence test for means-tested benefits (see p159).

Settled intention

For your residence to become habitual, you must have a settled intention to reside in the required area (see p156). This is not determined just by your declaring your intention, but depends on the evidence about all the factors that are relevant to it.[42]

Your settled intention to reside does not need to be permanent; it is enough that you intend to make the required area your home for the time being.

Do you have a settled intention?

The following factors are relevant when determining whether or not you have a settled intention.

1. Your reasons for moving. If there is one or more clear reason why you have moved to the required area (such as a family breakdown, a desire to study there or an offer of employment), this helps to show your settled intention.
2. The steps you took to prepare for moving – eg, the plans you made beforehand about where you would live, enquiries about work, making arrangements for your children to attend school, contacting people you know and settling your affairs in the country you were leaving, such as closing bank accounts, disposing of property and ending a tenancy.
3. The strength of your ties to the required area compared with your ties to other places (this is sometimes called your 'centre of interests') – eg, whether you are joining family or friends, whether you have registered with a doctor or joined any clubs or associations, whether your children are in school, whether you have begun a course of study, whether you have transferred your bank account, or whether you have rented accommodation. Similarly, if you have these sort of ties outside the required area, this may indicate a weaker settled intention.
4. The viability of your continued residence is a relevant factor, but not an additional requirement. This means that you do not need to separately show that you could survive without claiming the benefits to which the habitual residence test applies.[43] The viability of your residence is simply one factor that can be taken into account when considering whether you have a settled intention to reside,[44] and therefore you can be accepted as habitually resident in fact even though you have very few or no resources.
5. Your current immigration status and your future options. For example, applying for, or obtaining pre-settled status (limited leave granted under the European Union Settlement Scheme – EUSS) or settled status (indefinite leave granted under the EUSS), and the options that each gives you to lawfully reside in the UK, are evidence of a settled intention to reside in the UK.

As with the requirement to be resident (see p146), you must be seen to be making a home in the required area, but it need not be your only home or a permanent one.[45] Therefore, a long-standing intention to move outside the required area (eg, when debts are paid) does not prevent you from being habitually resident.[46]

Events after you claim benefit, or receive a decision, may confirm that your intention was always to reside in the UK – eg, if you are refused benefit because the DWP does not accept that you have a settled intention to stay in the UK, the fact that you are still here by the time of the appeal hearing may help show that you always intended to reside here.[47]

There is a close connection between 'settled intention' and 'appreciable period': the stronger your settled intention, the shorter the period you need to reside in order to count as 'habitually resident in fact'.[48]

Appreciable period

In most cases, you do not count as 'habitually resident in fact' until you have resided in the required area (see p156) for an 'an appreciable period of time'.[49]

However, your appreciable period is reduced or may not apply at all if you are:

- a returning resident in certain circumstances (see p166); *and/or*
- covered by the main European Union (EU) co-ordination rules (see p167).

There is no fixed period of time that amounts to an appreciable period and it depends on your circumstances.[50] Benefit authorities must not set a standard minimum period of residence, and any such policy should be challenged by judicial review. There is extensive caselaw on what constitutes an appreciable period of residence. Periods of between one and three months are frequently cited,[51] but decision makers should not put too much weight on any one decision, nor should any general rule about a specific time period be derived from it.[52]

The decision maker must consider whether you had been resident for an appreciable period on your date of claim, and also on each subsequent date down to the date their decision is made, since at some point during this time, your period of residence may have become appreciable, and your entitlement should begin from that date.[53]

Your appreciable period can include visits to prepare for settled residence made before that residence is taken up.[54]

The stronger your settled intention to make your home in the common travel area for the time being, the shorter your period of actual residence need be before you can be accepted as habitually resident in fact (and vice versa).[55]

Advance claims

You can claim carer's allowance, disability living allowance (DLA), attendance allowance (AA) or personal independence payment (PIP) in advance if in the next three months (six months for AA) you will have been resident for an appreciable period and so be 'habitually resident in fact'.[56] However, in practice, this is only relevant if, from that future date, you will satisfy, or be exempt from, the past presence test (see p302).

You can make an advance claim for child disability payment (CDP) or adult disability payment (ADP) if you are likely to satisfy the residence and presence requirements, including being habitually resident, within the next 13 weeks.[57]

Your claim for a Best Start grant can be treated as having been made up to 10 days after the date it was received if the decision maker considers you would only be entitled from that later date.[58]

You cannot make an advance claim for a young carer grant and you must therefore satisfy, or be exempt from, the habitual residence test on the day of your application.[59]

You cannot make an advance claim for housing benefit or pension credit for a future date when you will have been resident for an appreciable period because the rules prevent your claim from being treated as made on a future date if you do not satisfy the habitual residence test.[60] **Note:** this also applied to income support, income-based jobseeker's allowance (JSA), and income-related employment and support allowance (ESA), but it is no longer possible to make a new claim for these benefits.[61]

This exclusion does not apply to universal credit (UC), but you can only make a UC claim in advance if the DWP considers you will be entitled within the next month and you are in a group accepted by the DWP.[62] DWP guidance states this is limited to prisoners and care leavers.[63]

Returning residents

If you were living in the required area (see p155) in the past and you return to that area, you may count as 'habitually resident in fact' either immediately on your return or after a much shorter period of residence than would otherwise be the case.[64]

Are you a returning resident?

If you are a returning resident, you should consider the following issues.[65]

1. Were you habitually resident when you were previously in the area?
2. If so, did you cease to be habitually resident when you went abroad either immediately on departure or while you were abroad?
3. If so, when did you resume habitual residence? This may involve deciding when you resumed residence, and then when that residence became 'habitual'.

If you never stopped being habitually resident in fact, you continue to be habitually resident on your return. This could apply if you only went abroad for a short period – eg, for a short holiday. It could also apply if you were abroad for an extended holiday.[66] Similarly, it can apply if your absence abroad was only ever intended to be for a temporary period. For example, in one case, a man was held not to have ceased to be habitually resident on his return from a two-year Voluntary Service Overseas placement, during which time he had given up his tenancy in the UK and put his possessions in storage.[67] It may also apply if your absence abroad was involuntary. Guidance to decision makers states that people who leave, or remain away from, the UK because of a forced marriage are not considered to have lost their habitual residence as they were abroad through no fault of their own. They are therefore considered to be habitually resident from the date of their claim.[68]

If you have ceased to count as habitually resident in fact while abroad, whether or not you need to complete a further period of residence here on your return before you can resume your habitual residence depends on the following.[69]

- The circumstances in which your earlier habitual residence was lost. If you went abroad for a temporary or conditional reason and/or you stayed away longer because of circumstances beyond your control, you may be more likely to be found habitually resident immediately on your return.
- The links between you and the required area while abroad. This could include retaining property, bank accounts and membership of organisations, maintaining contact with family and friends and making visits back to the relevant area (their frequency, length and purpose are all relevant).
- The circumstances of your return. Evidence of your settled intention is relevant (see p164).

In two cases that were heard jointly, a commissioner applied the above factors and found both claimants to be habitually resident on the day of their return.[70]

Even if you are not able to resume your previous habitual residence immediately on your return, you may still be able to argue that your previous habitual residence here is a factor that reduces the period of time that counts as an appreciable period of actual residence.

If you are covered by the European Union co-ordination rules

If you are covered by the main EU co-ordination rules (see p379), the period of time you must be resident before you can be found to be 'habitually resident in fact' can be shorter than otherwise might be required, and can be outweighed by other factors that show you are habitually resident. The co-ordination rules can only assist you in this way if you are claiming a 'special non-contributory benefit' (see p397) – ie:

- pension credit (PC);
- DLA mobility component;
- PIP mobility component;[71]
- ADP mobility component (in Scotland);
- CDP mobility component (in Scotland).

Note: income-based JSA and income-related ESA are also special non-contributory benefits, but it is no longer possible to make a new claim for either.

The main co-ordination rules state that you are entitled to 'special non-contributory benefits' in the member state in which you are 'resident'[72] and define 'residence' as the place where you 'habitually reside' (see p401).[73]

The Court of Justice of the European Union (CJEU) has held that when deciding where someone habitually resides, their length of residence in the member state cannot be regarded as an intrinsic element of the concept of residence. The case concerned a British national who lived in the UK until he was 23 and then moved to France, where he worked for 14 years until he was made redundant. He returned to the UK and was refused benefit on the basis of not having completed an appreciable period of actual residence. The CJEU held that the claimant, who was covered by the EU co-ordination rules and was claiming a special non-contributory benefit, could not be deemed not to be habitually resident merely because the period of residence completed was too short.[74] Although the case concerned a returning resident, subsequent caselaw confirms that the principle applies to any claimant covered by the EU co-ordination rules.[75] So, while 'duration and continuity of presence' is one of the factors that should be considered when determining where you habitually reside, it is only one factor and can be outweighed by others. Therefore, you cannot be denied PC or the mobility component of PIP/ADP/DLA/CDP solely because you have not completed an 'appreciable period' of actual residence in the common travel area.

3. The right to reside

The right to reside requirement applies to:

- child benefit;
- child tax credit (CTC);
- housing benefit (HB);
- income support (IS);
- income-based jobseeker's allowance (JSA);
- income-related employment and support allowance (ESA);
- pension credit (PC);
- universal credit (UC).

The right to reside requirement also applies to council tax reduction (see p623).[76]

To satisfy the right to reside requirement, you need a right to reside *other than* one that is excluded for the benefit you are claiming. For child benefit and CTC, you need to have a right to reside in the UK and for the means-tested benefits, you need to have a right to reside in the common travel area (the UK, Ireland, Channel Islands and the Isle of Man).

The details of the right to reside requirement for the above benefits, including which residence rights are excluded for specific benefits, are covered in this section. For details of the circumstances in which you have a right to reside, see Chapter 12.

Note: if you have been claiming benefits in the UK since 2004, there are transitional rules that can mean you do not need a right to reside for the benefit you want to claim, but note these do not apply to UC (see p174 for means-tested benefits and p177 for child benefit and CTC).

Who does the right to reside test apply to

The right to reside test only applies to the claimant(s).

For **UC**, if you live with your partner you generally have to make a joint claim and the right to reside test applies to both claimants. If your partner does not have a right to reside, they fail the habitual residence test and, provided you are both under pension age, your joint claim is *treated as* a claim for UC as a single person, but your partner's income and capital are taken into account (see p158).

For **means-tested benefits, other than UC**, if your partner does not have a right to reside, you can still include them in your claim and you are still paid as a couple (see p157).

If you are claiming **income-based JSA as a 'joint-claim couple'** and your partner does not have a right to reside, see p158.

If you are receiving **CTC** on the basis of a joint claim, both you and your partner must have a right to reside (see p320). If your partner ceases to have a right to reside, your entitlement to CTC ends. As it is no longer possible to make a new claim for CTC (unless you have just been granted refugee leave) you must claim UC (see p158).

The right to reside requirement does not apply to any child included in your claim for any benefit.

Means-tested benefits

The right to reside requirement for means-tested benefits is part of the habitual residence test (see p155). Therefore, check whether you are exempt from the habitual residence test – if so, you do not need to demonstrate your right to reside (see p159). If you are not exempt from the habitual residence test, in addition to having a right to reside, you must also be 'habitually resident in fact' (see p163).

The type of residence right you need

To satisfy the right to reside requirement for UC, IS, income-based JSA, income-related ESA, PC and HB, you must have a right to reside in the common travel area (ie, the UK, Ireland, Channel Islands and Isle of Man), *other than:*[77]

- pre-settled status (limited leave granted under the European Union Settlement Scheme – EUSS). For exceptions to this exclusion, and ways to satisfy the right to reside requirement if you do have pre-settled status, see below;
- limited leave to enter as the holder of an EUSS family permit (see p68) or EUSS travel permit. See second bullet point in the note below;
- as a European Economic Area (EAA) national with an initial right of residence during your first three months in the UK (to have this you must have arrived before the end of 2020) (see p203);
- as a family member of someone in the bullet point above;
- as the 'primary carer' of a British citizen who is dependent on you and would have to leave the European Union (EU) if you left the UK (often called a 'Zambrano carer' – see p261). **Note:** to date, all legal challenges to this exclusion have failed;[78]
- (except for income-based JSA) as an EEA jobseeker;
- (except for income-based JSA) as a family member of an EEA jobseeker. **Note:** this exclusion does not apply if you are a former family member of a jobseeker and you have retained your right to reside (see p174).

Note:

- If you have one of the above rights to reside, you are only excluded from benefit if it is your *only* right to reside. If you have any other right to reside that is not listed above, you satisfy the requirement, and the benefit authorities often refer to this as having a 'qualifying' right to reside.
- If you have limited leave to enter as the holder of an EUSS family permit or EUSS travel permit, although this leave does not satisfy the right to reside requirement, once you have made a valid application for settled or pre-settled status under the EUSS you are in a protected group that can potentially have a free movement right to reside (see p188), so check whether you have such a free movement right (see p192), other than one of the excluded residence rights listed above.
- If you have a partner and claim UC and only your partner has a qualifying right to reside, your joint claim for UC is treated as a UC claim by your partner as a single person (see p158).[79]
- To be entitled to council tax reduction, you must have a non-excluded right to reside. The exclusions vary between England, Wales and Scotland (see p625).

Pre-settled status

If you have pre-settled status (limited leave granted under the EUSS – see p59), this does not satisfy the right to reside requirement by itself since this leave is listed as an excluded right to reside in each of the means-tested benefit regulations. However, there are several circumstances in which you may either have a qualifying right to reside while having pre-settled status or be exempt from the habitual residence test. The legislation in Steps 1 to 5 below is not in dispute.

However, the benefit authorities do not currently accept the arguments in Step 6.[80]

To obtain benefit as quickly as possible, it is helpful to work through the following steps.

Step 1: Are you an Irish citizen? If you are, your citizenship satisfies the right to reside requirement, and that is not altered by your having pre-settled status (see p182).

Step 2: Do you have a free movement right to reside? Having pre-settled status means you are in one of the protected groups (see p188) that can have a free movement right to reside (see p192). If you have such a right to reside, other than one listed above, you satisfy the right to reside requirement for the means-tested benefit(s) you want to claim.[81]

Step 3: Were you living in Ukraine immediately before 1 January 2022 and left due to the Russian invasion of 24 February 2022? If you did, your pre-settled status means you are exempt from the habitual residence test (see p159).

Step 4: Are you the family member of an EEA frontier worker? If you are the family member (see p240), other than an extended family member, of an EEA frontier worker (see p278), and you have pre-settled status, you are exempt from the habitual residence test (see p159).

Step 5: Are you the family member (other than an extended family member) of a 'relevant person of Northern Ireland' (see below) who *would* have a free movement right to reside under the EEA Regulations (see p192) (other than one of the excluded residence rights listed above) *if* they were an EEA national? If this applies, the regulations for each of the means-tested benefits do *not* exclude you.[82]

A **'relevant person of Northern Ireland'** is defined as a British or Irish citizen who was born in Northern Ireland and at the time of their birth at least one of their parents was a British or Irish citizen or had the right to reside in Northern Ireland without a time limit.[83]

Step 6: If you have pre-settled status but no other non-excluded right to reside, your pre-settled status does not satisfy the right to reside requirement because the regulations for each of the means-tested benefits list pre-settled status as an excluded right to reside.[84] However, you may be able to argue that this exclusion of pre-settled status is unlawful if the consequent refusal of benefit would mean you do not have sufficient resources to live in dignified conditions or you are at risk of destitution, based on one or more of the arguments below. Note that you can make these arguments if you do not have any qualifying free movement right to reside, or in addition to arguing that you do have a qualifying free movement right to reside. Furthermore, even if you did not make these arguments before your claim was refused, you can do so as part of your mandatory reconsideration request or appeal. You should provide as much information and evidence to support your arguments as you can, including details of why you cannot work and why any other potential resources are either not available or are insufficient.

It may be arguable that excluding pre-settled status as a qualifying right to reside for a means-tested benefit is unlawful if one or more of the following arguments apply.

- **If this exclusion means you cannot live in dignified conditions, and therefore breaches your rights under the EU Charter of Fundamental Rights.** This argument is based on a Court of Justice of the European Union (CJEU) judgment that held that an EU citizen who is lawfully resident in the UK on the basis of having pre-settled status can rely on the EU Charter of Fundamental Rights and, consequently, the benefit authority cannot refuse a benefit such as UC without first checking that refusal does not violate specific rights under the Charter, in particular to live in dignified conditions.[85] This argument was recently accepted by the Upper Tribunal in a decision that held the Charter continues to apply after the end of the transition period to those with rights under the Withdrawal Agreement.[86] The Upper Tribunal held that where refusal of UC would mean that a claimant and her child could not live in dignified conditions, the exclusion of pre-settled status as a qualifying right to reside must be disapplied to enable entitlement to UC. Dignified conditions was held to mean having sufficient resources to have adequate food, clothing, hygiene and accommodation, including heating. In assessing the risk of not living in dignified conditions, the benefit authority can take account of alternative support that is currently available, and the ability to get paid work, but not if these are only theoretical and not actually options in practice. The DWP's appeal to the Court of Appeal was, at the time of writing, due to be heard in March 2023.[87] The DWP policy is to 'stay' (not decide; 'sist' in Scotland) a decision on your claim or mandatory reconsideration request until the final outcome is known in this test case. However, DWP guidance states that a claim should not be stayed if this would cause hardship.[88] There is no right of appeal against a decision to stay, but you can request that your claim be decided, and the recent Upper Tribunal decision applied to your claim, because otherwise you would suffer hardship. If the DWP continues to stay making a decision, you should get advice on pursuing a judicial review (see p467). For further information including template letters, see cpag.org.uk/destitutepss.
- **If this exclusion means you are at risk of destitution and unlawfully discriminates against you under the Human Rights Act 1998.** This argument is based on comparing your circumstance of being excluded from benefits during a period of limited leave granted under the EUSS (pre-settled status), with a person excluded from benefits during a period of limited leave granted subject to a 'no recourse to public funds' condition due to this condition meaning they are defined as a 'person subject to immigration control' (see p93). The difference is that in the latter circumstance, the person may be able

to apply to have the condition lifted in specific circumstances that include being destitute or at risk of destitution (see p33). This argument was raised, but not considered, in the recent Upper Tribunal case referred to above.

- **If this exclusion means you are at risk of destitution and unlawfully discriminates against you under the Human Rights Act 1998 in the specific circumstances of domestic violence.** This argument is similar to the one above, but only applies if your pre-settled status was granted due to your relationship (already existing on 31 December 2020) with an EEA national in the UK since before the end of 2020, and that relationship has now broken down due to domestic violence or abuse. The comparison is with a person who has limited leave granted subject to a no recourse to public funds condition, granted on the basis of their relationship (eg, with an EEA national in the UK with settled status, which began *after* the end of 2020), whose relationship has broken down due to domestic violence or abuse. The difference is that in the latter circumstance, the person may be able to apply for destitution domestic violence concession leave, which provides access to benefits (see p104).
- **If this exclusion amounts to unlawful nationality-based discrimination under the Withdrawal Agreement.** This argument requires acceptance that the protection from nationality-based discrimination provided by the Withdrawal Agreement[89] is sufficiently different from the protections provided by the Treaty on the Functioning of the EU, which the CJEU and UK Supreme Court each held did not to apply.[90]

All of the above arguments are legally complex and, at the time of writing, cases relying on one or more of these arguments were due to be heard by the Upper Tribunal and the Court of Appeal. The outcome of all these cases will affect the arguments that can be made. See CPAG's *Welfare Rights Bulletin* and the online version of this *Handbook* on AskCPAG for updates. If your claim has been refused and you need to rely on any of these arguments, challenge the refusal, get advice and ask your adviser to contact CPAG.

Note:

- The CJEU and Upper Tribunal judgments referred to above do not apply if you have pre-settled status granted by virtue of having a right to reside as a 'Zambrano carer' (see p261) because these rights are not provided under the Withdrawal Agreement, which the Upper Tribunal held to be the reason the Charter of Fundamental Rights continues to apply beyond the end of the transition period.
- If you have pre-settled status, you should apply for settled status as soon as you become eligible. Settled status satisfies the right to reside requirement for all benefits that have it. For more details about moving from pre-settled to settled status, see p63.

Jobseekers

If your only right to reside is as an EEA jobseeker, you do not satisfy the right to reside test for any of the means-tested benefits except income-based JSA (and child benefit and CTC).

Note:

- Challenges to the exclusion from HB of those whose only right to reside is as an EEA jobseeker have failed.[91]
- It is arguable that UC is a benefit designed to facilitate access to the labour market, and that it is therefore unlawful to exclude someone whose only right to reside is as a jobseeker.[92] However, the Court of Appeal has rejected this argument in relation to income-related ESA (see p293).[93]

Family members of jobseekers

If your only right to reside is as a family member (see p239) of an EEA jobseeker, that does not satisfy the right to reside requirement for any of the means-tested benefits except income-based JSA, but *does* satisfy the requirement for child benefit and CTC.

If you previously had a right to reside as a family member of an EEA jobseeker and you retain that because the EEA jobseeker has died or no longer lives in the UK or your marriage or civil partnership them has been terminated, your retained right to reside as a former family member of an EEA jobseeker satisfies the right to reside requirement for *all* means-tested benefits, as well as for child benefit and CTC. This was confirmed by the Court of Session in Scotland.[94] For further details on former family members who can retain their residence rights, see p249.

If you have been getting benefit since April 2004

You do not need a right to reside to be entitled to any of the means-tested benefits, except UC, if you have been receiving any combination of the following benefits continuously since 30 April 2004:[95]

- council tax benefit (until it was abolished from 1 April 2013);
- HB;
- IS;
- income-based JSA;
- income-related ESA (only from 31 October 2011 – see below);
- PC.

This transitional protection means you do not need a right to reside in order to continue to receive that benefit, or if you make a new claim for HB or PC, provided the periods of entitlement have been continuous since 30 April 2004.

UC is not covered by this transitional protection. However, if you have been residing in the UK since 2004, and you are an EEA national, family member of an EEA national, or have had a derivative right to reside, check whether you can obtain settled status (indefinite leave to remain under the EUSS). This leave satisfies the right to reside requirement for all benefits that have it from the date the leave is granted, and while your EUSS application is pending, you are in a protected group that can potentially have one or more free movement residence rights (see p188). For details on eligibility for settled status, see p59. If you need immigration advice about applying to the EUSS, or about your other immigration options, see Appendix 2.

The rules on transitional protection did not apply to income-related ESA when ESA was introduced – it was only added from 31 October 2011.

If you were entitled to IS on the grounds of disability or incapacity for work and were reassessed and transferred to income-related ESA, you were exempt from the habitual residence test on the date of transfer.[96]

For transitional protection to apply, you must have been the claimant throughout the whole period of continuous entitlement, rather than a partner, child or parent of a claimant.[97]

The benefit authorities rarely check, or even ask, whether you have transitional protection. So, if you have been receiving one or more of the above benefits since 30 April 2004, you should always make this clear when you make your claim, and provide evidence.[98]

Example

Astrid is Swedish and came to the UK in January 2004. She had health problems and claimed IS on grounds of incapacity while living with friends. In 2008, she moved into a bedsit and claimed HB. In 2012, Astrid's IS was converted to income-related ESA. Four months ago, Astrid reached pension age and sought help to claim PC. The advice agency also helped her to apply to the EUSS and her application is still pending.

Astrid did not need to satisfy the right to reside requirement for any of these benefit claims because she had been in receipt of one or more of the relevant benefits for every day since 30 April 2004.

If Astrid were younger and needed to claim UC, rather than PC, she would not have transitional protection. She would not be entitled to UC as she does not have a right to reside. However, if she is granted settled status, she would have a right to reside that would enable her to be entitled to UC from the date that leave is granted.

Child benefit and child tax credit

For child benefit and CTC, the right to reside requirement is part of the presence test. This also requires you to be ordinarily resident (see p147) in the UK and to have lived in the UK for the past three months (see p143).

If you do not have a right to reside, you are treated as not present in the UK and therefore not entitled to child benefit or CTC.[99]

The type of residence right you need

To satisfy the right to reside requirement for child benefit and CTC, you must have a right to reside in the UK, *other than:*[100]

- pre-settled status (limited leave granted under the EUSS). For exceptions to this exclusion, and ways to satisfy the right to reside requirement if you have pre-settled status, see below;
- limited leave to enter as the holder of an EUSS family permit or travel permit (see p67). See the second bullet point in the note below; *or*
- as the primary carer of a British citizen who is dependent on you and who would have to leave the EU if you left the UK (often called a 'Zambrano carer' – see p261). However, you are not excluded on this basis if you are working in the UK and a national of Morocco, San Marino, Tunisia or Turkey (or Algeria if you made your claim before 1 January 2021[101]), because you are covered by agreements that provide for equal treatment in relation to family benefits that, therefore, override this exclusion (see p116).[102] To date, all other legal challenges to this exclusion have failed.[103]

Note:

- If you have one of the above rights to reside, you are only excluded if that is your *only* right to reside. If you have any other right to reside that is not listed above, you satisfy the requirement.
- If you have limited leave to enter as the holder of an EUSS family permit or EUSS travel permit, although this leave does not satisfy the right to reside requirement, once you have made a valid application for settled or pre-settled status under the EUSS you are in a protected group that can potentially have a free movement right to reside (see p188), so check whether you have such a free movement right (see p192), other than one of the excluded residence rights listed above.
- If you are not entitled to child benefit for a child living with you because you do not have a non-excluded right to reside, someone else who contributes to the cost of that child may be able to claim child benefit instead. To be entitled, they must contribute at least the amount of child benefit that would be payable for the child.[104] See CPAG's *Welfare Benefits and Tax Credits Handbook* for further details.
- The CJEU dismissed an application from the European Commission to declare the right to reside test for child benefit and CTC unlawful.[105] The Court of Appeal in Northern Ireland has also held that the right to reside requirement for child benefit is not unlawful.[106] See p413 for more information.

Pre-settled status

The child benefit and CTC regulations list pre-settled status as an excluded right to reside that does not, by itself, satisfy that requirement for either benefit. However, there are several circumstances in which you may have a qualifying right to reside while having pre-settled status (see Steps 1 to 3 below). **Note:** the exclusion of pre-settled status has been held not to be unlawfully discriminatory. For details and possible arguments, see Step 4 below.

To obtain benefit as quickly as possible, it is helpful to work through the following steps.

Step 1: Are you an Irish citizen? If you are, your citizenship satisfies the right to reside requirement, and that is not altered by your having pre-settled status (see p182).

Step 2: Do you have a free movement right to reside? Having pre-settled status means you are in one of the protected groups (see p188) that can have a free movement right to reside (see p192), and if you have such a right to reside, other than the one in the last bullet point listed above, that satisfies the right to reside requirement for child benefit and CTC.

Step 3: Are you the family member (see p240), other than an extended family member, **of a 'relevant person of Northern Ireland'** who *would* have a free movement right to reside under the EEA Regulations if they were are an EEA national (see p170)? If this applies, the regulations for child benefit and CTC do not exclude you on the basis of your pre-settled status.[107]

Step 4: If you have pre-settled status but no other non-excluded right to reside, your pre-settled status does not satisfy the right to reside requirement because the regulations for child benefit and CTC exclude this right to reside. For details of the legal challenges to the exclusion of pre-settled status for means-tested benefits and possible arguments that may also apply to CTC, and, in exceptional circumstances, to child benefit, see Step 6 on p170. Those arguments are unlikely to assist you to access child benefit because it is not a subsistence benefit, and is unlikely to significantly affect your ability to live in dignified conditions or your risk of destitution.

Note: if you are not entitled to child benefit for a child living with you, consider whether someone else who contributes to the cost of that child could be entitled claim child benefit instead.[108]

If you have been getting benefit since April 2004

The right to reside requirement only applies to child benefit and CTC claims made on or after 1 May 2004.[109]

If you are still receiving the same award of child benefit that began before 1 May 2004, you do not need a right to reside.

If you have been claiming CTC since before 1 May 2004, you also do not need a right to reside to continue to receive it. Although the tax credit rules treat you as making a new claim each year when you respond to your annual declaration (or when you receive a notice saying you will be treated as having made a declaration), this renewal claim does not require a right to reside.[110]

Note: if a change of circumstances ends your CTC entitlement, or you are invited to claim UC under 'managed migration', you need a right to reside to be entitled to UC. If you are an EEA national, or a family member of an EEA national, or you have a derivative right to reside, you may be able to obtain settled status (indefinite leave granted under the EUSS). This leave satisfies the right to reside requirement for all benefits that have it from the date the leave is granted, and while your EUSS application is pending, you are in a protected group that can potentially have one or more free movement residence rights (see p188). For details on eligibility for settled status, see p57, and if you need immigration advice about applying to the EUSS or about your other immigration options, see Appendix 2.

Notes

1. **The habitual residence test**

1 Sch para 21 CTRS(DS)E Regs; reg 12 CTRS(PR)E Regs; reg 16 CTR(SPC)S Regs; reg 16 CTR(S) Regs; reg 28 CTRSPR(W) Regs; Sch para 19 CTRS(DS)W Regs
2 See *Refugees and Asylum Seekers* at rightsnet.org.uk/universal-credit-guidance; see also House of Commons, *Hansard*, answer to Written Question 238412, 2 April 2019
3 Art 7(2)(b) and (3)(b) WRA(No.31)O; HB Circular A9/2019, paras 15-17; Vol 13 Ch 77 paras 77035, 77150-1 and 77160 note 2 DMG
4 ss3 and 4(1)(c) and (2) WRA 2012; regs 3(3) and 9 UC Regs
5 Regs 3(3) and 36(3) UC Regs
6 ss3 and 4(1)(e) WRA 2012; reg 3(3) UC Regs; reg 9 UC,PIP,JSA&ESA(C&P) Regs
7 Regs 3(3), 18(2) and 22(3) UC Regs
8 Sch 4 para 9(2)(b) UC Regs
9 Sch 4 paras 27 and 28 UC Regs
10 ss4(1)(d) and 19(6) WRA 2012; regs 4, 14(1)(c), 24 and 86 UC Regs
11 Regs 62(3) and (4) and 90 UC Regs
12 Art 7(1) and (2)(a) and (b) and (3)(b) WRA(No.31)O; HB Circular A9/2019, paras 15-17; Vol 13 Ch 77 paras 77035 note 2, 77150-1 and 77160 DMG
13 Reg 3E(1) and (2)(d) JSA Regs
14 **UC** Reg 9(4) UC Regs
IS Reg 21AA(4) IS Regs
JSA Reg 85A(4) JSA Regs
ESA Reg 70(4) ESA Regs
PC Reg 2(4) SPC Regs
HB Reg 10(3B) HB Regs; reg 10(4A) HB(SPC) Regs
15 See ADM Memo 14/21 and DMG Memo 11/21
16 See also ADM Memos 11/22 and 1/23; DMG Memo 8/22; HB Circular A4/2022
17 See also ADM Memo 19/20 and DMG Memo 17/20
18 Reg 10(3B)(k) HB Regs; reg 10(4A)(k) HB(SPC) Regs; *LB Hillingdon v MJ and Another (HB)* [2009] UKUT 151 (AAC)
19 Reg 3 HB(HR)A Regs
20 Reg 8(2) CA(YCG)(S) Regs
21 Sch 2 para 4(1)(b) and (2) and Sch 3 para 3(1)(b) and (2) and Sch 4 para 4(1)(b) and(2) EYA(BSG)(S) Regs
22 **AA** Regs 2(2) and (3A), and 2C SS(AA) Regs
DLA Regs 2(2) and (3A), and 2C SS(DLA) Regs
PIP Regs 19, 20 and 23A SS(PIP) Regs
CA Regs 9(3) and 9C SS(ICA) Regs
CDP Reg 5(6)-(7) and (10A) DACYP(S) Regs
ADP Regs 15(7)-(8) and 17 DAWAP(S) Regs
23 See ADM Memo 14/21 and DMG Memo 11/21

24 See also ADM Memo 11/22 and DMG Memo 8/22
25 Regs 3(3), 18(2), 22(3) and 36(3) UC Regs; reg 9 UC,PIP,JSA&ESA(C&P) Regs
26 **UC** Reg 9 UC Regs
PC Reg 2 SPC Regs
27 **IS** Regs 21 and 21AA and Sch 7 para 17 IS Regs
JSA Regs 85 and 85A and Sch 5 para 14 JSA Regs
ESA Regs 69 and 70 and Sch 5 para 11 ESA Regs
28 Reg 10(1) HB Regs; reg 10(1) HB(SPC) Regs
29 **AA** s64(1) SSCBA 1992; reg 2(1) SS(AA) Regs
DLA s71(6) SSCBA 1992; reg 2(1) SS(DLA) Regs
PIP s77(3) WRA 2012; reg 16 SS(PIP) Regs
CA s70(4) SSCBA 1992; reg 9(1) SS(ICA) Regs
YCG Reg 8 CA(YCG)(S)Regs
BSG Sch 2 para 1(c) and para 4 EYA(BSG)(S)Regs
CDP Reg 5 DACYP(S) Regs
30 Reg 3(9) SS&CS(DA) Regs; reg(5)(2) UC,PIP,JSA&ESA(DA) Regs; s12(8)(b) SSA 1998
31 s8(2) SSA 1998
32 Statement by the Secretary of State for Work and Pensions given as part of Cm 7073, May 2007, para 20, available at gov.uk/government/uploads/system/uploads/attachment_data/file/243307/7073.pdf
33 See, for example, *GE v SSWP (ESA)* [2017] UKUT 145 (AAC), reported as [2017] AACR 34, paras 52-58; and *SSWP v KK (JSA)* [2019] UKUT 313 (AAC), para 8
34 Confirmed in *EP v SSWP (JSA)* [2016] UKUT 445 (AAC), paras 24-25
35 Reg 8 UC(TP) Regs; s4(1)(a)-(d) WRA 2012
36 Reg 5(3) Univeral Credit (Transitional Provisions) Amendment Regulations 2022 No.752 omitted para (1)(b) of reg 8 UC(TP) Regs; see also ADM Memo 16/22, paras 14-16
37 *SK v HMRC and SSWP (UC)* [2022] UKUT 10 (AAC); *JL v Calderdale MBC and SSWP (UC)* [2022] UKUT 9 (AAC); see also different view taken in *HMRC v AB* [2021] UKUT 209 (AAC); see also CTC/923/2018, unreported, especially paras 39 and 52
38 *HMRC v DWP and SA (TC)* [2022] UKUT 350 (AAC); see also *HMRC v SSWP and GS(TC)* [2023] UKUT 9 (AAC)

2. **'Habitual residence in fact'**

39 R(IS) 6/96, para 15
40 CIS/15927/1996
41 *R v Barnet LBC ex parte Shah* [1983] 2 AC 309, p342; *Cameron v Cameron* [1996] SLT 306; R(IS) 9/99
42 *Nessa v Chief Adjudication Officer* [1999] UKHL 41
43 CIS/4474/2003, paras 15-16
44 R(IS) 2/00, para 28, followed in CIS/1459/1996 and CIS/16097/1996
45 R(IS) 6/96, para 19
46 *M v M (Abduction: England and Scotland)* [1997] 2 FLR 263
47 R(IS) 2/00, para 30
48 CJSA/1223/2006; R(IS) 7/06; CIS/1304/97 and CJSA/5394/98, paras 29-31
49 *Nessa v Chief Adjudication Officer* [1999] UKHL 41, reported in R(IS) 2/00
50 *Nessa v Chief Adjudication Officer* [1999] UKHL 41, reported in R(IS) 2/00; *Cameron v Cameron* [1996] SLT 306
51 CIS/4474/2003; R(IS) 7/06
52 CIS/1972/2003; CIS/2559/2005
53 R(IS) 2/00; CIS/11481/1995; *SSWP v KK (JSA)* [2019] UKUT 313 (AAC), para 8
54 *Nessa v Chief Adjudication Officer* [1999] UKHL 41, reported in R(IS) 2/00, para 26
55 CJSA/1223/2006; R(IS) 7/06; CIS/1304/97 and CJSA/5394/98, paras 29-31
56 **AA** s65(6) SSCBA 1992
CA Reg 13 SS(C&P) Regs
DLA Reg 13A(1) SS(C&P) Regs
PIP Reg 33(1) UC,PIP,JSA&ESA(C&P) Regs
57 Regs 5(9) and 24 DACYP(S) Regs; reg 35 DAWAP(S) Regs
58 Reg 4 EYA(BSG)(S) Regs
59 Reg 8 CA(YCG)(S) Regs
60 **PC** Reg 13D(4) SS(C&P) Regs
HB Reg 83(10) HB Regs; reg 64(11) HB(SPC) Regs
61 Reg 13(9) SS(C&P) Regs
62 Reg 32 UC,PIP,JSA&ESA(C&P) Regs
63 para A2048 ADM
64 *Nessa v Chief Adjudication Officer* [1999] UKHL 41, reported in R(IS) 2/00
65 CIS/1304/1997 and CJSA/5394/1998, para 11
66 *TC v SSWP (JSA)* [2017] UKUT 222 (AAC)
67 *KS v SSWP (SPC)* [2010] UKUT 156 (AAC)
68 HB/CTB Circular A22/2010, paras 11-12
69 CIS/1304/97 and CJSA/5394/98, paras 34-38

70 CIS/1304/97 and CJSA/5394/98, paras 40-41
71 *SSWP v DS* [2019] UKUT 238 (AAC); Ch C2 para C2097 and Appendix 1 para 4 ADM
72 Art 70(4) EU Reg 883/04
73 Art 1(j) EU Reg 883/04
74 *Swaddling v Chief Adjudication Officer*, C-90/97 [1999]
75 R(IS) 3/00

3. **The right to reside**

76 Reg 12 CTRS(PR)E Regs; reg 16 CTR(SPC)S Regs; reg 16 CTR(S) Regs; reg 28 CTRSPR(W) Regs; Sch para 19 CTRS(DS)W Regs
77 **UC** Reg 9(3) UC Regs
IS Reg 21AA(3) IS Regs
JSA Reg 85A(3) JSA Regs
ESA Reg 70(3) ESA Regs
PC Reg 2(3) SPC Regs
HB Reg 10(3A) HB Regs; Reg 10(4) HB(SPC) Regs
78 Most recently *R (on the application of HC) v SSWP and Others* [2017] UKSC 73
79 Regs 3(3), 18(2), 22(3) and 36(3) UC Regs
80 See, for example, DWP letter to the Work and Pensions Select Committee (15 July 2022) at committees.parliament.uk/publications/23183/documents/169469/default
81 ADM Memo 29/20, paras 24 and 87-114; DMG Memo 25/20, paras 23-35 and 92-119
82 **UC** Reg 9(3A) UC Regs
IS Reg 21AA(3B) IS Regs
JSA Reg 85A(3B) JSA Regs
ESA Reg 70(3B) ESA Regs
PC Reg 2(3B) SPC Regs
HB Reg 10(3AB) HB Regs; reg 10(4ZB) HB(SPC) Regs
Confirmed in ADM Memo 19/20 and DMG Memo 17/20
83 Appendix EU Annex 1, IR; see also ADM Memo 19/20, para 10 and DMG Memo 17/20, para 10
84 **UC** Reg 9(3)(c)(i) UC Regs
IS Reg 21AA(3A)(a) IS Regs
JSA Reg 85A(3A)(a) JSA Regs
ESA Reg 70(3A)(a) ESA Regs
PC Reg 2(3A)(a) SPC Regs
HB Reg 10(3AA)(a) HB Regs; reg 10(4ZA)(a)HB(SPC) Regs
85 *CG v Department for Communities NI*, C-709/20 [2021], paras 84-93; Art 1 EU Charter of Fundamental Rights
86 *SSWP v AT (Aire Centre and IMA Intervening)* [2022] UKUT 330 (AAC)
87 *SSWP v AT* case ref: CA-2023-000085 due to be heard 8 March 2023
88 DWP, *Suspension and Termination Guide*, paras 1001, 4053 and 4100-02
89 Art 12 WA 2019
90 *CG v Department for Communities NI*, C-709/20 [2021]; *Fratila and Tanase v SSWP* [2021] UKSC 53
91 Most recently, *Stach v Department for Communities and DWP* [2018] NIQB 93
92 *Vatsouras (C-22/08) and Koupatantze (C-23/08) v Arbeitsgemeinschaft (ARGE) Nurnberg* 900 [2009]
93 *Alhashem v SSWP* [2016] EWCA Civ 395
94 *Slezak v SSWP* [2017] CSIH 4, reported as [2017] AACR 21
95 Reg 6(1) SS(HR)A Regs, preserved by reg 11(2) SS(PA)A Regs
96 Reg 70(4)(l) ESA Regs; reg 10A ESA(TP)(EA) Regs
97 CIS/1096/2007
98 For example, see *AP v SSWP* [2018] UKUT 307 (AAC)
99 **CB** s146 SSCBA 1992; reg 23(4) CB Regs
CTC s3(3) TCA 2002; reg 3(5) TC(R) Regs
100 **CB** Reg 23(4) CB Regs
CTC Reg 3(5) TC(R) Regs
101 **CB** Regs 23(4A)(a) CB Regs
CTC Reg 3(5A)(a) TC(R) Regs
102 **CB** Regs 1(3) and 23(4)(b) and (4A) CB Regs
CTC Reg 3(5)(b)(ii), (5A) and (12) TC(R) Regs
HMRC v HEH and SSWP (TC and CHB) [2018] UKUT 237 (AAC)
103 Most recently, *R (on the application of HC) v SSWP and Others* [2017] UKSC 73
104 s143(1)(b) SSCBA 1992
105 *European Commission v UK*, C-308/14 [2016]
106 *Commissioners for HMRC v Aiga Spiridonova*, [2014] NICA 63
107 **CB** Regs 1(3) and 23(4B) CB Regs
CTC Reg 3(5B) and (11) TC(R) Regs
108 s143(1)(b) SSCBA 1992
109 **CB** Reg 23(4) CB Regs
CTC Reg 3(5)(a) TC(R) Regs
110 Reg 3(5)(a) TC(R) Regs

Chapter 12

Who has a right to reside

This chapter covers:

This chapter explains who has a right to reside. For information on the benefits and tax credits that require a right to reside, details of the requirement for each and the types of residency rights that are specifically excluded, see p168.

The right to reside requirement is only one of the residence and presence conditions that must be satisfied for some benefits and tax credits. For all the residence and presence rules for each benefit, see Chapter 13.

If you, your partner and child are *not* all British or Irish citizens, you also need to check whether your benefit entitlements are affected by being defined as a 'person subject to immigration control' (see Chapters 7 and 8).

1. Introduction

Whether or not you have a right to reside depends on your nationality, immigration status and your other particular circumstances, and also on the nationality, immigration status and other circumstances of your family members and certain people for whom you care. You may have more than one right of residence, or you may not have any.

Any residence right is sufficient to satisfy the right to reside requirement, unless it is specifically excluded for the particular benefit you want to claim (see p169 and p176).

The residence rights of some people are more complicated than others. In general, if you are a European Economic Area (EEA) national (see p53), or a family member or primary carer of an EEA national, and you began residing in the UK before 11pm on 31 December 2020, or you are the family member of such an EEA national and you have joined them in the UK since that date, your residence rights are more complex. The majority of this chapter therefore covers the rights of these groups.

Note: in this *Handbook,* all references to the EEA are to be read as including Switzerland. The EEA countries are listed on p53.

2. British, Irish and Commonwealth citizens

If you are a British citizen, including if you also hold another nationality, you have an automatic right of residence in the UK under UK law and, therefore, do not require leave to enter or remain in the UK.

British citizens do not automatically confer residence rights on their family members. If you are not a British citizen, but since before 31 December 2020 you have been, and continue to be, a family member of a British citizen or a dual British/European Economic Area (EEA) citizen, or the primary carer of a British citizen, you may, in limited circumstances, have a European free movement right to reside (see p192).

If you are a Commonwealth citizen and have been a long-term resident in the UK (eg, if you are part of the 'Windrush generation'), you may have a right of residence on the basis of having the right of abode (see p16), indefinite leave or British citizenship. If you are unsure of your status, or do not have documents to prove it, get immigration advice before contacting the Home Office as this is a complex area (see Appendix 2).

Irish citizens

If you are an Irish citizen, you have an automatic right to reside in the UK and do not require leave to enter or remain in the UK (unless you are subject to a deportation or exclusion order).[1] As an Irish citizen, you are not required to obtain leave under the European Union Settlement Scheme (EUSS – see p67), but you can if you began residing in the UK before 31 December 2020 and you wish to do so, for example, to make it easier for a family member to also get leave.

If you are the family member of an Irish citizen in the UK before 31 December 2020, you may have a free movement right to reside in the same way as family members of other EEA nationals (see p239). If you do not have leave to be in the UK, you need to apply for leave under the EUSS (see p184).

3. Changes due to the UK leaving the European Union

The UK left the European Union (EU) on 31 January 2020 and this was followed by a 'transition period' until 11pm on 31 December 2020. During this period, the European free movement residence rights described in this chapter continued to apply in the UK, but at the end of the transition period, European free movement rights were, in general, ended within UK law.[2] That included revoking the European Economic Area (EEA) Regulations, which were the main domestic legislation providing free movement residence rights in UK law. However, these regulations continue to have effect if you are covered by one of the protected groups that can use free movement rights (see p188).

Transition period

The transition period (also called the 'implementation period') was the period from the UK leaving the EU at 11pm on 31 January 2020 to 11pm on 31 December 2020.[3] During the transition period, in general, EU legislation and caselaw, as well as all EU-derived law (eg, the EEA Regulations) continued to have effect as it had done before the UK left the EU.[4] During the transition period, all references to the EU or EEA were treated as if they included references to the UK, and references to an EEA national or EU citizen were treated as if they included references to a UK national.[5] However, note that British citizens do not require European free movement residence rights, but can confer such rights on family members in limited circumstances (see p192).

If you are an EEA national arriving after the end of the transition period, unless you are joining an EEA national who was your family member on 31 December and continues to be, and who was, living in the UK before that date, you will need to obtain leave under the same rules as non-EEA nationals (see p67). Your benefit entitlements will depend primarily on your immigration status and whether you are defined as a 'person subject to immigration control' (see p93), and if you are, whether you are covered by an exempt group for the benefit you want to claim (see Chapter 8). To check your right to reside, see p187.

If you are an EEA national already living in the UK by the end of the transition period, or you are the family member of such an EEA national, or you lived in the UK with a derivative right to reside in the UK before the end of the transition period, you will, in general, be eligible to apply for leave under the European Union Settlement Scheme (EUSS). For details of the leave you can obtain under the EUSS, and its significance for claiming benefits that require a right to reside, see below.

For information on how the law on free movement residence rights operates after the UK left the EU, and after the end of the transition period, see p195.

Note: the UK leaving the EU and the ending of the transition period also affects the EU co-ordination rules (see p374).

European Union Settlement Scheme

You are, in general, eligible to apply for either settled status (indefinite leave) or pre-settled status (limited leave) under the EUSS if you are:

- an EEA national and began living in the UK by the end of the transition period (11pm on 31 December 2020); *or*
- the family member of an EEA national in the group above, and have been their family member since at least 31 December 2020 (whether you are an EEA national or not); *or*
- a non-EEA national and began living in the UK with a derivative right to reside before the end of the transition period.

For further information on who is eligible for settled and pre-settled status, see p55.

Although, in general, the **deadline** to apply for this leave was 30 June 2021,[6] you can apply after this date if you have 'reasonable grounds' for missing the deadline. The requirement for the UK to admit late applications with 'reasonable grounds' is specified in the Withdrawal Agreements.[7] The Home Office published extensive, but non-exhaustive, guidance on the circumstances in which an application will be admitted after 30 June 2021,[8] and currently interprets 'reasonable grounds' broadly. If you have missed the deadline, get urgent immigration advice to help you apply as soon as possible (see also p64). The deadline for applications is different if you are (and were on 31 December 2020) the family member of an EEA national already living in the UK by the end of the transition period, and you joined them in the UK after this date. If you entered with an EUSS family permit, the deadline is normally three months from your arrival in the UK, with applications made after this requiring 'reasonable grounds' for missing that deadline. The deadline is also different if you were living in an EEA country as the family member of a British citizen since before the end of the transition period. If this applies, the deadline to both return to the UK *and* to apply for settled or pre-settled status was 29 March 2022, with applications made after this requiring 'reasonable grounds' for missing those deadlines. The Home Office published separate guidance on these applications[9] (see p62).

If you have **settled status**, this satisfies the right to reside requirement for all benefits that have this requirement. If you are the 'family member' of someone with settled status, note that this leave does not confer a right to reside on you, but if they are an EEA national they may confer a free movement right to reside on you. For details and an example, see p239.

If you have **pre-settled status**, this leave does not, by itself, satisfy the right to reside requirement for any of the benefits that have this requirement because each of the benefit regulations list it as an excluded right to reside. However, having pre-settled status means you are in a protected group that can potentially have one or more free movement rights to reside (see p188). For the steps to work through if you have pre-settled status, including potential arguments if you do not have a qualifying free movement right to reside, see p170 for means-tested benefits and p176 for child benefit and child tax credit.

If you have a **pending application to the EUSS** for settled or pre-settled status (or appeal against, or administrative review of, a refusal) this means you are in a protected group that can potentially have one or more free movement rights to reside (see p188).

If you have been granted limited leave to enter the UK on the basis that you hold a valid **EUSS family permit** (see p67) or EUSS travel permit (see p68), this leave does not satisfy the right to reside requirement for any of the benefits that have that requirement because each of the benefit regulations list it as an excluded right to reside. However, once you apply to the EUSS for settled or pre-settled status, you are in the protected group above, and can therefore potentially have one or more free movement rights to reside (see p192).

Moving from pre-settled to settled status

Pre-settled status is granted for five years and you need to apply for settled status before it expires. However, you do not need to wait until it is due to expire and you can apply for settled status as soon as you have lived in the UK for five years (or earlier if you become eligible sooner – see p57).

If you apply for settled status before your pre-settled status expires, but you have not received a decision by the date it would have expired, your pre-settled status is extended while your application is pending (see p100).

If you do not apply for settled status before your pre-settled status expires then, as someone who requires leave but does not have it, you are defined as a person subject to immigration control (see p93) and you will be excluded from most benefits on this basis. However, once you make a valid EUSS application for settled status, you will cease to be a person subject to immigration control and will be in a protected group that can potentially have a free movement right to reside (see p95).

At the time of writing, the High Court had just held that the UK government's position that a person with pre-settled status must make a further application for settled status, and that all rights (including to benefits) are lost if the application for settled status is not made before their pre-settled status expires, is unlawful under the Withdrawal Agreements.[10] The Home Office obtained permission to appeal, but in February 2023 it announced it would not appeal. Changes need to be made to the EUSS to take account of the High Court judgment. The advice remains that you should ensure you apply for settled status before your pre-settled status expires. See CPAG's *Welfare Rights Bulletin* and the online version of this *Handbook* on AskCPAG for updates.

Proving status

If you are granted settled or pre-settled status under the EUSS, or leave to enter on the basis that you hold a valid EUSS family permit or travel permit, in most cases you are not issued with a physical document (unless, for example, you are a non-EEA national family member of an EEA national and did not already have a biometric residence card when you applied – see note below). Instead, you confirm your settled or pre-settled status by accessing your online profile. You can get a 'share code' to allow others, including the DWP, HM Revenue and Customs or a local authority, to view your status online.[11]

If you are unable to provide the benefit authority with a share code, you can provide a copy of the Home Office document emailed to you when you were granted leave under the EUSS. Although this is not proof of status by itself, the decision maker should accept this as supporting evidence and can then verify your status directly with the Home Office.

If you have made a valid application to the EUSS for settled or pre-settled status, the Home Office should have issued you with a 'Certificate of Application'. This should be visible on your online account and the benefit authority will be able to view this if you provide it with a share code. You should also have had a Certificate of Application emailed to you (or posted if you made a paper application) when you applied, and you can provide a copy of this if you are unable to provide a share code to the benefit authority. If the Home Office has not yet issued you with a Certificate of Application, provide the benefit authority with a copy of any email acknowledging your application and ask the decision maker to confirm directly with the Home Office that you have made a valid application which is still pending.

Further information is provided in the leaflet available at gov.uk, *Your immigration status: an introduction for EU, EEA and Swiss citizens*.

Note: If you have been issued with a biometric residence permit (often referred to as a BRP card) it may have a 'valid until' date of 31 December 2024, despite your having either indefinite leave in the UK or leave which expires after 2024. If this applies, you should explain to the benefit authority that this date relates to the card and not your leave. For more details, including how to prove the duration of your leave, see p79.

4. European and non-European nationals

Whether you are a European Economic Area (EEA) national or a non-EEA national, the following overview applies to you since 1 January 2021.

If you are a British or Irish citizen, you have a right to reside in the UK (see p182).

If you are *not* a British citizen, you have a right to reside if either:

- you are within a period of leave to enter or remain granted under UK immigration law. Any type of leave gives you a right to reside that satisfies the right to reside requirement for all benefits that have this requirement *except:*
  - pre-settled status (limited leave to enter or remain granted under the European Union Settlement Scheme – EUSS); *or*
  - limited leave to enter granted on the basis you hold a valid EUSS family permit or EUSS travel permit; *or*
- you are in one of the protected groups that can have a free movement right to reside (see below) *and* you have a free movement right to reside (see p192). To claim a benefit that requires a right to reside, you need to have a free movement right to reside that is not excluded for the benefit you want to claim (see p169 for means-tested benefits and p176 for child benefit and child tax credit (CTC)).

If you are within a period of immigration leave, you have a right to reside throughout the duration of that leave. However, check the following points about how the type of leave you have may affect your entitlement to benefits.

- If you have pre-settled status, that does not by itself satisfy the right to reside requirement, as it is an excluded right to reside for all benefits with that requirement. However, having pre-settled status means you are in a protected group that can use free movement rights (see p188). If you have such a free movement right to reside (see p192), it will satisfy the right to reside requirement for all benefits with that requirement, provided it is not excluded for the benefit you want to claim (see p169 for means-tested benefits and p176 for child benefit and CTC). If you do not have a qualifying free movement right to reside, for the steps to work through, and potential arguments that it may be unlawful to refuse you benefit, see p170 for means-tested benefits and p176 for child benefit and CTC.
- If you have limited leave granted on the basis that you hold a valid EUSS family permit or travel permit (see p67), that is an excluded right to reside for each of the benefits that require a right to reside. However, once you apply to the EUSS for settled or pre-settled status, and while your application (or appeal against,

or administrative review of, a refusal) is pending, you are in a protected group that can potentially have one or more free movement rights to reside (see below), and if you have such a right, you can access benefits provided your free movement right is not excluded for the benefit you want to claim (see p169 and p176).
- If you have settled status (indefinite leave granted under the EUSS), that satisfies the right to reside requirement for all benefits that require it.
- If you have time-limited leave that has been granted subject to a 'no recourse to public funds' condition, or if you have indefinite leave granted as the result of a maintenance undertaking, although your leave satisfies the right to reside requirement for all benefits that have it, you are defined as a 'person subject to immigration control' (see p93) and, unless you are in an exempt group, you are excluded from benefits on this basis (see Chapter 8).
- If you have refugee leave or humanitarian protection, you have a right to reside that satisfies the requirement for all benefits that require it, and you are not defined as a person subject to immigration control. Furthermore, you are exempt from some of the residence and presence requirements that can mean you are entitled to benefits more quickly (see p128). For details, including the duration of refugee leave and humanitarian protection, see p43.
- The Court of Appeal has held that having temporary admission as an asylum seeker does *not* give you a right to reside in the UK and this is likely to apply also to immigration bail, which has replaced temporary admission (see p14).[12]

5. Protected groups that can have European free movement residence rights

Since the end of the transition period (11pm on 31 December 2020), you can only have a free movement right to reside if you are in one of the protected groups below. If you are in one of these groups, the European Economic Area (EEA) Regulations continue to be available to you, for the purpose of claiming benefits, despite their having been revoked more generally as part of the ending of free movement rights within UK law at the end of the transition period.

If you need a free movement right to reside to claim a benefit that requires you to have a right to reside, you need to check whether:
- you are in a protected group; *and*
- you have a free movement right to reside (see p192), other than one that is excluded for the benefit you want to claim (see p168).

For details of free movement law, see p195.

For periods since 30 June 2021, you are in a protected group while you:

- have pre-settled status (limited leave granted under the European Union Settlement Scheme – EUSS) (see also note below);[13] *or*
- have made a valid application to the EUSS for settled or pre-settled status and that application (or appeal against, or administrative review of, a refusal) has not been finally determined, withdrawn or abandoned.

In practice, while either of the above groups apply to you, the benefit authorities will generally accept that you are in a protected group that can potentially have one or more free movement rights to reside. However, if it is not accepted that the second bullet point applies to you, or if you need to set out the basis of these rights (eg, at an appeal tribunal), you may need to refer to specific legislation and guidance, and this will vary depending on the details of your circumstances – see box on p190.

You will need to prove that you are covered by either of the protected groups above. For the second group, note that guidance states decision makers should accept you have made a valid EUSS application if you have received a Certificate of Application.[14] However, having a Certificate of Application is not itself a requirement for you to claim benefit, and the benefit authority can confirm that you have a pending valid EUSS application directly with the Home Office.

For information on how to prove that you are in either of the above protected groups, see p186.

Note: if you have pre-settled status, you remain in a protected group while you have that leave. This is granted for five years and you need to apply for settled status before it expires. If you do so, and if you do not receive a decision before your leave was due to expire, your pre-settled status is extended while your application is pending (see p100). During this time you continue to be in a protected group. If your application is then refused, and you submit an appeal against, or administrative review of, this refusal, the benefit authority may decide you are then a 'person subject to immigration control' and refuse or terminate your benefit on this basis. For details, including why this is arguably wrong, see p106. If your pre-settled status expires *before* you apply for settled status, you are then defined as a person subject to immigration control, because you require leave but do not have it, and you are excluded from benefits on this basis. For details, including a recent High Court case on the loss of rights when pre-settled status ends, see p98. If you submit an application for settled status *after* your pre-settled status has expired, you are then in the protected group in the second bullet point above, and are not a person subject to immigration control (although if you are a non-EEA national, see point 7 in the box below).

If you have a pending EUSS application (or appeal or administrative review)

If you need to check, or explain, that your pending EUSS application for settled or pre-settled status means you are in a protected group, note the following:

1. All references to having a 'pending EUSS application' in this box refer to you having made a valid EUSS application for settled or pre-settled status (or an appeal against, or administrative review of, a refusal) which has not been finally determined, withdrawn or abandoned.

2. You are in a protected group that potentially has a free movement right to reside while you have a pending EUSS application. These rights are provided directly under the Withdrawal Agreements and apply whether you made your EUSS application for settled or pre-settled status by or, if you have 'reasonable grounds', after the general deadline of 30 June 2021. These rights also apply if you have applied to the EUSS having come to the UK with an EUSS family permit to join your EEA national family member already living in the UK before the end of 2020 (note that your deadline will, in general, be three months after your date of arrival in the UK, but you can apply after this if you have 'reasonable grounds'). For details on EUSS applications, including deadlines, see p184.[15]

3. If your pending EUSS application was made on or before 30 June 2021, you may *also* have rights provided under UK regulations.[16] However, these regulations only apply if, on 31 December 2020, you either had a permanent right to reside or were resident in the UK with another free movement right to reside (or you were *treated as* having this – see point 5 below). If your benefit claim is refused on the basis that you did not have (and are not treated as having) a free movement right to reside on 31 December 2020, and therefore that you are not in a protected group that can currently have a free movement right to reside, challenge this decision. First, check whether you did have (or are treated as having) *any* free movement right to reside on 31 December 2020, and note that this can be a *different* free movement right than the one you have at the time of claiming benefit. For example, you may be an EEA national who entered the UK in the last three months of 2020 and therefore on 31 December 2020 had an initial right to reside (see p203), but now have a right to reside as a worker (see p211). However, if you cannot satisfy this additional requirement of the regulations, or as a second argument, explain that this additional requirement goes beyond what is required under the Withdrawal Agreements and therefore does not need to be satisfied, as the Withdrawal Agreements have direct effect. The Withdrawal Agreements provide continuing rights to those with a pending EUSS application, if you (or the EEA national family member that you have joined in the UK) had a free movement right to reside in the UK *at any time* before 31 December 2020.[17]

4. If your pending EUSS application was made *after* 30 June 2021 (and is therefore referred to as a 'late application'), it is unlikely that your benefit claim would be refused on the basis that you did not have a free movement right to reside on 31 December 2020, because the regulations referred to in the point above do not apply to late applications. However, if this is the reason given by a decision maker, you should challenge the decision and apply the arguments in the point above. It may also be helpful to refer to guidance specifically on the benefit rights of those with pending late applications.[18]

5. If you are seeking to show that you satisfy the requirements of the regulations referred to at point 3 above, note the following.
a. Under these regulations you are *treated as* having had a free movement right to reside on 31 December 2020, if you previously had a free movement right to reside in the UK and on that date you were absent from the UK, but your absence was in circumstances that did not break your continuity of residence – eg, if that absence, together with any other absences in the last 12-month period, was less than six months in total (see p271).[19]
b. Under these regulations you are *treated as* having a permanent right to reside in the UK on 31 December 2020 if you lost a previously acquired permanent right to reside in the UK, due to having been absent from the UK for more than two years (see p277), but your absence on that date was less than five years.[20]
c. As with all evidence of your benefit entitlement, you should provide sufficient evidence that you had a free movement right to reside on 31 December 2020 if you can. However, if you cannot, you should ask the benefit authority to make its own investigations (eg, by checking HM Revenue and Customs records) and you should provide sufficient information to enable the benefit authority to do so (see p499).[21]
6. While you have a pending EUSS application, you are not defined as a 'person subject to immigration control' (see p93). If you are an EEA national, this applies whether or not you currently have a free movement right to reside and this is clearly set out in regulations if your EUSS application was made by 30 June 2021.[22] If you are a non-EEA national, it may be arguable you do not need to currently have a free movement right to reside, but you should always provide evidence of one if you can. For further details, see p95.
7. The rights you have while you have a pending EUSS application are confirmed most clearly in Home Office guidance,[23] but are also covered in benefit guidance.[24] A useful summary of these rights was provided by a recent High Court decision. The Court held that a provision of the EEA Regulations,[25] which terminates a right to reside under those regulations if a decision has been made to remove that person on specified grounds, was of no effect while the EEA national was appealing a refusal to grant settled status (as well as appealing the removal decision), and therefore his right to reside under the EEA Regulations continued.[26]

Between 31 December 2020 and 30 June 2021 you were in a protected group if:

- you were covered by either of the two protected groups in the bulleted list above the box (see p189); *or*
- on 31 December 2020 you either had a permanent right to reside or were resident in the UK with another free movement right to reside (or you were *treated as* having this – see point 5 in the box above). It was not necessary for you to have applied to the EUSS during this period;[27] *or*
- you were defined as the 'relevant family member' (see below) of a person covered by the group above, and on 31 December 2020 neither they nor you had leave under the EUSS.[28]

You were a 'relevant family member' of a person ('P') if:[29]

- on 31 December 2020 you were a 'family member' (see p239) of P. That includes if you were an 'extended family member' and you held, and continued to hold, a valid residence document issued under the EEA Regulations (see p504); *or*
- on 31 December 2020 you were P's durable partner (whether or not you held a valid residence document issued under the EEA Regulations – see note below); *or*
- you became a 'family member' as defined under the EEA Regulations after 31 December 2020 due to being an extended family member on that date and at a later date, before 30 June 2021, being issued with a valid residence document under the EEA Regulations (see p504); *or*
- you were the spouse or civil partner of P and P is a Swiss national; *or*
- you are P's child and either:
  - the other parent is in either the second or third protected groups (that applied between 31 December 2020 and 30 June 2021) above, or has leave granted under the EUSS, or is a British citizen; *or*
  - you were born or adopted after 31 December 2020, and P is either an EEA or Swiss national living in the UK (or a British citizen living in an EEA state or Switzerland), with a right to reside in that state, since before 31 December 2020, and P has sole or joint custody of you.[30]

For periods before the end of 2020, you did not need to be in a protected group to have a free movement right to reside because free movement law continued to apply in the UK.

Note:

- Being defined as a 'relevant family member' could only assist you to be in a protected group, and therefore potentially have a free movement right to reside, between 31 December 2020 and 30 June 2021.
- For further details and an example of a 'relevant family member', see p180 of the 13th edition this *Handbook.*

6. European free movement residence rights

Since the end of 2020, you can only have a free movement right to reside if you are in a protected group, which means that either you have pre-settled status (limited leave granted under the European Union Settlement Scheme – EUSS) or you have a pending EUSS application for pre-settled or settled status (or pending appeal, or administrative review, of a refusal). For more details, including additional protected groups that applied during the period 31 December 2020 to 30 June 2021, see p188.

If you *are* in a protected group, then the European Economic Area (EEA) Regulations continue to be available to you. This means that you can potentially have one or more free movement rights, for specific purposes, including claiming benefits, despite their having been revoked more generally as part of the ending of free movement within UK law at the end of 2020 (see p183). Before the end of 2020 it was not necessary to be in a protected group to have a free movement right to reside, because free movement legislation continued to apply in the UK. For details of the legal sources of free movement rights, see p195.

If you are in a protected group, you *may* have European free movement residence rights if you are:

- an EEA national; *or*
- a family member of an EEA national (or, in limited circumstances, of a British citizen – see below) who has a right to reside. You do not need to be an EEA national yourself; *or*
- someone who was previously in the above group; *or*
- the primary carer of certain EEA nationals (or certain British citizens).

Whether or not you have one or more European free movement residence rights also depends on other factors set out in the relevant sections of this chapter.

Note: references to EEA nationals in this chapter should be read as *not* including British citizens (unless otherwise stated), including during periods before the UK left the European Union (EU) and during the transition period that followed (see p183). Although during the transition period, references to the EEA or EU were *treated as* if they included references to the UK, and references to EEA nationals or EU citizens were *treated as* if they included British citizens, for many EU law purposes, this did not apply for the purpose of European free movement residence rights.[31]

If you are a British citizen, you always have a right to reside in the UK under UK law. However, British citizens do not give free movement residence rights to their family members, except in limited circumstances. If you are the family member of a British citizen (including if you have dual citizenship), see p244. If you are the primary carer of a British citizen, see p253.

For a list of EEA member states, see p53.

In general, Swiss nationals have the same residence rights as EEA nationals, so references to EEA nationals in this *Handbook* include Swiss nationals.

Croatian, A2 and A8 nationals may have their current free movement residence rights affected by certain restrictions that applied in the past. For a list of these countries and details of the restrictions, see p197.

Free movement residence rights checklist

Since the end of 2020, you can only have a European free movement right to reside if you are in one of the following protected groups:

- you have pre-settled status; *or*

- you have made a valid application to the EUSS for settled or pre-settled status and that application (or appeal against, or administrative review of, a refusal) has not been finally determined, withdrawn or abandoned; *or*
- (during the period 31 December 2020 to 30 June 2021 only) you had not yet applied for leave under the EUSS and on 31 December 2020 you either had a permanent right to reside or were resident in the UK with another free movement right to reside, or you were the 'relevant family member' of a person who did.

For details of all the protected groups, see p188.

While you are in a protected group (or for periods before the end of 2020), to determine if you have (or had) one or more free movement rights to reside, check the following.

- **Option one:** (for periods before 1 April 2021 only) were you an EEA national who began residing in the UK *before* 11pm on 31 December 2020? If so, you had an initial right to reside for the first three months of your residence in the UK (see p203). If you were the family member (see p239) of such an EEA national, you had a right to reside while they had this initial right to reside.
- **Option two:** are you an EEA national with a right to reside as a 'qualified person'?[32] This term may apply if you are in the UK as a:
  - jobseeker (see p203);
  - worker (see p211), including if you have retained this status (see p222);
  - self-employed person (see p218), including if you have retained this status (see p222); *or*
  - self-sufficient person, including a self-sufficient student (see p232).
- **Option three:** are you a 'family member' (see p239) of an EEA national covered in Option two or Option four? You have this right to reside whether you are an EEA or non-EEA national. In limited circumstances, you may have a right to reside if you were the family member of someone in Option two but they have now died, left the UK or your marriage or civil partnership has been terminated (see p249).
- **Option four:** do you have a permanent right of residence (see p265)? In most cases this is acquired after five years of 'legal residence' in the UK (which can include periods with a right to reside under Options one, two or three above, but *not* under Option five below), but can sometimes be acquired before five years.
- **Option five:** do you have a 'derivative right to reside' through someone else's right to reside, but not as their family member? That covers certain children and certain primary carers, whether EEA or non-EEA nationals (see p253).

Note:

- If you have been granted settled status (indefinite leave granted under the EUSS – see p55), that gives you a right to reside from the date that leave was granted, which satisfies the right to reside requirement for all benefits that have that requirement. However, as the leave is not retrospective, it does not give you a right to reside for any period before the date it was granted. Note also that your settled status does *not* confer a right to reside on your family member(s) (seep239).

- If you have been granted pre-settled status, for the duration of this leave you are in a protected group that can potentially have one or more free movement residence rights under the EEA Regulations (see p188). Pre-settled status does *not* satisfy the right to reside requirement by itself because it is listed as an excluded right to reside for each of the benefits that have that requirement. For details of the steps to work through if you have pre-settled status, including, if you do not have a qualifying free movement right to reside, potential arguments that it may be unlawful to refuse you benefit, see p170 for means-tested benefits and p176 for child benefit and child tax credit.
- If you have limited leave to enter granted on the basis that you hold an EUSS family or travel permit (see p67), your leave does *not* satisfy the right to reside requirement for any of the benefits that require it. You are not able to use free movement residence rights until you make a valid application for settled or pre-settled status to the EUSS, which will bring you into a protected group (see p188).
- You can have more than one European free movement right to reside at a time – eg, you may be a self-employed person and also the family member of someone with a permanent right of residence.[33]
- If you are a Croatian, A2 or A8 national, a family member (see p240) of a Croatian, A2 or A8 national, or if you are the primary carer of a child of a Croatian, A2 or A8 national and may have a derivative right to reside (see p253), see p197 for the additional restrictions that can affect your right to reside.

Legal sources of European free movement residence rights

The UK left the EU at 11pm on 31 January 2020 and, in accordance with the Withdrawal Agreements, there followed a transition period until 11pm on 31 December 2020 (see p183). During this time, EU law and EU-derived law, such as the EEA Regulations (see below), continued to apply as they did before the UK left the EU.[34]

At the end of the transition period, EU law was converted into UK law and, together with EU-derived law, continues to apply in the UK as it did on 31 December 2020.[35] However, from this date, this 'retained EU law' can be amended or revoked.[36]

The law on European free movement rights was, in general, revoked within UK law from 11pm on 31 December 2020.[37] However, the Withdrawal Agreements provide protections for EEA nationals who were already living in the UK and

British citizens already living in EEA states, before the end of the transition period, and the family members of each.[38] New regulations were introduced to reproduce these protections, but when they fail to do so, the Withdrawal Agreements have direct effect in the UK. For details of these protected groups that can have free movement residence rights, including the duration of the protection, see p188.

The Withdrawal Agreements must be interpreted in accordance with EU law, including the Treaty on the Functioning of the European Union (TFEU).[39] Questions about the interpretation of these Withdrawal Agreement protections can be referred to the Court of Justice of the European Union (CJEU) for up to eight years from the end of the transition period.[40] If the protected rights are not already provided for in UK legislation, new UK legislation should be introduced, as happened, for example, to provide for the rights of 'frontier workers' (see p278).

In practice, for the purposes of establishing benefit entitlement on the basis of a European free movement right, either during a period before the end of the transition period or, if you are in one of the protected groups, after the end of the transition period, the starting point is the EEA Regulations (see below). However, these regulations must be interpreted in accordance with not only the Withdrawal Agreements but also the, now retained, EU law that they are intended to implement.[41] If this retained EU law is not significantly modified, then its interpretation must be in accordance with EU legal principles and CJEU caselaw decided before the end of the transition period, and *may* have regard to new EU law, decided or passed after 31 December 2020. However, specified courts may depart from CJEU caselaw. These specified courts include the Supreme Court, the level of courts below this, including the Court of Appeal, and equivalent-level courts across the UK.[42] If the retained EU law *is* modified, it is interpreted in accordance with EU caselaw (decided before the end of the transition period) and EU legal principles, *only* if doing so is consistent with the intention of the modifications.[43]

Whether the retained EU law is modified or not, it must implement the rights and protections contained in the Withdrawal Agreements.

The main EU legislation that continues to be relevant in determining European free movement residence rights of EEA nationals, their family members and those with derivative residence rights comes from the EU treaties, in particular the TFEU, or the EEA Agreement that provides similar rights for Norway, Iceland and Liechtenstein.

The rights provided by the TFEU include the right of EU nationals to move and reside freely within the EU. However, this right is subject to limitations and conditions set out in the TFEU and in other legislation that give effect to the treaty.[44] This means that people covered by the TFEU must satisfy certain conditions to have a right of residence. The most important secondary legislation that sets out residence rights and the conditions that must be satisfied is **EU Directive 2004/38**. This brings together most rights of residence under EU law into one piece of legislation and replaces many earlier directives and regulations, which previously set out EU residence rights. Directive 2004/38 has been in force since 30 April 2006 and was extended from 1 March 2009 to cover nationals of Norway, Iceland and Liechtenstein.[45] **Note:** while the EU Directive is the most important source of residence rights for EEA nationals and their family members, it is not the only one – eg, some derivative rights of residence (see p253) stem from other EU legislation.[46]

Swiss nationals and their family members are covered by a separate agreement that provides similar rights.[47]

The Immigration (European Economic Area) Regulations 2016, referred to in this *Handbook* as the 'EEA Regulations', reproduce in UK law most of the residence rights contained in EU Directive 2004/38 and some provided directly under the TFEU and other provisions of EU law. The EEA Regulations apply to all EEA nationals and Swiss nationals, but not British citizens (see p182).[48] The current EEA Regulations replaced very similar regulations from 1 February 2017.[49] **Note:** the EEA Regulations were, in general, revoked from the end of the transition period. However they continue to be applicable if you are in a protected group listed on p188.

Note: at the time of writing, the Retained EU Law (Revocation and Reform) Bill was going through parliament. This legislation, if passed, will give far reaching powers to repeal, replace and reform retained EU legislation, to repeal the principle of EU law supremacy, and to facilitate courts departing from retained EU caselaw. See CPAG's *Welfare Rights Bulletin* and the online version of this *Handbook* on AskCPAG for updates.

7. Croatian, A2 and A8 nationals

Since 30 June 2021, you can only have any free movement right to reside if you either have pre-settled status or you have a pending European Union Settlement Scheme (EUSS) application for settled or pre-settled status (or a pending appeal or administrative review of a refusal). For details of these protected groups and others that applied during the period 31 December 2020 to 30 June 2021, see p188. If you are in one of the protected groups (or for a period before the end of 2020), your current free movement residence rights could be affected by additional restrictions that *previously* applied to nationals of the countries, and for the periods listed below.

Croatia, A2 and A8 states

Croatia joined the European Union (EU) on 1 July 2013.

Restrictions applied until 30 June 2018.

The A2 states are: Bulgaria and Romania.

These states joined the EU on 1 January 2007.

Restrictions applied until 31 December 2013.

The A8 states are: Czech Republic, Estonia, Hungary, Latvia, Lithuania, Poland, Slovakia and Slovenia.

These states joined the EU on 1 May 2004.

Restrictions applied until 30 April 2009.

The treaties under which the above 'accession' states joined the EU allowed existing member states, including, at the relevant dates, the UK, to restrict accession nationals' access to their labour markets, and their residence rights as workers and jobseekers. The duration of these restrictions was limited to five years from the date the states joined the EU, but could be extended for a further two years if certain conditions were met. The UK government imposed the restrictions for five years and then extended them for A8 and A2 nationals for an additional two years. However, this extension of restrictions for A8 nationals from 1 May 2009 to 30 April 2011 has been held to be unlawful by the Supreme Court.[50] This means that, retrospectively, A8 nationals were not subject to restrictions during this two-year period.[51]

Although the restrictions on Croatian, A2 and A8 nationals ended some years ago, you need to know what the restrictions were if the free movement residence rights you, or another person, had during the relevant period of restriction affects your free movement at a later date. In particular, the restrictions may be relevant if you are seeking to establish permanent residence and you, or your family member whose free movement residence rights you need to rely on, are a Croatian, A2 or A8 national. The restrictions can also be relevant in determining whether you have a derivative right to reside as the primary carer of a child in education when the child's parent is a Croatian, A2 or A8 national who has worked in the UK (see p256).

Note: these restrictions do not affect your eligibility to apply for leave under the EUSS (see p184).

Restrictions on employment and residence rights

Between 1 July 2013 and 30 June 2018 (if you are a Croatian national) or between 1 January 2007 and 31 December 2013 (if you are an A2 national), unless you were in one of the exempt groups listed on p199, you must have obtained an 'accession worker authorisation document' (in most cases, an accession worker registration certificate if you are Croatian, or an accession worker card if you are an A2 national, specifying the employer you could work for) before taking up employment, and then have worked in accordance with it.[52] Your residence rights were restricted as follows.[53]

- You did not have a right to reside as a jobseeker.
- You were only defined as a 'worker' if you had an accession worker authorisation document and worked in accordance with it.

- You could not retain your 'worker' status when you stopped work in the ways other workers could (see p222).

If you are an A8 national, between 1 May 2004 and 30 April 2009, unless you were in one of the exempt groups listed on p200, you had to work for an 'authorised employer'.[54] In general, this meant you had to register each job you took with the Worker Registration Scheme (but see p201 for the precise meaning, because that can affect your residence rights). Your residence rights were restricted as follows.[55]

- You did not have a right to reside as a jobseeker.
- You were only defined as a 'worker' if you were working for an 'authorised employer' (see p202).
- You could not retain your 'worker' status when you stopped work in the ways other workers could (see p222).[56] However, if you lost your job within the first month of employment, you could retain your status in these ways until the end of the month. **Note:** the Court of Justice of the European Union held that the exclusion of an A8 national subject to restrictions from retaining worker status was not unlawful.[57]

The restrictions do not affect other residence rights you may have or had as a European Economic Area (EEA) national – eg, as a self-employed or self-sufficient person.[58] The Upper Tribunal has also held that the restrictions were not imposed on A8 nationals to limit their rights to permanent residence in less than five years and so periods of unregistered employment can count for this purpose (see p275).[59]

Other rights under EU law (eg, under the EU co-ordination rules covered in Chapter 16) were not affected.

Croatian and A2 nationals who were exempt from restrictions

Between 1 July 2013 and 30 June 2018 (if you are a Croatian national) or between 1 January 2007 and 31 December 2013 (if you are an A2 national), you were subject to worker authorisation and had additional restrictions on your residence rights (see above), *unless* you:[60]

- had on 30 June 2013 (Croatian) or 31 December 2006 (A2) leave to enter or remain with no restriction on employment;
- were 'legally working' (see p201) in the UK for 12 months without breaks of more than 30 days (in total), up to and including 31 December 2006 (A2) or 30 June 2013 (Croatian);[61]
- had 'legally worked' for 12 months (beginning before or after 31 December 2006 (A2) or 30 June 2013 (Croatian)), disregarding any breaks of less than 30 days (in total);[62]
- were a posted worker – ie, you were working in the UK providing services on behalf of an employer who was not established in the UK;

- were a member of a diplomatic mission (or the family member of such a person) or a person otherwise entitled to diplomatic immunity;
- had dual nationality with the UK or another (non-A2/Croatian) EEA state;
- were the spouse/civil partner (or, Croatian only, unmarried or same-sex partner) of a UK national or of a person with indefinite leave to enter or remain (see p30[63]) in the UK;
- were the spouse/civil partner (or, Croatian only, unmarried or same-sex partner) or child under 18 of a person with leave to enter or remain in the UK that allowed employment;
- had a permanent right of residence (see p265);
- were a student with a registration certificate that stated that you could not work more than 20 hours a week (unless it was part of vocational training or during vacations) and you complied with this. If the certificate confirmed you could work during the four months after the course ended, the exemption continued for this period;
- were a family member of an EEA national who had a right to reside, unless the EEA national was an A2 (or, if you are Croatian, a Croatian) national subject to worker authorisation (or, A2 only, the only reason they were not an A2 national subject to worker authorisation is because they were covered by the bullet point below);
- were a family member of an A2 (or, if you are Croatian, a Croatian) national subject to worker authorisation who had a right to reside (for an A2 national only, as a worker, student, self-employed or self-sufficient person). If you are a Croatian national (or an A2 national relying on an A2 worker), you were a 'family member' if you were the descendant and either under 21 or dependent, the spouse/civil partner, or (Croatians only) the unmarried or same-sex partner; *or*
- were a 'highly skilled person' – ie, you:[64]
  - met the points-based criteria in the Immigration Rules for entering the UK on this basis; *or*
  - had a qualification at degree level or higher in the UK, or Higher National Diploma in Scotland and, within 12 months of this award, you applied for a registration certificate confirming your unconditional access to the labour market.

A8 nationals who were exempt from restrictions

Between 1 May 2004 and 30 April 2009, if you are an A8 national, you were defined as 'requiring registration' and so any work you did had to be for 'an authorised employer' (see p201) and your residence rights were restricted (see p198) *unless* you:[65]

- had leave to enter or remain on 30 April 2004 that had no restriction on employment;

- were 'legally working' (see below) in the UK for 12 months, without breaks of more than 30 days (in total), up to and including 30 April 2004 (see also note below);[66]
- had 'legally worked' in the UK for 12 months (beginning before or after 30 April 2004), disregarding any breaks of less than 30 days (in total);[67]
- were the spouse/civil partner or child under 18 of a person with leave to enter or remain in the UK that allowed employment;
- had dual nationality with the UK and another (non-A2/A8) EEA state or Switzerland;
- were a family member of another EEA or Swiss national who had a right to reside under the EEA Regulations (other than an A2/A8 national subject to registration/authorisation if their only right to reside was for the first three months in the UK);
- were the member of a diplomatic mission (or the family member of such a person) or a person otherwise entitled to diplomatic immunity; *or*
- were a posted worker – ie, you were working in the UK providing services on behalf of an employer who was not established in the UK.

Note: the Upper Tribunal held that an A8 national who was not in one of the above exempt groups could be treated as if he were if the outcome would otherwise be 'disproportionate'. It ruled that it would be disproportionate to disregard the appellant's years of work and subsequent involuntary unemployment just because he failed to satisfy the second bullet point above because he was abroad (albeit still employed in the UK) on 30 April 2004 and had then failed to register his employment under the Worker Registration Scheme (as he believed he did not need to). The Upper Tribunal accepted that he had therefore acquired a permanent right to reside.[68]

Legally working

The phrase 'legally working' has a specific meaning and only refers to employment: periods of self-employment do not count as 'legally working' for the purpose of exempting you from restrictions.

If you are a Croatian or A2 national, you were 'legally working' before the restrictions ended (see p197) if:[69]

- you were working in accordance with your worker authorisation document; *or*
- you were working during a period when you were in one of the exempt groups on p199 (other than posted workers); *or*
- the work was done before 1 July 2013 (for Croatian nationals) or before 1 January 2007 (for A2 nationals), either in accordance with any leave you had under the Immigration Act 1971 or when you did not require leave (except work done with permission from the Home Office while you were an asylum seeker[70]).

If you are an A8 national, you were 'legally working' before the restrictions ended (see p197) if:[71]

- you were working for an authorised employer (see below); *or*
- you were working during a period when you were in one of the exempt groups listed above (other than if you were the spouse/civil partner or child of a person whose leave to enter or remain in the UK allowed employment); *or*
- the work was done before 1 May 2004 either in accordance with any leave you had under the Immigration Act 1971 or when you did not require leave (except work done with permission from the Home Office while you were an asylum seeker[72]).

Authorised employer for A8 nationals

If you were an A8 national subject to restrictions, you were defined as working for an **'authorised employer'** if:[73]

– you were within the first month of employment; *or*
– you applied for a worker's registration certificate under the Worker Registration Scheme within the first month of work, but did not yet have a certificate or refusal; *or*
– you had a valid worker's registration certificate issued under the Worker Registration Scheme for that employer; *or*
– you had been 'legally working' for that employer since 30 April 2004; *or*
– you began work at an agricultural camp between 1 May 2004 and 31 December 2004, and before 1 May 2004 you had been issued with leave under the Immigration Act 1971 as a seasonal worker at such a camp.

If you applied for a registration certificate after the first month of work, you only counted as working for an authorised employer from the date it was issued.[74]

Note: the Upper Tribunal has held that the restrictions on A8 nationals had not been imposed to limit their rights to permanent residence in less than five years and so all periods of employment count for this purpose, even if they were not for an authorised employer (see p275).[75]

If you were a Croatian, A2 or A8 national subject to restrictions and your employment ended, you stopped legally working, stopped being a 'worker' and, unless you were exempt, you could not retain your worker status. However, if you were still under a contract of employment, you continued to be legally working and a worker – eg, if you were on maternity leave, holiday leave, sick leave or compassionate leave (including if the leave was unpaid).[76]

If you need to provide evidence that your employment gave you worker status, in most cases you will need to show it was in accordance with your worker authorisation document (if you are a Croatian or A2 national), or that (beyond the first month) it was registered under the Worker Registration Scheme, if you are an A8 national. For details of how to obtain this evidence if you do not have it, see p512.

8. Initial right of residence

Until the end of the transition period at 11 pm on 31 December 2020, all European Economic Area (EEA) nationals had a right to enter the UK.[77] If you are an EEA national and you entered the UK before the end of the transition period, you also had an initial right of residence for the first three months of your stay, provided you held a valid identity card or passport,[78] and you were not an unreasonable burden on the UK's social assistance system during the three months.[79] You had this initial right of residence whether or not you were working or seeking work. As this right to reside must have begun on or before 31 December 2020, and only lasted for three months, it could only have applied during periods before 1 April 2021.

You also had a right of residence if you were a family member (see p239) of an EEA national who had this initial right of residence for three months (whether or not *you* are an EEA national), provided you held a valid passport.[80]

Note: you could have had another residence right (eg, as a family member of a worker and/or as a jobseeker) in addition to your initial right of residence – ie, you did not have to wait for the three months to end before you had another residence right.

If your *only* right of residence was on the basis of your (or your family member's) initial three-month right of residence, that did not satisfy the right to reside requirement for any of the means-tested benefits because it is one of the excluded residence rights for those benefits (see p168). However it may still assist you to be entitled to benefits at a later date because:

- you can count a period during which this was your only right to reside as part of the continuous five-year period required for permanent residence (see p266);
- if you (or the person you were a 'relevant family member' of – see p188) had this right to reside on 31 December 2020, that can mean you satisfied regulations on the protected groups who can, after that date, potentially have other free movement residence rights (and not be defined as a 'person subject to immigration control') (see p93).

Although this initial right to reside (or right to reside as the family member of someone who had an initial right to reside) is not an excluded right to reside for child benefit and child tax credit, it did not help in practice due to the requirement, for these benefits, to have been living in the UK for the past three months (see p143).

9. Jobseekers

Since 30 June 2021, you can only have any free movement right to reside, including as a jobseeker (or family member of a jobseeker), if you either have pre-settled status or you have a pending European Union Settlement Scheme (EUSS) application for settled or pre-settled status (or a pending appeal or administrative review of a refusal). For details of these protected groups and others that applied during the period 31 December 2020 to 30 June 2021, see p188.

If you are in one of the protected groups, or for a period before the end of 2020, you may have a right to reside as a 'jobseeker' if you are a European Economic Area (EEA) national looking for work in the UK (see below). You may also have a right to reside if you are a family member (see p239) of a jobseeker.

However, these residence rights only satisfy the right to reside requirement for child benefit, child tax credit (CTC) and income-based jobseeker's allowance (JSA) (see p209). You may have difficulty claiming these benefits over the longer term solely on the basis of your right to reside as a jobseeker because of the evidence requirements (see p205).

You should therefore always check whether you have a right of residence on some other basis.

Note:

- If you have previously been a 'worker' (see p211) or a self-employed person (see p218) and are now looking for work, in addition to having a right to reside as a jobseeker, you may also have a right to reside as someone who has retained worker or self-employed status (see p222), which is a right to reside that satisfies the right to reside requirement for all benefits that have it.
- Periods when you have a right to reside as a jobseeker count towards the five years required for permanent residency (see p266), which then satisfies the right to reside requirement for all benefits that have it.
- If, on 31 December 2020, you (or the person you were a 'relevant family member' of – see p188) had a right to reside as a jobseeker (or family member of a jobseeker) and, on that date, did not have leave granted under the EUSS, you were, until at least 30 June 2021, in one of the protected groups that could potentially have one or more *other* free movement residence rights. If you are an EEA national, these protections also meant that you were not defined as a 'person subject to immigration control' (see p93). For further details, including the duration of these protections, see p188.

Who has a right to reside as a jobseeker

If you are in one of the protected groups that can have a free movement right to reside (see p188), or during a period before the end of 2020, you have a right to reside as a jobseeker if you are an EEA national and:[81]

- you are in the UK and you can provide evidence that you are seeking employment and have a 'genuine chance of being engaged' (for details, including caselaw on when the latter requirement applies, see p205). **Note:** (under the EEA Regulations only) after 91 days, this evidence must be 'compelling' (see p205); *and*

- (rarely required by the benefit authorities) you entered the UK to seek employment, or (under the EEA Regulations only) you are present in the UK seeking employment immediately after having a right to reside as a worker (except if you retained worker status while involuntarily unemployed – see p223), a student or a self-sufficient person.

If you previously had a right to reside as a jobseeker for 91 days, or you retained either worker or self-employed status while involuntarily unemployed (see p223) for at least six months, in order to have a right to reside as a jobseeker under the EEA Regulations (unless you have been absent from the UK continuously for at least 12 months since having either residence right), you must:[82]

- provide 'compelling' evidence (see below) that you are seeking employment and have a genuine chance of being engaged from the start of your current period of residence as a jobseeker; *and*
- (rarely required by the benefit authorities) have since had an absence from the UK.

Note: if you are refused benefit because of a requirement that is in the EEA Regulations only, you may be able to challenge the decision on the basis that these regulations should be interpreted in accordance with European Union (EU) caselaw and legal principles (see p195) and the regulations cannot interpret the category of jobseeker more narrowly than the Court of Justice of the European Union (CJEU).[83]

Croatian, A2 and A8 nationals

If you are a Croatian, A2 or A8 national, you did not have a right to reside as a jobseeker during the period of restrictions, if these restrictions applied to you (see p197).[84] **Note:** the extension of the restrictions on A8 nationals from 30 April 2009 to 30 April 2011 has been held to be unlawful.[85] This means that if you are an A8 national, retrospectively, you were not excluded from having had a right to reside as a jobseeker during this two-year period.

For how long do you have a right to reside as a jobseeker

There is no time limit on how long you can have a right to reside as a jobseeker. It continues for as long as you can provide the required evidence that you are continuing to seek work and have a genuine chance of being engaged.[86] However, under the EEA Regulations, in order to continue to have a right to reside as a jobseeker for longer than 91 days, this evidence must be 'compelling' (see below).

Providing evidence

To have a right to reside as a jobseeker, you must provide evidence that you are seeking employment. The EEA Regulations also require you to provide evidence of having a genuine chance of being engaged. However, the CJEU held that this cannot be required until after a 'reasonable period', and that period could be six months from the date you register as a jobseeker with the relevant employment office (the DWP in the UK).[87] **Note:** it is not a requirement to register as a jobseeker in order to have a right to reside as a jobseeker (see p209). See below for the type of employment you must be looking for and have a genuine chance of obtaining and when you must show this genuine chance.

Under the EEA Regulations (but not under EU law), this evidence must be 'compelling':[88]

- in order to continue to have a right to reside as a jobseeker for more than 91 days;
- from the start of your period of residence as a jobseeker (but see note below) if you previously:
  - had a right to reside as a jobseeker for a total of 91 days; *or*
  - retained worker or self-employed status while involuntarily unemployed (see p223) for at least six months.

Note:

- If you have had an absence from the UK for a continuous period of at least 12 months, on your return you can have 91 days with a right to reside as a jobseeker before your evidence must be compelling.[89]
- If you previously had a right to reside as a jobseeker for at least 91 days, or you retained worker or self-employed status for at least six months, the EEA Regulations require you to have been absent from the UK before you can have a period with a right to reside as a jobseeker.[90] However, the benefit authorities have not been enforcing this requirement, except in very rare cases.

Providing compelling evidence: the 'genuine prospects of work test'

The **'genuine prospects of work test'** is a term used by the benefit authorities, including in their guidance. It refers to the above requirement in the EEA Regulations for the evidence that you are continuing to seek work and have a genuine chance of being engaged to be 'compelling' after 91 days as a jobseeker.

Note: guidance confirms this test no longer applies to those retaining worker or self-employed status on the basis of being involuntarily unemployed for longer than six months (see p223).[91]

Although the terms and the detail of the guidance emphasise the need for evidence that you have a 'genuine chance of being engaged' over the need for evidence that you are continuing to seek work, the EEA Regulations require both.

If you are asked to provide compelling evidence to satisfy the 'genuine prospects of work test', or you are told that you have failed to do so, note the following.

1. Check whether this test should be applied to you. If you have a right to reside other than as a jobseeker, this test does not apply to you at any point.[92] You can continue to receive the benefit or tax credit you are claiming for as long as your other residency right

continues. However, this is frequently overlooked. If you have another right to reside, make sure the DWP or HM Revenue and Customs (HMRC) is aware of this and make it clear that your other right to reside means that the test should not be applied to you. **Note:** if you are claiming benefit while working part time, provided this work gives you worker (see p211) or self-employed status (see p218), the guidance to decision makers confirms that you are not subject to the test.[93]

2. Argue that you cannot, following a CJEU judgment, be required to provide evidence, 'compelling' or otherwise, of having a genuine chance of being engaged until after a 'reasonable period' has been allowed to acquaint yourself with potentially suitable employment opportunities and to take the necessary steps to obtain employment. The CJEU held that six months from the date you register as a jobseeker would not be insufficient to count as a 'reasonable period'.[94]

3. Check whether the test has been applied to you at the right time. If your only right to reside is as a jobseeker, it applies after 91 days.[95] However, if you previously had a right to reside as a jobseeker for 91 days, the test will be applied to you from the first day of this current period of residence as a jobseeker, unless since then you have had an absence from the UK of a continuous period of 12 months. Although you are required to provide compelling evidence after 91 days of having a right to reside as a jobseeker, the DWP tends to follow guidance stating that only periods of entitlement to income-based or contribution-based JSA count towards the 91 days.[96] This guidance also states that certain periods can be disregarded when calculating the 91-day period, including up to 13 weeks when you are treated as being available for work because you have experienced domestic violence, periods of temporary absence when you are treated as being in Great Britain (see p343) and periods of sickness.[97]

4. The term 'compelling' is not defined in the legislation and, therefore, should have its ordinary, everyday meaning. The Upper Tribunal held that the requirement to provide 'compelling' evidence means you are required to provide evidence that shows, on the balance of probabilities, that you are seeking employment and have a genuine chance of being engaged, and that to require a higher standard of proof is contrary to EU law.[98] In a different case, the Upper Tribunal held that when determining whether you have a genuine chance of being engaged, a period of six months or more seeking employment without success is a relevant factor to be taken into account, but only one among others.[99]

5. Whether you have a genuine chance of being engaged requires looking forward, and so future events are also relevant.[100] Provide evidence of any qualifications and experience you expect to get in the near future. If you have appealed against a decision that you have not provided compelling evidence, the tribunal can draw conclusions from events that occurred after the time of the decision about circumstances at or before that time. For example, obtaining a job six weeks after the decision is evidence of your chance of being engaged on the date of the decision.[101] See also point 2 above.

6. In rare circumstances, if you have an offer of a job that you cannot take up immediately, but which is being held open for you and is due to start in less than three months, you may have a right to reside as a 'worker' (see p211).[102]

7. DWP guidance to decision makers includes lists of examples of relevant evidence.[103] This guidance wrongly emphasises the need for there to have been a change in your circumstances for your evidence to be accepted as compelling; the Upper Tribunal has held that a change of circumstances is just one factor to take into account. If the limited way in which the guidance is framed caused the decision maker to fail to ask all the relevant questions about your evidence and you appeal, the First-tier Tribunal may need to ask a broader range of questions.[104]

8. The introduction of universal credit (UC) has greatly reduced the relevance of this requirement for benefit claimants who are jobseekers. That is because a right to reside as a jobeeker only satisfies the right to reside requirement for income-based JSA (and most of these claims have now been terminated), child benefit and CTC. In practice, HMRC only requires compelling evidence from jobseekers claiming child benefit and CTC claims occasionally, and if HMRC does so, it should clearly request the evidence required from you.[105]

9. For further details on how this requirement has been held to operate, see p161 and pp178–81 of the 11th edition of this *Handbook.*

Employment you must seek and have a genuine chance of obtaining

To have a right to reside as a jobseeker, you must be looking for and (although see note below) have a genuine chance of obtaining employment that would count as sufficient for you to be a 'worker' (see p211) if you obtained it.[106]

Note:

- The CJEU held that a jobseeker cannot be required to show a 'genuine chance of being engaged' until after a 'reasonable period', which could be six months (see point 2 in the box above).[107]
- If you are only looking for work on a self-employed basis because you are establishing yourself as self-employed, you may have a right of residence as a self-employed person (see p218).

In most cases, you should be accepted as seeking employment and having a genuine chance of being engaged if you are 'signing on' and provide evidence that you are actively seeking and available for work for JSA or national insurance (NI) credits, or that you satisfy the work search and work availability requirements if you come under the UC system.

There are only be a few unusual circumstances in which you would satisfy these conditions and not be accepted as having a genuine chance of being engaged.[108] If the decision maker decides you do not have a genuine chance of being engaged, argue that your case is not one of these rare cases. It may help to look in detail at the requirements that you already satisfy. For example, if you have placed restrictions on your availability, but because you can still show you have reasonable prospects of securing employment these have been accepted for the purpose of your JSA claim, you may be able to argue that it is irrational to decide that you do not have a genuine chance of being engaged. This argument was discussed at the Upper Tribunal, but it was accepted that it did not apply in any of the cases in question, and so no decision was required.[109]

There is no change to the type of work you must be seeking and have a genuine chance of obtaining after 91 days, when you are required to provide compelling evidence of this (see p205).

If you have not claimed jobseeker's allowance

You do not need to have claimed or be receiving JSA, or to have registered as a jobseeker with the DWP, in order to have a right to reside as a jobseeker: you must simply be an EEA national and provide evidence that you are seeking employment and, arguably only after a 'reasonable period' (see p205), have a genuine chance of being engaged.[110]

The most straightforward way of demonstrating that you meet these requirements is to claim contribution-based JSA on the basis that you satisfy the work search and work availability requirements, or NI credits on the basis of unemployment.

However, if you are not eligible for benefit or NI credits, or you are waiting for a decision on your claim, or you have not made a claim, you can still have a right to reside as a jobseeker if you provide evidence that you are seeking employment and have a genuine chance of being engaged. This could be relevant, for example, if you want to claim child benefit, or you need to show you had a right to reside as a jobseeker in the past to count the period as part of the continuous five years required for permanent residence (see p266).

Benefit entitlement

Although having a right to reside as a jobseeker only satisfies the right to reside requirement for three benefits (see below), having this right to reside in the past can also assist with current entitlement to other benefits, if:

- the period during which you had a right to reside as a jobseeker was part of a continuous period of five years of residing in the UK with free movement residence rights, which can mean you now have a permanent right to reside (see p266); *or*
- you are seeking to show that you had a free movement right to reside on 31 December 2020, to satisfy regulations on the protected groups who can, after that date, potentially have free movement residence rights, and, if you are an EEA national, not be defined as a 'person subject to immigration control' (see p93). For further details, including the duration of these protections, see p188.

If you have a right to reside as a jobseeker, this satisfies the right to reside requirement for:

- child benefit;
- income-based JSA; *and*
- CTC.

In addition to having a right to reside:

- for child benefit and CTC, you must also have been living in the UK for the three months prior to your claim, unless you are exempt from this requirement (see p144);
- to continue to be entitled to income-based JSA, you must continue to be accepted as 'habitually resident in fact' (see p163).

Note: it is no longer possible to make a new claim for income-based JSA or (other than if you have just been granted refugee leave) CTC.

If you have a right to reside as a jobseeker, this does *not* satisfy the right to reside requirement for:

- UC;
- housing benefit (HB) (but see below);
- income support;
- income-related employment and support allowance (ESA);
- pension credit.

You must therefore have another right to reside to get one of the above benefits (other than another excluded right to reside – see p168).

Jobseekers have more limited benefit entitlement than most other groups with European free movement residence rights under EU law. Under EU Directive 2004/38, the UK is not obliged to provide entitlement to social assistance to those with a right to reside as a jobseeker.[111] However, it is required to give EEA jobseekers who have established real links with the UK labour market equal access to the financial benefits that are intended to facilitate access to that labour market as British citizens.[112]

Note: the CJEU has held that financial benefits intended to facilitate access to the UK labour market must be made available to EEA jobseekers on an equal basis to British citizens.[113] It may be arguable that UC is a benefit designed to facilitate access to the labour market, and that it is therefore unlawful to exclude someone whose only right to reside is as a jobseeker. However, the Court of Appeal rejected this argument in relation to income-related ESA as that benefit was held not to be one designed to facilitate access to the labour market and therefore excluding access to it was not unlawful.[114]

Housing benefit

If you have a right to reside as a jobseeker, this does not satisfy the right to reside requirement for HB.[115]

However, you are exempt from the habitual residence test for HB (see p159) if you are receiving income-based JSA and either you:

- have a right to reside other than one that is excluded for HB (see p169); *or*

- have been receiving both HB and income-based JSA since 31 March 2014. Your exemption on this basis ends when either you cease to be entitled to that income-based JSA or you make a new claim for HB.[116]

10. **Workers**

Since 30 June 2021, you can only have any free movement right to reside, including as a worker (or family member of a worker), if you either have pre-settled status or you have a pending European Union Settlement Scheme (EUSS) application for settled or pre-settled status (or a pending appeal or administrative review of a refusal). For details of these protected groups and others that applied during the period 31 December 2020 to 30 June 2021, see p188.

If you are in one of the protected groups, or for a period before the end of 2020, you may have a right to reside as a 'worker' if you are a European Economic Area (EEA) national working in the UK (see below). You may also have a right to reside if you are a family member (see p239) of a worker. Once you have established worker status, it is important to be clear when you cease to be a worker (see p217). In limited circumstances, you can retain your worker status after you stop being a worker (see p222).

If you have a right to reside as a worker, as someone who has retained worker status or as the family member of a worker, this satisfies the right to reside requirement for all benefits that have this requirement.

Who has a right to reside as a worker

If you are in one of the protected groups that can have a free movement right to reside (see p188), or during a period before the end of 2020, you have a right to reside as a worker if you are an EEA national in the UK and:[117]

- you are in an employment relationship (see p213); *and*
- the work you do entails activities that are 'genuine and effective', rather than 'marginal and ancillary' (see p215).

The EEA Regulations cross-refer to European Union (EU) law for the meaning of 'worker'.[118] However, the term 'worker' is not defined in EU legislation. Instead, the above conditions, and their meaning, have been established through EU caselaw, and this caselaw must be used to interpret the concept (see p195).

The reason why you moved to the UK is irrelevant, provided you meet the above conditions.[119] For example, if your main intention in coming to the UK was to study, that is not relevant when determining whether you are a worker.[120]

Your motives for seeking employment can be taken into account when determining whether you are pursuing activity as an employed person. However, once it is established that you are, your motives are irrelevant.

Note:

- If you have been a worker, you do not necessarily lose this status just because you stop working. For more information on when you cease being a worker, see p217, and for the circumstances in which you can retain your worker status, see p222.
- If you are an EEA national and on 31 December 2020, and continuously since then, you have been working in the UK while 'not primarily resident in the UK', you may have rights as a 'frontier worker' (see p278). These rights include being exempt from the habitual residence test for means-tested benefits (see p159).

Croatian, A2 and A8 nationals

If you are a Croatian or A2 national and during the period of restrictions (1 July 2013 to 30 June 2018 for Croatian, and 1 January 2007 to 31 December 2013 for A2 nationals) you were subject to worker authorisation, you did not have a right to reside as a worker unless you held an accession worker authorisation document and worked in accordance with it (see p201).[121]

If you were an A8 national and during the period of restrictions (1 May 2004 to 30 April 2009) you were required to register your work, you did not have a right to reside as a worker unless you were working for an 'authorised employer' (see p201).[122] The extension of restrictions on A8 nationals from 30 April 2009 to 30 April 2011 has been held to be unlawful (see p197).[123] This means that you can retrospectively be accepted as having had worker status during this two-year period, even if this would not have been accepted at the time because you were not working for an 'authorised employer'.[124]

Guidance to decision makers

Decision makers are advised to follow a two-stage process when determining whether you are, or were, a worker (or self-employed).[125] Although this guidance is not legally binding, it is helpful to know its content either to offset potential problems before your claim is decided or to challenge an incorrect decision more effectively.

The guidance advises decision makers first to establish whether your average gross earnings reach a minimum earnings threshold equal to the level at which you start to pay national insurance contributions. This is £242 a week (£1,048 a month) since 6 July 2022 (it was £190 a week and £823 a month between 6 April to 5 July 2022, and £183 a week/£797 a month in 2021/22). If your average gross earnings were at least this amount for a continuous period of three months immediately before you claim benefit, you are automatically accepted as a worker (or self-employed).

If your earnings did not meet this threshold, the guidance is clear that, in all cases, decision makers should then take into account all your circumstances in relation to the criteria set out below to establish whether your activity was genuine and effective, rather than marginal and ancillary, to determine whether you are (or were) a worker (or self-employed).[126]

You should not be told that you are not a worker (or self-employed) just because you have not met the minimum earnings threshold for three months. It may be useful to refer the decision maker or First-tier Tribunal to an Upper Tribunal decision, which held that a local authority was wrong to decide that a housing benefit claimant had ceased to be self-employed when her earnings decreased below the minimum earnings threshold, and that this error was due to the local authority failing to apply the second part of the guidance and take into account of all of the circumstances of her self-employment.[127]

Employment relationship

You count as being in an 'employment relationship' if you:[128]

- provide services;
- receive remuneration in return for those services (see below);
- perform your work under the direction of another person (see below).

The services you provide must entail activities that are 'genuine and effective' as opposed to 'marginal and ancillary' (see p215).

Although, in general, your employment must have started for you to be a worker, you may be a worker if you have moved to the UK to take up a job offer and it is not possible for you to begin work immediately but the offer is being held open for you.[129]

What counts as remuneration

In order to be a worker, you must receive 'remuneration' in return for the services you provide.

If you do voluntary work and receive payments for expenses, you are not a worker.[130] This is because the payments you receive are not provided in return for the services you perform, but rather to compensate you for the expenses you have incurred in providing them.

You can still count as a worker if the remuneration you receive is in the form of payment in kind rather than, or in addition to, money.[131]

Working under the direction of another person

To count as a worker, you must perform the services for, and under the direction of, someone else[132] – ie, there must be someone who tells you what work to do. If you provide services in return for remuneration and you are not under the direction of another person, you count as self-employed (see p218) rather than a worker.[133]

If you are taxed as a self-employed person, this by itself does not prevent you from being in an employment relationship, although it is a relevant factor. For example, many people who work in the construction industry and pay tax as subcontractors under the Construction Industry Scheme, provide services in return for payment and work under the direction of another person. They are therefore workers and not self-employed.

It does not matter whether the person or organisation that provides the remuneration is the same as the person or organisation to whom you provide services.[134]

'Cash in hand', agency and 'trafficked' work

You count as being in an employment relationship if you provide services in return for renumeration under the direction of another person. This is not affected by the fact that:

- you are paid 'cash in hand'. The concept of 'worker' is an economic status, rather than a legal one.[135] However, you must still provide evidence of your employment;
- you were 'trafficked' into the work. Even if you could get discretionary leave to remain in the UK as a result of the trafficking (which would mean you were exempt from the habitual residence test for means-tested benefits – see p159), that does not prevent you from having a free movement right to reside as a worker on the basis of your work.[136] You still need to provide evidence of your employment;
- you did not declare the work to the DWP at the time.[137] This is likely to be most relevant when you are relying on past periods of employment;
- the person or organisation to whom you provide the services is different from the person or organisation that pays you for these – eg, if you are 'employed' by an employment agency.[138] However, the activities entailed in your provision of services must still be accepted as genuine and effective rather than marginal and ancillary (see below and, in particular p216, regarding the regularity of the work). There is nothing inherent in working for an agency that would exclude your activities from being genuine and effective; that depends on the facts of each case.[139]

Example

Nora is a Hungarian national with pre-settled status. She is working as a care assistant 'employed' by an employment agency. The payment she receives is via the agency, but the services are provided to a private care home. The care home has a contractual relationship with the agency, rather than with Nora, and it pays the agency. Nora is still classed as a worker because she is providing services and doing so in return for remuneration, even though there is a separation between the care home where she provides the services and the agency that pays her.

For your worker status to be accepted, you must provide evidence of your employment and this may be harder to do in some of the circumstances above, such as if you are paid cash in hand or you were trafficked into the work. The benefit authority must take your own statements about your work into account as evidence, unless they are self-contradictory or inherently improbable (see p496). If you have provided details of your employment to another government agency and these have been accepted (eg, to the police as part of an investigation of trafficking), a record of these should be accepted as relevant evidence when determining whether you have worker status.[140] See Chapter 20 for more information on evidence requirements and p510 for evidence of your work.

'Genuine and effective', not 'marginal and ancillary'

You only have a right to reside as a worker if the services you provide entail activities that are 'genuine and effective', as opposed to those that are on such a small scale as to be regarded as 'marginal and ancillary'.[141]

When deciding this, the decision maker must assess, as a whole, all the circumstances of your case.[142] See p212 for details of the guidance issued to decision makers. Relevant factors that must be considered include:

- the number of hours you work;
- the duration of your employment;
- the level of earnings;
- whether the work is regular or erratic;
- other employment rights;
- whether the work is 'marginal and ancillary' – ie, is insignificant in scale, is not for the economic benefit of the employer or is just a small part of a more substantial relationship between you and the employer.

Number of hours worked

The number of hours you work in a given period is a relevant factor when determining whether your work is genuine and effective. There is no minimum number of hours you must work. Provided other factors indicate that the work is genuine and effective, even work for a few hours a week can count as genuine and effective.

In one case, the Court of Justice of the European Union (CJEU) held that, after an overall assessment of the employment relationship, the possibility could not be ruled out that someone who worked only 5.5 hours a week could be a worker.[143] However, in most circumstances, you must work for more than 5.5 hours a week for your activity to be accepted as genuine and effective. In one case, someone working as an au pair for 13 hours a week for £35 per week plus board and lodging, for a duration of 5.5 weeks, was held to be a worker.[144]

Duration of the employment

The duration of the employment is a relevant factor to consider when deciding whether or not your work is genuine and effective. However, it is not conclusive, so if your work only lasts a short time, this fact by itself cannot exclude you from being a worker.[145]

Provided other factors indicate that the work you do is genuine and effective, even very short periods of work can still be sufficient to mean you have worker status while doing this work. In one case, the Court of Appeal found that someone was a worker during employment that was (and was always known to be) of two weeks' duration.[146] Although a short duration of employment that was fixed from the outset may not prevent you from being a worker,[147] work that is curtailed prematurely may be more likely to be considered to be genuine and effective.[148] The CJEU recently held that employment of two weeks' duration, which was not a fixed-term contract but which ended because of involuntary unemployment, meant the person had acquired worker status that was then retained for six months because he had registered as a jobseeker (see p223).[149]

Level of earnings

If your earnings are very low, this may be a factor that indicates that your work is not genuine and effective. However, low earnings cannot, by themselves, prevent you from being a worker. Even if your earnings are so low that they do not meet your needs and you supplement them by claiming means-tested benefits, this does not prevent you from being a worker.[150]

Note: your earnings can include non-monetary payments in kind (see p213).

Irregular or erratic work

If you are in an employment relationship in which you are only occasionally called upon to work, this may indicate that your work is not genuine and effective. However, the decision maker must always look at all your circumstances. There is nothing inherent in an 'on-call' or 'zero-hour' contract that prevents you from being a worker; it depends on the work you actually do.[151] Similarly, there is nothing inherent in doing temporary work for an agency that prevents you from being a worker. If the work is regular, rather than intermittent, and for a prolonged period or with a high likelihood of further work being obtained, you may be a worker.[152]

Other employment rights

If you have rights in your contract of employment, for example to paid holidays and sick pay, or you are a member of a trade union recognised by your employer, these are factors that may contribute to your employment being genuine and effective.[153]

Work not for an economic purpose or part of a wider relationship

Work may count as 'marginal' or 'ancillary' if it is done as part of another relationship which is more significant – eg, if a lodger performs a small task for their landlord as part of the terms of their tenancy.[154]

Work may not count as 'genuine and effective' if its main purpose is not for the economic benefit of the employer. Fostering children or caring for a person with disabilities have been held not to be economic activities and receipt of a fostering allowance or carer's allowance have been held not to count as remuneration in a commercial sense.[155] However, in a subsequent case, which did not consider this earlier caselaw, the care provided while in receipt of carer's allowance was held to be genuine and effective, and not marginal and ancillary, and the carer was held to be a worker.[156]

When you cease to be a worker

You only cease to be a worker when the employment relationship (see p213) ends. While you are still under a contract of employment, you continue to be a worker. You are therefore still a worker if, for example, you are a woman on maternity leave (including unpaid maternity leave), or if you are on holiday, sick or compassionate leave (including if it is unpaid).[157] Similarly, you are still a worker during periods when you have been furloughed.

If you have ceased to be a worker, you may retain your worker status in certain circumstances (see p222).

Benefit entitlement

If you have a right to reside as a worker, or as a family member (see p239) of a worker, this satisfies the right to reside requirement for all benefits that have this requirement (see p168). You are also exempt from the habitual residence test for means-tested benefits (see p159) and therefore do not need to be 'habitually resident in fact' (see p163). You are also exempt from the requirement to have been living in the UK for the past three months for child benefit and child tax credit (see p144).

Your current entitlement to benefits can be assisted if you had a right to reside as a worker, or as a family member of a worker, in the past – specifically:

- if you (or the person you are a family member of) have retained that worker status (see p222); or
- if it was part of a period of five years of residing in the UK with free movement residence rights, which can mean you now have a permanent right to reside (see p265); *or*
- if you are seeking to show that you had a free movement right to reside on 31 December 2020, to satisfy regulations on the protected groups who can, after that date, potentially have free movement residence rights, and, if you are an EEA national, not be defined as a 'person subject to immigration control' (see p188). For further details, including the duration of these protections, see p188.

See p510 for information on providing evidence of work.

11. Self-employed people

Since 30 June 2021, you can only have any free movement right to reside, including as a self-employed person (or family member of a self-employed person), if you either have pre-settled status or you have a pending European Union Settlement Scheme (EUSS) application for settled or pre-settled status (or a pending appeal or administrative review of a refusal). For details of these protected groups and others that applied during the period 31 December 2020 to 30 June 2021, see p188.

If you are in one of the protected groups, or for a period before the end of 2020, you may have a right to reside as a 'self-employed person' if you are a European Economic Area (EEA) national undertaking self-employed activity in the UK. You may also have a right to reside if you are a family member (see p239) of a self-employed person. Once you have established your status as a self-employed person, it is important to be clear when you cease to be self-employed (see p220). In limited circumstances, you can retain your status as a self-employed person after you cease self-employed activity (see p222).

If you have a right to reside as a self-employed person, as someone who has retained status as a self-employed person, or as a family member of a self-employed person, this satisfies the right to reside requirement for all benefits that have this requirement.

Who has a right to reside as a self-employed person

If you are in one of the protected groups that can have a free movement right to reside (see p188), or during a period before the end of 2020, you have a right to reside as a self-employed person if you are an EEA national in the UK and:[158]

- you provide services;
- you receive remuneration in return for those services (see p213);
- you do not perform your work under the direction of another person (see p213); *and*
- the work you do entails activities that are 'genuine and effective', rather than 'marginal and ancillary' (see p215).

The EEA Regulations cross-refer to European Union (EU) law for the meaning of 'self-employed person'.[159] However, the term 'self-employed person' is not defined in EU legislation. Instead, the above requirements, and their meaning, have been established through EU caselaw, and this caselaw must be used to interpret the concept (see p195).

The meanings of the above conditions are the same as they are for workers. The main difference between the definition of a self-employed person and a worker is that the work a self-employed person does is *not* carried out under the direction of another person.

Whether or not you satisfy these requirements depends on all your circumstances. For example, in one case, the Upper Tribunal held that someone selling the *Big Issue* was self-employed, as the activities involved were 'genuine and effective'.[160] A subsequent case held that someone selling the *Big Issue* was not self-employed, as his activities were not genuine and effective (although this decision was largely due to there being insufficient evidence for the whole period and, arguably, the tribunal did not consider all the relevant circumstances adequately).[161] In a separate case, the Upper Tribunal has held that the First-tier Tribunal had not made an error of law in finding that someone selling the *Big Issue* was not self-employed because her activities were not genuine and effective. It held that the First-tier Tribunal *had* considered all the relevant factors and not, for example, just looked at the person's low level of earnings.[162] Recently, the Upper Tribunal held that a busker could not be considered to be a self-employed person due to the absence of an agreement on remuneration.[163] This finding arguably does not apply to all buskers or street musicians.

Fostering children and caring for a person with disabilities have both been held not to be self-employment because they are not economic activities and the fostering allowance or carer's allowance received is not remuneration in a commercial sense.[164] However, in a case that did not consider these earlier cases, an EEA national in receipt of carer's allowance was held to be a worker (see p216).[165]

Decision makers are advised in guidance to follow a two-stage process when determining whether you are, or were, self-employed (or a worker).[166] Although this guidance is not legally binding, it is helpful to know its content either to pre-empt potential problems before your claim is decided or to challenge an incorrect decision more effectively (see p212).

Note: if you are an EEA national and on 31 December 2020, and continuously since then, you have been self-employed in the UK while 'not primarily resident in the UK', you may have rights as a 'frontier worker' (see p278). These rights include being exempt from the habitual residence test for means-tested benefits (see p151).

Croatian, A2 and A8 nationals

If you are a Croatian, A2 or A8 national and were self-employed during the relevant period of restrictions (see p197), your residence rights as a self-employed person were exactly the same as for nationals of any other EEA country – there were no restrictions for self-employed people.

When you become and cease to be self-employed

Whether you have become self-employed or you have ceased to be self-employed can be harder to determine than whether you have become, or ceased to be, a worker. Unlike a person who is employed, a person who is self-employed does not have a contract of employment that starts and ends on a particular date. You may count as self-employed when you are setting yourself up to work as a self-employed person and continue to count as self-employed, despite the fact that you have no work coming in for the time being.

When you become self-employed

The EEA Regulations define you as a self-employed person if you are established in the UK in order to pursue activity as a self-employed person within the meaning of (or, until 31 December 2020, 'in accordance with'[167]) Article 49 of the Treaty on the Functioning of the European Union.[168] The treaty prohibits restrictions on the freedom of establishment, including 'the right to take up and pursue activities as a self-employed person and to set up and manage undertakings'.[169]

However, you must have more than an intention to pursue self-employed activity, and you must provide evidence of the steps you have taken or the ways in which you have set yourself up as self-employed.[170] Exactly what steps you must take depends on your particular circumstances. It helps if you have registered with HM Revenue and Customs (HMRC) as self-employed. However, if you have not registered, this does not necessarily mean you are not self-employed.[171]

Relevant steps include:

- advertising your services;
- researching opportunities to find customers;
- setting up your accounts;
- registering with HMRC as self-employed for purposes of national insurance contributions and taxes;
- obtaining equipment required for the work you intend to do;
- setting up a website for your business.

The above steps are only examples; you do not have to take any of these particular steps, but the more steps you have taken, the more likely it is that you will be accepted as having a right to reside as a self-employed person.

Note: if you are told that you do not have residence rights as a self-employed person until you have been earning money from your self-employed activity for three months, and/or earning a certain amount of money, this is incorrect. It is likely to be based on an incorrect interpretation of decision makers' guidance (see p212).

For more information on evidence of self-employment, see p510.

When you cease to be self-employed

If you have stopped all your self-employed activity and do not intend to resume that activity, it is clear that you have ceased to be a self-employed person. However, some situations are less clear – eg, if you are in a temporary lull, you can continue to be a self-employed person despite having no current work. Whether you continue to be a self-employed person during a period when you have little or no work depends on your particular circumstances and the evidence you provide.[172]

Factors that are relevant in determining whether or not you have ceased self-employment include:[173]

- the amount of work you have coming in;
- steps you are taking to find new work;
- whether you are continuing to market your services;
- whether you are developing your business in new directions;
- whether you are maintaining your accounts;
- if you were entitled to a payment from the Self-Employment Income Support Scheme (payable if your self-employed income had been reduced due to your activity, capacity or demand being affected by the coronavirus pandemic, and entitlement requiring a declaration that you intended to continue trading);
- your motives and intentions.

Which factors are relevant depends on the nature of your self-employment and all your circumstances. However, the more factors that show you are still undertaking self-employed activity, the stronger your argument that you have not ceased to be a self-employed person.

If you have ceased to be self-employed, you may be able to retain your self-employed status in certain circumstances (see p222).

Pregnancy

If you are working on a self-employed basis and you become pregnant, you may, depending on your circumstances, continue to count as self-employed during your maternity period when you do no self-employed work, but you intend to resume your self-employment at the end of your maternity period.[174] The Upper Tribunal, in two linked cases, emphasised the need for careful fact finding to establish whether self-employment is maintained during maternity leave. This includes establishing whether the self-employment was 'genuine and effective' before the start of maternity leave and what steps are being taken to maintain that self-employment, taking into account all the circumstances, even if little, or no, actual work is done. Only one of the women in these cases was found, due to her particular circumstances, to have maintained her self-employed status during her maternity period.[175] The question of whether the other woman could *retain* her self-employed status, taking into account European caselaw on retaining worker status when stopping work because of late pregnancy,[176] was referred to the Court of Justice of the European Union, which held that she did (see p229).[177]

Benefit entitlement

If you have a right to reside as a self-employed person, or as a family member (see p239) of a self-employed person, this satisfies the right to reside requirement for all benefits that have this requirement (see p168). You are also exempt from the habitual residence test for means-tested benefits (see p159), and therefore do not need to be 'habitually resident in fact' (see p163). You are also exempt from the requirement to have been living in the UK for the past three months for child benefit and child tax credit (see p144).

Your current entitlement to benefits can be assisted if you had a right to reside as a self-employed person, or as a family member of a self-employed person, in the past – specifically:

- if you (or the person you are a family member of) have retained that self-employed status (see below); or
- if it was part of a period of five years of residing in the UK with free movement residence rights, which can mean you now have a permanent right to reside (see p265); *or*
- if you are seeking to show that you had a free movement right to reside on 31 December 2020, to satisfy regulations on the protected groups who can, after that date, potentially have free movement residence rights, and, if you are an EEA national, not be defined as a 'person subject to immigration control' (see p93). For further details, including the duration of these protections, see p188.

See p510 for information on providing evidence of self-employment.

12. **Retaining worker or self-employed status**

Since 30 June 2021, you can only have any free movement right to reside, including retained worker or self-employed status (or a family member of an European Economic Area (EEA) national with either), if you either have pre-settled status or you have a pending European Union Settlement Scheme (EUSS) application for settled or pre-settled status (or a pending appeal or administrative review of a refusal). For details of these protected groups and others that applied during the period 31 December 2020 to 30 June 2021, see p188.

If you are in one of the protected groups, or for a period before the end of 2020, you can retain the status of 'worker' or 'self-employed', even though you are no longer working, if:[178]

- you are involuntarily unemployed and registered as a jobseeker (see p223);
- you are undertaking vocational training (see p227);
- you are temporarily unable to work because of an illness or accident (see p228);
- you are unable to work because you are in the late stages of pregnancy or have just given birth (see the note below).[179]

Before arguing that you have retained your worker or self-employed status, check whether you have actually ceased to be a worker (see p217) or self-employed (see p220). For example, if you are employed and off work on unpaid sick leave, but you can return to your job when you are better, you are still a worker and so do not need to argue that you have retained your worker status. Similarly, you may still count as self-employed if you are in a temporary period with little or no work.

Note:

- Following a decision by the Court of Justice of the European Union (CJEU) that a self-employed man could retain his self-employed status when he was involuntarily unemployed and registered as a jobseeker,[180] the EEA Regulations were amended from 24 July 2018 to include the right of self-employed people to retain their status in the same circumstances as workers. If these circumstances applied to you before 24 July 2018, you can rely on the CJEU judgment.[181]
- It may also be possible to argue that you can retain your worker or self-employed status in other circumstances than those listed above. The CJEU has held that European Union (EU) Directive 2004/38 does not provide an exhaustive list of such circumstances.[182] However, the Upper Tribunal held that a man who had been required, for a temporary period, to stop work to care for his children did not retain his worker status.[183]

Croatian, A2 and A8 nationals

If you are a Croatian or A2 or A8 national who was subject to restrictions (see p198), you could not retain your worker status during the relevant period of restrictions in the ways described in this section. However, if you were an A8 national subject to restrictions and you stopped working during the first month of employment, you could retain your worker status in the ways described in this section for the remainder of that month.[184]

The extension of the restrictions on A8 nationals from 30 April 2009 to 30 April 2011 has now been held to be unlawful (see p197).[185] This means that if you would have been accepted as having retained your worker status during these two years were it not for your being subject to restrictions at that time, you can retrospectively be accepted as having retained your worker status during this period.[186]

If you are a Croatian, A2 or A8 national and were self-employed during the relevant periods of restrictions, you could retain your self-employed status in exactly the same way as nationals of any other EEA country – there were no restrictions on retaining self-employed status.

You are involuntarily unemployed and registered as a jobseeker

You retain your status as a worker or self-employed person if you:[187]

- are recorded as involuntarily unemployed (see p224); *and*
- have registered yourself as a jobseeker with the relevant employment office (see p225); *and*

- provide evidence that you are seeking employment (or, to retain self-employed status, seeking either employment or self-employment).

In addition to the above, the EEA Regulations contain requirements that are very rarely enforced by benefit authorities that in order to:[188]

- retain worker status:
  - you must have entered the UK to seek employment; *or*
  - you must be present in the UK seeking employment immediately after having a right to reside as a worker (except if you retained your worker status on this basis), a student or a self-sufficient person;
- retain self-employed status:
  - you must have entered the UK as a self-employed person or in order to seek self-employment; *or*
  - you must be present in the UK seeking self-employment immediately after having a right to reside as a self-employed person (except if you retained your self-employed status on this basis), a student or self-sufficient person.

The EEA Regulations also continue to require that to retain your worker or self-employed status beyond six months, your evidence that you are continuing to seek employment (or, to retain self-employed status, continuing to seek either employment or self-employment) must be 'compelling'. However, that was held to be unlawful by the Upper Tribunal.[189] Guidance confirms that since this judgment (on 14 February 2020), this requirement no longer applies, and if you are claiming universal credit (UC), you should continue to be accepted as retaining your worker or self-employed status while you are meeting your work-search requirements.[190]

Involuntary unemployment

You are 'involuntarily unemployed' if you are seeking and are available to take up employment (or self-employment, to retain your status as a self-employed person). This depends on your remaining in the labour market. The circumstances in which you left your last job, or ceased your self-employment, including whether you did so voluntarily, are relevant in determining whether you have remained in the labour market. However, they are just one factor and all your actions and circumstances, both at the time of leaving, or ceasing, work and since then, must also be taken into account.[191]

Example

Karl is German and has pre-settled status. He was working at a food processing factory for seven months. The shift times changed recently, which meant that when he was on late shifts he had to catch three buses to get home from work. He found this commute exhausting and asked his employer if he could just do the early shift when the bus connections were better. His employer said that all employees must work both early and late shifts, so Karl handed in his notice. Even while working his notice, Karl looked for other alternative work closer to home. He did not find any, but now his job has ended he spends more time contacting potential employers. Karl counts as involuntarily unemployed, despite the fact that he left his previous employment voluntarily.

Most of the caselaw covers the circumstances in which you are involuntarily unemployed for the purpose of retaining worker status because it was decided before the CJEU confirmed that self-employed people can also retain their status on this basis (see p222). However, in the case in which this was confirmed, the CJEU accepted that the man's self-employed activity had ceased because of a lack of work due to the economic downturn, and as this was due to reasons beyond his control, it was 'involuntary unemployment'.[192] More recently, the Upper Tribunal accepted the concession from the DWP that the principles established in caselaw also apply to retaining self-employed status and held that a self-employed driver who lacked the means to obtain a reliable vehicle was involuntarily unemployed.[193]

Registering as a jobseeker

You must register as a jobseeker with the 'relevant employment office'. In the UK, this is Jobcentre Plus, which is part of the DWP.

The best way to register as a jobseeker is to claim UC on the basis that you are searching, and are available, for work and/or jobseeker's allowance (JSA), and show that you continue to satisfy the work search and work availability requirements (or the requirements to be available for and actively seeking work for JSA). Be clear when completing the habitual residence test for UC that you are currently seeking work. If you are not entitled to benefit, contact the job centre and claim national insurance credits on the basis of unemployment. You do not need to receive UC or JSA in order to be registered as a jobseeker.

You may also satisfy the requirement to register as a jobseeker if you claim a benefit that does not require you to look for work (eg, UC while you are the responsible carer of a child under three, or pension credit (PC)) and you declare to the job centre in the course of making your claim that you are looking for work – eg, you provide a written statement as part of your habitual residence test.[194] You must provide evidence of your work search. **Note:** this way of registering as a jobseeker is only relevant for retaining your worker or self-employed status and claiming benefit on the basis of having a right to reside as a worker or self-employed person. It does not enable you to claim benefits, such as UC or PC, if your only right to reside is as a jobseeker (as this is an excluded right to reside for those benefits – see p169).

If there was a gap between when your work ended and when you registered as a jobseeker, see p230.

For how long can you retain worker or self-employed status

The length of time you can retain your worker or self-employed status while involuntarily unemployed depends on whether or not you have already been employed or self-employed in the UK for more than a year.

If you were employed or self-employed for more than a year, you can retain your worker or self-employed status on this basis indefinitely, until there is an event that indicates that you have entirely withdrawn from the labour market.[195] Receipt of maternity allowance by a woman who remained registered with employment agencies has been held *not* to be such an event.[196]

You do not need to have been employed in one continuous job. Also, small gaps between jobs (eg, around two weeks) do not necessarily mean that you were not employed for more than a year.[197] The same principles should also apply to small gaps in self-employed activity.

Although the EEA Regulations continue to state that, to retain your worker or self-employed status on this basis for longer than a continuous period of six months, you must provide 'compelling' evidence of continuing to seek work, this requirement, together with the requirement to provide evidence of having a 'genuine chance of being engaged', were held to be unlawful by the Upper Tribunal.[198] The regulations were amended with effect from 1 January 2021 to omit the latter requirement, but note that for earlier periods you can rely on the Upper Tribunal decision. Guidance confirms that since the Upper Tribunal judgment (on 14 February 2020), there are no additional evidence requirements after six months, and, if you are claiming UC, you should continue to be accepted as retaining your worker or self-employed status while you are meeting your work search requirements.[199]

If you were employed for less than a year, the EEA Regulations limit the period during which you can retain your worker or self-employed status while involuntarily unemployed to a maximum of six months.[200] The EU Directive allows you to retain worker status for no less than six months.[201] The CJEU held that worker status could be retained for six months following employment of two weeks' duration, which was not a fixed-term contract and that ended due to involuntary unemployment, provided the person registered as a jobseeker.[202] Applying this decision, the Upper Tribunal recently held that a First-tier Tribunal had been wrong to decide that a man who became involuntarily unemployed could not retain his self-employed status because he had been self-employed for less than a year.[203]

Once you can no longer retain your worker or self-employed status on this basis, you may have a right to reside as a jobseeker (see p203). If so, note that under the EEA Regulations, you must (although these requirements are not always enforced):[204]

- have a period of absence from the UK since you retained your worker or self-employed status on the basis of being involuntarily unemployed (although the benefit authorities have not been enforcing this requirement, other than in very few cases); *and*

- (unless you were absent from the UK for at least 12 continuous months) provide 'compelling' evidence of seeking employment and having a genuine chance of being engaged from the start of your period of residence as a jobseeker (see p205).

Note: having a right to reside as a jobseeker only satisfies the right to reside requirement for child benefit, child tax credit (CTC) and income-based JSA, but periods when you had a right to reside as a jobseeker count towards the five-year period of residing with a free movement right to reside in the UK, needed to obtain a permanent right to reside (see p266). Also, if you had a right to reside as a jobseeker on 31 December 2020, this will assist if you are seeking to show you satisfy regulations on protected groups that can, after that date, potentially have other free movement residence rights (see p188).

You have started vocational training

You retain your worker or self-employed status, if you have either:[205]

- started vocational training related to your previous employment or, to retain self-employment, related to your previous occupation; *or*
- started vocational training and you are 'involuntarily unemployed' (see p224). This applies if you have to retrain in order to find work that is reasonably equivalent to your former employment.[206]

In general, you should be able to argue that any training or study that can assist you in obtaining employment counts as vocational training. This can include a course leading to a qualification for a particular profession, trade or employment or a course that provides the necessary training or skills.[207] A course can be vocational for you even if it is not vocational for someone else – eg, a photography course if you want to work as a photographer.

Training related to your previous employment or occupation

If you are not involuntarily unemployed, your vocational training must be related to your previous employment for you to retain your worker status or related to your previous occupation for you to retain your self-employed status. For this to apply, there must be a relationship between the purpose of your studies and your previous occupational activity.[208] The decision maker must take into account all your previous occupational activity in the UK, not just your most recent employment.[209] If you consider that the course you are pursuing is related to any of your previous employment in the UK, explain this relationship in detail to the decision maker and provide evidence.

You are temporarily unable to work because of an illness or accident

You can retain your worker or self-employed status if you are temporarily unable to work as a result of an illness or accident.[210]

Always check whether you have actually ceased to be a worker (see p217) or self-employed (see p220). For example, if you are off work on unpaid sick leave but you can return to your job when you are better, you are still a worker and so do not need to argue that you have retained your worker status.

As a result of an illness or accident

To retain your worker or self-employed status on this basis, your inability to work must be as a result of an illness or accident.

The test of your inability to work is unrelated to any test in the benefits system – eg, you do not need to show you have 'limited capability for work' or that you are 'incapable of work'. Instead, the test is whether you can be fairly described as unable to do the work you were doing or, if it follows a period in which you were seeking work, the sort of work you were seeking.[211]

You do not need to have claimed a benefit payable on grounds of illness or disability, such as employment and support allowance, or any benefit at all, to retain your right to reside as a worker on this basis.[212] However, if you *have* received benefit paid on the basis of your illness or disability, this is evidence of your inability to work for that period. Otherwise, you need to provide other evidence of your inability to work, such as a medical certificate from your GP.

Your inability to work must be caused by your own illness or accident – eg, you cannot retain your worker status if you are unable to work because you are looking after a child who is ill.[213]

Temporary inability to work

Your inability to work must be temporary. This simply means not permanent.[214] It is your inability to work that must be temporary, not your health condition, so you can retain your worker or self-employed status on the basis of a permanent illness or effect of an accident if this fluctuates and causes temporary periods when you are unable to work.[215]

You are considered temporarily unable to work if, taking into account all the available evidence, there is a realistic prospect of your being able to work again and re-enter the labour market.[216]

Note: if there is no reasonable prospect of your being able undertake *any* work again (whether the same as, or different to, the work you did previously), then you cannot *retain* your worker or self-employed status. However, you may have acquired a permanent right to reside on the basis of your permanent incapacity (see p275).

You are pregnant or have recently given birth

If you have established worker or self-employed status and you are now not working because you are pregnant or have recently given birth, you may still count as a worker or as self-employed, or you may be able to retain your worker or self-employed status.

You do not cease to be a worker while you are still under a contract of employment (see p217). You are therefore still a worker while on maternity leave, whether or not it is paid. **Note:** this also applied to Croatian, A2 and A8 nationals who established worker status during the period of restrictions (see p197).[217]

You can remain a self-employed person if you intend to resume your self-employment after your maternity period. This depends on whether you can show that you have remained engaged in genuine and effective self-employed activity, even though you are not working while in your maternity period (see p220).[218]

If you have ceased to be a worker or self-employed, you may retain your worker or self-employed status if you have a pregnancy-related illness that prevents you from working on the basis that you are temporarily unable to work because of an illness or accident (see p228).[219] You can also retain your worker or self-employed status on this basis if you have another illness, unrelated to your pregnancy, that results in your being temporarily unable to work. **Note:** pregnancy itself does not mean you are temporarily unable to work because of an illness or accident.[220]

Stopping work during the late stages of pregnancy or after childbirth

You retain your worker or self-employed status if you stop work (or stop seeking work if you retained your worker or self-employed status while involuntarily unemployed – see p223) because of the physical constraints of the late stages of pregnancy and the aftermath of childbirth, provided you intend to start work again (or start seeking work and thereby retain your worker or self-employed status while involuntarily unemployed) within a 'reasonable period' after the birth of your child.[221]

The Upper Tribunal has held that, in most cases, a 'reasonable period' is 52 weeks, although this may differ if your circumstances are unusual.[222] The Upper Tribunal also held that, in most cases, your 'reasonable period', and therefore the period during which you retain your worker or self-employed status on this basis, starts 11 weeks before your due date. However, in exceptional cases, it could be earlier if the physical constraints of your pregnancy require you to stop work (or to stop seeking work if you have retained worker or self-employed status) sooner, and you can provide evidence of this – eg, if you have a multiple pregnancy or if you can no longer carry out particular requirements of your work.[223]

Note: most of the principles established in caselaw concerning the retention of status on this basis concern workers because this was established several years before it was confirmed that a self-employed woman in comparable circumstances also retains status, but these principles apply equally to retaining worker or self-employed status.[224]

If you intend to work again within a 'reasonable period', you should always make this clear to the decision maker. However, you should be accepted as retaining worker or self-employed status on this basis unless you state that you have absolutely no intention of returning to work under any circumstances.[225]

If the basis on which you retain your worker or self-employed status changes

You can continue to retain your worker or self-employed status if you are in one of the groups on p222 and move into another category.[226]

Example

Nikolas is Greek and has pre-settled status. He worked for 13 months in a hotel until he was made redundant. He claimed UC while he looked for another job. Five months later, Nikolas became unwell and was unable to carry on looking for work. He provided medical evidence to the DWP confirming that he was currently too ill to work. Nikolas is entitled to UC because he has retained his right to reside as a worker – initially, as someone who was involuntarily unemployed and who had registered as a jobseeker, and then because of his temporary inability to work as a result of his illness.

There is no limit to the number of times you can change the basis on which you retain worker or self-employed status. However, if you lose your worker or self-employed status, you cannot regain it without undertaking further employment or self-employment that gives you worker or self-employed status.

Gaps

If you cease to be a worker or self-employed and do not retain that status, you cannot regain it again. To be a worker or self-employed in the future, you must acquire that status afresh. However, if there is just a gap between your having worker or self-employed status and your being covered by one of the groups that can retain that status on p222, you may not have lost that status. This depends on all your circumstances, including the length of the gap.

Several Upper Tribunal decisions have confirmed that a gap between your employment ending and your registering as a jobseeker while involuntarily unemployed does not necessarily mean that you lose your worker status. The same principles should apply to any gap between your self-employed activity ceasing and your registering as a jobseeker. These decisions have held that the significance of a gap depends on whether the length of the gap, and the reasons for it, indicate that you have left the labour market.[227] If the delay is for more than a few days, all your circumstances (including the reasons for the gap and what you did during that time) should be considered to establish whether there are reasonable grounds for the delay, so that it is not considered an 'undue delay'.

There is no fixed period of gap that will be considered an 'undue delay'. Gaps of two months or less, during which there is clear evidence of looking for work, are generally accepted by First-tier Tribunals as not amounting to an 'undue delay', without the DWP seeking to appeal the decisions. However, the longer the gap, the more compelling the reasons must be.[228]

Arguably, you should be able to retain your worker or self-employed status if there is a gap between your ceasing work and your being temporarily unable to work because of an illness or accident, since there is no requirement for the illness or accident to be the reason for your ceasing work. You do not need to have been receiving any benefit while you were temporarily unable to work, so if there was a delay before you claimed benefit, this does not necessarily mean there was a gap between your being a worker or self-employed and retaining your worker or self-employed status on the basis of your temporary inability to work.[229]

Example

Rita is a Portuguese national who came to the UK in 2019 and obtained pre-settled status a year ago. She completed a 10-month fixed-term contract of full-time work. The day after this job finished, she was seriously injured in a cycling accident and so could not look for work. She did not claim any benefits as she lived with her partner who supported her. Seven months later she separated from her partner and made a single claim for UC, because she is still unable to work because of her injuries. Rita provides the DWP with a medical certificate that confirms her inability to work since the date of her accident. She satisfies the right to reside requirement for UC since she retains her worker status because she is temporarily unable to work as a result of her accident. There was no gap between her retaining her worker status on this basis and her last day of employment.

You can also retain your worker or self-employed status during a short gap between two different bases on which you can retain that status. Whether the gap is relevant also depends on your circumstances, the bases you are switching between, the length of the gap and your actions during it.

Benefit entitlement

If you retain your worker or self-employed status, this satisfies the right to reside requirement for all benefits that have this requirement (see p168).

If you are a family member (see p239) of someone who retains their worker or self-employed status, your residence rights are the same as if you were the family member of someone who *is* a worker or self-employed, and, therefore, you satisfy the right to reside requirement for all the benefits that have this requirement.

If you retain worker or self-employed status (or you are a family member of someone who does), you are also exempt from the habitual residence test for means-tested benefits (see p159), and therefore do not need to be 'habitually resident in fact' (see p163). You are also exempt from the requirement to have been living in the UK for the past three months for child benefit (see p144).

Your current entitlement to benefits can be assisted if you had retained worker or self-employed status, or were a family member of someone who had either status, in the past – specifically:

- if it was part of a period of five years of residing in the UK with free movement residence rights, which can mean you now have a permanent right to reside (see p265); *or*
- if you are seeking to show that you had a free movement right to reside on 31 December 2020, to satisfy regulations on the protected groups who can, after that date, potentially have free movement residence rights, and, if you are an EEA national, not be defined as a 'person subject to immigration control' (see p93). For further details, including the duration of these protections, see p188.

13. **Self-sufficient people and students**

Since 30 June 2021, you can only have any free movement right to reside, including as a self-sufficient person (or family member of a self-sufficient person), if you either have pre-settled status or you have a pending European Union Settlement Scheme (EUSS) application for settled or pre-settled status (or a pending appeal or administrative review of a refusal). For details of these protected groups and others that applied during the period 31 December 2020 to 30 June 2021, see p188.

If you are in one of the protected groups, or for a period before the end of 2020, you have a right of residence as a self-sufficient person if you are a European Economic Area (EEA) national and you, and any family members who do not have an independent right to reside, have:[230]

- sufficient resources (see p233) not to become a burden on the social assistance system of the UK during your period of residence (see p234); *and*
- comprehensive sickness insurance cover in the UK (see p235).

You have a right to reside as a student if you are an EEA national and:[231]

- you are enrolled as a student in a government-accredited college;
- you provide an assurance that you have sufficient resources (see p233) for yourself, and any family members who do not have an independent right to reside, not to become a burden on the UK social assistance system during your intended period of residence (see p234);
- you, and any family members who do not have an independent right to reside, have comprehensive sickness insurance cover in the UK (see p235).

Because the requirements to have a right to reside for students and self-sufficient people are very similar, this chapter refers to those who have a right to reside as a student as 'self-sufficient students'. The specific differences that apply to students are on p236.

You can also have a right to reside if you are a family member of a self-sufficient person or self-sufficient student.

Periods when you have a right to reside as a self-sufficient person or student, or a family member of either, count as periods of having 'resided legally' for acquiring permanent residence after five years (see p266).

Croatian, A2 and A8 nationals

If you are a Croatian, A2 or A8 national, your residence rights as a self-sufficient person or self-sufficient student during the relevant period of restrictions were the same as other EEA nationals – ie, there were no restrictions for self-sufficient people.

Note: certain students were exempt from the restrictions that applied to Croatian and A2 nationals. You were not subject to worker authorisation if you were a student with a registration certificate which stated that you could not work more than 20 hours a week (unless it was part of vocational training or during vacations) and you complied with this. If the certificate confirmed that you could work during the four months after the course finished, the exemption continued for this period (see p199). If that applied to you and you worked no more than 20 hours a week, you may have had a right to reside as a 'worker' (see p211). In addition, you counted as 'legally working' and, after a year of legally working (see p201), you were no longer subject to worker authorisation.

If you were employed during the relevant period of restrictions, but your work was not in accordance with your worker authorisation document (or, if you are an A8 national, for an 'authorised employer'), you cannot rely on those earnings as your resources for the purpose of having a right to reside as a self-sufficient person.[232]

For further details of the restrictions that previously applied to Croatian, A2 and A8 nationals, see p197.

Sufficient resources

Your resources must be 'sufficient' to avoid you, and any family member whose right to reside depends on their being your family member, becoming a burden on the social assistance system of the UK (see p234).[233] The government cannot set a fixed amount that it regards as 'sufficient' and must take your personal situation into account.[234]

Your resources are 'sufficient' if they:[235]

- are more than the maximum level you (and your family) can have to be eligible for 'social assistance' (see below); *or*

- are not more than that level, but the decision maker considers that they are sufficient, taking into account your personal circumstances (and those of any family member whose right to reside depends on their being your family member).

The 'maximum level' is the equivalent of your means-tested benefit applicable, or maximum, amount, including any premiums or elements you would be entitled to. Your resources also include your accommodation, so if your resources are more than your applicable, or maximum, amount plus your rent, they should be sufficient. You may also be self-sufficient if your resources are more than your applicable, or maximum, amount and you are provided with free and stable accommodation by friends or family.[236]

You do not need to own the resources that make you self-sufficient. It is enough if you have access to them – eg, if you are supported by someone else.[237]

The source of the resources does not matter.[238] However, you cannot rely on your earnings from your employment in the UK to give you self-sufficient status.[239] (In most circumstances, this does not matter as your employment means you have a right to reside as a 'worker', but it is relevant if, for example, you did not have worker status because you did not satisfy the additional conditions imposed on you as a Croatian, A2 or A8 national – see p197). However, if you are employed and have worker status in an EEA state, but you live in the UK, you can rely on your earnings in the EEA state to have a right to reside as a self-sufficient person in the UK.[240] You can also rely on the earnings of your non-EEA national spouse/civil partner.[241] An EEA national child can rely on the earnings of their non-EEA parent, even if that parent's employment in an EEA country is unlawful due to a lack of residence card and work permit.[242]

Not a burden on the social assistance system

You count as self-sufficient if you have sufficient resources 'not to become a burden on the social assistance system of the UK during your period of residence'.

'Burden' has been held to be an 'unreasonable burden'.[243]

The 'social assistance system of the UK' includes all means-tested benefits.[244] In its guidance, the DWP does not include child tax credit (CTC), but lists all the means-tested benefits (although in the universal credit (UC) guidance, only UC and pension credit (PC) are listed).[245]

You must not be automatically regarded as not self-sufficient just because you make a claim for a means-tested benefit. Although a claim could indicate that you do not have sufficient resources to avoid becoming an unreasonable burden on the social assistance system of the UK, the decision maker must carry out an assessment of the specific burden that awarding you the benefit you have claimed would make on the system as a whole. This assessment must take all your circumstances into account, including the likely duration of your claim,[246] at the point you make your claim for benefit on the basis of your right to reside as a self-sufficient person. You do not need to have had sufficient resources at the start of your period of residence. However, from the point the assessment is carried out, you must show sufficient resources for your intended period of residence, including for five years if permanent residence is sought.[247] **Note:** the Upper Tribunal held that the 'open-ended' nature of a claim for PC was a factor in deciding that claim represented an 'unreasonable burden' and so the claimant did not therefore have a right to reside as a self-sufficient person.[248] However, it is arguable that the tribunal should have limited the assessment period to the point at which she would have acquired a permanent right to reside. At the time of writing, the Upper Tribunal had just heard a separate case on the circumstances in which a claim for UC would not amount to an 'unreasonable burden'.[249] See CPAG's *Welfare Rights Bulletin* and the online version of this *Handbook* on AskCPAG for updates.

Although you should always provide any evidence you have that shows that the award of benefit would *not* mean you would become an 'unreasonable burden', the onus is on the decision maker to prove the specific burden that would be caused by an award (see p496).[250]

Comprehensive sickness insurance

To have a right of residence as a self-sufficient person, in addition to having sufficient resources (see p233) you must also have comprehensive sickness insurance cover in the UK.

In March 2022, the Court of Justice of the European Union (CJEU) held that the requirement to have comprehensive sickness insurance cover in the UK was satisfied by being able to use the UK's free National Health Service (NHS).[251] This judgment was then applied by the Upper Tribunal, which held that an EEA national had acquired a permanent right to reside following five years of supporting himself while having access to the NHS.[252]

Prior to the CJEU judgment, the UK courts had held that access to NHS treatment where the UK bears the cost did not satisfy the requirement to have comprehensive sickness insurance cover in the UK.[253] The European Commission had stated it considered this to be unlawful and, in October 2020, began infringement proceedings requiring the UK to amend the relevant rules.[254] **Note:** the European Commission can bring such proceedings within four years of the transition period ending on 31 December 2020, and any resulting judgment from the CJEU remains binding in the UK (see p195).[255]

The UK courts had, however, held that the requirement *is* satisfied if the UK can be reimbursed by an EEA state for any NHS costs incurred while in the UK.[256] This usually applies if you are covered by the European Union co-ordination rules (see p379) and an EEA state continues to be your 'competent state' (see p399) – eg, if you are:

- resident in the UK, but you are working or self-employed in an EEA state;

- resident in the UK and receive a pension from an EEA state (and you do not also receive a pension from the UK, and you are not working or self-employed in the UK (see p404);[257]
- living temporarily in the UK (eg, you are a student on a course in the UK) and during your stay in the UK you are entitled to health treatment in an EEA state because you are insured there.[258]

Note: although in these circumstances you may have been issued with a European health insurance card (EHIC) (and/or an S1 card) by the country in which you were last insured, holding such a card does not, in itself, confirm that your NHS costs will be reimbursed. As with other residence documents (see p504), the card only confirms your rights on the date it was issued; it does not mean you retain those rights if your circumstances change and your competent state changes from the state that issued the EHIC to the UK.[259]

It has also been accepted for a long time that the requirement to have comprehensive sickness insurance cover is satisfied if you have private health insurance.[260] Furthermore, it was held to be disproportionate to deny a right to reside solely on the basis that sickness insurance cover was not 'comprehensive'.[261] Although other arguments that it is disproportionate to insist on this requirement when the person did not have *any* sickness insurance have failed,[262] these cases were decided before the most recent CJEU case held that access to free NHS care satisfies the requirement. Specifically, in the recent case, the CJEU noted that it would be disprortionate to deny the EEA national child, one of whose parents had worked and paid tax in the UK, a right to reside as a self-sufficient person on the sole ground that he (and his primary carer – see next paragraph) could access free NHS care, as this did not constitute an unreasonable burden on the UK's public finances.[263]

The recent CJEU case also held that the requirement to have comprehensive sickness insurance cover applies to the primary carer of a self-sufficient child, as well as to that child, for that primary carer to have a derivative right to reside (see p260).

The question of whether being covered by the common travel area reciprocal arrangements on health insurance satisfies the requirement for comprehensive sickness insurance cover was also referred to the CJEU as part of the same case. However, this question was deemed inadmissible by the CJEU and so was not answered. It had also not been addressed by the Advocate General's opinion.[264]

Self-sufficient students

You have a right to reside as a self-sufficient student if you are an EEA national and:[265]

- you are enrolled as a student in a government-accredited establishment for the principal purpose of following a course of study (including vocational training); *and*

- you provide an assurance that you have sufficient resources for yourself, and any family members (see below) who do not have an independent right of residence, not to become a burden on the UK social assistance system during your intended period of residence (see below); *and*
- you, and any family members who do not have an independent right of residence, have comprehensive sickness insurance (see above).

The conditions for having a right of residence as a student are very similar to those for a self-sufficient person. The only differences are as follows.

- To have the right to reside as a self-sufficient student, you must be enrolled on a course of study.[266]
- The requirement to have sufficient resources is met by providing an assurance that you have 'sufficient resources'.[267] The assessment of what counts as 'sufficient resources' is the same as for a self-sufficient person (see p233) and it is not clear what practical difference it makes to provide an assurance of this. Although you may be more easily accepted as having a right to reside if you provide an assurance of your resources at the start of your studies, this does not prevent you from losing your right of residence if your circumstances change. However, such a loss is never automatic and always depends on your circumstances.[268] Also, if you are only likely to need to claim benefits on a temporary basis, depending on the length of your course, it may be easier to argue that your claim does not amount to an unreasonable burden on the social assistance system of the UK (see p234).
- The definition of family member is different.

Family members

Family member of a self-sufficient student

You are the **'family member'** of a self-sufficient student (once they have been in the UK for three months) if you are:[269]

– their spouse or civil partner; *or*

– their dependent child (regardless of your age); *or*

– the dependent child (regardless of your age) of the student's spouse or civil partner.

The above definition of family member is narrower than that which generally applies (see p240), and only applies if the student does not have another right to reside that can confer a right of residence on you.

If you are the parent/grandparent of a self-sufficient student who has been in the UK for at least three months, or a parent/grandparent of their spouse or civil partner, you may be able to be treated as a family member on the basis of being an extended family member if you have the relevant documentation (see p243).[270]

When assessing whether you have sufficient resources, you do not need to take account of anyone who does *not* come within this definition of family member after you have lived in the UK for three months – eg, your resources do not need to be sufficient for your non-dependent children under 21 or dependent parent living in the UK.

Benefit entitlement

If you have a right to reside as a self-sufficient person, a self-sufficient student, or family member of either, that satisfies the right to reside requirement for all benefits that have such a requirement (see p168).

The most common way in which periods of residence as a self-sufficient person or student (or family member of either) can assist you to access benefits that require a right to reside, is when such periods are in the past (see below). That is because, during your period of self-sufficiency, your resources often exclude you from means-tested benefits. However, if they do not, it cannot automatically be decided that you are not self-sufficient just because you have claimed a means-tested benefit (see p234).

Note:

- During your period of residence as a self-sufficient person you may be entitled to child benefit, as this is not a means-tested benefit, and CTC, for which your resources can be greater than for other means-tested benefits.
- You may have a right to reside if you are the primary carer of a self-sufficient child.

Your current entitlement to benefits can be assisted if you had a right to reside as a self-sufficient person, a family member of a self-sufficient person or as a student or family member of a student, in the past, or you are the primary carer of a child who had such a right to reside in the past – specifically:

- if your previous right to reside based on your self-sufficiency was part of a period of five years of residing in the UK with free movement residence rights, which can mean you now have a permanent right to reside (see p265); *or*
- if you are the primary carer of a child who has acquired a permanent right to reside, you may have a derivative right to reside (see p263);
- if you are seeking to show that you had a free movement right to reside on 31 December 2020, to satisfy regulations on the protected groups who can, after that date, potentially have free movement residence rights, and, if you are an EEA national, not be defined as a 'person subject to immigration control' (see p93). For further details, including the duration of these protections, see p188.

14. Family members of European Economic Area nationals

Since 30 June 2021, you can only have any free movement right to reside, including as a family member of a European Economic Area (EEA) national with one of the residence rights listed below, if you have either pre-settled status or a pending European Union Settlement Scheme (EUSS) application for settled or pre-settled status (or a pending appeal or administrative review of a refusal). For details of these protected groups and others that applied during the period 31 December 2020 to 30 June 2021, see p188.

If you are in one of the protected groups, or for a period before the end of 2020, you have a right to reside if you are a 'family member' (see p240) of an EEA national who has:[271]

- a right to reside as a 'qualified person' – ie, a:[272]
  - jobseeker (see p203);
  - worker (see p211), including if they have retained this status (see p222);
  - self-employed person (see p218), including if they have retained this status (see p222);
  - self-sufficient person, including a self-sufficient student (see p232); *or*
- a permanent right of residence (see p265); *or*
- an initial right to reside (see p203).

You have this right to reside as a family member of an EEA national with one of the free movement residence rights listed above, whether or not you are an EEA national yourself.

You have a right to reside for as long as you remain in a protected group, and as long as the EEA national has one of the above residence rights and as long as you remain their family member. In general, if they cease to have a relevant right to reside or if you cease to be their family member, your right to reside ends. However, there are some limited circumstances in which you can continue to have residence rights as a former family member (see p249).

If the EEA national, whom you are a family member of, has immigration leave, this does *not* confer a right to reside on you. However, having immigration leave also does not *prevent* that EEA national conferring a free movement right to reside on you if they would have one of the residence rights above, other than for the fact of not being in one of the protected groups.

Example

Mira is a Hungarian national who has been living in the UK since 2017 and working for the last year. She has settled status. Her Hungarian husband, Ivan, joined her in the UK in 2020 and he has pre-settled status. Ivan has never worked in the UK. Mira's hours are reduced and so the couple make a joint claim for universal credit (UC). They are entitled to be paid as a couple because neither is defined as a 'person subject to immigration control' (see p93), each is habitually resident in fact (see p163) and each has a qualifying right to reside. Mira's settled status satisfies the right to reside requirement for UC for her, but does *not* confer a right to reside on her husband. Ivan's pre-settled status does not, by itself, satisfy the right to reside requirement for UC, because the UC regulations list it as an excluded right to reside (see p169). However, Ivan's pre-settled status means he is in a protected group that can use free movement rights to claim benefits (see p188), and because, as her spouse, he is defined as a 'family member' (see below) of Mira who is an EEA worker (see p211), he has a free movement right to reside that entitles him to UC.

Note:

- The type of right to reside you have depends on the type of free movement right to reside your family member has, and can affect which benefits you can be entitled to (see p252). However, all periods when you have a right to reside as the family member of an EEA national with one of the free movement rights above count towards the five-year period required to acquire a permanent right to reside (see p266), which then satisfies the right to reside requirement for all benefits that have it.
- British citizens only give free movement residence rights to their family members in limited circumstances (see p244).
- If you have leave to enter the UK as the holder of an EUSS family permit, this leave does *not* satisfy the right to reside requirement for any of the benefits that have it. However, once you make a valid EUSS application for settled or pre-settled status, you are *then* in a protected group that can potentially have one or more free movement rights, including as the family member of an EEA national with one of the free movement rights above.

Croatian, A2 and A8 nationals

If you are a Croatian, A2 or A8 national and during the relevant period of restrictions you were a family member of an EEA national with one of the residence rights listed above, you have a right to reside in the same way as family members of other EEA nationals. In addition, this may mean that you were exempt from the restrictions (see p199 for Croatian and A2 nationals and p200 for A8 nationals). However, if you are relying on the past residence rights of your family member who is a Croatian, A2 or A8 national, note that their residence rights may have been affected by these restrictions.

For further details of the restrictions that previously applied to Croatian, A2 and A8 nationals, see p197.

Who is a family member

If you are in one of the protected groups that can have a free movement right to reside (see p188), or during a period before the end of 2020, you have a right to reside as a family member of an EEA national who has a relevant free movement right to reside (see p239), if you come within the definition of 'family member' below.

Family member

You are a **'family member'** of an EEA national if you are their:[273]

- spouse or civil partner;
- child, grandchild or great-grandchild (or the child, grandchild or great-grandchild of the EEA national's spouse or civil partner) and you are under 21;
- child, grandchild or great-grandchild (or the child, grandchild or great-grandchild of the EEA national's spouse or civil partner) and you are dependent on them;
- parent, grandparent or great-grandparent (or the parent, grandparent or great-grandparent of the EEA national's spouse/civil partner) and you are dependent on them.

If you are not covered by the above definition, you can be *treated as* a family member and have residence rights on that basis if:[274]

- you are an 'extended family member'; *and*
- you have been issued with an EEA family permit, a registration certificate or a residence card under the EEA Regulations. If you do not have this documentation, or it no longer remains in force, you are not treated as a family member.

For the meaning of 'extended family member' and information on these residence documents, see p243.

Note:

- A wider definition of 'relevant family member' applied for the purpose of being in one of the protected groups that could use free movement rights during the period 31 December 2020 to 30 June 2021. See p188 for that definition.
- A narrower definition applies to family members of students (see p237).

Spouses and civil partners

Spouses and civil partners are family members. If you are not married to, or in a civil partnership with, your partner, they can only confer a right to reside on you in very limited circumstances (see p243).

You remain a spouse or civil partner if you have separated, including while you are in the process of getting divorced or dissolving a civil partnership. It is only once you are legally divorced (ie, in the UK, when the decree nisi is given) or the civil partnership has been legally terminated that you cease to count as the spouse or civil partner of the other person.[275]

If your marriage or civil partnership has been terminated (or if your spouse/civil partner dies or leaves the UK), in certain circumstances you may continue to have a right to reside as a former family member (see p249).

Aged under 21

You count as a family member of an EEA national if you are their child (or grandchild or great-grandchild), or you are a child of the EEA national's spouse/civil partner, and you are aged under 21.

You do not need to show that you are dependent on the person in order to count as their family member. Therefore, you do not need to live with, or show you are receiving support from, that person, and it is irrelevant whether you do or not.[276]

Example

Greta is a Lithuanian national who moved to the UK as a teenager with her Lithuanian father on 29 December 2020. They were each granted pre-settled status in July 2021. Greta's father worked in the UK, but just after Greta turned 18 and finished school, her father's hours were cut to 20 hours a week and he moved to a smaller flat where there was no room for Greta. She moved in with a friend and receives no support from her father. While looking for work, Greta claims UC. Greta is entitled to UC as her father is an EEA worker and she is defined as his family member because she is his daughter and is aged under 21. Greta does not need to show she is dependent on her father.

For information on providing evidence of your age, see p509.

Dependent

In some situations, to count as a family member of an EEA national, you must be dependent on that person – eg, if you are their parent or grandparent, or child aged 21 or older.

'Dependence' is not defined in the legislation, but caselaw has established a number of principles.[277]

There are only three things you must show in order to establish that you are dependent on a person.

- You receive support from that person.
- The support you receive is 'material'. If the person is providing you with financial help, paying your bills, buying you food or providing your meals, providing you with accommodation or caring for you because you are ill or disabled, this all counts as 'material support'. Translation, emotional and social support do not count.[278]
- The support *contributes to* your essential needs (the 'basic necessities of life'). It is not necessary for this to be your only source of support.

It is irrelevant if there are alternative sources of support, including savings or potential employment, available to you, either in your country of origin or in the UK.[279]

The Court of Appeal recently agreed that, in principle, education can be an 'essential need', but may not always be.[280]

If you only became dependent on the EEA national in the UK, this does not prevent you from being classed as a family member. It is sufficient that you are dependent at the point when your claim for benefit is decided.[281] (**Note**: if you are an extended family member on the basis of dependency/member of household, you must have been dependent on/member of the household of the EEA national in the country you have come from – see below.)

You can be dependent on someone even if you receive benefit, and your dependency should be considered independently of any benefit you claim. A decision maker should not make the 'circular' decision that you are not entitled because awarding you a benefit that relies on your residence rights as a dependent family member would mean you would to cease to be dependent. Whether you are dependent while receiving a benefit depends on whether or not your evidence shows the three things listed above.[282]

Extended family members

If you do not come within the definition of 'family member' on p240, but you have a partner or relative in the UK who is an EEA national with a relevant free movement right to reside (see p239), you can be *treated as* their family member, and therefore have residence rights on that basis, if you:[283]

- are an 'extended family member' (see below); *and*
- have been issued with an EEA family permit, a registration certificate or a residence card under the EEA Regulations and it remains in force. In most cases, you had to apply for this residence document before the end of the transition period (11pm on 31 December 2020). However, there was a later deadline of 30 June 2021 to apply for an EEA family permit to enter the UK if on 31 December 2020 you were a partner, in a durable relationship, of an EEA national living in the UK by that date. For details of these documents, including their status since 30 June 2021, see p504.

Extended family member

You are an **'extended family member'** of an EEA national if they are your:[284]

- partner and you are in a durable relationship[285] with them (or you are the child, under 18, of the partner); *or*
- non-adoptive legal guardian (under the law of the country in which the guardianship order was granted), you are under 18, dependent on them and have lived with them since they became your legal guardian;[286] *or*
- relative and:

– you have serious health problems that require their (or their spouse or civil partner's) day-to-day care;[287] *or*

– you were dependent on them (or you were a member of their household) in another country and you accompanied or joined them in the UK (or you wish to join them in the UK) and you continue to be dependent on them (or to be a member of their household).[288] Your previous connection does not need to have been the same as it is now – eg, you may have been a member of their household before coming to the UK and then be dependent on them on your arrival;[289] *or*

– you would meet the requirements (other than those relating to entry clearance) of the Immigration Rules for indefinite leave as their dependent relative.

The term 'dependent' is not defined in the legislation and its meaning is the same as that for a family member (see p242).

Before 1 February 2017, you were also defined as an extended family member if you were a relative of the EEA national's spouse or civil partner and:

- you had serious health problems that required their care. The spouse or civil partner of this category was then added back into the definition from 15 August 2019 following a judgment of the Court of Justice of the European Union (CJEU);[290] *or*
- you were previously dependent on them (or you were a member of their household) in another country and you accompanied or joined them in the UK (or you wished to join them in the UK) and you continued to be dependent on them (or to be a member of their household).

If you were issued with a residence document on this basis, you continue to be defined as an extended family member, provided you have been continuously resident in the UK since 1 February 2017.[291]

Family members of British citizens

British citizens do not generally confer free movement residence rights on their family members. That is because, in most cases, an EEA national can only confer European free movement residence rights on family members if the EEA national had moved to, or was residing in, an EEA country (or the UK until the end of 2020) *other than* the one of which they are a national.[292] However, in the limited circumstances covered below, a British citizen can confer a free movement right to reside on a family member. These rights continue to apply while you are in one of the protected groups that can have a free movement right to reside (see p188).

If you are the family member of a British citizen and you have pre-settled status, or a pending EUSS application for settled or pre-settled status (or a pending appeal or administrative review of a refusal) (or for periods before 30 June 2021, see p188), that British citizen can confer a right of residence on you if they:

- were residing, with a right to reside as a worker, self-employed person, self-sufficient person or self-sufficient student, or a permanent right to reside, in an EEA state and you resided there with them as their family member, and you have both returned to the UK (see below);
- are self-employed and carry out some of their business activities in an EEA state (see p247); *or*
- are a dual British/EEA citizen (see p247).

Note:

- If you are the primary carer of a British citizen who would not be able to continue to live anywhere in the EEA if you were required to leave the UK, you may have a 'derivative right to reside'. However, that is an excluded right to reside for each of the benefits that have that requirement (see p261).
- If you have joined your British family member in the UK, and you have been given leave by the Home Office (eg, as a spouse or civil partner) that is subject to a 'no recourse to public funds' condition, you are defined as a 'person subject to immigration control' (see p101) and excluded from all the benefits listed on p111, unless you are exempt (see p113).

The British citizen has resided in another state

If you are a family member (see p240) of a British citizen, you have a right to reside as their family member if, on or before 31 December 2020:[293]

- the British citizen is, or immediately before returning to the UK was, residing in an EEA state with a right to reside as a worker, self-employed person, self-sufficient person, self-sufficient student or a permanent right to reside; *and*
- you resided as their family member (including as an 'extended family member'[294]) with them in that state, your family life was created or strengthened there, and your residence there together was 'genuine' (see below).

On returning to the UK together, the British citizen confers a free movement right to reside on you, regardless of whether they are working on return to the UK (see below for details).

Note: the British citizen can confer a right to reside on you even if they only returned to the UK after 31 December 2020, provided the above bullet points applied to you by that date.[295] However, to obtain pre-settled (or settled) status as the family member of a British citizen on this basis, the deadline to return to the UK and to apply for pre-settled (or settled) status was 29 March 2022, although late applications can be accepted if you have 'reasonable grounds' for missing these deadlines (see p62).

You do not have a right to reside on this basis if you only became the British citizen's family member after they returned to the UK.[296]

The EEA Regulations have interpreted these rights more restrictively than the CJEU, and some of these restrictions have been confirmed to be unlawful by the Upper Tribunal, with amendments being made to the regulations as a result. For periods before these amendments, you can rely directly on the Upper Tribunal decisions and the CJEU caselaw to which they refer. For information on the continuing requirement to interpret free movement residence rights in accordance with CJEU caselaw, see p195.

Since the end of 2020, the returning British citizen is, under the EEA Regulations, *treated as* satisfying any requirement to be a 'qualified person' (see p193).[297] This amendment to the EEA Regulations followed an Upper Tribunal decision and earlier caselaw from the CJEU, which held that an EEA national who had been a worker in a different EEA state and then returned to their own state did not need to be undertaking an economic activity in their own state in order for their family member to have a right to reside.[298] Prior to the end of 2020, the EEA Regulations only gave you a right to reside as a family member of a British citizen while they had a right to reside in the UK under the regulations in the same ways as EEA nationals (with minor easements).

If you were an 'extended family member' of a British citizen in the EEA state, the EEA Regulations require you to have been lawfully resident in that state.[299] This does not necessarily mean you had been granted the relevant EEA residence document by that state; your residence may instead have been lawful under domestic immigration law.[300]

The British citizen's and your residency in the EEA state must have been 'genuine', which has been held to mean real, substantive or effective, and more than mere physical presence.[301] The EEA Regulations list the following as being relevant when considering whether residence is 'genuine':[302]

- the length of your joint residence in the EEA state;
- the nature and quality of your joint accommodation in the EEA state and whether it was the British citizen's principal residence;
- the degree of your and the British citizen's integration in the EEA state;
- whether the residence in the EEA state was your first lawful residence in the European Union (EU).

Until the end of 2020, the EEA Regulations also required the British citizen to have transferred their 'centre of life' to the EEA state. However, this was then removed from the EEA Regulations following an Upper Tribunal decision confirming that this was not a requirement under EU law.[303] **Note:** when considering whether residence was genuine, the CJEU has focused on whether residence enabled the creation or strengthening of family life in that state and whether the conditions for the relevant residence right were satisfied.[304]

The EEA Regulations exclude you from having a right to reside on the basis of being a family member of a British citizen who has resided in an EEA country if you are a non-EEA national and the purpose of your residence in the EEA state was to circumvent the immigration laws.[305]

The British citizen lives in the UK and carries out activities in another state

Until the end of the transition period (11pm on 31 December 2020), if you were the family member (see p240) of a British citizen who was employed or self-employed in the UK and whose business involved them undertaking some activities in an EEA state, you could have a right of residence, depending on your circumstances. This right was not covered in the EEA Regulations or EU Directive 2004/38 but was confirmed by the CJEU as coming directly from the Treaty on the Functioning of the European Union (TFEU). The cases concerned a non-EEA spouse of a British citizen providing services in EEA countries from a business in the UK,[306] and a non-EEA family member of a Dutch national residing in the Netherlands but working in another EEA country.[307]

If you are a non-EEA national and began living in the UK as the family member of a British citizen, in these circumstances, before the end of the transition period, you may be able to obtain leave under the EUSS. However, you should get urgent immigration advice, because your application could be complex and you may also have other immigration options.

If you are granted settled status (indefinite leave granted under the EUSS), that satisfies the right to reside requirement for all benefits that have that requirement.

If you are granted pre-settled status (limited leave granted under the EUSS), this does not satisfy the right to reside requirement, but does mean you are in a protected group that can potentially have one or more free movement rights to reside (see p188).

The British citizen also has citizenship of a European Economic Area state

If you are the family member of a British citizen who also has citizenship of an EEA state, you may have a right to reside in the same circumstances as if you were the family member of an EEA national, provided that before acquiring British citizenship they had a free movement right to reside in the UK as either a 'qualified person' (see p192) or a permanent right to reside (see p265).

These rights are not provided under EU Directive 2004/38 as that does not apply to British citizens living in the UK, including citizens of EEA states who only acquired British citizenship after moving to the UK, and so it cannot provide rights to that person's family member. Instead they are provided by the TFEU, as confirmed by the CJEU, which held that an EEA national who moved to the UK, resided here as a worker, acquired permanent residence and then dual British nationality, continued to have citizenship rights under the TFEU, including the right to build a family life with the non-EEA national she subsequently married.[308] Consequently, the CJEU held that her spouse had a right to reside in the UK on conditions which must not be stricter than those that would apply to a family member of another EEA national.[309] The nationality of the family member does not affect these rights and they apply equally to EEA or non-EEA family members.[310]

The EEA Regulations were amended on 24 July 2018 following this decision, but interpret the rights more restrictively (see below). If you do not have a right to reside under the EEA Regulations, you may be able to rely on the above CJEU judgment. Challenge any refusal of benefit if this is not accepted and get specialist advice.

If you are the family member of a dual British/EEA citizen, you can have a right to reside under the EEA Regulations provided they had a right to reside as a national of a state that was at that time an EEA state,[311] either as a qualified person or a permanent right to reside (or as a family member of an EEA national with either) before they became a British citizen.[312] If they currently have a right to reside as a qualified person, they must have had such a right at the time of acquiring British citizenship, and continuously since then, for you to have a right to reside as their family member. If you are a non-EEA national, they must have had a right to reside as a qualified person or a permanent right to reside in the UK under the EEA Regulations at the time they acquired British citizenship.[313]

Note: although these rights have only been included in the EEA Regulations since 24 July 2018, they are treated as if they were in force before this date.[314] Similarly, the CJEU judgment confirms rights that previously existed.[315] This means you may be able to rely on these rights to acquire permanent residence and to challenge earlier decisions refusing you benefit.

In an earlier case, the CJEU held that a dual British/EEA state citizen did not have rights under EU law as she had never moved between EEA states, but had lived all her life in the UK. Therefore, she could not confer any residence rights on her family members.[316]

Following this judgment, the definition of 'EEA national' in the EEA Regulations was amended to exclude anyone who was also a British citizen.[317] Although this definition was amended again from 24 July 2018, the more recent amendments do not treat family members of dual British/ EEA citizens the same as family members of EEA citizens in all circumstances. You may therefore need to rely on the limited transitional protection that was given to family members of dual nationals who had residence rights before 16 October 2012, when family members of dual British/EEA nationals did have the same rights as family members of EEA nationals.[318] If you had such a right to reside before this date, it continues in limited circumstances.[319] See p1604 of the 2013/14 edition of CPAG's *Welfare Benefits and Tax Credits Handbook* for details.

Former family members who retain their right to reside

In general, if you are the family member of an EEA national who confers a right to reside on you, your right to reside ceases if they:

- are no longer your family member (see p240); *or*
- no longer have a relevant right to reside.

However, you can *retain* your right to reside in certain circumstances. Whether or not these apply to you depends on the type of right to reside your family member has. **Note:** several of these circumstances may mean that you have another free movement right to reside that could be easier to prove or may apply instead (see p251).

When you may retain your right to reside

You may retain your right to reside if the EEA national who confers this right on you dies or leaves the UK, or if your marriage or civil partnership to them is terminated. These rights are in EU Directive 2004/38 but are not exactly reproduced in the EEA Regulations (see below). The decision maker is more likely to accept that you retain your right to reside if you satisfy the requirements of the EEA Regulations, so you should check these requirements first. If you cannot satisfy these, check whether you satisfy the requirements of the EU Directive (see p250), because the EEA Regulations should be implementing these (see p195). **Note:** under the EEA Regulations, you can count periods of residence spent as a former family member who retains their right of residence towards the five years of residence required for permanent residence (see p266).

European Economic Area Regulations

If you are in one of the protected groups (see p188) that can have a free movement right to reside, or for a period before the end of 2020, you retain your right to reside under the EEA Regulations if you are a family member of a 'qualified person' (see p193) or a person with a permanent right to reside (see p265) and:[320]

- that person dies and you are:
  - not an EEA national, but if you were you would be a worker, or a self-employed or self-sufficient person (or jobseeker[321]), or you are the family member of such a non-EEA national, and, for at least a year immediately before they died, you:
    - (for periods before the end of 2020 and after that date if you are in a protected group *other than* having pre-settled status) resided in the UK with a right to reside under the EEA Regulations; *or*
    - (for periods after the end of 2020, while you have pre-settled status) resided 'lawfully'. This could potentially include periods when you did not have a free movement right to reside but, for example, did have pre-settled status; *or*

  - their child or grandchild (or the child or grandchild of their spouse or civil partner) and you were in education (see p257) immediately before their death and you remain in education; *or*
  - a parent with custody of a child in the previous bullet point; *or*
- that person leaves the UK and you are:
  - their child or grandchild (or the child or grandchild of their spouse or civil partner) and you were in education (see p257) immediately before they left the UK and you remain in education; *or*
  - a parent with custody of a child in the previous bullet point; *or*
- your marriage or civil partnership to that person is terminated, and they were a qualified person (or had a permanent right to reside) at least until the termination proceedings began,[322] and you are not an EEA national, but if you were, you would be a worker or a self-employed or self-sufficient person (or jobseeker[323]), or you are the family member of such a non-EEA national, and you were residing in the UK with a right to reside under the EEA Regulations at the date of the termination and:
  - the marriage/civil partnership had lasted for at least three years with you both residing in the UK for at least one of those years; *or*
  - you have custody of the qualified person's child; *or*
  - you have a right of access to the qualified person's child, which a court has said must take place in the UK; *or*
  - your continued right of residence in the UK is warranted by particularly difficult circumstances, such as your (or another family member's) being subject to domestic violence during the period of the marriage/civil partnership. Your rights are not retained in this way if your spouse or civil partner left the UK before the termination proceedings began.[324]

You have a right to reside on this basis for as long as the conditions apply to you,[325] until you can acquire a permanent right of residence (see p265).[326] For details on using periods with this residence right to acquire permanent residency, see p269.

European Union Directive 2004/38

If you do not satisfy the requirements of the EEA Regulations above, but you satisfy the requirements of the EU Directive 2004/38 below, you can argue that the EEA Regulations should be treated as if the requirements were the same. For more information on the continued relevance of the EU Directive for interpreting rights under the EEA Regulations after the end of the transition period, see p195.

You can retain your right to reside under EU Directive 2004/38 if you are a family member of an EEA national who has a right to reside as a worker, self-employed or self-sufficient person, or as a self-sufficient student and:

- the EEA national dies and you have lived in the UK as their family member for at least a year before their death and you are a non-EEA national; [327] *or*

- the EEA national leaves the UK and you are:[328]
  - their child, grandchild or great-grandchild and in education; *or*
  - the parent with custody of a child in education; *or*
- your marriage or civil partnership to the EEA national is terminated, and they had a right to reside as a worker, self-employed or self-sufficient person, or as a self-sufficient student at least until the termination proceedings began,[329] and:[330]
  - before the termination proceedings were started, the marriage/civil partnership had lasted for at least three years with you both residing in the UK for at least one of these years. Your rights are not retained in this way if your spouse or civil partner left the UK before the termination proceedings began;[331] *or*
  - you have custody of their child; *or*
  - you have a right of access to their child, which a court has said must take place in the UK; *or*
  - your continued right of residence in the UK is warranted by particularly difficult circumstances, such as your being subject to domestic violence during the period of the marriage/civil partnership. Your rights are not retained in this way if your spouse or civil partner left the UK before the termination proceedings began.[332]

It may be arguable that if you are an EEA national, you can retain your right to reside in each of the three circumstances above without needing to satisfy any other conditions.[333] However, two Upper Tribunal decisions rejected this interpretation and took the view that the provisions in the directive just confirm that any independent residence rights that an EEA national may have had are not affected by the above changes.[334] It is arguable that these parts of each decision are not legally binding as each case failed on other grounds, but they will be persuasive until further caselaw decides the issue.

Periods when you have retained your right to reside as a former family member are not, on their own, sufficient to enable you to acquire a permanent right of residence after five years, because you are also required to show that you are a worker, or a self-employed or a self-sufficient person, or you are the family member of such a person.[335]

Other residence rights

If you are covered by any of the circumstances that enable you to retain your right to reside as a family member, under either the EEA Regulations or the EU Directive, or if your circumstances are similar but you do not fit within these rules, check whether similar free movement residence rights could apply to you. The main ones that might apply are the following.

- If you have had a right to reside in the UK as the family member of an EEA national who has conferred a right to reside on you for five years, you may have a permanent right to reside (see p266).
- If you were the family member of an EEA national who has died and they were a worker or a self-employed person, you may have a permanent right to reside (see p275).
- If you are the child of a worker and you are in education, or you are the primary carer of such a child, you may have a 'derivative right to reside' (see p253).

Benefit entitlement

Whether your right to reside as the family member of an EEA national satisfies the right to reside requirement depends on:

- the type of free movement right to reside the EEA national has; *and*
- the benefit you want to claim.

Your right to reside is the equivalent of the EEA national's right to reside. This means the following.

- If you are the family member of a **worker or self-employed person** (including if this status has been retained), you have the same residence rights as if you were a worker or a self-employed person yourself. That satisfies the right to reside requirement for all benefits that have such a requirement (see p168). You are also exempt from the habitual residence test for means-tested benefits (see p159) and, therefore, do not need to be 'habitually resident in fact' (see p163). You are also exempt from the requirement to have lived in the UK for three months for child benefit (see p144).
- If you are the family member of a **self-sufficient person** or self-sufficient student, you have the same residence rights as if you were a self-sufficient person or student yourself. That satisfies the right to reside requirement for all benefits that have such a requirement (see p168).
- If your *only* right to reside is as the family member of an EEA national who has a right to reside as a **jobseeker**, you have the same residence rights as if you were a jobseeker yourself. If this is your only right to reside, that does not satisfy the right to reside requirement for any of the means-tested benefits (except income-based jobseeker's allowance – see p169) but does satisfy the requirement for child benefit and CTC.
- If you were the family member of an EEA national who had an **initial right of residence** for three months that began before the end of 2020, you had an equivalent right to reside. If this was your only right to reside, that did not satisfy the right to reside requirement for any of the means-tested benefits (see p169).
- If you are the family member of an EEA national who has a **permanent right of residence**, your right to reside satisfies the right to reside requirement for all

benefits that have such a requirement (see p168). You only have a *permanent* right to reside yourself once you have been residing in the UK with this right to reside (or another free movement right to reside other than a derivative right) for five years or you are the family member of an EEA national who acquired this permanent residency in less than five years (see p275) (and, in the latter case only, you are exempt from the habitual residence test – see p159).

- If you have a right to reside as a **former family member** (see p249), your right to reside satisfies the right to reside requirement for all benefits that have such a requirement (see p168).

Note: periods when you had a right to reside as the family member of an EEA national in any of the above circumstances count towards the five-year period required to acquire a permanent right to reside (see p266), which then satisfies the right to reside requirement for all benefits that have it.

If you are seeking to show that you had a free movement right to reside on 31 December 2020, to satisfy regulations on the protected groups who can, after that date, potentially have free movement residence rights (and, if you are an EEA national, not be defined as a person subject to immigration control – see p93), you may be able to satisfy these regulations if on 31 December 2020:

- any of the above bullets applied to you; *or*
- you had a permanent right to reside (or had lost it due to being absent from the UK for more than two years, but your absence was less than five years on that date); *or*
- you were the 'relevant family member' (see p192, and note the term is wider than 'family member' on p240) of an EEA national who, on that date, had any free movement right to reside. However, this only enabled you to be in a protected group until 30 June 2021.

For further details of all the protected groups, see p188.

15. **Derivative residence rights**

Since 30 June 2021, you can only have any free movement right to reside, including a derivative right to reside, if you either have pre-settled status or you have a pending European Union Settlement Scheme (EUSS) application for settled or pre-settled status (or a pending appeal or administrative review of a refusal). For details of these protected groups and others that applied during the period 31 December 2020 to 30 June 2021, see p188.

You may be able to 'derive' a right to reside from someone with a right to reside without being their family member. These rights are not listed in European Union (EU) Directive 2004/38, but are based on other provisions of EU law, as interpreted by caselaw. The European Economic Area (EEA) Regulations list these rights as 'derivative rights of residence'. However, they interpret them more narrowly and impose some additional conditions. If these mean you do not have a right to reside, you can rely on the rights confirmed by EU caselaw.

Note:

- You cannot count periods when you have a derivative right to reside towards the five years of residence required for permanent residency (see p266).
- Some of the circumstances below are similar to those that enable you to retain a right to reside if you are a former family member of an EEA national who conferred a right to reside on you and who has now died or left the UK, or your marriage or civil partnership to them has been terminated (see p249). Check whether this may apply to you because it may make it easier to have your residence rights accepted by the benefit authorities and, in certain circumstances, you can count periods with a right to reside as a former family member towards the five years required for permanent residence.
- If you do not fit into any of the groups below, but your circumstances are similar, it may still be arguable that you have a right to reside (see p264).

Who has a derivative right to reside

If you are in one of the protected groups that can have a free movement right to reside (see p188), or for a period before the end of 2020, you have a derivative right to reside if you are not an 'exempt person' (see below) and you are:[336]

- the child of an EEA national who was a 'worker' in the UK (see p211) while you were living in the UK, and you are currently in education (see p256);[337] *or*
- the primary carer of a child in the above bullet point and the child would be unable to continue their education in the UK if you left the UK for an indefinite period (see p259);[338] *or*
- the primary carer of a self-sufficient child who is an EEA national, who would be unable to remain in the UK if you left for an indefinite period (see p260);[339] *or*
- the primary carer of a British citizen residing in the UK who would be unable to reside in the UK or an EEA state if you left the UK for an indefinite period (see p261).[340] **Note:** this right to reside does not satisfy the right to reside requirement for any of the benefits that have this requirement, except for child benefit and child tax credit (CTC) in limited circumstances, if you are a national of Morocco, San Marino, Tunisia, Turkey, or, for claims made before 1 January 2021, Algeria (see p176); *or*
- aged under 18 and your primary carer is covered by either the second, third or fourth bullet points above and they would be prevented from residing in the UK if you left the UK for an indefinite period, and you do not have leave to enter or remain in the UK (other than under the EUSS) (see p262); *or*
- (not in the EEA Regulations) the primary carer of a child with a permanent right to reside, who would be unable to remain in the UK if you left the UK.[341]

Note: it is strongly arguable that you have a derivative right to reside if you are the child of an EEA national who was a 'self-employed person' in the UK (see p218) while you were living in the UK, and you are currently in education, or if you are the primary carer of such a child (see p259).

Who is an 'exempt person'

Under the EEA Regulations, you are excluded from having a derivative right to reside if you are an 'exempt person'.[342] You are an exempt person if you have a right to reside:[343]

- under any other provision of the EEA Regulations. If this other right to reside is excluded for the benefit you want to claim (eg, as a jobseeker if you are claiming a means-tested benefit), see below;
- as a British citizen or as a Commonwealth citizen with a right of abode;
- as a person with indefinite leave (other than under the EUSS); *or*
- under provisions that exempt certain people from the requirement to have leave – eg, specified aircrew and diplomats.

Have you been refused universal credit on the basis that you are an exempt person?

If you have a derivative right to reside as the primary carer of a worker's child in education, and the DWP refuses your claim for universal credit (UC), or another means-tested benefit, on the grounds that you do not have this derivative right to reside because you have a right to reside as an EEA jobseeker and are therefore an 'exempt person', you should challenge the decision.

1. You can only have a right to reside as a jobseeker if you are looking for work. If you are not looking for work and your claimant commitment does not require you to satisfy the work search and work availability requirements, you do not have a right to reside as a jobseeker and so you are not excluded from having a derivative right to reside. This would apply, for example, if you are not seeking work and you are the responsible carer of a child under three years old, if you have limited capability for work or (for 13 weeks) if you have experienced domestic violence. For details of the work-related requirements for UC, see CPAG's *Welfare Benefits and Tax Credits Handbook*.

2. If your claimant commitment requires you to search for and be available for work, your right to reside as a jobseeker means you are an exempt person under the EEA Regulations. However, this exclusion has been held to be unlawful because the EEA Regulations must be interpreted in accordance with the EU law they are intended to implement (see p195), and there is no requirement in EU law that to access subsistence benefits on the basis of this derivative right to reside you must not have *another* right to reside. The Court of Justice of the European Union (CJEU) held that a similar exclusion in German law was unlawful.[344] The Upper Tribunal then applied this CJEU judgment to hold that having a right to reside as a jobseeker does not preclude having a derivative right to reside as the primary carer of a worker's child in education, and the latter satisfies the right to reside requirement for housing benefit.[345] It is also arguable that excluding you from UC on the basis that, as a

jobseeker you are an exempt person, and therefore do not have rights as a primary carer of a worker's child in education, infringes the requirement of the UK to encourage all efforts to enable that child to attend their education under the best possible conditions.[346] This argument was already being accepted by First-tier Tribunals in several appeals, without the DWP seeking to appeal the decisions, and is strengthened by the recent caselaw of both the CJEU and Upper Tribunal.

Croatian, A2 and A8 nationals

The restrictions on when a Croatian, A2 or A8 national could have 'worker' status during the relevant periods of restrictions may affect you if you are seeking to derive your right to reside from being a worker's child in education, the primary carer of such a child, or a child of such a primary carer, and the child in education's parent was a Croatian, A2 or A8 national.

If a Croatian or A2 national was subject to restrictions (see p198), the work they did only gave them worker status if it was done in accordance with their worker authorisation document. Therefore, if you are the child of a Croatian or A2 national and you are in education (or you are the primary carer of such a child, or the child of such a primary carer), the work done by the parent must have been done in accordance with a worker authorisation document for it to enable you to have a derivative right to reside.[347]

If an A8 national was subject to restrictions (see p198), the work they did during the period of restrictions (see p197) only gave them worker status if it was done for an 'authorised employer' (see p201). Therefore, if you are the child of an A8 national and you are in education (or you are the primary carer of such a child, or the child of such a primary carer), the work done by the parent must have been for an 'authorised employer' for you to have a derivative right to reside. This includes a period when the parent had a valid worker's registration certificate for their employer, but they did not complete 12 months of working for an 'authorised employer'.[348] It also includes a period in which the parent was in their first month of employment. This is because the first month of any employment, even if it was never registered, counted as working for an 'authorised employer' provided the A8 national satisfied the requirements of being a worker, including that their work was accepted as 'genuine and effective' (see p211).[349]

For further details of the restrictions that previously applied to Croatian, A2 and A8 nationals, see p197.

Worker's child in education

A child has a right to reside if:[350]

- they were living in the UK at a time when one of their parents (or the parent's spouse or civil partner) had a right to reside in the UK as a worker (see p258); *and*
- they are now in education (see p257).

The purpose of this right of residence is to enable a child to take up their right to be educated in the EEA state where their (step-)parent is (or has been) employed, if the child is also living in that state.[351] For this right to education to be effective, the child must have a right of residence as long as they are in education. As the child's right of residence continues until they have *completed* their education (see below), there is no upper age limit. This *Handbook* refers to a 'child' in education, because they must have been a child when the education began.[352]

There must have been a common period when the child was in the UK and one of their parents (or step-parents) was a worker in the UK.[353] A child is not considered to have been in the UK before they are born.[354] However, if a woman with worker status stops work because of the physical constraints of the late stages of pregnancy or aftermath of childbirth, she can retain worker status (see p229). If that applies, once the child is born, it is arguable that they are then the child of a worker (see p258).

The (step-)parent does not need to have continued to be a worker, or have been in the UK, when the child started school or at any time since then.[355]

It is the child's parent, or their parent's spouse or civil partner, who must have been an EEA worker in the UK while the child was also in the UK.[356] A child does not have this type of right to reside if the EEA worker is their grandparent,[357] their parent's partner (rather than spouse or civil partner),[358] or their non-parent legal guardian.[359] However, it may be arguable that the question of which rights are conferred on a child by their legal guardian should be reconsidered following a recent judgment of the CJEU, which held that a child is the 'extended family member' of their non-adoptive legal guardian (see p243).[360]

Note: the Court of Appeal held that you cannot have a right to reside on this basis if your parent was a self-employed EEA national rather than a worker.[361] However, it is strongly arguable that the Withdrawal Agreements provide for a right to reside on this basis.[362] The DWP accepts this *if* the parent has been a 'frontier worker' in the UK on the basis of being self-employed person (or worker) (see p278), and, significantly, the guidance confirming this notes the right of a child of a self-employed person as an example of a *new* right to reside provided by the Withdrawal Agreement.[363] At the time of writing, this right had been accepted by a First-tier Tribunal in an appeal about the rights of the primary carer of such a child (see p259).

Who is 'in education'

Caselaw has confirmed that the definition of 'education' excludes nursery education,[364] and that a child's rights begin when they start compulsory education at around the age of five (and therefore excludes preschool),[365] and that can include reception class, despite the child being under five years old.[366]

The definition in the EEA Regulations excludes nursery education, but does not exclude education received before the compulsory school age if this is equivalent to the education received at or after the compulsory school age.[367]

Differences in Scotland may affect when residence rights begin. Although there is no reception class in Scotland, it may still be arguable that a child can be 'in education' when they are approaching age five. Furthermore, as the Scottish Curriculum for Excellence starts at the age of three, it maybe arguable that a child in Scotland can be in education well before the age of five.

Residence rights apply to the child and their primary carer until at least the age of 'majority' while the child remains in education. The *child's* residence rights can continue beyond this age until they have completed their education. This includes all forms of education, whether vocational or general, and can include university courses. Whether or not the residence rights of the child's *primary carer* continue after the child reaches the age of majority depends on whether the child continues to need the presence or care of the primary carer to continue and complete their education.[368]

Who is a 'worker'

The child's parent or step-parent who was employed in the UK must have been an EEA national to enable them to have had a right to reside as a worker.

The EEA Regulations state that, for this purpose, 'worker' does not include a jobseeker or someone who retains their worker status (see p222).[369] It is arguable that the latter exclusion is wrong. The EU regulation that gives a child the right to be educated in a state does so for the child of a national of one EEA state 'who is or has been employed' in another EEA state.[370] Caselaw confirms that a child has a right to reside if they are now in education and were in the EEA state during a time when one of their parents was exercising rights of residence in that state as a 'worker' or a 'migrant worker'.[371] It appears from the wording of EU Directive 2004/38 that a person who retains their status as a worker resides in a country as a 'migrant worker', as they have equivalent rights to 'workers', provided they satisfy the conditions for retaining worker status. Also, family members of someone who has retained their status as a worker have residence rights equivalent to those of family members of workers.

Absence of the child from the UK

A child may lose their right to reside as a worker's child in education if they leave the UK but then return. However, this depends on all the circumstances. DWP guidance suggests that a child may lose this right to reside if they have become habitually resident in another EEA state for a substantial period, but not if the absence from the UK is just temporary.[372] However, it may be arguable that what matters is whether the child's studies undertaken on their return are a continuation of their earlier education. The CJEU has held that a worker's child in education continued to have his rights, despite an absence during which the child went back to his country of origin, because he returned to continue his studies which he could not pursue in his own country.[373]

Primary carer of a worker's child in education

You have a derivative right to reside under the EEA Regulations if you:[374]

- are the 'primary carer' (see below) of a child of a worker who is in education; *and*
- the child would be unable to continue to be educated in the UK if you were required to leave (see p260).

The basis of this right builds on the residence rights of the child, which are necessary in order to be educated in the country where their parent is, or was, employed.[375] It is assumed that the child needs an adult to look after them and, consequently, their primary carer must also have a right of residence.[376] Your rights as the primary carer continue until the child reaches at least the age of majority, and beyond that if they continue to need your presence and care in order to pursue and complete their education (see p257).[377]

You can have a right to reside as the primary carer of a worker's child in education if you were that worker or if the worker was someone else.

Neither you nor the child need be self-sufficient in order to have residence rights.[378]

Your nationality (except if you are British, because you would then be excluded from a derivative right to reside as an 'exempt person' – see p255) and the nationality of the child do not affect this right of residence.[379] However, the child's parent (or step-parent) who had the right to reside as a worker must be an EEA national.

If the child in education is British, that does not prevent you from having a derivative right to reside as their primary carer, provided they are the child of an EEA worker. Although the EEA Regulations define the child as an 'exempt person' (see p255), that only prevents them from having a derivative right to reside under those regulations; it does not prevent you from having a derivative right to reside as their primary carer.[380]

Note: the Court of Appeal held that you cannot have a right to reside on this basis if the parent of the child in education was a self-employed EEA national rather than a worker.[381] However, it is strongly arguable that the Withdrawal Agreements provide a right to reside if you are the primary carer of a child in education, if one of the child's parents had, during a common period when the child was in the UK, been a self-employed EEA national in the UK.[382] DWP guidance confirms this right if the parent has been a 'frontier worker' in the UK on the basis of being a self-employed person (or worker) (see p278), and, significantly, notes the right of a child of a self-employed person as an example of a new right to reside provided by the Withdrawal Agreements.[383] At the time of writing, a First-tier Tribunal had accepted that the primary carer of the child of a self-employed EEA national had a right to reside on this basis.

Who is a primary carer

You are a 'primary carer' of someone if you are their direct relative or legal guardian, and either you:[384]

- have primary responsibility for that person's care; *or*
- share equally the responsibility for that person's care with one other person (see p255).

Note: if you do not come within the above definition of 'primary carer', you may be able to argue that you have rights based on EU caselaw (see p253) – eg, if you are the primary carer of someone who is dependent on you, but you are not their direct relative or legal guardian.

You are not regarded as someone's primary carer solely on the basis of a financial contribution you make towards their care.[385]

Is the child dependent on you

The decision of whether or not a child would be unable to continue their education or remain in the UK, or if British, whether they would be unable to reside in the EEA, if you were to leave the UK, must take account, in the best interests of the child, of all their specific circumstances.[386]

If you share equally the responsibility of caring with another person, the question of whether the child would be unable to continue their education or remain in the UK, or whether the British citizen would be unable to reside in the EEA, must be decided on the basis that you would both leave the UK, unless the person with whom you share the care had already acquired a derivative right to reside before the responsibility for care became shared.[387]

Primary carer of a child who is self-sufficient

You have a derivative right to reside under the EEA Regulations if:[388]

- you are the 'primary carer' (see above) of a child under 18 who is residing in the UK as a self-sufficient person (see p232); *and*
- the child would be unable to remain in the UK if you were required to leave (see above).

The basis of this right of residence is to make effective the rights of the child, as it is assumed that they need an adult to look after them, and so their primary carer must also have a right of residence.[389]

Note: the EEA Regulations treat the primary carer as a 'family member' of the child. Therefore, the child's resources must be sufficient for both you and them (see p233 for what counts as sufficient) and you must both have comprehensive sickness insurance cover (see p235).[390] The CJEU recently confirmed that, although the primary carer is not a 'family member' of the child, the requirements to have both sufficient resources and comprehensive sickness insurance cover apply to the primary carer as well as the child. The Court held that the latter requirement was satisfied in that case because both the child and his primary carer were affiliated to the UK's system of health insurance offered free by the NHS.[391] The CJEU also held that once the child had acquired a permanent right of residence, having had a right to reside as a self-sufficient person for a continuous period of five years, the requirements to have sufficient resources and comprehensive sickness insurance cover cease to apply to either the child or his primary carer.[392] Note that once the child has a permanent right to reside, their primary carer may have a derivative right to reside on that basis (see p263).

Your nationality does not affect this right of residence. However, the child must be an EEA national to have a right to reside as a self-sufficient person.

Primary carer of a British citizen

You have a derivative right to reside under the EEA Regulations if you:[393]

- are the 'primary carer' (see p260) of a British citizen who is residing in the UK; *and*
- the British citizen would be unable to reside in the UK or an EEA state if you left the UK for an indefinite period (see p260). Other than in exceptional circumstances, this residence right only applies to non-EEA nationals.

This right of residence (often referred to as a 'Zambrano carer') is based on the right provided by Article 20 of the Treaty on the Functioning of the European Union (TFEU) for all nationals of EU member states to be citizens of the EU, and for every EU citizen to have the right to move and reside freely within the EU. If an EU citizen is dependent on another person who is a non-EEA national to make this right effective, the non-EEA national as the EU citizen's primary carer must be given a right of residence.[394] However, the EEA Regulations only provide these rights when the dependent person is British. If you are the primary carer of an EEA national who is not British, you can rely directly on EU law, but as these arguments can be complex, you should get specialist advice.

Note: in most cases when this right to reside applies, the British citizen is a dependent child but, in exceptional cases, could be a dependent adult.[395]

Having a right to reside on the basis of being the primary carer of a British citizen only entitles you to child benefit and CTC if you (or the family member you are living with) are a national of Morocco, San Marino, Tunisia, Turkey or (if you claimed before 1 January 2021) Algeria, and you (or the family member you are living with) are lawfully working in the UK (see p446). Otherwise, having a right to reside on the basis of being the primary carer of a British citizen does not enable you to be entitled to any benefit that requires a right to reside, because that is listed as an excluded right of residence in each of the benefit regulations (see p168). However, if you have a pending EUSS application for settled or pre-settled status and you have this derivative right to reside, it does mean that you are not defined as a 'person subject to immigration control' (see p95). You may therefore be able to claim one or more of the disability and carers' benefits, provided you meet all the other presence and residence requirements (see p302). You may also be entitled to working tax credit (WTC), since you have a right to work.

Note: if this was your only right of residence in the UK, your eligibility for leave under the EUSS is complicated by recent legal challenges (see p61). If you do not already have leave, you should urgently obtain specialist immigration advice on the type(s) of immigration leave you can apply for, and which would be best in your circumstances. You may be entitled to immigration leave on the basis of your right to family life (see p45). If this leave is granted without the condition that you have 'no recourse to public funds', you are not excluded from benefits, because you are not defined as a person subject to immigration control (see p93) and you have a non-excluded right to reside (see p187). You may be entitled to leave under the EUSS (see p55), which is never granted subject to a no recourse to public funds condition. If you are granted settled status (indefinite leave granted under the EUSS), that satisfies the right to reside requirement for benefits. If you are granted pre-settled status, this leave does not satisfy the right to reside requirement in any of the benefits that have it. The recent legal challenge to the exclusion of pre-settled status does not apply to pre-settled status granted by virtue of having a right to reside as a 'Zambrano carer' (see p261), because this right is not provided under the Withdrawal Agreements. For details of the legal challenges, and other information if you have pre-settled status, see p170 for means-tested benefits and, for child benefit and CTC, see p176.

Child of a primary carer

You have a derivative right to reside under the EEA Regulations if:[396]

- you are aged under 18 and your primary carer has a derivative right to reside as the primary carer of:
  - a worker's child in education (see p256); *or*
  - a child under 18 who is residing in the UK as a self-sufficient person (see p260); *or*
  - a British citizen who would be unable to reside in the UK or an EEA state if the primary carer left the UK (see above); *and*
- you do not have leave to enter or remain in the UK, *other than* pre-settled status (or settled status, which would itself mean you have a qualifying right to reside); *and*
- your primary carer would be prevented from residing in the UK if you left the UK for an indefinite period.

The basis of this right of residence is to make effective the rights of the primary carer and the other child for whom they are caring. Your nationality does not affect this right of residence.

Example

Veronika is a Czech national and has lived in the UK with her mother and brother since 2019. All members of the family have pre-settled status. Veronica is aged 16, has learning difficulties and is eight months pregnant. She has stopped attending school. Veronika's mother last worked in the UK in 2020 when she stopped work to care for her children and did not retain her worker status. Veronika's mother has a right to reside as the primary carer of Veronika's younger brother, Patrik, who is nine years old and in school. Veronika has a derivative right to reside because her mother has to look after her, and if Veronika left the UK, so too would her mother. This right to reside enables Veronika to be entitled to UC on the basis of her pregnancy. When Veronika's baby is born, she will be able to claim child benefit and continue to be entitled to UC on the basis that she will be responsible for a child.

Primary carer of a child with a permanent right to reside

You have a derivative right to reside if you are the primary carer of a child with a permanent right to reside. This derivative right to reside is not included in the EEA Regulations, but has been confirmed in caselaw. In two separate cases, it has been held that the non-EEA primary carer of a child who had acquired a permanent right to reside, after living in the UK for five years as a self-sufficient EEA national, must have a derivative right to reside to ensure the effectiveness of the child's right to reside. Once the child has acquired a permanent right to reside, their primary carer is no longer required to have comprehensive sickness insurance cover.[397]

If you are the primary carer of a child who has a permanent right to reside, you can have this derivative right to reside whether you are an EEA or non-EEA national and regardless of how the child acquired their permanent right to reside.

Example

Lisandra and her boyfriend Rasmus are Estonian nationals who have lived in the UK since August 2020. In June 2021 Lisandra gave birth to their baby, Oleg, and six months later she began working full time while Rasmus cared for Oleg. All three were granted pre-settled status in October 2021. In December 2022 Lisandra was in a car accident, and her level of injury meant her doctors have stated she will never be able to work again. Lisandra and Rasmus make a joint claim for UC and are entitled to be paid as a couple because both parents have a qualifying right to reside. Lisandra has acquired a permanent right to reside because she ceased her activity as a worker due to permanent incapacity, having resided in the UK for more than two years (see p275). Oleg, as the 'family member' of his mother, has also acquired a permanent right to reside and this means that Rasmus, as Oleg's primary carer, has a derivative right to reside.

Other derivative rights

It is arguable that you may have a right to reside if your circumstances do not exactly fit the criteria for the derivative rights on p254, but they are similar and the legal principles underlying derivative residence rights could be applied. For example, you may be able to argue that you have a right to reside in the following situations.

- You are the primary carer of a worker's child who is under school age. Such a child has a clear right to reside as the family member of a worker and it may be arguable that you must have a right to reside to make the child's right effective. The Upper Tribunal held that the primary carer does not have a right to reside in this situation.[398] However, a different decision may be reached if this argument were made again, due to more recent caselaw, which held that the primary carer of a child with a permanent right to reside must have a right to reside to ensure the child's right is effective (see above).
- You are aged under 21 (but not under 18) and you are dependent on a primary carer with a derivative right to reside and they would be prevented from residing in the UK if you left the UK for an indefinite period, and you do not have leave to enter or remain in the UK. The EEA Regulations only give a derivative right to reside in this situation if you are under 18.[399]
- You are the child of a self-employed person in education, or you are the primary carer of such a child. The Court of Appeal held that you cannot have a right to reside on this basis and permission to appeal to the Supreme Court was refused.[400] However, it may be arguable that the Withdrawal Agreements do provide for residence rights on this basis.[401] The DWP accepts that you can have an equivalent right to reside while you are in education if you had been in the UK while your parent had been a 'frontier worker' in the UK on the basis of being *either* a worker or self-employed person (see p278), and the guidance confirming that notes it as an example of a new right to reside.[402]

There may be other circumstances in which you need a right to reside to make effective someone else's residence rights. The strength of your argument always depends on your circumstances and those of the other relevant people.

Benefit entitlement

If you have a derivative right to reside (other than on the basis of being the primary carer of a British citizen – see below), this satisfies the right to reside requirement for any of the benefits that require it (see p168).

If your derivative right to reside is on the basis of your being the primary carer of a British citizen, this right to reside is specifically excluded for each of the benefits with that requirement (see p168). To date, all legal challenges to this general exclusion have failed. However, the Upper Tribunal held that a Moroccan national, whose only right to reside in the UK was as the primary carer of a British citizen, was entitled to child benefit and CTC because she was lawfully working in the UK and was therefore covered by the association agreement between the EU and Morocco that provides for equal treatment in relation to family benefits.[403] For details of these agreements, see p446.

If you had a derivative right to reside in the past, note the following.

- The period of time when you have a derivative right to reside does *not* count towards the five years of residence required for permanent residence (see below). If you have lived in the UK for five years, check whether you can obtain settled status (indefinite leave to remain in the UK under the EUSS), because that requires actual residence, not residence with a right to reside (see p55).
- If you had a derivative right to reside on 31 December 2020, this can assist you if you are seeking to show that you had a free movement right to reside on that date, to satisfy regulations on the protected groups who can, after that date, potentially have free movement residence rights, and, if you are an EEA national, not be defined as a 'person subject to immigration control' (see p93). For further details, including the duration of these protections, see p188.

16. Permanent right to reside

Since 30 June 2021, you can only have any free movement right to reside, including a permanent right to reside, if you either have pre-settled status or you have a pending European Union Settlement Scheme (EUSS) application for settled or pre-settled status (or a pending appeal or administrative review of a refusal). For details of these protected groups and others that applied during the period 31 December 2020 to 30 June 2021, see p188.

If you are in one of the protected groups, or for a period before the end of 2020, you can have a permanent right to reside either:

- after five years if you have resided in the UK with a free movement right to reside (other than a derivative right to reside) for a continuous period of five years, disregarding certain gaps (see p266); *or*
- after less than five years if you have resided in the UK with a free movement right to reside as a European Economic Area (EEA) worker, or EEA self-employed person, or family member of either and certain other circumstances apply (see p275).

Once you have a permanent right to reside, you do not need to satisfy any ongoing conditions[404] (eg, you do not also need to be a worker) and this right of residence satisfies the right to reside requirement for all the benefits that have this requirement.

Other than in exceptional circumstances, you only lose your permanent right of residence if you are absent from the UK for more than two consecutive years (see p277).[405]

Note:

- If you do not already have settled status (indefinite leave under the EUSS), check whether you can obtain it. If you have pre-settled status, you need to apply for settled status before your pre-settled status expires, but you do not need to wait until then if you are eligible before (see p185). You may be eligible for settled status if either:
  - you have resided in the UK for five years (not necessarily with a right to reside, but if you are not an EEA national you will need to have been a family member of an EEA national or had a derivative right to reside); *or*
  - you satisfy the criteria for obtaining this leave after less than five years, which are broadly the same as those to acquire permanent residence in less than five years (see p275).
- If you have settled status, this satisfies the right to reside requirement for all the benefits that have it. For information on the criteria for settled status, see p57.
- If you have a permanent right to reside, this confers a right to reside on anyone defined as your family member (see p239). In contrast, if you are granted settled status, this does not in itself provide anyone defined as your family member with a right to reside, although they may be able to obtain their own grant of settled status.
- If you have pre-settled status, it may be easier for you to obtain a permanent right to reside, because the quality of residence required for some of the five years may be easier to satisfy (see p267).
- If you are seeking to show that you had a free movement right to reside on 31 December 2020, to satisfy regulations on the protected groups who can, after that date, potentially have free movement residence rights (and, if you are an EEA national, to not be defined as a 'person subject to immigration control'), note that you are *treated as* having a permanent right to reside on that date if you had lost a previously acquired permanent right to reside due to being absent from the UK for more than two years, but your absence on that date was less than five years.[406] For further details, including the duration of these protections, see p188.

Permanent residence after five years

If you are in one of the protected groups (see above), or for a period before the end of 2020, you have a permanent right to reside if you have 'resided legally' (see below) for a continuous period of five years (see p271).[407]

You can have permanent residence, whether you are an EEA national or non-EEA national, provided you satisfy the criteria. However, if you are a non-EEA national, there are fewer ways in which you count as having resided legally (see p270). If you are a Croatian, A2 or A8 national, additional restrictions may affect you during the years after your country joined the European Union (EU) and you can only count periods of residence in the UK before your country joined the EU in limited circumstances (see p270).

Resided legally

The precise quality of residence that you are required to have had for a continuous period of five years in the UK may vary depending on the legislation you are relying on. In most cases, it makes no difference, and so the phrase 'resided legally' is used in this section. However, check the quality of residence you are required to have in case this could affect your rights.[408]

- Other than, potentially, if the bullet point below applies to you, the EEA Regulations require you to have resided 'in accordance with these regulations' (or previous regulations).
- For periods after the end of the transition period, while you have pre-settled status, the EEA Regulations are amended such that you are required to have resided 'lawfully'. This could potentially include periods when you did not have a free movement right to reside, but, for example, did have pre-settled status.

EU Directive 2004/38 requires you to have resided 'legally'. This means that you must have had a residence right under the directive or under any of the earlier EU legislation that it replaced. You count as residing legally during periods when you have a free movement right to reside:[409]

- as a worker (see p211), including if you have retained this status (see p222);
- as a self-employed person (see p218), including if you have retained this status (see p222);
- as a self-sufficient person, including a self-sufficient student (see p232);
- as a family member of any of the above (see p269);
- (EEA Regulations only) as a jobseeker, or family member of a jobseeker, since 30 April 2006 (see below); *or*
- (EEA Regulations only) based on your, or your family member's, initial right of residence, since 30 April 2006 (see p269).

Most periods when you have a free movement residence right, other than a derivative right to reside, can count, but periods with rights other than those above can be more complicated.

Note: if you have lived in the UK for five years, even if you did not have a right to reside for all or any of that period, check whether you can obtain settled status (indefinite leave granted under the EUSS). That only requires actual residence, not residence with a right to reside. From the date you are granted settled status, you have a right to reside that satisfies the right to reside requirement for all the benefits that have it. However, it does not in itself provide your family members with a right to reside, but each may be able to obtain their own grant of settled status. In contrast, anyone defined as your family member does have a right to reside if you have a permanent right to reside (see p239).

Periods before 30 April 2006

The right of permanent residence was only introduced on 30 April 2006 when EU Directive 2004/38 and the EEA Regulations 2006 came into force. However, you can still count periods when you had a right of residence before 30 April 2006 towards the required five years, if your residence was on the basis of one or more of those points listed above (other than the last two bullet points: jobseeker or initial right to reside, or as a family member of an EEA national with either).

If you completed five years' legal residence before 30 April 2006 and then had a gap of less than two years when you were either out of the UK or residing in the UK but not 'residing legally', this does not affect you acquiring permanent residency.[410] If you completed five years' legal residence and then had a gap of two or more years when you were not residing in accordance with the EEA Regulations, see p274. If you completed five years' legal residence and were then absent from the UK for more than two continuous years, you lost your right of permanent residence (see p277).

Jobseekers

You can count periods when you had a right to reside as a jobseeker (see p203), or as a family member of a jobseeker, from 30 April 2006 towards your five years of 'residing in accordance with the EEA Regulations'.[411] You cannot count periods before this date, as jobseekers did not have a right to reside under earlier regulations. If you need to rely on periods when you were seeking work before 30 April 2006, check whether you had another residence right at that time – eg, if you retained worker status.

Guidance to decision makers confirms that if you have had a right to reside as a jobseeker, including if you have been awarded income-based jobseeker's allowance (JSA) on the basis of this right to reside for a continuous period of five years, this is sufficient for you to acquire permanent residence.[412] It further states that if your JSA is disallowed, the continuity of your legal residence is broken.[413] This is not necessarily correct, as you can have a right to reside as a jobseeker without receiving JSA (see p209).[414] The guidance also confirms that a period when your income-based JSA is not paid because of a sanction does not affect your continuity of residence as a jobseeker.[415]

Note: periods when your only right of residence was as a jobseeker, or as a family member of a jobseeker, do not count as 'residing legally' under the EU Directive.[416] However, this is rarely a problem in practice since you can count such periods under the EEA Regulations.

Initial right of residence

You can count periods after 30 April 2006 when you had an initial right of residence for the first three months after your arrival in the UK (see p203), or as the family member of someone with an initial right of residence, towards your five years of residing in accordance with the EEA Regulations.[417] You cannot count such periods under the EU Directive.[418] There was no initial right of residence before 30 April 2006.

Family members

You can count periods when you have a right to reside as the family member (see p240) of a 'qualified person' (see p193) towards your five years of 'residing legally', including if you are an 'extended family member' with the relevant residence document.[419]

If you are the family member of a person who has acquired permanent residency after residing legally in the UK for five years, you have a right to reside for as long as you remain their family member.[420] Under the EEA Regulations, you can also use periods as a family member of a person with a permanent right of residence towards your five years of residing in accordance with those regulations, and so acquire a permanent right of residence yourself.[421] This is in addition to any other periods when you have a right to reside through being a family member of an EEA national with a right to reside – eg, as a worker (see p267).

Note:

- If you are a non-EEA national, see p270.
- If you are the family member of a person who has acquired permanent residency in less than five years, you may have permanent residency yourself (see p275).

Former family members

In certain circumstances, you can count periods since 30 April 2006 when you retained a right to reside as a former family member under the EEA Regulations towards your five years of residence required for permanent residence. If you are a non-EEA national, you must have a right to reside as a former family member at the end of your five-year period to acquire a permanent right to reside under the EEA Regulations.[422]

The circumstances in which your retained right to reside as a former family member count towards your five years are if you are also a worker or a self-employed or self-sufficient person, or the family member of such a person.[423] However, if you were the child of the qualified person and were in education immediately before the qualified person died or left the UK, or you were the parent with custody of such a child, you do not have to meet this additional requirement.[424]

For further details on retaining your residence rights as a former family member, see p249.

Non-European Economic Area nationals

Periods when you are in the UK with leave to enter or remain do not count as periods of 'residing legally' under the EU Directive. They also do not count under the EEA Regulations as they are not periods in which you resided in accordance with those regulations and so do not count towards the five years required for permanent residency.[425] However, for periods since the end of the transition period, it may be arguable that periods when you did not have a free movement right to reside, but did have pre-settled status, can count if you currently have pre-settled status, because the EEA Regulations were amended to require that for the five-year period you simply resided 'lawfully' see p267.[426]

If you are a non-EEA national, you cannot have a right of residence as a worker, self-employed person, person who retains either of these statuses, a self-sufficient person or a self-sufficient student. However, you can have a right of residence as the family member of an EEA national who is in one of these groups.

In practice, therefore, unless the argument above is accepted, as a non-EEA national the only way you can obtain a permanent right of residence after five years of residing legally is by either:

- residing for a five-year period as the family member of an EEA national who is legally residing; *or*
- retaining the right as a former family member on the basis of either the death of your spouse or civil partner or the termination of your marriage or civil partnership (see p250).[427]

Note:

- If you are the family member of a dual British/EEA citizen, you can only acquire a permanent right to reside as their family member under the EEA Regulations if, at the time they acquired British citizenship, they were either a 'qualified person' (see p193) or had a permanent right to reside under those regulations.[428]
- In limited circumstances, you can also acquire a right of permanent residence in less than five years if you are the family member of an EEA national who has acquired a permanent right of residence in less than five years (see p275).

Croatian, A2 and A8 nationals

If you are a Croatian, A2 or A8 national, you can acquire permanent residency after five years of residing legally in the same way as any other EEA national. However, note the following.

- If you are relying on periods when you were subject to additional restrictions on your residence rights, these may affect whether you had a right to reside as a jobseeker or a worker, or retained worker status (see p197). **Note:** the Court of Appeal has held that the restrictions on A8 nationals ended on 30 April 2009 and their extension to 30 April 2011 was unlawful.[429] This means that if at the time you would not have had a right to reside as a jobseeker, a worker or retained your worker status during this two-year period because of the restrictions, you can retrospectively be accepted as having had these residence rights and count this period as one when you were residing legally.

- The Upper Tribunal held that it was 'disproportionate' to disregard the years of work by an A8 national and his subsequent involuntary unemployment just because he had not complied with the restrictions, and accepted that he had acquired permanent residency (see p200).[430]
- If you are relying on periods when you were living in the UK before your country joined the EU, you do not count as having resided legally just on the basis that you had leave to enter or remain in the UK. However, you count as residing legally if:[431]
  - you had leave to enter or remain in the UK; *and*
  - you would have had a right of residence as a worker, self-employed person, person who retains one of those statuses, a self-sufficient person or self-sufficient student, except for the fact that you were not an EU national at the time.

Derivative right to reside

Periods when you have resided with a derivative right to reside (see p253) do not count as periods of residing legally, and so you cannot count them towards your five years for the purposes of acquiring permanent residency under either the EEA Regulations or the EU Directive.[432]

Continuity of residence

You acquire permanent residency when you have been 'residing legally' (see p267) for a continuous period of five years.[433] However, the continuity of your residence is not affected by certain absences from the UK (see below). It is also arguable that the continuity of your residence is not affected by certain gaps during the five years when you were in the UK, but did not count as 'residing legally' (see p272).

Note: if you are seeking to show that you had a free movement right to reside on 31 December 2020, to satisfy regulations on the protected groups that can potentially have free movement residence rights after that date, these regulations *treat* you as having had such a right to reside if one of the absences below applied to you on that date. For details of these protections, including their duration, see p188.[434]

Absence from the UK

Temporary absences from the UK do not affect the continuity of your residence if:[435]

- they add up to less than six months a year in total;
- it is one absence of up to 12 consecutive months for important reasons – eg, pregnancy and childbirth, serious illness, study or vocational training, or a posting abroad. If you have one absence of up to 12 months for a similar important reason, it should also not affect the continuity of your residence;[436] *or*

- they are for compulsory military service.

If you have one or more of the above temporary absences from the UK, you can count the time spent abroad as part of your five continuous years.[437] However, you are likely to need to make this argument to the benefit authority, as guidance to decision makers only refers to earlier caselaw that held that time spent abroad during a temporary absence does *not* count towards your five continuous years.[438] In support of your argument, note that the guidance is not legally binding and that the approach of the most recent caselaw (each heard by a two-judge panel rather than a single commissioner) should be followed. The Upper Tribunal summarised these alternative approaches, noting that the most recent caselaw has held that the absences abroad counted towards the five years.[439]

Example

Miroslav is a Slovakian national. In November 2017, he came to the UK and began working as a self-employed carpenter. He obtained pre-settled status in 2020, and in November 2021 he returned to Slovakia. Miroslav was then offered a job in the UK, and he returned to take this up in March 2022. In January 2023, Miroslav left his job to care for his British girlfiend and claimed universal credit (UC) as her carer. Miroslav satisfied the right to reside right requirement for UC as his pre-settled status meant he was in a protected group that could have a free movement right to reside (see p188) *and* when he claimed UC he had a permanent right to reside because he had legally resided in the UK for a continuous period of five years, including the five months he was in Hungary. Miroslav can also now apply for settled status under the EUSS.

Your continuity of residence is broken if you are subject to a deportation or exclusion order, or you are removed from the UK.[440] However, this *may* not apply if you appeal the removal decision and also have a pending EUSS application for settled or pre-settled status (or a pending appeal or administrative review of a refusal). In a decision about a *different* provision of the EEA Regulations (which terminates a right to reside under those if a decision has been made to remove the person on specified grounds),[441] the High Court held this provision was of no effect while the EEA national was appealing both the removal decision and a refusal to grant settled status. Consequently, his right to reside continued.[442] If you are subject to a removal decision, get urgent immigration advice.

Gaps while in the UK

Between the periods when you are residing legally in the UK, you may have one or more temporary periods when you remain in the UK, but you are not 'residing legally'. These periods are not covered in the EU Directive or the EEA Regulations, but have been considered in caselaw.[443]

You may be able to argue that the continuity of your residence is not affected by a period in which you remain in the UK, but do not count as residing legally, on the grounds that it should be treated as equivalent to a period abroad, which does not affect continuity of residence.[444] This argument was rejected by the Court of Appeal, which held that acquiring a permanent right of residence depends on continuous residence with a qualifying status.[445] However, it is arguable that the Court of Appeal did not adequately consider all the arguments and relevant caselaw, and also that the decision only applies in cases where the facts are comparable to the ones in that case, which concerned a non-EEA national who could not provide evidence of five years' residence as a dependent family member.[446] Since this decision, the Upper Tribunal stated that the legislation on continuity should be interpreted as requiring continuity of residence, not necessarily continuity of having 'resided legally', provided the total period of having legally resided is at least five years.[447] However, a more recent Upper Tribunal decision held that the previous Upper Tribunal decision was decided without referring to the Court of Appeal's decision and that the latter interpretation should be followed.[448]

It is, therefore, important to identify a right to reside in any potential gaps in your five years if possible. You should also check whether you can obtain settled status, but note that this leave only gives you a right to reside from the date it is granted.

Guidance to decision makers states that you can have a cumulative gap of up to 30 days in any 12-month period between periods of residence on different bases – eg, a gap between having a right to reside as a self-employed person and then as a worker. However, it goes on to state that a gap between two periods of the same type of residence (eg, as a jobseeker) breaks the continuity of residence.[449] The guidance gives no legal basis for this and, as guidance, it is not legally binding.

The guidance also correctly notes that if you have been given a benefit sanction, the continuity of your residence is not affected.[450] However, it also states that if your UC or JSA is disallowed, the continuity of your legal residence is broken.[451] This is not necessarily correct, as you can have a right to reside as a jobseeker, or with worker status retained while involuntarily unemployed and registered as a jobseeker, without receiving UC or JSA (see p209 and p225).[452]

If you stopped work to care for someone, you may be able to argue that you retained your worker or self-employed status (see p222).

If the gap was while you were serving a sentence in prison, that may interrupt the continuity of your residence and mean you cannot count the time spent in prison towards your five years. The Court of Justice of the European Union (CJEU) found that taking time spent serving a prison sentence into account when calculating the five years is contrary to the EU Directive's aim of strengthening social cohesion. This aim was a key factor behind establishing the right of permanent residency and was also the reason why permanent residency depends not just on the duration but also the quality of residence, relating to the level of integration in the member state. Receiving a prison sentence was considered to show the person's non-compliance with the values of that state.[453] However, subsequent caselaw emphasises the need to take an overall assessment of the level of the person's integration in the host state, and whether that was broken by being in prison, taking account of the nature of the offence, length of sentence and attitude while in prison.[454]

This approach suggests that *other* gaps in your five-year period should be treated differently, particularly if they do not call into question your level of integration in the UK – eg, periods when you temporarily ceased to be a worker or self-employed because you were caring for someone.

Being detained in a secure mental health unit under a hospital order made by a criminal court does not break continuity of residence.[455]

Note: if you were in prison on 31 December 2020, and you are seeking to show that you had a free movement right to reside on that date, to satisfy regulations on the protected groups who can, after that date, potentially have free movement residence rights, it is likely that the benefit authorities will not accept that you had a free movement right to reside on that date.[456] For details of these protected groups, including their duration, see p188. If you are refused benefit on this basis, challenge the decision and seek specialist advice.

Gaps after five years

If you have a gap, during which you were in the UK but not residing in accordance with the current or previous regulations, of at least two continuous years after a five-year period during which you resided either:[457]

- in accordance with previous regulations (see p267) – ie, before the current regulations came into force on 1 February 2017; *or*
- before the country of which you are a national joined the EU (see p270),

you cannot count those periods of residence under the EEA Regulations.

However, it is arguable that discounting these periods of residence, which would otherwise result in permanent residence, is not compatible with EU law: the EU Directive is clear that permanent residence is only lost if you are absent from the UK for more than two consecutive years (see p277).[458] The CJEU has held that a gap of *less* than two years which follows the five-year period does not affect the acquisition of permanent residence.[459] However, this does not necessarily mean that a gap of *more* than two years does affect it. In addition, the CJEU judgment concerned periods wholly before the right of permanent residence existed (ie, before 30 April 2006), whereas the exclusion in the EEA Regulations also covers periods since then. For residence before 30 April 2006, see p268.

Permanent residence in less than five years

If you are in one of the protected groups (see p188), or for a period before the end of 2020, you can, in the circumstances below, acquire a permanent right of residence in less than five years.

You have a permanent right to reside if you:[460]

- were a worker (see p211) or self-employed person (see p218) and at the time you ceased working, you:
  - had reached pension age, or (workers only) had taken early retirement,[461] and you either:
    - had a spouse or civil partner who is a British citizen (or who lost that nationality by marrying you); *or*
    - had worked in the UK for the preceding year and resided in the UK continuously (see p276) for more than three years. Under the EEA Regulations, this residence must have been immediately before you stopped working; *or*
  - stopped your activity as a worker or self-employed person in the UK because of a permanent incapacity (see below) and:
    - you had a spouse or civil partner who is a British citizen (or who lost that nationality by marrying you); *or*
    - you had resided in the UK continuously (see p276) for more than two years; *or*
    - the incapacity was as a result of an accident at work or occupational disease that resulted in benefit entitlement – eg, industrial injuries disablement benefit; *or*
  - were a worker or self-employed in another EEA country while residing in the UK and returned, as a rule, at least once a week, following (under the EEA Regulations, immediately following) three years of continuous employment or self-employment, and residence, in the UK; *or*
- are the family member of a worker or self-employed person in any of the above groups and satisfy other conditions (see p277); *or*
- are the family member of a worker or self-employed person who died while still working and who did not acquire a permanent right of residence as a result of being in one of the above groups and:
  - they had resided (see p276) in the UK for two years; *or*
  - the death resulted from an accident at work or an occupational disease; *or*
  - (EU Directive only) you lost your UK nationality as a result of marrying them.

Note: these circumstances can enable you to obtain settled status (indefinite leave to remain under the EUSS) in less than five years (see p55).

Permanent incapacity

'Permanent incapacity' is the opposite of temporary incapacity,[462] and means there is no reasonable prospect of your being able undertake any work again.

If your incapacity is *not* permanent, you may be able to retain your worker or self-employed status on the basis that you are temporarily unable to work due to illness or accident.

For further details, including on the meanings of a 'temporary' and 'permanent' incapacity, see p228.

What can be treated as a period of work

If the basis on which you acquire a permanent right to reside in less than five years requires you to have worked for a period of time, in addition to the periods when you are actually working, the following are treated as periods of activity as a worker or self-employed person:[463]

- periods when you were not working for reasons not of your making;
- periods when you were not working because of an illness or accident;
- periods of involuntary unemployment (see p224) recorded by the relevant employment office – ie, Jobcentre Plus. **Note:** the EEA Regulations limit this basis to workers, but it is strongly arguable it should also apply to self-employed persons, given the CJEU caselaw confirming that self-employed people as well as workers can retain status on this basis (see p223).

Under the EEA Regulations, you must meet the requirements for retaining worker status during these periods (see p222). If you are a Croatian, A2 or A8 national, the EEA Regulations also require you to have complied with the additional restrictions that affected whether you could have, or retain, worker status in order to count periods as periods of work (see p197).[464] However, the Upper Tribunal has held that the UK did not impose restrictions on the right of A8 nationals to permanent residence in under five years and, therefore, periods of employment count for this purpose, even if they did not comply with the restrictions – eg, if your work was not registered under the Worker Registration Scheme.[465]

Note: if you retire or become permanently incapable of work while you are in one of the above situations, since you are treated as being in a period of activity as a worker or self-employed person, provided you satisfy the other requirements you can acquire permanent residence on that basis. This approach was followed by the Court of Appeal, which held that a permanent right to reside can still be acquired, if permanent incapacity is preceded by temporary incapacity rather than actual employment, provided the person has resided in the UK (see below) for more than two years at the date the incapacity became permanent.[466]

Residing in the UK

Some of the ways in which you can acquire permanent residence in less than five years require you to have resided in the UK continuously for specified periods. This has been held to mean factual residence, not necessarily with a free movement right to reside.

The Supreme Court has held that to acquire permanent residency in less than five years following retirement, 'residence' means 'factual residence' rather than the 'legal residence' required for acquiring permanent residence after five years,[467] and that earlier caselaw that interpreted 'residence' as 'legal residence' should not be followed.[468] In a subsequent case, the Upper Tribunal has held that this meaning of 'residence' also applies for acquiring permanent residence in less than five years following permanent incapacity.[469]

It is also arguable that when calculating the period of your continuous residence, certain absences should not affect your continuity of residence in the same way as for acquiring permanent residence after five years (see p271).

Family members

You acquire permanent residence in less than five years if you are living in the UK and are the family member (see p240) of someone who has acquired a permanent right to reside under the first bullet point about permanent residence on p275. The requirements of the EU Directive and the EEA Regulations differ on the circumstances in which you have this right to reside.

- **Under the EU Directive,** you must 'reside with' the family member in the UK. This does not mean you have to live with the person; it is sufficient that you are living in the UK now.[470] You do not have to have lived in the UK for the same period as them, and you do not need to have been their family member throughout this time.[471]
- **Under the EEA Regulations, since 1 February 2017,** you must have had a right to reside on the basis of being their family member at the point they ceased activity as a worker or self-employed person.[472]

If you are refused benefit on the grounds that you do not satisfy the EEA Regulations but you do satisfy the EU Directive, you should challenge the decision on the basis that the EEA Regulations have to be interpreted in accordance with the, now retained, EU law that they are intended to implement, which includes the directive (see p195).

Loss of permanent right to reside

Once you have a permanent right to reside (either because you have resided legally in the UK for five years or under the rules that enable you to acquire permanent residence in less than five years), you only lose this right if you are absent from the UK for more than two consecutive years.[473]

Note:

- In exceptional circumstances, your residence rights can be revoked or cancelled on grounds of public policy, public security or public health (see p71).[474] If you are told this has happened or will happen to you, get specialist immigration advice immediately.
- If you are seeking to show that you had a free movement right to reside on 31 December 2020, to satisfy regulations on the protected groups who can, after that date, potentially have free movement residence rights, note that these regulations *treat you as* having a permanent right to reside in the UK on that

date if you lost a previously acquired permanent right to reside due to being absent from the UK for more than two years, but your absence on that date was less than five years.[475] For further details, including the duration, of these protections, see p188.

Benefit entitlement

If you have a permanent right to reside, this satisfies the right to reside requirement for all the benefits that have this requirement (see p168).

If you acquired a permanent right to reside in less than five years, you are exempt from the habitual residence test for means-tested benefits (see p159), and therefore do not need to be 'habitually resident in fact' (see p163).

To claim benefit on the basis of your permanent residence, you must provide evidence of this. It may help you to refer to decision makers' guidance, including sections on evidence, if this supports your situation.[476] You should always provide as much documentary evidence that you satisfy the conditions for permanent residence as you can. However, if you are unable, for example, to prove you worked for a relevant period, the decision maker should use additional records available to them – eg, national insurance contribution records.[477] This is covered in more detail on p499. For more information on evidence, see Chapter 20.

17. Frontier worker

You may have rights as a frontier worker in the UK if you are a European Economic Area (EEA) national and on 31 December 2020, and continuously since then, you have been 'not primarily resident in the UK', and you have:[478]

- been a worker in the UK (see p211); *or*
- been a self-employed person in the UK (see p218); *or*
- retained your worker or self-employed status (see p222).

If you changed between the three situations above, this does not affect your rights.[479]

You are treated as 'not primarily resident in the UK' if you have either:[480]

- been present in the UK for less than 180 days in the last 12 months; *or*
- returned to your country of residence at least once in the last six months, or at least twice in the last 12 months, unless there are exceptional reasons for your not doing so.

The rights that you have as a frontier worker include rights to means-tested benefits without nationality-based discrimination.[481] Consequently, if you are a frontier worker, or if you have been granted pre-settled status and you are a family member of a frontier worker, you are exempt from the habitual residence test for all means-tested benefits (see p159). **Note:** you still have to satisfy all the other conditions of entitlement, including the requirement to be present in Great Britain (other than for specified temporary absences – see p339).[482]

If you are the child of a frontier worker, whether on the basis of being a worker or self-employed person, you have a right to reside in the UK to complete your education. Your primary carer also has a right to reside until you reach the age of majority or, if you continue to need a primary carer beyond then, until you complete your education. These rights are similar to the derivative residence rights that the child of a worker in education, and their primary carer, can have (see p259).[483]

18. Other European freedom of movement residence rights

Until the end of the transition period (11pm on 31 December 2020), if you did not have a right to reside in the UK under the European Economic Area (EEA) Regulations or European Union (EU) Directive 2004/38, it was possible in limited circumstances to argue that despite not meeting all of the specific conditions required in those pieces of legislation, you still had a free movement right to reside by applying principles that have been accepted in other cases.

In particular, it has been accepted that you may have residence rights directly from the Treaty on the Functioning of the European Union, if these are necessary for someone else's rights not to be infringed.[484] For example, for a British citizen not to have been deterred from moving freely and working in an EEA country before the end of the transition period, it may be necessary for their family members to have a right to reside if they accompanied the British citizen on their return to the UK (see p244).[485] A different example is that to give effect to a child's right of permanent residence, it may be necessary for their primary carer to have a right to reside (see p263). In other cases, it has been accepted that you can have a right to reside to make another person's EU citizenship meaningful – eg, a British child may require their primary carer to have a right to reside (see p261).[486]

It may be possible to argue that despite not meeting every requirement, you should still have a right to reside if this would be 'proportionate' in your circumstances. See p200 for an example of when this was accepted in relation to an A8 national who had not fully complied with his employment restrictions.

See p235 for an example of this argument in relation to the requirement to have comprehensive sickness insurance cover in order to have a right to reside as a self-sufficient person. However, arguments based on this proportionality principle are complex and have been held not to apply, except possibly in exceptional circumstances.[487]

Get specialist advice to make these arguments, due to their legal complexity.

Notes

2. **British, Irish and Commonwealth citizens**

1 s3ZA IA 1971

3. **Changes due to the UK leaving the European Union**

2 s1 and Sch 1 ISSCA 2020; reg 4 ISSCA(C) Regs
3 Arts 2(e), 126 and 127 WA 2019; ss1A, 1B, 8A and Sch 2 Part 1A EU(W)A 2018
4 ss 1A and 1B EU(W)A 2018
5 s1B(3)(d) and (e) EU(W)A 2018
6 Reg 2 CR(ADTP) Regs, and Articles of the Withdrawal Agreements cited
7 Art 18(d) WA 2019; Art 17(1)(d) UK-EFTA; Art 16(1)(d) UK-Swiss Agreement
8 gov.uk/government/publications/eu-settlement-scheme-caseworker-guidance
9 *EU Settlement Scheme: family member of a qualifying British citizen,* available at gov.uk/government/publications/eu-settlement-scheme-caseworker-guidance
10 *R (on the application of the IMA) v SSHD* [2022] EWHC 3274 (Admin)
11 gov.uk/view-prove-immigration-status

4. **European and non-European nationals**

12 *Yesiloz v LB Camden and Another* [2009] EWCA Civ 415

5. **Protected groups that can have European free movement residence rights**

13 Reg 83 and Sch 4 paras 1-4 ISSC Regs; ADM Memo 29/20, paras 24 and 87-114; DMG Memo 25/20, paras 23-35 and 92-119
14 DMG Memo 14/21, para 8; ADM Memo 19/21, para 8; HB Circular A10/2021, para 12
15 Arts 4, 10 and 18(3) WA 2019; Arts 4, 9 and 17(3) UK-EFTA; Arts 4, 10 and 16(3) UK-Swiss Agreement; ss7A-7C EU(W)A 2018
16 Regs 3 and 4 CR(ADTP) Regs; ADM Memo 30/20, esp paras 12-13; DMG Memo 26/20, esp paras 12-13
17 Arts 4, 10 and 18(3) WA 2019; Arts 4, 9 and 17(3) UK-EFTA; Arts 4, 10 and 16(3) UK-Swiss Agreement; ss7A-7C EU(W)A 2018
18 HB Circular A10/2021, paras 8 and 11-13; DMG Memo 14/21, paras 8 and 9; ADM Memo 19/21, paras 8 and 9; Home Office, *Public Funds: migrant access to public funds, including social housing, homelessness assistance and social care* (version 18), 20 August 2021, p30
19 Regs 3(5)(b) and 4(6)(c) CR(ADTP) Regs; reg 3 I(EEA) Regs
20 Regs 3(5)(c) and 4(6)(d) CR(ADTP) Regs
21 Reg 13 CR(ADTP) Regs; *Kerr v DSDNI* [2004] UKHL 23, paras 62-69; ADM Memo 30/20, para 42; DMG Memo 26/20, para 42; see also comments in *FN v SSWP (UC)* [2022] UKUT 77 (AAC), paras 4-8
22 Regs 3(4)-(6), 4(2) and (5)-(8) and 12(1)(i) CR(ADTP) Regs; DMG Memo 26/20, paras 36, 37 and 41; ADM 30/20, paras 36, 37 and 41; DMG Memos 6/21 and 7/21; ADM Memos 7/21 and 8/21
23 Home Office, *Public Funds: migrant access to public funds, including social housing, homelessness assistance and social care* (version 18), 20 August 2021, pp5, 27 and 30
24 In particular: ADM Memo 30/20; DMG Memo 26/20; ADM Memo 19/21; DMG Memo 14/21; HB Circular A10/2021
25 Reg 23(9) I(EEA) Regs
26 *Silva v SSHD* CO/2344/2021 – see insights.doughtystreet.co.uk/post/102hevp/deportation-order-does-not-terminate-eu-right-to-reside
27 Reg 3 CR(ADTP) Regs; ADM Memo 30/20, paras 10 and 11; DMG Memo 26/20, paras 10 and 11
28 Reg 3 CR(ADTP) Regs; ADM Memo 30/20, paras 9 and 11; DMG Memo 26/20, paras 9 and 11
29 Regs 3(6) CR(ADTP) Regs; ADM Memo 30/20, para 9; DMG Memo 26/20, para 9

30 Reg 3(6)(g)(iii) and (iv) CR(ADTP) Regs and provisions of the Withdrawal Agreements cited

6. **European free movement residence rights**

31 This approach was taken in the I(EEA) Regs: see reg 2(1), definition of 'EEA national', I(EEA) Regs
32 Regs 6 and 14(1) I(EEA) Regs. The term 'qualified person' appears in these regulations, but is not used in the EU Directive, although the same groups of people are covered: Arts 7 and 14 EU Dir 2004/38.
33 See, for example, *SSWP v JB (JSA)* [2011] UKUT 96 (AAC)
34 ss1A and 1B EU(W)A 2018
35 ss2-5 EU(W)A 2018
36 For a recent official summary of these changes, see paras 7.1-7.4 Explanatory Memo to The Cessation of EU Law Relating to Prohibitions on Grounds of Nationality and Free Movement of Persons Regulations 2022 No.1240
37 s1 and Sch 1 ISSCA 2020; reg 4 ISSCA(C) Regs
38 Part 2 WA 2019; Part 2 UK-EFTA; UK-Swiss Agreement
39 Arts 2 and 4 WA 2019; Arts 2 and 4 UK-EFTA; Art 4 UK-Swiss Agreement
40 Art 158 WA 2019
41 For helpful discussion, see *Geci (EEA Regs: transitional provisions, appeal rights) Albania* [2021] UKUT 285 (IAC)
42 s6 EU(W)A 2018; The European Union (Withdrawal) Act 2018 (Relevant Court) (Retained EU Case Law) Regulations 2020 No.1525
43 s6 EU(W)A 2018
44 Arts 20 and 21 TFEU
45 EEA Joint Committee Decision No.158/2007
46 EU Reg 492/2011
47 *Agreement between the European Community and its Member States, of the one part, and the Swiss Confederation, of the other, on the free movement of persons*, Cmd 5639, 21 June 1999 (in force on 1 June 2002)
48 Reg 2(1) I(EEA) Regs
49 Reg 1(2) I(EEA) Regs – except reg 9, which was replaced from 25 November 2016

7. **Croatian, A2 and A8 nationals**

50 *SSWP v Gubeladze* [2019] UKSC 31 dismissed the SSWP's appeal from *SSWP v Gubeladze* [2017] EWCA Civ 1751, which had dismissed the SSWP's appeal from *TG v SSWP (PC)* [2015] UKUT 50 (AAC); see also para C1838 ADM; Vol 2 Ch 7 part 3, para 073502 DMG
51 See, for example, *AM v SSWP (ESA)* [2019] UKUT 215 (AAC) and *SSWP v KK (JSA)* [2019] UKUT 313 (AAC)
52 **Croatia** Reg 8 AC(IWA) Regs
A2 Reg 9 A(IWA) Regs
53 **Croatia** Regs 4 and 5 AC(IWA) Regs
A2 Reg 6 A(IWA) Regs; reg 7B I(EEA) Regs 2006, as saved by reg 45 and Sch 4 para 2 I(EEA) Regs
54 Reg 7 A(IWR) Regs
55 Reg 5 A(IWR) Regs; reg 7A I(EEA) Regs 2006, as saved by reg 45 and Sch 4 para 2 I(EEA) Regs
56 The CJEU has held that excluding an A8 national subject to restrictions from retaining worker status is not unlawful: *Prefeta v SSWP*, C-618/16 [2018]
57 *Prefeta v SSWP*, C-618/16 [2018]
58 CIS/1042/2008; *SSWP v JB* [2011] UKUT 96 (AAC)
59 *NZ v SSWP (ESA) (Third interim decision)* [2017] UKUT 360 (AAC); see also *SSWP v NZ (ESA) (Final decision)* [2019] UKUT 250 (AAC)
60 Reg 2 AC(IWA) Regs; reg 2 A(IWA) Regs; *OB v SSWP (ESA)* [2017] UKUT 255 (AAC)
61 *SSWP v LM (ESA) (Interim decision)* [2017] UKUT 485 (AAC), paras 20-21, which confirms that reg 2(8) A(IWR) Regs requires you to have been legally working at the beginning and end of the 12-month period
62 *SSWP v LM (ESA) (Interim decision)* [2017] UKUT 485 (AAC), paras 20-21, which confirms that reg 2(8) A(IWR) Regs requires you to have been legally working at the beginning and end of the 12-month period
63 s33(2A) IA 1971
64 Reg 3 AC(IWA) Regs; reg 4 A(IWA) Regs
65 Reg 2 A(IWR) Regs
66 *SSWP v LM (ESA) (Interim decision)* [2017] UKUT 485 (AAC), paras 20-21, which confirms that reg 2(8) A(IWR) Regs requires you to have been legally working at the beginning and end of the 12-month period

67 *SSWP v LM (ESA) (Interim decision)* [2017] UKUT 485 (AAC), paras 20-21, which confirms that reg 2(8) A(IWR) Regs requires you to have been legally working at the beginning and end of the 12-month period
68 *JK v SSWP (SPC)* [2017] UKUT 179 (AAC); see also *SSWP v LM (ESA) (Interim decision)* [2017] UKUT 485 (AAC), paras 22-24
69 Reg 2(5) AC(IWA) Regs; reg 2(12) A(IWA) Regs
70 *Miskovic and Another v SSWP* [2011] EWCA Civ 16
71 Reg 2(7) A(IWR) Regs
72 *Miskovic and Another v SSWP* [2011] EWCA Civ 16
73 Reg 7 A(IWR) Regs
74 *SSWP v ZA* [2009] UKUT 294 (AAC); *Szpak v SSWP* [2013] EWCA Civ 46
75 *NZ v SSWP (ESA) (Third interim decision)* [2017] UKUT 360 (AAC)
76 *BS v SSWP* [2009] UKUT 16 (AAC)

8. **Initial right of residence**

77 Reg 11 I(EEA) Regs
78 Reg 13(1) I(EEA) Regs; Art 6(1) EU Dir 2004/38
79 Reg 13(2) I(EEA) Regs; Art 6(2) EU Dir 2004/38
80 Reg 13(2) I(EEA) Regs; Art 6(2) EU Dir 2004/38

9. **Jobseekers**

81 Art 45 TFEU; Art 14 EU Dir 2004/38; *The Queen v Immigration Appeal Tribunal, ex parte Antonissen*, C-292/89 [1991]; reg 6 I(EEA) Regs
82 Reg 6(1) and (8)-(10) I(EEA) Regs
83 Art 45 TFEU; *The Queen v Immigration Appeal Tribunal, ex parte Antonissen*, C-292/89 [1991]
84 **Croatia** Reg 5 AC(IWA) Regs
A2 Reg 6 A(IWA) Regs
A8 Regs 4(2) and (4) and 5(2) A(IWR) Regs
85 *SSWP v Gubeladze* [2017] EWCA Civ 1751 dismissed the SSWP's appeal from *TG v SSWP (PC)* [2015] UKUT 50 (AAC)
86 *The Queen v Immigration Appeal Tribunal, ex parte Antonissen*, C-292/89 [1991], para 21; confirmed in *SSWP v MB (JSA) (and linked cases)* [2016] UKUT 372 (AAC), reported as [2017] AACR 6, para 49
87 *G.M.A. v État belge*, C-710/19 [2020]
88 Reg 6 I(EEA) Regs
89 Reg 6(8) I(EEA) Regs
90 Reg 6(1), (8) and (9) I(EEA) Regs
91 paras C1302 and C1403-4 ADM; DMG Memo 27/20, paras 11 and 14
92 Confirmed in Vol 2 Ch 7 para 073080 DMG
93 Vol 2 Ch 7 para 073120 DMG
94 *G.M.A. v État belge*, C-710/19 [2020]
95 Reg 6(1) and (5)-(8) I(EEA) Regs
96 Vol 2 Ch 7 para 073107 DMG
97 Vol 2 Ch 7 para 073108 DMG
98 *KS v SSWP* [2016] UKUT 269 (AAC) and ECJ caselaw cited; Vol 2 Ch 7 paras 073096-073100 DMG
99 *SSWP v MB (JSA) (and linked cases)* [2016] UKUT 372 (AAC), reported as [2017] AACR 6, paras 49-60, especially paras 49 and 57
100 *SSWP v MB (JSA) (and linked cases)* [2016] UKUT 372 (AAC), reported as [2017] AACR 6, para 47
101 *OS v SSWP (JSA)* [2017] UKUT 107 (AAC), paras 5-7 and caselaw cited
102 *SSWP v RR (IS)* [2013] UKUT 21 (AAC), reported as [2013] AACR 20
103 Vol 2 Ch 7 paras 073099-073100 DMG
104 *SSWP v MB (JSA) (and linked cases)* [2016] UKUT 372 (AAC), reported as [2017] AACR 6, paras 61, 91 and 127
105 *DD v HMRC and SSWP (CB)* [2020] UKUT 66 (AAC)
106 CH/3314/2005
107 *G.M.A. v État belge*, C-710/19 [2020]
108 R(IS) 8/08, para 6; *SSWP v MB (JSA) (and linked cases)* [2016] UKUT 372 (AAC), reported as [2017] AACR 6, in particular paras 32-33; CIS/1951/2008, para 21; see also *Shabani v SSHD (EEA – jobseekers; nursery education)* [2013] UKUT 315 (IAC)
109 s7 JSA 1995; reg 8 JSA Regs. This argument was discussed in *SSWP v MB (JSA) (and linked cases)* [2016] UKUT 372 (AAC), reported as [2017] AACR 6, paras 63-79. However, it did not apply in any of the cases in question and so no decision was required.
110 *The Queen v Immigration Appeal Tribunal, ex parte Antonissen*, C-292/89 [1991], para 21; R(IS) 8/08, para 5; *GE v SSWP (ESA)* [2017] UKUT 145 (AAC), reported as [2017] AACR 34, para 46; see also *Cardiff CC v HM (HB)* [2019] UKUT 271 (AAC), paras 6 and 18, and *SSWP v KK (JSA)* [2019] UKUT 313 (AAC), para 9

111 Art 24(2) EU Dir 2004/38; see also *Jobcentre Berlin Neukölln v Alimanovic*, C-67/14 [2015]; *Vestische Arbeit Jobcenter Kreis Recklinghausen v García-Nieto*, C-299/14 [2016]
112 *Vatsouras and Koupatantze v Arbeitsgemeinschaft Nürnberg*, C-23/08 [2009], paras 40 and 45
113 *Vatsouras and Koupatantze v Arbeitsgemeinschaft Nürnberg*, C-23/08 [2009], para 40
114 *Alhashem v SSWP* [2016] EWCA Civ 395. The case is not being appealed further.
115 The exclusion of jobseekers from HB was held not to be unlawful in *Stach v The Department for Communities and DWP* [2018] NIQB 93
116 Reg 3 HB(HR)A Regs

10. **Workers**
117 Regs 4(1)(a), 6(1) and 14(1) I(EEA) Regs; Arts 7(1)(a) and 14(2) EU Dir 2004/38; Art 45 TFEU
118 Reg 4(1)(a) I(EEA) Regs
119 *Levin v Staatssecretaris van Justitie*, C-53/81 [1982]
120 *LN v Styrelsen for Videregaende Uddannelser og Uddannelsesstøtte*, C-46/12 [2013]
121 **Croatia** Reg 5 AC(IWA) Regs
A2 Reg 6 A(IWA) Regs
122 Reg 5(2) A(IWR) Regs
123 *SSWP v Gubeladze* [2019] UKSC 31 dismissed the SSWP's appeal from *SSWP v Gubeladze* [2017] EWCA Civ 1751, which had dismissed the SSWP's appeal from *TG v SSWP (PC)* [2015] UKUT 50 (AAC)
124 See, for example, *AM v SSWP (ESA)* [2019] UKUT 215 (AAC)
125 Vol 2 Ch 7 paras 073031-58 DMG; paras C1480-C1509 ADM; HB A3/2014; HMRC, *Child Benefit and Child Tax Credit: right to reside establishing whether an EEA national is/was a worker or a self-employed person under EU law*, February 2014
126 Vol 2 Ch 7 para 073040 DMG; para C1489 ADM; HB A3/2014, para 15; HMRC, *Child Benefit and Child Tax Credit: right to reside establishing whether an EEA national is/was a worker or a self-employed person under EU law*, February 2014, para 7
127 *RF v LB Lambeth* [2019] UKUT 52 (AAC); see also *DDCC v HMRC and SSWP (CB)* [2020] UKUT 66 (AAC), para 26
128 *Raulin v Minister van Onderwijs en Wetenschappen*, C-357/89 [1992], para 10
129 *SSWP v RR (IS)* [2013] UKUT 21 (AAC), reported as [2013] AACR 20
130 CIS/868/2008; CIS/1837/2006; see also *VW v SSWP (PC)* [2014] UKUT 573 (AAC)
131 *Steymann v Staatssecretaris van Justitie*, C-196/87 [1988] ; R(IS) 12/98; *Trojani v CPAS*, C-456/02 [2004]
132 *Lawrie-Blum v Land Baden-Württemberg*, C-66/85 [1986], para 17
133 *Jany v Staatssecretaris van Justitie*, C-268/99 [2001], para 34
134 *SSWP v KP (JSA)* [2011] UKUT 241 (AAC); *SSWP v MM (IS)* [2015] UKUT 128 (AAC), paras 31 and 36
135 *Bettray v Staatssecretaris van Justitie*, C-344/87 [1989], para 16; *JA v SSWP (ESA)* [2012] UKUT 122 (AAC); *EP v SSWP (JSA)* [2016] UKUT 445 (AAC), para 21
136 *EP v SSWP (JSA)* [2016] UKUT 445 (AAC), para 22
137 *Barry v London Borough of Southwark* [2008] EWCA Civ 1440, para 45; *NE v SSWP* [2009] UKUT 38 (AAC), para 4
138 *Bettray v Staatssecretaris van Justitie*, C-344/87 [1989]; *SSWP v KP (JSA)* [2011] UKUT 241 (AAC)
139 *NE v SSWP* [2009] UKUT 38 (AAC), para 9; *SSWP v MM (IS)* [2015] UKUT 128 (AAC), paras 31 and 36
140 *EP v SSWP (JSA)* [2016] UKUT 445 (AAC), para 21
141 *Levin v Staatssecretaris van Justitie*, C-53/81 [1982], para 17
142 *Ninni-Orasche v Bundesminister für Wissenschaft, Verkehr und Kunst*, C-413/01 [2003], para 27
143 *Genc v Land Berlin*, C-14/09 [2010]
144 R(IS) 12/98
145 *Ninni-Orasche v Bundesminister für Wissenschaft, Verkehr und Kunst*, C-413/01 [2003], para 25
146 *Barry v London Borough of Southwark* [2008] EWCA Civ 1440
147 *Ninni-Orasche v Bundesminister für Wissenschaft, Verkehr und Kunst*, C-413/01 [2003], para 19
148 In *NE v SSWP* [2009] UKUT 38 (AAC), para 9; R(IS) 12/98
149 *Tarola v Minister for Social Protection*, C-483/17 [2019]

150 *Kempf v Staatssecretaris van Justitie*, C-139/85 [1986]; *Vatsouras and Koupantze v Arbeitsgemeinschaft (ARGE) Nürnberg 900*, C-22/08 [2009] and C-23/08 [2009], paras 27-28 and caselaw cited
151 *Raulin v Minister van Onderwijs en Wetenschappen*, C-357/89 [1992]
152 *NE v SSWP* [2009] UKUT 38 (AAC); CIS/1793/2007; *SSWP v MM (IS)* [2015] UKUT 128 (AAC)
153 *Genc v Land Berlin*, C-14/09 [2010]
154 *Barry v London Borough of Southwark* [2008] EWCA Civ 1440, para 20
155 *SSWP v SY (IS)* [2012] UKUT 233 (AAC); *JR v SSWP (IS)* [2014] UKUT 154 (AAC); *JR v Leeds City Council (HB)* [2014] UKUT 154 (AAC)
156 EA/02300/2016
157 *BS v SSWP* [2009] UKUT 16 (AAC); CIS/4237/2007

11. **Self-employed people**

158 Regs 4(1)(b) and 6(1)(c) I(EEA) Regs; Art 7(1)(a) EU Dir 2004/38; Art 49 TFEU; *Aldona Malgorzata Jany and Others v Staatssecretaris van Justitie*, C-268/99 [2001]
159 Reg 4(1)(b) I(EEA)Regs
160 *Bristol City Council v FV (HB)* [2011] UKUT 494 (AAC)
161 *HMRC v IT (CTC)* [2016] UKUT 252 (AAC), paras 25-28
162 *DV v SSWP* [2017] UKUT 155 (AAC)
163 *N v HMRC (CHB)* [2021] UKUT 28 (AAC)
164 *SSWP v SY (IS)* [2012] UKUT 233 (AAC); *JR v SSWP (IS)* [2014] UKUT 154 (AAC); *JR v Leeds City Council (HB)* [2014] UKUT 154 (AAC)
165 EA/02300/2016
166 Vol 2 Ch 7 paras 073031-58 DMG; paras C1480-C1509 ADM; HB A3/2014; HMRC, *Child Benefit and Child Tax Credit: right to reside establishing whether an EEA national is/was a worker or a self-employed person under EU law*, February 2014
167 Amended by reg 5(c) CR(ADTP) Regs and Sch 4 para 4(c) ISSC Regs
168 Reg 4(1)(b) I(EEA) Regs – until 31 December 2020
169 Art 49 TFEU; R(IS) 6/00
170 R(IS) 6/00, para 31
171 *TG v SSWP* [2009] UKUT 58 (AAC), para 5
172 *SSWP v JS (IS)* [2010] UKUT 240 (AAC), paras 5 and 8; *RJ v SSWP (JSA)* [2011] UKUT 477 (AAC), paras 9 and 17; *HMRC v HD (Interim decision) and HMRC v GP* [2017] UKUT 11 (AAC)
173 *SSWP v JS (IS)* [2010] UKUT 240 (AAC), para 5; Vol 2 Ch 7 para 072842 DMG; para C1452 ADM
174 CIS/1042/2008
175 *HMRC v HD (Interim decision) and HMRC v GP* [2017] UKUT 11 (AAC); see also *HMRC v HD (CHB) (Second interim decision)* [2018] UKUT 148 (AAC), paras 2 and 3
176 *Saint Prix v SSWP*, C-507/12 [2014]
177 *HMRC v HD (CHB) (Second interim decision)* [2018] UKUT 148 (AAC); *HMRC v Dakneviciute*, C-544/18 [2019]

12. **Retaining worker or self-employed status**

178 Art 7(3) EU Dir 2004/38; *Gusa v Minister for Social Protection (Ireland)*, C-442/16 [2017]; reg 6 I(EEA) Regs
179 *Saint Prix v SSWP*, C-507/12 [2014]; *HMRC v Dakneviciute*, C-544/18 [2019]
180 *Gusa v Minister for Social Protection (Ireland)*, C-442/16 [2017]
181 See, for example, *SB v SSWP (UC)* [2019] UKUT 219 (AAC)
182 *Saint Prix v SSWP*, C-507/12 [2014], paras 31 and 38; *Tarola v Minister for Social Protection*, C-483/17 [2019], para 26; *HMRC v Dakneviciute*, C-544/18 [2019], para 28; see also *Gusa v Minister for Social Protection (Ireland)*, C-442/16 [2017] AG Opinion, 26 July 2017, paras 67-79
183 *JS v SSWP (IS)* [2019] UKUT 135 (AAC)
184 Reg 5(4) A(IWR) Regs; reg 7A(4) I(EEA) Regs 2006, as saved by reg 45 and Sch 4 para 2 I(EEA) Regs
185 *SSWP v Gubeladze* [2019] UKSC 31 dismissed the SSWP's appeal from *SSWP v Gubeladze* [2017] EWCA Civ 1751, which had dismissed the SSWP's appeal from *TG v SSWP (PC)* [2015] UKUT 50 (AAC)
186 See, for example, *AM v SSWP (ESA)* [2019] UKUT 215 (AAC)
187 Art 7(3)(b) and (c) EU Dir 2004/38; *Gusa v Minister for Social Protection (Ireland)*, C-442/16 [2017]; reg 6(2)(b) and (c), (3), (4)(b) and (c) and (4A) I(EEA) Regs
188 Reg 6(2)(b) and (c), (3), (4)(b) and (c) and (4A)-(7) I(EEA) Regs
189 *KH v Bury MBC and SSWP* [2020] UKUT 50 (AAC), esp paras 4, 26, 36, 39 and 67

190 paras C1302 and C1403-4 ADM; DMG Memo 27/20, paras 11 and 14
191 CH/3314/2005, para 11; confirmed in *SSWP v EM (IS)* [2009] UKUT 146 (AAC), para 10; *SSWP v MK* [2013] UKUT 163 (AAC), paras 44-47; *SB v SSWP (UC)* [2019] UKUT 219 (AAC), paras 8-13
192 *Gusa v Minister for Social Protection (Ireland)*, C-442/16 [2017], paras 17 and 31
193 *SB v SSWP (UC)* [2019] UKUT 219 (AAC), paras 8-13
194 *SSWP v Elmi* [2011] EWCA Civ 1403; paras 072826-27 DMG
195 Art 7(3)(b) EU Dir 2004/38; *SSWP v MM (IS)* [2015] UKUT 128 (AAC), paras 53-54; *KH v Bury MBC and SSWP* [2020] UKUT 50 (AAC), paras 40-43
196 *SSWP v MM (IS)* [2015] UKUT 128 (AAC), paras 53-58
197 *SSWP v MM (IS)* [2015] UKUT 128 (AAC), paras 45-46
198 Reg 6(1)(e), (2)(b), (4)(b), (4C) and (7) I(EEA) Regs; *KH v Bury MBC and SSWP* [2020] UKUT 50 (AAC), esp paras 4, 26, 36, 39-44 and 67
199 paras C1302 and C1403-4 ADM; DMG Memo 27/20, paras 11 and 14
200 Reg 6(1), (2)(c), (3), (4)(c) and (4A) I(EEA) Regs
201 Art 7(3)(c) EU Dir 2004/38
202 *Tarola v Minister for Social Protection*, C-483/17 [2019]
203 *SB v SSWP (UC)* [2019] UKUT 219 (AAC)
204 Reg 6(1) and (7)-(10) I(EEA) Regs
205 Art 7(3)(d) EU Dir 2004/38; reg 6(1), (2)(d) and (e) and (4)(d) and (e) I(EEA)Regs
206 *SSWP v EM (IS)* [2009] UKUT 146 (AAC), para 10; see also *OB v SSWP (ESA)* [2017] UKUT 255 (AAC), para 32
207 *Brown v Secretary of State for Scotland*, C-197/86 [1988]
208 *Lair v Universität Hannover*, C-39/86 [1988], para 37
209 *Raulin v Minister van Onderwijs en Wetenschappen*, C-357/89 [1992], paras 18 and 19
210 Art 7(3)(a) EU Dir 2004/38; reg 6(2)(a) and (4)(a) I(EEA) Regs
211 CIS/4304/2007, para 35
212 *HK V SSWP (ESA)* [2017] UKUT 421 (AAC)
213 CIS/3182/2005
214 *SSHD v FB* [2010] UKUT 447 (IAC), para 23; *LM v HMRC (CHB)* [2016] UKUT 389 (AAC); *SSWP v LM (ESA)* [2017] UKUT 485 (AAC), paras 31-34
215 CIS/3890/2005
216 *De Brito v SSHD* [2012] EWCA Civ 709; *Konodyba v Royal Borough of Kensington and Chelsea* [2012] EWCA Civ 982; *Samin v Westminster CC* [2012] EWCA Civ 1468 (this part of the decision was not in dispute in the further appeal to the Supreme Court); *LM v HMRC (CHB)* [2016] UKUT 389 (AAC); *SSWP v LM (ESA)* [2017] UKUT 485 (AAC), paras 31-34
217 CIS/4237/2007
218 CIS/1042/2008; *HMRC v HD (Interim decision) and HMRC v GP* [2017] UKUT 11 (AAC); see also *HMRC v HD (CHB) (Second interim decision)* [2018] UKUT 148 (AAC), para 2
219 CIS/731/2007
220 CIS/4010/2006
221 *Saint Prix v SSWP*, C-507/12 [2014]; *SSWP v SFF and others* [2015] UKUT 502 (AAC), reported as [2016] AACR 16; *HMRC v Dakneviciute*, C-544/18 [2019]
222 *SSWP v SFF and Others* [2015] UKUT 502 (AAC), reported as [2016] AACR 16, para 35; confirmed in Vol 2 Ch 7 paras 073224 and 073230 DMG and para C1521 ADM
223 *SSWP v SFF and others* [2015] UKUT 502 (AAC), reported as [2016] AACR 16, para 26; *Weldemichael and Another v SSHD* [2015] UKUT 540 (IAC), paras 22-23
224 *HMRC v Dakneviciute*, C-544/18 [2019], paras 39-42; Vol 2 Ch 7, paras 073214-5 DMG; para C1528-9 ADM
225 *SSWP v SFF and Others* [2015] UKUT 502 (AAC), reported as [2016] AACR 16, paras 24 and 25
226 CIS/4304/2007, para 34; *SSWP v IR* [2009] UKUT 11 (AAC); *SSWP v SFF and Others* [2015] UKUT 502 (AAC), reported as [2016] AACR 16, para 40; *GE v SSWP (ESA)* [2017] UKUT 145 (AAC), reported as [2017] AACR 34, para 41
227 CIS/1934/2006; *SSWP v IR (IS)* [2009] UKUT 11 (AAC)
228 *SSWP v MK* [2013] UKUT 163 (AAC); *VP v SSWP (JSA)* [2014] UKUT 32 (AAC), reported as [2014] AACR 25, paras 56-61; *SSWP v MM (IS)* [2015] UKUT 128 (AAC), paras 47-52; *SSWP v LM (Interim decision) (ESA)* [2017] 485 (AAC), para 23; *FT v LB Islington and SSWP (HB)* [2015] UKUT 121 (AAC); *KH v Bury MBC and SSWP* [2020] UKUT 50 (AAC)
229 *HK V SSWP (ESA)* [2017] UKUT 421 (AAC), para 7

13. **Self-sufficient people and students**

230 Art 7(1) EU Dir 2004/38; regs 4(1)(c) and (2)-(4), 6(1) and 14(1) I(EEA) Regs
231 Art 7(1) EU Dir 2004/38; regs 4(1)(d) and (2)-(4), 6(1) and 14(1) I(EEA) Regs
232 *VP v SSWP (JSA)* [2014] UKUT 32 (AAC), reported as [2014] AACR 25, paras 88-97
233 Reg 4 I(EEA)Regs
234 Art 8(4) EU Dir 2004/38
235 Reg 4 I(EEA) Regs
236 *SG v Tameside MBC (HB)* [2010] UKUT 243 (AAC)
237 *Zhu and Chen v SSHD*, C-200/02 [2004]; *AMS v SSWP (PC)* [2017] UKUT 48 (AAC), para 62
238 *Commission of the European Communities v Kingdom of Belgium*, C-408/03 [2006]; *Zhu and Chen v SSHD*, C-200/02 [2004]
239 *VP v SSWP (JSA)* [2014] UKUT 32 (AAC), reported as [2014] AACR 25, paras 88-97
240 *VP v SSWP (JSA)* [2014] UKUT 32 (AAC), reported as [2014] AACR 25, para 94
241 *Singh and Others v Minister of Justice and Equality*, C-218/14 [2015]; see also *VI v HMRC*, C-247/20 [2022], para 26
242 *Bajratari v SSWP*, C-93/18 [2019]
243 *Pensionsversicherungsanstalt v Brey*, C-140/12 [2013], paras 54-57
244 CH/1400/2006; *SG v Tameside MBC (HB)* [2010] UKUT 243 (AAC); *Pensionsversicherungsanstalt v Brey*, C-140/12 [2013]
245 Vol 2 Ch 7 para 073244 DMG; para C1729 ADM
246 *Pensionsversicherungsanstalt v Brey*, C-140/12 [2013], paras 64 and 75-78; *AMS v SSWP (PC)* [2017] UKUT 48 (AAC)
247 *VP v SSWP (JSA)* [2014] UKUT 32 (AAC), reported as [2014] AACR 25, paras 77, 84 and 94
248 *AMS v SSWP (PC) (Final decision)* [2017] UKUT 381 (AAC), reported as [2018] AACR 27; see also *HK v SSWP (PC)* [2020] UKUT 73 (AAC), para 41
249 UA-2021-1684-USTA *SSWP v WV* heard 7 November 2022, awaiting judgment
250 See, for example, confirmation of this in relation to evidence of collective impact: *AMS v SSWP (PC) (Final decision)* [2017] UKUT 381 (AAC), reported as [2018] AACR 27, para 23
251 *VI v HMRC*, C-247/20 [2022], paras 66-70
252 *WH v Powys County Council and SSWP* [2022] UKUT 203 (AAC)
253 *FK (Kenya) v SSHD* [2010] EWCA Civ 1302; *VP v SSWP (JSA)* [2014] UKUT 32 (AAC), reported as [2014] AACR 25; *SSWP v LL (SPC)* [2014] UKUT 136 (AAC); *Ahmad v SSHD* [2014] EWCA Civ 988; see also *Cardiff CC v HM (HB)* [2019] UKUT 271 (AAC), para 19
254 European Commission press release, *Commission urges UK to ensure a comprehensive sickness insurance for EU citizens*, 30 October 2020; see also *A v Latvijas Republikas Veselibas ministrija*, C-535/19 [2021]
255 Art 87 WA 2019
256 *SG v Tameside MBC (HB)* [2010] UKUT 243 (AAC); *VP v SSWP (JSA)* [2014] UKUT 32 (AAC), reported as [2014] AACR 25; *SSWP v HH (SPC)* [2015] UKUT 583 (AAC); Vol 2 Ch 7 para 073246 DMG; para C1730 ADM
257 *SSWP v HH (SPC)* [2015] UKUT 583 (AAC); *AMS v SSWP (PC) (Final decision)* [2017] UKUT 381 (AAC), reported as [2018] AACR 27, paras 2 and 4-5; Vol 2 Ch 7 para 073246 DMG; para C1730 ADM
258 Arts 1(j) and (k) and 19 EU Reg 883/2004; *I v Health Services Executive*, C-255/13 [2014], para 59
259 *SSWP v GS (PC)* [2016] UKUT 394 (AAC), reported as [2017] AACR 7, paras 13-40; Vol 2 Ch 7 para 073246 DMG; para C1730 ADM; see also Decision S1 of 12 June 2009 of the Administrative Commission for the Co-ordination of Social Security Systems, C-106/08 [2010]
260 *W (China) and Another v SSHD* [2006] EWCA Civ 1494
261 *Baumbast and R v SSHD*, C-413/99 [2002]
262 *KS v SSWP* [2016] UKUT 269 (AAC), para 6; *SSWP v GS (PC)* [2016] UKUT 394 (AAC), reported as [2017] AACR 7, paras 42-46R; *B v SSWP* [2017] UKUT 472 (AAC), paras 72-73; see also *Cardiff CC v HM (HB)* [2019] UKUT 271 (AAC), para 19
263 *VI v HMRC*, C-247/20 [2022], para 70
264 *VI v HMRC*, C-247/20 [2022] paras 73-77, AG Opinion, 30 September 2021, para 53
265 Art 7(1) EU Dir 2004/38; regs 4(1)(d) and (2)-(5), 6(1) and 14(1) I(EEA) Regs
266 Reg 4(1)(d)(i) I(EEA) Regs
267 Reg 4(1)(d)(iii) I(EEA) Regs

268 *Grzelczyk v Centre Public d'aide Sociale d'Ottignies-Louvain-la-Neuve*, C-184/99 [2001]
269 Art 7(4) EU Dir 2004/38; reg 7(2) I(EEA) Regs
270 Art 7(4) EU Dir 2004/38

14. **Family members of European Economic Area nationals**

271 Arts 6(2) and 7(1)(d) and (2) EU Dir 2004/38; *Clauder*, C-E-4/11 [2011] EFTACR 216, para 43; regs 13(2) and 14(2) I(EEA) Regs
272 Regs 6 and 14(1) I(EEA) Regs. The same groups are covered in Arts 7 and 14 EU Dir 2004/38, although the term 'qualified person' is not used.
273 Art 2(2) EU Dir 2004/38; reg 7(1) I(EEA) Regs
274 Regs 7(3) and 8 I(EEA) Regs
275 *Aissatou Diatta v Land Berlin*, C-267/83 [1985] ECR I-00567
276 CF/1863/2007
277 CIS/2100/2007, which considers the findings of *Centre Public d'Aide Sociale de Courcelles v Lebon*, 316/85 [1987], *Zhu and Chen v SSHD*, C-200/02 [2004] and *Jia v Migrationsverket*, C-1/05 [2007]; *SSWP v MB (JSA) (and linked cases)* [2016] UKUT 372 (AAC), paras 132-39
278 *SSWP v MF (SPC)* [2018] UKUT 179 (AAC)
279 *Reyes v Migrationsverket*, C-423/12 [2014]; *Centre Publique d'Aide Social de Courcelles v Lebon* C-316/85 [1987] ECR 02811; *ECO v Lim (EEA dependency)* [2013] UKUT 437 (IAC)
280 *Singh v SSHD* [2022] EWCA Civ 1054
281 *Pedro v SSWP* [2009] EWCA Civ 1358. Arguably, this remains good law despite the assumptions made in *Reyes v Migrationsverket*, C-423/12 [2014].
282 *Centre Publique d'Aide Social de Courcelles v Lebon*, C-316/85 [1987] ECR I-02811, para 20; *SSWP v MB (JSA) (and linked cases)* [2016] UKUT 372 (AAC), reported as [2017] AACR 6, paras 132-39
283 Reg 7(3) I(EEA) Regs; CPC/3588/2006; *SS v SSWP (ESA)* [2011] UKUT 8 (AAC); *SSWP v LZ (SPC)* [2014] UKUT 147 (AAC); *Macastena v SSHD* [2018] EWCA Civ 1558; *SSHD v Aibangbee* [2019] EWCA Civ 339; *MW v SSWP (UC)* [2019] UKUT 184 (AAC); *AM v SSWP and CC Swansea Council* [2019] UKUT 361 (AAC), paras 19-21; para C1738 ADM; Vol 2 Ch 7 paras 073293-5 DMG; see also *Celik v SSHD* [2022] UKUT 220 (IAC)
284 Reg 7(3) and 8 I(EEA) Regs; the same groups are covered in Art 3 EU Dir 2004/38, but the term is not used
285 See CIS/612/2008 for discussion of the meaning of 'durable relationship'; *Singh (EEA, EFM)* [2021] UKUT 319 (IAC)
286 *SM v Entry Clearance Officer, UKVI*, C-129/18 [2019]
287 *TR (reg 8(3) EEA Regs 2006) Sri Lanka* [2008] UKAIT 4
288 *SSHD v Rahman and Others*, C-83/11 [2012]; *Oboh and Others v SSHD* [2013] EWCA Civ 1525; *Soares v SSHD* [2013] EWCA Civ 575; *AA (Algeria) v SSHD* [2014] EWCA Civ 1741; *Chowdhury v SSHD* [2021] EWCA Civ 1220; *Begum v SSHD* [2021] EWCA Civ 1878; *Sohrab and Others (continued household membership) Pakistan* [2022] UKUT 157 (IAC)
289 *Dauhoo (EEA Regs – Reg 8(2)) v SSHD* [2012] UKUT 79 (IAC)
290 *SM v Entry Clearance Officer, UKVI*, C-129/18 [2019]; reg 2(5)(c), I(EEA)A Regs 2019
291 Reg 8(7) I(EEA) Regs; see also *Soares v SSHD* [2013] EWCA Civ 575, in particular para 26; *SSHD v Rahman and Others*, C-83/11 [2012]; Recital 6 and Art 3(2) EU Dir 2004/38
292 Art 3(1) EU Dir 2004/38
293 Regs 1, 7(4) and Reg 9 I(EEA) Regs since 1 February 2017, and reg 4 and Sch 5 I(EEA) Regs for prior period from 25 November 2016; Art 21(1) TFEU; Arts 7(1) and (2) and 16(1) and (2) EU Dir 2004/38; *R v IAT and Singh ex parte SSHD*, C-370/90 [1992]; *Minister voor Vreemdelingenzaken en Integratie v Eind*, C-291/05 [2007]; *O and B v Minister voor Immigratie, Intergratie en Asiel*, C-456/12 [2014]; *Coman and Others v Inspectoratul General pentru Imigrari and Others*, C-673/16 [2018]
294 *SSHD v Banger*, C-89/17 [2018]
295 Reg 9 I(EEA) Regs; Reg 5(h) CR(ADTP) Regs; Sch 4 para 4(h) ISSC Regs
296 Confirmed in *B v SSWP* [2017] UKUT 472 (AAC), which reviews the relevant caselaw
297 Reg 5(h) CR(ADTP) Regs; Sch 3 para 6(h) and Sch 4 para 4(h) ISSC Regs

298 *HK v SSWP (SPC)* [2020] UKUT 73 (AAC); see also *FN v SSWP (UC)* [2022] UKUT 77 (AAC); *Minister voor Vreemdelingenzaken en Integratie v Eind*, C-291/05 [2007], para 45. The case relates to an earlier EU regulation, but the same reasoning applies to Art 7(2) EU Dir 2004/38. For an additional summary of *Eind*, see *B v SSWP* [2017] UKUT 472 (AAC), paras 33-39. See also DMG Memo 21/20 and ADM Memo 24/20.
299 Reg 9(1A) and (2)(d) I(EEA) Regs
300 *SSHD v Christy* [2018] EWCA Civ 2378
301 *O and B v Minister voor Immigratie, Integratie en Asiel*, C-456/12 [2014]; *ZA (Reg 9 EEA Regs; abuse of rights) Afghanistan* [2019] UKUT 281 (IAC), para 75; *VW v SSWP (PC)* [2014] UKUT 573 (AAC)
302 Reg 9(3) I(EEA) Regs
303 *ZA (Reg 9 EEA Regs; abuse of rights) Afghanistan* [2019] UKUT 281 (IAC)
304 *O and B v Minister voor Immigratie, Intergratie en Asiel*, C-456/12 [2014], in particular paras 51-56
305 Reg 9(4) I(EEA) Regs
306 *Mary Carpenter v SSHD*, C-60/00 [2002], para 46; *S and G v Minister voor Immigratie, Integratie en Asiel*, C-457/12 [2014]
307 *S and G v Minister voor Immigratie, Integratie en Asiel*, C-457/12 [2014]
308 Art 21(1) TFEU
309 *Lounes v SSHD*, C-165/16 [2017]
310 *AS v SSWP (UC)* [2018] UKUT 260 (AAC); *ODS v SSWP (UC)* [2019] UKUT 192 (AAC)
311 *Kovacevic (British citizen – Art 21 TFEU) Croatia* [2018] UKUT 273 (IAC)
312 Reg 2(1) I(EEA) Regs
313 Reg 9(A) I(EEA) Regs; reg 5(l) CR(ADTP) Regs; Sch 3 para 6(1)(i) and Sch 4 para 4(i) ISSC Regs
314 Reg 3 I(EEA)A Regs 2018
315 *Lounes v SSHD*, C-165/16 [2017]; *AS v SSWP (UC)* [2018] UKUT 260 (AAC); *ODS v SSWP (UC)* [2019] UKUT 192 (AAC); *Kovacevic (British citizen – Art 21 TFEU) Croatia* [2018] UKUT 273 (IAC)
316 *McCarthy v SSHD*, C-434-09 [2011]
317 Reg 2(1) I(EEA) Regs
318 *AA v SSWP* [2009] UKUT 249 (AAC); *HG v SSWP (SPC)* [2011] UKUT 382 (AAC)
319 Sch 3 I(EEA)A Regs 2012 up to, and Sch 6 para 9 I(EEA) Regs since, 1 February 2017; reg 10(e) CR(ADTP) Regs
320 Regs 10 and 14(3) I(EEA) Regs; reg 5(j) CR(ADTP) Regs; Sch 3 para 6(1)(j) and Sch 4 para 4(j) ISSC Regs
321 *Gauswami v SSHD* [2018] UKUT 275 (IAC)
322 *Baigazieva v SSHD* [2018] EWCA Civ 1088
323 *Gauswami v SSHD* [2018] UKUT 275 (IAC)
324 *SSHD v NA*, C-115/15 [2016]; reg 10(5)(b) I(EEA) Regs
325 Reg 14(3) I(EEA) Regs
326 Reg 10(8) and (9) I(EEA) Regs; *MK v SSWP (ESA)* [2020] 235 (AAC), para 11
327 Art 12 EU Dir 2004/38
328 Art 12 EU Dir 2004/38
329 *Baigazieva v SSHD* [2018] EWCA Civ 1088
330 Art 13 EU Dir 2004/38
331 *Singh and Others v Minister of Justice and Equality*, C-218-14 [2015]
332 *SSHD v NA*, C-115/15 [2016]
333 Arts 12(1) and 13(1) EU Dir 2004/38
334 *JP v SSWP (ESA)* [2018] UKUT 161 (AAC), paras 12-21; *GA v SSWP (SPC)* [2018] UKUT 172 (AAC), paras 27-44
335 Arts 12, 13 and 18 EU Dir 2004/38; *Ziolkowski and Szeja*, joined cases C-424/10 and C-425/10 [2011], para 44

15. **Derivative residence rights**
336 Reg 16 I(EEA) Regs
337 See also *London Borough of Harrow v Ibrahim and SSHD*, C-310/08 [2010]; *Teixeira v London Borough of Lambeth and SSHD*, C-480/08 [2010]; *GBC Echternach and A Moritz v Minister van Onderwijs en Wetenschappen*, joined cases 389/87 and 390/87 [1989]; *Baumbast and R v SSHD*, C-413/99 [2002]
338 See also *London Borough of Harrow v Ibrahim and SSHD*, C-310/08 [2010]; *Teixeira v London Borough of Lambeth and SSHD*, C-480/08 [2010]; *GBC Echternach and A Moritz v Minister van Onderwijs en Wetenschappen*, joined cases 389/87 and 390/87 [1989]; *Baumbast and R v SSHD*, C-413/99 [2002]
339 See also *Zhu and Chen v SSHD*, C-200/02 [2004]; *SSHD v NA*, C-115/15 [2016]
340 See also *Zambrano v ONEm*, C-34/09 [2011]; *Dereci and Others v Bundesministerium für Inneres*, C-256/11 [2011]
341 *FE v HMRC (CHB)* [2022] UKUT 4 (AAC); *VI v HMRC*, C -247/20 [2022]

342 Reg 16(1) I(EEA) Regs
343 Reg 16(7)(c) I(EEA) Regs
344 *JD v Jobcenter Krefeld*, C-181/19 [2020], especially paras 64, 71 and 79; see also *Fratila and Tanase v SSWP* [2020] EWCA Civ 1741, especially paras 42-55
345 *Sandwell MBC v KK and SSWP (HB)* [2022] UKUT 123 (AAC)
346 Art 10 EU Reg 492/2011 (before 1 June 2012, Art 12 EC Reg 1612/68 was in identical terms). See the emphasis on the state's duties in *MA v Department for Social Development (JSA)* [2011] NICom 205, para 13. See also comment in *HK v SSWP* [2017] UKUT 421 (AAC), para 10, which was cited in support in *AV v SSWP (UC)* CUC/1190/2019, paras 6-11.
347 *HMRC v IT (CTC)* [2016] UKUT 252 (AAC)
348 *SSWP v JS (IS)* [2010] UKUT 347
349 *DJ v SSWP* [2013] UKUT 113 (AAC)
350 Reg 16(3) I(EEA) Regs
351 Art 10 EU Reg 492/2011 (before 1 June 2012, Art 12 EC Reg 1612/68 was in identical terms)
352 *Baumbast and R v SSHD*, C-413/99 [2002]
353 *Bolton MBC v HY (HB)* [2018] UKUT 103 (AAC), reported as [2018] AACR 31, and caselaw cited
354 *Brown v The Secretary of State for Scotland*, C-197/86 [1988] ECR I-03205
355 *Teixeira v LB Lambeth and SSHD*, C-480/08 [2010], para 74; *Baumbast and R v SSHD*, C-413/99 [2002], para 63; *SSHD v NA*, C-115/15 [2016]
356 *Baumbast and R v SSHD*, C-413/99 [2002] ECR I-07091, para 57; *Alarape and Tijani (Article 12, EC Reg 1612/68) Nigeria* [2011] UKUT 413 (IAC), paras 28-29
357 *JS v SSWP (ESA)* [2016] UKUT 314 (AAC)
358 *IP v SSWP (IS)* [2015] UKUT 691 (AAC)
359 *MS v SSWP (IS)* [2016] UKUT 348 (AAC)
360 *SM v Entry Clearance Officer, UKVI*, C-129/18 [2019]
361 *Hrabkova v SSWP* [2017] EWCA Civ 794 – permission to appeal to UKSC refused
362 Arts 24(1)(h) and (2) and 25(1)(b) and (2) WA 2019; Arts 23(1)(h) and (2) and 24(1)(b) and (2) UK-EFTA
363 ADM Memo 33/20, para 53; DMG Memo 29/20, para 53
364 CIS/3960/2007
365 *SSWP v IM (IS)* [2011] UKUT 231 (AAC), paras 17 and 28
366 *Shabani v SSHD* [2013] UKUT 315 (IAC)
367 Reg 16(7)(a) I(EEA) Regs
368 Art 10 EU Reg 492/2011; *Landesamt für Ausbildungsförderung Nordrhein-Westfalen v Lubor Gaal*, C-7/94 [1995], paras 24 and 25; *Teixeira v LB Lambeth and SSHD*, C-480/08 [2010], paras 76-87; *Alarape and Tijani v SSHD*, C-529/11 [2013], paras 24, 25 and 31
369 Reg 16(7)(b) I(EEA)Regs
370 Reg 10 EU Reg 492/2011 (before 1 June 2012, Art 12 EC Reg 1612/68 was in identical terms)
371 *London Borough of Harrow v Ibrahim and SSHD*, C-310/08 [2010]; *Teixeira v London Borough of Lambeth and SSHD*, C-480/08 [2010] ECR I-01107; *Baumbast and R v SSHD*, C-413/99 [2002]; *SSWP v Czop* and *SSWP v Punakova*, joined cases, C-147/11 and C-148/11 [2012]; *Landesamt für Ausbildungsförderung Nordrhein-Westfalen v Lubor Gaal*, C-7/94 [1995]
372 Vol 2 Ch 7 para 073400-1 DMG
373 *Echternach and Moritz v Netherlands Minister for Education and Science*, joined cases 389/87 and 390/87 [1989], paras 18-23
374 Reg 16(1) and (4) I(EEA) Regs
375 Art 10 EU Reg 492/2011 (before 1 June 2012, Art 12 EC Reg 1612/68 was in identical terms)
376 *Baumbast and R v SSHD*, C-413/99 [2002]
377 *Teixeira v LB Lambeth and SSHD*, C-480/08 [2010], paras 84-86; *Alarape and Tijani v SSHD*, C-529/11 [2013]
378 *Teixeira v LB Lambeth and SSHD*, C-480/08 [2010], para 3
379 *Baumbast and R v SSHD*, C-413/99 [2002], para 75; see also *SSWP v RR (IS)* [2013] UKUT 21 (AAC), reported as [2013] AACR 20, paras 75-76
380 Reg 16(1),(3),(4) and (7)(c) I(EEA) Regs
381 *Hrabkova v SSWP* [2017] EWCA Civ 794 – permission to appeal to UKSC refused
382 Arts 24(1)(h) and (2) and 25(1)(b) and (2) WA 2019; Arts 23(1)(h) and (2) and 24(1)(b) and (2) UK-EFTA
383 ADM Memo 33/20, para 53; DMG Memo 29/20, para 53
384 Reg 16(8) I(EEA) Regs
385 Reg 16(11) I(EEA) Regs
386 *Chavez-Vilchez and Others v Raad van bestuur van de Sociale verzekeringsbank*, C-133/15 [2017]; Vol 2 Ch7 paras 073385 and 073389 DMG; paras C1829 and C1833 ADM; see also *Patel and Shah v SSHD* [2019] UKSC 59

387 Reg 16(8)-(10) I(EEA) Regs; *MA v Department for Social Development (JSA)* [2011] NICom 205, para 13; Vol 2 Ch7 paras 073386 and 073403 DMG; paras C1830-1 and C1834 ADM
388 Regs 4(c) and 16(1) and (2) I(EEA) Regs
389 *Zhu and Chen v SSHD*, C-200/02 [2004]; see also *Alokpa and Moudoulou v Ministre du Travail, de l'Emploi et de l'Immigration*, C-86/12 [2013], paras 27-29; *SSHD v NA*, C-115/15 [2016]; *Bajratari v SSHD*, C-93/18, AG Opinion, 19 June 2019
390 Reg 4(3) and (5) I(EEA) Regs; Vol 2 Ch 7 Part 3 para 073387 DMG; para C1832 ADM
391 *VI v HMRC*, C-247/20 [2022], in particular paras 61-72
392 *VI v HMRC*, C-247/20 [2022], in particular paras 53-60; see also AG Opinion, 30 September 2021
393 Reg 16(1) and (5) I(EEA) Regs
394 *Zambrano v ONEm*, C-34/09 [2011]; *Dereci and Others v Bundesministerium für Inneres*, C-256/11 [2011]
395 *A v Belgium*, C-82/16 [2018]; *Patel and Shah v SSHD* [2019] UKSC 59; see, for example, *DM v SSWP (PIP)* [2019] UKUT 26 (AAC)
396 Reg 16(1) and (6) I(EEA) Regs
397 *FE v HMRC (CHB)* [2022] UKUT 4 (AAC); *VI v HMRC*, C-247/20 [2022], esp paras 58-60
398 *AM v SSWP and CC Swansea Council* [2019] UKUT 361 (AAC), selected for reporting as [2020] AACR 17, paras 49-64
399 Reg 16(6) I(EEA) Regs
400 *Hrabkova v SSWP* [2017] EWCA Civ 794
401 Arts 24(1)(h) and (2) and 25(1)(b) and (2) WA 2019; Arts 23(1)(h) and (2) and 24(1)(b) and (2) UK-EFTA
402 ADM Memo 33/20, para 53; DMG Memo 29/20, para 53
403 *HMRC v HEH and SSWP (TC and CHB)* [2018] UKUT 237 (AAC)

16. **Permanent right to reside**
404 Art 16(1) EU Dir 2004/38
405 Art 16(4) EU Dir 2004/38; reg 15(3) I(EEA) Regs
406 Regs 3(5)(c) and 4(6)(d) CR(ADTP) Regs
407 Art 16(1) and (2) EU Dir 2004/38; reg 15(1) I(EEA) Regs
408 Art 16(1) and (2) EU Dir 2004/38; reg 15(1)(a) and (b) and Sch 6 para 8 I(EEA) Regs; reg 6(e) CR(ADTP) Regs; Sch 4 para 4(m) ISSC Regs
409 Arts 7 and 16(1) and (2) EU Dir 2004/38; regs 6, 7, 14 and 15 I(EEA) Regs; *Ziolkowski and Szeja v Land Berlin*, joined cases C-424/10 and C-425/10 [2011]
410 *SSWP v Lassal*, C-162/09 [2010]; *SSWP v Dias*, C-325/09 [2011]; Sch 6 para 8(4) I(EEA) Regs
411 Regs 6(1)(a), 7, 14(1) and (2) and 15(1) and Sch 6 para 8 I(EEA) Regs; *GE v SSWP (ESA)* [2017] UKUT 145 (AAC), reported as [2017] AACR 34
412 Vol 2 Ch 7 para 073428 DMG; para C1807 ADM; HB Circular A8/15, para 19
413 Vol 2 Ch 7 para 073443 DMG; HB Circular A8/15, para 27
414 *GE v SSWP (ESA)* [2017] UKUT 145 (AAC), reported as [2017] AACR 34, para 46
415 Vol 2 Ch 7 para 073442 DMG; HB Circular A8/15, para 26
416 *Ziolkowski and Szeja*, joined cases C-424/10 and C-425/10 [2011]
417 Regs 13 and 15(1) I(EEA) Regs; *GE v SSWP (ESA)* [2017] UKUT 145 (AAC), reported as [2017] AACR 34
418 *Ziolkowski and Szeja*, joined cases C-424/10 and C-425/10 [2011]; *GE v SSWP (ESA)* [2017] UKUT 145 (AAC), reported as [2017] AACR 34, paras 59-66
419 *Macastena v SSHD* [2018] EWCA Civ 1558; *SSHD v Aibangbee* [2019] EWCA Civ 339; *MW v SSWP (UC)* [2019] UKUT 184 (AAC)
420 Reg 14(2) I(EEA) Regs; *Clauder*, C-E-4/11 [2011] EFTACR 216, para 43
421 Regs 14(2) and 15(1)(a) and (b) I(EEA) Regs
422 Reg 15(1)(f) I(EEA) Regs
423 Reg 10(6) I(EEA) Regs; Arts 12, 13 and 18 EU Dir 2004/38; *Ziolkowski and Szeja*, joined cases C-424/10 and C-425/10 [2011]
424 Reg 10(3) and (4) I(EEA) Regs
425 *Ziolkowski and Szeja*, joined cases C-424/10 and C-425/10 [2011]
426 Sch 4 para 4(m) ISSC Regs; reg 15 I(EEA) Regs
427 Arts 12(2), 13(2) and 18 EU Dir 2004/38
428 Reg 9A(3) and (4) I(EEA) Regs
429 *SSWP v Gubeladze* [2019] UKSC 31 dismissed the SSWP's appeal from *SSWP v Gubeladze* [2017] EWCA Civ 1751, which had dismissed the SSWP's appeal from *TG v SSWP (PC)* [2015] UKUT 50 (AAC)

430 *JK v SSWP (SPC)* [2017] UKUT 179 (AAC); see also *SSWP v LM (ESA) (Interim decision)* [2017] UKUT 485 (AAC), paras 22-24
431 *Ziolkowski and Szeja*, joined cases C-424/10 and C-425/10 [2011]; Sch 6 para 8(1) and (3) I(EEA) Regs; *SSWP v LS (IS)* [2012] UKUT 207 (AAC)
432 *Oakfor and Others v SSHD* [2011] EWCA Civ 499; *Alarape and Tijani v SSHD*, C-529/11 [2013]; *Bee and Another v SSHD* [2013] UKUT 83 (IAC); reg 15(2) I(EEA) Regs
433 Art 16(1) EU Dir 2004/38; reg 15(1) I(EEA) Regs
434 Regs 3(5)(b) & 4(6)(c) CR(ADTP) Regs; reg 3 I(EEA) Regs
435 Art 16(3) EU Dir 2004/38; reg 3 I(EEA) Regs
436 *Babajanov v SSHD* [2013] UKUT 513 (IAC)
437 *Idezuna v SSHD* [2011] UKUT 474 (IAC); *Babajanov v SSHD* [2013] UKUT 513 (IAC)
438 Vol 2 Ch 7 paras 073360 and 073417 DMG; para C1796 ADM; HB Circular A8/2015, para 7; CIS/2258/08
439 *OB v SSWP (ESA)* [2017] UKUT 255 (AAC), para 28
440 Reg 3(3) I(EEA) Regs; Sch 3 para 6(1)(b) and Sch 4 para 4(b) ISSC Regs
441 Reg 23(9) I(EEA) Regs
442 *Silva v SSHD* CO/2344/2021 – see insights.doughtystreet.co.uk/post/102hevp/deportation-order-does-not-terminate-eu-right-to-reside
443 *OB v SSWP (ESA)* [2017] UKUT 255 (AAC), paras 29-30 and 34; see also *AP v SSWP (IS)* [2018] UKUT 307 (AAC), paras 15-18, and *ODS v SSWP (UC)* [2019] UKUT 192 (AAC), para 22
444 Following *SSWP v Dias*, C-325/09 [2011] ECR I-06387; see also *Saint Prix v SSWP*, C-507/12 [2014], paras 45 and 46, and *HMRC v Dakneviciute*, C-544/18 [2019], para 40
445 *SSHD v Ojo* [2015] EWCA Civ 1301, para 20
446 For example, there is no discussion of *Saint Prix v SSWP*, C-507/12 [2014], paras 45 and 46
447 *OB v SSWP (ESA)* [2017] UKUT 255 (AAC), paras 29-30 and 34; see also *AP v SSWP (IS)* [2018] UKUT 307 (AAC), paras 15-18, and *ODS v SSWP (UC)* [2019] 192 (AAC), para 22
448 *Cardiff CC v HM (HB)* [2019] UKUT 271 (AAC)
449 Vol 2 Ch 7 paras 073433-35 DMG; paras C1812-14 ADM; HB Circular A8/2015, paras 20-22
450 Vol 2 Ch 7 para 073442 DMG; para C1820 ADM; HB Circular A8/15, para 26
451 Vol 2 Ch 7 para 073443 DMG; para C1821 ADM; HB Circular A8/15, para 27
452 *GE v SSWP (ESA)* [2017] UKUT 145 (AAC), reported as [2017] AACR 34, para 46; *SSWP v WN (rule 17)* [2018] UKUT 268 (AAC)
453 *Onuekwere v SSHD*, C-378/12 [2014], esp paras 24-26
454 reg 3(1), (3)(a) and (4) I(EEA) Regs; Art 28(3) EU Dir 2004/38; *Vomero v SSHD* and *B v Land Baden-Württemberg*, joined cases, C-424/16 and C-316/16 [2019]; *SSHD v Viscu* [2019] EWCA Civ 1052
455 *SSHD v JO (Qualified person – hospital order – effect) Slovakia* [2012] UKUT 237 (IAC)
456 Regs 3(5)(b) and 4(6)(c) CR(ADTP) Regs; reg 3(3)(a) and (4) I(EEA) Regs
457 Sch 6 para 8(4) I(EEA) Regs
458 Art 16(4) EU Dir 2004/38
459 *SSWP v Dias*, C-325/09 [2011]; see also *SSWP v Lassal*, C-162/09 [2010]
460 Regs 5 and 15 I(EEA) Regs; Art 17 EU Dir 2004/38
461 *JP v SSWP (ESA)* [2018] UKUT 161 (AAC), paras 2, 4, 23-40 and 24
462 *SSHD v FB* [2010] UKUT 447 (IAC), para 23; *LM v HMRC (CHB)* [2016] UKUT 389 (AAC); *SSWP v LM (ESA)* [2017] UKUT 485 (AAC); see also *BL v SSWP (ESA)* [2019] UKUT 364 (AAC), paras 20-23
463 Reg 5(7) I(EEA) Regs; Art 17(1) EU Dir 2004/38
464 Regs 5(7) and 6(2) I(EEA) Regs; regs 7A(3) and 7B(3) I(EEA) Regs 2006, as saved by reg 45 and Sch 4 para 2 I(EEA) Regs
465 *NZ v SSWP (ESA) (Third interim decision)* [2017] UKUT 360 (AAC); see also *SSWP v NZ (ESA) (Final decision)* [2019] UKUT 250 (AAC)
466 *De Brito v SSHD* [2012] EWCA Civ 709
467 *SSWP v Gubeladze* [2019] UKSC 31; see also *AT v Pensionsversicherungsanstalt*, C-32/19 [2020]
468 *ID v SSWP (IS)* [2011] UKUT 401 (AAC), paras 17 and 18
469 *SSWP v NZ (ESA) (Final decision)* [2019] UKUT 250 (AAC)
470 *PM (EEA – spouse – 'residing with') Turkey* [2011] UKUT 89 (IAC)

471 Art 17(3) EU Dir 2004/38; see also *RM (Zimbabwe) v SSHD* [2013] EWCA Civ 775, para 56 – cited in *TG v SSWP (PC)* [2015] UKUT 50 (AAC), para 33, and *JP v SSWP (ESA)* [2018] UKUT 161 (AAC), paras 5 (footnote 1) and 42; paras 62-64 of the AG's Opinion in *Givane*, C-257/00 [2003], although the ECJ did not address the issue itself
472 Reg 15(1)(d) I(EEA) Regs
473 Art 16(4) EU Dir 2004/38; reg 15(3) I(EEA) Regs – note that the words 'only' and 'consecutive' were removed from these regulations from 1 February 2017, but EU law has not changed and should be followed
474 Part 4 I(EEA) Regs
475 Regs 3(5)(c) and 4(6)(d) CR(ADTP) Regs
476 Vol 2 Ch 7 paras 073350-68 and 073414-43 DMG; paras C1750-77 and C1793-824 ADM; HB Circular A8/2015
477 Vol 2 Ch 7 paras 073429-32 DMG; para C1810 ADM

17. **Frontier worker**

478 Regs 3 and 4 CR(FW) Regs; Arts 45 and 49 TFEU; Arts 24 and 25 WA 2019; Arts 23 and 24 UK-EFTA; Arts 20 and 23 UK-Swiss Agreement; ADM Memo 33/20; DMG Memo 29/20
479 Regs 3(2) CR(FW) Regs
480 Regs 3(3) CR(FW) Regs
481 Arts 24 and 25 WA 2019; Arts 23 and 24 UK-EFTA; Arts 20 and 23 UK-Swiss Agreement; Arts 45 and 49 TFEU; EU Reg 492/2011
482 ADM Memo 33/20, para 51; DMG Memo 29/20, para 51
483 Arts 24(1)(h) and (2) and 25(1)(b) and (2) WA 2019; Arts 23(1)(h) and (2) and 24(1)(b) and (2) UK-EFTA; EU Reg 492/2011; ADM Memo 33/20, paras 35 and 53; DMG Memo 29/20, paras 35 and 53

18. **Other European freedom of movement residence rights**

484 Arts 20 and 21 TFEU
485 For discussion of this principle of deterrence, see *B v SSWP* [2017] UKUT 472 (AAC), paras 25-29, 39, 49 and 62-63
486 *Sanneh v SSWP (and linked cases)* [2015] EWCA Civ 49, paras 6-7 and 71-3; see also *LO v SSWP (IS)* [2017] UKUT 440 (AAC)
487 *Mirga v SSWP* [2016] UKSC 1; see also *MM v SSWP (ESA)* [2017] UKUT 437 (AAC); *LO v SSWP (IS)* [2017] UKUT 440 (AAC); *JS v SSWP (IS)* [2019] UKUT 135 (AAC)

Chapter 13

Residence and presence: rules for individual benefits

This chapter covers:

This chapter explains the residence and presence rules for each benefit. It also covers how you may be assisted by the European Union (EU) co-ordination rules. Further information on the different residence and presence tests is in Chapter 10, further information on the habitual residence and right to reside tests is in Chapter 11 and further information on the EU co-ordination rules is in Chapter 16. This chapter does not explain the rules on being paid while you are abroad. These are covered in Part 5.

1. Means-tested benefits

To be entitled to **universal credit (UC), income support (IS), income-based jobseeker's allowance (JSA), income-related employment and support allowance (ESA), housing benefit (HB) and pension credit (PC)**, you (and your partner for joint-claim JSA or UC) must:

- be present in Great Britain (although for HB see below) (see p142);[1] *and*
- satisfy the habitual residence test (see p156), unless you are exempt (see p159).[2]

To satisfy the habitual residence test for these benefits, you must:

- be 'habitually resident in fact' in the common travel area (the UK, Ireland, Channel Islands and the Isle of Man);
- have a right to reside in the common travel area (but see p174 if you have been receiving benefit since April 2004).

Although it is no longer possible to make a new claim for IS, income-based JSA or income-related ESA, if you are already receiving one of these benefits you must continue to satisfy the above requirements to remain entitled.

To be entitled to HB, although there is no requirement to be present in Great Britain, the HB rules on occupying your home have the same effect and mean that you can cease to be entitled if you go abroad.[3] However, in certain circumstances you are treated as occupying your home while you are temporarily absent from your home and outside Great Britain, and your entitlement can therefore continue while you are abroad for limited periods (see p335).

For the means-tested benefits other than HB, in certain circumstances you are treated as present in Great Britain during a temporary absence, so you can continue to receive these benefits while you are abroad for limited periods (see p339).

For all means-tested benefits, the habitual residence test applies to the claimant.

If you live with a partner and claim UC or joint-claim JSA, the habitual residence test applies to both of you, as you are both claimants.

If you satisfy the habitual residence test but your partner does not:

- for UC if you are both under pension age, or you are under pension age and your partner has reached pension age, your joint claim is treated as a claim for UC as a single person, but your partner's income and capital are taken into account (see p158);
- for UC if you have reached pension age and your partner is under pension age, your claim is not treated as a single claim for UC. Instead, you can claim PC and HB and you are treated as a single person for each of these claims (see p158);
- for joint-claim JSA, you do not need to make a joint claim and are still paid as a couple (see p158).

Note:

- To be entitled to the carer element in UC, you must satisfy all the conditions of entitlement to carer's allowance (except the earnings limit), including the 'past presence test' (see p302).[4]
- If you receive a benefit paid by another state, for the purpose of calculating UC this is treated in the same way as a UK benefit, if the foreign benefit is 'analogous to' the UK benefit or is a state retirement pension.[5]

- If you claimed UC before 25 July 2022, and it was refused on the basis that you failed the habitual residence test, it may be arguable that this did not terminate an existing award of HB, IS, child tax credit (CTC) or working tax credit (WTC) (see point 11 on p162).[6]

If your partner is abroad

If your partner is abroad, the effect this has on your benefit depends on whether the separation is permanent or, if temporary, whether you still count as members of the same household.

If you separate permanently (ie, you do not intend to resume living together), you no longer count as a couple and must claim as a single person.[7] Your partner's income and capital no longer affect your benefit.

If you are still regarded as a couple, your partner's absence abroad can affect your benefit in two ways.

- At some point, you will cease to be paid an amount of benefit for your partner.
- Your partner's capital and income can continue to affect your entitlement.

If you and your partner are living apart temporarily, you continue to count as a couple because you are still treated as members of the same household, unless:[8]

- **for UC**, you have been separated (or expect to be separated) for more than six months;
- **for IS, income-based JSA, income-related ESA, PC and HB**, you are likely to be separated for more than 52 weeks. However, you still count as a couple if you are unlikely to be separated for 'substantially' longer than 52 weeks and there are exceptional circumstances, such as a stay in hospital, or if you have no control over the length of the absence;
- **for IS, income-based JSA, income-related ESA and PC**, you or your partner are detained in custody or in a high-security psychiatric hospital, or are on temporary release, or are living permanently in a care home.

Your partner's absence is from *you*, not from the family home, so these rules can apply even if your partner has never lived in your current home, and your former household need not have been in this country.[9] However, you must have been living with your partner in the same household before you can be treated as continuing to be members of that household.[10]

If the question of whether you or your partner intend to resume living together is relevant, your intention must be 'unqualified'. This means that it must not depend on a factor over which you have no control – eg, the right of entry to the UK being granted by the Home Office[11] or the offer of a suitable job.[12]

If you still count as a couple, you may be able to continue to receive an amount of benefit for your partner while they are abroad for a limited period. The rules vary between the different means-tested benefits (see Chapter 15).

Once you stop being paid for your partner because these rules do not apply, or at the end of the limited period:

- **for UC**, you cease to be entitled as joint claimants and must notify the DWP. Your award is based on the maximum amount for a single person, but your partner's income and capital are taken into account until you have been, or you expect to be, apart for six months (as then you cease to be treated as a couple).[13] **Note:**
  - if your partner's absence abroad means they are no longer habitually resident in the common travel area, your joint claim is then *treated as* a claim by you as a single person and you are paid allowances as a single person, but your partner's income and capital are taken into account (see p158), *until* you have been, or you expect to be, apart for six months (because then you cease to be treated as a couple). Once you cease to be treated as a couple, you are treated as having claimed as a single person;[14]
  - if you are claiming UC jointly with your partner who is under pension age and you have reached pension age, once they stop being treated as present in the UK or cease to be habitually resident in the common travel area, you stop being entitled to UC. Instead you can claim PC and HB, and you are treated as a single person for each of these claims;[15]
- **for IS, income-based JSA, income-related ESA and HB**, your applicable amount no longer includes an amount for your partner. However, your partner's capital, income and work are still taken into account as they are still treated as part of your household;[16]
- **for PC**, you are paid as a single person. Your partner's income and capital are ignored because they are no longer treated as part of your household.[17]

Note: if you have reached pension age and your partner is under pension age and you cease to be paid PC or HB for your partner because they are abroad, when they return you will need to make a joint claim for UC. However, note that if your partner fails the habitual residence test, you will not be entitled to UC, but you can instead claim PC and HB, and you are treated as a single person for each of these claims (see p158).[18]

If your child is abroad

If you have a child who is abroad, the effect this has on your benefit depends on whether, for **UC and PC**, you are still treated as responsible for them, or for the **other means-tested benefits**, they are still treated as being part of your household despite temporarily living away from you.

If your child ceases to be included in your claim, you are no longer paid benefit for them. Other aspects of your benefit entitlement may also be affected if you no longer have a child included in your claim – eg, your work-related requirements may change or the number of bedrooms you are allowed in your UC housing costs or HB calculation may change. For further details, see CPAG's *Welfare Benefits and Tax Credits Handbook*.

For UC, you cease to be responsible for a child if they are absent from your household and the absence exceeds, or is expected to exceed, one month or, in limited circumstances, two or six months (see p341).[19]

For PC, you cease to be responsible for a child if they are, or are expected to be, absent from Great Britain for four weeks or, in limited circumstances, eight or 26 weeks (see p349).[20]

For the **other means-tested benefits**, they cease to be treated as part of your household if:[21]

- **for IS, JSA, ESA and HB**, they are not living with you and:
  - have no intention of resuming living with you; *or*
  - are likely to be absent for more than 52 weeks, unless there are exceptional circumstances, such as being in hospital, or if you have no control over the length of absence and the absence is unlikely to be substantially longer than 52 weeks;
- **for IS, JSA and ESA**, they are not living with you and have been abroad for more than:
  - four weeks; *or*
  - eight weeks (26 weeks for ESA) to get medical treatment;
- there are other reasons that are not related to residence or presence, such as being fostered. See CPAG's *Welfare Benefits and Tax Credits Handbook* for more information.

For IS or income-based JSA, once your child stops being treated as part of your household, they are no longer included in your applicable amount. If they return to your household, you must, unless you have another child included in your applicable amount, claim UC instead. See p343 for IS and p345 for income-based JSA.

Note: you can only be paid means-tested benefits and CTC for your third and subsequent child in limited circumstances (due to the 'two-child limit'). These include (for UC and HB) certain transitional rules which may no longer apply if your child returns from abroad after payments for them (or your claim) ended because they were no longer part of your household, although HB is always paid for a child for whom you receive a CTC element.

For HB, UC, IS and income-based JSA, if you have adopted a child or they have been placed with you for adoption, this is generally an exception that means you can be paid for the child even if they are your third or subsequent child. However, this does not apply if you adopted the child under the law of another country before the adoption under UK law.[22]

The rules on the 'two-child limit' and the exceptions vary between the benefits. Check the details of the benefit you are claiming in CPAG's *Welfare Benefits and Tax Credits Handbook*.

European Union co-ordination rules

If you are covered by the main European Union (EU) co-ordination rules (see p379), these can assist you to satisfy the habitual residence test for **PC** sooner. That is because you cannot be denied this category of benefit solely on the basis that your length of actual residence is too short, since the period of your residence is only one relevant factor in determining whether you are 'habitually resident in fact' and can be outweighed by others (see p167).[23]

UC, IS and HB are not covered by the main EU co-ordination rules and neither the UK–EU Protocol nor the UK–Ireland Convention can assist you to be entitled to any of the means-tested benefits (see p392). However, other equal treatment provisions of EU law may assist (see p414).

Reciprocal agreements

Most means-tested benefits are not covered by reciprocal agreements. One exception is the agreement between Great Britain and Northern Ireland which, since 6 April 2016, has covered income-related ESA (as well as contributory ESA) and, since 27 November 2016, has covered income-based JSA (as well as contribution-based JSA)[24] and, since 24 July 2020, has covered UC.[25] See p435 for further details.

2. Bereavement benefits

To be entitled to bereavement support payment, you must be ordinarily resident (see p147) in Great Britain (or Sark – see p441) on the date your spouse or civil partner died.[26]

You do not need to satisfy any residence or presence rules to be entitled to widowed parent's allowance.

European Union co-ordination rules

If you are covered by the main European Union (EU) co-ordination rules or the UK–EU Protocol or, for situations involving the UK and Ireland only, the UK–Ireland Convention (see p379), and the UK is your 'competent state' (see p399):[27]

- you can, if necessary, rely on national insurance contributions paid by your late spouse or civil partner in one or more European Economic Area (EEA) countries (EU if relying on the UK–EU Protocol, or Ireland if you are relying on the UK–Ireland Convention) to calculate your entitlement to bereavement benefits (under the 'aggregation principle' – see p416); *and*
- the bereavement support payment requirement to be ordinarily resident in Great Britain on the date your spouse or civil partner died does not apply if you were resident in an EEA country (EU country/Ireland) on that date.

If you have moved to the UK from an EEA state (or EU state or Ireland) that was paying you a bereavement benefit, you may be able to continue to receive this (referred to as 'exporting' the benefit – see p419) if that state remains the competent state to pay that benefit.

Reciprocal and other international agreements

If your late spouse or civil partner lived and worked in a country with which the UK has a reciprocal agreement (see p433), periods of insurance paid in that country can count towards your bereavement benefit entitlement.

If the agreement treats you as being present in the UK while in the other country and you were ordinarily resident in that country on the date your spouse or civil partner died, you are treated as ordinarily resident in Great Britain on that date.[28] Guidance lists the relevant countries.[29]

Note: the reciprocal agreements were amended to include, from 6 April 2017, bereavement support payment.[30]

If your late spouse or civil partner was covered by an international agreement between the EU and another country, you may be able to count periods of insurance they paid in the relevant country towards your bereavement benefit entitlement (see p445).

For more information on reciprocal and other international agreements, see Chapter 17.

3. Child benefit, Scottish child payment and guardian's allowance

Child benefit

To be entitled to child benefit, you and your child(ren) must be present in Great Britain (see p142).[31]

You (but not your child) are treated as not present and, therefore, not eligible for child benefit if:[32]

- you are not ordinarily resident in the UK (see p147); *or*
- you do not have a right to reside in the UK (see p168); *or*
- you have not been living in the UK for the three months prior to your claim, unless you are exempt (see p143).

Note: you do not need to have a right to reside if you claimed child benefit before 1 May 2004 and you have been receiving it continuously since that date (see p177).

You are treated as present if you are:[33]

- a Crown servant posted overseas and:
  - you are, or immediately before your posting abroad you were, ordinarily resident in the UK; *or*
  - immediately before your posting you were in the UK in connection with that posting; *or*
- the partner of a Crown servant posted overseas and in the same country as them, or temporarily absent from that country under the same exceptions that enable child benefit to continue during a temporary absence from Great Britain (see p351).

You are treated as ordinarily resident if you are in the UK as a result of your being deported or legally removed from another country.[34]

You and/or your child can be treated as present for limited periods during a temporary absence (see p351).

While you are treated as present, you continue to satisfy that condition of entitlement. This means that you can continue to receive child benefit if it is already being paid and you can also make a fresh claim during your, or your child's, absence. If you, or your child, spend longer abroad than the permitted periods (see p351), you (or they) cease to satisfy the presence condition and your entitlement to child benefit ends.

Note: if you or your child are treated as present, you must satisfy all the other conditions of entitlement including, if your child is not living with you, contributing to the costs of the child at least the amount of child benefit that would be payable for them.[35]

Scottish child payment

To be entitled to a Scottish child payment, you must be ordinarily resident (see p147) in Scotland[36] in addition to receiving a qualifying benefit (a means-tested benefit or tax credit).

Guardian's allowance

Entitlement to guardian's allowance depends on entitlement to child benefit, so you must meet the above conditions for child benefit. In addition, at least one of the child's parents must have:[37]

- been born in the UK or a European Economic Area (EEA) country; *or*
- spent a total of 52 weeks in any two-year period in Great Britain at some time after reaching the age of 16.

In order to satisfy the second condition above, you are treated as being present in Great Britain during any absence abroad which is due to your employment as a serving member of the armed forces, an airman or airwoman, mariner or continental shelf worker.

European Union co-ordination rules

If you are covered by the main European Union (EU) co-ordination rules or, for situations involving the UK and Ireland only, the UK–Ireland Convention (see p379), you may be able to:

- use certain periods of residence in an EEA country (Ireland, if relying on the convention) to satisfy the child benefit requirement to have been 'living in' the UK for the past three months (under the 'aggregation principle' – see p416). For further information, including on HM Revenue and Customs guidance that suggests this only applies to residence in four EEA countries, see p144;
- use time spent in an EEA country (Ireland, if relying on the convention) to satisfy the guardian's allowance requirement to have spent 52 weeks in any two-year period in Great Britain (under the 'aggregation principle' – see p416). It may also be arguable that this condition should not apply to you if you are covered by the co-ordination rules and have a 'genuine and sufficient link to the UK' (see p307);[38]
- be paid for a child resident in an EEA country (Ireland, if relying on the convention) without their needing to satisfy the UK rules on temporary absences. However, you must still satisfy all the other conditions of entitlement, including contributing to the costs of the child an amount at least equal to the amount of child benefit payable for that child;[39]
- continue to receive a family benefit from an EEA state (Ireland, if relying on the convention), if you were receiving it before you moved to the UK (referred to as 'exporting' the benefit – see p419) and that state continues to be the 'competent state' to pay that benefit (see p399).

Child benefit and guardian's allowance are categorised under the main EU co-ordination rules, and listed under the UK–Ireland Convention, as 'family benefits'. For more details on the payment of 'family benefits', see p420.

Scottish child payment has been categorised as a special non-contributory benefit (see p397) and so the last two bullet points above do not apply to that benefit.

If you are not covered by either the main EU co-ordination rules or the UK–Ireland Convention, but you are covered by the UK–EU Protocol, that will not assist you in the ways above because that protocol does not cover family benefits.

Reciprocal and other international agreements

If you are covered by a reciprocal agreement, that may allow periods of residence and/or presence in the other country to be treated as residence and/or presence in Great Britain in order to be entitled to child benefit and guardian's allowance.

Arguably, it could also enable you to to use periods of residence in the other country to satisfy the requirement for child benefit to have been living in the UK for the past three months. For more information on reciprocal agreements, see p443.

There are agreements with Albania and Israel that can assist in ways that are similar to the EU co-ordination rules. For more information on these agreements, see p447.

4. Disability and carers' benefits

For **attendance allowance (AA), personal independence payment (PIP), adult disability payment (ADP), disability living allowance (DLA), child disability payment (CDP) and carer's allowance (CA)**, you must:[40]

- be present in Great Britain (for CDP and ADP, the common travel area – the UK, Ireland, Channel Islands and the Isle of Man) at the time of your claim;
- satisfy the 'past presence test' (see also the bulleted list below) by having been present in:
  - (CDP and ADP only) the common travel area for at least 26 weeks in the last 52, but see below for a child under three;
  - (DLA only) Great Britain for at least 26 weeks in the last 52 – see below;
  - (PIP, AA and CA) Great Britain for at least 104 weeks in the last 156 – see also the note on CA below; *and*
- be habitually resident in the common travel area (see p163, but also the exemptions below); *and*
- (CDP and ADP only) be ordinarily resident in Scotland.

In relation to the **past presence test**, note the following.

- If a **child under three is claiming DLA or CDP**, the past presence test is reduced to 13 weeks if the claimant is a baby under six months old, and that continues to apply until the child is 12 months old. For a child claiming DLA or CDP when aged six months to 36 months old, the past presence test is 26 weeks in the last 156 weeks for DLA, or in the last 52 weeks for CDP.[41]
- If you are **aged between three and 16 claiming DLA**, the past presence test is 26 weeks in the last 52. This is due to the Upper Tribunal decision which held that increasing the duration of the past presence test in 2013 was, for children aged three to 16, unlawful and that the previous requirement to have been present for 26 weeks out of the last 52 must be treated as continuing for this age group.[42] At the time of writing, the DLA regulations had not been amended but the shorter period is confirmed in guidance.[43]
- If you are claiming **CA** as the carer of a child awarded DLA or CDP after being present for 26 weeks out of the last 52, it is arguable that the past presence test for CA must also be 26 weeks out of the last 52. This was accepted at a First-tier

Tribunal (and the DWP did not appeal). For details and a template letter written for the carer of a child receiving DLA, see cpag.org.uk/welfare-rights/legal-test-cases/disability-living-allowance-2-year-past-presence-test.

- (For CDP or ADP only) if you do not satisfy the past presence test (or other residence and presence requirements), but will within 13 weeks, your claim may be treated as an advance claim from the date you satisfy this requirement.[44]
- **Challenges** that the past presence requirement for a child breaches public sector equality duties have, to date, failed.[45]
- Periods when you are **treated as present** count for the past presence test (see below).
- If you are covered by an **exemption from the past presence test**, you do not need to satisfy it (see p304).

Note: a child's residence, but *not* their presence or past presence, is generally determined by the residence of the person responsible for them (see p147).

To be entitled to the **carer's allowance supplement**, you must be in receipt of CA and resident (see p146) in Scotland on the qualifying date.[46]

To qualify for a **young carer grant**, on the day of your application you must be:[47]

- ordinarily resident in Scotland; *and*
- habitually resident in the UK, Channel Islands, Isle of Man or the European Economic Area (EEA) (see p156), or be exempt from this requirement (see p159).

To be entitled to **child winter heating assistance,** you must be under 19 and in receipt of the higher rate of the care component of DLA or CDP, or the enhanced rate of the daily living component of PIP or ADP, and on any day in the qualifying week you must be:[48]

- resident (see p146) in Scotland; *or*
- habitually resident (see p163) in an EEA state (other than Cyprus, France, Greece, Malta, Portugal or Spain) or Switzerland *and* have a 'genuine and sufficient link to Scotland' (see p307).

For **employment and support allowance (ESA) in youth, incapacity benefit (IB) in youth and severe disablement allowance (SDA)**, you must:[49]

- be present in Great Britain at the time of your claim (see p142);
- have been present in Great Britain for not less than 26 weeks in the last 52 weeks (the 'past presence' test – see p143);
- be ordinarily resident in Great Britain (see p147).

For ESA in youth, IB in youth and SDA, once you satisfy these tests, you do not need to do so again while you are in the same period of limited capability for work or incapacity for work.[50]

When you can be treated as present

You are treated as being present during certain absences (see p354). Any period when you are treated as present can be counted to satisfy both the presence and the past presence tests.

Exemptions from habitual residence and past presence test

For **AA, PIP, ADP, DLA, CDP and CA**, the **past presence test** and the **habitual residence requirement** do not apply if you:[51]

- have been granted refugee leave or humanitarian protection, or you have leave as the dependent family member of someone who has such leave – eg, because you joined them under the family reunion provisions. For details of these types of leave, including their duration, see p43;[52]
- (from 22 March 2022) were living in Ukraine immediately before 1 January 2022 and you left in connection with the Russian invasion of 24 February 2022, *and* you have leave, or a right of abode, in the UK (including if you are British) or you are Irish;[53]
- (from 15 September 2021) have leave in the UK granted under the Afghan Citizens Resettlement Scheme, or granted by virtue of the Afghan Relocations and Assistance Policy (ARAP) or the scheme for locally employed staff in Afghanistan ('LES Scheme'), or discretionary leave as the dependant of a person with leave under either of the last two schemes;[54] *or*
- (except CA) (exemption from past presence test only) are terminally ill. The definition of 'terminal illness' is the same as applies for other purposes for these benefits – ie, that you have a progressive disease and your death as a result of that disease can reasonably be expected (other than for CDP and ADP) within a set period, which at the time of writing was six months, but was due to increase to 12 months;[55]
- (CDP and ADP only) are abroad as a serving member of the armed forces or a civil servant, provided you satisfied the residence and presence requirements (other than the past presence test) immediately prior to the start of this employment; or are living with someone who is abroad as a serving member of the armed forces or civil servant, and you are their spouse, civil partner (or living together as if you were either), son, stepson, daughter, stepdaughter, or child in their care, or, for ADP only, father, stepfather, father-in-law, mother, stepmother or mother-in-law. You are treated as being present for both the presence requirement and the past presence test, and also treated as habitually resident and ordinarily resident;
- (CDP and ADP only) (treated as meeting the presence and past presence conditions only) are an aircraft worker, mariner or continental shelf worker;
- (AA, DLA, PIP and CA only) (exempt from the habitual residence test only, but also treated as present in Great Britain) are abroad as a serving member of the armed forces, or are living with someone who is abroad as a serving member of

the armed forces and they are your spouse, civil partner, son, stepson, daughter, stepdaughter, or father, stepfather, father-in-law, mother, stepmother or mother-in-law.

These exemptions are not always picked up by the DWP, so you will need to explain why the past presence test does not apply to you when you make your claim.

In relation to **CDP and ADP**, note the following.

- CDP and ADP require past presence and habitual residence in the common travel area (the UK, Ireland, Channel Islands and the Isle of Man) and, therefore, periods of residence in Ireland can assist in satisfying these requirements. In addition, if you are covered by the UK–Ireland Convention (see p387) and have a 'genuine and sufficient link to Scotland', the requirement to be 'ordinarily resident' in Scotland is disapplied;[56]
- if you do not satisfy the past presence test (or other residence and presence requirements), but will within 13 weeks, your claim may be treated as an advance claim, and decided from the date you satisfy this requirement.[57]

European Union co-ordination rules

If you are covered (see p379) by the main European Union (EU) co-ordination rules or, for situations involving the UK and Ireland only, the UK–Ireland Convention, or for ADP and CDP in situations involving the UK and Gibraltar only, the agreement between the UK and Gibraltar (see p436):

- the UK must be your 'competent state' (see the first note below) for you:[58]
  - to be entitled to AA, PIP daily living component, DLA care component or CA;
  - to disapply the past presence test for ADP or CDP (see below);
  - while habitually resident in a member state (see the second note below), to make a new claim for, or continue to be entitled to, ADP daily living component, CDP care component, a young carer grant or carer's allowance supplement;
- you may be able to claim AA, DLA, PIP, ADP, CA and CDP more quickly, either because the past presence test does not apply to you (see below) or because periods of residence in a member state can be used to satisfy the test (under the 'aggregation principle' – see p308);
- even if you cannot be entitled to the benefits in the first bullet point due to the UK not being your competent state, you may still be entitled to the mobility component of PIP, ADP, DLA or CDP, and may be entitled sooner than you would otherwise be (see p309);
- you may be able to make a new claim for AA, the care component of DLA or CDP, the daily living component of PIP or ADP, CA, young carer grant and carer's allowance supplement if you live in a member state (see p308);

- if you have moved to the UK from a member state, you may continue to receive a sickness or invalidity benefit (or long-term care benefit, if relying on the UK–Ireland Convention) (referred to as 'exporting' the benefit – see p419), if that state continues to be the competent state to pay that benefit (see p399).

Note:
- The UK might not be your **competent state** (see p399) if you (or your family member who brings you within the co-ordination rules) receive a contributory benefit (classed as a 'pension') paid by a member state, or if your family member is working in a member state (see p404).
- '**Member state**' in the bullet points above means an EEA state if you are covered by the main EU co-ordination rules, Ireland if you are relying on the UK–Ireland Convention or, for ADP and CDP only, Gibraltar if you are relying on the agreement between the UK and Gibraltar.
- If you are only covered by the UK–EU Protocol, that will not assist you in the ways above because it does not cover disability and carers' benefits.[59]

When the past presence test does not apply

The past presence test does not apply to AA, DLA, PIP, ADP, CA and CDP if:[60]
- (ADP or CDP only) you are ordinarily resident in Scotland; *and*
- you are covered by the main (or the old) EU co-ordination rules (see p379 and the first note below) or, for ADP or CDP only, the agreement between the UK and Gibraltar (see p436); *and*
- you are habitually resident in Great Britain (the UK, for ADP or CDP); *and*
- (other than for the mobility component of PIP and DLA) the UK is the competent state (see p399); *and*
- (other than for ADP or CDP) you can demonstrate 'a genuine and sufficient link' to the UK.

Note:
- It is strongly arguable that the second bullet point above applies to you if you are not, or no longer, covered by the Withdrawal Agreement protections (see p380), but you are covered by the *partial* Withdrawal Agreement protections (see p384). This is because the benefit regulations require that a relevant EU regulation[61] 'applies to you', and if you are covered by the partial Withdrawal Agreement protections then the aggregation principle of the relevant EU regulation applies to you, so if you also satisfy the other requirements listed above, the past presence test should not apply to you. However, you should always, if possible, *also* argue that you can aggregate periods of residence in an EEA state with periods of presence in Great Britain (or the common travel area for ADP and CDP) and thereby satisfy the past presence test (see below). See the example on p385.
- 'Habitual residence', in this context, is interpreted in the same way as 'residence' is interpreted under the EU co-ordination rules (see p401).[62]

- You may be able to make a new claim if you are habitually resident in an EEA country (see p308).

Genuine and sufficient link

The phrase **'genuine and sufficient link to the UK'** (for Scottish benefits, see the note below) is not defined in regulations, but comes from a case decided by the Court of Justice of the European Union (CJEU).[63] The way this phrase is interpreted must therefore be consistent with this judgment.

Although the regulations require you to demonstrate a 'genuine and sufficient link to the UK *social security system*', the Court of Appeal has held that the last three words must be disregarded as they are not authorised by the CJEU's judgment.[64] The DWP guidance memos about this have been removed from gov.uk, but at the time of writing the DWP had not updated the main guidance.[65]

The circumstances that applied in the CJEU case and which were held to have amounted to a 'genuine and sufficient link to the UK' are relevant, but they are not exhaustive. Many factors can be relevant to determining whether you have a genuine and sufficient link to the UK, depending on your circumstances and the benefit you are claiming, and include:[66]

- whether you have worked in the UK;
- whether you have spent a significant part of your life in the UK;
- whether you are receiving a UK contributory benefit;
- evidence of your motives, intentions and expectations;
- if you are claiming a disability benefit, whether your carer would be entitled to CA;
- whether you are dependent on a family member who has worked in the UK and/or receives a UK contributory benefit. 'Family member' in this context is not limited to the definition of 'member of the family' in the co-ordination rules (see p390). The Upper Tribunal has held that a child claiming DLA had a 'genuine and sufficient link to the UK' on the basis that he was dependent on his sister who had worked in the UK for at least five years.[67] This principle that your link can be established through someone else's link to the UK was also accepted by the Court of Appeal in a subsequent case.[68]

The Upper Tribunal has held that your presence in Great Britain is also a factor, and the closer your period of presence comes to satisfying the two-year past presence requirement, the more significance should be attached to this factor. This part of the decision did not need to be addressed by the Court of Appeal, which merely noted that it is highly unlikely that presence alone would ever be the sole factor demonstrating a 'genuine and sufficient link' to the UK.[69]

Note: the requirement to demonstrate a **'genuine and sufficient link to Scotland'**, which applies in specific circumstances as part of satisfying elements of the residence and presence requirements for ADP, CDP, child winter heating assistance (see p302 for all three), carer's allowance supplement and young carer grant (see p308 for both), must be interpreted in a way consistent with the caselaw referred to above, but in relation to Scotland. For ADP, CDP, carer's allowance supplement and young carer grant, the regulations state that a link is sufficient, if not granting that benefit would be incompatible with the relevant co-ordination rules that apply.[70]

When the co-ordination rules can help you satisfy the past presence test

If you are covered by the main EU co-ordination rules, or the UK–Ireland Convention (see p379), you may be able to satisfy the past presence test by adding certain periods of residence in an EEA state (Ireland, if relying on the convention) to periods of presence in Great Britain (or, for ADP or CDP, the common travel area) under the 'aggregation principle'.[71] **Note:** the circumstances in which you can use the aggregation principle of the main co-ordination rules include if you are only covered by partial Withdrawal Agreement protections (see p384).

If you are claiming AA, PIP, DLA or CA you should, if possible, provide evidence to show both that the past presence test does not apply to you due to your 'genuine and sufficient link' to the UK (see above) *and* that you satisfy the past presence test by aggregating your residence in an EEA state with your presence in Great Britain, in case one basis for your entitlement is not accepted (see the example on p385). However, this is not required if you are claiming ADP or CDP while ordinarily resident in Scotland, because the past presence test is disapplied simply by your being covered by the main EU co-ordination rules or the agreement between the UK and Gibraltar. **Note:** because ADP and CDP require past presence in the common travel area, which includes Ireland, reliance on aggregation of residence in Ireland under the UK–Ireland Convention is not necessary.

Note: the Upper Tribunal has held that 'mere residence' in an EEA country cannot be aggregated in order to satisfy the past presence test under the main EU co-ordination rules and that only periods of residence during which you were 'insured' can be aggregated under the UK–Ireland Convention.[72]

For further details on the 'aggregation principle', see p416.

Making a new claim while living in another European Economic Area state

If you are living in an EEA state, you can make a new claim (or continue to be paid an existing award – see p356) for **AA, CA, the daily living component of PIP or ADP, the care component of DLA or CDP** without needing to satisfy the usual habitual residence, presence and past presence (and, for ADP or CDP only, ordinary residence) requirements if the UK is your 'competent state'[73] (see p399) and:[74]

- you are covered by the main EU co-ordination rules (see p379) or, for ADP or CDP, the UK–Ireland Convention (see p387) or the agreement between the UK and Gibraltar (see p436); *and*
- you are habitually resident in an EEA state (or Gibraltar if relying on the agreement with Gibraltar, and Ireland if relying on the UK–Ireland Convention, for ADP or CDP); *and*
- you can demonstrate a 'genuine and sufficient link' to the UK (to Scotland, for ADP or CDP) (see p307).

You can make a new claim (including for a backdated period if you *would have* been entitled had these rules been in force at the time) for **carer's allowance supplement** or a **young carer grant** without needing to satisfy the requirement to be resident or ordinarily resident in Scotland if:[75]

- you have a 'genuine and sufficient link' to Scotland (see p307); *and*
- the UK is your 'competent state' to pay this benefit; *and*
- you are either:
  - resident in an EEA state and covered by the main EU co-ordination rules (see p379); *or*
  - resident in Ireland and covered by the UK–Ireland Convention (see p387); *or*
  - resident in Gibraltar and covered by the agreement between the UK and Gibraltar (see p436).

Disability and carers' benefits are not covered by the UK–EU Protocol at all.

Mobility component

You are only entitled to the mobility component of DLA, PIP, ADP or CDP if you are habitually resident in the UK (common travel area for ADP or CDP, and for ADP or CDP you also have to be ordinarily resident in Scotland). That is because under the main EU co-ordination rules, DLA mobility component is listed as, PIP mobility component is accepted as, and the mobility payment for ADP and CDP is treated as, a special non-contributory benefit and, therefore, not 'exportable' (see p397).[76] You can only be paid these in the state where you are resident, which means where you 'habitually reside'.[77]

The UK–Ireland Convention does not cover these mobility components at all.

If you are covered by the main EU co-ordination rules (see p379), these can still assist you to be entitled to the DLA, PIP, ADP or CDP mobility component sooner than you would otherwise be because:

- the past presence test does not apply to you if you are covered by the rules on p306; *and*
- you cannot be found to be not habitually resident and denied benefit solely on the basis that you have not been actually resident for an 'appreciable period' of time. Your length of actual residence is only one relevant factor in determining whether you are 'habitually resident in fact' and can be outweighed by other factors (see p167).

Note: the requirement for the UK to be your competent state does not apply to the mobility components of PIP or DLA. Consequently, even if you are not entitled to PIP daily living component or DLA care component because the UK is not the competent state to pay these benefits, you may still be entitled to the mobility component.

Reciprocal agreements

At the time of writing, the UK had reciprocal agreements that refer to the disability and carers' benefits with few countries and, other than the agreement between Northern Ireland and Great Britain, none had been updated to include PIP. See Appendix 5 for a list of the countries that have reciprocal agreements and p433 for more information on those agreements. However, the agreement between the UK and Gibraltar (see p436) can assist with claims for a young carer grant, carer's allowance supplement, ADP and CDP.

The reciprocal agreement between Northern Ireland and Great Britain provides for periods of residence and presence in one territory to count as residence and presence in the other territory for the purpose of entitlement to AA, DLA, PIP and CA.[78]

5. Industrial injuries benefits

Industrial injuries benefits are:
- industrial injuries disablement benefit;
- reduced earnings allowance;
- retirement allowance;
- constant attendance allowance;
- exceptionally severe disablement allowance.

To be entitled to any of these benefits, you must have been:
- in Great Britain when the accident at work happened;[79] *or*
- engaged in Great Britain in the employment that caused the disease (even if you have also been engaged outside Great Britain in that employment);[80] *or*
- paying UK national insurance (NI) contributions, either at class 1 rate or at class 2 rate as a volunteer development worker, when the accident at work happened or you contracted the disease. Benefit is not payable until you return to Great Britain.[81]

There are exceptions to these rules, which mean you can qualify for benefit in respect of an accident which happens, or a disease which is contracted, outside Great Britain while you are:[82]
- employed as a mariner or airman or airwoman;
- employed as an apprentice pilot on board a ship or vessel;
- on board an aircraft on a test flight starting in Great Britain in the course of your employment.

In these cases, there are also more generous rules for defining when accidents arise 'out of and in the course of' your employment, and for complying with time limits under the benefit rules.[83]

European Union co-ordination rules

If you are covered by the main European Union (EU) co-ordination rules (which cover the UK and the European Economic Area states) or similar co-ordination rules contained in the UK–EU Protocol (which cover the UK and the EU states), or, for situations involving the UK and Ireland only, the UK–Ireland Convention (see p379), you can, if necessary, rely on periods of employment and NI paid in member states to qualify for industrial injuries benefits in the UK (under the 'aggregation principle' – see p416).

Industrial injuries benefits are classed as 'benefits for accidents at work and occupational diseases' under these co-ordination rules (see p392).

If you have an accident while travelling abroad in another member state, that can be deemed, under the co-ordination rules, to have occurred in the state liable to pay benefits for accidents at work and occupational diseases. If one state determines that you have had an accident or contracted a disease, that should be accepted by the state liable to pay benefit in respect of that accident or disease. These outcomes are achieved under the principle of equal treatment of facts or events (see p414).[84]

If you have worked in two or more member states in jobs that gave you a prescribed industrial disease, you get benefit from the state in which you last did work that, by its nature, is likely to cause that disease and which recognises that disease under its industrial injuries scheme.[85] If you make your claim to the state that does not have responsibility under this rule, your claim and all supporting evidence must be forwarded to the relevant institution in the correct state without delay.[86]

Reciprocal agreements

The UK has reciprocal agreements with several countries that cover industrial injuries benefits. The agreements determine which country is responsible for determining and paying your entitlement, and if and how you can combine injuries or take account of new accidents or diseases. For more information, see p441.

6. Contribution-based jobseeker's allowance and contributory employment and support allowance

To be entitled to contribution-based jobseeker's allowance (JSA) or contributory employment and support allowance (ESA), you must be in Great Britain.[87] The rules about when you can be paid during a temporary absence abroad are covered on p343 for JSA and p346 for ESA. There are no residence conditions (the only exception is contributory ESA in youth – see p303).

Note: looking for work abroad does not count towards satisfying the JSA requirement that you be 'actively seeking employment'.[88]

European Union co-ordination rules

Contribution-based jobseeker's allowance

If you are covered by the main European Union (EU) co-ordination rules, which cover the UK and the European Economic Area (EEA) states, or similar co-ordination rules contained in the UK–EU Protocol, which cover the UK and the EU states, or, for situations involving the UK and Ireland only, the UK–Ireland Convention (see p379), you can, if necessary, rely on the equivalent of national insurance (NI) contributions paid in a member state to entitle you to contribution-based JSA in the UK (under the 'aggregation principle' – see p416). However, in most cases, because it is an unemployment benefit, you can only aggregate your contributions if your most recent period of paying or being credited with those contributions was in the UK.[89] See p418 for more details.

If you are coming to, or returning to, the UK to look for work and you are covered by the main EU co-ordination rules and have been insured in an EEA state (and obtain a U2 form authorising you to export your unemployment benefit), or if you are covered by the UK–Ireland Convention and have been insured in Ireland, you may be able to continue to receive (referred to as 'exporting') that state's unemployment benefit for up to three months, if:[90]

- you were getting that unemployment benefit immediately before coming to the UK;
- you have been registered as available for work for four weeks (or less if the other state's rules allow) in the other state;
- you claim JSA within seven days after you were last registered in the other state; *and*
- you meet the relevant jobseeking requirements for JSA.

The three months can be extended to a maximum of six months if the state from which you are claiming the unemployment benefit agrees.[91]

You cannot 'export' unemployment benefit under the UK–EU Protocol.[92]

For general information on 'exporting' benefits, see p419.

Contributory employment and support allowance

If you are covered by any of the EU co-ordination rules (see p379), you can, if necessary, rely on the equivalent of NI contributions paid in an EEA state (EU if relying on the UK–EU Protocol, and Ireland if relying on the UK–Ireland Convention) to entitle you to contributory ESA in the UK (under the 'aggregation principle' – see p416).

If you are covered by any of the EU co-ordination rules (see p379) and have moved to the UK from an EEA state (EU if relying on the UK–EU Protocol, and Ireland if relying on the UK–Ireland Convention), you may be able to continue to receive a sickness or (unless you are only covered by the protocol) an invalidity benefit from that state (referred to as 'exporting' the benefit – see p419) if that state continues to be your 'competent state' for paying that benefit (see p399). These rules operate broadly as they do if you move *to* an EEA state *from* the UK, except in reverse – see p360.

Reciprocal and other international agreements

If you have lived and worked in a country with which the UK has a reciprocal agreement (see p433), you may be able to count periods of insurance paid in that country towards your entitlement to contribution-based JSA or contributory ESA in the UK if the agreement covers you and that benefit. Similarly, if you are covered by another type of international agreement between the EU and another country, you may be able to do the same (see p445).

Although most reciprocal agreements do not cover income-based JSA or ESA (see p433), the reciprocal agreement between Northern Ireland and Great Britain was extended to cover income-based JSA (as well as contribution-based JSA) from 27 November 2016 (see p435) and contributory ESA (as well as income-related ESA) from 6 April 2016.[93] For details, including the policies if you moved between Northern Ireland and Great Britain while claiming ESA before this date, see p435.

7. Maternity allowance

Entitlement to maternity allowance (MA) is based on past employment. In general, you must have been employed or self-employed in Great Britain.[94] However, you can count weeks during which you were employed abroad before you returned to Great Britain if, throughout the whole period of your absence, you remained ordinarily resident in Great Britain and you paid, or would have been liable to pay were it not for a reciprocal agreement, class 1 national insurance contributions.[95]

There are no residence requirements for MA. However, in general you are disqualified if you are absent from Great Britain.[96] See p361 for the rules allowing you to be paid during a temporary absence.

European Union co-ordination rules

If you are covered by the main European Union (EU) co-ordination rules, which cover the UK and the European Economic Area states, or the UK–EU Protocol, which cover the UK and the EU states, or, for situations involving the UK and Ireland only, the UK–Ireland Convention (see p379) and the UK is your 'competent state' (see p399), you can, if necessary, rely on periods of employment or self-employment in one or more member states to satisfy the employment and earnings conditions to qualify for MA in the UK (under the 'aggregation principle' – see p416).

If you are covered by any of the EU co-ordination rules and have moved to the UK from another member state, you may be able to continue to receive a maternity or paternity benefit from that other state (referred to as 'exporting' the benefit – see p419) if that state continues to be your competent state for paying that benefit (see p399).

8. **Retirement pensions**

Retirement pensions, other than a category D retirement pension, do not have any residence or presence conditions. They can be paid without time limit, whether or not you are present in Great Britain. However, going abroad can mean you are not paid the annual uprating, can be relevant to decisions on deferring your retirement and can prevent you from 'de-retiring' while you are abroad (see p363).[97]

To be entitled to a category D retirement pension, you must have been:[98]

- resident in Great Britain for at least 10 years in any continuous period of 20 years ending on or after your 80th birthday; *and*
- ordinarily resident (see p147) in Great Britain on either:
  - your 80th birthday; *or*
  - the date on which you claimed the category D pension, if later.

European Union co-ordination rules

If you are covered by the main European Union (EU) co-ordination rules, which cover the UK and the European Economic Area (EEA) states, or the UK–EU Protocol, which covers the UK and the EU states, or, for situations involving the UK and Ireland only, the UK–Ireland Convention (see p379), you can:

- continue to receive an 'old age' pension if you were receiving it from a member state before you moved to the UK (referred to as 'exporting' the pension – see p419), and it will be uprated as normal, if the state that pays the pension continues to be the 'competent state' to pay that benefit (see p399);
- rely, if necessary, on the equivalent of national insurance (NI) contributions paid in one or more of the member states (see below) to calculate your entitlement to retirement pensions from the UK and from the member state(s); *and*
- rely, if necessary, on certain periods of residence in EEA countries to meet the residence requirement for a category D pension.

The last two bullet points above are each achieved under the 'aggregation principle' (see p416). You may receive pension payments from the UK and one or more member states, because your total award may be made in proportions that reflect the proportion of years of contributions paid, or periods of residence completed, in the UK and other member states, out of the total years of contributions paid or periods of residence completed in all member states.[99]

The requirement to be ordinarily resident for a category D retirement pension may not apply to you if you are covered by the EU co-ordination rules and you can show that you have a 'genuine and sufficient link to the UK' (see p307).[100]

Although the main co-ordination rules were, in general, revoked in UK law from the end of the transition period and now only apply to those covered by the Withdrawal Agreement protections (see p379), note the following.

- The provisions of the main co-ordination rules relating to the uprating of, and aggregation of NI contributions for entitlement to, UK retirement pensions, were saved and continue to apply.[101]
- If you are not, or no longer, covered by the Withdrawal Agreement protections, but you are covered by the *partial* Withdrawal Agreement protections (see p384), you may be able to rely on the aggregation principle to calculate your entitlement to retirement pensions.[102]
- The UK–EU Protocol also contains rules on aggregation and uprating exported old age pensions, but the protocol does not cover Iceland, Norway, Liechtenstein or Switzerland. Although the UK government continues to seek an agreement with these four countries that these rules on old age pensions continue to apply between these states,[103] this has not yet been reached. However, bilateral agreements have been secured between Norway and the UK, and between Switzerland and the UK (see p437). Also, the main co-ordination rules may continue to apply due to the two bullet points above.

Reciprocal and other international agreements

If you have lived and worked in a country with which the UK has a reciprocal agreement (see p433), you may be able to count periods of residence or insurance paid in that country towards your UK retirement pension entitlement. For further information on reciprocal agreements and retirement pensions, see p441.

Similarly, if you remain covered by an association agreement between the EU and another country, or you are covered by a replacement agreement, you may be able to do the same (see p445).

9. Social fund and other payments

Funeral payments

To qualify for a **funeral expenses payment** from the social fund you must live in England and Wales,[104] and to qualify for a **funeral support payment** you must be ordinarily resident (see p147) in Scotland on the date you make your application.[105] For either benefit, you must also satisfy the conditions below.

- The person who has died must have been ordinarily resident (see p147) in the UK at the date of their death (this does not apply for funeral support payment if they were a stillborn child).[106]
- The funeral must usually take place in the UK. However, it can take place in a European Economic Area (EEA) country or the UK if you or your partner:[107]
  - are an EEA national with a right to reside as a 'worker' (see p211) or self-employed person (see p218), including if you have retained either status (see p222); *or*
  - have a right to reside as a family member (other than an 'extended family member') of one of the above (see p239); *or*
  - have a permanent right of residence acquired in less than five years (see p275); *or*
  - (funeral support payment only) have pre-settled status or settled status granted under the European Union Settlement Scheme (EUSS – see p57);
  - arguably, are a person with any other free movement right of residence in the UK (see below).

Note:

- Since the end of 2020, you can only have one of the free movement residence rights listed above if you are in a protected group (see p188).
- It is arguable that you can also qualify for a funeral expenses payment for a funeral held in an EEA state if you have *any* free movement right to reside in the UK. That is because the relevant law on residence rights has developed since the above rules were introduced and now covers additional groups of EEA nationals and their family members. The above rules were introduced following a case in which the Court of Justice of the European Union (CJEU) held that requiring a funeral to be in the UK was unlawfully discriminatory against European Union (EU) migrant workers.[108] Arguably, the same applies to other groups who can now have free movement residence rights but who are not listed in the funeral payment regulations – eg, people who have a permanent right of residence following five years of legal residence in the UK. For the continuing relevance of EU caselaw, see p195.[109]

If you are responsible for the costs of a funeral of a child aged under 18 or a stillborn baby, you may be entitled to:

- a **children's funeral fund payment** in England. The burial or cremation must take place in England, but there are are no residence (or immigration status) requirements;[110]
- a **child funeral fund payment** in Wales. The child's family home must be in Wales, but there are no other residence (or immigration status) requirements.[111]

Winter fuel and heating payments

To qualify for a **winter fuel payment** from the social fund, if you have reached pension age, you must be ordinarily resident (see p147) in Great Britain on any day in the qualifying week.[112]

The qualifying week

The **'qualifying week'** is the week beginning on the third Monday in September before the winter you want to be paid for.

To qualify for a **winter heating payment**, if you get a qualifying benefit, you must be resident (see p146) in Scotland on any day in the qualifying week.[113]

To qualify for **child winter heating assistance** if you are under 19 and in receipt of the higher rate of the care component of disability living allowance or child disability payment, or the enhanced rate of the daily living component of personal independence payment or adult disability payment, on any day in the qualifying week, you must be:[114]

- resident (see p146) in Scotland; *or*
- habitually resident (see p163) in an EEA state (other than Cyprus, France, Greece, Malta, Portugal or Spain) *and* have a 'genuine and sufficient link' to Scotland (see p307). If that applies, you need to claim using a specific form.[115]

European Union co-ordination rules

You are not required to be ordinarily resident in Great Britain to be entitled to a winter fuel payment if, on any day in the qualifying week, you are:[116]

- covered by either the Withdrawal Agreement protections (see p380) or the UK–Ireland Convention (see p387);
- habitually resident (see p163) in an EEA country (other than Cyprus, France, Gibraltar, Greece, Malta, Portugal or Spain); *and*
- can demonstrate a 'genuine and sufficient link to the UK' (see p307).

Winter fuel payments are not covered by the UK–EU Protocol or, other than to overcome the requirement to be ordinarily resident in Great Britain as above, the UK–Ireland Convention.[117]

Was your application for a winter fuel payment refused before September 2013?

The EU rules were only included in the UK regulations from 16 September 2013. However, they are based on a judgment of the CJEU, dated 21 July 2011.[118] If you had your winter fuel payment refused because, at the relevant time, you were not ordinarily resident in Great Britain, but you satisfied the above rules, you can request that the decision be revised. The DWP will revise its decision on the grounds of official error if it was made on or after 21 July 2011.[119] If the decision was made before this date, the DWP's position is that it can only be revised if another ground for revision is available.[120] For a discussion of similar issues in relation to previous refusals of disability benefits, see p356.

Maternity grant payments

To qualify for a **Sure Start maternity grant** from the social fund, you must live in England or Wales.[121]

To qualify for a **Best Start grant**, you must be ordinarily resident in Scotland.[122] In addition, if neither you nor your partner receive a qualifying benefit (a means-tested benefit or tax credits), but you qualify for a grant because you are aged under 20, you must also satisfy one of the following:[123]

- you are habitually resident (see p156) in the UK, Channel Islands or Isle of Man; *or*
- you, or your partner, are habitually resident in the EEA *and* have a right to reside in the UK either as a qualified person or a family member (other than an extended family member) of a qualified person or a permanent right to reside (see p192), or have pre-settled status or settled status granted under the EUSS; *or*
- you are exempt from this habitual residence test (see p159).

10. Tax credits

You can only make a new claim for tax credits if you have been granted refugee leave and you are making a backdated claim (see p131). To make such a claim, or if you are already entitled to tax credits, to continue to be entitled you must satisfy the residence and presence rules below. **Note:** if you already have an award of one type of tax credit and you become entitled to the other, this is treated as a change of circumstances so a new claim is not required and you can begin to receive both tax credits.

To be entitled to **child tax credit** (CTC), you (and your partner in a joint claim) must:[124]

- be present in the UK (see p142); *and*
- be ordinarily resident in the UK (see p147); *and*
- have a right to reside in the UK (see p168); *and*

- have been living in the UK for the three months prior to your claim (unless you are exempt – see p143).

To be entitled to **working tax credit** (WTC), you (and your partner in a joint claim) must be:[125]
- present in the UK (see p142); *and*
- ordinarily resident in the UK (see p147).

There are, however, some exceptions: in particular, note the following.[126]
- You can be treated as present for either eight or 12 weeks during a temporary absence, or while you or your partner are a Crown servant posted overseas (see p366). While you are treated as present, you continue to satisfy the conditions of entitlement to tax credits. This means that you can continue to receive tax credits that are already being paid and can make a renewal claim during your absence. If you spend longer abroad than the permitted periods, you cease to satisfy the presence condition and your tax credit entitlement ends.
- You do not need to have a right to reside for CTC if you claimed CTC before 1 May 2004 and you have been receiving it since then (see p177).
- You are treated as ordinarily resident in the UK for CTC and WTC and, for CTC, you are not required to have been living in the UK for the past three months, if you have been deported or otherwise legally removed from another country to the UK.
- You are treated as ordinarily resident in the UK for WTC if you have a free movement right to reside (see p192), but note that, in practice, being accepted as ordinarily resident is rarely a problem.
- You are exempt from the requirement to have been living in the UK for three months prior to your CTC claim if you are in an exempt group (see p144).

You can be entitled to the childcare element of WTC if your childcare is provided outside the UK if either:[127]
- it is provided in an European Economic Area (EEA) country and is regulated by the relevant authorities of that country;[128] *or*
- you are are employed by the Ministry of Defence and the childcare is regulated in accordance with the requirements of the Department for Education.

Note:
- If you are a self-employed EEA national, the definition of 'self-employed' for WTC purposes[129] is different from, and does not affect, the meaning of 'self-employed' for the purpose of having a right to reside that satisfies that requirement for CTC (see p218).
- If you are responsible for a child but do not have a right to reside and so are not entitled to CTC, the number of hours you need to work to be entitled to WTC is still determined on the basis that you are responsible for a child.[130] If HM

Revenue and Customs (HMRC) tells you that you are not entitled to WTC unless you work 30 hours because you do not receive CTC, that is wrong.

Being absent (other than while you are treated as present), ceasing to be ordinarily resident or losing your right to reside are all changes that you must notify to HMRC within one month. Failure to do so may result in your being overpaid and/or being given a penalty.

Couples and children

If you are a member of a couple and are entitled on the basis of a joint tax credit claim, you must both satisfy the residence requirements. Your entitlement to tax credits as a couple ends if either you or your partner:

- are abroad for longer than a permitted temporary absence of eight or 12 weeks (see p366);
- (for CTC only) lose the right to reside;
- cease to be ordinarily resident.

Note: the person who continues to satisfy the residence rules cannot make a new single claim for CTC or WTC, but may be entitled to universal credit instead.

If you or your partner are abroad (even for a permitted temporary absence of less than eight or 12 weeks) and you (or they) were the only partner in full-time work, you may lose entitlement to WTC if the requirement to be in full-time work is no longer satisfied.

If at any point HMRC considers that you and your partner have separated and this is likely to be permanent, your entitlement to tax credits on the basis of your joint claim ends.[131]

You have a duty to notify HMRC of any of the above changes within one month of their taking place. Failure to do so may result in your being overpaid or being given a penalty.

There are no presence or residence requirements for any child in your claim, but you must be responsible for them. You count as being responsible if the child normally lives with you or, if there are competing claims, you have main responsibility for them.[132]

If your partner or child is a non-EEA national, also check the rules in Part 3. In particular, see p123 if:

- your child is a non-EEA national with leave that is subject to a 'no recourse to public funds' condition; *and/or*
- your partner is a non-EEA national who does not have leave to enter or remain in the UK and does not have a right to reside.

You can only be paid CTC for your third and subsequent child in limited circumstances (due to the 'two-child limit'). These include if the child was born before 6 April 2017 or if an exception applies. One exception is if you have adopted the child or they have been placed with you for adoption. However, this exception does not apply if you adopted the child under the law of another country before the adoption under UK law.[133] For details of the 'two-child limit' rule, including the exceptions, see CPAG's *Welfare Benefits and Tax Credits Handbook*.

European Union co-ordination rules

You may be assisted in the ways below if you are covered by the main European Union (EU) co-ordination rules or, for situations involving the UK and Ireland only, the UK–Ireland Convention (see p379). The UK–EU Protocol does not apply to CTC or WTC.

CTC is classed as a 'family benefit' under the main co-ordination rules and the UK–Ireland Convention. If you are covered by either, you may be able to be paid CTC for a partner or child resident in an EEA country (or in Ireland, if relying on the convention). However, you still have to satisfy all the other conditions for CTC, including that the child is 'normally living with' you.[134] For more details on the payment of family benefits, see p420.

WTC is not covered by any of the EU co-ordination rules. Therefore, if your partner is in Ireland or another EEA country, although you may be entitled to CTC on the basis of a joint claim, you are only entitled to WTC on the basis of a single claim.[135] In this case, or if you are a single claimant entitled to claim for a child in an EEA country, your CTC entitlement is in accordance with the relevant co-ordination rules, but your WTC entitlement is solely under UK legislation. If you or your partner are working in an EEA country but live in the UK and therefore remain present and ordinarily resident in the UK, this work can count for the purposes of your WTC claim.[136]

In any of the circumstances above, your claim(s) is likely to be deemed 'complex' and processed by the 'international team' at HMRC. If you experience difficulties, you can refer to guidance for decision makers on how these claims should be administered,[137] and get an advice agency to help.

Although the co-ordination rules do not apply to WTC, other provisions of EU law mean that you cannot be refused the childcare element of WTC:

- if your partner receives a benefit from an EEA state that is substantially similar to a UK benefit that is accepted as evidence of incapacity (see p414).[138] Since the Upper Tribunal held this to be the case, the WTC regulations have been amended;[139]
- in respect of childcare costs solely because the childcare provider is located in an EEA state.[140] Since the Northern Irish commissioners held this to be the case, the WTC regulations have been amended.[141]

Notes

1. Means-tested benefits

1 **UC** s4(1)(c) WRA 2012
IS s124(1) SSCBA 1992
JSA s1(2)(i) JSA 1995
ESA s1(3)(d) WRA 2007
PC s1(2)(a) SPCA 2002

2 **UC** Reg 9 UC Regs
IS Regs 21-21AA IS Regs
JSA Regs 85-85A JSA Regs
ESA Regs 69-70 ESA Regs
HB Reg 10 HB Regs; reg 10 HB(SPC) Regs
PC Reg 2 SPC Regs

3 s130(1)(a) SSCBA 1992; reg 7 HB Regs; reg 7 HB(SPC) Regs

4 Reg 30 UC Regs; para F6203 ADM

5 Reg 66(1)(c) and (da) and (2)(a) UC Regs; see also *LR v SSWP (UC)* [2022] UKUT 65 (AAC) and reg 83(2)(d) UC Regs

6 s4(1)(a)-(d) WRA 2012; reg 9 UC Regs; reg 8 UC(TP) Regs; *HMRC v AB* [2021] UKUT 209 (AAC); but see different view taken in *SK v HMRC and SSWP (UC)* [2022] UKUT 10 (AAC) and *JL v Calderdale MBC and SSWP (UC)* [2022] UKUT 9 (AAC)

7 **UC** Reg 3(6) UC Regs
IS Reg 16(2)(a) IS Regs
JSA Reg 78(2)(a) JSA Regs
ESA Reg 156(3)(a) ESA Regs
PC Reg 5(1)(a)(i) SPC Regs
HB Reg 21(2)(a) HB Regs; reg 21(2)(a) HB(SPC) Regs

8 **UC** Reg 3(6) UC Regs
IS Reg 16(1)-(3) IS Regs
JSA Reg 78(1)-(3) JSA Regs
ESA Reg 156(1)-(4) ESA Regs
PC Reg 5 SPC Regs
HB Reg 21(1) and (2) HB Regs; reg 21(1) and (2) HB(SPC) Regs

9 CIS/508/1992

10 *Broxtowe Borough Council v CS(HB)* [2014] UKUT 186 (AAC)

11 CIS/508/1992; CIS/13805/1996

12 CIS/484/1993

13 Regs 3(3) and (6), 18(2), 22(3) and 36(3) UC Regs; Reg 9(1) UC,PIP,JSA&ESA(C&P) Regs

14 Regs 3(3), 9, 18(2), 22(3) and 36(3) UC Regs; reg 9(1) and (6) UC,PIP,JSA&ESA(C&P) Regs

15 Art 7(2)(b) and (3)(b) WRA(No.31)O; HB Circular A9/2019, paras 15-17; Vol 13 Ch 77 paras 77035 note 2, 77150-1 and 77160 DMG

16 **IS** Regs 4, 16 and 21 and Sch 7 paras 11 and 11A IS Regs
JSA Regs 78 and 85 and Sch 5 paras 10 and 11 JSA Regs
ESA Reg 156 and Sch 5 paras 6 and 7 ESA Regs
HB Reg 21 HB Regs; reg 21 HB(SPC) Regs

17 Regs 3-5 SPC Regs

18 s4(1A) SPCA 2002; Arts 4(2), 6(2)(a), 7(1), (2)(a) and (b) and (3)(b) and 8 WRA(No.31)O; HB Circular A9/2019; Vol 13 Ch 77 paras 77035 note 2, 77150-1 and 77160 DMG

19 Reg 4(7) UC Regs

20 Sch IIA para 7 SPC Regs

21 **IS** Reg 16 IS Regs
JSA Reg 78 JSA Regs
ESA Reg 156 ESA Regs
HB Reg 21 HB Regs; reg 21 HB(SPC) Regs

22 **UC** Sch 12 para 3 UC Regs; Ch F1 para F1018-19 ADM
IS/JSA Regs 5 and 6 The Social Security (Restrictions on Amounts for Children and Qualifying Young Persons) Amendment Regulations 2017 No.376
HB Reg 22 HB Regs; reg 22 HB(SPC) Regs

23 *Swaddling v Chief Adjudication Officer*, C-90/97 [1999]

24 SS(NIRA) Regs; SS(GBRA)(NI) Regs; SS(NIRA)(A) Regs; SS(GBRA)(A)NI Regs

25 **UC** SS(NIRA) Regs; see also ADM Memo 18/20

2. Bereavement benefits

26 s30(1) PA 2014 – Sark is the only 'specified territory'

27 Arts 5, 6, 7, 42 and 43 EU Reg 883/04; Arts 5, 6, 7 and 43 UK-IC; Arts SSC 6, 7, 8, 37 and 38 UK-EUP

28 Sch 1 para 4 The Social Security (Reciprocal Agreements) Order 2017 No.159; Vol 2 Ch 7 Part 6 paras 077080-83 DMG
29 DMG Vol 2 Ch 7 Part 6 paras 077110-24 DMG
30 The Social Security (Reciprocal Agreements) Order 2017 No.159; SS(NIRA)(A) Regs; SS(GBRA)(A)NI Regs

3. **Child benefit, Scottish child payment and guardian's allowance**
31 s146 SSCBA 1992
32 Reg 23 CB Regs
33 Regs 23, 30 and 31 CB Regs
34 Reg 23(3) CB Regs
35 s143(1)(b) SSCBA 1992
36 Regs 18(d) and 19(2)(c) SCP Regs
37 Reg 9 GA(Gen) Regs
38 *Stewart v SSWP*, C-503/09 [2011] ; *SSWP v JG (IS)* [2013] UKUT 298 (AAC); *SSWP v Garland* [2014] EWCA Civ 1550
39 s143(1)(b) SSCBA 1992; *RK v HMRC (CHB)* [2015] UKUT 357 (AAC); *JL v HMRC (CHB)* [2017] UKUT 193 (AAC)

4. **Disability and carers' benefits**
40 **AA** Reg 2 SS(AA) Regs
PIP Reg 16 SS(PIP) Regs
ADP Reg 15 DAWAP(S) Regs
DLA Reg 2 SS(DLA) Regs and *TS and EK v SSWP (DLA)* [2020] UKUT 284 (AAC), reported as [2021] AACR 4
CDP Reg 5 DACYP(S) Regs
CA Reg 9 SS(ICA) Regs
41 **CDP** Reg 5(2) and (3) DACYP(S) Regs
DLA Reg 2(5)-(7) SS(DLA) Regs
42 *TS and EK v SSWP (DLA)* [2020] UKUT 284 (AAC), reported as [2021] AACR 4
43 Vol 2 Ch 7 Part 2 para 071721 DMG; see also gov.uk/disability-living-allowance-children/eligibility
44 Regs 5(9) and 24 DACYP(S) Regs; reg 35 DAWAP(S) Regs
45 *FM v SSWP (DLA)*[2017] UKUT 380 (AAC), reported as [2019] AACR 8; *TS and EK v SSWP (DLA)* [2020] UKUT 284 (AAC), reported as [2021] AACR 4
46 s81 SS(S)A 2018
47 Reg 8 CA(YCG)(S) Regs
48 Reg 4(1) and Sch WHACYP(S) Regs
49 **ESA** Reg 11 ESA Regs; reg 12 ESA Regs 2013
IB Reg 16 SS(IB) Regs
SDA Reg 3 SS(SDA) Regs
50 **ESA** Reg 11(4) ESA Regs; reg 12(4) ESA Regs 2013
IB Reg 16(6) SS(IB) Regs
SDA Reg 3(3) SS(SDA) Regs
51 **AA** Regs 2(2),(3) and (3A) and 2C SS(AA) Regs
PIP Regs 19, 20, 21 and 23A SS(PIP) Regs
ADP Regs 15(6)-(8), 17, 18, 21 DAWAP(S) Regs
DLA Regs 2(2), (3A) and (4) and 2C SS(DLA) Regs
CDP Reg 5(6), (7), (8), (10), (10A) and (11) DACYP(S) Regs
CA Regs 9(3) and 9C SS(ICA) Regs
52 See also *MM and IS v SSWP (DLA)* [2016] UKUT 149 (AAC), reported as [2016] AACR 38
53 See also ADM Memo 11/22, ADM Memo 1/23 and DMG Memo 8/22
54 See also ADM Memo 14/21 and DMG Memo 11/21
55 **AA** s35(2C) SSA 1975
DLA s66(2) SSCBA 1992
PIP s82(4) WRA 2012
ADP Reg 26 DAWAP(S) Regs
CDP Reg 15(6) DACYP(S) Regs
AA, DLA, PIP To be amended by Social Security (Special Rules for End of Life) Act 2022
56 Reg 5(1) and (4) DACYP(S) Regs; reg 15(1) and (3) DAWAP(S) Regs
57 Regs 5(9) and 24 DACYP(S) Regs; reg 35 DAWAP(S) Regs
58 **AA** s65(7) SSCBA 1992
DLA s72(7B) SSCBA 1992
PIP s84 WRA 2012
ADP Regs 15(3)(c), 19(c)(ii) and 20(2)(ii) DAWAP(S) Regs
CA s70(4A) SSCBA 1992
CDP Regs 5(4)(c)(ii), 8(c)(ii) and 9(2)(a)(i) DACYP(S) Regs
YCG Reg 8(3)-(10) CA(YCG)(S) Regs
CAS s81(2A) and (9)-(15) SS(S)A 2018
59 Art SSC3(4) and Annex SSC-1, Parts 1 and 2 UK-EUP
60 **AA** Reg 2A SS(AA) Regs
DLA Reg 2A SS(DLA) Regs
PIP Reg 22 SS(PIP) Regs
ADP Reg 19 DAWAP(S) Regs
CA Reg 9A SS(ICA) Regs
CDP Regs 8 DACYP(S) Regs
61 Defined as either EU Reg 883/04 or EU Reg 1408/71 (s84 WRA 2012; Reg 2 DACYP(S) Regs; reg 2 DAWAP(S) Regs)

62 *SSWP v MM and BK v SSWP* [2016] UKUT 547 (AAC), reported as [2019] AACR 21, para 33; Art 1(j) EU Reg 883/04; Art 11 EU Reg 987/09
63 *Stewart v SSWP*, C-503/09 [2011]
64 *Kavanagh and Another v SSWP* [2019] EWCA Civ 272, para 68 – see also para 32: the DWP dropped this part of its appeal against *SSWP v MM and BK v SSWP* [2016] UKUT 547 (AAC), reported as [2019] AACR 21, paras 28-31
65 ADM Memo 11/19 and DMG Memo 8/19 are no longer available
66 *Stewart v SSWP*, C-503/09 [2011]; *Kavanagh and Another v SSWP* [2019] EWCA Civ 272; *SSWP v JG (IS)* [2013] UKUT 298 (AAC); *SSWP v Garland* [2014] EWCA Civ 1550
67 *PB v SSWP (DLA)* [2016] UKUT 280 (AAC)
68 *Kavanagh and Another v SSWP* [2019] EWCA Civ 272
69 *SSWP v MM and BK v SSWP* [2016] UKUT 547 (AAC), reported as [2019] AACR 21, para 32; *Kavanagh and Another v SSWP* [2019] EWCA Civ 272, paras 86-90
70 **ADP** Regs 15 and 20 DAWAP(S) Regs
CDP Regs 5 and 9 DACYP(S) Regs
CAS s81(2A) and (9)-(15) SS(S)A 2018
YCG Reg 8(3)-(10) CA(YCG)(S) Regs
All see also paras 96-102 SSS DMG ADP(R and P) and paras 94-100 SSS DMG CDP(R and P)
71 Art 6 and Annex XI UK entry para 2 EU Reg 883/04; Art 6 UK-IC
72 *SSWP v MM and BK v SSWP* [2016] UKUT 547 (AAC), reported as [2019] AACR 21, paras 18-27 and 35. The challenge to this part of the decision was dropped – see *Kavanagh and Another v SSWP* [2019] EWCA Civ 272, paras 30-31; Art 19 UK-IC.
73 ss65(7), 70(4A) and 72(7B) SSCBA 1992; s84 WRA 2012; regs 5(4) and 9 DACYP(S) Regs; regs 15(3) and 20 DAWAP(S) Regs
74 **AA** Reg 2B SS(AA) Regs
DLA Reg 2B SS(DLA) Regs
PIP Reg 23 SS(PIP) Regs
ADP Regs 15(3) and 20 DAWAP(S) Regs
CA Reg 9B SS(ICA) Regs
CDP Regs 5(4) and 9 DACYP(S) Regs
All See also DMG Memo 16/20, paras 14 and 18-21, and ADM Memo 17/20, paras 14 and 18-21
75 **CAS** s81(2A) and (9)-(15) SS(S)A 2018
YCG Reg 8(3)-(10) CA(YCG)(S) Regs
76 *Bartlett and Others v SSWP*, C-537/09 [2011]; *SSWP v DS* [2019] UKUT 238 (AAC); para C2097 and Appendix 1 para 4 ADM; para 71 SSS DMG ADP(R and P); para 67 SSS DMG CDP(R and P)
77 Arts 1(j) and 70 EU Reg 883/04; *Swaddling v Adjudication Officer*, C-90/97 [1999]
78 Sch para 2(1) SS(NIRA) Regs; Sch para 2(1) SS(GBRA)(NI) Regs

5. Industrial injuries benefits

79 s94(5) SSCBA 1992
80 Reg 14 SS(IIPD) Regs
81 Reg 10C(5) and (6) SSB(PA) Regs
82 Reg 2 SS(II)(AB) Regs; reg 2 SS(II)(MB) Regs
83 Regs 3, 4, 6 and 8 SS(II)(MB) Regs; regs 3 and 6 SS(II)(AB) Regs
84 Art 5 EU Reg 883/04; Art 5 UK-IC; Art SSC 6 UK-EUP
85 Art 38 EU Reg 883/04; Art 36 EU Reg 987/09; *SSWP v OF (by MF) (II)* [2011] UKUT 448 (AAC); Art SSC 33 UK-EUP
86 Art 36(2) EU Reg 987/09; Art SSC 33 UK-EUP

6. Contribution-based jobseeker's allowance and contributory employment and support allowance

87 **JSA** s1(2)(i) JSA 1995
ESA ss1(3)(d) and 18(4)(a) WRA 2007
88 *GP v SSWP (JSA)* [2015] UKUT 476 (AAC), reported as [2016] AACR 14
89 Art 61(2) EU Reg 883/04; Art 21(1) and (2) UK-IC; Art SSC 56 UK-EUP
90 Art 64 EU Reg 883/04; Arts 7 and 21 UK-IC
91 Art 64(3) EU Reg 883/04; Art 21(4(c) UK-IC
92 Art 3(1) and (4) and 8 UK-EUP
93 SS(NIRA) Regs; SS(GBRA)(NI) Regs

7. Maternity allowance

94 s2(1) and s35(1) SSCBA 1992
95 The Social Security (Maternity Allowance) (Work Abroad) Regulations 1987 No.417; Vol 2 Ch 7 paras 075570-73 DMG
96 s113(1) SSCBA 1992

8. Retirement pensions

97 s113 SSCBA 1992; reg 4(1) SSB(PA) Regs
98 Reg 10 SS(WB&RP) Regs

99 Arts 51, 52 and 58 EU Reg 883/04; for example, see Vol 2 paras 075771 and 076060-64 DMG; Arts 25 and 26 UK-IC; Arts SSC 45, 46 and 47 UK-EUP
100 *Stewart v SSWP*, C-503/09 [2011]; *SSWP v Garland* [2014] EWCA Civ 1550, paras 14 and 28
101 Regs 5 and 9 The Social Security Co-ordination (Revocation of Retained Direct EU Legislation and Related Amendments) (EU Exit) Regulations 2020 No.1508
102 Art 32 WA 2019; Art 31 UK-EFTA; Art 26a UK-Swiss Agreement; see also DWPWAG, Ch 1 paras 43-52; DMG Memo 11/22, paras 13-15; ADM Memo 15/22, paras 13-15
103 para 7.12 Explanatory Memo to The Social Security Co-ordination (Revocation of Retained Direct EU Legislation and Related Amendments) (EU Exit) Regulations 2020 No.1508

9. **Social fund and other payments**
104 Reg 7(9A) SFM&FE Regs
105 Reg 9(1) FEA(S) Regs
106 **FEP** Reg 7(5) SFM&FE Regs
FSP Reg 9(2)(a) and (6) FEA(S) Regs
107 **FEP** Reg 7(9) and (10) SFM&FE Regs
FSP Reg 9(2)(b), (3) and FEA(S) Regs
108 *O'Flynn v Adjudication Officer*, C-237/94 [1996]; R(IS) 4/98
109 Art 24 EU Dir 2004/38
110 The Social Fund (Children's Funeral Fund for England) Regulations 2019 No.1064; *The Children's Funeral Fund for England – technical guidance*, Ministry of Justice, March 2020, paras 1.7 and 1.8
111 gov.wales/child-funeral-and-other-related-costs-information
112 Reg 2 SFWFP Regs
113 Reg 4(2) WHA(LI)(S) Regs
114 Reg 4(1) and Sch WHACYP(S) Regs
115 mygov.scot/child-winter-heating-assistance-for-children-who-no-longer-live-in-scotland
116 Reg 2 SFWFP Regs
117 Art SSC 3(4) UK-EUP; Art 3 UK-IC
118 *Stewart v SSWP*, C-503/09 [2011]
119 Reg 3(5)(a) SS&CS(DA) Regs; para 73245 and Vol 2 Part 6 Appendix 1 para 10 DMG
120 Vol 2 Part 6 Appendix 1 para 11 DMG
121 Reg 5(6) SFM&FE Regs
122 Sch 2 para 4(1)(a), Sch 3 para 3(1)(a) and Sch 4 para 4(1)(a) EYA(BSG)(S) Regs
123 Sch 2 para 4(1)(b) and (2), Sch 3 para 3(1)(b) and (2) and Sch 4 para 4(1)(b) and(2) EYA(BSG)(S) Regs

10. **Tax credits**
124 s3(3) TCA 2002; reg 3(1) and (5) TC(R) Regs
125 s3(3) TCA 2002; reg 3(1) TC(R) Regs
126 Reg 3 TC(R) Regs
127 Reg 14(2)(d) WTC(EMR) Regs; HMRC leaflet WTC5, *Working Tax Credit: help with the costs of childcare*, 2019, p8
128 For periods before 21 March 2019, see *NB v HMRC (TC)* [2016] NICom 47
129 Reg 2(1) WTC(EMR) Regs
130 Regs 2(2) and 4 (2nd condition) WTC(EMR) Regs
131 s3(5A) TCA 2002
132 s8(2) TCA 2002; reg 3(1) CTC Regs
133 Reg 11(2) CTC Regs
134 *RI v HMRC (TC)* [2019] UKUT 306 (AAC)
135 CCM paras 20090, 20160, 20170 and 20260; TCTM paras 09374 and 09376
136 TCM para 0288580; see also *GC v HMRC (TC)* [2014] UKUT 251 (AAC)
137 CCM para 20000
138 *AS v HMRC* [2017] UKUT 361 (AAC)
139 Reg 13(6)(K) WTC(EMR) Regs
140 *NB v HMRC (TC)* [2016] NICom 47; Art 56 TFEU
141 Reg 14(2)(d) WTC(EMR) Regs

Part 5

Benefits while abroad

Chapter 14

Going abroad

This chapter covers:

This chapter provides an overview of the way your entitlement to benefits and tax credits is affected if you, or a partner or child for whom you claim, go abroad. It explains how particular presence and residence conditions are affected by going abroad. The specific information about individual benefits and tax credits is in Chapter 15.

1. Introduction

Most benefits and tax credits are affected if you, or your partner or child, go abroad. The rules vary between different benefits and tax credits. Some can always be paid abroad, some can only be paid in certain circumstances and for limited periods, and some benefits have rules affecting the amount that can be paid if you are abroad.

Note: some benefits are affected if you leave Great Britain, others are affected if you leave the UK, and Scottish benefits can be affected if you leave Scotland.

Your entitlement while you, or your partner or child, are abroad depends on the following factors:

- the benefit or tax credit you are claiming (see Chapter 15);
- the reason for going abroad;
- whether the absence is temporary or permanent;
- the length of time the absence will last;
- the country to which you, or they, are going;
- whether you are covered by any of the European Union (EU) co-ordination rules, and if so, which rules;
- whether you are covered by a reciprocal agreement the UK has with the country you, or they, are going to.

In addition to the above factors, other changes that occur indirectly as a consequence of your being abroad can also affect your entitlement – eg, if your income changes, or you cease to count as being in full-time work for the benefit or tax credit you are claiming. Further details on the way these other changes affect your entitlement are covered in CPAG's *Welfare Benefits and Tax Credits Handbook.*

Before you go abroad

If you are thinking about going abroad, check how your entitlement will be affected well in advance of your departure, because that could affect your decisions, including on the duration of your absence. It also ensures you have sufficient time to take any necessary action before you leave. Notify each of the benefit authorities that pay your benefit(s) before you leave, providing details of your destination, purpose and expected duration of your absence. If it is possible for you get your UK benefit paid abroad, you should give the relevant benefit authority as much notice as possible, because it may be very slow in making these arrangements.

To see how going abroad affects your entitlement, check which rules apply (see below) and then check the rules for the specific benefit or tax credit you are claiming (see Chapter 15).

If you might want to claim a benefit from the country you are going to, it is worth checking what the conditions of entitlement are, and take relevant documents with you – eg, a statement of the national insurance contributions you have paid, which you can obtain from HM Revenue and Customs, or proof of your past employment. **Note:** check whether claiming a benefit in another country could affect your entitlement to benefits paid abroad by the UK – eg, if you claim a benefit in a European Economic Area (EEA) country, this could mean that the UK is no longer the 'competent state' responsible for paying a different benefit to you in that country (see p399).

Which rules apply

Your entitlement to UK benefits or tax credits while you, or a family member, are abroad can be affected by three different sets of rules.

- **The UK benefit and tax credit legislation** contains rules about how absence from the UK affects entitlement (see below). Check these rules first. If you can be paid the benefits you want when you or your family member go outside Great Britain (or the UK, for tax credits, or the common travel area (see p331), for adult disability payment and child disability payment) under these rules, you do not generally need to check the other rules. However, if you want to be paid a disability or carers' benefit when you go to an EEA country and you are covered by the EU co-ordination rules, check whether these affect your entitlement.
- If you or your family member go to an EEA country (listed on p53), even if you are not entitled under UK legislation, you may be able to receive UK benefits if

the **EU co-ordination rules** apply to you (not all the rules apply in all the EEA countries) (see p379).

- **Reciprocal agreements** exist between the UK and some other countries (see p337). These can assist in similar ways to the EU co-ordination rules and, in general, only apply if the EU co-ordination rules do not help you. There are also reciprocal agreements between Great Britain and Northern Ireland.

2. How your benefits and tax credits are affected

UK law

There are different ways in which the UK benefits and tax credits rules affect your entitlement when you (or your partner or child) go abroad. The main ways in which they result in your not receiving benefit (or not being paid for your partner or child) are *if*:

- during your (or their) absence, you (or they) stop meeting the requirement to:
  - be present in Great Britain, the UK or the 'common travel area' – ie, the UK, Ireland, Channel Islands and the Isle of Man (see below);
  - be ordinarily resident in Scotland or Great Britain or the UK (see p333);
  - be habitually resident in the common travel area (see p333); *or*
  - have a right to reside in the UK or common travel area (see p334);
- your partner's absence abroad means you no longer count as a couple (see p334);
- your child's absence abroad means they are no longer included in your claim (see p334);
- you stop being covered by the rules that allow you to receive housing costs for a certain period while you are absent from your home (see p335).

All of the above rules have exceptions. In particular, you can be treated as present in certain circumstances, provided (in most cases) your absence is temporary (see below).

Presence and absence

Most benefits require you to be present in Great Britain (the UK for tax credits, and the common travel area for adult disability payment (ADP) and child disability payment (CDP)). You can be treated as present and, therefore, continue to be entitled to the benefit or tax credit, during a temporary absence in specified circumstances (see below). You are disqualified from entitlement to some benefits if you are absent from Great Britain (or the UK or common travel area), although there are exemptions.

Presence and absence

'**Presence**' means being physically present in Great Britain (or the UK or common travel area) and '**absence**' means 'not physically present'.

You count as present on the day you return from an absence. For many decades it has been accepted that you also count as present on the day you leave to go abroad. However, the Upper Tribunal recently held in a housing benefit (HB) case that the day you leave Great Britain counts as the first day of your absence. It is arguable that this decision only applies to HB, as its reasoning was partly based on the specific wording of the HB regulations. The DWP continues to state that both the day you leave and the day you return count as days of presence.[1]

Other than ADP and CDP, Scottish benefits require residence, or ordinary residence, rather than presence.

Temporary absence

You can be treated as present, and therefore entitled to most benefits and tax credits, in specified circumstances if your absence counts as a 'temporary absence'. Your entitlement therefore depends on:

- whether your absence counts as 'temporary' for the benefit or tax credit you are claiming (see below); *and*
- how long (if at all) the rules for that benefit or tax credit treat you as present while you are absent (see Chapter 15).

Temporary absence

For attendance allowance (AA), disability living allowance (DLA), personal independence payment (PIP), ADP, CDP, tax credits and (for the claimant's, but not the child's, absence) child benefit, you are '**temporarily absent**' from Great Britain (the UK, for tax credits, and the common travel area for ADP and CDP) if, at the beginning of the period, your absence is unlikely to exceed 52 weeks.[2]

For all other benefits, temporary absence is not defined. It is your responsibility to demonstrate that your absence will be temporary. You should therefore provide full details of why you are going abroad, how long you intend to be away and what you intend to do while you are abroad.[3] However, although your intentions are relevant, they are not decisive.[4] The nature of an absence can also change over time: if your absence is found to be temporary at the beginning of the period, it does not mean that it will always remain temporary. If your circumstances change while you are abroad (eg, you go abroad for one reason and decide to stay for a different purpose), your absence may no longer be regarded as temporary.[5] Although there is no set period for a temporary absence (except for tax credits, child benefit, AA, DLA, PIP, ADP and CDP), as a general rule, absences of more than 12 months are not considered to be temporary unless there are exceptional circumstances.[6] If the purpose of your trip abroad is obviously temporary (eg, for a holiday, to visit friends or relatives or for a particular course of medical treatment) and you buy a return ticket, your absence should be viewed as temporary.

If your absence counts as temporary for the benefit or tax credit you are claiming, you are entitled to receive the benefit or tax credit for a specified period. This period varies for each benefit or tax credit and according to your circumstances. Many of the rules that entitle you to benefit during a specified period only do so if certain circumstances apply, but some simply state a maximum period.

See Chapter 15 for rules on absences for the specific benefit you are claiming.

Note: for many benefits and tax credits, your intended absence still counts as temporary even if it is longer than the maximum period for which the benefit or tax credit is payable.

Example

Mohsen receives PIP. He goes to visit family in Iran, having bought a return ticket to come back after seven months. Mohsen is entitled to PIP for the first 13 weeks of his absence (the maximum period in these circumstances – see p354). Although his intended period of absence is longer than this maximum period, it is still a temporary absence, because when it began it was unlikely to exceed 52 weeks (which is how a temporary absence is defined for PIP – see box above).

Ordinary residence

In order to be entitled to some benefits and tax credits, you must be ordinarily resident in Great Britain (the UK, for child benefit and tax credits, and Scotland for most Scottish benefits). See p147 for a list of benefits and tax credits that require you to be ordinarily resident and an explanation of what 'ordinary residence' means. If, by going abroad (or leaving Scotland), you cease to be ordinarily resident, your entitlement to any benefit or tax credit that requires you to be ordinarily resident ends. However, if your absence abroad is temporary and you intend to return to Great Britain (or the UK or Scotland), your ordinary residence is not usually affected.[7]

Ceasing to be ordinarily resident is rarely the reason why your entitlement ends when you go abroad. It is more likely that your entitlement ends simply because you are absent (see p331). If you receive a decision that your entitlement to a benefit or tax credit has ended because you have ceased to be ordinarily resident, ask for the decision to be looked at again and get specialist advice.

If you are moving from Scotland to another part of the UK (or vice versa), there are specific rules to enable you to switch from ADP to PIP or vice versa, or from CDP to DLA or vice versa (see p354).

Habitual residence

In order to be entitled to some benefits, you must be habitually resident in a specified area, or be exempt from this requirement. See p155 for which benefits require you to be habitually resident, an explanation of what this means, including the required area for each benefit, and who is exempt. If, by going abroad, you cease to be habitually resident, your entitlement to any benefit that requires you to be habitually resident ends. However, ceasing to be habitually resident will rarely be the reason why your entitlement ends, which is more likely to be simply due to your being absent (see p331) or, for HB, absent from your home (see p335).

Note: if you need to make a new claim when you return from abroad, you will not usually have ceased to be habitually resident if your absence was temporary and you intended to return to the common travel area[8] (the UK, Ireland, Channel Islands and the Isle of Man). However, you may need to explain that to the decision maker.

Right to reside

In order to be entitled to some benefits and tax credits, you must have a right to reside in either the UK or the common travel area (the UK, Ireland, Channel Islands and the Isle of Man). See p168 for which benefits and tax credits require a right to reside. If, by going abroad, you lose your right to reside, your entitlement to any benefit or tax credit that requires you to have a right to reside ends. However, an absence does not necessarily mean you lose your right to reside – it depends on your circumstances.

Couples and children living apart

There are general rules on when you continue to count as a couple despite living apart from your partner and when a child living elsewhere is still included in your claim. These rules are not specific to absences abroad, but if your partner or child is abroad, they can affect your entitlement.

If your partner goes abroad, this can affect your benefit or tax credit in the following ways.

- For universal credit (UC) and tax credits, you may no longer be entitled on the basis of your joint claim as a couple and may need to make a new single claim. If you were getting tax credits, this will mean you now have to claim UC.
- Depending on the circumstances, including the permanence or duration of your partner's absence, at some point you will stop being paid for your partner.
- Even if you are not paid for your partner, in some circumstances their income and capital can still affect your entitlement.

If your child goes abroad, depending on the circumstances, including the duration, they can stop being part of your claim. This can affect your entitlement – either you stop being paid for them or your entitlement ends altogether.

Note: you can only be paid means-tested benefits and child tax credit for your third and subsequent child in limited circumstances (due to the 'two-child limit'). These include (for UC and HB) certain transitional rules which may cease to apply when your child returns from abroad after payments for them, or your claim, ended because they were abroad. The rules and exceptions vary between benefits, so check the details of the benefit you are claiming in CPAG's *Welfare Benefits and Tax Credits Handbook*.

For further details of the rules about couples and children for means-tested benefits, see p295, and for tax credits, see p320.

Absence from your home

If you are temporarily absent from your normal home, you can be treated as occupying it for a period. These rules apply to HB and to housing costs in UC, income support (IS), income-based jobseeker's allowance (JSA), income-related employment and support allowance (ESA) and pension credit (PC). They mean you can continue to receive payments during your temporary absence.

The absence rules are not (except for HB) specific to your being outside Great Britain, but can still affect you if you are absent from your home when abroad. For further details, see CPAG's *Welfare Benefits and Tax Credits Handbook*.

A new period of absence starts if you return home, even for a short stay, and then leave again. A stay of at least 24 hours before you leave again may be enough.[9]

If you are temporarily absent from your home, you can continue to be paid **UC** housing costs for up to six months while you are absent for any reason. You are no longer treated as occupying your home once your absence has lasted, or is expected to last, longer than six months.[10] The main exception to this is if you are absent because of a fear of domestic violence, in which case you can be treated as occupying your home for up to 12 months.[11] However, your entitlement to UC may cease before six months if you are absent from your home because you are abroad (see p340).

If you are temporarily absent from home, have not rented out your home and intend to return to it, you can continue to be paid housing costs in your **IS, income-based JSA, income-related ESA or PC** for up to:

- **13 weeks** while you are absent, whatever the reason. You must be unlikely to be away for longer than this;[12]
- **52 weeks** in specific circumstances.[13] These include if you, your partner or child are in hospital, if you are undergoing or recovering from medical treatment, or if you are absent from home because of domestic violence. See CPAG's *Welfare Benefits and Tax Credits Handbook* for more details.

For **HB**, the above 13- or 52-week rule only applies if your absence is in Great Britain.[14]

If you are temporarily absent from home while abroad, have not rented out your home and intend to return to it, you can continue to be paid **HB** for up to:[15]

- **four weeks**, if you are absent outside Great Britain and the absence is not expected to exceed this;
- **eight weeks,** if the absence abroad is in connection with the death of your partner, your (or your partner's) close relative, or a child for whom you (or

your partner) are responsible: the above four weeks are extended by up to four weeks if the decision maker considers it unreasonable for you to return within the first four weeks;

- **26 weeks in specific circumstances.** These include if you, your partner or child are in hospital, if you are undergoing or recovering from medical treatment, or if you are absent from home because of domestic violence. See CPAG's *Welfare Benefits and Tax Credits Handbook* for more details. Your absence abroad must be unlikely to exceed (or in exceptional circumstances, substantially exceed) 26 weeks;
- **26 weeks,** if you are a member of the armed forces posted overseas, a mariner or a continental shelf worker. Your absence abroad must be unlikely to exceed 26 weeks.

Note:

- When counting the period of absence for HB, the day of departure counts as a day of absence from Great Britain, but the day of return does not.[16]
- The 13- or 52-week period for which you can be paid HB while you are absent from your home but in Great Britain continues to run during any absence abroad. You may, therefore, be able to return to Britain and continue to be paid HB while absent from your home for the remainder of the 13- or 52-week period. However, if your entitlement has ended as a result of your absence abroad, you cannot qualify for HB again until you return home,[17] but note that unless you are over pension age (and do not have a partner under pension age), in most cases you will now need to claim UC instead of HB.
- HB guidance contains a useful table summarising when you can receive HB during different periods of absence, both in Great Britain and abroad.[18]
- If you have a European free movement right to reside in the UK and go abroad to a European Economic Area (EEA) state, it may be arguable that the shorter period of time during which you remain entitled to HB while temporarily absent abroad is discriminatory under European Union (EU) law and should not apply (see p349).
- If you are temporarily absent from your home, you can continue to be entitled to council tax reduction in certain circumstances (see p627).

European Union co-ordination rules

If you go to an EEA country, you may be able to benefit from the EU co-ordination rules. If these apply to you, they can override the specific UK rules that prevent you from being entitled to benefit outside the UK and mean you can be paid your UK benefit in that EEA country for longer than would be the case under the UK rules described above.

There are three main sets of co-ordinating rules that may apply. The main EU co-ordination rules provide the greatest protections across the greatest number of benefits and all of the EEA countries, and the UK–Ireland Convention has similar rules but for situations involving the UK and Ireland only. The UK–EU Protocol contains fewer protections, covers fewer benefits and only covers the EU countries. The rules you are covered by can be affected by your nationality, the country you are going to and other circumstances, including the date you or your family member went abroad (see p379).

See Chapter 15 for information on the individual benefits and tax credits and Chapter 16 for further information on the co-ordination rules.

Reciprocal and other international agreements

The UK has reciprocal agreements with several EEA and non-EEA countries. For a list of these and further information, see p433. In general, a reciprocal agreement only applies if the EU co-ordination rules do not assist you (see p436). They can also apply if you are moving between Great Britain and Northern Ireland or between the UK and the Channel Islands, the Isle of Man or Gibraltar. In addition, there are international agreements between EU and specific non-EU countries, which can continue to apply to existing claimants, and replacement agreements between the UK and those non-EU countries that can also affect your entitlement. See Chapter 17 for further information on all the agreements.

For more information on reciprocal agreements with EEA states since the UK left the EU, see p437.

Notes

2. How your benefits and tax credits are affected

1 R(S)1/66; *Slough BC v PK* [2019] UKUT 128 (AAC); Vol 2 Ch 7 para 070642 DMG; Ch C1 paras C4008 and C1122 ADM

2 **AA** Reg 2(3C) SS(AA) Regs
DLA Reg 2(3C) SS(DLA) Regs
PIP Reg 17(2) SS(PIP) Regs
ADP Reg 16(2)(a) DAWAP(S) Regs
CDP Reg 7(2)(a) DACYP(S) Regs
CB Reg 24(2) CB Regs
TC Reg 4(2) TC(R) Regs

3 *Chief Adjudication Officer v Ahmed and Others*, 16 March 1994, CA, reported as R(S) 1/96

4 *Chief Adjudication Officer v Ahmed and Others*, 16 March 1994, CA, reported as R(S) 1/96

5 R(S) 1/85

6 R(U) 16/62

7 *R v Barnet London Borough Council ex parte Shah* [1983] 2 AC 309, p342D

8 *KS v SSWP (SPC)* [2010] UKUT 156 (AAC)

9 *R v Penwith District Council ex parte Burt* [1988] 22 HLR 292 (QBD); para A3/3.460 GM

10 Sch 3 para 9(1) UC Regs

11 Sch 3 paras 6 and 9(3) UC Regs

12 **IS** Sch 3 para 3(10) IS Regs
JSA Sch 2 para 3(10) JSA Regs
ESA Sch 6 para 5(10) ESA Regs
PC Sch 2 para 4(10) SPC Regs

Notes

13 **IS** Sch 3 para 3(11)-(13) IS Regs
JSA Sch 2 para 3(11)-(13) JSA Regs
ESA Sch 6 para 5(11)-(13) ESA Regs
PC Sch 2 para 4(11)-(13) SPC Regs
14 Reg 7(13), (16), (17) and (18) HB Regs; reg 7(13), (16), (17) and (18) HB(SPC) Regs
15 Reg 7(13A)-(13G), (16), (17A)-(17D) and (18) HB Regs; reg 7(13A)-(13G), (16), (17A)-(17D) and (18) HB(SPC) Regs
16 *Slough BC v PK* [2019] UKUT 128 (AAC)
17 Reg 7(13B) and (17B) HB Regs; reg 7(13B) and (17B) HB(SPC) Regs
18 **HB** Circular A7/2016

Chapter 15

Going abroad: rules for individual benefits

This chapter covers:

This chapter explains the UK benefit and tax credit rules on being paid when you, or your family members, are abroad. It also covers the ways in which the European Union (EU) co-ordination rules may affect whether you can be paid benefit. See Chapter 14 for an overview of how your entitlement is affected when you go abroad and see Chapters 16 and 17 for more details on the EU co-ordination rules and international agreements.

1. Means-tested benefits

You cannot usually receive means-tested benefits when you are abroad, because the rules for each benefit require you to be present in Great Britain or, for housing benefit (HB – see p349) and council tax reduction (see p627), to occupy your home. However, you can be treated as present (or as occupying your home for HB and council tax reduction) in certain circumstances. The rules differ between the different benefits.

Note: if you were receiving income support (IS), income-based jobseeker's allowance (JSA), income-related employment and support allowance (ESA) or, in many circumstances, HB and it stopped because you went abroad, when you return you will be unable to reclaim that benefit, but may be able to claim universal credit (UC) instead, *unless* you are in one of the circumstances that mean you can make a new claim for HB – eg, if you are pension age or you live in temporary accommodation. For details, see CPAG's *Welfare Benefits and Tax Credits Handbook.*

Universal credit

You cannot usually be paid UC if you (and your partner, if it is a joint claim) are not in Great Britain.[1] However, if you were entitled to UC immediately before leaving Great Britain and you are temporarily absent, you can continue to be entitled for:[2]

- **one month** if your absence is not expected to exceed, and does not exceed, one month; *or*
- **two months** if your absence is in connection with the death of your partner or child, or a close relative of yours (or of your partner or child), and it would be unreasonable for you to return to Great Britain within the first month;
- **six months** if your absence is not expected to exceed, and does not exceed, six months and you are a mariner or continental shelf worker; *or*
- **six months** if your absence is not expected to exceed, and does not exceed, six months and is solely in connection with you undergoing (or you are accompanying your partner or child who is undergoing):
  - treatment of an illness or impairment, by, or under the supervision of, a qualified practitioner; *or*
  - medically approved care or convalescence as a result of an illness or impairment that you had before leaving Great Britain.

Note:

- You are automatically exempt from the work search requirement and are treated as 'able and willing immediately to take up work' during the six-month period following the death of your partner or child or while the fourth bullet above applies.[3]
- Since 24 July 2020, periods of temporary absence in Northern Ireland are ignored due to reciprocal arrangements between Great Britain and Northern Ireland that treat periods of presence and residence (and also employment) in one territory as having the same effect on UC as if it had occurred in the other territory.[4]
- To be entitled to the carer element in your UC while you are abroad, you must satisfy the rules for being paid carer's allowance abroad (see p354).
- The limited capability for work element was abolished for new UC claims from 3 April 2017. If your entitlement to UC ends because you are abroad, you

cannot be entitled to this element in a future claim unless extremely limited circumstances apply. See CPAG's *Welfare Benefits and Tax Credits Handbook*.

If your partner is abroad

If you have a joint claim for UC and both you and your partner go abroad, your entitlement is not affected while one of the above situations applies to both of you. After this time, if you both remain abroad, your entitlement ends.

If you stay in Great Britain while your partner is abroad, their absence does not affect your entitlement during the one-, two- or six-month period if one of the above circumstances applies to them. After this time, unless your partner is in Northern Ireland (see note above), you cease to be entitled as joint claimants and your joint claim is treated as a claim by you as a single person.[5] However, if you and your partner have been, and expect to be, apart for less than six months you are still treated as a couple, so although you are awarded the elements for a single person, your partner's income and capital are taken into account.[6] Once you have been, or expect to be, apart for six months, you stop being treated as a couple[7] and your entitlement as a single person is unaffected by your absent partner.

If your partner's absence abroad means that they stop being habitually resident (including if they no longer have a right to reside) in the common travel area (the UK, Ireland, Channel Islands and the Isle of Man), they are treated as no longer present. Your joint claim is treated as a claim by you as a single person, but your partner's income and capital are taken into account (unless you are no longer being treated as a couple, as described above). For further details on such claims, see p158.[8]

If you have reached pension age, and your partner is under pension age, once their absence exceeds the periods above, your entitlement to UC ends. As a single person, you are not entitled to UC once you have reached pension age, but you can claim pension credit (PC) and HB and you are treated as a single person for each of these claims.[9]

If your child is abroad

If your child is abroad (unless they are in Northern Ireland – see p340), you cease to be entitled for them if their absence is, or is expected to be, longer than the one-, two- or six-month periods allowed in the circumstances above. The circumstances must apply to your child.[10] **Note:** the rules that restrict payment of UC for your third or subsequent child in limited circumstances (the 'two-child limit') may affect you when your child returns. For further details, see p296.

European Union co-ordination rules

The DWP considers that UC is not a 'social security benefit' under the main European Union (EU) co-ordination rules or the UK–EU Protocol. The UK–Ireland Convention lists UC as 'social assistance' and the only co-ordinating rules that apply relate to the recovery of overpayments (see p398).

Therefore, none of these rules can assist you to be paid UC if you go to Ireland, or an EU or European Economic Area (EEA) country. You can only be paid UC under the UK rules above.

Income support

You cannot usually get IS if you are not in Great Britain.[11] However, if you were entitled to IS immediately before leaving Great Britain and you are temporarily absent, your entitlement can continue:[12]

- **indefinitely** if your absence is for NHS treatment at a hospital or other institution outside Great Britain;
- during the first **four weeks** of your absence, if it is unlikely to exceed 52 weeks and:
  - you are in Northern Ireland; *or*
  - you and your partner are both abroad and they satisfy the conditions for one of the pensioner premiums, a disability premium or a severe disability premium; *or*
  - you are entitled to statutory sick pay (SSP) and are abroad for the sole purpose of receiving treatment (see below) for the incapacity that entitles you to SSP; *or*
  - you have been (or are treated as) continuously entitled to SSP before you go abroad for 364 days (or 196 days if you are terminally ill or receiving the highest rate of the care component of disability living allowance or child disability payment, the enhanced rate of the daily living component of personal independence payment or adult disability payment, or armed forces independence payment). Two or more periods of entitlement to SSP are treated as continuous if the break between them is not more than 56 days each time; *or*
  - you are not:
    - entitled to SSP (unless you are covered by either group above); *or*
    - in 'relevant education'; *or*
    - involved in a trade dispute, or have returned to work for 15 days or less following the dispute; *or*
- during the first **eight weeks** of your absence, if it is unlikely to exceed 52 weeks and is solely in connection with arrangements made for the treatment (see below) of a disease or disablement of a child or qualifying young person (for whom you count as responsible under the IS rules).

'**Treatment**' must be carried out by, or under the supervision of, a person qualified to provide medical treatment, physiotherapy or similar treatment.

If you are entitled to housing costs in your IS, your temporary absence from your home can mean that you cease to be entitled to receive these (see p335).

Note: if your entitlement to IS ends because you go abroad, when you return you cannot reclaim IS and must claim UC instead.

If your partner is abroad

If you are the IS claimant and you stay in Great Britain, your IS applicable amount includes an amount for your partner who is temporarily absent from the UK for:[13]

- the first **four weeks**; *or*
- the first **eight weeks**, if they meet the conditions of the eight-week rule above.

If both you and your partner are temporarily absent from the UK, your IS includes an amount for your partner for the first eight weeks if both of you meet the conditions of the eight-week rule above.[14]

After this four- or eight-week period, your benefit is reduced because your applicable amount is calculated as if you have no partner. However, your partner is still treated as being part of your household and, therefore, their work, income and capital affect your IS entitlement, unless you are no longer treated as a couple (see p334).[15]

If your child is abroad

If you were getting an amount in your IS for your child before they went abroad, you continue to be paid for them for:[16]

- the first **four weeks**; *or*
- the first **eight weeks**, if your child meets the conditions of the eight-week rule above.

After this four- or eight-week period, you are no longer paid IS for your child. When they return to Great Britain, unless you have continued to be paid IS for another child, you will not be able to receive a personal allowance for them within your IS, and to receive benefit for them you will need to claim UC. (If you are already receiving IS for two or more children and your returning child was born after 6 April 2017, you may not be able to receive IS for them due to the 'two-child limit' – see p296.)

European Union co-ordination rules

IS is not covered by any of the EU co-ordination rules (except, to co-ordinate the recovery of overpayments, the UK–Ireland Convention – see p398). This means that these rules cannot assist you if you go to Ireland, or an EU or EEA country. You can only be paid IS under the UK rules above.

Income-based jobseeker's allowance

You cannot usually get JSA if you are not in Great Britain.[17] However, if you are temporarily absent from Great Britain, both income-based and contribution-based JSA can continue to be paid:[18]

- **indefinitely** if you are entitled to JSA immediately before leaving Great Britain and your absence is for NHS treatment at a hospital or other institution outside Great Britain;

- for up to **four weeks** if you are entitled to JSA immediately before leaving Great Britain and:
  - your absence is unlikely to exceed 52 weeks, you continue to satisfy the conditions of entitlement and you are in Northern Ireland. **Note:** the reciprocal agreements between Great Britain and Northern Ireland can mean that after four weeks, the administration of your claim moves to Northern Ireland – you do not have to make a new claim[19] (see p435); *or*
  - your absence is unlikely to exceed 52 weeks, you continue to satisfy the conditions of entitlement and your partner is also abroad with you and satisfies the conditions for one of the pensioner premiums, a disability premium or a severe disability premium; *or*
  - you get a specified type of training allowance that means you do not have to satisfy the JSA jobseeking conditions;[20]
- for up to **eight weeks** if you are entitled to JSA immediately before leaving Great Britain and your absence is unlikely to exceed 52 weeks and is solely in connection with arrangements made for the treatment of a disease or disablement of a child or qualifying young person. The treatment must be carried out by, or under the supervision of, a person qualified to provide medical treatment, physiotherapy or similar treatment and you must count as responsible for the child or young person in the same way as for the similar rule on temporary absence for IS (see p342);
- for an absence of up to **seven days** if you are attending a job interview and you notified your work coach before you left (in writing if required). On your return, you must satisfy them that you attended the interview as stated;
- for an absence of up to **15 days** for the purpose of training as a member of the reserve forces.

You can be treated as available for work and actively seeking work during certain temporary absences abroad (these are similar to those listed above).[21] If you are getting contribution-based JSA under the UC system, you are exempt from the work search requirement and are treated as 'able and willing immediately to take up work' during these absences.[22] See CPAG's *Welfare Benefits and Tax Credits Handbook* for details.

If you are entitled to housing costs in your income-based JSA, your temporary absence from your home can mean that you cease to be entitled to receive these (see p335).

Note: if your entitlement to income-based JSA stops because you go abroad, when you return you cannot reclaim income-based JSA and must claim UC instead.

Joint-claim jobseeker's allowance if your partner is abroad

If you are a member of a 'joint-claim couple' (see CPAG's *Welfare Benefits and Tax Credits Handbook* for what this means) and your partner goes abroad *after* you claimed JSA, and their absence is for NHS treatment at a hospital or other institution outside Great Britain, you are paid as a couple for up to four weeks.[23]

After this four-week period, or from the date they leave Great Britain if none of those circumstances apply, your JSA is reduced because your applicable amount is calculated as if you have no partner.[24] However, your partner is still treated as part of your household while they are abroad for treatment. Therefore, their work, income and capital affect your joint-claim JSA entitlement, unless they stop being treated as part of your household for another reason (see p295).[25]

If your partner is no longer treated as part of your household, you can continue to receive income-based JSA as a single person.

Income-based jobseeker's allowance if your partner is abroad

If you are the income-based JSA claimant and you stay in Great Britain, your applicable amount includes an amount for your partner while they are temporarily absent from the UK for:[26]

- the first **four weeks** of a temporary absence; *or*
- the first **eight weeks** if your partner meets the conditions of the eight-week rule (see p344).

If both you and your partner are temporarily absent from the UK, your applicable amount includes an amount for your partner for the first eight weeks if both of you meet the conditions of the eight-week rule (see p344).[27]

After this four- or eight-week period, your benefit is reduced because your applicable amount is calculated as if you have no partner. However, your partner is still treated as part of your household and, therefore, their work, income and capital affect your income-based JSA entitlement, unless you are no longer treated as a couple (see p295).[28]

Income-based jobseeker's allowance if your child is abroad

If you were getting JSA for your child before they went abroad, you can continue to be paid for them for:[29]

- the first **four weeks**; *or*
- the first **eight weeks** if your child meets the conditions of the eight-week rule on p344.

After this four- or eight-week period, the income-based JSA paid in respect of your child stops. When they return to Great Britain, unless you have continued to be paid income-based JSA for another child, you cannot receive a personal allowance for them within your income-based JSA and to receive benefit for them you will need to claim UC. If you are already receiving income-based JSA for two or more children and your returning child was born after 6 April 2017, you may not be able to receive income-based JSA for them due to the 'two-child limit' (see p296).

European Union co-ordination rules

Income-based JSA is classed as a 'special non-contributory benefit' under the main EU co-ordination rules and the UK–EU Protocol (see p397) and 'social assistance' under the UK–Ireland Convention (see p398). This means that it cannot be 'exported' and, if you go to Ireland, or an EU or EEA country, the co-ordination rules cannot assist you. You can only be paid income-based JSA abroad under the UK rules explained above.

However, if you are covered by the main EU co-ordination rules or the UK–Ireland Convention, these may enable you to be paid contribution-based JSA for up to three months if you go to an EEA country (Ireland, if relying on the convention) – see p359.

Income-related employment and support allowance

You cannot usually get ESA if you are not in Great Britain.[30] However, if you were entitled to ESA immediately before leaving Great Britain and you are temporarily absent, you can continue to be entitled to both income-related and contributory ESA:[31]

- **indefinitely** if:
  - your absence is for NHS treatment at a hospital or other institution outside Great Britain; *or*
  - you are living with your spouse, civil partner, son, daughter, stepson, stepdaughter, father, father-in-law, stepfather, mother, mother-in-law or stepmother who is a serving member of the armed forces;
- for the first **four weeks**, if your absence is unlikely to exceed 52 weeks;
- for the first **26 weeks**, if your absence is unlikely to exceed 52 weeks and is solely in connection with arrangements made for the treatment of:
  - your disease or disablement that is directly related to your limited capability for work which began before you left Great Britain; *or*
  - the disease or disablement of a dependent child who you are accompanying.

The treatment must be carried out by, or under the supervision of, a person qualified to provide medical treatment, physiotherapy or similar treatment.

If you are due to have a medical examination to assess your limited capability for work when you go abroad, you can ask for this to be carried out in the other country, or to be postponed until you return. If your request is refused and you go abroad and miss your medical, your ESA is terminated, unless it is accepted that you had a good cause for not attending. In deciding whether you had good cause, the decision maker must take all your circumstances into account, including the fact that you were outside Great Britain.[32] See CPAG's *Welfare Benefits and Tax Credits Handbook* for further details.

If you appeal against a decision on your limited capability for work-related activity while abroad, the tribunal should consider the hypothetical work-related activity that applies in the area of the UK where the tribunal hearing is held, unless you object. This area is usually Newcastle if you opt for a paper hearing.[33]

If you are entitled to housing costs in your income-related ESA, your temporary absence from your home can mean that you cease to be entitled to receive these (see p335).

Note: if your entitlement to income-related ESA stops because you go abroad, when you return you cannot reclaim income-related ESA and must claim UC instead.

If your partner is abroad

If you are the claimant, you stay in Great Britain and your partner is temporarily absent from the UK, your income-related ESA includes an amount for them for:[34]

- the first **four weeks**; *or*
- the first **26 weeks** if they are accompanying a child abroad for treatment and meet the conditions of the 26-week rule above.

If both you and your partner are temporarily absent from the UK, your income-related ESA includes an amount for your partner for the first 26 weeks if both of you are accompanying a child abroad for treatment and you both meet the conditions of the 26-week rule above.[35]

After this four- or 26-week period, your benefit is reduced because your applicable amount is calculated as if you have no partner. However, your partner is still treated as part of your household and, therefore, their work, income and capital affect your income-related ESA entitlement, unless you are no longer treated as a couple (see p334).[36]

European Union co-ordination rules

Income-related ESA is listed under the main co-ordination rules and the UK–EU Protocol as a 'special non-contributory benefit' (see p397) and under the UK–Ireland Convention as 'social assistance'. This means that it cannot be 'exported' and, if you go to Ireland, or an EU or EEA country, the co-ordination rules cannot assist you. You can only be paid income-related ESA abroad under the UK rules explained on p346.

However, each of the co-ordination rules may enable you to continue to be paid contributory ESA if you go to live in an EEA country, but note the UK–EU Protocol only assists during the assessment phase and only in EU states (see p359).

Reciprocal agreements

Reciprocal agreements have not been updated to include ESA (see p433), with the following exceptions.

- The reciprocal agreements between Northern Ireland and Great Britain have included ESA (both income-related and contributory) since 6 April 2016.[37] The purpose of these agreements is to ensure you do not lose out if you move from one territory to the other while claiming ESA. For more information on arrangements between Great Britain and Northern Ireland, including if you moved before 6 April 2016, see p435.

- If your award of contributory ESA was converted from an award of incapacity benefit, it is covered by each of the agreements (with the exception of the Isle of Man, Israel and Switzerland) that cover incapacity benefit (see Appendix 5).[38]

Pension credit

You cannot usually get PC if you are not in Great Britain.[39] However, if you were entitled to PC immediately before leaving Great Britain and you are temporarily absent, your entitlement can continue:[40]

- for up to **four weeks**, provided your absence is not expected to exceed that;
- for up to **eight weeks**, provided your absence is not expected to exceed that, the decision maker considers it unreasonable for you to return to Great Britain within four weeks and the absence is in connection with the death of:
  - your partner;
  - a child who normally lived with you; *or*
  - a close relative of you, your partner or child who normally lives with you;
- for up to **26 weeks**, provided your absence is not expected to exceed that and is solely in connection with medical treatment or medically approved convalescence or care as a result of medical treatment, for you, or your partner or a child who you are accompanying and who normally lives with you.

If you are entitled to housing costs in your PC, your temporary absence from home can mean that you cease to be entitled to receive these (see p335).

If your partner is abroad

If your partner is abroad and you are entitled to PC, either while in Great Britain or abroad because you are covered by the above rules, your PC only includes an amount for them if they are also covered by the above rules. After this, they are not treated as part of your household, you are paid as a single person and their income and capital do not affect your claim.[41]

Note: if your partner is under pension age and you stop being paid PC for them while they are abroad, on their return your entitlement to PC ends, but you can make a joint claim for UC instead. However, if your partner fails the habitual residence test, you will not be entitled to UC, but, until your partner satisfies the habitual residence test, you remain entitled to PC and HB, and you are *treated as* a single person for each of these claims.[42]

For further information about your partner going abroad, see p334.

If your child is abroad

If your child is temporarily absent from Great Britain, you continue to be entitled to an amount in your PC for them:[43]

- **for up to four weeks**, if their absence is not expected to exceed this; *or*
- **for up to eight weeks**, if their absence is not expected to exceed this and is in connection with the death of your partner, a child or qualifying young person who normally lives with you, or a close relative of theirs, yours or your partner's, and the DWP considers it unreasonable for them to return to Great Britain within four weeks; *or*
- **for up to 26 weeks**, if their absence is not expected to exceed this and it is solely in connection with their or your or your partner's medical treatment, or medically approved convalescence.

European Union co-ordination rules

PC is classed as a 'special non-contributory benefit' under the main EU co-ordination rules and the UK–EU Protocol (see p397) and as 'social assistance' under the UK–Ireland Convention. This means that it cannot be 'exported' and, if you go to Ireland, or an EU or EEA country, the co-ordination rules cannot assist you. You can only be paid PC abroad under the UK rules on p348.

Housing benefit

You cannot normally get HB if you are not in Great Britain due to the requirements for you to be occupying your home, except during certain temporary absences. The length of temporary absence you are allowed is shorter if you go abroad than if you were absent from your home but remained in Great Britain.[44]

Provided you meet the other conditions of entitlement, you have not rented out your home and you intend to return to it, you can continue to be paid HB when you are temporarily absent from Great Britain for:[45]

- **up to four weeks**, if your absence is not expected to exceed this;
- **up to eight weeks**, if the absence abroad is in connection with the death of your partner, your (or your partner's) close relative, or a child for whom you (or your partner) are responsible – the above four weeks are extended by up to four weeks if the decision maker considers it unreasonable for you to return within the first four weeks;
- **up to 26 weeks in specific circumstances**. These include if you, your partner or child are in hospital, if you are undergoing or recovering from medical treatment, or if you are absent from home because of domestic violence. See CPAG's *Welfare Benefits and Tax Credits Handbook* for more details. Your absence abroad must be unlikely to exceed (or in exceptional circumstances, substantially exceed) 26 weeks;
- **26 weeks**, if you are a member of the armed forces posted overseas, a mariner or a continental shelf worker. Your absence abroad must be unlikely to exceed 26 weeks.

Note:

- When counting the period of absence for HB, the day of departure counts as a day of absence from Great Britain, but the day of return does not.[46]
- Unless you have reached pension age (and do not have a partner younger than pension age), or in another of the limited circumstances when you can make a new claim for HB (eg, if you are in temporary accommodation), if your entitlement to HB stops because you go abroad, when you return you cannot reclaim HB and must claim UC instead.
- DWP guidance states your HB can continue if you were unable to return from abroad within the periods above due to coronavirus pandemic travel restrictions, although there has been no change to the regulations.[47]
- If you have a European free movement right to reside in the UK (see p192) and you go abroad to an EEA country, it is arguable that the shorter period during which you can be entitled while abroad should not apply as it is indirect discrimination and potentially unlawful under EU law (see p413). The Court of Justice of the European Union accepted a similar argument in relation to funeral payments, ruling that requiring the funeral to take place in the UK unlawfully discriminated against EU migrant workers (see p316).[48]

For further details on the rules on absence from your home, see p335.

If your partner or child is abroad

Whether or not you have amounts included in your HB for your partner or child who is abroad depends on whether they are treated as part of your household (see p295 for partner and p296 for child). The amount of your HB may also depend on whether they are treated as occupying the home (see p335).

You can only be paid HB for your third or subsequent child in limited circumstances (due to the 'two-child limit'). These include if you have been receiving an amount for the child in your HB since 5 April 2017. However, these transitional rules may cease to apply when your child returns from abroad if payments for them, or your claim, stopped because they were abroad. For further details, see p296.

European Union co-ordination rules

HB is not covered by any of the EU co-ordination rules (see p398). This means that these rules cannot assist you. If you go to an EEA country, you can only be paid under the UK rules above.

2. Bereavement benefits

In general, bereavement benefits are payable while you are abroad. However, if you are receiving widowed parent's allowance because your spouse or civil partner died before 6 April 2017, your benefit is not uprated each year if, on the day before the annual uprating takes place, you have ceased to be 'ordinarily resident' (see p147) in Great Britain (unless you have gone to an European Economic Area (EEA) country and you are covered by the European Union (EU) co-ordination rules, or you can rely on a reciprocal agreement – see below).

You may be entitled to a bereavement support payment if you were ordinarily resident in Great Britain on the date your spouse or civil partner died. If you were abroad on that date, see p150 for whether your absence meant that you had ceased to be ordinarily resident.

European Union co-ordination rules

Bereavement benefits are classed as 'survivors' benefits' under each of the EU co-ordination rules (see p393) and are, therefore, fully 'exportable' (see p419). If you are covered by any of these rules (see p379) and the UK is your 'competent state' (see p399):[49]

- and you go to stay or live in an EEA country (or EU country if relying on the UK–EU Protocol, or Ireland if relying on the UK–Ireland Convention), you can be paid your bereavement support payment or widowed parent's allowance for as long as you would receive it if you remained in Great Britain, including any annual uprating; *and*
- for bereavement support payment, the requirement to be ordinarily resident in Great Britain on the date your spouse or civil partner died does not apply if you were resident in an EEA state (or EU state if relying on the protocol, or Ireland if relying on the convention) on that date.

Reciprocal agreements

If you are covered by a reciprocal agreement, this can assist in a similar way to the EU co-ordination rules (see above) in respect of the relevant country.[50] The reciprocal agreements were amended to include bereavement support payment from 6 April 2017.[51] For more information on reciprocal agreements, see Chapter 17.

---

3. Child benefit, Scottish child payment and guardian's allowance

Child benefit

You and your child can be treated as present in Great Britain and, therefore, you can continue to be entitled to child benefit for a limited period during a 'temporary absence' (see p332).

Provided you are 'ordinarily resident' (see p147), you are treated as present during a temporary absence for:[52]

- the first **eight weeks**; *or*
- the first **12 weeks** of any period of absence, or any extension to that period, which is in connection with:
  - the treatment of an illness or disability of you, your partner, a child for whom you are responsible, or another relative of yours or your partner's; *or*
  - the death of your partner, a child or qualifying young person for whom you or your partner are responsible, or another relative of yours or your partner's.

'Relative' means brother, sister, parent, grandparent, great-grandparent or child, grandchild or great-grandchild.[53]

Your child is treated as present during a temporary absence for:[54]

- the first **12 weeks** of any period of absence; *or*
- **any period** during which they are absent for the specific purpose of being treated for an illness or disability which began before their absence began; *or*
- **any period** when they are in Northern Ireland; *or*
- **any period** during which they are absent only because they are:
  - receiving full-time education at a school or college in a European Economic Area (EEA) country; *or*
  - engaged in an educational exchange or visit made with the written approval of the school or college they normally attend; *or*
  - a child who normally lives with a Crown servant posted overseas who is either in the same country as them or is absent from that country for one of the reasons in the two bullet points immediately above.[55]

If a child is born outside Great Britain during the eight- or 12-week period in which you were treated as present in Great Britain, they are treated as being in Great Britain for up to 12 weeks from the start of your absence.[56]

While you and your child are present, or treated as present, you satisfy that condition of entitlement. This means that you can continue to receive any child benefit already being paid and can also make a fresh claim during your, or their, absence. **Note:** if you or your child are treated as present, you must satisfy all the other conditions of entitlement including, if your child is not living with you, contributing at least the amount of child benefit that would be payable for the costs of that child.[57] For information on all the conditions of entitlement for child benefit, see CPAG's *Welfare Benefits and Tax Credits Handbook*.

Scottish child payment

You cease to be entitled to a Scottish child payment the week after you cease to be ordinarily resident in Scotland (see p147).[58]

Guardian's allowance

Entitlement to guardian's allowance generally depends on entitlement to child benefit, so you can be paid guardian's allowance abroad for the same period as child benefit (see p351). For the limited circumstances in which you can be entitled to guardian's allowance because you are *treated* as entitled to child benefit, including if you are receiving a family benefit from another country, see CPAG's *Welfare Benefits and Tax Credits Handbook*.

Your guardian's allowance is not uprated each year if you have ceased to be ordinarily resident (see p147) in Great Britain on the day before the annual uprating takes place,[59] unless you have gone to an EEA country and you are covered by the main European Union (EU) co-ordination rules or you can rely on a reciprocal agreement.

European Union co-ordination rules

If you are covered by the main EU co-ordination rules or, for situations involving the UK and Ireland only, the UK–Ireland Convention (see p379), and the UK is your 'competent state' (see p399):

- you can be paid child benefit and guardian's allowance for a child resident in an EEA country (Ireland, if you are relying on the convention). The child does not have to be in education. However, you must still satisfy all the other conditions of entitlement, including contributing to the costs of the child an amount at least equal to the amount of child benefit payable for them; *and/or*
- you can 'export' (continue to be paid) child benefit and guardian's allowance (and arguably Scottish child payment) if you go to stay or live in an EEA country (Ireland, if you are relying on the convention) provided the UK continues to be your competent state (see p399), and your benefit is uprated in the normal way.

These rules can be complicated in certain circumstances – eg, if there is entitlement to family benefits in more than one state.

Child benefit and guardian's allowance are categorised under the main EU co-ordination rules and listed under the UK–Ireland Convention as 'family benefits'. For more information on the payment of 'family benefits', see p420.

Scottish child payment has been categorised as a special non-contributory benefit (see p397) and so the EU co-ordination rules above do not apply.

If you are not covered by either the main EU co-ordination rules or the UK–Ireland Convention, but you are covered by the UK–EU Protocol, that will not assist you in the ways above because the protocol does not cover family benefits.

Reciprocal and other international agreements

If you are covered by a reciprocal agreement, this may enable periods of residence and/or presence in the other country to be treated as residence and/or presence in

Great Britain in order to be entitled to child benefit and guardian's allowance. For more information on reciprocal agreements, see p443.

There are agreements with Albania and Israel that can assist in ways that are similar to the EU co-ordination rules (see above). For more information on these agreements, see p447.

4. Disability and carers' benefits

Provided you continue to be habitually resident (see p163), if you go abroad you are treated as being present in Great Britain (or for adult disability payment (ADP) and child disability payment (CDP), in the common travel area of the UK, Ireland, Channel Islands and the Isle of Man), and can continue to receive, or make a new claim for,[60] **attendance allowance (AA), disability living allowance (DLA), CDP, personal independence payment (PIP), ADP and carer's allowance (CA)**:[61]

- (except CA) for the first **13 weeks** of a 'temporary absence' (see p332);
- (except CA) for the first **26 weeks** of a 'temporary absence' (see p332), if the absence is solely in connection with medical treatment for your illness or disability that began before you left Great Britain (common travel area for ADP and CDP);
- (for CA only) for up to **four weeks** if your absence is (and was when it began) for a temporary purpose and does not exceed four weeks. If you are not accompanied by the disabled person for whom you are caring, you must satisfy the rules that entitle you to CA during a break from caring. See CPAG's *Welfare Benefits and Tax Credits Handbook* for more information;
- (for CA only) if your absence is temporary and for the specific purpose of caring for a disabled person who is also absent from Great Britain and who continues to receive AA, DLA care component paid at the highest or middle rate, the daily living component of PIP, armed forces independence payment or constant attendance allowance (at the time of writing, amendments to include the daily living component of ADP and the care component of CDP in this list were expected[62]);
- while you are abroad as an aircraft worker or mariner or continental shelf worker (for ADP and CDP, you are also treated as satisfying the 'past presence test' (see p143));
- (for AA, DLA, PIP and CA) while you are a serving member of the armed forces or are living with someone who is abroad as a serving member of the armed forces and they are your spouse, civil partner, son, stepson, daughter, stepdaughter, or father, stepfather, father-in-law, mother, stepmother or mother-in-law. **Note:** you are also treated as habitually resident if you are in this group; *or*

- (for ADP or CDP) while you are a serving member of the armed forces or a civil servant, and immediately prior to the start of either employment you satisfied the residence and presence conditions (other than the past presence test), or you are living with someone who is abroad as a serving member of the armed forces or civil servant, and you are their spouse, civil partner, or living together as if married/civil partners, or son, stepson, daughter, stepdaughter, or a child in the care of, or (for ADP only) father, stepfather, mother, stepmother, mother-in-law or father-in-law of that person. **Note:** you are also treated as habitually resident, ordinarily resident, and as satisfying the past presence test if you are in this group.

ADP and CDP entitlement *also* ends 13 weeks after you cease to be ordinarily resident in Scotland due to moving to another part of the UK (or, for CDP only, if notification is given less than 13 weeks after that date, 13 weeks after the date of notification). If you are in receipt of PIP or DLA when you become ordinarily resident in Scotland, you should notify the DWP about your change of address. The DWP should then notify Social Security Scotland who will determine your entitlement to ADP or CDP without a claim being required. Your PIP or DLA continues until the decision on your ADP or CDP.[63]

If your entitlement to **PIP** ended because you went abroad, the above rules did not apply for the whole period you were away and you return to Great Britain within 12 months, a new claim for PIP can be assessed on the basis of the information held about your last claim if your needs have not changed. The DWP refers to this as a 'rapid reclaim'.[64]

If you lose your entitlement to **CA**, you should still be eligible for a carer premium in your income support, income-based jobseeker's allowance, income-related employment and support allowance and housing benefit for a further period of eight weeks, provided you remain entitled to these benefits while you are away.[65] If you lose your entitlement to CA while you are abroad and the disabled person you care for is staying in the UK, they may instead become entitled to a severe disability premium in their benefit during your absence. For further information on premiums, see CPAG's *Welfare Benefits and Tax Credits Handbook*.

You can continue to be paid an **increase in your CA** for your spouse/civil partner or dependent adult while they are abroad if:[66]

- you are entitled to CA; *and*
- you are residing with them. **Note:** you can be treated as residing together during a temporary absence from each other.[67]

If you are under 19, in receipt of DLA or CDP higher rate care component, or PIP or ADP enhanced rate daily living component, and have a 'genuine and sufficient link' to Scotland while habitually resident in particular European Economic Area (EEA) countries, you may qualify for **child winter heating assistance** (see p317).

European Union co-ordination rules

You may be able to receive these benefits while abroad if you are covered (see p379) by the main European Union (EU) co-ordination rules or, in situations involving the UK and Ireland only, the UK–Ireland Convention, or for ADP or CDP in situations involving the UK and Gibraltar only, the agreement between the UK and Gibraltar (see p436). If you are only covered by the UK–EU Protocol, that will not assist you in the ways below because it does not cover disability and carers' benefits.[68]

Since April 2013, if you move to, and become habitually resident in, an EEA country (Ireland if relying on the UK-Ireland Convention, or, for ADP or CDP only, Gibraltar), you can continue to be paid **AA, DLA or CDP care component, PIP or ADP daily living component, and CA** without needing to satisfy the usual presence and residence requirements (see p302) if:[69]

- you are covered by the main EU co-ordination rules (or, if you are resident in Ireland, the UK–Ireland Convention) (see p379) (or, for ADP or CDP, the agreement between the UK and Gibraltar – see p436); *and*
- you are habitually resident in an EEA state (Ireland if relying on the UK–Ireland Convention, or for ADP or CDP only, Gibraltar if relying on the agreement with Gibraltar); *and*
- you can demonstrate a 'genuine and sufficient link' to the UK (to Scotland for ADP or CDP) (see p307).

Note:

- To continue to be paid your benefit, or to make a new claim (see p308), while the above bullets apply, the UK must be your 'competent state' to pay that benefit (see p399).[70] You can then continue to be paid for as long as the UK remains your competent state.
- For ADP or CDP while in Ireland, the above rules assist by overcoming the requirement to be ordinarily resident in Scotland (the habitual residence, presence and past presence requirements can be satisfied in Ireland as this is part of the common travel area).

You can make a new claim (including for a backdated period if you would have been entitled if these rules had been in force at the time) for **carer's allowance supplement** or a **young carer grant** without needing to satisfy the requirement to be resident or ordinarily resident in Scotland if:[71]

- you have a 'genuine and sufficient link to Scotland' (see p307); *and*
- the UK is your 'competent state' to pay this benefit; *and*
- you are either:
  - resident in an EEA state and covered by the main EU co-ordination rules (see p379); *or*
  - resident in Ireland and covered by the UK–Ireland Convention (see p387); *or*

- resident in Gibraltar and covered by the agreement between the UK and Gibraltar (see p436).

Whether or not you could be paid in an EEA country **before April 2013** depends on the date your entitlement began, as AA, DLA and CA have been categorised in different ways under the co-ordination rules at different times.

Before 1 June 1992, AA, DLA and CA were classed as 'invalidity benefits' (see p393). If your entitlement began before this date, you can continue to be paid benefit in any EEA state.

From 1 June 1992, the UK government categorised AA, DLA and CA as 'special non-contributory benefits' (see p397). These are not 'exportable'. However, the Court of Justice of the European Union (CJEU) declared that this was wrong and that these benefits (except DLA mobility component) were 'sickness benefits'.[72] This means they are 'exportable' and you should continue to receive the benefit if you are covered by the main EU co-ordination rules, for as long as the UK remains your competent state (see p402).[73] The CJEU has reconfirmed that DLA care component is a sickness, and not an invalidity, benefit.[74] The daily living component of PIP/ADP and the care component of CDP are treated as 'sickness benefits'.

Under the **main EU co-ordination rules, DLA mobility component** is listed as, **PIP mobility component** is accepted as, and **the mobility components of ADP and CDP** are treated as 'special non-contributory benefits' (see p397).[75] You can only be paid the mobility component in the state where you are resident under the co-ordination rules.[76] See p401 for details on where you are considered 'resident'.

The UK–Ireland Convention and UK–EU Protocol do not cover these mobility components at all.

You cannot make a new claim for the mobility components of DLA, PIP or ADP after you reach pension age, so if you lose your entitlement because you go abroad, you cannot re-establish this when you return to the UK if you have then reached pension age. The Upper Tribunal has held that this rule is *not* contrary to EU law in a case concerning a man who returned to the UK after living in France for several years.[77] **Note:** if you lose your entitlement to DLA, PIP or ADP because you went abroad and you reached pension age before your entitlement ended, you can become entitled again (including, if you were previously entitled, to the mobility component, despite being pension age or over), provided you make a new claim within 12 months of the previous award ending.[78] For further details on DLA and PIP entitlement criteria and the rules on renewal claims, see CPAG's *Welfare Benefits and Tax Credits Handbook*.

If you receive CA while in the UK and the main EU co-ordination rules apply to you (see p379), you may be able to continue to be paid an addition for an adult or child if they go to stay or live in an EEA country. These additions count as 'family benefits' under the co-ordination rules (see p420).

Was your benefit stopped because you moved to another European Economic Area state on or after 8 March 2001?

If your AA, DLA care component or CA was stopped solely because you moved to an EEA state on or after 8 March 2001, this decision was wrong.[79]

The DWP can restore your entitlement and pay arrears from 18 October 2007 (or the date your payment was stopped, if this is later).[80] The DWP pays arrears from this date because this was when the CJEU decided these benefits had been wrongly categorised.

To get your entitlement restored and arrears paid for any period between 8 March 2001 and 18 October 2007, see p266 of the 10th edition of this *Handbook*.

Reciprocal agreements

Most reciprocal agreements do not cover disability and carers' benefits. However, the agreements with Denmark, Germany, Guernsey, Jersey and the Isle of Man have provisions in relation to AA and DLA, and (Isle of Man only) CA. From 6 April 2016, the reciprocal arrangements between Great Britain and Northern Ireland provide for periods of presence and residence in Northern Ireland to count as presence and residence in Great Britain (and vice versa) for AA, DLA, PIP and carer's allowance.[81]

For general information on these agreements, see p435.

5. Industrial injuries benefits

Industrial injuries benefits are:

- disablement benefit;
- reduced earnings allowance (REA);
- retirement allowance;
- constant attendance allowance;
- exceptionally severe disablement allowance.

Disablement benefit and retirement allowance are not affected if you go abroad.[82]

Constant attendance allowance and exceptionally severe disablement allowance are payable for the first six months of a temporary absence, or a longer period that the DWP may allow.[83]

REA can be paid while you are temporarily absent abroad for the first three months (or longer if the DWP allows) if:[84]

- your absence from Great Britain is not in connection with employment, trade or business; *and*
- your claim was made before you left Great Britain; *and*
- you were entitled to REA before going abroad.

Note: REA has been abolished. If you break your claim, you may no longer be eligible for benefit.

European Union co-ordination rules

Industrial injuries benefits, with the exception of retirement allowance, are classed as 'benefits for accidents at work and occupational diseases' under each of the European Union (EU) co-ordination rules (see p393) and are, therefore, fully 'exportable'. If you are covered by these rules (see p379) and you go to stay or live in a European Economic Area country (EU country if relying on the UK–EU Protocol, or Ireland if relying on the UK–Ireland Convention), you can be paid without any time limit and the benefits will be fully uprated each year. See p419 for more details.

Reciprocal agreements

The UK has reciprocal agreements with several countries that cover industrial injuries benefits. These can enable you to continue to be paid benefit indefinitely when you go to a relevant country, and contain provisions for determining entitlement when more than one country is involved. For more information on reciprocal agreements covering industrial injuries benefits, see p441.

6. Contribution-based jobseeker's allowance and contributory employment and support allowance

You cannot usually get jobseeker's allowance (JSA) or employment and support allowance (ESA) if you are not in Great Britain.[85] However, contribution-based JSA can be paid when you are temporarily absent from Great Britain in the same circumstances as income-based JSA (see p343), and contributory ESA can be paid when you are temporarily absent from Great Britain in the same circumstances as income-related ESA (see p346).

European Union co-ordination rules

You may be able to be paid contribution-based JSA or contributory ESA when you go abroad if you are covered by the main European Union (EU) co-ordination rules, or, for situations involving the UK and Ireland only, the UK–Ireland Convention, or, arguably contributory ESA (see p393), if you go to an EU state and are covered by the UK–EU Protocol. The specific rules differ under each set of co-ordination rules, so you need to check which you are covered by (see p371).

Contribution-based jobseeker's allowance

Contribution-based JSA is classed as an unemployment benefit under each of these co-ordination rules (see p393). However, the **UK–EU Protocol** does not provide for unemployment benefits to be 'exported'.[86]

If you are covered by the main co-ordination rules or, if you are going to Ireland, the **UK–Ireland Convention** (see p379) and the UK is your 'competent state' (see p399), you can continue to be paid (referred to as 'exporting') contribution-based JSA for up to three months if:[87]

- you satisfied the conditions for contribution-based JSA before you left the UK for at least four weeks (in total, which need not be continuous[88]), unless the DWP authorised you to go abroad before then; *and*
- you register as unemployed in Ireland, if you are relying on the UK–Ireland Convention, or the European Economic Area (EEA) country you go to, within seven days, and comply with its procedures.

Contributory employment and support allowance

If you are covered by the **main co-ordination rules** (see p379) and you go to live in an EEA country, in most cases, you can continue to be paid ('export') contributory ESA, while the UK remains your competent state (see p399).

Exportability can be affected by how the benefit is classed. 'Invalidity benefits' are fully exportable under the main co-ordination rules, whereas 'sickness benefits' can be subject to limitations on exportability. Contributory ESA is initially classed as a 'sickness benefit' during at least the 91-day 'assessment phase',[89] and potentially, the first 365 days,[90] and then as an 'invalidity benefit' thereafter. However, in most cases 'sickness benefits' are exportable in similar circumstances to 'invalidity benefits', and DWP guidance confirms you can continue to receive assessment phase ESA while staying temporarily in, or if you have moved to, an EEA country.[91] If the DWP terminates your contributory ESA due to your moving to an EEA country, challenge the decision and get advice. If you have a long-term or permanent disability, it is arguable that contributory ESA during the assessment phase should be regarded as an 'invalidity benefit'.[92]

If you are covered by the **UK–Ireland Convention** (see p387), you can continue to be paid your ESA during and after the assessment phase if you go to stay or live in Ireland, while the UK remains your competent state.

If you are covered by the **UK–EU Protocol** (see p388), DWP guidance states that contributory ESA is treated as an invalidity benefit from the outset and is therefore not exportable because, under the protocol, invalidity benefits are not exportable.[93] However, it may be arguable that contributory ESA under the protocol should be classed in the same way as it is under the main co-ordination rules, and therefore that you should be able to export if you move to an EU country and the UK remains your competent state.

If you can export your contributory ESA, the DWP continues to assess your limited capability for work and your limited capability for work-related activity.

However, any checks and medicals take place in the state in which you are living, with reports then sent to the DWP.[94]

If you appeal against a decision on your limited capability for work-related activity while abroad, the tribunal should consider the hypothetical work-related activity that applies in the area of the UK where the tribunal hearing is held, unless you object. This area is usually Newcastle if you opt for a paper hearing.[95]

Reciprocal agreements

If the country you are going to has a reciprocal agreement that covers contribution-based JSA (see Appendix 5), check whether you are covered by it. Such agreements can, for example, enable you to be paid a contribution-based benefit for a limited period and/or to use periods of employment completed, or national insurance contributions paid, in Great Britain to entitle you to unemployment benefits in the country you are going to. See p440 for further information.

Most reciprocal agreements do not cover contributory ESA (see p440). The exceptions are:

- the agreement with Northern Ireland, which, since 6 April 2016, covers contributory ESA (as well as income-related ESA). For details, including the policy if you moved between Great Britain and Northern Ireland while claiming ESA before this date, see p435;[96] *and*
- if your award of contributory ESA was converted from incapacity benefit, it is covered by the agreements (except the Isle of Man, Israel and Switzerland) that cover incapacity benefit (see Appendix 5).[97]

7. Maternity allowance, incapacity benefit and severe disablement allowance

In general, you are disqualified from maternity allowance (MA), incapacity benefit (IB) and severe disablement allowance (SDA) if you are absent from Great Britain.[98] However, if you are temporarily absent from Great Britain, you can continue to be paid MA, IB and SDA, if:[99]

- you are receiving attendance allowance (AA), disability living allowance (DLA), personal independence payment (PIP) or armed forces independence payment. For when AA, DLA or PIP can be paid abroad, see p354; *or*
- the DWP certifies that you should continue to be paid. You can then receive the benefit for the first 26 weeks of your temporary absence; *or*
- you are the spouse, civil partner, son, stepson, daughter, stepdaughter, father, stepfather, father-in-law, mother, stepmother or mother-in-law of a serving member of the armed forces and you are abroad only because you are living with them.

In addition:

- when you left Great Britain, you must have been continuously incapable of work for six months and have been continuously incapable since your departure; *or*
- your absence from Great Britain must be for the specific purpose of being treated for an incapacity which began before you left Great Britain; *or*
- for IB only, your incapacity for work is the result of a personal injury caused by an accident at work and your absence from Great Britain is for the specific purpose of receiving treatment for that injury.

If you are due to have a medical examination, this can be arranged abroad.

Note: most IB and SDA claims have been reassessed for transfer to employment and support allowance (ESA). If your award of IB or SDA is converted to contributory ESA, you do not need to resatisfy the national insurance (NI) contribution conditions. However, if you are getting IB or SDA and lose entitlement because you go abroad for more than 26 weeks, you do not requalify for IB or SDA on your return to Great Britain, and you can only get contributory ESA if you satisfy all the conditions of entitlement, including the NI contribution conditions. Losing entitlement because you go abroad could therefore result in a loss of potential future benefit.

You can continue to be paid an increase in your IB or SDA for your spouse/civil partner or dependent adult while they are abroad if you are residing with them.[100] **Note:** you can be treated as residing together during a temporary absence from each other.[101]

European Union co-ordination rules

If you are covered by the main European Union (EU) co-ordination rules or, for situations involving the UK and one or more EU states, the UK–EU Protocol, or, for situations involving the UK and Ireland only, the UK–Ireland Convention (see p379), and the UK continues to be your 'competent state' to pay the relevant benefit (see p399), you can:

- be paid **MA** if you go to live or stay in a European Economic Area (EEA) country (EU country if relying on the protocol, or Ireland if relying on the convention). This is referred to as 'exporting' your MA.[102] MA is classed as a 'maternity benefit' under each of the co-ordination rules (see p393);
- (only if you are covered by the main EU co-ordination rules) continue to receive your **long-term IB and SDA**, including any uprating if you go to live in an EEA country. This is referred to as 'exporting' your IB or SDA. The DWP continues to determine your incapacity for work, but any checks and medicals take place in the state in which you live and the reports are then sent to the paying state.[103] IB and SDA are classed as 'invalidity benefits' under the main EU co-ordination rules (see p393). The UK–EU Protocol does not provide for

invalidity benefits to be 'exported', and the UK–Ireland Convention does not cover these two benefits;

- (only if you are covered by the main co-ordination rules) if you remain in the UK, continue to be paid an increase for an adult or child if they go to stay or live in an EEA country. These increases are classified as 'family benefits'. See p420 for details about when you can receive these for a family member living abroad.

See p419 for details on 'exporting' benefits.

Reciprocal agreements

The UK has reciprocal agreements with several countries that cover incapacity, sickness and maternity benefits. If you are going to one of these countries, the agreement may enable you to:

- continue to be paid benefit; *or*
- make a new claim for MA; *or*
- use NI contributions paid, or periods of employment completed, in the UK to qualify for benefit in the country you are going to.

For more information on reciprocal agreements covering maternity benefits, see p441, and for sickness and invalidity benefits, see p440.

8. Retirement pensions

All retirement pensions are payable without any time limit while you are abroad.[104] However, if you are not ordinarily resident (see p147) in Great Britain:[105]

- on the day before the annual uprating takes place, your benefit is not uprated that year;[106]
- when you claim state pension (for people who reach pension age on or after 6 April 2016) that you have deferred, the upratings that occurred while you were abroad are ignored when calculating both the deferral increase and rate payable;
- you cannot stop claiming ('de-retire') your 'old' retirement pension (for people who reached pension age before 6 April 2016) in order to accrue a deferral payment.[107]

The above does not apply if you go to a European Economic Area (EEA) state and you are covered by the European Union (EU) co-ordination rules, or you can rely on a reciprocal agreement (see below).

Although category D retirement pension is payable if you are abroad, you must meet the residence requirements at the date you make your claim (see p314).

If you live abroad, your retirement pension can be paid into a bank in either the country where you live or in the UK.

You can continue to be paid an increase in your category A retirement pension for your spouse/civil partner or dependent adult while they are abroad if:[108]

- you are entitled to the pension; *and*
- you are residing with them. You can be treated as residing together during a temporary absence from each other.[109]

European Union co-ordination rules

If you are covered by the main EU co-ordination rules (which cover the UK and the EEA states), or the UK–EU Protocol (which covers the UK and the EU states), or, for situations involving the UK and Ireland only, the UK–Ireland Convention (see p379), and the UK is your 'competent state' (see p399), and you go to live in a member state:

- you can 'export' (ie, continue to be paid) your retirement pension without time limit;
- your retirement pension is paid at the same rate as if you were still in the UK, including your annual uprating; *and*
- (if you reached pension age before 6 April 2016) you can opt to stop claiming your pension ('de-retire') in order to accrue a deferral payment while living in a member state.

Retirement pensions are classed as 'old age benefits' under each of the co-ordination rules (see p393).

See also the note on continued pension uprating (and aggregation of national insurance contributions) for those not otherwise covered by the main co-ordination rules (see p314).

If you are covered by the **main EU co-ordination rules** and you remain in the UK, you may be able to continue to be paid an increase for an adult or child if they go to stay or live in an EEA state. These increases count as 'family benefits' under these co-ordination rules. See p420 for more details.

Reciprocal agreements

If you are covered by a reciprocal agreement (see p433) that provides for uprating, you can continue to be paid your pension at the same rate as if you were still in the UK. **Note:** the agreements with Canada and New Zealand, and the former agreement with Australia, do not provide for uprating. For further information on reciprocal agreements and retirement pensions, see p441.

9. Statutory payments

There are no presence or residence rules for statutory sick pay (SSP), statutory maternity pay (SMP), statutory adoption pay (SAP), statutory paternity pay (SPP), statutory shared parental pay (SSPP) and statutory parental bereavement pay (SPBP). You remain entitled to these benefits if you go abroad, provided you meet the usual rules of entitlement, including those relating to being an employee.[110]

Although you are generally required to be employed in Great Britain to count as an 'employee', you count as an employee for the purpose of these benefits, even while employed abroad, in certain circumstances, including if:[111]

- your employer is required to pay secondary class 1 national insurance (NI) contributions for you; *or*
- you are a continental shelf worker or, in certain circumstances, an airman/woman or mariner; *or*
- you are employed in a European Economic Area (EEA) country and had you been employed in Great Britain you would be considered an employee, and the UK is the 'competent state' under the European Union (EU) co-ordination rules (see p399).

Your employer is not required to pay you SSP, SMP, SAP, SPP, SSPP or SPBP if:[112]

- your employer is not legally required to pay employer class 1 NI contributions (even if these contributions are, in fact, made) because, at the time they become payable, your employer:
  - is not resident or present in Great Britain; *and*
  - does not have (or is treated as not having) a place of business in Great Britain; *or*
- because of an international treaty or convention, your employer is exempt from the Social Security Acts, or they are not enforceable against your employer.

European Union co-ordination rules

The DWP has considered that these statutory payments are treated as wages and not social security benefits under the main co-ordination rules,[113] and it was expected the same view would be taken under the UK–EU Protocol. It has always been arguable that SSP is a 'sickness benefit' and SMP, SAP, SPP, SSPP and SSBP are 'maternity/paternity benefits' under the main co-ordination rules[114], and recent guidance has listed them as such, under each of these co-ordination rules.[115] However, due to the absence of residence and presence requirements for these benefits, it is unlikely you need to rely on the co-ordination rules. The DWP accepts you can be paid all these statutory payments if you go to stay or live in an EEA state under the UK rules above.

The UK–Ireland Convention prevents these statutory payments being paid at the same time as Irish sickness, maternity, paternity or invalidity benefits.[116]

10. Tax credits

Provided you are ordinarily resident (see p147), you can be treated as being present and, therefore, entitled to child tax credit (CTC) and working tax credit (WTC) during a 'temporary absence' (see p332) for:[117]

- the first **eight weeks**; *or*
- the first **12 weeks** of any period of absence, or any extension to that period, which is in connection with:
  - the treatment of an illness or disability of you, your partner, a child for whom you are responsible, or another relative (see below) of either you or your partner; *or*
  - the death of your partner, a child or qualifying young person for whom you or your partner are responsible, or another relative (see below) of you or your partner.

'**Relative**' means brother, sister, parent, grandparent, grandchild or great-grandparent or child.[118]

You are also treated as present if you are:[119]

- a Crown servant posted overseas and:
  - you are, or immediately before your posting abroad you were, ordinarily resident in the UK; *or*
  - immediately before your posting you were in the UK in connection with that posting; *or*
- the partner of a Crown servant posted overseas and in the same country as them or temporarily absent from that country under the same exceptions that enable tax credits to continue during a temporary absence from Great Britain.

While you are treated as present in any of the above ways, you continue to satisfy that condition of entitlement. This means that you can continue to receive any tax credits that are already in payment, and can make a renewal claim during your absence. It also means that if you are receiving CTC or WTC and become entitled to the other, you can start to receive this during your absence (you are not required to claim universal credit (UC)).

If your childcare provider is located outside the UK, you can still be entitled to the childcare element of WTC (see p318).

Your tax credit entitlement ends if:

- you (or your partner, in a joint claim) spend longer abroad than the permitted temporary absence periods, as you cease to satisfy the presence condition; *or*
- you (or your partner, in a joint claim) cease to be ordinarily resident; *or*
- you are entitled to tax credits on the basis of a joint claim and you separate from your partner in circumstances in which the separation is likely to be permanent, as you cease to count as a couple.[120]

If your entitlement to tax credits on the basis of a joint claim ends, you cannot make a new single claim, but may be able to claim UC instead.

European Union co-ordination rules

You may be assisted in the ways below if you are covered by the main European Union (EU) co-ordination rules, or, for situations involving the UK and Ireland only, the UK–Ireland Convention. The UK–EU Protocol does not apply to CTC or WTC.

CTC is classed as a 'family benefit' under the main EU co-ordination rules and the UK–Ireland Convention (see p393). If either of these rules apply to you (see p379) and the UK is your 'competent state' (see p399), you can be paid CTC:

- if you go to stay or live in a European Economic Area (EEA) state (Ireland, if relying on the convention); *and/or*
- for a child resident in an EEA state (Ireland, if relying on the convention) – provided you meet the other conditions of CTC, including that the child is 'normally living with' you.[121]

See p420 for more details on the payment of family benefits under the EU co-ordination rules.

WTC is not covered by any of the EU co-ordination rules. Therefore, if your partner is in an EEA country, although you may have a joint claim for CTC as a couple, you can only be entitled to WTC on the basis of a single claim.[122]

If you or your partner are working in an EEA country but live in the UK and, therefore, remain present and ordinarily resident in the UK, this work can count for the purposes of your WTC claim.[123]

Notes

1. **Means-tested benefits**
   1 ss3 and 4(1)(c) WRA 2012
   2 Reg 11 UC Regs; see also paras C1986-95 ADM
   3 Reg 99(1)-(3) UC Regs
   4 Sch para 2 UC(NIRA) Regs; see also ADM Memo 18/20, para 3
   5 Regs 3(3) UC Regs; reg 9(1) UC,PIP,JSA&ESA(C&P) Regs
   6 Regs 3, 18, 22 and 36 UC Regs
   7 Reg 3(6) UC Regs
   8 Regs 3(3), 9, 18(2), 22(3) and 36(3) UC Regs; reg 9(1) UC,PIP,JSA&ESA(C&P) Regs
   9 Art 7(1), (2)(a) and (b) and (3)(b) WRA(No.31)O; HB Circular A9/2019, paras 15-17; Vol 13 Ch 77 paras 77035 note 2, 77150-1 and 77160 DMG
   10 Reg 4(7) UC Regs
   11 s124(1) SSCBA 1992
   12 Reg 4 IS Regs
   13 Reg 21 and Sch 7 paras 11 and 11A IS Regs
   14 Reg 21 and Sch 7 para 11A IS Regs
   15 Reg 16 IS Regs
   16 Reg 16(5) IS Regs
   17 s1(2)(i) JSA 1995
   18 s21 and Sch 1 para 11 JSA 1995; reg 50 JSA Regs; reg 41 JSA Regs 2013
   19 Sch para 2 SS(NIRA) Regs; Sch para 2 SS(GBRA)(NI) Regs
   20 Regs 50(4) and 170 JSA Regs
   21 Regs 14 and 19 JSA Regs
   22 Reg 16 JSA Regs 2013
   23 Regs 3E(1) and (2)(c), 50(6B) and 86C JSA Regs
   24 Regs 50(6B) and 78(1A) and (3)(c) and Sch 5A para 7 JSA Regs
   25 Reg 78 JSA Regs
   26 Reg 85 and Sch 5 paras 10 and 11 JSA Regs
   27 Reg 85 and Sch 5 para 11 JSA Regs
   28 Reg 78 JSA Regs
   29 Reg 78(5) JSA Regs
   30 ss1(3)(d) and 18(4)(a) WRA 2007
   31 Regs 151-55 ESA Regs; regs 88-92 ESA Regs 2013
   32 Reg 24 ESA Regs; reg 20 ESA Regs 2013
   33 *BB v SSWP (ESA)* [2015] UKUT 545 (AAC); see also *KC and MC v SSWP (ESA)* [2017] UKUT 94 (AAC)
   34 Regs 69 and 156 and Sch 5 paras 6 and 7 ESA Regs
   35 Regs 69 and 156 and Sch 5 para 7 ESA Regs
   36 Reg 156 ESA Regs
   37 SS(NIRA) Regs; SS(GBRA)(NI) Regs
   38 SS(RA)O
   39 s1(2)(a) SPCA 2002
   40 Regs 3 and 4 SPC Regs
   41 Reg 5 SPC Regs
   42 s4(1A) SPCA 2002; Arts 4(2), 6(2)(a), 7(1), (2)(a) and (b) and (3)(b) and 8 WRA(No.31)O; HB Circular A9/2019; Vol 13 Ch 77 paras 77035 note 2, 77150-1 and 77160 DMG
   43 Sch IIA para 7 SPC Regs
   44 s130(1)(a) SSCBA 1992; reg 7 HB Regs; reg 7 HB(SPC) Regs
   45 Reg 7 HB Regs; reg 7 HB(SPC) Regs
   46 *Slough BC v PK* [2019] UKUT 128 (AAC)
   47 LA Welfare Direct 6/2020 (updated 11 December 2020)
   48 Art 18 TFEU; Art 24 EU Dir 2004/38; *O'Flynn v Adjudication Officer*, C-237/94 [1996]; R(IS) 4/98

2. **Bereavement benefits**
   49 Arts 5, 7, 42 and 43 EU Reg 883/04; Arts 5, 7 and 43 UK-IC; Arts 6, 8, 37 and 38 UK-EUP
   50 Reg 5 SSB(PA) Regs
   51 The Social Security (Reciprocal Agreements) Order 2017 No.159; SS(NIRA)(A) Regs; SS(GBRA)(A)NI Regs

3. **Child benefit, Scottish child payment and guardian's allowance**
   52 Reg 24 CB Regs
   53 Reg 24(1) CB Regs
   54 Reg 21 CB Regs
   55 Reg 32 CB Regs
   56 Reg 21(2) CB Regs
   57 s143(1)(b) SSCBA 1992
   58 Reg 19 SCP Regs
   59 Reg 5 SSB(PA) Regs

4. **Disability and carers' benefits**

60 Confirmed in ADM Memo 9/20 and DMG Memo 12/20

61 **AA** Reg 2(2), (3B) and (3C) SS(AA) Regs
DLA Reg 2(2), (3B) and (3C) SS(DLA) Regs
PIP Regs 17-20 SS(PIP) Regs
CA Reg 9(2) and (3) SS(ICA) Regs
CDP Regs 5(6)-(8) and 7 DACYP(S) Regs
ADP Regs 16, 17 and 18 DAWAP(S) Regs

62 Scottish Government email to CPAG, 5 October 2022

63 **DLA** Reg 2(1ZB) SS(DLA) Regs
CDP Regs 35, 36 and 41 and Sch Part 3 DACYP(S) Regs; see also DMG Memo 10/21, para 4
PIP Reg 23ZA(2) SS(PIP) Regs
ADP Regs 52, 53 and 60 and Sch 2 Part 3 DAWAP(S) Regs

64 'Disability', House of Commons, *Hansard*, Written statement HCWS603, 20 April 2017; confirmed by emails to CPAG, November 2020

65 **IS** Sch 2 para 14ZA IS Regs
JSA Sch 1 para 17 JSA Regs
ESA Sch 4 para 8 ESA Regs
HB Sch 3 para 17 HB Regs

66 Reg 13 SSB(PA) Regs; Sch 2 para 7 SSB(Dep) Regs

67 Reg 2(4) SSB(PRT) Regs

68 Art SSC3(4) and Annex SSC-1, Parts 1 and 2 UK-EUP

69 **AA** Reg 2B SS(AA) Regs
DLA Reg 2B SS(DLA) Regs
CDP Regs 5(4)-(5) and 9 DACYP(S) Regs
PIP Reg 23 SS(PIP) Regs
ADP Regs 15(3)-(4) and 20 DAWAP(S) Regs
CA Reg 9B SS(ICA) Regs
All Art 7 EU Reg 883/04; see also ADM Memos 9/20 and 17/20, and DMG Memos 12/20 and 16/20

70 **AA** s65(7) SSCBA 1992
DLA s72(7B) SSCBA 1992
CDP Regs 5(4)(c)(ii) and 9(2)(a)(ii) DACYP(S) Regs
PIP s84 WRA 2012
ADP Regs 15(3)(c)(ii) and 20(2)(ii) DAWAP(S) Regs
CA s70(4A) SSCBA 1992
All See also ADM Memo 17/20 and DMG Memo 16/20

71 **CAS** s81(2A) and (9)-(15) SS(S)A 2018
YCG Regs 4(7), 8(3)-(10) and 12(1A) CA(YCG)(S) Regs

72 *Commission of the European Communities v European Parliament and Council of the European Union*, C-299/05 [2007], 18 October 2007

73 ss65(7), 70(4A) and 72(7B) SSCBA 1992; s84 WRA 2012

74 *SSWP v Tolley*, C-430/15 [2017]. This case relates to the old co-ordination rules, but on this point has been held to apply also to the current co-ordination rules: *LD v SSWP* [2017] UKUT 65 (AAC).

75 *Bartlett and Others v SSWP, C-537/09* [2011]; see also *NG v SSWP(DLA)* [2012] UKUT 26 (AAC), reported as [2012] AACR; *SSWP v DS* [2019] UKUT 238 (AAC); para C2097 and Appendix 1 para 4 ADM

76 Art 70 EU Reg 883/04; *Swaddling v AO*, C-90/97 [1999]

77 *GS v SSWP (DLA)* [2015] UKUT 687 (AAC)

78 **DLA** Sch 1 paras 3 and 5 SS(DLA) Regs; Vol 10, para 61558 DMG
PIP Regs 15 and 26 SS(PIP) Regs; para P4082 ADM
ADP Reg 23 DAWAP(S) Regs

79 *Commission of the European Communities v European Parliament and Council of the European Union*, C-299/05 [2007], 18 October 2007

80 Reg 6(35)-(37) SS(C&P) Regs; reg 7(9A) SS&CS(DA) Regs

81 Sch para 2(1) SS(NIRA) Regs; Sch para 2(1) SS(GBRA)(NI) Regs

5. **Industrial injuries benefits**

82 Reg 9(3) SSB(PA) Regs

83 Reg 9(4) SSB(PA) Regs

84 Reg 9(5) SSB(PA) Regs

6. **Contribution-based jobseeker's allowance and contributory employment and support allowance**

85 s1(2)(i) JSA 1995; ss1(3)(d) and 18(4)(a) WRA 2007

86 Arts SSC3(1) and (4) and SSC8 UK-EUP

87 Art 64 EU Reg 883/04; Arts 7 and 21 UK-IC

88 *Arbetsmarknadsstyrelsen v Rydergard*, C-215/00 [2002]

89 Annex VI EU Reg 883/04 – for awards before 1 April 2016; Vol 2 Ch 7 Part 1 paras 070152, 070280 and 070401 and Appendix para 18 DMG; para C4119 ADM

90 Annex VI EU Reg 883/04 – for awards since 1 April 2016; DWPWAG, Fig 4

91 paras C4142-3 ADM

92 *Stewart v SSWP*, C-503/09 [2011]
93 DWPWAG, Fig 4; Arts SSC3(1) and SSC8 UK-EUP
94 Arts 5, 46 and 82 EU Reg 883/04; Arts 27, 46, 49 and 87 EU Reg 987/2009; Art 59(7) UK-IC; Art 63 UK-EUP
95 *BB v SSWP (ESA)* [2015] UKUT 545 (AAC); see also *KC and MC v SSWP (ESA)* [2017] UKUT 94 (AAC)
96 SS(NIRA) Regs; SS(GBRA)(NI) Regs
97 s179(3), (4) and (5) SSAA 1992; SS(RA)O

7. **Maternity allowance, incapacity benefit and severe disablement allowance**
98 s113(1) SSCBA 1992
99 Reg 2 SSB(PA) Regs
100 Reg 13 SSB(PA) Regs; reg 14 SS(IB-ID) Regs
101 Reg 2(4) SSB(PRT) Regs
102 Arts 7 and 21 EU Reg 883/04; Art 7 UK-IC; Art 8 UK-EUP
103 Arts 5, 46 and 82 EU Reg 883/04; Arts 27, 46, 49 and 87 EU Reg 987/2009

8. **Retirement pensions**
104 s113 SSCBA 1992; reg 4(1) SSB(PA) Regs
105 Regs 4(3) and 5 SSB(PA) Regs; ss18 and 20 PA 2014; regs 21-23 The State Pension Regulations 2015 No.173
106 Vol 2 Ch 7 Part 5 paras 075780-1 and 075795 DMG
107 Reg 6 SSB(PA) Regs
108 Reg 13 SSB(PA) Regs; reg 10 SSB(Dep) Regs
109 Reg 2(4) SSB(PRT) Regs

9. **Statutory payments**
110 **SSP** Reg 10 SSP(MAPA) Regs
SMP Reg 2A SMP(PAM) Regs
SAP/SPP Reg 4 SPPSAP(PAM) Regs
SSPP Reg 6 SSPP(PAM) Regs
SPBP Reg 6 SPBP(PAM) Regs
111 **SSP** s163(1) SSCBA 1992; reg 16 SSP Regs; regs 5-10 SSP(MAPA) Regs
SMP s171(1) SSCBA 1992; regs 2, 2A, 5, 7 and 8 SMP(PAM) Regs
SAP/SPP ss171ZJ(2)-(3) and 171ZS(2)-(3) SSCBA 1992; regs 3, 4, 8 and 9 SPPSAP(PAM) Regs
SSPP s171ZZ4(2) SSCBA 1992; regs 5, 6, 7, 9, 10 SSPP(PAM) Regs
SPBP s171ZZ(14)(2)-(3) SSCBA 1992; regs 5-10 SPBP(PAM) Regs
112 **SSP** Reg 16(2) SSP Regs
SMP Reg 3 SMP(PAM) Regs; reg 17(3) SMP Regs
SAP/SPP Reg 2 SPPSAP(PAM) Regs; reg 32(3) SPPSAP(G) Regs; reg 24(4) ASPP(G) Regs
SSPP Reg 33(5) SSPP(G) Regs; reg 4 SSPP(PAM) Regs
SPBP Reg 4 SPBP(PAM) Regs
113 See, for example, Vol 2 Part 7 Ch 1 para 070153 DMG
114 *Caisse nationale des prestations familiales v Hiddal and Bernard*, C-216/12 and C-217/12 held that a parental leave allowance was a family benefit under EU Reg 1408/71
115 DWPWAG, Fig 4
116 Arts 16 and 17 UK-IC

10. **Tax credits**
117 Reg 4 TC(R) Regs
118 Reg 2(1) TC(R) Regs
119 Regs 3, 5 and 6 TC(R) Regs
120 s3(5A) TCA 2002
121 s143(1)(b) SSCBA 1992; *RK v HMRC (CHB)* [2015] UKUT 357 (AAC), reported as [2016] AACR 4; *JL v HMRC (CHB)* [2017] UKUT 193 (AAC); *RI v HMRC (TC)* [2019] UKUT 306 (AAC)
122 CCM paras 20090, 20160 and 20170; TCTM paras 09374 and 09376
123 TCM 0288580; see also *GC v HMRC (TC)* [2014] UKUT 251 (AAC)

Part 6

European co-ordination rules and international agreements

Chapter 16

European Union co-ordination rules

This chapter covers:

This chapter describes how European Union (EU) social security co-ordination rules can affect your entitlement to benefits. It covers how to determine which (if any) of the rules apply, and the ways that the rules can either assist you to be entitled to benefit, either in the UK or after you (or a family member) move to an European Economic Area state, or prevent entitlement.

The residence and presence conditions for the individual benefits that affect your entitlement while you are in Great Britain, including if the EU co-ordination rules apply, are covered in Part 4. The rules that affect your entitlement to individual benefits if you go abroad, including if the EU co-ordination rules apply, are covered in Part 5.

If you are not a British or Irish citizen, check Part 3 first because your immigration status may exclude you from the benefit you want to claim.

1. Introduction

The phrase 'European Union (EU) co-ordination rules' is used in this *Handbook* to refer to four different pieces, or collections, of legislation, which provide broadly similar social security rights and require broadly similar conditions to be met. However, the rules contain important differences in terms of which people, which European countries and which benefits are covered by each, and the ways they affect benefit entitlements. These differences are covered in this chapter.

The specific rules that apply to you can depend on your nationality, the country you have moved to or from, the date you (or, in some cases, a member of your family) moved to or from the UK, and what you have been doing in the UK or another country. How you determine which rules apply to you is covered in section 2 of this chapter.

Note:

- In this *Handbook* all references to the European Economic Area (EEA) are to be read as including Switzerland. The EEA and EU states are listed on p53.
- The phrase **'member state'**, when used in the context of the co-ordination rules in this *Handbook*, means those states covered by the specific rules being referred to. The **main co-ordination rules** and the **old co-ordination rules** cover the UK, all EEA states plus Switzerland, the **UK–EU Protocol covers** the UK and EU states, and the **UK–Ireland Convention** covers the UK and Ireland.

The co-ordination rules can affect whether you qualify for benefits in the UK. In most cases, the co-ordination rules make it easier to satisfy the UK rules (eg, by enabling you to count periods of residence, insurance and employment in another member state) towards meeting the conditions of entitlement. However, in limited circumstances the co-ordination rules can prevent you from claiming a UK benefit – eg, if the UK is not the 'competent state' to pay that benefit. For the ways in which the co-ordination rules can affect whether you qualify for individual UK benefits, see Chapter 13.

The co-ordination rules can also help you to be paid a UK benefit in another member state for longer than you would be able to do under UK law alone. See Chapter 15 for the ways the co-ordination rules can help you claim, or continue to receive, individual UK benefits if you or your member of your family are in an EEA country.

Overview

The original aim of the EU co-ordination rules was to secure and promote European freedom of movement, by ensuring that those covered by the rules do not lose out on social security protection as a result of moving between EEA member states. The rules do not seek to harmonise the social security systems of individual states – their sole objective is to co-ordinate the different social security schemes.

Changes due to the UK leaving the European Union

The UK left the EU on 31 January 2020. However, the main EU co-ordination rules and the European caselaw that has interpreted their meaning, together with other parts of EU law relating to European free movement, continued to apply to the UK *as if* it was still an EEA state until the end of the transition period.

Transition period

The transition period (also called the 'implementation period') was the period from the UK leaving the EU at 11pm on 31 January 2020 to 11pm on 31 December 2020.[1] During the transition period, in general, all EU and EU-derived legislation and caselaw, including the main EU co-ordination rules, continued to have effect as before the UK left the EU.[2] For the purposes of the EU co-ordination rules, during the transition period all references to the EEA were treated as if they included references to the UK, and any references to an EEA national or EU citizen were treated as if they included references to a UK national.[3]

From the end of the transition period, in general, the main EU co-ordination rules ceased to apply within UK law.[4] However, the Withdrawal Agreements provide protections for people in certain situations to continue to be able to use these co-ordination rules (see p380). For people not covered by these Withdrawal Agreement protections, a new UK–EU Protocol on Social Security came into force from the end of the transition period, providing more limited co-ordination of social security for people moving between the EU and UK. For people moving between the UK and Ireland, a new bilateral agreement, the UK–Ireland Convention on Social Security, came into force from the end of the transition period, providing broadly the same level of co-ordination as under the main co-ordination rules just between these two countries.

From the end of the transition period, there are four sets of co-ordination rules that may apply, and these are covered in this chapter.

- The **main co-ordination rules**[5] can continue for EEA nationals and British citizens (and family members of either) covered by the **Withdrawal Agreement protections.** In broad terms, these protections may apply if, on 31 December 2020, your situation involved both an EEA state and the UK – eg, if on that date you were an EEA national living and working in the UK or a British citizen living and working in an EEA state. For people who remain covered by the main co-ordination rules, they apply as if the UK were still a member of the EEA. Note that the main co-ordination rules can also apply in limited ways if you are covered by the partial Withdrawal Agreement protections.
- The **old co-ordination rules**[6] can continue for those covered by the **Withdrawal Agreement protections** (or, in limited ways, the partial Withdrawal Agreement protections), in specific circumstances, mainly for claims made before June 2012 and non-EEA (and non-British) nationals.
- A new **UK–EU Protocol on Social Security** was agreed in December 2020, and was brought into force from the end of the transition period.[7] This protocol mirrors the structure of the main co-ordination rules (see p377), but only applies to the UK and EU states and provides more limited social security co-ordination for those not covered by Withdrawal Agreement protections.

- A new **UK–Ireland Convention on Social Security** was agreed in February 2019, and was brought into force from the end of the transition period.[8] This convention mirrors the structure of the main co-ordination rules (see p377) and broadly reproduces their principles and effects but is limited to the UK and Ireland and to specified benefits of each country.

For details on who is covered by each of the four sets of rules, see p379. For details of the benefits covered by each of the sets of rules, see p392.

Note:

- If you are not covered by the Withdrawal Agreement protections (or partial Withdrawal Agreement protections) and therefore cannot be covered by the main co-ordination rules (or the old co-ordination rules), you may be covered by reciprocal agreements between the UK and specific EEA countries (see p433). In particular, if your situation only involves the UK and Switzerland, you may be covered by the new UK–Switzerland Convention, which broadly reproduces the principles and effects of the main co-ordination rules, but is limited to the UK and Switzerland and covers fewer categories of benefits (see p437).
- The UK leaving the EU also affects residence rights – see p183.

How to check whether the co-ordination rules apply

To check whether and how the co-ordination rules apply to you, work through the following steps.

- **Step one:** check which, if any, of the sets of co-ordination rules you are covered by. Follow the steps on p379.
- **Step two:** check whether the particular benefit you want to claim is covered by the relevant co-ordination rules, and into which category the benefit falls (see p392).
- **Step three:** check which state is the 'competent state' to pay the benefit you are claiming (see p399).
- **Step four:** check the principle you want to apply – eg, the aggregation principle or exporting benefits (see below for a list and cross references to each principle), and check whether that principle applies under the rules that you are covered by, and to the benefit you want to claim.
- **Step five:** check how that principle can affect your entitlement to an individual benefit while you are in the UK (see the section on 'EU co-ordination rules' at the end of each specific benefit in Chapter 13) or allows you to be paid that benefit when you or a member of your family are in a member state (see the section on 'EU co-ordination rules' at the end of each specific benefit in Chapter 15).

Note:

- You may be entitled to benefit under UK social security legislation and not need to rely on the co-ordination rules. Check the individual benefit rules in

Chapter 13 if you want to be paid in the UK, or Chapter 15 if you want to be paid a benefit when you or a member of your family are in an EEA country.
- In many circumstances, the co-ordination rules can help you be entitled to benefit, or be paid benefit longer if you or a member of your family go abroad, but they can also prevent you from being entitled to some UK benefits – eg, if you are claiming particular disability or carers' benefits and the UK is not your competent state.

The co-ordination principles

The following principles are contained in the main co-ordination rules in relation to the EEA and UK, in the UK–EU Protocol in relation to the EU and UK, and in the UK–Ireland Convention in relation to Ireland and the UK.

- **The single state principle.** You can generally only claim a particular category of benefit from one state at any one time. The state responsible for paying your benefit is referred to as the 'competent state' (see p399).
- **Equal treatment of people.** Discrimination on the grounds of nationality in terms of access to, or the rate of payment of, the benefits that are covered is prohibited (see p413).
- **Equal treatment of benefits, income, facts and events.** If receipt of a benefit, or a fact or an event, has a legal consequence in one state, this must be recognised in the same way by other member states (see p414).
- **Aggregation.** Periods of residence, insurance and employment in any of the member states can be used towards entitlement to benefit in another (see p416).
- **Exportability of certain benefits.** You can continue to be paid certain benefits abroad if you go to another of the states. These rules generally mean that you can be paid your UK benefit if you go to another member state for longer than under the UK rules (see p419).
- **Administrative co-operation.** Member states undertake to co-operate in the administration of the co-ordination rules.

There are exceptions and limitations to these general principles for specific categories of benefits and, in some cases, there are more detailed provisions on how the above principles should apply in certain circumstances.

Legal sources of the co-ordination rules

The main co-ordination rules

The main EU co-ordination rules were converted into UK law from the end of the transition period (11pm on 31 December 2020).[9] In general, these rules were then immediately revoked and, therefore, ceased to apply to the UK from the end of the transition period.[10] However, for people covered by the **Withdrawal Agreement** protections (see p380) or, for specific provisions, covered by the partial Withdrawal Agreement provisions (see p384), the co-ordination rules continue to form part of UK law and continue to apply in the same way as they did before the end of the transition period.[11] In addition, the provisions relating to aggregation of national insurance contributions for entitlement to UK retirement pensions, and their uprating while you live in an EEA country, were saved and continue to apply.[12] The legislation setting out the main co-ordination rules is below.

Article 48 of the Treaty on the Functioning of the European Union (TFEU) requires the European Parliament and the Council of Ministers to make such rules in the field of social security:

> 'as are necessary to provide freedom of movement for workers; to this end, they shall make arrangements to secure for employed and self-employed migrant workers and their dependants:
> (a) aggregation, for the purpose of acquiring and retaining the right to benefit and of calculating the amount of benefit, of all periods taken into account under the laws of the several countries;
> (b) payment of benefits to persons resident in the territories of Member States.'

Under this article, the following further legislation has been made.

- **EU Regulation 883/2004** sets out the rules for co-ordinating the different social security systems of the various EU states. The structure of this regulation is as follows.
  - **Preamble.** This contains numbered 'recitals' that explain the purpose of the regulation and the principles it contains. These recitals can be used as an aid to interpret the subsequent articles.
  - **General Provisions.** Article 1 contains important definitions. Article 2 explains the 'personal scope' of the regulation – ie, the people to whom it applies (see p379). Article 3 sets out the 'material scope' – ie, the categories of benefits to which the regulation applies (see p392). Articles 4 to 10 contain the general principles of the regulation.
  - **Determination of the Legislation Applicable.** Articles 11 to 16 contain the general rules for working out which is the competent state (see p399).
  - **Special Provisions Concerning the Various Categories of Benefits.** Articles 17 to 70 contain more specific rules for different categories of benefits and are divided into chapters, one for each category of benefits.
  - **Administrative Commission and Advisory Committee.** Articles 71 to 75 establish organisations to oversee and implement the working of the regulation.
  - **Miscellaneous Provisions.** Articles 76 to 86 contain various rules on practical issues of administration.
  - **Transitional and Final Provisions.** Articles 87 to 91 provide for the implementation of the regulation and transitional measures.
  - **Annexes.** These contain further rules, most of which concern specific rules for individual member states.
- **EU Regulation 987/2009** contains procedures for implementing EU Regulation 883/2004.

The old co-ordination rules

EU Regulation 883/2004 succeeds **Regulation 1408/71**, which (together with its implementing regulation, EU Regulation 574/72) came into force on 1 April 1973 and is referred to in this *Handbook* as the **'old co-ordination rules'**. The current co-ordination rules build on these, taking into account developments in European caselaw and national legislation to modernise and simplify the rules and extend their personal scope (see below).[13] However, the old co-ordination rules continue to apply to limited groups of people (see p388). As the majority of claims are now determined under the current co-ordination rules, this *Handbook* only covers current rules. For further information on the old co-ordination rules, see the 2012/13 edition of CPAG's *Welfare Benefits and Tax Credits Handbook*.

The UK–Ireland Convention on Social Security

The UK–Ireland Convention on Social Security was agreed in February 2019. It was brought into force from the end of the transition period (11pm on 31 December 2020).[14] The convention broadly mirrors the above structure of the main EU co-ordination rules and broadly reproduces their principles and effects but is limited to the UK and Ireland, to specified benefits of each country and, in most cases, to nationals of each country.

The UK–EU Protocol on Social Security Co-ordination

The UK–EU Protocol on Social Security Co-ordination was agreed in December 2020 and forms part of the Trade and Co-operation Agreement between the UK and EU. The protocol was brought into force from the end of the transition period (11pm on 31 December 2020).[15] It broadly mirrors the above structure of the main EU co-ordination rules and broadly reproduces their principles and effects. However, the protocol is more limited. It only applies to the UK and EU states (not Iceland, Norway, Liechtenstein or Switzerland), covers fewer categories of benefits and does not apply some of the principles to as many categories of benefits as the main co-ordination rules.

2. **Who is covered**

In this *Handbook* you are 'covered by the co-ordination rules' if you are covered by one or more of the four different sets of rules that co-ordinate the social security systems throughout all or part of the European Economic Area (EEA) and UK. It can be important to identify which, if any, of the sets of rules you are covered by, as some of the specific provisions are different and you may only be covered by a set of rules for specific 'principles' (see Step 2 below, and p377 for a list of the principles). If more than one set of rules appears to apply to you, in general, you will be covered by the main co-ordination rules (exceptions to this are noted when they arise). Check which rules apply by working through the following steps.

Step 1: are you covered by the Withdrawal Agreement protections? These may apply if on 31 December 2020, you were an EEA national living in the UK, or a British citizen living in an EEA country, or you are a member of the family of either, or, in specific circumstances, you are a non-EEA national. For the details of who is covered, see below. The Withdrawal Agreement protections mean you can potentially be covered by the **main co-ordination rules**, and in most cases it is likely you are covered, but you need to check (see p386). The Withdrawal Agreement protections can also mean that you can potentially be covered by the **old co-ordination rules.** These rules could apply to you if either you have been receiving benefit under them since before June 2012, or you are a non-EEA (and non-British) national and, before the end of 2020, your circumstances involved both the UK and an EEA state. For details of the old co-ordination rules, see p388.

Step 2: are you covered by the partial Withdrawal Agreement protections? These can apply if you are not, or are no longer, covered by the Withdrawal Agreement protections. They mean you can make use of specific provisions of the main or old co-ordination rules, in particular the aggregation principle, *if* you are covered by these rules – so you need to check. For the partial Withdrawal Agreement protections, see p384.

Step 3: are you covered by the UK–Ireland Convention? This can apply if you are (or you are a member of the family of) an Irish or British citizen, or a refugee, and live in either Ireland or the UK (see p387).

Step 4: are you covered by the UK–European Union (EU) Protocol? This can apply if you have only moved between the UK and the EU since the end of 2020; or if, for another reason, the other co-ordination rules do not apply; or, if you are covered by the partial Withdrawal Agreement protections, the main co-ordination rules only apply in limited ways (see p388).

Note: If you are covered by both the main co-ordination rules and the UK–Ireland Convention, you can rely on whichever is the more generous.[16]

Withdrawal Agreement protections

Since the end of the transition period (31 December 2020 – see p374), you can only be covered by the main co-ordination rules (or, in limited circumstances, the old co-ordination rules) if you are covered by the protections provided by one or more of the three Withdrawal Agreements which the UK made with the EU, the European Free Trade Association (EFTA) states and Switzerland. Since these protections are broadly the same in each of the three agreements, they are referred to collectively in this *Handbook* as the Withdrawal Agreement protections, and the relevant parts of the three agreements are referenced in the endnotes (see also final note on p382).

You are covered by the Withdrawal Agreement protections if *both*:

- on 31 December 2020, one of the situations listed in the bullet points below applied to you; *and*
- since 31 December 2020, the Withdrawal Agreement protections have not ceased to apply to you (see below).

You can be covered by the Withdrawal Agreement protections if, at the end of the transition period (ie, on 31 December 2020), you were:[17]

- an EEA national 'subject to the legislation of' (see p389) the UK – eg, a Polish national working in the UK; *or*
- a UK national 'subject to the legislation of' an EEA state; *or*
- an EEA national 'subject to the legislation of' an EEA state while residing in the UK – eg, a French national living in the UK receiving a French social security benefit; *or*
- a UK national 'subject to the legislation of' the UK while residing in an EEA state; *or*
- a refugee or stateless person residing in the UK or an EEA state and 'subject to the legislation of' the UK or an EEA state; *or*
- a member of the family (see first note below and p390) or survivor of someone in one of the above categories; *or*
- (other than under the EFTA or Swiss agreements) a non-EEA national covered by the old co-ordination rules (see p388) and legally resident in, and 'subject to the legislation' of, the UK or an EEA state;
- if none of the above apply, an EEA national with a European free movement right to reside in the UK (see p192) or a UK national with an EU free movement right to reside in an EEA state; *or*
- a family member (see first note below) of a person covered by the bullet point above.

If one or more of the above groups applies to you, you then need to check whether these protections *continue* to apply to you (see below). If they do, it means that the main co-ordination rules (or, in limited circumstances, the old co-ordination rules) are potentially available to you. Therefore, your next step is to check whether you are *also* covered by the main co-ordination rules (see p386) (or, in limited circumstances, the old co-ordination rules – see p388). **Note:** although the criteria for who is covered by the main co-ordination rules are similar to the circumstances in the first six bullet points above, the criteria are not exactly the same and do not apply in all cases.

Note:

- Although the Withdrawal Agreements use the phrase 'family member' throughout, the meaning of this phrase differs depending on the context. When determining whether you are covered by the last bullet point above – ie, the 'family member' of an EEA national with a right to reside in the UK (or a

UK national with a right to reside in an EEA state) – the meaning is that which applies to free movement residence rights (see p240).[18] However, when determining whether you are covered by the sixth bullet point – ie the member of the family of a person covered by one of the first five groups above – the phrase has the narrower meaning set out in the main co-ordination rules (see p390), thus 'member of the family' is used in these contexts in this *Handbook*, including in the sixth bullet point above.[19]

- For the last bullet point above to apply to you, you must have been the family member of the person in the second last bullet point on 31 December 2020, whereas you can be covered by the sixth bullet point even if you only became a member of the family (eg, by becoming a spouse) *after* 31 December 2020.[20] To be covered by the last bullet point as an 'extended family member' (see p243) you must have been living, on 31 December 2020, in the same state as the person who confers rights on you *and* you must have either obtained or applied for a free movement residence document by that date. However, other than if you are an extended family member, to be covered by either the sixth or the last bullet point above, you do *not* need to have been living, on 31 December 2020, in the same state as the person who confers rights on you, provided you have now joined them. Guidance provides a table summarising the requirements for 'family member' groups under the Withdrawal Agreement co-ordination provisions.[21]
- If you are not covered by either of the last two bullet points in the list above, and one of the first seven bullet points did not apply on 31 December 2020, but had applied at an earlier date, or if the bullet points in the list above did not apply to you on 31 December 2020, but on that date you were receiving a family benefit for a child living abroad, check whether you are covered by the **partial Withdrawal Agreement protections**, which only enable you to use limited aspects of the main co-ordination rules – see p384.
- Guidance sets out examples of situations in which EEA and British citizens have Withdrawal Agreement protections. Some guidance refers to this as being in 'full scope' (of the Withdrawal Agreement and, therefore, of the main EU co-ordination rules)[22] and other guidance refers to both those with Withdrawal Agreement protections and partial Withdrawal Agreement protections as the 'protected cohort'.[23] Much of the guidance refers to the relevant articles of the Withdrawal Agreement: Article 30(1) for the first seven bullet points above and Article 30(3) for the last two bullet points above.[24] **Note:** the details in these guidance documents are not always consistent. Like all guidance, it is not legally binding, but referring to specific paragraphs can be useful – eg, the interpretation given in guidance of the requirement to have been 'subject to the legislation' of a state on 31 December 2020 (see p389).
- Although the UK concluded separate withdrawal agreements with the EU, with the EFTA states (Iceland, Liechtenstein, Switzerland and Norway) and with Switzerland, each agreement has provisions to ensure that social security

co-ordination can continue between the EU, UK and the EFTA states, and between the EU, UK and Switzerland.[25]

How long the Withdrawal Agreement protections apply

The Withdrawal Agreement protections summarised above continue to apply for as long as:

- **(if you are covered by one of the first seven bullet points on p381)** you continue 'without interruption' to be in one of the situations listed.[26] Examples could include if you continue to be an EEA national residing and working or claiming social security benefits in the UK, or a British citizen residing and working or claiming social security benefits in an EEA country. You can move between the situations listed, but there must not be an 'interruption' during which none of the situations apply.[27] Legislation does not define 'interruption'. DWP guidance states that an 'absence' of 30 days or less will not constitute an 'interruption' and an 'absence' of 31 days or more will be considered on a case-by-case basis. The guidance states that when a Polish national who had been working in the UK on 31 December 2020 moved back to Poland to begin work on a 12-month contract, this would constitute an 'interruption'.[28] Until new caselaw is established on the meaning of an 'interruption' to your situation, it may be relevant to refer to the caselaw on the meaning of the 'relevant situation remains unchanged', which can determine when the main co-ordination rules apply in place of the old (see p388). If you cease to be in one of the situations listed in the first seven bullet points, but you are covered by one of the last two bullet points, the Withdrawal Agreement protections continue for as long as the bullet point below applies to you;[29]
- **(if you are covered by one of the last two bullet points on p381)** you continue to have a free movement right to reside, or a right to work, as an EEA national in the UK, or a British citizen in an EEA country, or you continue to be a family member (see p240) of a person who does.[30] In particular, your continuing to have a free movement right to reside may be affected by:
  - whether you have complied with the Withdrawal Agreement residence scheme in the country in which you are residing.[31] For example, if you are an EEA national residing in the UK, you must have either obtained leave under the EU Settlement Scheme (EUSS) or have a pending valid application for settled or pre-settled status (or a pending appeal or administrative review of a refusal). If you are a British citizen residing in an EEA country, you will need to have complied with the residence scheme in that country. Details of the scheme for each EEA country are available on the EU Commission website: europa.eu/youreurope/citizens/residence/brexit-residence-rights/uk-nationals-living-in-eu.
  - absences from the country in which you are residing. Your continuity of residence for this purpose is not broken by absences abroad totalling less than six months in a year, or up to a year in specific circumstances (these

rules are the same as for absences ignored when calculating the five years to acquire a permanent right to reside – see p271). If you have obtained a permanent right to reside under the Withdrawal Agreement (eg, if you are in the UK, once you have obtained settled status under the EUSS), an absence will only cause the Withdrawal Agreement protections to end if you are absent for more than five years.[32]

While the Withdrawal Agreement protections continue to apply, you can potentially be covered by the main co-ordination rules (or, in limited circumstances, the old co-ordination rules).

If you are not, or no longer, covered by one of the nine bullet points on p381, check whether you are covered by the partial Withdrawal Agreement protections below.

Note:

- Guidance suggests that it may be accepted that the Withdrawal Agreement protections continue to apply to you solely on the basis that you have complied with the Withdrawal Agreement residence scheme in the country in which you are residing, and have not subsequently lost these rights due to absence. For example, DWP guidance states that if the Polish national referred to in the first main bullet point on p383 had obtained settled status under the EUSS, the Withdrawal Agreement protections would continue to apply despite their returning to work in Poland, provided they were not absent from the UK for more than five years.[33]
- Determining how long Withdrawal Agreement protections apply in specific circumstances can be complex. Until new caselaw is established, the correct interpretation of the Withdrawal Agreements remains arguable. If your claim is refused or your award is terminated on the basis that the Withdrawal Agreement protections have ceased to apply, challenge the decision and ask your adviser to contact CPAG.

Partial Withdrawal Agreement protections

If you are not, or are no longer, covered by the Withdrawal Agreement protections, you may be able to use the 'aggregation principle' (see p416) of the main co-ordination rules to satisfy benefit rules that require past periods of residence, insurance or employment, or you may be able to continue to receive family benefits for family members living in another member state. These partial Withdrawal Agreement protections are referred to in guidance as being in 'partial scope' (of the Withdrawal Agreement and, therefore, of the main EU co-ordination rules).[34] However, note that the guidance appears to interpret these protections too restrictively. For example, the guidance suggests that an EEA national in the first (or a UK national in the second) bullet point below must have moved back to the EEA (or UK) by 31 December 2020,[35] but moving back by this date is not a requirement – eg, a UK national may have only just moved back from an EEA state to the UK.

The **aggregation principle** is potentially available to you if you are not, or are are no longer, covered by the Withdrawal Agreement protections (see p380) and *before* the end of the transition period (31 December 2020) you were:[36]

- an EEA national 'subject to the legislation of' (see p389) the UK; *or*
- a UK national 'subject to the legislation of' an EEA state; *or*
- a refugee or stateless person 'subject to the legislation of' the UK and currently residing in an EEA state, or 'subject to the legislation of' an EEA state and currently residing in the UK; *or*
- (other than under the EFTA or Swiss agreements) a non-EEA national covered by the old co-ordination rules (see p388), 'subject to the legislation of' the UK and currently legally resident in an EEA state, or 'subject to the legislation of' an EEA state and currently legally resident in the UK; *or*
- a member of the family (see p390) or survivor of someone in one of the above categories.

If this applies, you may be able to add together periods of residence, insurance or employment/self-employment completed in one or more EEA states or the UK to satisfy the requirements for a particular benefit, whether the periods were completed before or after the end of the transition period.[37] If you can potentially receive benefit as a result of this, you are also subject to some of the provisions of the main co-ordination rules about sickness benefits, including the requirement that the UK be the 'competent state' in order for you to be entitled to attendance allowance (AA), carer's allowance (CA), the daily living component of personal independence payment (PIP), the care component of disability living allowance (DLA) and, in specific circumstances only, the daily living component of adult disability payment (ADP) and the care component of child disability payment (CDP) (see p404).[38]

Note: If you are covered by the partial Withdrawal Agreement protections above and you are covered by the main co-ordination rules (see p386) or the old co-ordination rules (see p388), in addition to aggregating periods of residence to enable you to satisfy the past presence test for AA, CA, DLA, CDP, PIP and ADP, you may also be able to *disapply* this test (see example below and p306).

You may be able to continue to receive **family benefits** for family members living in another member state, if you are not, or or are no longer, covered by the Withdrawal Agreement protections, in limited circumstances – see p421.

Example

David is a British citizen who moved to Italy to take up a job in June 2019 when he was aged 52. In August 2021 David had a stroke, which left him with right-sided paralysis. In December 2021, he ended the tenancy on his flat in Italy and moved back to England, to live in his sister's house and be cared for by her. In February 2022, he claimed PIP. His claim was refused on the basis that he had not been present in the UK for two out of the past three years. David requested a mandatory reconsideration and in his letter he explained that the decision to refuse his claim was wrong for the following reasons.

1. On 31 December 2020, he was subject to the legislation of Italy (due to his being employed there). Although this situation had ceased by the date he claimed PIP, and therefore he was no longer covered by the Withdrawal Agreement protections, David is covered by the *partial* Withdrawal Agreement protections.
2. Consequently, he can potentially use the aggregation principle of the main co-ordination rules if he is covered by those rules, which he is as a British citizen who moved to an EEA country before 31 December 2020 and who was subject to the legislation of at least one EEA country.
3. He can therefore aggregate (add together) his 22 months of residence in Italy and his two months of presence in the UK to satisfy the past presence test. Note that David's residence in Italy can be aggregated for the purpose of satisfying the past presence test because it was *not* 'mere residence', due to his working in Italy. For details on aggregation, see p416.
4. In addition, the past presence test should be disapplied (see p306) because:
   a. the main co-ordination rules apply to David (due to points 1 and 2 above); *and*
   b. he is habitually resident in Great Britain (see p163). To ensure this is accepted, David details relevant aspects of his circumstances, including that he has been actually resident for two months, that he is a returning resident (see p166), and evidence of his settled intention to live in the UK for the time being – eg, his one way ticket to Great Britain and evidence of ending his tenancy in Italy; *and*
   c. David can demonstrate a 'genuine and sufficient link' to the UK. This includes his previous periods of residence in the UK, any previous periods of work in the UK, his dependence on his sister for care, his future intentions and expectations (see p307).
5. Finally, David notes in his letter that the UK is the competent state to pay the daily living component of PIP. This is because it is the state where he is resident, and he is not working in, or receiving a pension from, any other state (see p404).

David's request was successful and the DWP revised its decision.

Who is covered by the main co-ordination rules

Since the end of the transition period (31 December 2020 – see p374), you can only be covered by the main co-ordination rules if you are covered by the Withdrawal Agreement protections (see p380) or, for specific limited purposes, you are covered by the partial Withdrawal Agreement protections (see above).

If these protections apply to you (or applied for a period before the end of the transition period), you are covered by the main co-ordination rules if you fall within the range of people to whom they apply, which is known as being within the '**personal scope**' of these co-ordination rules.

In addition, your situation must involve either the UK and one or more EEA states, or at least two EEA states. That generally means that you must have moved between an EEA state and the UK (or another EEA state), or you live in one and work in another, or you live in one and are the national of another.[39]

Note: Until the end of the transition period, the UK was treated as an EEA member state for the purpose of these co-ordination rules, and continues to be so treated for people covered by the Withdrawal Agreement protections, or partial Withdrawal Agreement protections.

You are within the 'personal scope' of the main co-ordination rules if:[40]

- you are:
  - an EEA national; *or*
  - a British citizen; *or*
  - a refugee; *or*
  - a stateless person; *and*
- you are residing in the UK or an EEA state and you have been 'subject to the legislation of' one or more EEA states or the UK (see p389); *or*
- you are a 'member of the family' (see p390) or a survivor of someone covered in the above bullet point. **Note:** the old co-ordination rules defined 'survivor' in terms of national legislation, so in the UK it meant a widow, widower or surviving civil partner.[41] However, there is no definition in the main co-ordination rules, so it might be possible to argue a wider meaning could apply.

If you are covered by the main co-ordination rules, check whether the benefit you are claiming or want to claim is covered by the co-ordination rules (see p392) and then check which is the competent state for that benefit (see p399).

Who is covered by the UK–Ireland Convention on Social Security

You are covered by the UK–Ireland Convention on Social Security if you come within the range of people to whom it applies, which is known as being within the **'personal scope'** of this convention.

In addition, your situation must involve both the UK and Ireland. That generally means that you have moved between the two states, or you live in one and work in the other, or you live in one and are the national of the other.

You are within the 'personal scope' of the UK–Ireland Convention on Social Security if:[42]

- you are:
  - an Irish citizen; *or*
  - a British citizen; *or*
  - a refugee; *or*
  - a stateless person; *and*
- you are residing in the UK or Ireland and you are or have been 'subject to the legislation of' the UK or Ireland (see p389); *or*

- you are a 'member of the family' (see p390) or a survivor of someone covered in the above bullet point. '**Survivor**' is defined as a surviving spouse or civil partner or child to whom a survivor's benefit or death grant is payable under Irish, or (not including for a child) UK, legislation.[43]

Note: If you are covered by both the UK–Ireland Convention and the main co-ordination rules (which is only possible if you are covered by the Withdrawal Agreement protections – see p380), you can rely on whichever is the more generous.[44]

Who is covered by the UK–EU Protocol

You are covered by the UK–EU Protocol if you are or have been 'subject to the legislation of' (see p389) the UK or an EU state, or you are the 'member of the family' (see p390) or survivor (not defined) of someone who has.[45]

In addition, your situation must involve either the UK and one or more EU states, or at least two EU states. That generally means that you must have moved between an EU state and the UK (or another EU state), or you live in one and work in another, or you live in one but are the national of another.[46]

Note:

- You can be covered by the protocol regardless of your nationality. The protocol applies to 'persons, including stateless persons and refugees' who satisfy the above requirements.[47]
- The protocol is between the UK and the EU. Unlike the main EU co-ordination rules, the protocol does not extend to Iceland, Liechtenstein, Norway and Switzerland. Although the UK government has sought similar co-ordination provisions with these four states,[48] at the time of writing it was understood that the only agreements in force were on a bilateral basis with Norway and Switzerland (see p437).

When the old co-ordination rules apply

If you are covered by the Withdrawal Agreement protections (see p380), in the vast majority of situations the main co-ordination rules[49] will be the rules most likely to apply to you. However, the old co-ordination rules[50] (see p379) can apply if any of the following applies to you.

- You are receiving a benefit because you claimed it before the main rules came into force.[51] That depends on your nationality (see the relevant dates below). However, if you claimed your benefit before the main rules came into force but did not need to rely on the co-ordination rules until after that date (eg, when moving between states), the main rules apply.[52] If the old rules apply to you, they continue to do so during a transitional period of up to 10 years, provided your 'relevant situation remains unchanged',[53] which is decided by the state administering your benefit claim, with reference to its national social security legislation.[54] What amounts to a change in your 'relevant situation' that brings you under the main co-ordination rules depends on your circumstances. In one case, a change was making a 'renewal' claim for DLA after the relevant date (see below).[55] In another case, a change was moving to another EEA country after the relevant date.[56] However, in one case, the Upper Tribunal held that the old rules continued to apply because the claimant started employment in another EEA country *before* the relevant date and so moving there *after* the relevant date was not a relevant change.[57] The transitional period is intended to protect anyone who might otherwise lose benefit under the main rules. However, you can ask to be transferred and considered under the main rules if that would be better for you. If so, the main rules take effect from the start of the following month.[58] **Note:** it is possible that the old co-ordination rules applied to you and then, subsequently, the main rules applied, so a decision maker or First-tier Tribunal may need to consider both.[59]

- You are a non-EEA (and non-British) national (other than a refugee or member of the family of an EEA or British citizen who is covered by the main rules) who is legally resident in an EEA country or the UK.[60] You must have been employed or self-employed and subject to the legislation of an EEA state or the UK because you have paid (or should have paid) national insurance (NI) contributions, or a student and subject to the legislation of the UK or an EEA state. You continue to be covered by the old co-ordination rules if the UK is one of the states where you have legally resided. That is because the UK obtained an opt-out, allowing it not to extend the main rules to nationals of non-EEA states.[61]

Relevant dates

The main co-ordination rules apply to nationals (and members of their family) of:[62]
- the EU member states (and refugees and stateless people) from 1 May 2010;
- Switzerland from 1 April 2012;
- Iceland, Liechtenstein and Norway from 1 June 2012.

As very few claims are now determined under the old co-ordination rules, this *Handbook* does not cover these. For further information on the old co-ordination rules, see the 2012/13 edition of CPAG's *Welfare Benefits and Tax Credits Handbook*.

Common terms

'Subject to the legislation of'

The requirement that you (or the person whose family you are a member of) have been 'subject to the legislation of' one of the member states to which the relevant Withdrawal Agreement, or relevant co-ordination rules, applies is essential to being covered by any of the co-ordinating rules.

'Subject to the legislation of'

You have been **'subject to the legislation of'** a state if you have worked in and paid (or should have paid) the equivalent of NI contributions to that state, or you have paid contributions to that state on interest from assets,[63] or you have received any 'social security benefit' (see first note below) or 'special non-contributory' benefit (see p397) from that state. You may also be subject to the legislation if you are potentially eligible for any social security benefit or special non-contributory benefit.

'Legislation' is defined as the legislation of each member state relating to the 'social security branches covered' (or under the UK–Ireland Convention, the 'benefits specified') in the relevant set of co-ordination rules.[64]

Note:

- The benefits referred to in this definition include UK benefits that are intended to assist you in the event of one of the risks covered by the co-ordination rules (see p393).[65] Under the main co-ordination rules and the UK–Ireland Convention, examples include AA, DLA, PIP, CA, child benefit and child tax credit. None of these depend on your being an employee or self-employed at any time. Potentially, therefore, even if you have never worked, including in some circumstances if you are a child, you can be covered by these co-ordination rules. DWP guidance confirms that the personal scope of the main co-ordination rules includes non-economically active people.[66]
- Recent DWP guidance suggests that for the purpose of being covered by the Withdrawal Agreement protections, or partial Withdrawal Agreement protections, you can be considered to have been 'subject to the legislation of' a state on 31 December 2020 solely on the basis of having been resident (see p401) in that state on that date.[67]

Member of the family

A member of the family of someone covered by the each of the co-ordination rules can also rely on, and be affected by, the rules that cover that person (which can vary depending on which rules they are covered by and the type of benefit claimed).[68]

'Member of the family' is defined in broadly the same way in each of the co-ordination rules, and the Withdrawal Agreements[69] cross-refer to the definition in the main co-ordination rules for the purpose of determining who is covered by Withdrawal Agreement protections (see p380).

Note:

- The definition of 'member of the family' is different to, and in general narrower than, the definition of a 'family member' within free movement residence rights law (see p239). Note, also, the definition can be affected by national social security legislation, so can vary among member states.
- Although the legislation does not consistently use the phrase 'member of the family', and in some instances uses the phrase 'family member', in this *Handbook* the phrase 'member of the family' is used when the narrower meaning applies, which is in matters relating to social security co-ordination.

- You may be covered under the main co-ordination rules and the UK–Ireland Convention, and possibly the UK–EU Protocol, even if you are economically inactive, including in some circumstances if you are a child. Consequently, if you are covered directly, you may not *need* to rely on being a member of someone else's family. If you are both a member of the family of a person covered by the rules and also covered by the rules yourself, you can usually rely on either coverage. **Note:** the consequences of being a member of someone's family are not always favourable – eg, if they change which state is competent to pay your benefit (see p399).

Member of the family

You are a **'member of the family'** of a person covered by the co-ordination rules if you are:[70]

- defined or recognised as a member of the family, or designated as a member of the household, by the legislation under which benefits are provided; *or*
- if the legislation under which benefits are provided does not make a distinction between the members of the family and other people to whom it applies, the covered person's spouse or child who is either under the age of majority (18 in England, Wales and Northern Ireland; 16 in Scotland) or older but dependent on the person covered.

If, under the legislation in either bullet point above, you are only considered to be a member of the family or member of the household if you are living in the same household as the person, this condition is considered to be satisfied if you are mainly dependent on them.

The 'legislation under which benefits are provided' in the above definition covers the legislation providing for the particular benefit you are claiming. Although it may be arguable that a broader category of social security legislation should apply, that has not been accepted to date.

Upper Tribunal decisions

In a case concerning child benefit, the Upper Tribunal found that the relevant legislation was the child benefit legislation and held that the claimant's niece and nephew living in a different EU state did not count as members of the claimant's family.[71] Although this case concerned the old co-ordination rules, it was cited in support of a more recent child benefit decision in which the Upper Tribunal held that the claimant's stepson, for whom it was accepted the claimant was responsible, was not a member of the claimant's family under the main co-ordination rules because the stepson was not the claimant's biological child.[72]

In a case concerning DLA for a child, the Upper Tribunal found that the relevant legislation was the DLA legislation and therefore held that the claimant's sister did not count as a member of his family. However, that did not affect his entitlement because he was covered by the main co-ordination rules himself.[73]

In a case concerning CA, the Upper Tribunal found that the relevant legislation was the CA legislation and since that does not define any particular people as members of the family or household, the claimant's spouse was held to be a member of the family, despite being separated and living in another EEA state.[74]

Note: if you are claiming 'sickness benefits' (eg, AA, CA, the daily living component of PIP or ADP and the care component of DLA or CDP), in limited circumstances a slightly different definition of 'member of the family' can be relevant under the main co-ordination rules, and rules can apply to determine whether your rights as a member of the family, or any independent rights you have, take priority (see p408).

3. Which benefits are covered

The benefits to which the co-ordination rules apply are referred to as being within the **'material scope'** of the rules.

Each of the rules refers to categories of benefits designed to cover certain 'risks', such as 'old age' or 'maternity'. The UK–Ireland Convention lists the benefits of each state considered to assist with each risk.[75] Under the main co-ordination rules and the UK–European Union (EU) Protocol, most benefits are not specified in the legislation, but member states are required to list the benefits considered to assist with each risk, and those are published by the EU.[76] However, the categorisation of a benefit can be challenged, because ultimately categorisation depends on the benefit's characteristics rather than on how an individual state lists the benefit.

Benefits are also divided into the following types, depending on the conditions of eligibility:
- social security benefits (see p393);
- (except under the UK–Ireland Convention) special non-contributory benefits (see p397);
- social and medical assistance (social assistance under the UK–Ireland Convention) (see p398).

Those benefits categorised as social security benefits have the most rights. Special non-contributory benefits provide fewer rights under the main co-ordination rules and are not covered under the UK–EU Protocol. Social and medical assistance is not covered by the co-ordination rules, and the UK–Ireland Convention only covers social assistance in relation to recovery of overpayments.

Social security benefits

Social security benefits are categorised according to the risk against which they are designed to provide financial protection.[77]

The main co-ordination rules and the UK–EU Protocol do not list the benefits that assist with each risk within the legislation, but the UK–Ireland Convention does.[78]

The table below lists the benefits that are accepted as categorised for each risk under the main co-ordination rules (with disputes noted) and the benefits listed in the UK–Ireland Convention. Under the UK–EU Protocol, benefit categorisation should follow that of the main co-ordination rules, unless the protocol specifically provides otherwise. That is confirmed in recent guidance, which lists UK benefits into categories for both the main co-ordination rules and the UK–EU Protocol (but see the note on contributory employment and support allowance (ESA) below the table).[79]

The UK–EU Protocol is the only set of rules that lists benefits which are *not* covered.

The UK–EU Protocol does not apply to:[80]

- family benefits;
- long-term care benefits. These are listed as attendance allowance (AA), disability living allowance (DLA) care component, personal independence payment (PIP) daily living component, carer's allowance (CA), carer's allowance supplement and young carer grant[81] (although adult disability payment (ADP) daily living component and child disability payment (CDP) care component are not listed, each is expected to be treated as a long-term care benefit);
- winter fuel or cold weather payments;
- special non-contributory benefits (see p397);
- social and medical assistance (see p398).

Risk	*UK benefits listed under main co-ordination rules*	*UK benefits listed under UK–Ireland Convention*
Sickness	AA DLA care component PIP daily living component CA Carer's allowance supplement (Scotland) Young carer grant (Scotland) ADP (Scotland) daily living component CDP (Scotland) care component Child winter heating assistance (Scotland) Statutory sick pay Contributory ESA in the assessment phase or for the first 365 days (see the note on p396)	Contributory ESA in the assessment phase
Long-term care benefits	Treated as sickness benefits[82]	AA DLA care component PIP daily living component CA (ADP daily living component and CDP care component are not listed but are expected to be treated as long-term care benefits)
Maternity and paternity	Maternity allowance (MA) Statutory maternity, adoption, paternity and shared parental pay See also the note on p396	MA

Invalidity	AA, DLA care and mobility components and CA if you were in receipt of benefit before 1 June 1992. If you claimed after this date, see p396. Long-term incapacity benefit Severe disablement allowance Contributory ESA after the assessment phase or after the first 365 days (or arguably before – see the note on p396)	Contributory ESA after the assessment phase
Old age	State pension Category A, B and D retirement pensions Additional pension Graduated retirement benefit Winter fuel payments Increments – eg, to pensions Increases of retirement pension for an adult Age addition in pensions	State retirement pension
Pre-retirement	None	None
Survivors	Bereavement benefits	Widowed mother's allowance Widow's pension Widowed parent's allowance
Death grants	Bereavement support payment (lump-sum payment)	Bereavement support payment
Accidents at work and occupational diseases	Industrial injuries disablement benefit Constant attendance allowance Exceptionally severe disablement allowance Reduced earnings allowance Retirement allowance	Industrial injuries benefits

Unemployment	Contribution-based jobseeker's allowance (JSA)	Contribution-based JSA
Family benefits (see p420)	Child benefit Guardian's allowance Child tax credit (CTC) Increases in other benefits for an adult or a child	Child benefit Guardian's allowance CTC

Note:

- **Contributory ESA** is classed, under the main co-ordination rules, initially as a sickness benefit during at least the 91-day 'assessment phase',[83] and potentially the first 365 days,[84] and then as an invalidity benefit thereafter. Under the UK–EU Protocol, DWP guidance classes it as an invalidity benefit from the outset.[85] This is significant because invalidity benefits cannot be exported under the UK–EU Protocol. For more details on exporting your contributory ESA, including an argument as to why the DWP guidance may be wrong, see p360.
- The DWP had considered **statutory maternity, adoption, paternity and shared parental pay** to be pay rather than social security or special non-contributory benefits.[86] However, it has always been arguable that these benefits should be classed as maternity and paternity benefits, and recent guidance lists them as such (see also p365).[87]
- The DWP considers **universal credit** (UC) to be neither a social security nor a special non-contributory benefit and so the co-ordination rules do not apply to UC.[88] It is arguable that UC should be listed as a social security benefit – eg, the child elements are arguably a family benefit. Get specialist advice if you want to make this argument. Note that UC is listed as 'social assistance' in the UK–Ireland Convention (see p398).

Disability and carers' benefits

Under the **main co-ordination rules**, AA, DLA care component, CDP care component, PIP daily living component, ADP daily living component and CA are categorised as sickness benefits. However, these benefits have been categorised as assisting with different risks at different times. Under the old co-ordination rules and then the main co-ordination rules, these benefits were categorised as invalidity benefits until 1 June 1992. They were then categorised as special non-contributory benefits until that was held to be wrong and they were re-categorised as sickness benefits.[89] The Court of Justice of the European Union has reconfirmed that DLA care component should be categorised as a sickness, not an invalidity, benefit.[90] For the relevance of the changing categorisations on whether you can be paid one of these benefits in a European Economic Area state, see p356.

The mobility component of DLA continues to be listed as a special non-contributory benefit and that has been held to be lawful.[91] The mobility components of PIP and ADP and CDP are each accepted as special non-contributory benefits (see below).

Carer's allowance supplement and young carer grant have been classified as 'cash sickness benefits' by the EU Administrative Commission and that has been accepted by the Scottish government.[92]

The **UK–Ireland Convention** categorises AA, DLA care component, PIP daily living component and CA as long-term care benefits, but then treats them in broadly the same way as sickness benefits are treated under the main co-ordination rules.[93] Although ADP daily living component, CDP care component, young carer grant and carer's allowance supplement are not listed under the convention, the regulations enable you to make a new claim for these benefits while resident in Ireland in certain circumstances if you are covered by the convention (see p308).[94]

The **UK–EU Protocol** categorises AA, DLA care component, PIP daily living component, CA, carer's allowance supplement and young carer grant as long-term care benefits, and the mobility components of DLA and PIP as special non-contributory benefits, and lists both categories as ones to which the protocol does not apply.[95] ADP and CDP are not listed in the UK–EU Protocol, but ADP daily living component and CDP care component are treated as long-term care benefits and the mobility components are treated as special non-contributory benefits, therefore neither component of ADP or CDP is covered by the protocol.

Special non-contributory benefits

The **main EU co-ordination rules** and the **UK–EU Protocol** define 'special non-contributory benefits' as:[96]

- intended to provide supplementary or ancillary cover against the risks on p393 and guarantee a minimum subsistence income, or provide specific protection for disabled people closely linked to a person's social environment in the state concerned; *and*
- funded solely from general taxation and not dependent on having made contributions as a condition of entitlement; *and*
- listed as such by each state in an annex to main legislation. The UK benefits listed, or treated as listed, are in the table below.

In the **main EU co-ordination rules**, the UK government has only listed pension credit (PC), income-based JSA, income-related ESA and the mobility component of DLA as special non-contributory benefits.[97] It has applied for the mobility component of PIP to be listed and that has been agreed by the Administrative Commission for the Co-ordination of Social Security Systems, but the listing of PIP has been delayed. Consequently, and since the component satisfies all other conditions, the Upper Tribunal recently held that the mobility component of PIP is a special non-contributory benefit.[98] In any case, the DWP has been treating the mobility component of PIP as such.[99] The mobility components of ADP and CDP are treated as special non-contributory benefits.[100] Income-related ESA replaced income support (IS) in the list from 28 June 2012.

The **UK–EU Protocol** lists as special non-contributory benefits[101] all the benefits in the right-hand column of the table below, except Scottish child payment and the mobility components of ADP and CDP, which are treated as such.

Special non-contributory benefits under main co-ordination rules	*Special non-contributory benefits under UK–EU Protocol*
Income-related ESA	Income-related ESA
Income-based JSA	Income-based JSA
PC	PC
DLA mobility component	DLA mobility component
PIP mobility component	PIP mobility component
ADP mobility component	ADP mobility component
CDP mobility component	CDP mobility component
Best Start grants	Best Start grants
Best Start foods payment	Best Start foods payment
Funeral support payment	Funeral support payment
Scottish child payment	Scottish child payment

The **main co-ordination rules** state that special non-contributory benefits can only be paid in the state in which you are 'resident'[102] (see p401 for details of when you count as resident). However, although you cannot 'export' special non-contributory benefits, all the other co-ordination principles apply.[103]

In contrast, under the **UK–EU Protocol**, *none* of the principles apply because the protocol lists special non-contributory benefits as benefits to which the protocol does not apply.[104]

The **UK–Ireland Convention** does not refer to special non-contributory benefits at all, but defines the three means-tested benefits as 'social assistance' (see below) and does not refer to the others at all.

Social and medical assistance

Under the **main co-ordination rules** and the **UK–EU Protocol**, benefits which are neither 'social security' nor 'special non-contributory' benefits are considered to be social assistance and are excluded from the co-ordination rules.[105]

The UK government does not specify which benefits it considers to be social assistance under either legislation but has made it clear that it does not consider UC to be either a social security or a special non-contributory benefit.[106] The Scottish government has categorised job start payment as social assistance.

It has also been decided that housing benefit[107] and working tax credit[108] are not social security or special non-contributory benefits. It is likely that the UK government might argue that IS is now also outside the scope of the EU co-ordination rules, since the removal of IS from the list of special non-contributory benefits on 28 June 2012.

Under the **UK–Ireland Convention**, 'social assistance' is defined in relation to UK benefits as UC, PC, IS, income-related ESA and income-based JSA.[109] The only provisions made by the convention for 'social assistance' relate to the recovery of overpayments. If you, or members of your family, have received social assistance in the UK while you were entitled to that assistance under Irish legislation, the convention provides for the UK to request that the Irish benefit authorities recover this 'overpayment' from ongoing payments of the Irish benefit and then forward that to the UK (and vice versa).[110]

4. **Principles of co-ordination**

The co-ordination rules set out several general principles (see p377). These principles are often the starting point in deciding how the co-ordination rules affect your entitlement.[111] However, there are exceptions to these principles for specific categories of benefits and, in some cases, there are more detailed provisions on how the principles should apply in certain circumstances. The following information provides an overview of the principles, because it is beyond the scope of this *Handbook* to cover all the exceptions and additional provisions in detail. You should, therefore, get specialist advice about the way in which the co-ordination rules apply to your particular circumstances.

The single competent state

In general, under each of the co-ordination rules you can only claim a particular category of benefit from one member state, and are only liable to pay national insurance (NI) contributions (or their equivalent) to one state, at any one time. That is expressed as the general principle that you can only be subject to the legislation of a single member state.[112] **Note:** the UK–Ireland Convention refers to the 'parties' of the UK and Ireland rather than 'states', and 'competent party' rather than 'competent state', but the same principle applies.

The competent state and competent institution

The **'competent state'** is the state responsible for paying your benefit and to which you must pay NI contributions. It is the state in which the 'competent institution' is situated.[113] The **'competent institution'** is broadly the institution responsible for paying your benefit and to which you are liable to pay NI contributions.[114] In the UK, the competent institutions are the DWP and HM Revenue and Customs.

The general rule is that the **competent state** is the one in which you are:[115]

- employed or self-employed (see the notes below);
- a civil servant;
- (other than for the UK–EU Protocol) resident while receiving an unemployment benefit under specific provisions;[116] *or*
- (other than for the UK–EU Protocol) a conscripted member of the armed forces or someone doing compulsory civilian service.

If none of the above bullet points apply, the competent state is the state in which you are 'resident' (see p401 for how this is determined). However, in certain circumstances other co-ordination rules may mean that a different state is deemed competent.[117] In particular, there are exceptions for 'sickness benefits' if you (or the member of your family who brings you within the co-ordination rules) receive a pension from a state other than the one in which you reside, or a member of your family is working in a state other than the one in which you reside (see p404). There are also exceptions for family benefits if you receive a pension (see p421).

Note:

- For your competent state to be determined on the basis of your employment or self-employment, your earnings do not need to exceed the threshold at which you are liable to pay NI contributions.[118]
- You are treated as still employed or self-employed if, as a result of that activity, you are receiving cash benefits (other than for the risks of old age, occupational diseases and accidents at work or, except under the UK–Ireland Convention, invalidity, sickness or being a survivor).[119]
- If you work simultaneously in the UK and one or more of the European Economic Area (EEA) states, you are subject to the legislation of the state of residence if you pursue a substantial part (generally, at least 25 per cent) of your activities there.[120]
- If your employer's business is normally in one state, but you are sent to another to work and it is anticipated that the posting will last for no more than 24 months, you remain subject to the legislation of the first state. Similarly, if you are self-employed in one state and go to another state to pursue a similar activity as a self-employed person, you remain subject to the legislation of the first state, provided the anticipated duration of your activity in the other state is not more than 24 months.[121] Under the UK–EU Protocol, you are referred to as a 'detached worker', and all the European Union (EU) states have 'opted in' to follow these rules in relation to the UK.[122]
- If you have moved to another EEA state, you may continue to be subject to the legislation of the state where you previously lived and were self-employed if you continue to be self-employed in that previous state.[123]

- If you make a claim, declaration or appeal to the institution in a state that takes the view it is not your competent state, it must forward your claim without delay to the relevant institution of the state the institution considers *is* competent. Your claim, declaration or appeal is treated as if it had been submitted to the competent state on the date it was originally submitted.[124] For further information, including if there is a dispute between states over which is your competent state, see p403.

How residence is determined

'**Residence**' is defined in each of the co-ordination rules as 'the place where a person habitually resides'.[125] The Withdrawal Agreements cross-refer to this definition in the main co-ordination rules for the purpose of determining who is covered by Withdrawal Agreement protections (see p380).[126]

Under the **UK–Ireland Convention**, this term is interpreted in accordance with the legislation of the state in which you reside.[127]

Under the **main co-ordination rules** and the **UK–EU Protocol**, the following factors should be considered when determining where you habitually reside. Although this list of factors is in a rule that explains what should be done if there is a difference of views between two states or institutions about where you are resident, it should also be used if there is no such dispute. Firstly, it should be established by common agreement where your centre of interests lies. This is based on an overall assessment of the relevant facts, including:[128]

- the duration and continuity of presence in the state(s) concerned;
- your personal situation, including:
  - the nature and specific characteristics of any activity pursued, in particular the place where such activity is habitually pursued, the stability of the activity and the duration of any work contract;
  - your family status and family ties;
  - any unpaid activity, such as voluntary work;
  - if you are a student, the source of your income;
  - your housing situation, in particular how permanent it is;
  - the member state in which you are deemed to reside for tax purposes.

If there is still a dispute about your place of residence, your intentions should be considered, especially the reasons why you moved. That is decisive in establishing your actual place of residence.[129]

If there is a dispute between states over which is your competent state, see p403.

When the competent state changes

If you are subject to the legislation of a member state, it continues to be your competent state until a change means that another member state becomes competent.[130]

The main factors that change the competent state are if:

- you start to work in another member state;[131] *or*
- (for 'sickness' or 'family' benefits) you start to receive a 'pension' from another member state (unless you are already receiving a pension in the state you are resident in);
- in some circumstances, a member of your family starts working in, or receiving a pension from, another member state;
- in some circumstances, you move to an EEA state and become resident there.

When the competent state changes can be affected by which co-ordination rules you are covered by and the category of benefit being paid. For example, the Court of Appeal recently held that the UK ceased to be the competent state for child benefit when the claimant moved, with her child, to reside in Spain. Consequently, entitlement to child benefit ceased, and this was not altered by the UK continuing to be the competent state for the child's disability living allowance (DLA) care component, which is a different category of benefit.[132] If you are covered by the main co-ordination rules and are receiving a 'sickness benefit' (see p404) from the UK because the UK is the competent state on the basis of your residence in the UK, and you then begin receiving a 'pension' from an EEA state (see p407), this generally means that your competent state ceases to be the UK and becomes the state that pays the pension.[133] On the other hand, if you are covered by the main co-ordination rules and are receiving a 'sickness benefit' from the UK and also a 'pension' from the UK and then you move to an EEA country, the UK remains your competent state. That was confirmed by the Upper Tribunal, which held that a woman continued to be entitled to the care component of DLA when she moved from the UK to Finland because she was receiving contributory employment and support allowance (ESA). **Note:** the same decision also held that when her entitlement to contributory ESA expired after a year, she continued to be entitled to DLA care component while living in Finland.[134] Recent guidance on adult disability payment (ADP) suggests ADP continues to be paid for the remaining duration of an award if the claimant moves from Scotland to France, but that a new claim would then be directed to the French authorities as France has become the competent state on the basis of residence.[135]

The point at which the UK stops being responsible for paying your benefit if you move to another state is not always clear and much of the caselaw has considered the old co-ordination rules, which differ in significant respects from the main co-ordination rules (see p377).[136] Also, there is no caselaw yet on the UK–Ireland Convention or the UK–EU Protocol. However, in general, under each of the co-ordination rules, *if* you continue to be entitled to a UK benefit when you move to an EEA state, the UK remains the competent state for paying *that* benefit until either you become employed/self-employed in the other state or, in certain circumstances, you start to receive a benefit from that state.[137] If you were self-employed in the UK and it is accepted that you continue to be so when you move to live in an EEA state, the UK remains your competent state.[138]

If the decision maker decides the UK is not the competent state

If, when you claim a UK benefit, the decision maker decides the UK is not the competent state to pay that benefit, they must, under the main co-ordination rules, forward the claim to the relevant institution in the state that is considered competent without delay, unless there is evidence that state takes a different view (see next paragraph). The date you submitted your claim (or appeal) to a state that is not competent is treated as your date of claim (or appeal) by the state that is competent.[139]

If there is a 'difference of views' between the institutions of two (or more) states on which is the competent state for paying a cash benefit or meeting the cost of a benefit in kind, while the issue is being resolved you can, if you meet the other rules of entitlement, get provisional payments. These payments are made by, and under the legislation of, the state in which you are resident (or, for family benefits under the UK–Ireland Convention, the state in which the child resides[140]) or (other than under the UK–Ireland Convention) the state where you first applied if you are not resident in any of the states concerned.[141]

If no agreement is reached between the states after one month, the matter can be referred to the EU Administrative Commission (under the main co-ordination rules) or the UK–EU Specialised Committee on Citizens' Rights (under the protocol), which aims to reconcile disputes within six months.[142] The process is slightly different under the UK–Ireland Convention: an arbitration tribunal gets appointed to resolve the dispute.

If it is established that the state that made provisional payments is not the competent state, it can be reimbursed by the state that is competent, if the latter has a comparable benefit.[143]

Caselaw decided under the main co-ordination rules has established the following points about provisional payments. The rules on provisional payments apply if forwarding your claim triggers a different view and also if there is evidence of a different view when the claim is received, in which case it should not be forwarded.[144] The legislation only requires there to be a 'difference of views'; legislation says nothing about the form in which the view must be expressed, nor the evidence required to prove the difference. If you have written confirmation that the institution of another state takes a different view of which state is competent, provide that to the decision maker (or tribunal).[145] However, the Court of Appeal has held that oral evidence can be accepted if it is sufficient to satisfy the decision maker (or tribunal) that two states hold different views on the issue of competence. The Court of Appeal has also confirmed that the requirement to make provisional payments is unaffected by whether a comparable benefit is paid in the other state or whether the payments would be recouped.[146]

Note: DWP guidance, which states that provisional payments need not be made if the other state does not have a similar benefit, has not been updated since the Court of Appeal decision and should not be followed.

Even if there is clear evidence of a 'difference of views', the benefit authorities do not always comply with their duty to make provisional payments, so you may need to request these in writing, and refer to the relevant legislation and caselaw.

In most cases, the issue is which state is competent to make the payment, but if there is a difference of views between states on which legislation applies, you are provisionally subject to the legislation of one state in the following order of priority:[147]

- if you only work in one state, the state where you work;
- if you either work in two or more states and live in one of them, or do not work, the state where you reside;
- (except under the UK–Ireland Convention) in all other cases, of the states in which you work, the state to which you first applied.

Sickness benefits

Under the **main co-ordination rules**, attendance allowance (AA), the daily living component of personal independence payment (PIP), the daily living component of ADP, the care component of DLA, the care component of child disability payment (CDP), carer's allowance (CA), carer's allowance supplement and young carer grant are all classed as 'sickness benefits' (see p396).

If you are covered by the main co-ordination rules (see p379), the UK must be the competent state for paying your 'cash sickness benefits' for you to be entitled to:[148]

- AA, PIP daily living component, DLA care component or CA; *or*
- ADP daily living component or CDP care component if either you are resident in an EEA state or if you are only entitled because the past presence test has been disapplied under the rules on p306; *or*
- a young carer grant or carer's allowance supplement if you are resident in an EEA state.

The UK must be the competent state to pay *your* sickness benefits. So, for example, for you to receive CA, the UK must be the competent state to pay you CA, even if there is a different competent state for paying a sickness benefit to the person for whom you care.[149]

The **UK–Ireland Convention** categorises AA, DLA care component, PIP daily living component and CA as long-term care benefits, but then treats them in broadly the same way as sickness benefits are treated under the main co-ordination rules.[150] Although not listed under the convention, the regulations for ADP, CDP, young carer grant and carer's allowance supplement require the UK to be the competent state if you are resident in Ireland when you make a new claim while covered by the convention (see p308).[151]

The **UK–EU Protocol** categorises AA, DLA care component, PIP daily living component, CA, carer's allowance supplement and young carer grant as long-term care benefits, and the mobility components of DLA and PIP as special non-contributory benefits, and lists both categories as ones to which the protocol does not apply.[152]

The care components of ADP and CDP are treated as long-term care benefits and the mobility components of ADP and CDP are treated as special non-contributory benefits under the UK–EU Protocol, and therefore the protocol does not apply to these components.

Determining the competent state for sickness benefits

In most cases, the competent state is determined under the general rule explained on p399. However, in specific circumstances, the competent state can be altered by other factors.

If you are covered by the **UK–Ireland Convention**, the competent state to pay 'sickness benefits' (which under the convention are categorised as 'long-term care benefits') can be affected by you, or a member of your family, receiving a pension from either the UK or Ireland (see p407).

If you are covered by the **main co-ordination rules**, and the only basis for the UK being the competent state to pay your 'sickness benefits' is that you are resident in the UK, 'other provisions' of those co-ordination rules may mean that another state is deemed competent.[153] The 'other provisions' that arise most often can apply if either you (or a member of your family) receive a 'pension' from a member state other than the one where you reside (see below) or a member of your family is working in a member state other than the one where you reside (see text beneath the note below).

The rules to determine which member state is the competent state to pay your sickness benefit can be complex. It can therefore be helpful to start with the DWP's 'simple hierarchy':[154]

1. the state in which you are working;
2. the state from which you are receiving a pension;
3. the state in which a member of your family is working;
4. the state from which a member of your family is receiving a pension;
5. the state in which you are residing.

Note:

- This 'simple hierarchy' is contained in DWP guidance memos that summarise caselaw on the competent state for sickness benefits.[155] Like all guidance, it is not binding. If legislation or caselaw provides that your competent state does not follow this 'simple hierarchy', the law, rather than the guidance, must be followed.
- The DWP's main guidance also contains sections on *Deciding the Competent State to Pay Cash Sickness Benefits.*

- Recent guidance on ADP and CDP contains a similar 'order of priority', together with examples. It does not include options 3 or 4, but for CDP suggests that where the child has parents living in separate countries, the 'order of priority' should still be used and if this fails to identify the competent state, then it should be where the child lives.[156] However, note that the question of how to determine the competent state for a child who has one parent working in another member state is due to be decided by the Court of Appeal (see immediately below).

If you are resident in a state, the benefit authorities may decide that state is not the competent state to pay your sickness benefits if a member of your family (see p390) is working, and therefore 'insured', in another member state. This is how the 'other provision' of Article 21 of the main co-ordination rules has been interpreted to apply. Article 21 provides that an insured person and members of their family residing or staying in a state other than the competent state shall be entitled to cash benefits provided by the competent state.[157] The Upper Tribunal held that this provision meant the UK was not the competent state to pay CA to a woman resident in the UK because her husband (from whom she was separated but not divorced) was working, and therefore 'insured', in the Netherlands. Since the Netherlands was his competent state, and she was a member of his family residing in another state, the Netherlands was held to be the competent state for her 'sickness' benefit.[158] Similarly, in a different case, the Upper Tribunal held that the UK was not the competent state to pay DLA care component to a child resident in the UK with her mother who was not working, because her father was self-employed, and therefore 'insured', in Belgium. Consequently, Belgium was held to be the competent state for the child's 'sickness' benefit. At the time of writing, the claimant's appeal to the Court of Appeal was due to be heard in February 2023.[159]

An arguably different approach to Article 21 was adopted in a separate Upper Tribunal case in which it was held that this provision only applies *after* the competent state has been identified and only if that state is not the state of residence. The only circumstance in which it was suggested this could apply is if you are resident in one state and receive a pension from another – ie, if your competent state is determined by *separate* 'other provisions' of the main co-ordination rules.[160] In the further appeal from one of these cases, the Court of Appeal also took the view that Article 21 could not apply to the appellant who had claimed CA while resident in Cyprus at a time when he did not work or receive any benefits. That was because his competent state was Cyprus, as his state of residence, and furthermore he was not 'insured' (a finding not altered by his having paid sufficient NI contributions to be entitled, in future, to a UK retirement pension).[161]

Note: two linked cases on whether the claimants' competent state is affected by a member of their family being employed in another state have been due to be heard by the Upper Tribunal for a few years and it is understood they will still be heard.[162] See CPAG's *Welfare Rights Bulletin* and the online version of this *Handbook* on AskCPAG for updates, and get specialist advice if you think this could affect your entitlement.

If you or a member of your family receive a pension from another member state

If you, or the member of your family who brings you within the **main co-ordination rules**, receive a 'pension' (see below) from a member state other than the one in which you reside, that can mean the competent state to pay your 'sickness benefits' is the state that pays the pension. This is because, under the main co-ordination rules, the competent state for paying your cash sickness benefits is the one responsible for meeting the cost of your sickness benefits in kind – eg, in the UK, NHS treatment.[163] **Note:** although you receive sickness benefits in kind in the state where you are resident, the *cost* of these treatments can be borne by another state. This means that to work out which state is competent for paying a cash sickness benefit, you must establish which state must bear the cost of sickness benefits in kind. Various scenarios are set out on p409.

If you are covered by the **UK–Ireland Convention** and you, or a member of your family, receive a 'pension', the competent state is:[164]

- the state in which you, or the member of your family who receives the pension, are employed or self-employed; *or*
- if the bullet above does not apply, the state:
  - that pays the pension if there is only one pension in payment; *or*
  - the state in which you were subject to the legislation for longest if both the UK and Ireland are paying a pension or, if the relevant periods are the same, the state to whose legislation you (or the member of your family who receives the pension) were subject most recently.

Pension and pensioner

'Pension', for the purpose of the **main co-ordination rules**, includes more than old age pensions. It includes lump-sum benefits that can be substituted for pensions and reimbursement of contributions, and can include revaluation increases and supplementary allowances.[165] It refers to state payments made under the legislation of an EEA state and does not include private or occupational pensions. Under the old co-ordination rules, it was accepted that a pension can include incapacity benefit (IB), ESA, DLA and severe disablement allowance (SDA).[166] However, a more recent case has held that the care component of DLA is not a pension under the current co-ordination rules. It also held that the term 'pension' must have the same meaning throughout the EU regulations and that a Dutch survivor's benefit is a pension.[167] A further case confirmed that the mobility component of DLA is also not a pension.[168] It may be arguable that the term 'pension' includes pension credit (PC) since this is a supplementary allowance.[169] Although the Upper Tribunal commented that PC is not a 'pension', as it is a special non-contributory benefit (see p397),[170] the argument was not considered in depth, and the Court of Justice of the European Union (CJEU) has held that a benefit can be both a special non-contributory benefit and a supplementary allowance.[171] However, the most recent Upper Tribunal decisions have focused on the need for a benefit to be contributory for it to be considered a pension[172] (although contributory ESA awarded on conversion from IB in youth was still accepted as a pension, despite the claimant's not having paid contributions).[173] Recent DWP guidance confirms that receipt of contributory ESA, IB, SDA, retirement pension (other than category D), industrial injuries disablement benefit and bereavement benefit (other than a lump-sum bereavement support payment) are all considered UK 'pensions'.[174] **Note:** it is strongly arguable that the guidance is wrong to exclude a category D pension, and that this should count as a 'pension'. If this is the reason for you being refused AA or CA, challenge that decision and get advice to argue that your category D pension means that the UK is your competent state.

Under the **UK–Ireland Convention**, 'pension' is defined as an old age benefit, invalidity benefit or a survivor's benefit.[175]

'Pensioner' is not defined under the main co-ordination rules, but refers to someone receiving a 'pension'.[176]

Under the UK–Ireland Convention, 'pensioner' is defined as a person receiving a pension.[177]

Who is a member of the family for sickness benefits in kind

Under the main EU co-ordination rules, the definition of 'member of the family' for sickness benefits in kind is slightly different to the general definition (see p390). The difference is highlighted below in *italics*.

You are a member of the family of a person covered by the main co-ordination rules for the purpose of sickness benefits in kind, if:[178]

- you are a person defined or recognised as a member of the family, or designated as a member of the household, by the legislation, under which benefits are provided, *of the member state in which you reside*; or
- the legislation under which benefits are provided does not make a distinction between the members of the family and other people to whom it applies, and you are the covered person's spouse or child who is either under the age of majority (18 years old in England, Wales and Northern Ireland; 16 years old in Scotland) or older but dependent on the person covered.

If, under the legislation in either bullet point above, you are only considered to be a member of the family or member of the household if you are living in the same household as the person, this condition is considered to be satisfied if you are mainly dependent on them.

If you have a right to benefits in kind as a member of the family, as well as an independent right to benefits in kind, your independent right takes priority unless this is only based on residence.[179] Examples are given below.

Scenarios if a pension is paid by another member state

If you are covered by the **main co-ordination rules** and you, or the member of your family (see p390) who brings you within those rules, receive a 'pension' (see p407) from an EEA (or UK) state other than the one you are living in, check the possible scenarios, and exceptions, to determine which state is competent for paying your cash sickness benefits. These are AA, DLA care component, PIP daily living component, CA, ADP daily living component, CDP care component, carer's allowance supplement and young carer grant (**note:** the requirement for the UK to be the competent state only applies in certain circumstances for the last four Scottish benefits – see p404).

If you reside in the UK (or another state in which entitlement to sickness benefits in kind is on the basis of residence, rather than insurance or employment) and you (or the member of your family who brings you within the co-ordination rules) receive a 'pension' from another state, *but not* from the UK (or the other state of residence), the cost of sickness benefits in kind received in the UK (or other state) is borne by the state that pays the pension, to the extent that you would be entitled to receive sickness benefits in kind from that state if you lived there. Therefore, the state that pays your pension, rather than the state in which you reside, is responsible for paying your cash sickness benefit.[180] If you are already receiving a UK cash sickness benefit and then start receiving a pension from another state, your entitlement to the UK sickness benefit ends.[181] Similarly, if you are living in an EEA state, receiving its cash sickness benefit and start to receive retirement pension from the UK, the UK would become the competent state.[182]

Example

Emil is a Swedish national with settled status who has been living in the UK for nine years. He was working in the UK until a few months ago, but stopped when he turned 62 and became eligible for a small Swedish old-age state pension. Due to long-term health problems, Emil claims the daily living component of PIP. As he receives a pension from another state (Sweden), that state is responsible for reimbursing the UK for the cost of any NHS treatment he has. Consequently, provided Emil would be entitled to sickness benefits in kind (eg, healthcare) if he were resident in Sweden, he is not entitled to the daily living component of PIP (but may be able to claim a Swedish cash sickness benefit). If the DWP decides that the UK is not the competent state, and considers Sweden to be the competent state, it must forward Emil's claim to the relevant institution in Sweden without delay (see p403).

Recent guidance for decision makers covers examples of these rules applying to claimants living in EEA states.

- The receipt of a UK pension by a French national residing in France means the competent state to pay their cash sickness benefits is the UK, and therefore they are able to receive AA.[183]

– The receipt of a UK pension by a UK national residing in Spain means the competent state to pay their cash sickness benefits is the UK, and therefore they are able to make a new claim for the daily living component of ADP.[184]

If you receive a pension from two or more states and one of them is the state in which you reside, that state is responsible for the cost of your sickness benefits in kind (and is therefore the competent state for paying cash sickness benefits).[185]

Example

Emil claims contributory ESA. He now receives a 'pension' from two or more states, including the one in which he resides (the UK). The state which is *both* the one in which he resides and the one that pays his 'pension' (the UK) is the state that is responsible for the cost of his NHS treatment, and is therefore the competent state to pay his cash sickness benefit. Consequently, Emil can now be entitled to the daily living component of PIP.

If you reside in the UK (or another state in which entitlement to sickness benefits in kind is on the basis of residence) and you receive a pension from two or more states other than the UK (or other state of residence), the cost of your healthcare in kind is met by the state in which you were subject to pensions legislation for the longest period (or if that is more than one state, the state in which you were last subject to its pensions legislation).[186] That state is therefore the competent state for paying your cash sickness benefits.

Example

Jonas is a German national with pre-settled status. He worked for 10 years in Germany and 18 years in France. Since 2019 he has been residing in the UK and receiving pensions from both Germany and France. France is the state responsible for the cost of any NHS treatment he has while he lives in the UK and so France is the competent state for paying cash sickness benefits.

If you are the member of the family of a person receiving a pension and reside in a different state to them, whichever state must meet the cost of the sickness benefits in kind for them must also meet the cost of sickness benefits in kind for you (and is therefore the competent state for paying cash sickness benefits).[187]

However, check whether you also have an independent right to benefits in kind and, if so, whether these take priority. See the second bullet point below.

Example

Reka is a Dutch national with settled status who moved to the UK in 2016 to join her Dutch husband, Roland, who had been living and working in the UK most of his life. In 2020

Roland retired and began receiving a UK pension and Reka began receiving AA. In 2022 she moved to back to the Netherlands. Reka continues to be entitled to AA as the UK continues to be the competent state to pay her cash sickness benefits. This is because the UK is the state that must meet the cost of the sickness benefits in kind for Roland and, therefore, is also the state that must meet these costs for Reka.

The above rules do not apply in the following cases.

- You (or the member of your family who is a pensioner) are entitled to benefits under the legislation of a state because that state is the competent one on the basis of an activity as an employed or self-employed person.[188] **Note:** the DWP accepts that undertaking activity as an employed or self-employed person in the UK is sufficient to mean that the UK is the competent state for paying cash sickness benefits.[189]

Example

Sophia is Portuguese with settled status. Since 2017 she has been living in the UK and receiving a small pension from Portugal. Sophia works part time as a self-employed cleaner and claims child benefit and child tax credit (CTC) for her disabled granddaughter who lives with her and receives DLA middle rate care component. Sophia can claim CA, as the UK is the competent state for paying benefits to her on the basis of her self-employment here.

- You have an independent right to benefits in kind, either under the legislation of a state or under the co-ordination rules, and also a right derived from being a member of the family of, for example, a pensioner. Your independent right takes priority, unless it exists solely because of your residence in that state.[190]

Examples

Krista is Latvian and has been residing in the UK with her Latvian husband Andris since 2015. They each have settled status. Andris receives a pension from Latvia and Krista receives contributory ESA from the UK. Krista wants to claim the daily living component of PIP. She can do this as her contributory ESA is classed as a 'pension' (see p407),[191] and therefore her independent rights take priority over the rights she has as a member of her husband's family. The UK is the state responsible for the cost of her sickness benefits in kind, and is therefore the competent state for paying her cash sickness benefits.

Ryan is a 13-year-old Irish national living in the UK since 2019 with his Irish mother Megan who receives an invalidity pension from Ireland. They each have pre-settled status. Ryan wants to claim the care component of DLA. However, because his independent rights are only based on his residence in the UK, the rights he has as the member of his mother's family take priority. Therefore, Ireland is the state responsible for the cost of his sickness benefits in kind, and is therefore the competent state for paying his cash sickness benefits.

To check the sickness benefits payable by EEA states, search for 'Your rights country by country' at ec.europa.eu/social.

If the rules exclude you

If you are residing in the UK and you receive a decision that the rules determining the competent state for sickness benefits exclude you from entitlement to AA, DLA care component, CDP care component, the daily living component of PIP, the daily living component of ADP, or CA, or you think these rules might exclude you, check the following.

Are you excluded from 'sickness benefits'?

1. Check whether the rules on competent state actually apply to you. These rules can only apply if you are covered by either the UK–Ireland Convention (see p387) or the main co-ordination rules, and note the latter can only apply if you are covered by either the Withdrawal Agreement protections (see p380) or you are both covered by the partial Withdrawal Agreement protections *and* relying on the main co-ordination rules to either satisfy or disapply the past presence test (see p384). Furthermore, note that competent state rules only apply to the care component of CDP or the daily living component of ADP in limited circumstances – see p404.
2. If it is suggested that you (or the member of your family who brings you within the co-ordination rules) are receiving a pension from an EEA state (Ireland, if you are covered by the UK–Ireland Convention), check whether it is a state payment classed as a 'pension'. Private and occupational pensions should not bring you within the above rules. See p407 for the meaning of 'pension'.
3. Do, or could, you (or your family member who brings you within the co-ordination rules) receive a pension from the UK as well as from the EEA state (or Ireland)? If so, the UK is responsible for the cost of your NHS treatment and so is the competent state for paying sickness benefits (see the examples of Emil on p409 and Krista on p411).
4. Do, or could, you (or your family member who brings you within the co-ordination rules) work in the UK? The DWP accepts that undertaking activity as an employed or self-employed person in the UK is sufficient to mean that the UK is the competent state for paying cash sickness benefits (see the example of Sophia on p411). **Note**: your earnings do not need to exceed the threshold at which you are liable to pay NI contributions.[192]
5. Do not withdraw your (or the member of your family's) claim for a pension from the other state without getting specialist advice, because that could leave you worse off. Firstly, it could affect your (or their) future pension entitlement or you may lose the option to reclaim. Secondly, recent caselaw suggests the DWP may continue to treat the state that paid your pension as the competent state to pay your cash sickness benefit (see p402).[193]
6. If the DWP has decided that the UK is not the competent state, see p403.
7. If you are covered by the main co-ordination rules, it may be possible to argue that your particular circumstances mean that the exclusion from AA, DLA care component, CDP

care component, the daily living component of PIP or the daily living component of ADP on the basis that the UK is not your competent state does not apply.

- If you are the dependent family member of an EEA worker, the exclusion is prohibited by the principle of equal treatment (see below) if the refusal of a disability benefit reduces or impedes their ability to work or disadvantages them in relation to a British worker.[194] The Upper Tribunal rejected an argument that refusal of AA was disproportionate and discriminatory, but arguably did not fully consider this discrimination argument.[195] However, the argument was considered in a subsequent case when it was put in broad terms.[196] Although the judge dismissed the argument as presented, he left open the possibility that the principle of equal treatment could prohibit excluding a worker's family member from sickness benefits in particular circumstances. Such an argument may be accepted if there is no equivalent sickness benefit payable by the competent state and exclusion would result in your being deprived of any entitlement at all.[197] **Note:** this argument was rejected in relation to a child refused DLA, because the competent state was held to be Belgium where her father was self-employed, and not the UK where she lived with her mother, but the appeal from this case is due to be heard in the Court of Appeal.[198]
- If you have previously worked and paid taxes in the UK, the co-ordination rules should not deprive you of entitlement to a benefit paid for by taxation. If this would be the result of the co-ordination rules, a state is not prevented from awarding the benefit, even when it is not the competent state for paying it.[199] The Upper Tribunal has considered this line of argument, developed through EU caselaw, but decided it did not apply in that particular case as the person had not contributed through general taxation.[200] In the circumstances of this case, it held that the UK was not prevented from excluding the claimant from entitlement to AA if the UK was not the competent state to pay cash sickness benefits.[201]

Equal treatment of people

If you are covered by any of the co-ordination rules, you are entitled to the same benefits under the legislation of the 'competent state' (see p399) as a national of that state.[202] Equal treatment is one of the fundamental rights of EU law,[203] and the principle of non-discrimination prohibits discrimination based on your nationality. Both direct discrimination and, if it cannot be justified as proportionate and in pursuit of a legitimate aim, indirect discrimination are prohibited.

Direct discrimination arises when one person is treated less favourably than another in the same situation. Indirect discrimination arises when apparently neutral and non-discriminatory rules have, in practice, a greater adverse impact on some people than others – eg, non-nationals of the competent state over nationals of the competent state. For example, the right to reside test in UK law appeared, when the UK was a member of the EU, to apply equally to all EEA nationals. However, British and Irish citizens always have a right to reside in the common travel area (the UK, Ireland, Channel Islands and the Isle of Man) and therefore satisfy the test for means-tested benefits, whereas other EEA nationals only satisfy it in certain circumstances. Therefore, the test is indirectly discriminatory. However, the Supreme Court decided in a case concerning PC that this discrimination is justified and, therefore, legal.[204] Similarly, the CJEU has held that the right to reside test for child benefit and CTC was not directly discriminatory and, although indirectly discriminatory, this was justified.[205] Although a different view was taken by the Northern Ireland Chief Commissioner, who found that the right to reside test for child benefit was directly and indirectly discriminatory, that decision was overturned by the Court of Appeal in Northern Ireland.[206]

In 2021, the CJEU considered whether the exclusion from universal credit (UC) of EU nationals who have been granted pre-settled status (limited leave) under the EU Settlement Scheme, and who have no other right to reside, was unlawfully discriminatory. The CJEU held that this exclusion was not discriminatory.[207] That is because, rather than considering whether the regulations discriminated on nationality grounds contrary to the equal treatment provisions of the Treaty on the Functioning of the EU (TFEU),[208] the CJEU considered whether the regulations were contrary to the EU Directive 2004/38, but found that as the claimant did not have a right to reside under that directive she could not rely on its equal treatment provisions.[209]

In an earlier separate case, on the same question, the Court of Appeal had held that the equal treatment provisions of TFEU did apply and meant that the exclusion of pre-settled status was direct discrimination on nationality grounds and therefore unlawful.[210] That Court of Appeal judgment overturned the decision of the High Court that this exclusion was only indirect discrimination and was lawful because it was justified.[211] However, the DWP appealed the decision of the Court of Appeal to the Supreme Court, which allowed the appeal as the question was held to have already been answered definitively by the CJEU.[212]

It may be arguable that the exclusion of pre-settled status as a qualifying right to reside is unlawfully discriminatory under the equal treatment provisions of the Withdrawal Agreement.[213] This argument requires these provisions to be distinguished from the equal treatment provisions of the TFEU, which the CJEU and Supreme Court already held do not apply. For this and other potential arguments that may now apply since the judgments of the CJEU and Supreme Court discussed above, see p170.

Equal treatment of facts and events

Each of the co-ordination rules provide for the 'equal treatment of benefits, income, facts or events'.[214] This provision is sometimes referred to as the 'principle of the assimilation of facts'. This principle is designed to ensure that if the competent state regards the receipt of a particular benefit or income, or the occurrence of certain facts or events, as producing certain legal effects, it should regard the receipt of an equivalent benefit or income from another member state, or the occurrence of particular facts or events in another member state, as producing the same effect. For example, if one state has determined that a person has had an industrial accident, that fact must be accepted, for the purpose of awarding benefit, in another member state.

A benefit paid by a member state is 'equivalent' to a benefit paid by another member state if they are comparable, taking account of the aim of each benefit and the legislation under which they are established. Receipt of a Polish benefit paid on the basis that the claimant was incapable of independent living was accepted in one Upper Tribunal case as equivalent to the middle or higher rate of DLA care component and therefore entitled the claimant's carer to CA, and in a separate case as equivalent to AA and therefore entitled the claimant to a severe disability addition within her PC.[215]

The Upper Tribunal has held that this principle does not apply to the effects on working tax credit (WTC) because WTC is not a benefit covered by the co-ordination rules (see p392). However, because *other* EU regulations require workers from EEA states to have the same 'social advantages' as national workers,[216] the regulations on entitlement to the childcare element must be interpreted so as to accept a Dutch invalidity benefit as evidence of a claimant's incapacity.[217] Following this judgment, the WTC regulations were amended to include any benefit paid by an EEA state which is substantially similar to any of the UK benefits listed as evidence of incapacity.[218]

Note: the UC regulations treat a benefit paid by another state in the same way as a UK benefit that counts as unearned income, if the foreign benefit is 'analogous to' the UK benefit or is a state retirement pension.[219]

There are exceptions to the general principle of the assimilation of facts, some of which are set out in the co-ordination rules, and others arise as a result of a conflict between this principle and other principles of the co-ordination rules. For example, the assimilation of facts cannot render another member state competent.[220] The competent state should first be determined (see p399) and then that state should assimilate the facts for the purposes of its own legislation.

The assimilation principle should also not interfere with the principle of aggregation (see below).[221] So, the competent state should count periods of insurance in another EEA state (under the aggregation principle) without needing to address the question of whether they count as periods of insurance for the assimilation principle to apply. If it counts as a period of insurance under the legislation of the state in which it took place, that period can be aggregated.

Aggregation

The principle of aggregation for the purpose of acquiring and calculating entitlement to benefits is a key co-ordinating principle in each of the co-ordination rules.[222] To ensure and promote freedom of movement, the aim of this principle is to remove disadvantages that arise when claiming benefit after moving from one member state to another.

'Aggregation' means adding together periods of insurance (eg, periods in which you have paid NI contributions in the UK), residence or employment/self-employment completed under the legislation of one or more member states to satisfy the conditions of entitlement for a benefit. For example, if you want to claim a UK contribution-based benefit such as contributory ESA, but you have not paid sufficient NI contributions in the UK, you can rely on periods of insurance in one or more other member states to satisfy the UK contribution rules.

The competent institution must contact the competent institutions in the other relevant states to determine the periods completed under their legislation.[223]

What constitutes a period of residence, employment or insurance is determined by the legislation of the state in which it took place.[224]

The aggregation principle is particularly important in calculating entitlement to retirement pensions if you have worked in more than one EEA country or the UK and an EEA country. You claim in the country where you are living (or where you last worked if that was not where you are living), but your total pension may be made up of pensions paid by more than one state. If you are claiming in the UK you should contact the International Pension Centre (see Appendix 3) and see p314. Note that differing retirement ages can affect when a state pays its proportion of your pension.

Note: the main co-ordination rules were, in general, revoked in UK law from the end of the transition period and now only apply to those covered by the Withdrawal Agreement protections (see p380). However, even if these protections do not, or no longer, apply to you, and therefore you cannot rely on other aspects of the main co-ordination rules, you may still be able to rely on their aggregation principle if:

- you are covered by the *partial* Withdrawal Agreement protections (see p384).[225] This is particularly important if you need to rely on aggregating past periods of residence to satisfy the 'past presence test' for the disability and carers' benefits, because the UK–EU Protocol does not cover these benefits (see below);
- you need to aggregate insurance contributions to be entitled to a UK retirement pension, because these provisions, together with those on the uprating of pensions, were saved and continue to apply (see p314).[226]

If you cannot rely on the aggregation principle of the main co-ordination rules, check whether you are covered by any of the other co-ordination rules, but note that the UK–EU Protocol does not cover disability, carers' or family benefits.

Example

Sancha is a Portuguese national who has worked for many years in Portugal. She leaves her job in Portugal and moves to the UK. She works for three weeks before being made redundant. Sancha is expecting a baby in two months' time and claims maternity allowance (MA). She can be entitled to MA because she can add her periods of employment in Portugal to her period of employment in the UK to satisfy the employment condition of having worked for 26 out of the last 66 weeks.

Note: if Sancha had moved to, and begun working in, the UK before 31 December 2020, she would be covered by the main co-ordination rules; if she moved after 31 December 2020, she would be covered by the UK–EU Protocol, but the aggregation principle would apply in either case.

Disability and carers' benefits

The **main co-ordination rules** provide for 'residence' in a member state to be aggregated with presence in Great Britain to satisfy the past presence test for AA, CA, PIP, ADP, DLA and CDP (see p302).[227]

Note:

- The Upper Tribunal has held that 'mere residence' in an EEA country cannot be aggregated under the main co-ordination rules for the purpose of satisfying the past presence test in disability and carers' benefits. Although in these cases it was not necessary to decide what qualities the residence must have in order to count, it was suggested that insurance-based, or contribution-based, residence would count.[228] The appeal against this part of the judgment was dropped when the appeal was heard by the Court of Appeal.[229]
- You can rely on the aggregation principle of the main co-ordination rules if you are covered by the Withdrawal Agreement protections (see p380), or if these do not, or no longer, apply, the *partial* Withdrawal Agreement protections (see p384).[230] However, if you can potentially receive benefit as a result of aggregating past periods of residence, the rules on the competent state for sickness benefits then apply to your claim for AA, CA, PIP daily living component, DLA care component and, in specific circumstances only, the ADP daily living component and the CDP care component (see p404).
- If you may not be able to aggregate your residence in an EEA state due to it being 'mere residence', or in addition to *satisfying* the past presence test through aggregation, always check whether the test can be *disapplied* due to your being covered by the main co-ordination rules (see p306).

The **UK–Ireland Convention** states that, if the UK is your competent state for these benefits, you can be entitled to AA, DLA care component, PIP daily living component and CA while resident in Ireland. However, when determining this entitlement, only periods of residence in Ireland during which you were insured may count towards the past presence requirement.[231] **Note**: because ADP and CDP require past presence in the common travel area, which includes Ireland, reliance on aggregation of residence in Ireland under the UK–Ireland Convention is not necessary.

The **UK–EU Protocol** does not cover these disability and carers' benefits (see p392).[232]

Unemployment benefits

When determining entitlement to unemployment benefits, your periods of insurance (if entitlement depends on insurance) or employment/self-employment (if entitlement depends on employment/self-employment) completed in all member states are only aggregated if you were last insured or you last worked (whichever is required) under the legislation of the state from which you are claiming benefit.[233]

Example

Tomasz is Polish and after working and being insured in Poland for four years became unemployed, and so he moved to the UK to look for work and to join his Polish wife (who has been working in the UK since 2020 and has pre-settled status). If Tomasz claims contribution-based jobseeker's allowance (JSA), he cannot use his periods of insurance from Poland to satisfy the NI contribution conditions. However, if he takes two weeks' full-time temporary work in the UK and then claims contribution-based JSA, he can then aggregate his periods of insurance in Poland and the NI contributions paid in the UK to be able to qualify for contribution-based JSA.

However, this additional condition does not apply if, during your last period of employment or self-employment, you resided in a state other than your competent state. In this case, if you claim an unemployment benefit in the state in which you continue to reside (or have returned to), you *can* aggregate periods of insurance or employment or self-employment in order to be entitled to that benefit.[234]

Example

Monique is a Belgian national who was employed and insured in Belgium for three years. In December 2020 she got a job in France that she could do while working from home, and so she moved to the UK, where she now has pre-settled status. In December 2022 she was made redundant and immediately claimed contribution-based JSA. She was entitled to this because she could aggregate the contributions paid in both Belgium and France.

Exporting benefits

Each of the co-ordination rules allows you to 'export' certain social security benefits from one member state to another if you cease to be resident in the state in which your entitlement arose.

This means that certain benefits may not be reduced, modified, suspended, withdrawn or confiscated just because you go to live in a different member state.[235] The rules for exporting vary according to the benefit concerned: some are fully exportable, some may be exportable on a temporary basis, and some are not exportable at all.

Check the individual benefit rules in Chapter 15 to see whether that benefit can be exported. If it can, you should contact the office that pays your benefit well in advance so that arrangements can be made to pay you in the state you are going to. The rules covering periodic reassessments still apply – so, for example, if you export contributory ESA, the DWP continues to assess your limited capability for work and your limited capability for work-related activity. However, any checks and medicals take place in the state in which you are living, with reports then sent to the DWP.[236]

Under the **main co-ordination rules**, and the **UK–Ireland Convention**, all UK benefits categorised as social security benefits are exportable, provided the UK remains the competent state for the payment of that benefit (see p399). However, the **UK–EU Protocol** excludes invalidity and unemployment benefits from export provisions and does not cover family or long-term care benefits.[237] See p393 for a list of the UK benefits covered.

The following benefits can be exported indefinitely:

- old age benefits;
- survivor's benefits;
- pensions for accidents at work or occupational diseases;
- (not under the UK–EU Protocol) invalidity benefits;
- (not under the UK–EU Protocol) family benefits (see p420);
- death grants.

The following benefits can be exported for a limited period or subject to certain restrictions:

- (not under the UK–EU Protocol) unemployment benefits;
- sickness, maternity and paternity benefits. However, in most cases, these benefits are exportable in a similar way to the fully exportable benefits.

Special non-contributory benefits (see p397) cannot be exported. Under the main co-ordination rules they are paid only in the state in which you are 'resident'.[238] See p401 for details of when you count as resident.

Overlapping benefit rules

A general principle of each of the co-ordination rules is that you should not use one period of compulsory insurance to obtain more than one benefit derived from that period of insurance.[239] In general, you are only insured in one member state for any one period, so you cannot use insurance from that one period to obtain entitlement to benefits of the same kind from more than one state. Usually, benefits are adjusted to ensure that either only one state (the 'competent state' – see p399) pays the benefit, taking into account periods of insurance in other member states, or the benefit is paid pro rata according to the lengths of the periods of insurance in different states.[240]

In certain cases, however, you may be paid both the full level of a UK benefit and a proportion of a benefit from another state, accrued as a result of having been insured in that state for a sufficient period. Member states are not allowed to prevent their own benefits overlapping with those of other states if this would reduce what you would have received under national law from your periods of contributions in the first state alone.[241]

There are particular overlapping rules on specific categories of benefits – eg, old age and survivor's benefits,[242] and, under the main co-ordination rules and the UK–Ireland Convention, family benefits (see p423)[243] – and the UK–Ireland Convention prevents entitlement to statutory payments by one state at the same time as sickness, invalidity, maternity or paternity benefits by the other state.[244]

5. Family benefits

Under the **main co-ordination rules**, family benefits in the UK include child benefit, child tax credit (CTC), guardian's allowance and child dependants' additions in other benefits.

Scottish child payment has been categorised as a special non-contributory benefit, so the rules below do not apply.

If you are covered by the main co-ordination rules, you can:

- export family benefits without any time limit *provided* the 'competent state' to pay your family benefits has not changed (see p402).[245] If you export family benefits, they are uprated in the normal way;
- be entitled to benefits paid in respect of a 'member of your family' (see p390) living in another member state (see below).[246] If you are entitled to family benefits from more than one European Economic Area (EEA) state in respect of the same person and for the same period, there are rules that determine which state has priority if your entitlements overlap (see p423).

To be covered by the main co-ordination rules, you need to be covered by the Withdrawal Agreement protections (see p380). HM Revenue and Customs guidance summarises these rules.[247] If you are not, or are no longer, covered by these protections, but you were receiving a family benefit for a family member living in another member state on 31 December 2020, you can continue to receive this (see below).

Note:

- Working tax credit (WTC) has been held not to be a social security benefit or a special non-contributory benefit under the co-ordination rules and, therefore, these rules do not apply to WTC (see p392).[248] However, other provisions of European Union (EU) law can assist you in being paid the childcare element of WTC (see p321 and p414).[249]
- The DWP does not accept that universal credit (UC) is a family benefit and takes the view that the co-ordination rules do not apply to UC. It is arguable that the child elements of UC are a family benefit. Get specialist advice if you want to make this argument.

Under the **UK–Ireland Convention**, family benefits are listed as child benefit, CTC and guardian's allowance.[250] It contains similar provisions as the main co-ordination rules, but only in relation to the UK and Ireland.[251]

The **UK–EU Protocol** does not apply to family benefits.[252]

Members of your family resident in another state

If you are covered by the main co-ordination rules (see second note on p422) or, for situations involving only the UK and Ireland, if you are covered by the UK–Ireland Convention, you are entitled to receive family benefits from your competent state, even when the member of your family for whom you are claiming is resident in another state, because they are *treated as* if they were resident in the competent state.[253] You must satisfy the other conditions for that benefit – see the first note on p422.

In general, unless you are receiving a pension (see below the first example), your competent state is determined in the usual way (see p399).[254] It is not necessary for you to be employed or self-employed in the competent state for you to be entitled to the family benefits paid by that state.[255] HMRC has often incorrectly stated, in decisions and appeal submissions, that you need to be working and paying national insurance in the UK to be covered by the current co-ordination rules, and that has been confirmed to be wrong by the Upper Tribunal.[256] For details on who is covered by the co-ordination rules, see p379.

Example

Carla is Italian. Since August 2020, she has been working in the UK and sending money to her two children who live in Italy with their grandmother. Carla obtained pre-settled status the month after she arrived in the UK. Carla has been entitled to child benefit for her children since she first claimed in September 2020 (as an EEA worker, she was exempt from the requirement to have lived in the UK for three months – see p144). Two months ago, Carla was made redundant and claimed UC. She is awarded UC since she has pre-settled status and so, firstly, is not defined as a person subject to immigration control (see p93) and secondly, she is in a protected group that can have free movement right to reside (see p188), and she has retained her worker status (see p223) and so satisfies the right to reside requirement. She is not paid elements for her children as they do not normally live with her. She continues to be entitled to child benefit.

However, if you are receiving a 'pension', the state that is competent for paying this is the one from which you claim family benefits.[257] See p407 for the definition of 'pension'.[258]

Example

Julien is a French national with settled status. He has been living in the UK and receiving a state pension from France since 2016. Julien's 15-year-old twin daughters live with their uncle (Julien's brother) in Germany, but Julien supports his daughters financially. Julien is not entitled to child benefit for his daughters because he receives a pension from France, and so he is only entitled to claim French family benefits.

Note: although your child is treated as resident in the competent state, you still have to satisfy all the other conditions for that benefit. For CTC, this includes that the child is 'normally living with' you, although this is not referred to in HMRC's leaflet on tax credits.[259] For child benefit, this includes, if the child is not living with you, that you are contributing to the costs of that child an amount at least equal to the amount of child benefit payable for them.[260]

Note: in general, to rely on the main co-ordination rules you need to be covered by the Withdrawal Agreement protections (see p380). However, if these do not, or no longer, apply to you, you can continue to receive a family benefit that you were entitled to, as a result of the main co-ordination rules, on 31 December 2020 for a family member living in:[261]

- an EEA country while you were 'subject to the legislation of' (see p389) the UK, if you are a British citizen (or refugee, or stateless person or non-EEA national legally resident in the UK); *or*
- the UK while you were 'subject to the legislation of' an EEA country, if you are an EEA national (or refugee, or stateless person or non-EEA national legally resident in that EEA country).

This is referred to in this *Handbook* as being covered by partial Withdrawal Agreement protections (see p384). If you cease to be entitled to the family benefit, or your entitlement ceases to be as a result of the main co-ordination rules, this partial Withdrawal Agreement protection ends.[262] Guidance states that this protection only applies to the family member that you were receiving benefit for on 31 December 2020.[263] However, it may be arguable that the protection also allows you to claim for subsequent family members since these partial Withdrawal Agreement protections apply to the claimant and to the award of benefit, rather than to the family member claimed for.

Example

Tony is a British citizen and lives in the UK, and his wife Isabella is a Spanish citizen and lives in Portugal with their son. Tony has been claiming child benefit for his son since he was born in September 2020. Tony sends money to Isabella and visits regularly. Tony benefits from the partial Withdrawal Agreement protections and continues to be entitled to child benefit for his son. Last month, Isabella gave birth to their second child. It may be arguable that Tony should also be entitled to child benefit for his second child. See also the first example on p424.

Priority when family benefits overlap

There may be entitlement to family benefits under the legislation of more than one EEA state (or, under the UK–Ireland Convention, the legislation of both the UK and Ireland) in respect of the same family member and for the same period. This can arise when two people are entitled to benefit for the same child (eg, if a mother resides in one state and the father in another and both can claim family benefits for their child) or if you have an entitlement from more than one state – eg, if you live in one state with your children, but work in another.

To ensure that equivalent family benefits are not paid by more than one state in respect of the same family member for the same period, the main co-ordination rules and the UK–Ireland Convention set out which state has 'priority' – ie, must pay the family benefits.

Note: these priority rules *only* need to be considered if there is an actual overlap of entitlement because a claim has been made for a family benefit in another state (unless entitlement does not require a claim to have been made) – see the note at the end of this section.

The way the priority rules work depends on the basis on which each family benefit is paid and, in some cases, the state in which the child lives.[264]

Different states have different criteria for entitlement. In some, you must reside in that state (family benefits payable on the basis of 'residence'); in others, you must work in that state (family benefits payable on the basis of 'employment or self-employment'); and some states require you to receive a pension (family benefits payable on the basis of 'receipt of a pension'). It can be difficult to work out the basis on which a family benefit is paid, but the European Commission has online information on the conditions for each state.[265] In the majority of states, including the UK, family benefits are mostly payable on the basis of residence –

eg, there are no employment conditions or a requirement to receive a pension in order to obtain child benefit or CTC.

If the family benefits from each state are payable on a *different* basis, the state which has priority (ie, must pay) is the one whose family benefits are payable on the first of the following bases:[266]

- activity as an employed or self-employed person. This can include temporary periods not working for reasons such as sickness, maternity or unemployment, provided you receive either wages or benefits other than a 'pension' (see p407);[267]
- receipt of a pension (see p407);
- residence.

If the family benefits from each state are payable on the *same* basis, the state which has priority (ie, must pay) is as follows.[268]

- If family benefits are based on employment/self-employment in both states, the state with priority is the one where the child resides, if you (or if there is another potential claimant, they) work there; otherwise, it is the state that pays the highest amount.[269]
- If family benefits are based on receipt of a pension in both states, the state with priority is the one where the child resides if that state also pays the pension; otherwise, it is the state where you (or the other potential claimant) have been insured or resided for the longest period.
- If family benefits are based on residence, the state with priority is the one where the child resides.

If there is an entitlement to family benefits from the state that has priority, the entitlement to family benefits from the other state(s) with lower priority is suspended up to the amount provided under the legislation of the priority state. If this suspension does not wipe out all your entitlement, a supplement is paid to 'top up' the family benefits paid by the priority state.[270] However, this top-up need not be paid for children residing in another state when entitlement to family benefits in both states is based on residence only.[271]

Examples

Marie and her two children moved to the UK from Belgium in November 2020, and Marie began working immediately. They all obtained pre-settled status. The children's father, Arnaud, remained living and working in Belgium. He continued to receive the Belgian family benefit and sends this money to Marie for the children. Arnaud continues to be entitled to this family benefit since he is covered by the partial Withdrawal Agreement protections (see above).

Two months ago, Marie was made redundant and claimed UC while she looks for another job (she, therefore, retained her worker status). Marie also claimed child benefit. However, the Belgian family benefit, which is payable on the basis of employment, has priority over the UK family benefit, since the latter is based on residence. If the UK family benefits are more than the Belgian family benefits, Marie should be paid the difference to top up the Belgian family benefits.

Alicia moved to the UK to start work in November 2020 and immediately obtained pre-settled status. Her children remained with their father, Jozef, in Slovakia. When Alicia was made redundant two months ago, she claimed UC and child benefit. Jozef receives Slovakian family benefits, which are payable on the basis of residence. Since child benefit in the UK is also payable on the basis of residence, Slovakia has priority because the children live there. The UK does not need to pay a top-up if its family benefits are more generous than the Slovakian ones.

Note: if entitlement to a family benefit in one state depends on a claim having been made and no claim has been made, entitlement to the family benefit that has been claimed in another state cannot be suspended.[272] It is therefore not necessary to consider whether family benefits in another state have priority or are payable at a higher rate if a claim is required for entitlement but no claim has been made.[273]

If family benefits are paid to someone who is not using them to maintain the member(s) of their family, the EEA state paying the benefit can make payments to the person who is, in fact, maintaining the member(s) of the family. This is done at the request of, and through, the relevant institution in the state where the person who is maintaining the family member lives.[274]

Administration of family benefits

There are rules that cover the administration of claims for family benefits in which more than one state could potentially be involved.[275]

If a claim is submitted to the relevant institution in a state whose legislation is applicable but which does not have priority under the rules above, that institution should make a provisional decision on the priority rules and then forward the claim to the relevant institution in the state with priority without delay. The date of claim is the date it was made to the first state. The relevant institution in the other state should then make a decision within two months. If it fails to do so, benefit should be awarded on the basis of the provisional decision, including any 'top-up' from the state where the benefit was claimed.[276] However, if there is a difference of view between the states about which has priority, provisional payments must be made by the state in which the child resides (or where the benefit was first claimed if the child does not reside in any of the relevant states). If agreement is not reached between the states within a month, the matter may be referred to the EU Administrative Commission for the Co-ordination of Social Security Systems to resolve within six months.[277]

If you are claiming in the UK and HMRC advises you that another state has priority, you may need to remind HMRC of its duty to forward the claim to the relevant institution in the other state. If this has been done and there is evidence of a difference of view between HMRC and the relevant institution in the other state, remind HMRC of its duty to make provisional payments. Although the Upper Tribunal caselaw on provisional payments under the EU co-ordination rules has concerned sickness benefits, it can still be helpful to refer to because it sets out how the rules on provisional payments work (see p403).[278]

The **UK–Ireland Convention** contains similar rules on the administration of claims for family benefits, including making provisional payments if there is a delay in deciding, or dispute over, whether the UK or Ireland has priority.[279]

Notes

1. **Introduction**

1 Arts 2(e), 126 and 127 WA 2019; ss1A, 1B, 8A and Sch 2 Part 1A EU(W)A 2018
2 ss1A and 1B EU(W)A 2018
3 s1B(3)(d) and (e) EU(W)A 2018
4 s6 ISSCA 2020; regs 3-4 The Social Security Co-ordination (Revocation of Retained Direct EU Legislation and Related Amendments) (EU Exit) Regulations 2020 No.1508; regs 7-8 The Social Security Co-ordination (EU Exit) (Scotland) (Amendments etc.) Regulations 2020 No.399
5 EU Reg 883/04
6 EU Reg 1408/71
7 s26 European Union (Future Relationship) Act 2020; reg 2 European Union (Future Relationship) Act 2020 (Commencement No.1) Regulations 2020 No.1662
8 Art 65 UK-IC; notification was sent from Ireland on 22 December 2020 and from the UK on 31 December 2020; Explanatory Memo to UK-IC
9 s3 EU(W)A 2018
10 s6 ISSCA 2020; regs 3-4 The Social Security Co-ordination (Revocation of Retained Direct EU Legislation and Related Amendments) (EU Exit) Regulations 2020 No.1508
11 Title III WA 2019; Title III UK-EFTA; Part 3 UK-Swiss Agreement; ss 7A and 7B EU(W)A 2018; s13 EU(W)A 2020
12 Regs 5 and 9 The Social Security Co-ordination (Revocation of Retained Direct EU Legislation and Related Amendments) (EU Exit) Regs 2020 No.1508
13 *Bogatu v Minister for Social Protection*, C-322/17 [2019], paras 26-27
14 Art 65 UK-IC; notification was sent from Ireland on 22 December 2020 and from the UK on 31 December 2020; Explanatory Memo to UK-IC
15 s26 European Union (Future Relationship) Act 2020; reg 2 European Union (Future Relationship) Act 2020 (Commencement No.1) Regulations 2020 No.1662

2. **Who is covered**

16 Art 3 (4) UK-IC; DWPWAG, Ch 1 para 5
17 Art 10 and Title III WA 2019, esp Art 30; Title III UK-EFTA, esp Art 29; Part 3 UK-Swiss Agreement, esp Art 25; ss7A and 7B EU(W)A 2018; s13 EU(W)A 2020

18 Arts 9(a), 10 and 30(3) WA 2019; Arts 8(a), 9 and 29(3) UK-EFTA; Arts 9(a), 10 and 25(3) UK-Swiss Agreement; DWPWAG, Ch 1 para 21; DMG Memo 11/22, para 7; ADM Memo 15/22, para 7
19 Art 30(5) WA 2019; Art 29(5) UK-EFTA; Art 25(5) UK-Swiss Agreement
20 Confirmed in DWPWAG, Ch 2 para 64
21 DWPWAG, Fig 3
22 DWPWAG
23 para 73 SSS DMG ADP(R and P); para 69 SSS DMG CDP(R and P)
24 DWPWAG; DMG Memo 11/22; ADM Memo 15/22
25 Art 33 WA 2019; Art 32 UK-EFTA; Art 26b UK-Swiss Agreement; see also DWPWAG, Ch 2 paras 115-21
26 Art 30(2) WA 2019; Art 29(2) UK-EFTA; Art 25(2) UK-Swiss Agreement
27 Confirmed in DWPWAG, Ch 1 paras 28, 53, 61 and 62; DMG Memo 11/22, para 6; ADM Memo 15/22, para 6
28 DMG Memo 11/22, para 6, including example; ADM Memo 15/22, para 6, including example
29 Art 30(3) WA 2019; Art 29(3) UK-EFTA; Art 25(3) UK-Swiss Agreement; DWPWAG, Ch 1 para 29
30 Art 30(4) WA 2019; Art 29(4) UK-EFTA; Art 25(4) UK-Swiss Agreement. See also Arts 10, 13, 24 and 25 WA 2019; Arts 9, 12, 23 and 24 UK-EFTA; Arts 10, 12, 19 and 20 UK-Swiss Agreement; DMG Memo 11/22, para 8; ADM Memo 15/22, para 8; DWPWAG, para 25
31 Arts 13(4), 18 and 30(4) WA 2019; Arts 12(4), 17 and 29(4) UK-EFTA; Arts 12(3), 16 and 25(4) UK-Swiss Agreement
32 Arts 11 and 15 WA 2019; Arts 10 and 14 UK-EFTA; Art 11 UK-Swiss Agreement; DWPWAG, paras 25-27
33 DMG Memo 11/22, para 7, including example; ADM Memo 15/22, para 7, including example. See also SSS DMG CDP(R and P), for example paras 76-77 and the examples between paras 81 and 82, and SSS DMG ADP(R and P), for example paras 80-81 and the examples between paras 85 and 86
34 DWPWAG, for example Ch 1 paras 43-52 and Ch 2 paras 86-95
35 DWPWAG, for example Ch 1 paras 44 and 52, examples (a) and (b)
36 Art 32 WA 2019; Art 31 UK-EFTA; Art 26a UK-Swiss Agreement; DWPWAG, paras 43-52 ; DMG Memo 11/22, paras 13-15; ADM Memo 15/22, paras 13-15
37 Art 32(1)(a) WA 2019; Art 31(1)(a) UK-EFTA; Art 26a(1)(a) UK-Swiss Agreement; DMG Memo 11/22, para 15; ADM Memo 15/22, para 15 ; DWPWAG, Chap 1 para 46
38 **AA** s65(7) SSCBA 1992
DLA s72(7B) SSCBA 1992
PIP s84 WRA 2012
CA s70(4A) SSCBA 1992
CDP Reg 8(c) and 9(2) DACYP(S) Regs
ADP Regs 19(c) and 20(2) DAWAP(S) Regs
All Art 32(2) WA 2019; Art 31(2) UK-EFTA; Art 26a(2) UK-Swiss Agreement; Ch 1, Title III EU Reg 883/04; DMG Memo 11/22, para 16; ADM Memo 15/22, para 16
39 *Petit v Office National de Pensions*, C-153/91 [1992]
40 Art 2 EU Reg 883/04
41 Art 1(g) EU Reg 1408/71
42 Art 2 UK-IC
43 Art 1 UK-IC
44 Art 3(4) UK-IC; DWPWAG, Ch 1 para 5
45 Art SSC2 UK-EUP
46 *Petit v Office National de Pensions*, C-153/91 [1992]
47 Art SSC2 UK-EUP
48 See, for example, Home Office policy paper: *Updated Impact Assessment for EU Social Security Co-ordination*, 2 March 2021, para 16
49 EU Reg 883/04
50 EU Reg 1408/71
51 Art 87(8) EU Reg 883/04*; Recital (2), Decision H1 of 12 June 2009 of the Administrative Commission for the Coordination of Social Security Systems* [2010] OJ C-106/13; *SSWP v PW (CA)* [2013] UKUT 296 (AAC)
52 *KG v SSWP (DLA)* [2015] UKUT 146 (AAC)
53 Art 87(8) EU Reg 883/04
54 *Jeltes, Peeters and Arnold v Raad van bestuur van het Uitvoeringsinstituut Werknemersverzekeringen*, C-443/11 [2013], para 59
55 *SSWP v SO*[2019] UKUT 55 (AAC)
56 *KR v SSWP (DLA)* [2019] UKUT 85 (AAC), reported as [2019] AACR 22, paras 10-12
57 *SSWP v MC (DLA)* [2019] UKUT 84 (AAC), paras 6 and 21
58 Art 87(8) EU Reg 883/04

59 For example, *SL v SSWP (DLA)* [2014] UKUT 108 (AAC)
60 Art 1 EU Reg 859/2003
61 Recital 18 EU Reg 1231/2010; DWPWAG, Ch 3 para 4(e) and glossary
62 The UK's attempt to challenge this extension of the co-ordination rules failed in relation to:
Switzerland: *UK v Council of the European Union*, C-656/11 [2014]
Iceland, Liechtenstein and Norway: *UK v Council of the European Union*, C-431/11 [2013]
63 *Ministre de l'Économie et des Finances v Ruyter*, C-623/13 [2015]
64 Art 1(l) EU Reg 883/04; Arts 1 and 3 UK-IC; Art SSC1(q) UK-EUP
65 Art 3 EU Reg 883/04; Art 3 UK-IC; Art SSC3 UK-EUP
66 Vol 2 Ch 7 Part 1 Appendix, para 5 DMG
67 DMG Memo 11/22, para 2 example 3; ADM Memo 15/22, para 2 example 3; see also DWPWAG, paras 53 and 61
68 Art 2 EU Reg 883/04; Art 2 UK-IC; Art SSC2 UK-EUP
69 Arts 30(5) and 31(2) WA 2019; Arts 29(5) and 30(2) UK-EFTA; Arts 25(5) and 26(2) UK-Swiss Agreement
70 Arts 1(i) and 2 EU Reg 883/04; Art 30(5) WA; Art 29(5) UK-EFTA; Art 25(5) UK-Swiss Agreement; DMG Memo 11/22, para 9; ADM Memo 15/22, para 9; Art 1(1) UK-IC; Art SSC1(s) UK-EUP
71 *KT v HMRC (CB)* [2013] UKUT 151 (AAC)
72 *HMRC v MB* [2018] UKUT 162 (AAC), reported as [2018] AACR 32
73 *PB v SSWP (DLA)* [2016] UKUT 280 (AAC), paras 8-10
74 *AM v SSWP* [2017] UKUT 26 (AAC), para 15

3. **Which benefits are covered**

75 Art 3 UK-IC
76 Arts 1(l), 3 and 9 EU Reg 883/04; Arts SSC1(q) and SSC3 UK-EUP
77 Art 3 EU Reg 883/04; Art 3 UK-IC; Art SSC3 UK-EUP
78 Art 3 UK-IC
79 DWPWAG, Fig 4
80 Art SSC3(4) UK-EUP
81 Annex SSC-1 Part 2(i) UK-EUP
82 Confirmed in Art 34 EU Reg 883/04
83 Annex VI EU Reg 883/04 – for awards before 1 April 2016; Vol 2 Ch 7 Part 1 paras 070152, 070280 and 070401 and Appendix, para 18 DMG; para C4119 ADM
84 Annex VI EU Reg 883/04 – for awards since 1 April 2016; DWPWAG, Fig 4
85 DWPWAG, Fig 4
86 para 070153 DMG
87 DWPWAG, Fig 4; note also *Caisse nationale des prestations familiales v Hiddal and Bernard*, C-216/12 and C-217/12 held that a parental leave allowance was a family benefit under EU Reg 1408/71
88 SSAC, *Universal Credit and Related Regulations Report and Government Response*, December 2012
89 *Commission of the European Communities v European Parliament and Council of the EU*, C-299/05 [2007]
90 *SSWP v Tolley*, C-430/15 [2017]. This case relates to the old co-ordination rules, but on this point has been held to also apply to the current co-ordination rules in: *LD v SSWP* [2017] UKUT 65 (AAC); *JM v SSWP (CA)* [2018] UKUT 329 (AAC), para 8; *KR v SSWP (DLA)* [2019] UKUT 85 (AAC), reported as [2019] AACR 22, para 2; *SSWP v TG (DLA)* [2019] UKUT 86 (AAC), para 3; and *GK v SSWP (CA)* [2019] UKUT 87 (AAC), para 3.
91 *Bartlett and Others v SSWP*, C-537/09 [2011]
92 p2 Policy Note to CASYCG(R)(S) Regs
93 Arts 3, 16, 19 and 20 UK-IC
94 **ADP** Reg 15(3) and (4) DAWAP(S) Regs
CAS s81(2A) and (13) SS(S)A 2018
CDP Reg 5(4)-(5) DACYP(S) Regs
YCG Reg 8(3) and (6) CA(YCG)(S) Regs
95 SSC3(4) and Annex SSC-1, Parts 1 and 2 UK-EUP
96 Art 70(1) and (2) and Annex X EU Reg 883/04; Art SSC1(bb) and Annex SSC-1 Part 1 UK-EUP
97 Annex X EU Reg 883/04
98 *SSWP v DS* [2019] UKUT 238 (AAC)
99 para C2097 and Appendix 1 para 4 ADM
100 para 71 SSS DMG ADP(R and P); para 67 SSS DMG CDP(R and P)
101 Annex SSC-1 Part 1 UK-EUP
102 Art 70 EU Reg 883/04
103 Art 3(3) EU Reg 883/04; *Dano v Jobcenter Leipzig*, C-333/13 [2014], paras 46-55
104 Art SSC3(4)(a) and Annex SSC-1 Part 1 UK-EUP
105 Art 3(5)(a) EU Reg 883/04; Art SSC3(4)(b) UK-EUP

106 SSAC, *Universal Credit and Related Regulations Report and Government Response,* December 2012
107 CH/1400/2006, paras 37-40
108 *MR v HMRC (TC)* [2011] UKUT 40 (AAC), para 17
109 Art1(1) UK-IC
110 Art 47 UK-IC

4. **Principles of co-ordination**
111 For example, see *J McG v (1) SSWP, (2) HMRC* [2018] UKUT 2 (AAC), paras 19-24
112 Art 11 EU Reg 883/04; Art 9 UK-IC; Art SSC10 UK-EUP
113 Art 1(s) EU Reg 883/04; Art SSC1(i) UK-EUP
114 Art 1(q) EU Reg 883/04; Art SSC1(h) UK-EUP
115 Art 11 EU Reg 883/04; Art 9 UK-IC; Art SSC10 UK-EUP
116 Art 65 EU Reg 883/04; Art 22 UK-IC
117 Art 11(3)(e) EU Reg 883/04; Art 9(4)(e) UK-IC; Art SSC10(3)(c) UK-EUP
118 *JS v SSWP* [2019] UKUT 239 (AAC); ADM Memo 1/20 and DMG Memo 3/20
119 Art 11(2) EU Reg 883/04; Art 9(2) and (3) UK-IC; Art SSC10(2) UK-EUP
120 Art 13 EU Reg 883/04; Art SSC12 and Annex SSC-7, Art SSCI.13(1)-(4) UK-EUP
121 Art 12 EU Reg 883/04; Art 10 UK-IC
122 Art SSC 11 and Annex SSC7, Art SSCI.13(1)-(4) UK-EUP
123 *AR v HMRC (CHB)* [2014] UKUT 553 (AAC); *HB v HMRC (CHB)* [2014] UKUT 554 (AAC), paras 37-39
124 **Main co-ordination rules:** Arts 67, 68 and 81 EU Reg 883/04; Arts 2, 45 and 60 EU Reg 987/2009; *SSWP v AK (AA)* [2015] UKUT 110 (AAC), reported as [2015] AACR 27; *MGL v SSWP (ESA)* [2018] UKUT 352 (AAC)
UK-IC: Art 60
UK-EUP: Art SSC62
125 Art 1(j) EU Reg 883/04; Art 1(1) UK-IC; Art SSC1(aa) UK-EUP
126 Art 30(5) WA 2019; Art 29(5) UK-EFTA; Art 25(5) UK-Swiss Agreement
127 Art 1(1) UK-IC
128 Art 11 EU Reg 987/2009; Annex SSC-7, Art SSCI.10 UK-EUP
129 Art 11(2) EU Reg 987/09; Annex SSC-7, Art SSCI.10(3) UK-EUP
130 Arts 11-16 EU Reg 883/04; Arts 9-13 UK-IC; Arts SSC 10-13 UK-EUP
131 See, for example, *SSWP v MC (DLA)* [2019] UKUT 84 (AAC)
132 *Carrington v HMRC and SSWP* [2021] EWCA Civ 1724
133 *LD v SSWP* [2017] UKUT 65 (AAC) – PTA to CA refused; *KS v SSWP* [2018] UKUT 121 (AAC)
134 *KR v SSWP (DLA)* [2019] UKUT 85 (AAC), reported as [2019] AACR 22, paras 18-24
135 para 94 example of Jimmy, SSS DMG ADP(R and P)
136 *Kuusijärvi v Riksförsäkringsverket,* C-275/96 [1998]; *AR v HMRC (CHB)* [2014] UKUT 553 (AAC); *HB v HMRC (CHB)* [2014] UKUT 554 (AAC)
137 See, for example, *Kuusijärvi v Riksförsäkringsverket,* C-275/96 [1998]; *AR v HMRC (CHB)* [2014] UKUT 553 (AAC); *HB v HMRC (CHB)* [2014] UKUT 554 (AAC); *SSWP v Tolley,* C-430/15 [2017]; *SSWP v MC (DLA)* [2019] UKUT 84 (AAC); *KR v SSWP (DLA)* [2019] UKUT 85 (AAC), reported as [2019] AACR 22
138 *AR v HMRC(CHB)* [2014] UKUT 553 (AAC); *HB v HMRC (CHB)* [2014] UKUT 554 (AAC), paras 37-39
139 **Main rules:** Art 81 EU Reg 883/2004; Art 2 EU Reg 987/2009; *SSWP v AK (AA)* [2015] UKUT 110 (AAC), reported as [2015] AACR 27; see also *MGL v SSWP (ESA)* [2018] UKUT 352 (AAC); Vol 2 Ch 7 Part 2 Appendix 4 DMG; Ch C2 Appendix 2 ADM
UK-IC: Art 60
UK-EUP: Art SSC62
140 Art 40(2) UK-IC
141 Art 6(2) EU Reg 987/2009; Art 63(2) UK-IC; Annex SSC-7, Art SSCI.6 UK-EUP; *SSWP v HR (AA)* [2014] UKUT 571 (AAC), reported as [2015] AACR 26; *SSWP v SO* [2019] UKUT 55 (AAC)
142 Art 6(3) EU Reg 987/2009; Annex SSC-7, Art SSCI.6(3) UK-EUP
143 Arts 6(4)-(5) and 73 EU Reg 987/2009; Art 63(5) UK-IC; Annex SSC7, Arts SSCI.6(5) and SSCI 57 and Title IV UK-EUP
144 *SSWP v AK (AA)* [2015] UKUT 110 (AAC), reported as [2015] AACR 27, paras 29-30
145 *SSWP v Fileccia* [2017] EWCA Civ 1907, para 46; see also *SSWP v HR (AA)* [2014] UKUT 571 (AAC), reported as [2015] AACR 26, paras 16-19, and *AH v SSWP* [2020] UKUT 53 (AAC), paras 7-19 – being appealed to CA, heard February 2023, awaiting judgment – case ref: CA-2020-000391 *Harrington v SSWP*

146 *SSWP v Fileccia* [2017] EWCA Civ 1907, para 45; see also *SSWP v HR (AA)* [2014] UKUT 571 (AAC), reported as [2015] AACR 26, para 18; see also *AH v SSWP* [2020] UKUT 53 (AAC), paras 7-19 – being appealed to CA, heard February 2023, awaiting judgment – case ref: CA-2020-000391 *Harrington v SSWP*
147 Art 6(1) EU Reg 987/2009; Art 63 UK-IC; Annex SSC-7, Art SSCI.6 UK-EUP
148 **AA** s65(7) SSCBA 1992
ADP Regs 19(c)(ii) and 20(2)(a)(ii) DAWAP(S) Regs
DLA s72(7B) SSCBA 1992
PIP s84 WRA 2012
CA s70(4A) SSCBA 1992
CDP Regs 8(c)(ii) and 9(2)(a)(i) DACYP(S) Regs
CAS s81(2A) and (9)-(15) SS(S)A 2018
YCG Reg 8(3)-(10) CA(YCG)(S) Regs
149 *SSWP v AH* [2016] UKUT 148 (AAC); linked cases: *JGv SSWP* [2019] UKUT 83 (AAC), paras 41-43; *Konevodv SSWP* [2020] EWCA Civ 809, paras 52-54
150 Arts 3, 16, 19 and 20 UK-IC
151 **ADP** Reg 15(3)(c) DAWAP(S) Regs
CDP Reg 5(4) DACYP(S) Regs
CAS s81(2A) and (13) SS(S)A 2018
YCG Reg 8(3) and (6) CA(YCG)(S) Regs
152 Arts SSC3(4) and Annex SSC-1, Part 1 and Part 2 UK-EUP
153 Art 11(3)(e) EU Reg 883/04
154 DMG Memo 16/20, para 37; ADM Memo 17/20, para 38
155 DMG Memo 16/20; ADM Memo 17/20
156 paras 90-94 SSS DMG ADP(R and P); paras 86-92 SSS DMG CDP(R and P)
157 Art 21(1) EU Reg 883/04
158 *AM v SSWP* [2017] UKUT 26 (AAC)
159 *AH v SSWP* [2020] UKUT 53 (AAC) – being appealed to CA, heard February 2023, awaiting judgment – case ref: CA2020-000391 *Harrington v SSWP;* ADM Memo 17/20, paras 6 and 34-36; DMG Memo 16/20, paras 6 and 33-35
160 Linked cases: *SSWP v TG (DLA)* [2019] UKUT 86 (AAC), paras 7-8 and 13-18; *GK v SSWP (CA)* [2019] UKUT 87 (AAC), paras 6-7 and 12-17 (appealed to CA: *Konevod v SSWP* [2020] EWCA Civ 809)
161 *Konevod v SSWP* [2020] EWCA Civ 809, paras 39-43; ADM Memo 17/20; DMG Memo 16/20
162 CSDLA/136/2017 and CSG/95/2017
163 Art 29 EU Reg 883/04
164 Art 20 UK-IC
165 Art 1(w) EU Reg 883/04
166 *JS v SSWP (DLA)* [2012] AACR 7, para 14; *KS v SSWP (DLA)* [2014] UKUT 19 (AAC), para 81; both in relation to EU Reg 1408/71
167 *LD v SSWP* [2017] UKUT 65 (AAC) – PTA to CA refused
168 *SSWP v SO* [2019] UKUT 55 (AAC), paras 11-12
169 *Perry v Chief Adjudication Officer* [1998]; *EC v SSWP (SPC)* [2010] UKUT 95 (AAC), para 40
170 *IG v SSWP* [2016] UKUT 176 (AAC), reported as [2016] AACR 41, para 25; see also *KS v SSWP* [2018] UKUT 121 (AAC), para 6
171 *Skalka v Sozialversicherungsanstalt der Gewerblichen Wirtschaft,* C-160/02 [2004]; *Naranjo v CRAM Nord-Picardie,* C-265/05 [2007]
172 *SSWP v SO* [2019] UKUT 55 (AAC); *SSWP v TG (DLA)* [2019] UKUT 86 (AAC), para 17; *GK v SSWP (CA)* [2019] UKUT 87 (AAC), para 16
173 *KR v SSWP (DLA)* [2019] UKUT 85 (AAC), reported as [2019] AACR 22, paras 6 and 13-17
174 para C2124 ADM; Vol 2 Ch 7 Part 2 para 071771 DMG; ADM Memo 17/20, para 13 and para 20 examples 1 and 2; DMG Memo 16/20, para 13
175 Art 1(1) UK-IC
176 *SSWP v SO* [2019] UKUT 55 (AAC), para 10
177 Art 1(1) UK-IC
178 Art 1(i)(1) and (ii), (2) and (3) EU Reg 883/04
179 Art 32(1) EU Reg 883/04
180 Arts 25 and 29 EU Reg 883/04; *SSWP v AK (AA)* [2015] UKUT 110 (AAC), reported as [2015] AACR 27; *KR v SSWP (DLA)* [2019] UKUT 85 (AAC), reported as [2019] AACR 22, paras 13-17
181 *LD v SSWP* [2017] UKUT 65 (AAC) – PTA to CA refused; *KS v SSWP* [2018] UKUT 121 (AAC)
182 ADM Memo 17/20, para 13; DMG 16/20, para 13
183 DMG Memo 11/22, para 16; ADM Memo 15/22, para 16
184 para 94 example of Theo, SSS DMG ADP(R and P)
185 Art 23 EU Reg 883/04; *SSWP v HR (AA)* [2013] UKUT 66 (AAC); *SL v SSWP (DLA)* [2014] UKUT 108 (AAC)
186 Arts 24(2)(b) and 25 EU Reg 883/04; *Helder and Farrington v College voor Zorgverzekeringen,* C-321/12 [2013]
187 Art 26 EU Reg 883/04

188 Art 31 EU Reg 883/04
189 Art 11(3)(a) EU Reg 883/04; *JS v SSWP* [2019] UKUT 239 (AAC); Vol 2 Ch 7 Part 2 Appendix 3 DMG, note to para 22; Ch 2 Appendix 1 ADM, note to para 22; ADM Memo 1/20; DMG Memo 3/20
190 Art 32(1) EU Reg 883/04
191 ADM Memo 17/20, para 13 and para 24 examples 1 and 2; DMG Memo 16/20, para 13 and para 24 examples 1 and 2
192 *JS v SSWP* [2019] UKUT 239 (AAC); ADM Memo 1/20 and DMG Memo 3/20
193 *KR v SSWP (DLA)* [2019] UKUT 85 (AAC), reported as [2019] AACR 22, paras 18-24
194 *INASTI v Hervein and Others,* C-393/99 and C-394/99 [2002], para 51; *Leyman v INAMI,* C-3/08 [2009], para 45
195 *SSWP v AK (AA)* [2015] UKUT 110 (AAC), paras 11-12
196 *IG v SSWP* [2016] UKUT 176 (AAC), reported as [2016] AACR 41, paras 11-12
197 *IG v SSWP* [2016] UKUT 176 (AAC), reported as [2016] AACR 41, paras 32 and 40-42 and caselaw cited
198 *AH v SSWP* [2020] UKUT 53 (AAC) – being appealed to CA, heard February 2023, awaiting judgment – case ref: CA-2020-000391 *Harrington v SSWP*
199 *Hudzinski and Wawrzyniak v Agentur für Arbeit Wesel – Familienkasse,* joined cases C-611/10 and C-612/10 [2012]
200 *IG v SSWP* [2016] UKUT 176 (AAC), reported as [2016] AACR 41, para 32 and caselaw cited
201 *IG v SSWP* [2016] UKUT 176 (AAC), reported as [2016] AACR 41, para 42; see also *JMcG v (1) SSWP, (2) HMRC* [2018] UKUT 2 (AAC) and *KS v SSWP* [2018] UKUT 121 (AAC), paras 14-16
202 Art 4 EU Reg 883/04; Art 4 UK-IC; Art SSC5 UK-EUP
203 Art 18 TFEU; Art 24 EU Dir 2004/38; Art 7 EU Reg 492/2011; Arts 12 and 23 WA 2019; Arts 11 and 22 UK-EFTA; Art 7 UK-Swiss Agreement
204 *Patmalniece v SSWP* [2011] UKSC 11
205 *European Commission v UK,* C-308/14 [2016]
206 *Commissioners for HMRC v Aiga Spiridonova,* 13/115948
207 *CG v Department for Communities NI,* C-709/20 [2021]; see also AG Opinion (June 2021)
208 Art 18 TFEU
209 Art 24 EU Dir 2004/38
210 *Fratila and Tanase v SSWP* [2020] EWCA Civ 1741
211 *Fratila and Tanase v SSWP* [2020] EWHC 998 (Admin)
212 *Fratila and Tanase v SSWP* [2021] UKSC 53
213 Arts 12 and 23 WA 2019
214 Art 5 EU Reg 883/04; Art 5 UK-IC; Art SSC6 UK-EUP
215 *Knauer v Landeshauptmann von Vorarlberg* C-453/14 [2016]; CG/1346/2018; *HT v SSWP* [2020] UKUT 57 (AAC); Vol 10 Ch 60 para 60033 point 8 DMG (also referred to by para F6013 ADM)
216 Art 7(1) and (2) EU Reg 492/11
217 *AS v HMRC* [2017] UKUT 361 (AAC), reported as [2018] AACR 14
218 Reg 13(6)(K) WTC(EMR) Regs
219 Regs 66(1)(c) and (da) and (2)(a) UC Regs; for example, see *LR v SSWP (UC)* [2022] UKUT 65 (AAC); see also Reg 83(2)(d) UC Regs
220 Recital 11 EU Reg 883/04
221 Recital 10 EU Reg 883/04
222 Art 6 EU Reg 883/04; see also Annex XI UK entry, para 2, and Art 48 TFEU; Art 6 UK-IC; Art SSC7 UK-EUP
223 Art 12 EU Reg 987/09; see *PB v SSWP (DLA)* [2016] UKUT 280 (AAC), para 10, second ground of appeal
224 Arts 1(t)(u) and (v) and 6 EU Reg 883/04; *Decision H6 of 16 December 2010 of the Administrative Commission for the Coordination of Social Security Systems* [2011] OJ C-45/04; Art 6(2) UK-IC; Art SSC7 UK-EUP
225 Art 32 WA 2019; Art 31 UK-EFTA; Art 26a UK-Swiss Agreement; see also DWPWAG, Ch 1 paras 43-52; DMG Memo 11/22, paras 13-15; ADM Memo 15/22, paras 13-15
226 Regs 5 and 9 The Social Security Co-ordination (Revocation of Retained Direct EU Legislation and Related Amendments) (EU Exit) Regulations 2020 No.1508
227 Art 6 and Annex XI UK entry para 2 EU Reg 883/04; *SSWP v MM and BK v SSWP* [2016] UKUT 547 (AAC), reported as [2019] AACR 21, para 25
228 *SSWP v MM and BK v SSWP* [2016] UKUT 547 (AAC), reported as [2019] AACR 21, paras 18-27 and 35
229 *Kavanagh and Another v SSWP* [2019] EWCA Civ 272
230 Art 32 WA 2019; Art 31 UK-EFTA; Art 26a UK-Swiss Agreement; see also DWPWAG, Ch 1 paras 43-52
231 Art 19 UK-IC

232 SSC3(4) and Annex SSC-1, Part 2 UK-EUP
233 Art 61 EU Reg 883/04; see, for example, *ONEM v M and M v ONEM*, C-284/15 [2015]; Art 21(1) and (2) UK-IC; Art SSC56 UK-EUP
234 Arts 61(2) and 65(2) and (5)(a) EU Reg 883/04; Art 21(1) and (2) UK-IC; Art SSC 56(2) UK-EUP; see also *Decision U2 of 12 June 2009 of the Administrative Commission for the Coordination of Social Security Systems* [2012] OJ C-106/12
235 Art 7 EU Reg 883/04; Art 7 UK-IC; Art SSC8 UK-EUP
236 Arts 5, 46 and 82 EU Reg 883/04; Arts 27, 46, 49 and 87 EU Reg 987/2009; Art 59(7) UK-IC; Art SSC63 UK-EUP
237 Arts SSC3(1) and (4) and SSC8 UK-EUP
238 Art 70 EU Reg 883/04
239 Art 10 EU Reg 883/04; Arts 8 and 31-33 UK-IC; Arts SSC9 and SSC48-50 UK-EUP
240 See, for example, *JMcG v (1) SSWP, (2) HMRC* [2018] UKUT 2 (AAC), paras 15 and 26-31
241 *Teresa and Silvana Petroni v Office National des Pensions Pour Travailleurs Salariés (ONPTS), Bruxelles* 24-75 [1975]
242 Arts 53-55 EU Reg 883/04; Art 31 UK-IC; Art SSC48(3) UK-EUP
243 Art 68 EU Reg 883/04; Art 39 UK-IC
244 Arts 16 and 17 UK-IC

5. **Family benefits**
245 Arts 7 and 67 EU Reg 883/04; *HB v HMRC (CHB)* [2014] UKUT 554 (AAC); *Carrington v HMRC and SSWP* [2021] EWCA Civ 1724
246 Art 67 EU Reg 883/04; *HMRC v Ruas* [2010] EWCA Civ 291
247 TCTM para 02015; para 10015 CBTM
248 *MR v HMRC (TC)* [2011] UKUT 40 (AAC), para 17
249 *NB v HMRC (TC)* [2016] NICom 47; Art 56 TFEU
250 Art 3(x) UK-IC
251 Arts 38-42 UK-IC
252 Arts SSC1(k) and SSC3(4)(g) UK-EUP
253 Art 67 EU Reg 883/04; *HMRC v Ruas* [2010] EWCA Civ 291; Art 38 UK-IC
254 *Bogatu v Minister for Social Protection*, C-322/17 [2019]
255 *Bogatu v Minister for Social Protection*, C-322/17 [2019]
256 *BM v HMRC* [2015] UKUT 526 (AAC)
257 Art 67 EU Reg 883/04, second sentence; *Würker v Familienkasse Nurnberg*, C-32/13 [2014]; Art 38(2) UK-IC
258 Art 1(w) EU Reg 883/04; Art 1(1) UK-IC
259 **WTC**/FS6: *Tax credits for people leaving the UK* (April 2021); see also gov.uk/tax-credits-if-moving-country-or-travelling
260 s143(1)(b) SSCBA 1992; s8 TCA 2002; reg 3(1) CTC Regs; *RK v HMRC (CHB)* [2015] UKUT 357 (AAC), reported as [2016] AACR 4; *JL v HMRC (CHB)* [2017] UKUT 193 (AAC); *RI v HMRC (TC)* [2019] UKUT 306 (AAC); *MZ v HMRC* [2020] UKUT 65 (AAC)
261 Art 32(1)(d) WA 2019; Art 31(1)(d) UK-EFTA; Art 26a(1)(d) UK-Swiss Agreement; see also DWPWAG, Ch 1 paras 87-95 and TCTM para 02015
262 DWPWAG, Ch 1 para 91
263 DWPWAG, Ch 1 paras 89, 90 and 95(a)(iii)
264 Art 68 EU Reg 883/04; Art 60 EU Reg 987/09; Art 39 UK-IC
265 Search for 'Your rights by country' at ec.europa.eu/social
266 Art 68(1)(a) EU Reg 883/04; Art 60 EU Reg 987/09; Art 39(2) UK-IC
267 *Decision F1 of 12 June 2009 of the Administrative Commission for the Coordination of Social Security Systems* [2010] OJ C-106/04
268 Art 68(1)(b) EU Reg 883/04; Art 60 EU Reg 987/09; Art 39(3) UK-IC
269 See also Art 58 EU Reg 987/2009
270 Art 68(2) EU Reg 883/04; see for example, *Slanina v Unabhängiger Finanzsenat, Aubenstelle Wien*, C-363/08 [2009], distinguished in *MZ v HMRC* [2020] UKUT 65 (AAC); Art 39(4) UK-IC
271 Art 68(2) EU Reg 883/04; Art 60 EU Reg 987/09; Art 39(4)(b) UK-IC
272 *Gudrun Schwemmer v Agentur für Arbeit Villingen-Schwenningen – Familienkasse*, C-16/09 [2010]; *Bundesagentur für Arbeit – Familienkasse Sachsen v Trapkowski*, C-378/14 [2015]
273 *JL v HMRC (CHB)* [2017] UKUT 193 (AAC); see also *WC v HMRC* [2019] UKUT 289 (AAC), paras 1, 8 and 9 – but note this decision was set aside on other grounds in *Carrington v HMRC and SSWP* [2021] EWCA Civ 1724
274 Art 68a EU Reg 883/04
275 Art 68(3) EU Reg 883/04; Arts 6 and 58-61 EU Reg 987/2009; see also *MZ v HMRC* [2020] UKUT 65 (AAC), para 12
276 Art 68(3) EU Reg 883/04; Art 60(2) and (3) EU Reg 987/2009
277 Arts 6(2)-(3) and 60(4) EU Reg 987/2009
278 Art 6(2) EU Reg 987/09
279 Arts 39-42 UK-IC

Chapter 17

International agreements

This chapter covers:

The rules in this chapter may help you to obtain benefits in the UK, or to get your benefit paid in another country. However, if you are moving to or from or within the European Economic Area (EEA), one or more of the sets of European Union co-ordination rules may apply to you instead. These co-ordination rules are covered in Chapter 16 and are cross-referred to in this chapter where relevant.

In this *Handbook* all references to the EEA are to be read as including Switzerland. The EEA states are listed on p53.

1. Reciprocal agreements

A reciprocal agreement is a two-way agreement made between two countries. The purpose of social security reciprocal agreements is to reduce the differences in your entitlements to benefits if you move from one country that is a party to an agreement to the other.[1] A reciprocal agreement can help you qualify for certain benefits by allowing periods of residence and contributions paid in each country to be added together (this is similar to the 'aggregation principle' in the European Union (EU) co-ordination rules – see p416). An agreement can also mean that you are paid more generously when you go abroad than you would be under the UK rules. In addition, some agreements specify that you must receive equal treatment with nationals of the country to which you have moved. Reciprocal agreements made between the UK and another country are part of UK law.

In general, a reciprocal agreement only applies if the EU co-ordination rules do not assist you (see p436). Therefore, if you are moving to or from a European Economic Area (EEA) country, you should first check whether you are covered by any of the EU co-ordination rules, whether they apply to the country you are going to or coming from, and whether they assist with the benefit you are claiming – for the steps to follow, see p376.

You do not need to first check the EU co-ordination rules if you are moving to or from a non-EEA country, Northern Ireland, the Channel Islands or the Isle of Man.

Reciprocal agreements differ in terms of the benefits and people covered and the provisions made. It is therefore crucial to check the individual agreement. You can find the agreements at legislation.gov.uk – search under the relevant country. However, most of the agreements on the website have not been fully updated, so also check for any amendments.

See Appendix 5 for a list of all the countries and the benefits covered.

The following benefits are not covered by any reciprocal agreement (with exceptions noted):

- adult disability payment (ADP) (in Scotland);
- child disability payment (CDP) (in Scotland);
- housing benefit;
- income support;
- income-based jobseeker's allowance (JSA) (except the agreement with Northern Ireland – see p435);
- employment and support allowance (ESA) (but see below);
- pension credit;
- personal independence payment (PIP) (but see below);
- social fund payments;
- universal credit (UC) (except the agreement with Northern Ireland – see p435);
- child tax credit;
- working tax credit.

Although amendments have been made enabling reciprocal agreements to be extended to include **ESA and PIP**,[2] in general, the necessary amendments to the individual agreements have not been made. However, the agreements with Northern Ireland cover both ESA and PIP (see p435). Most agreements cover your award of contributory ESA if it was converted from incapacity benefit (IB – see p440). It may be arguable that the agreement with the countries of the former Yugoslavia (see next paragraph) does not need to be amended to cover ESA and PIP because it contains a provision for cover to be extended to 'amendments, supplements and consolidations of listed legislation', provided the parties agree.[3]

The reciprocal agreement between the UK and the former Yugoslavia is a single agreement,[4] but is treated as separate agreements with Bosnia-Herzegovina, Croatia, Kosovo, North Macedonia, Montenegro, Serbia and Slovenia. **Note:** Croatia and Slovenia are members of the EU and therefore the main EU co-ordination rules or UK–EU Protocol may apply.

Agreements with non-European Economic Area countries

The UK has reciprocal agreements with some countries outside the EEA.

Each reciprocal agreement is different in terms of who is covered, which benefits are included and what arrangements are provided.

For a full list of the countries and the benefits covered, see Appendix 5.

Agreements with Ireland, Northern Ireland, the Channel Islands, the Isle of Man and Gibraltar

The rules on most social security benefits only apply in Great Britain – ie, England, Wales and Scotland. This does not include Northern Ireland, the Channel Islands, the Isle of Man or Gibraltar, which have their own social security legislation. There are reciprocal agreements between all these territories, which are intended to ensure you do not lose out if you move between them.[5]

If your situation involves **the UK and Ireland** (eg, you are moving between the two, or you live in one and work in the other), check whether you are covered by the main EU co-ordination rules, the UK–Ireland Convention on Social Security or the UK–EU Protocol on Social Security Co-ordination (see p379) and, if so, whether the benefit you want to claim is covered (see p392).

There is also an agreement with Ireland that applies across the **common travel area** (the UK, Ireland, Channel Islands and the Isle of Man).[6] This agreement only applies if none of the EU co-ordination rules apply to you or to your situation – eg, if you have been working in the Channel Islands or Isle of Man, or moving between either and Ireland.[7]

The Memorandum of Understanding on the Common Travel Area confirms the right of British citizens in Ireland, and Irish citizens in the UK, to the same social security rights as citizens of that state.[8]

Not all benefits and circumstances are covered by any specific agreement, so always check the provisions of the relevant agreement.

Note: although the reciprocal agreement between the UK and the Channel Islands does not cover Sark, there are regulations to ensure you are not disadvantaged by being there.[9]

See p441 for information on retirement pensions and bereavement support payment and Sark and the Isle of Man.

Agreements with Northern Ireland

Reciprocal 'arrangements' between Northern Ireland and Great Britain aim to co-ordinate the social security systems, creating a coherent system of social security throughout the UK.[10] The purpose of the arrangements is to ensure that when you move between the two, you are entitled to the same rights and benefits paid at the same rates, you do not need to make a new claim for the same benefit, and you do not need to return to the previous territory if you appeal a decision made there.[11] The Upper Tribunal considered the operation of the reciprocal agreements in the case of a woman who had moved to Great Britain and was appealing a decision made in Northern Ireland. The judge confirmed her appeal must be heard by the First-tier Tribunal in Great Britain, but that the relevant legislation was that of Northern Ireland.[12]

The reciprocal arrangements between Northern Ireland and Great Britain were replaced on 6 April 2016.[13] The replacement arrangements updated and extended the previous ones.

Although some benefits (many means-tested benefits, tax credits and all statutory payments) are still not covered, the new arrangements now include, from 6 April 2016, ESA (both contributory and income-related), PIP (in addition to attendance allowance, disability living allowance and carer's allowance that continue to be covered), state pension from 27 November 2016, income-based JSA (contribution-based JSA was already covered) from 6 April 2017, bereavement support payment[14] and, from 27 July 2020, UC.[15]

There is also guidance aimed at ensuring smooth and efficient co-operation between the DWP, in Great Britain, and the Department for Communities, in Northern Ireland.[16]

Before the agreements were extended to ESA, the DWP policy was to pay extra-statutory payments to make up any loss of ESA that resulted from having to make a new claim when moving from Northern Ireland to Great Britain or vice versa.[17] These extra-statutory payments continued after 6 April 2016. If you were receiving extra-statutory payments on this basis up to 27 November 2016, and do not satisfy the contributory conditions for entitlement to contributory ESA, you are treated as satisfying these conditions and as having made a claim for ESA from 27 November 2016, and your period of limited capability for work is treated as continuous.[18]

Agreements with Gibraltar

Gibraltar is a British overseas territory and the only one which is part of the EU. As the UK is responsible for Gibraltar's external relations, EU law treats Gibraltar as part of the UK for the purposes of the EU social security co-ordination.[19] However, Gibraltar and Great Britain have separate social security systems. The reciprocal agreement between Gibraltar and Great Britain provides for you to be treated as having the same rights and liabilities under the main EU co-ordination rules (except for family benefits) as you would have if the UK and Gibraltar were separate EEA states.[20] Saving regulations ensure that social security co-ordination with Gibraltar continues on the same basis as before the end of the transition period (see p374) until any new agreement is negotiated between the UK and Gibraltar.[21]

If you are covered by this reciprocal agreement and resident in Gibraltar, you can make a new claim for carer's allowance supplement, young carer grant, ADP and CDP, if you can demonstrate a 'genuine and sufficient link' to Scotland and the UK is your 'competent state' (see p308 and p356).

Agreements with European Economic Area states

The UK has reciprocal agreements with most of the EEA member states. For a list of the states with which the UK has social security agreements and the benefits covered by each, see Appendix 5.

In general, until the end of the transition period (see p374), reciprocal agreements could be relied on by EEA nationals if the main (or old) EU co-ordination rules did not apply.[22] This meant that, in most cases, you could not qualify for benefits using a reciprocal agreement if you were covered by the main (or old) co-ordination rules (see p379) *and* acquired your right to benefit on, or after, the date those EU co-ordination rules applied.[23] However, it is less clear if you can rely on reciprocal agreements between EEA states if you are not covered by the main (or old) EU co-ordination rules, but you *are* covered by the UK–EU Protocol. Get specialist advice if this could affect you. **Note:** the UK–EU Protocol only covers the EU states, and not Iceland, Liechtenstein, Norway and Switzerland. Furthermore, since the end of the transition period, UK agreements with Norway and Switzerland have been amended or replaced – see below.

Changes due to the UK leaving the European Union

The UK left the EU on 31 January 2020, but the main EU co-ordination rules continued to apply until the end of the transition period at 11pm on 31 December 2020.

From the end of the transition period:

- you can only be covered by the main EU co-ordination rules if you are covered by the Withdrawal Agreement protections (see p380);
- if your situation involves only the UK and **Ireland**, you may be covered by the UK–Ireland Convention, which came into force on 1 January 2021. This convention broadly reproduces the principles and effects of the main co-ordination rules but is limited to the UK and Ireland and to specified benefits of each country. The UK–Ireland Convention is covered in Chapter 16 – see p387;
- if your situation involves only the UK and **Switzerland**, you may be covered by the new UK–Switzerland Convention.[24] This agreement has been provisionally in force since 1 November 2021, which is therefore the effective start date of the convention.[25] It replaces an earlier UK–Switzerland convention,[26] *other than* for claims made before that date, or if you are moving between Switzerland and the Channel Islands or Isle of Man.[27] The new convention broadly reproduces the principles and effects of the main co-ordination rules but is limited to the UK and Switzerland. The benefits covered are limited in a similar way to the benefits covered by the UK–EU Protocol – eg, family, disability and carers' benefits are not covered at all and the principle of exportability does not apply to unemployment or invalidity benefits;[28]
- if your situation involves only the UK and **Norway**, you may be covered by the UK–Norway Convention, which reproduces many of the principles and effects of the main co-ordination rules, but is limited to the UK and Norway.[29] This convention was significantly amended from 1 January 2021, and the categories of benefits covered became more limited for claims made from that date.[30] The UK–Norway Convention covers Norway, the UK, the Isle of Man and Jersey, but since 1 January 2021 many of the provisions are limited to Norway, the Isle of Man and Jersey;[31]

- if you are not covered by the Withdrawal Agreement protections and the main EU co-ordination rules, you may be covered by the UK–EU Protocol, which covers the UK and all the **EU member states**, but not Iceland, Liechtenstein, Norway and Switzerland (see p388).

If you are not covered by any of the above bullet points, you should check whether a reciprocal agreement with the relevant country covers you and the benefit you are claiming.

For more details on the operation of the EU co-ordination rules after the transition period, and how to check whether they apply, see p374.

People covered by the agreements

Some of the reciprocal agreements cover nationals of the contracting countries, while others apply to 'people going from one member state to another'. This may be particularly significant if you are not covered by the Withdrawal Agreement protections and, therefore, the main (or old) co-ordination rules cannot apply and the UK–EU Protocol does not apply to either you or your situation (see p379).

The agreements with Belgium, Denmark, France, Italy and Luxembourg only cover nationals.[32] The convention with the Netherlands covers people who have been 'subject to the legislation of' (this phrase is likely to be interpreted as it is under the co-ordination rules – see p389) one or both member states, and their family members and survivors.[33]

The new UK–Switzerland Convention covers you if you have been 'subject to the legislation of' (see p389) the UK or Switzerland and you are a UK national, Swiss national, EU national, stateless person or refugee, or a family member or survivor of such.[34]

The reciprocal agreements define who is counted as a national for the purpose of the agreement, when nationality is an issue. In most agreements, a UK national is defined as a 'citizen of the United Kingdom and Colonies'.[35] This category of people disappeared on 1 January 1983 when the British Nationality Act 1981 came into force. On this date, if you previously had citizenship of the UK and Colonies, you might have become:

- a British citizen;
- a British overseas territories citizen (subsequently renamed British dependent territories citizen); *or*
- a British overseas citizen.

You might also have become one of the above after 1 January 1983, including if you were born after this date. The rules on this are beyond the scope of this *Handbook*. Get immigration advice if this is relevant to you.

For the purpose of the conventions with Belgium, Denmark, France, Italy and Luxembourg, a UK national now includes anyone in one of the above categories.

The definition of nationality in the agreements with Denmark, Italy and Luxembourg is simply that of a 'Danish' or 'Italian' or 'Luxemburger' national.[36] You have no rights under these agreements if you are not a national of one of these states. The agreement with Belgium, however, covers a 'person having Belgian nationality or a native of the Belgian Congo or Ruanda-Urundi'. The agreement with France refers to 'a person having French nationality' and 'any French-protected person belonging to French Togoland or the French Cameroons'.

When these agreements came into force in 1958, the Belgian Congo and Ruanda-Urundi, French Togoland and the French Cameroons were Belgian and French territories. Which Belgian and French nationals are covered by the agreements is a matter for the Belgian and French authorities. If you come from one of these countries (present-day Democratic Republic of Congo, Rwanda, Burundi, Togolese Republic and the Republic of Cameroon), check with the Belgian or French authorities whether you are covered by these agreements.

The agreements give equal treatment to nationals of the contracting countries, stating that a 'national of one contracting party shall be entitled to receive the benefits of the legislation of the other contracting party under the same conditions as if he were a national of the latter contracting party'.[37]

The reciprocal agreements with Finland, Iceland, Ireland, Portugal, Spain and Sweden are not confined to nationals but give rights to:

- in relation to the Ireland and the UK, persons not covered by the EU co-ordination rules, and in relation to Ireland and Jersey, Guernsey and the Isle of Man, people who have been 'subject to the legislation of' (this phrase is likely to be interpreted as it is under the co-ordination rules – see p389), and their family members and survivors;[38]
- 'a person subject to the legislation of one contracting party who becomes resident in the territory of the other party' (Portugal);
- 'a national of one contracting party, or a person subject to the legislation of that party, who becomes resident in the territory of the other contracting party' (Spain);
- 'a national of the state and person deriving their rights from such nationals and other people who are, or have been, covered by the legislation of either of the states and people deriving their rights from such a person' (Sweden).

The agreement with Norway extends beyond nationals of the relevant countries to include anyone who is 'subject to the legislation of' (see p389) the relevant state, and resident or present in the relevant country.[39] However, since 1 January 2021 many provisions of the agreement with Norway only apply to Jersey and the Isle of Man and not the UK (see p437).

The agreement with Germany is not restricted to nationals of either contracting country insofar as social security benefits are concerned. However, a nationality provision applies to contribution liability.

Benefits covered by the agreements

The following benefits are covered by some of the reciprocal agreements. See Appendix 5 for a full list of which benefits apply to which countries.

Unemployment benefits

The relevant benefit in the UK is contribution-based JSA and, for the agreements between Great Britain and Northern Ireland only, also income-based JSA (see p435).

The agreements between Great Britain and Northern Ireland, and between the UK and the Isle of Man, allow you to continue to be paid JSA while absent in the other territory.[40] However, none of the other agreements allow you to receive unemployment benefits outside the country in which you have paid your national insurance (NI) contributions.[41]

Some of the agreements allow insurance contributions paid in one country to count towards satisfying the conditions of entitlement in another. That is the case with the UK agreements with Austria, Canada, Cyprus, Finland, Iceland, the Isle of Man, Jersey, Guernsey, Malta, New Zealand, Norway, Switzerland and the agreement with the states of former Yugoslavia (see p434), as well as the agreements between Great Britain and Northern Ireland. **Note:** the new agreement with Switzerland only permits this if you were last insured, or employed or self-employed, in the state in which you are claiming the unemployment benefit.[42]

Sickness and invalidity benefits

In the UK, the relevant sickness benefit was short-term IB and the relevant invalidity benefit was long-term IB. In 2008, IB was abolished for new claims and replaced by ESA. There are now very few remaining claimants of IB, but if you still receive this, the agreements continue to apply.

Although reciprocal agreements can be amended to apply to ESA,[43] in general, the necessary amendments to the individual agreements have not been made.[44] There are three exceptions. The reciprocal agreements cover:

- contributory ESA if your award was converted from IB. Your ESA is covered by each of the agreements (except the Isle of Man, and Israel) that cover invalidity benefits (see Appendix 5);[45]
- contributory ESA under the new agreement with Switzerland (this covers sickness and invalidity benefits, unless the benefit is specifically listed as not covered[46]);
- both contributory and income-related ESA under the agreement between Great Britain and Northern Ireland (see p435).

It may be arguable that the agreement with the states of former Yugoslavia (see p434) does not need to be amended in order to cover ESA. This is because it allows for the agreement to be extended to 'amendments, supplements and consolidations of listed legislation', provided the contracting parties agree.[47]

The agreements on sickness and invalidity benefits vary. For example, some enable you to be paid in another country, and some enable contributions paid under one country's scheme to be taken into account to help you satisfy the conditions of entitlement in another. The agreements with Austria, Cyprus, Iceland and Sweden allow you to continue to receive your IB in these countries, subject to medical checks being undertaken in the agreement country. Similarly, you can receive the other country's invalidity benefits in the UK. The agreement with Barbados allows a certificate of permanent incapacity to be issued, permitting you to receive your invalidity benefit without medical checks. The new agreement with Switzerland does not enable invalidity benefits to be exported.[48]

Maternity benefits

In the UK, the relevant maternity benefit is maternity allowance (MA).

If you are entitled to maternity benefits, some of the agreements allow you to receive your benefit in another country. You may be entitled to MA, or continue to be paid MA, when absent from the UK, under the reciprocal agreements with Barbados, Cyprus, Ireland, the Isle of Man, Jersey and Guernsey, Switzerland, Turkey and the countries of former Yugoslavia (see p434), and when you have moved from Great Britain to Northern Ireland or vice versa. The circumstances under which you may be able to claim or retain MA differ from agreement to agreement.

Benefits for industrial injuries

The relevant benefits in the UK are industrial injuries disablement benefit (including constant attendance allowance or exceptionally severe disablement allowance), reduced earnings allowance and retirement allowance.

Most of the agreements include industrial injuries benefits. The arrangements determine which country's legislation applies to new accidents or diseases, depending on where you are insured at the time. Many of the agreements allow you to combine industrial injuries incurred in each country when assessing the degree of your latest injury. Also, if you work in one country and remain insured under the other country's scheme and you have an industrial injury, you can be treated as though the injury arose in the country in which you are insured. Most agreements include arrangements to allow you to receive all three UK benefits for industrial injuries indefinitely in the other country.

Retirement pensions and bereavement benefits

All the agreements include retirement pensions and, except Canada, bereavement benefits. In the UK, the relevant benefits are retirement pensions, bereavement support payment and widowed parent's allowance. All the agreements have been amended to include the UK state pension from its introduction on 6 April 2016.[49] Most agreements have been amended to include bereavement support payment from 6 April 2017, but not Barbados, Bermuda, Canada, Mauritius, Iceland, Malta or Sweden.[50]

There is a reciprocal agreement between the **Isle of Man** and the UK covering arrangements for all retirement pensions.[51] The UK state pension does not apply in the Isle of Man, so if you reach retirement age on or after 6 April 2016 and have paid contributions in both the UK and the Isle of Man, you must make two claims under the two different systems. If you receive a UK pension while resident in the Isle of Man, or an Isle of Man pension while resident in the UK, it is uprated as if you were resident in the territory that pays the pension.[52] The reciprocal agreement has been amended to include the Manx state pension, which is payable if you reach retirement age on or after 6 April 2019.[53] See gov.im for more details of the Isle of Man and Manx pensions and if you are resident in the Isle of Man.

Note: although the reciprocal agreement between the UK and the Channel Islands does not cover **Sark**, you are entitled to state pension and bereavement support payment if you are ordinarily resident in Sark.[54]

The provisions of the reciprocal agreements vary. In most cases, the agreements can enable you to receive a retirement pension or bereavement benefit in the agreement country at the same rate as you would be paid in the country where you are insured. However, the agreements with **Canada, New Zealand** and (for those still covered by the agreement revoked on 1 March 2001, subject to limited savings provisions[55]) **Australia** do not permit these benefits to be uprated. If you go to live in one of these countries, your retirement pension (and any other long-term benefit) is 'frozen' at the rate payable either when you left the UK or when you became entitled to your pension abroad.

The agreements with **Canada, New Zealand** and (for those still covered by the agreement revoked on 1 March 2001, subject to limited savings provisions[56]) **Australia**, allow you to be treated as having paid NI contributions in the UK during periods when you were resident in that country.[57] From 1 April 2015, periods of habitual residence in an EEA member state or Switzerland count as periods of residence in the UK, for the purpose of these calculations, if you:[58]

- are an EEA or UK national (see p53);
- are covered by the main EU co-ordination rules or, from 31 July 2021, by the Withdrawal Agreement protections or the UK–EU Protocol (see p379); *and*
- have a 'genuine and sufficient link' to the UK (see p307).

However, these rules were revoked from 31 December 2021 *unless* you were habitually resident in an EEA country or Switzerland on that date and have remained habitually resident in the same country since then.[59]

The agreement with **Chile** is limited and relates to the continuing liability to pay NI contributions to your home country if you go to work in the other country for a period of up to five years.[60]

If you do not qualify for a retirement pension or bereavement benefit from either the UK or the other country, or you qualify for a pension or bereavement benefit from one country but not the other, the agreements with the following countries allow you to be paid basic old age and bereavement benefits on a pro rata basis, with your insurance under both schemes taken into account: Austria, Barbados, Bermuda, Cyprus, Finland, Iceland, Israel, Jamaica, Malta, Mauritius, Norway, the Philippines, Sweden, Switzerland, Turkey, the USA and the countries of the former Yugoslavia (see p434).[61]

Family benefits

In the UK, the relevant family benefits are child benefit and guardian's allowance. The provisions concerning these two benefits enable periods of residence and/or presence in the other country to be treated as residence and/or presence in Great Britain. Arguably, these provisions could enable you to to use periods of residence in the other country to satisfy the requirement for child benefit to have been living in the UK for the past three months (see p143). The extent to which reciprocity exists varies, however, according to the particular agreement. For example, residence or contributions paid in Cyprus, Jamaica, Jersey/Guernsey, the Isle of Man, Israel, Mauritius and Turkey count towards your satisfying UK residence conditions for guardian's allowance.

If you are a 'person subject to immigration control' (see p93) and you are covered by a reciprocal agreement for child benefit, your immigration status does not exclude you from entitlement to child benefit (see p117). You must still meet the other conditions of entitlement, including the residence and presence requirements (see p299).

At the time of writing, HM Revenue and Customs guidance[62] confirms that this applies if you are covered by the agreements with Barbados, Canada, Israel, Mauritius or the countries of the former Yugoslavia (see p434). However, the guidance had not been updated to include the EEA countries with reciprocal agreements (Austria, Belgium, Denmark, France, Germany, Portugal, Spain, Sweden and, for claims made before 1 January 2021 only, Norway).

The new agreement with Switzerland does not cover family benefits, but if your claim began before 1 November 2021, it continues to be covered by the previous agreement with Switzerland (see p437).

Dependants' benefits

In the UK, a dependant's benefit is an increase to the benefit covered by the agreement. Dependants' increases can be paid if the dependant is in either country to the agreement.

2. Council of Europe conventions and agreements

There are a number of European conventions and agreements, prepared and negotiated within the Council of Europe – eg, the European Convention on Human Rights (ECHR). The purpose of these conventions is to address issues of common concern in economic, social, cultural, scientific, legal and administrative matters and in human rights. The agreements and conventions are not legally binding in the UK unless they are incorporated into UK law, or legislation is enacted to give specific effect to the treaty obligations in question – eg, the Human Rights Act incorporates the rights set out in the ECHR into UK law. They are statements of intent of the individual countries that are signatories. The UK is a signatory to a number of these agreements, including two that are significant for social security, and which continue to apply in the UK after having left the European Union (EU).

The **European Convention on Social and Medical Assistance** has been in force since 1954. It requires ratifying states to provide social assistance in cash and in kind to nationals of other ratifying states who are lawfully present in their territories and who are without sufficient resources on the same conditions as their own nationals. It also prevents ratifying states from repatriating a lawfully present national of other ratifying states simply because they are in need of assistance.

The **1961 European Social Charter** is a similar agreement, giving similar access to UK social security benefits to nationals of ratifying states who are lawfully present. It is only the 1961 Charter that has the effect below. If you are a national of a country that has signed a later charter only, that will not assist you.

The countries that have ratified one or both of these agreements are all the European Economic Area (EEA) countries (*except* Bulgaria, Liechtenstein, Lithuania, Romania and Slovenia), as well as the non-EEA countries of Turkey and North Macedonia. For a list of the EEA countries, see p53.

Effect on benefit entitlements

The main advantage for benefit claimants of the above agreements is if you are defined as a 'person subject to immigration control' (see p93). If you are a national of one of the countries that has ratified either of the above agreements and you are lawfully present, you are exempt from being excluded, on the basis that you are a person subject to immigration control, from working tax credit (WTC – see p118) or any of the means-tested benefits, provided you claimed before the dates below.

You must have already claimed:

- universal credit (UC) before 1 January 2021;

- housing benefit or pension credit before 3 May 2022;
- income support, income-related employment and support allowance, income-based jobseeker's allowance or WTC. There is no date by which you need to have claimed because it is no longer possible for anyone to make a new claim for these benefits.

For details, including on council tax reduction, see p114.

You can only benefit from the above agreements if you are **'lawfully present'** in the UK. In practice, this means you must be within a period in which you have leave to enter or remain in the UK.

Note: if your leave is subject to a 'no recourse to public funds' condition, claiming benefit (other than council tax reduction) as a result of being covered by this exemption is *not* regarded by the Home Office as having recourse to public funds and so does *not* breach that condition (see p101).[63]

You still must satisfy the other conditions of entitlement, including, for means-tested benefits, having a right to reside other than one that is excluded for the benefit claimed (see p168).[64] However, in practice this requirement will be satisfied by the leave that you must have to be 'lawfully present'.

Note: although the House of Lords held that an asylum seeker with temporary admission is 'lawfully present' and so potentially able to benefit from this exemption,[65] temporary admission does not give you a right to reside.[66] (Temporary admission was replaced by immigration bail from 15 January 2018, but the same arguments are likely to apply.)

3. European association agreements and their replacements

The Treaty on the Functioning of the European Union provides for agreements to be made with countries outside the European Union (EU).[67] The EU has a number of co-operation and association agreements, which can be divided into those that include a rule on equal treatment and have quite a wide scope and those that do not include an equal treatment rule and whose scope is much narrower – eg, Albania and Israel (see p447 and p448).

These co-operation and association agreements were directly applicable in UK law until the end of the transition period (31 December 2020), and their effect continues if your benefit claim began before then. Since then, most of these have been replaced by new trade and continuity agreements, which are intended to replicate the effects of the previous agreements with bilateral agreements with the UK that reproduce similar provisions in relation to social security rights.

Agreements with equal treatment provisions

The EU agreements that most directly affected benefit entitlement in the UK are those with Algeria,[68] Morocco,[69] San Marino, Tunisia and Turkey.[70] These agreements are relevant for claims made before 1 January 2021. New agreements between these countries and the UK are relevant for claims made since that date (other than, at the time of writing, for Algeria).

All these agreements specify that there must be equal treatment for those covered by the agreement in matters of 'social security'. They also contain provisions for aggregating, for the purposes of entitlement to certain social security benefits, periods of insurance or employment completed in one or more EU countries when someone covered by the agreement moves between EU states.

The Court of Justice of the European Union (CJEU) found, in one case, the Turkish agreement and, in another, the Algerian agreement, to be inspired by the old EU co-ordination rules and that these rules should be looked to for guidance in interpreting the agreements. The CJEU held that the benefits covered by these agreements were those classed as 'social security benefits' under the co-ordination rules.[71] See p393 for a full list of these benefits.

If your benefit claim began before 1 January 2021 and you were defined as a 'person subject to immigration control' (see p93), but you were covered by one of the above agreements, you are exempt from the exclusion from the main disability and carers' benefits and child benefit (see p115) and tax credits (see p117) that would otherwise apply. Although these agreements ceased to have direct effect in the UK from the end of the transition period (11pm on 31 December 2020), transitional rules mean that, provided your claim began before 1 January 2021, you continue to be entitled as if the agreements were still in force.[72]

If your benefit claim began on or after 1 January 2021 and you are covered (see p447) by new agreements between the UK and **Morocco, San Marino, Tunisia or Turkey**, which have similar provisions on benefits, you are not excluded from the above benefits despite being defined as a 'person subject to immigration control'.

At the time of writing, the UK had not concluded an agreement with **Algeria**, but it was expected that would be concluded and would have a similar effect. Check whether such an agreement has been reached if that could affect you.

The Upper Tribunal held that the equal treatment provisions in relation to family benefits meant that a Moroccan national who was lawfully working in the UK, and therefore covered by the agreement, could not be excluded from child benefit and child tax credit (CTC) on the basis that her only right to reside in the UK was as the primary carer of a British citizen (see p176).[73] As a result of this decision, the child benefit and CTC regulations were amended, and have been subsequently further amended to take account of the changing agreements.[74]

Who is covered

To benefit from the previous or current agreements, you must, at the relevant time, be within their 'personal scope' – ie, you must be a national of Morocco, Tunisia, San Marino or Turkey (or, for claims made before 1 January 2021, Algeria) and you must be lawfully working in the UK.

Note: HM Revenue and Customs (HMRC) guidance states this also applies for child benefit and CTC if you are lawfully working and a national of Albania (see below).

Lawfully working

'Lawfully working' in the previous agreements was equated with being an 'insured person' under the old EU co-ordination rules. In broad terms, this means that you must have been insured by paying, or being credited with, national insurance (NI) contributions.[75] However, this interpretation does not necessarily apply to the new agreements. It is likely that you will only be accepted as 'lawfully working' if your work does not breach any work restrictions attached to your leave or, if you are an asylum seeker, you have permission to work from the Home Office.

Other agreements

The EU also has numerous agreements with other countries. After leaving the EU, the UK has sought to continue the effects of these agreements by negotiating either replacement agreements or supplementary agreements that incorporate the EU agreement and need to be read alongside.

In general, most of the EU agreements, and their replacement UK agreements, do not contain any provisions on the co-ordination of social security schemes, but two notable exceptions are the agreements with Albania and Israel.

Albania

The EU agreement with Albania does not contain equal treatment provisions in matters of 'social security', but does contain some co-ordinating measures for Albanian nationals legally working in, and family members legally resident in, an EU state as well as equivalent provisions for EU nationals in Albania.[76] This agreement ceased to apply in the UK at the end of 2020 when the transition period ended. However, its effects are reproduced in the new Partnership, Trade and Cooperation Agreement,[77] which incorporates the previous agreement subject to some modifications.[78]

These agreements provide that for Albanian nationals legally working in the UK or an EU state and for their family members legally living in the UK:[79]

- periods of residence, insurance and employment completed in the UK and the EU states are added together for the purpose of working out your entitlement to the benefits covered (old age, invalidity and death benefits);

- the benefits covered (old age, death, industrial accident, occupational disease, or invalidity resulting therefrom – except non-contributory benefits) can be exported to Albania (or the UK or the EU state); *and*
- those legally working can receive family benefits for the members of their family legally resident in the UK (or EU state or Albania) – see the following note.

Note: Since the new Partnership, Trade and Cooperation Agreement came into effect in 2021, HMRC guidance has stated that if you are an Albanian national lawfully working in the UK, and you are defined as a 'person subject to immigration control', you are exempt from the exclusion from child benefit and CTC that would otherwise apply (see p116).[80]

Israel

The agreement with Israel covers nationals of the European Economic Area (EEA) and Israel who are legally working in the EEA (for Israelis) or Israel (for EEA nationals) and members of their family who are legally resident.[81]

It covers benefits designed to protect against the risks of old age, invalidity and accidents at work, benefits for survivors and family benefits. The interpretation of these categories is similar to the EU co-ordination rules (see p393).

This agreement would have ceased to apply at the end of the transition period. However, its effects are reproduced in a new Trade and Partnership Agreement which incorporates the previous agreement, subject to some modifications.[82]

If you are covered by the agreement:[83]

- for Israelis, all your periods of residence, insurance and employment in the UK and EEA states are added together for the purpose of working out your entitlement to the benefits covered;
- the benefits covered (except non-contributory benefits) can be exported to (for Israelis) Israel or (for UK and EEA nationals) from Israel to the UK or EEA.

Israel also has a reciprocal agreement with the UK.[84] See Appendix 5 for the benefits covered.

Notes

1. **Reciprocal agreements**

1 s179 SSAA 1992
2 s179(3), (4) and (5) SSAA 1992
3 Art 2 FANIII(Y)O
4 FANIII(Y)O
5 For example, The Social Security (Isle of Man) Order 1977 No.2150
6 The Social Security (Ireland) Order 2007 No.2122
7 Art 2 The Social Security (Ireland) Order 2007 No.2122; DWPWAG, Ch 1 paras 4-6; Explanatory Memo to UK-IC
8 *Memorandum of Understanding between Ireland and the UK concerning the Common Travel Area and associated reciprocal rights and privileges*, May 2019, para 10
9 In particular, reg 12 SS(PA) Regs
10 s87 Northern Ireland Act 1998; SS(NIRA) Regs; SS(GBRA)(NI) Regs
11 Sch para 2 SS(NIRA) Regs; Explanatory memorandum to SS(NIRA) Regs, para 4.2; see also *AG v The Department for Communities (DLA)* [2017] UKUT 442 (AAC), paras 15-24
12 *AG v The Department for Communities (DLA)* [2017] UKUT 442 (AAC), paras 15-24
13 SS(NIRA) Regs; SS(GBRA)(NI) Regs
14 SS(NIRA)(A) Regs; SS(GBRA)(A)NI Regs; see also DMG Memo 1/17
15 **UC**(GBRA) Regs; UC(NIRA) Regs; see also ADM Memo 18/20
16 *Concordat between the Department for Work and Pensions and the Department for Communities*, 4 June 2018
17 DWP guidance, *Extra-statutory Payments for Claimants Moving from Northern Ireland to Great Britain*, available at cpag.org.uk/welfare-rights/resources/article/dwp-guidance-relating-extra-statutory-payments-esa-claimants-who
18 Sch Arts 2A-2B SS(NIRA) Regs; Sch Arts 2A-2B SS(GBRA)(NI) Regs; see also DMG Memo 1/17, paras 4-7
19 Art 355(3) TFEU; Vol 2 Ch 7 para 070040 DMG; para C1005 ADM; para 80 SSS DMG CDP(R and P); para 84 SSS DMG ADP(R and P)
20 Sch para 2 The Family Allowances, National Insurance and Industrial Injuries (Gibraltar) Order 1974 No.555; see also Vol 2 Ch 7 paras 070044 and 070331 DMG; para C1005 ADM; *SSWP v Garland* [2014] EWCA Civ 1550, para 33
21 Reg 8 The Social Security Co-ordination (Revocation of Retained Direct EU Legislation and Related Amendments) (EU Exit) Regulations 2020 No.1508
22 See, for example, Art 8 EU Reg 883/04, Art 2 The Social Security (Ireland) Order 2007 No.2122 and the Explanatory Memo to UK-IC
23 *Walder v Bestuur der Sociale Verzekeringsbank*, C-82/72 [1973]; *Galinsky v Insurance Officer*, C-99/80 [1981]; R(P) 1/81; *Jean-Louis Thévenon and Stadt Speyer-Sozialamt v Landesversicherungsanstalt Rheinland-Pfalz*, C-475/93 [1995]; *Balazs v Casa Judeteana de Pensii Cluj*, C-401/13 [2015]
24 UK-Switzerland Convention; The Social Security (Switzerland) Order 2021 No.1088; The Social Security (Switzerland) (Further Provision in respect of Scotland) Order 2021 No.345
25 Art 73 UK-Switzerland Convention
26 Convention on Social Security between the UK and Northern Ireland and Switzerland, 21 February 1968
27 Art 77 UK-Switzerland Convention
28 Arts 6(4) and 11 and Annex 2 UK-Switzerland Convention
29 UK-Norway Convention
30 The Social Security (Norway) Order 2020 No.1597; see Art 2(7) UK-Norway Convention; note that The Social Security (Norway) Order 1992 No.3212 is revoked as now redundant
31 See, for example, Art 4 para 1 UK-Norway Convention
32 Art 3 to each of the relevant reciprocal agreements
33 Art 2 The Social Security (Netherlands) Order 2007 No.631
34 Art 2 UK-Switzerland Convention

35 Art 1 to each of the relevant reciprocal agreements
36 Art 1 to each of the relevant reciprocal agreements
37 Art 1 to each of the relevant reciprocal agreements
38 Sch 1 Art 2 The Social Security (Ireland) Order 2007 No.2122
39 Art 3 Convention on Social Security between UK and Norway (19 June 1990), reproduced as Sch to The Social Security (Norway) Order 1991 No 767
40 Sch para 2 SS(NIRA) Regs; Sch para 2 SS(GBRA)(NI) Regs; Sch 1 para 2(1) The Social Security (Isle of Man) Order 1977 No.2150
41 Confirmed in Vol 2 Ch 7 para 070338 DMG
42 Art 56 UK-Switzerland Convention
43 s179(3), (4) and (5) SSAA 1992
44 para 070312 DMG
45 SS(RA)O
46 Art 6 and Annex 2 UK-Switzerland Convention
47 Art 2 FANIII(Y)O
48 Arts 6(1)(c) and 11(b) UK-Switzerland Convention
49 SS(NIRA) Regs
50 The Social Security (Reciprocal Agreements) Order 2017 No.159
51 The Social Security (Reciprocal Agreement) (Isle of Man) Order 2016 No.157
52 Art 10 The Social Security (Reciprocal Agreement) (Isle of Man) Order 2016 No.157
53 The Social Security (Reciprocal Agreement) (Isle of Man) (Amendment) Order 2018 No.1359
54 Reg 8 The Bereavement Support Payment Regulations 2017 No.410
55 s299 Pensions Act 2004
56 s299 Pensions Act 2004
57 For the relevance of this for periods of residence in Australia before 1 March 2001, see *FE v SSWP (RP)* [2019] UKUT 61 (AAC)
58 The Social Security (Application of Reciprocal Agreements with Australia, Canada and New Zealand) (EEA States and Switzerland) Regulations 2015 No.349; see also *BB v SSWP (RP)* [2021] UKUT 141 (AAC)
59 Regs 1, 3 and 4 The Social Security (Reciprocal Agreements) (Miscellaneous Amendments) (EU Exit) Regulations 2021 No.811
60 Convention on Social Security Between the Government of the United Kingdom of Great Britain and Northern Ireland and the Government of the Republic of Chile, reproduced as Schedule to The Social Security (Contributions) (Republic of Chile) Order 2015 No.828
61 FANYIII(Y)O; *AP v SSWP (RP)* [2011] UKUT 64 (AAC)
62 para 10140 CBTM

2. **Council of Europe conventions and agreements**
63 para 6.2, notes under 'public funds' definition, IR
64 *Yesiloz v London Borough of Camden and DWP* [2009] EWCA Civ 415
65 *Szoma v SSWP* [2005] UKHL 64; [2006] 1 All ER 1, reported as R(IS) 2/06; *Yesiloz v London Borough of Camden* [2009] EWCA Civ 415
66 R(IS) 3/08

3. **European association agreements and their replacements**
67 Art 217 TFEU
68 Euro-Mediterranean Agreement establishing an Association between the European Community and its Member States, of the one part, and the People's Democratic Republic of Algeria, of the other part, 2005/690/EC, 18 July 2005
69 Euro-Mediterranean Agreement between the European Communities and the Kingdom of Morocco, 26 February 1996
70 Decision No.3/80 of the Council of Association, set up under the EEC-Turkey Association Agreement (sometimes referred to as the 'Ankara Agreement')
71 *Sema Sürül v Bundesanstalt für Arbeit,* C-262/96 [1999]; *Babahenini v Belgian State,* C-113/97 [1998]; see also CFC/2613/1997
72 Reg 1(3) SSCBCTC(A) Regs
73 *HMRC v HEH and SSWP (TC and CHB)* [2018] UKUT 237 (AAC)
74 **CB** Regs 1(3), 23(4)(b) and (4A) CB Regs
CTC Reg 3(5)(b)(ii), (5A) and (12) TC(R) Regs
75 *Sema Sürül v Bundesanstalt für Arbeit,* C-262/96 [1999], in particular paras 85-86 and 93

76 Stabilisation and Association Agreement between the European Communities and their Member States, of the one part, and the Republic of Albania of the other part, 28 April 2009
77 Partnership, Trade and Cooperation Agreement between UK and Albania (5 February 2021)
78 Partnership, Trade and Cooperation Agreement between UK and Albania (5 February 2021), relevant modifications in Annex I para 6
79 Art 48 Stabilisation and Association Agreement between the European Communities and their Member States, of the one part, and the Republic of Albania, of the other part, 28 April 2009
80 para 10140 CBTM; TCTM para 02108
81 Euro-Mediterranean Agreement establishing an Association between the European Communities and their Member States, of the one part, and the State of Israel, of the other part, 2000/384/EC, 20 November 1995 – in force 1 June 2000; The European Communities (Definition of Treaties) (Euro-Mediterranean Agreement establishing an Association between the European Communities and their Member States and the State of Israel) Order 1997 No.863
82 The Trade and Partnership Agreement between the UK and Israel (18 February 2019), relevant modifications in Annex II para 3
83 Title VIII Euro-Mediterranean Agreement
84 The National Insurance and Industrial Injuries (Israel) Order 1957 No.1879

Part 7

Benefit claims and getting paid

Chapter 18

Delays

This chapter covers:

1. Dealing with delays

Benefit authorities should act promptly to process your claim, to process any challenge you make to a decision and to issue payments due to you.

Although all benefit claimants can experience delays in the administration of their benefits and tax credits, you are more likely to experience delays if you are a migrant or if someone included in your claim is a migrant.

If you experience a delay, to resolve the matter it can be helpful if you:

- can establish the reasons for the delay (see below);
- are clear at which stage the delay has occurred (see p456).

The reasons for the delay

There can be many reasons for delays in benefit and tax credit administration. These are broadly due to decision makers needing to have sufficient information, which can take time to collect, and the volume of work that decision makers have.

If you or your family member have moved to or from the UK or are not British, a delay in the administration of your benefit or tax credit could be because of the following.

- The complexity of the rules on immigration status, residence and presence, and the effect of the European Union (EU) co-ordination rules (see Chapter 16), means that decisions may be made by specialist decision makers, who often have a backlog.
- The initial benefit or tax credit claim form may not ask for all the information that the decision maker needs to determine the effect of the rules on immigration status, residence, presence and EU co-ordination. They may

therefore need to write to you or to other agencies requesting further information, and this takes extra time.

- You may have difficulties providing evidence that the decision maker has requested – eg, about your immigration status or residence rights. See Chapter 20 for more details on this and what you can do in this situation.
- If you are covered by the EU co-ordination rules (see Chapter 16), information may need to be obtained from benefit authorities in European Economic Area countries, and that can take a long time.
- There may be a query about whether you need or have, or have applied for, a national insurance (NI) number. See Chapter 19 for more information on NI numbers.

When the delay occurs

What you can do to resolve a delay depends on the benefit you have claimed and the stage at which the delay occurs. Delays can occur when:

- you have made a claim for benefit and are waiting for a decision (see below);
- you have challenged a decision about your entitlement (see p468);
- you are awaiting payment (see p474).

Note: although the information in this chapter focuses on delays in decisions on claims, challenges to refusals of claims and payments, similar issues arise if there is a delay in deciding whether to supersede your award – eg, to increase your benefit after you report a child joining your household. For information about supersessions, including the date they take effect, see CPAG's *Welfare Benefits and Tax Credits Handbook.*

2. Waiting for a decision on a claim

If you have been waiting for a decision on your claim, what you can do depends on which benefit or tax credit you have claimed.

Are you waiting for a decision on your claim?

1. Check that your claim has been received by the benefit authority. If not, if possible provide a copy of the claim and/or any evidence you previously submitted. If you have no copy, submit a new claim and ask for it to be backdated. See CPAG's *Welfare Benefits and Tax Credits Handbook* for details on the backdating rules for the different benefits and tax credits.
2. If your claim has been received but not dealt with, ask why.
3. If the decision maker is not making a decision on your claim because there is a test case pending, see p468.
4. It is helpful to show the history of your previous contact when trying to resolve delays, so keep a copy of any letters sent or received and screenshots of any communication

online with the benefit authorities. Take the name and job title of anyone you speak to on the telephone and note the date and time.

5. In all communication, give your national insurance (NI) number (if you have one).

Note: administrative policy guidance is sometimes issued to decision makers on the processes to be followed when determining claims from particular groups of migrants – eg, to fast-track certain claims or accept certain standard pieces of evidence. It can be helpful to refer to this guidance to ensure that it is properly applied. For an example of such a policy on the habitual residence test, see p157. Although this guidance is often internal, organisations that work with particular groups (such as recently arrived refugees) may be able to give you details of current decision-making policies and practices.

Benefits administered by the DWP and HM Revenue and Customs

The rules about making decisions on claims for benefits and tax credits administered by the DWP or HM Revenue and Customs (HMRC) do not state how long it should take to determine a claim and issue a decision – ie, all benefits except housing benefit (HB – see p464) and those devolved to the Scottish government (see p465). However, the decision maker must decide claims for benefit within 'a reasonable time'.[1]

Whether or not the decision maker has taken longer than 'a reasonable time' to make a decision on your claim depends on:

- the volume of claims waiting to be decided and number of available decision makers;[2]
- the facts of your case, including how long you have waited for a decision and the effect of that wait. For example, if you have no income while you wait, this delay is more serious than if the benefit would top up an existing income. Similarly, it may be relevant if you or a family member have a health condition that is exacerbated by the lack of income.

If there are specific reasons why the delay is making things particularly difficult for you or your family, tell the benefit authority and suggest that it is not appropriate for your claim to be dealt with by the decision maker as part of a normal queuing system (whereby claims are determined in the order they are received).

If a delay continues, you could:

- request a universal credit (UC) advance or other short-term advance (certain benefits only) (see p459);
- request an interim payment of child benefit and guardian's allowance (see p463);
- apply for help from your local welfare assistance scheme (see p628);

- make a formal complaint, follow the complaints procedure and consider requesting help from your MP (see p465);
- obtain legal advice about possible judicial review (see p467);
- check whether you can get provisional payments if the delay is due to a dispute about which is the 'competent state' to pay your benefit or tax credit under the European Union (EU) co-ordination rules (see p403).

You can pursue more than one of these options – eg, you can make a complaint and if that does not resolve the delay, obtain legal advice about judicial review.

Is the delay due to the DWP determining whether you have a right to reside for universal credit?

If you are making a new claim for UC and have been receiving one of the benefits that UC replaces, your right to reside has already been accepted by a decision maker, unless you are receiving only working tax credit (WTC) or you had transitional protection (see p177). Therefore, unless your circumstances have changed such that you lost the right to reside, or it is a right to reside that is excluded for UC (see p169), the fact that you have already been accepted as having a right to reside should be taken into account by the decision maker when deciding whether you have a right to reside for UC. If you are applying for a UC advance, it must *appear* to the decision maker that you are entitled to UC, so your previously determined right to reside is relevant.

Note: if you had been receiving income support (IS), HB, child tax credit or WTC and before 25 July 2022, claimed UC and it was refused on the basis that you did not have a right to reside, see p295.

Official targets

If there are published targets for the time in which a claim should be processed, it can be helpful to refer to these. They should be taken into account when determining whether or not your claim has been dealt with as soon as is reasonably practicable.

HMRC publications state that its target for processing new child benefit and tax credit claims and changes of circumstances for UK claimants is within an average of 22 days, and for international claimants within an average of 92 days.[3] The DWP previously stated that its claim processing time was five days for IS and 10 days for jobseeker's allowance (JSA) and employment and support allowance. For UC, the target was to make a full first payment on time after the first monthly assessment period.[4] Current DWP publications only cite the percentage of claims processed within planned timescales but not what those current timescales are.[5]

You may be able to argue (in a judicial review) that policy stating that it will take substantially longer to deal with non-UK national claims is unlawful if you are either covered by the EU co-ordination rules (see p379) or you are a European Economic Area national exercising your rights as a 'worker' (see p211). The argument is that you should receive equal treatment and/or should not be deterred from exercising your rights as a worker.[6] For more information on equal treatment, see p413.

Advance payments

If you are waiting for a decision on your claim or to be paid (either your first or increased payments) and you are in 'financial need' (see p460), you may be able to get an advance payment of your future benefit award. For UC, this is called a 'universal credit advance' and, for other benefits, a 'short-term advance'.

Advance payments are discretionary (ie, the decision maker does not *have to* give you an advance *but must* take all the circumstances of your case into account when making their decision) and therefore it is helpful to refer to the DWP's guidance.[7]

Note: the decision maker should always determine your benefit claim and pay any benefit due, if possible, before considering an advance.[8] Consequently, requesting an advance can be a way of getting your claim processed and benefit paid.

The decision maker can only make an advance payment if:[9]

- you have made a claim for a benefit for which you can be paid an advance (see below). The only exception to this requirement is if you are not required to make a claim for benefit to be entitled, which only applies in limited circumstances; *and*
- you are in 'financial need' (see p460). **Note:** if you are moving to UC from one of the benefits it replaces, you do not need to show you are in financial need to get an advance;[10] *and*
- either:
  - your claim has not been decided, but it appears likely to the decision maker that you are entitled to the benefit; *or*
  - your claim has been decided and you have been awarded benefit but:
    - you are waiting for your first payment; *or*
    - you have received your first payment, but it was paid for a shorter period than subsequent payments will be and you are waiting for your next payment; *or*
    - you have had a change of circumstances that increases your entitlement, but your benefit has not yet been increased and paid to you; *or*
    - you are entitled to a payment, but it is impracticable to pay some or all of it on the date on which it is due.

You cannot get an advance payment if there is an appeal pending about the benefit in respect of which the advance would otherwise be paid.[11]

You can get an advance payment of any benefit *except*:[12]

- HB, although if your HB is delayed and you are a private or housing association tenant, you might be able to get a 'payment on account' (see p464);

- attendance allowance;
- disability living allowance;
- personal independence payment;
- child benefit or guardian's allowance, although you might be able to get an interim payment (see p463);
- statutory sick pay, statutory maternity pay, statutory adoption pay, statutory paternity pay or statutory shared parental pay;
- tax credits.

Financial need

'Financial need' means that there is a serious risk of damage to your or a member of your family's health or safety.[13] Guidance notes that situations which are considered 'serious risk' are not easily defined, but gives examples such as fleeing domestic violence and being without money for food or for gas/electricity meters.[14] The examples given in the information on UC advances on the gov.uk website are if you cannot afford to pay your rent or buy food.[15]

'Family' means your partner and any child in your household for whom you or your partner are responsible.[16]

Applications and decisions

Provided you have verified your identity, you can apply for a UC advance at your initial interview, at a subsequent meeting with your work coach or by telephoning the UC helpline on 0800 328 5644 (textphone 0800 328 1344). If you are in your first assessment period and have had your initial interview, you can also apply via your online account.[17]

You can request a short-term advance of other benefits in person at, or by writing (by post, fax or email) to, your local job centre, or by telephoning the number for the specific benefit (see gov.uk/short-term-benefit-advance).

Explain in your application how you meet the criteria. You should give the relevant history of your benefit claim and explain how you satisfy all the conditions of entitlement, including the immigration status, residence and presence requirements. Provide evidence for any areas where there may be a doubt – eg, the basis of your right to reside (see Chapter 12 and also p462) or the reason why you are not a 'person subject to immigration control' (see Chapter 7). You must also explain why you are in financial need (see above).

Before considering your application, DWP guidance confirms that the decision maker should always check whether they can simply decide your claim and issue payment. If so, the DWP should telephone you to let you know.[18] If your benefit cannot be paid, the decision maker should decide your application for an advance and give you the decision, usually on the same day or by 10am the next day.[19] This decision is notified via your online UC journal, or the DWP contacts you by telephone (or text) for other benefits to either tell you the decision or request more information.[20] If you do not have a telephone, provide the DWP with the number of a friend or relative. If you cannot, the DWP will tell you to call the benefit enquiry line after a certain period of time for an update on your request.[21]

If you are offered an advance, you are asked to accept the amount and the repayment terms. You should explain any problems with these. If you do not accept the offer, you are not given the advance.

There are no rules on how much an advance payment should be. However, the DWP considers how much you have asked for, how much you can afford to repay within the time period (see below) and what your benefit entitlement will be. Usually you can get a UC advance of up to 100 per cent of your estimated award (or estimated increase in your award due a change of circumstances).[22] The potential maximum short-term advance of other benefits is usually based on 60 per cent of your daily personal allowance multiplied by the number of days until your benefit is due to be paid.[23]

Repayments

Advance payments are recovered either in one lump-sum deduction from your next benefit payment or by smaller deductions from your regular benefit payments. You (and your partner if it is an advance of UC) must be notified of your liability to repay the advance.[24]

A UC advance is usually recovered within 24 months.[25] From April 2021, DWP policy is to recover at up to 25 per cent of your monthly UC standard allowance. However, the regulations only provide for recovery at a rate of 15 per cent of your UC standard monthly allowance, or 25 per cent if you have earned income (unless it is a 'benefit transfer' advance paid because you have recently moved from one of the benefits that UC replaces).[26] In 'exceptional circumstances' you can request that recovery of a new claim advance be deferred for up to three months, or request a change of circumstances advance for one month.[27] 'Exceptional circumstances' are not defined, so you should contact the UC helpline and explain how a one- or three-month deferment would help.

A short-term advance of other benefits is usually recovered within 12 weeks at no more than 25 per cent of your benefit.[28] Recovery can be deferred by up to 12 weeks if you are fleeing domestic violence.[29] In exceptional circumstances, you can request that recovery be rescheduled, over a maximum of 24 weeks. The DWP guidance gives a list of examples, including if your benefit has been reduced as a result of a sanction or separation from a partner, and an unforeseen and unavoidable event.[30]

There is no right of appeal against a decision on the rate of repayments of advances (unless it is a UC benefit transfer advance).[31] You can ask for the rate of recovery to be reconsidered, but if refused, your only legal remedy is judicial review (see p467). If your advance is recovered as a lump sum from arrears of benefit, you can appeal against this decision.[32]

If you are refused an advance payment

You cannot appeal against a refusal to award you an advance payment, unless it is a 'benefit transfer' advance when you move to UC from one of the benefits it replaces.[33] The only legal remedy is judicial review (see p467). However, you can ask for the decision to be reconsidered. If you are notified of the decision by telephone, ask for it to be reconsidered during that call; if you wait until later, you could be asked to make a new application instead.[34] If possible, provide any additional information to support your application, and if you are aware that the decision was based on incorrect information, correct that during the call. The decision maker should then reconsider your application based on the revised information.

You can also make a complaint to the DWP (see p466), including if you were prevented from requesting an advance, and that can be effective in either obtaining an advance or in getting your claim processed.

You can contact your MP to see whether they can help with either a complaint or to get the decision reconsidered.

Note: you may be able to get help from your local welfare assistance scheme (see p628) as well as, or instead of, an advance. However, you should not be prevented from requesting an advance just because local welfare assistance is available.

Are you having problems getting an advance payment?

1. Be aware of the DWP's guidance on advance payments and refer to it when helpful.
2. There is no minimum period of time you must wait before applying.
3. You may be told to seek help from your local welfare assistance scheme (see p628) or you may be referred to a food bank (see p642) instead. If you consider that you meet the criteria for an advance payment, insist on your application being passed to a decision maker. Decisions on advances must be made by a decision maker, not frontline staff.
4. The decision maker who considers your application may not be an expert on the rules for migrants. This lack of expertise can be a problem because an advance payment can only be made if it *appears* you are likely to be entitled to the benefit. It can assist your application if you set out clearly how you satisfy the relevant immigration status, residence and presence conditions.
5. If you are told you cannot receive an advance because the habitual residence test has not yet been applied to you, explain how you satisfy (or are exempt from) this and ask the decision maker to reconsider their decision. Although DWP guidance includes an outstanding habitual residence test as an example of when it is likely someone would not be entitled to benefit and an advance refused,[35] decision makers should not refuse your request without considering all your circumstances. Taking such a 'blanket' approach is contrary to earlier paragraphs in the guidance and is arguably unlawful.[36] If you are making a new claim for UC and have been receiving one of the means-tested benefits that UC replaces, your habitual residence (including your right to reside) will have previously been accepted by a decision maker. That is relevant to your application for a UC advance since

it must *appear* to the decision maker that you are entitled to UC (see p458 for more information).

6. If your claim cannot be processed because you are waiting for evidence showing that you meet all the conditions of entitlement, it may help to explain the cause of the delay, summarise any other evidence that you have already submitted and explain how it is consistent with the evidence you are waiting for. For more information on the evidence required for the immigration status and residence tests, see Chapter 20.

7. The decision maker may say you are not entitled to an advance because you do not have an NI number. If that happens, point out that the DWP guidance states that a short-term advance should still be considered, provided you can prove your identity and are complying with other requests for evidence.[37] The guidance also states that the DWP must ensure that all necessary action to allocate an NI number is taken promptly to ensure the claim can be finalised and paid.[38] See Chapter 19 for further information on the NI requirement.

8. If you are, or think you might be, refused an advance because you cannot repay it within the usual timescale, note the following.
- The regulations do not require you to be able to repay an advance within any particular period.
- DWP guidance covers circumstances in which the standard repayment rates can be varied. For example, you can agree to make higher repayments to pay back the advance over a shorter period and, in exceptional circumstances, recovery can be rescheduled over a longer period or deferred (see p461).[39]
- Make sure the decision maker is aware if your circumstances are likely to change in the future and improve your ability to repay the advance.

Interim payments of child benefit and guardian's allowance

An interim payment of child benefit or guardian's allowance can be made if it appears to HMRC that you may be entitled to benefit and:[40]

- you have not claimed correctly and it is impracticable for a claim to be made immediately; *or*
- you have claimed correctly and all the conditions of entitlement are satisfied *except* the NI number requirement (see p482) and it is impracticable for that to be satisfied immediately; *or*
- you have claimed correctly, but it is impracticable for the claim to be dealt with immediately; *or*
- you have been awarded benefit, but it is impracticable to pay you immediately, other than by an interim payment.

Note:

- You cannot appeal against a refusal to award you an interim payment. The only legal remedy is judicial review (see p467). You can ask HMRC to reconsider

its refusal and you can complain. You can also contact your MP to see whether they can help to get the decision reconsidered.
- An interim payment can be deducted from any later payment of the benefit and, if it is more than your actual entitlement, the overpayment can be recovered. You should be notified of this in advance.[41]
- An interim payment cannot be paid if you have an appeal pending.[42]

Housing benefit

Your HB claim must be determined within 14 days (or as soon as reasonably practicable after that) of your submitting a valid claim and providing all the information and evidence requested and reasonably required by the local authority.[43]

What counts as 'as soon as reasonably practicable' is the same as for benefits administered by the DWP and HMRC (see p457). In addition, the fact that your home may be at risk of repossession if the rent is not paid can often be a relevant factor in determining how long it should take to make a decision.

If you experience a delay in the local authority deciding your claim for HB, you can:

- request a 'payment on account' if you are a private or housing association tenant (see below);
- make a formal complaint (see p467);
- obtain legal advice about a judicial review (see p467).

You can pursue more than one of these options – eg, you can complain and if that does not resolve the delay, get legal advice about seeking a judicial review.

Note: HB guidance advising local authorities to refer claimants from the 'Windrush generation' (see p82) who are unable to provide evidence of their immigration status to the Home Office taskforce and then 'wait at least two weeks' before processing their claims is unlawful.[44] CPAG had been advised that the DWP was reviewing its procedures and taking legal advice on this point.[45] If you are a Commonwealth citizen and do not have documents showing your right to remain in the UK, get specialist immigration advice *before* contacting the Home Office as the rules are complex (see p82).

Payments on account

The local authority must make an interim payment (a 'payment on account') if:[46]

- you have claimed HB as a private or housing association tenant; *and*
- it is impracticable for it to make a decision on your claim within 14 days of its being made; *and*
- you have provided any information and evidence requested, or there is a good cause for your failure to do so.

A payment on account is *not* discretionary. The local authority *must* pay the amount it considers reasonable based on the information it has about your circumstances. If your actual entitlement is less, the local authority recovers the overpayment, or pays arrears if your entitlement is greater.[47] The local authority must notify you of the amount of a payment on account and that it can recover any overpayment resulting from your actual HB entitlement being lower.[48]

You should not need to ask the local authority to make a payment on account or make a separate claim.[49] However, in practice, it is often necessary to request a payment on account, and/or make a complaint (see below), and/or write to the solicitor for the local authority and threaten judicial review (see p467) in order to get a payment.

Scottish benefits

The rules for making decisions about benefits administered by Social Security Scotland (SSS) do not state how long it should take to determine a claim and issue a decision. However, SSS aims to make decisions on Best Start grants and Best Start foods applications in 30 days, funeral support payments in 10 days (or request further information), young carer grants in 14 days (or request further information) and child disability payments (CDP) in six to eight weeks (seven days in terminal illness cases for both CDP and adult disability payment).[50] There are no rules that allow advance or interim payments if SSS takes longer to make a decision on your application, but you can make a complaint.

Making a complaint

Making a complaint when there is an ongoing problem (such as a claim that has not been decided) is different from making a complaint about a situation that you think should not have happened but which is no longer producing a problem – eg, if your claim has been decided, but you are unhappy it took so long. The information in this section is aimed at enabling you to use the complaints process to get the situation resolved (ie, to get a decision on your claim), rather than at seeking compensation or highlighting to the decision maker the hardship it has caused after a delay has been resolved.

When you make a complaint to try to resolve an ongoing delay, it is important to highlight that the problem persists and that this is therefore an urgent matter, and be clear what you want to be done about it – eg, ask for your claim to be determined within X number of days. If the complaint is about your UC housing costs or HB claim, include any relevant details of steps your landlord is taking to obtain possession of the property as a consequence of the rent arrears arising from the delay.

The DWP, HMRC and SSS have different procedures for complaining. Local authorities should have their own complaints procedures. These procedures are outlined briefly below, but see CPAG's *Welfare Benefits and Tax Credits Handbook* for more detailed information about making a complaint.

Sometimes your local MP or councillor can help when there are problems with your claim or if you are getting no response to a complaint. If you want to complain about the DWP or HMRC to the Ombudsman, you must first ask your MP for help. If you do not know who your local MP is or how to contact them, you can telephone 0800 112 4272 or 020 7219 4272 or see members.parliament.uk. If your complaint is about SSS, your MSP may be able to help (see parliament.scot/msps). You should be able find out who your local councillors are and how to contact them by contacting your local authority.

Complaints about the DWP

If you want to complain about how the DWP has dealt with your case, first contact the office that is dealing with your claim. If you are unsure which office is dealing with your claim, contact numbers and information about the complaints procedure are provided on the DWP website.[51] You can also make a complaint about UC or JSA online at makeacomplaint.dwp.gov.uk.

If you are still unhappy after you get the initial response to your complaint, you can ask that your complaint be passed to the DWP Complaints Team. A dedicated complaints handler may contact you to discuss your complaint, which should normally be dealt with within 15 working days.

If you are still not satisifed, see CPAG's *Welfare Benefits and Tax Credits Handbook* for information about escalating your complaint to the Independent Case Examiner or the Parliamentary and Health Service Ombudsman.

Complaints about HM Revenue and Customs

You can complain about how HMRC has dealt with your claim for tax credits, child benefit or guardian's allowance online, by telephone or in writing. See gov.uk/complain-about-hmrc.

If you are not happy with the initial response, ask HMRC to review your complaint. If you are still not satisifed, see CPAG's *Welfare Benefits and Tax Credits Handbook* for information about escalating your complaint to the Adjudicator's Office or the Parliamentary and Health Service Ombudsman. If your complaint is about tax credits, also see CPAG's *Tax Credits and Complaints* factsheet.[52]

Complaints about Social Security Scotland

You can complain about how SSS has dealt with your application for a Scottish benefit, or if you feel an SSS policy affects you unfairly or that you have received poor advice from SSS. Complaints can be made by phone or in writing. Complaints must normally be made within six months. See mygov.scot/complain-social-security-scotland.

If you have had your final response from SSS but remain unsatisfied, you can take your complaint to the Scottish Public Services Ombudsman.

If SSS refuses to accept a benefit application because it decides you did not claim or ask for a redetermination in the right way, or you did not provide the required evidence, or did not have a good reason for missing the time limit to request a redetermination, you can appeal instead. These are called 'process decision' appeals.[53] You do not need to ask for a redetermination first, but otherwise the rules are mostly the same as for appeals against Scottish benefit entitlement decisions, except that you have no right to appeal to the Upper Tribunal if the First-tier Tribunal does not uphold your appeal. Your only option if it does not is to seek judical review (see below).

Complaints about housing benefit

Local authorities make HB decisions. They must have an effective complaints procedure, which should be made available to the public.

If you are unhappy about the actions of your local authority and wish to make a complaint, ask for a copy of its complaints policy. If you are unable to get the policy or there is no formal complaints procedure, contact the supervisor of the person dealing with your claim, making it clear why you are dissatisfied.

If you do not receive a satisfactory reply, take up the matter with someone more senior in the department and, ultimately, the principal officer. Send a copy of any correspondence to your ward councillors and to the councillor who chairs the relevant committee responsible for HB.

If this does not produce results, or if the delay is causing you severe hardship, consider a complaint to the Local Government and Social Care Ombudsman in England or the Public Services Ombudsman in Scotland and Wales, or obtain legal advice about a judicial review (see below). Government departments also monitor local authorities, so you could contact your MP (see p466) or write to the relevant minister.

Judicial review

Judicial review is a process by which you can ask a court to look at an action (or, in the case of delay, inaction) of any public authority that affects you, on the grounds that such (in)action is unlawful. If the High Court (Court of Session in Scotland) accepts that the (in)action is unlawful, it can order the decision maker to determine your benefit claim or otherwise resolve the issue.

Get legal advice as soon as possible if you are considering a judicial review. The time limit in England and Wales is 'promptly and in any event within three months after the grounds to make the claim first arose'.[54] The time limit in Scotland is also within three months, although there is limited discretion for the court to extend this limit.[55] It is strongly advisable that you only take judicial review proceedings with legal help. The process is complex and you risk having to pay the legal costs of the benefits authority (which could be thousands of pounds) if your challenge is unsuccessful.

However, in cases of benefit delay, often a 'pre-action letter', in which your adviser states that judicial review action will start *unless* your claim is determined by a certain date, can lead to your claim being decided promptly. The letter should be sent to the solicitor for the DWP, HMRC, SSS or local authority, together with a copy to the manager of the section responsible for dealing with your claim. Although a pre-action letter is currently only a statutory requirement in England and Wales, it can also be used in Scotland to help resolve delays.

A template for a pre-action letter (for use in England and Wales) is available online.[56] See also CPAG's Judicial Review Project (cpag.org.uk/welfare-rights/judicial-review) for more information and advice about judical review and a series of template pre-action letters for use in England and Wales (with notes about how to adapt them for use in Scotland) and how to use them effectively.

Pending test cases

The general rules on deciding your claim do not apply if there is an appeal pending against a decision of the Upper Tribunal or a court in a test case that deals with issues relevant to your claim. If this applies, the decision maker must consider whether it is possible that the outcome of the test case would mean you would have no entitlement. If so, the decision maker can postpone ('stay', or 'sist' in Scotland) making a decision on your claim (or revision or supersession request) until the test case is decided.[57] This prevents you appealing until a decision is made in the test case. Once a decision is made in the test case, the decision maker then makes a decision on your claim (or revision or supersession).[58]

If you would be entitled to benefit even if the test case were decided against you, the decision maker can make a decision.[59] This is done on the assumption that the test case has been decided in the way that is most unfavourable to you. This means that you are at least paid something while you wait for the result of the test case. Then, if the decision in the test case is in your favour, the decision maker revises their decision.

If you already have a decision in your favour, the decision maker can suspend payment of your benefit (see p476).

If you have already appealed to the First-tier Tribunal, see p470.

3. Delays when challenging a decision

If you have challenged a decision about your entitlement to a benefit or tax credit, there can be a delay while the:

- decision maker considers whether or not to revise (or review or redetermine) the decision (see below); *or*
- decision maker prepares the appeal to send to the First-tier Tribunal (see p470); *or*
- appeal is with the First-tier Tribunal waiting for a hearing date.

For benefits other than housing benefit (HB), if you want to appeal to the First-tier Tribunal, you usually have to first apply for a revision (or for tax credits, a review, or for Scottish benefits, a redetermination) of the decision.[60] The DWP and HM Revenue and Customs (HMRC) call this a 'mandatory reconsideration'.

The DWP or HMRC sends you a 'mandatory reconsideration notice', telling you the result of your application for a revision or review. The notice is proof that it has accepted and considered your application. You usually must send a copy of this to the tribunal when you appeal. If the DWP or HMRC only provides a mandatory reconsideration notice after a long delay, that may put you at a disadvantage – eg, if the delay makes it difficult to obtain evidence to support your appeal. The tribunal should take that into account if you subsequently appeal, so you should explain how you think the delay has affected your chances of winning your appeal.[61] You can appeal if Social Security Scotland (SSS) has failed to make a redetermination within 56 calendar days for child disability payment (CDP) and adult disability payment (ADP), or 16 working days for other Scottish benefits. For further information on challenging decisions, see CPAG's *Welfare Benefits and Tax Credits Handbook.*

Delay in carrying out a revision

Make it clear to the DWP that you are asking for a 'revision' when you request one, including the fact that the DWP calls a revision a 'mandatory reconsideration'. The dispute resolution team should then decide whether or not to revise the decision and send you the mandatory reconsideration notice. If the DWP responds to your revision request with a letter telling you that the decision has been looked at again, but not changed, and either inviting you to now request a mandatory reconsideration or informing you that it is only now being forwarded to a dispute resolution team, you should argue that you can now appeal. However, to safeguard your appeal rights, you should also continue with the mandatory reconsideration process and resubmit a further revision request, explaining what has happened and clearly asking that it be sent immediately to a dispute resolution team. You should also submit a complaint, because you should not need to request a mandatory reconsideration twice.

There are no specified legal time limits for how long a decision maker should take to carry out a revision (or, for tax credits, a review). However, revision requests should be dealt with within a reasonable time and tax credit reviews should be carried out as soon as is 'reasonably practicable'.[62] See p457 for the factors that are relevant when determining what is reasonable. You should ensure that you highlight any specific circumstances of your case that mean it is urgent for you, and therefore not appropriate for your request to be dealt with in the order in which it was received.

If a delay in carrying out a revision or review continues, the options for resolving it are the same as those for resolving a delay in determining a claim (see p457 for benefits administered by the DWP or HMRC and p464 for HB). However, you can also make an appeal application. Normally, you need a mandatory reconsideration notice before you can appeal, but if you have done everything correctly and your case is urgent and either there is an unreasonable delay in carrying out the revision (or review) or sending you the mandatory reconsideration notice, the tribunal can waive the normal rules, if it would be in the interest of justice to do so.[63] It might also use its powers to issue a direction requiring the DWP to provide a mandatory reconsideration notice.[64] Make sure that your application clearly states that it is being made without a mandatory reconsideration notice, that you want the tribunal to use its power to either waive that requirement or to issue a direction requiring the DWP or HMRC to provide one, *and* that you want this request to be considered by a tribunal judge rather than the clerk. You can find adaptable template letters for making an appeal application without a mandatory reconsideration notice at cpag.org.uk/welfare-rights/template-letters.

For CDP and ADP there is a time limit of 56 calendar days, and for other Scottish benefits 16 working days, in which SSS should make its redetermination.[65]

Note:

- The decision maker can postpone making a decision on your request for a revision if there is a test case pending (see p468).
- The DWP publishes quarterly statistics online that show average clearance times for work capability assessment mandatory reconsiderations.[66]
- HMRC has a target of processing all post and online forms within 15 days.[67]

Delay while an appeal is prepared

The time in which the decision maker must send their response to the First-tier Tribunal, and the possible solutions if there are delays, depends on whether or not you were required to request a mandatory reconsideration or redetermination before appealing.

If your appeal concerns your rights under European Union (EU) law (eg, your right to reside under EU law or the effect of the EU co-ordination rules – see p379), see also p477 for a possible argument that some payments should be made to you while you wait for your appeal to be heard.

Delay following a mandatory reconsideration or redetermination

Once you have sent your appeal to HM Courts and Tribunals Service (HMCTS), you may experience a delay in it being progressed.

You should first establish what stage the appeal has reached. If you have requested an oral hearing, you can register for an email and text notification service called 'Track Your Appeal' by telephoning 0300 123 1142 (Welsh speakers: 0300 303 5170; Scotland: 0300 790 6234). For all other appeals (or if the stage of your appeal is not clear from the notifications), contact HMCTS and check whether:

- your appeal has been received. You may wish to obtain proof of receipt – eg, by sending the appeal by a service that requires a signature or using the Royal Mail tracking service. Once your appeal has been received by the tribunal, it is responsible for ensuring that the case is dealt with 'fairly and justly', which includes 'avoiding delay so far as compatible with proper consideration of the issues';[68]
- your appeal has been sent on to the DWP, HMRC or SSS and, if so, on what date;
- the benefit authority has responded (see below). A copy of this response should be sent to you and/or your representative;
- you have been sent an enquiry form or, if you have returned this, whether it has been received; *and*
- if you have requested an oral hearing, your appeal is ready to be listed for a hearing date.

The decision maker must send their response to your appeal to the First-tier Tribunal within 28 days (31 days if SSS) of having received the appeal.[69] If the DWP/HMRC/SSS has not responded to your appeal, you can ask the tribunal to make a direction that the DWP/HMRC/SSS do so within a further short period, after which time the appeal is listed and the DWP/HMRC/SSS is barred from taking any further part in proceedings.[70]

If your situation is particularly urgent, you can ask the tribunal to 'expedite' matters by shortening the 28-day (or 31-day) time limit.[71]

If the DWP/HMRC/SSS applies for a direction to extend the time limit, you should be notified of this in writing and you can then also apply for a direction setting this direction aside.[72]

If you apply for a direction, explain the consequences for you of a continuing delay and why it would be fair and just to determine the case more quickly than would otherwise happen.

If you request that your appeal be dealt with quickly in this way, you must also be as flexible as possible in preparing your case quickly and making yourself, and any representative, available for hearings at short notice.

If the tribunal refuses to expedite your appeal, and it is arguable that this means your case is not being dealt with fairly and justly, get advice on whether there are grounds for a judicial review (see p467).

If your appeal is delayed because of a pending test case, see p473.

Delay without a mandatory reconsideration

You do not need to request a revision of an HB decision before appealing. Instead, you send your appeal to the decision maker in the local authority. It is a good idea to keep a copy of your application and any documents accompanying it. If there is a delay in your appeal being processed, first establish what stage it has reached. Contact the local authority and check whether:

- your appeal has been received;
- the decision maker has written their response and sent it to HMCTS. A copy should also be sent to you and/or your representative;
- you have been sent an enquiry form or, if you have returned this, whether it has been received; *and*
- your appeal is ready to be listed for a hearing date.

The decision maker must send their response to your appeal to HMCTS as soon as reasonably practicable. You are entitled to have your appeal heard within a reasonable period of time, so the decision maker should prepare the response and send it to the First-tier Tribunal without delay.[73] Following a complaint about an HB appeal, the Ombudsman said that the local authority should forward an appeal within 28 days.[74]

If your appeal has been received but has not been sent to HMCTS, request that this be done. You can complain about the delay (see p465).

If a DWP decision does not say you have to ask for a revision or mandatory reconsideration first before having a right to appeal, you can apply for permission to appeal directly to HMCTS.[75] Note that following a High Court decision, you do not need to ask for a mandatory reconsideration of some employment and support allowance decisions before appealing.[76] If you then experience delays with how HMCTS handles your appeal, see above.

If there are special reasons why your appeal should be dealt with urgently or there has already been significant delay, write to the First-tier Tribunal asking it to direct the decision maker to produce the response and/or list the appeal for a hearing.[77] Set out the history of the appeal, what you have done to try to get the matter resolved and the effect of the delay on you and your family as clearly as possible and include all documents that you have about the decision. Bear in mind that the tribunal expects normal procedures to be followed in the vast majority of cases, but, if necessary, can deal with your appeal differently. This includes admitting the appeal directly if it has not yet been received from the decision maker or prioritising the hearing date, so it is not listed in the order in which the appeal was received.

How should you ask the tribunal to deal with your appeal if it has not been sent by the decision maker?

If you write to the First-tier Tribunal, the tribunal clerk may be confused if they receive documents concerning an appeal that the decision maker has not told the tribunal about. To minimise the chances of confusion, do the following.

1. Clearly title your letter 'Application for a Direction under Rule 6 of the Tribunal Procedure Rules' and mark it 'urgent'.
2. Explain at the start of the letter that the papers have not been sent by the decision maker and you would like the case to be referred to a tribunal judge to give a direction to resolve this problem.

3. Set out the history of when your appeal was submitted to the decision maker and the contact you have had with the benefit authority since then. If possible, enclose a copy of your appeal request and any accompanying documents.
4. Refer to the caselaw that confirms that HMCTS has the power to issue directions in relation to an unnotified appeal.[78]
5. Clearly explain the consequences for you and your family of a continuing delay and why it would be fair and just to determine the case more quickly than would otherwise happen.
6. Follow up your letter with a phone call to the tribunal to establish that it has been received and passed to a judge.
7. See CPAG's website for a sample letter, which you may want to adapt.[79] This does not specify timescales, because what is reasonable depends on the facts of your case and the consequences of the continued delay. For example, if you are at imminent risk of losing your home because HB or universal credit housing costs have not been awarded, the timescale should reflect that.

If you request that your appeal be dealt with quickly in this way, you must then be as flexible as possible in preparing your case quickly and making yourself, and any representative, available for hearings at short notice.

If a tribunal judge refuses to direct the decision maker to submit their response to the tribunal and to expedite the appeal, you should consider whether there are grounds for a judicial review against this refusal (see p467). Depending on the particular facts, it may be arguable that a failure to give such directions has resulted in procedural impropriety because the tribunal has failed to deal with your case fairly and justly as required.[80]

Appeal delayed because of a pending test case

If you have appealed to the First-tier or Upper Tribunal and there is a test case pending against a decision of the Upper Tribunal or a court that deals with issues raised in your case, the decision maker can serve a notice requiring the tribunal in your appeal:[81]

- not to make a decision and to refer your case back to them; *or*
- to deal with your appeal by either:
  - postponing making a decision (known as 'stay' or, in Scotland, 'sist') until the test case is decided; *or*
  - deciding your appeal as if the test case had been decided in the way most unfavourable to you, but only if this is in your interests – eg, you will get some benefit paid as opposed to none. If that happens and the test case is eventually decided in your favour, the decision maker must make a new decision superseding the decision of the tribunal in the light of the decision in the test case.

If the decision on your appeal has been postponed, once a decision has been made in the test case, the decision is made on your appeal.

If your appeal concerns European law, see p477.

4. Delays getting paid

Once you have a positive decision stating that you are entitled to benefit, there may be delays in the benefit authority implementing it and making any payments due.

It is important to check first that a decision has been made to award you a specified amount of benefit (see below). If so, unless payments can be suspended (see p475), payment should be made to you as soon as reasonably practicable.[82]

For DWP-administered benefits, if you do not have a bank account you should be paid through the payment exception service, which enables you to collect your payment from a PayPoint outlet.[83]

If benefit is not paid promptly, you can start action in the county court (England and Wales) or sheriff court (Scotland) for payment of the money owed.[84] However, it is extremely rare that this action is required to obtain benefit that has been awarded but not paid.

The decision awarding you benefit

In most cases, it is clear that there has been a decision awarding you a specified amount of benefit. However, in some cases, you may get a *determination* that does not award benefit but only decides one or more conditions of entitlement. For example, if you appeal against the DWP's decision that it cannot pay you universal credit (UC) because you do not have a right to reside, although the tribunal can decide that you do have a right to reside (and so you win your appeal), that is not a decision awarding you benefit because it only relates to one condition of entitlement. The tribunal's decision is sent to the DWP and the decision maker must then decide whether you meet all the other conditions of entitlement to UC and whether to award you a specified amount of benefit. 'Process decision' appeals against Scottish benefits decisions are not about entitlement so if your appeal is upheld, the decision is sent to Social Security Scotland (SSS) to decide your entitlement.

If your appeal about one condition of your entitlement is allowed and there is then a delay in a decision being made to award you benefit, do the following.

- Check whether the decision maker has received notification of the tribunal's decision.
- If the decision maker has received notification, establish the cause of the delay. A long time may have elapsed since your initial claim was made, and so to ensure that you have met the other conditions of entitlement since your date of claim, the decision maker may write asking you to confirm this, often by completing a claim or review form. Any further delays can be reduced if you provide the information or complete and return any forms as soon as you can.
- If you are advised that the decision maker has all the information they require, but there is still a delay in deciding your claim, your options are the same as for

someone who experiences a delay in getting a decision on an initial claim (see p456). You should include in any correspondence the fact that you have already had a significant wait while your appeal was determined.

Suspension of benefit

In certain circumstances, a decision maker can suspend payment of part, or all, of your benefit or tax credits. In this case, you have no right to the payment (and so cannot appeal). See CPAG's *Welfare Benefits and Tax Credits Handbook* for all the circumstances in which benefit can be suspended. Note that there are currently no rules in force that allow payments of Scottish benefits to be suspended.

The situations when payment of benefit or tax credits can be suspended that are most relevant for migrants are:

- because the decision maker wants more information to decide whether you continue to be entitled to benefit (see below); *or*
- while an appeal against a positive decision is pending (see p476).

Has your benefit been suspended?

1. You cannot appeal to the First-tier Tribunal against the decision to suspend your benefit. The only way to change the decision is to negotiate to get your benefit reinstated or to challenge the decision by a judicial review (see p467).
2. If you receive a letter telling you that your benefit has been suspended, write explaining how the suspension affects you and your family and ask for the suspension decision to be reconsidered. There may be other arguments why your benefit should not be suspended, based on the information below.
3. The decision maker may be willing to continue to pay your benefit, or at least some of it, if you can show that you and your family will experience hardship otherwise. Guidance to decision makers is clear that, in almost all decisions to suspend benefit, consideration must be given to whether hardship would result and whether that would make the suspension unacceptable. In addition, the decision to suspend your benefit can be reconsidered if the decision maker receives additional information.[85]

The decision maker requires further information

You can be required to supply information or evidence if the decision maker needs this to determine whether your award of benefit should be revised or superseded.[86]

If you do not provide the information and evidence, payment of all or part of your benefit can be suspended if:[87]

- a question has arisen about your entitlement or whether a decision should be revised or superseded;[88] *or*
- you apply for a revision or supersession; *or*
- you do not provide certificates, documents, evidence or other information about the facts of your case as required.[89]

If the decision maker wants you to provide information or evidence, they must notify you in writing. Within 14 days (or one month for child benefit, guardian's allowance and housing benefit (HB), seven days for contribution-based jobseeker's allowance if you come under the UC system, or by the date specified, which must not be less than 30 days after the date of the notice, for tax credits) of being sent the request, you must:

- supply the information or evidence.[90] You can be given more time if the decision maker is satisfied that this is necessary; *or*
- satisfy the decision maker that the information does not exist or you cannot obtain it.[91]

If the decision maker has not already done so, your benefit can be suspended if you do not provide the information or evidence within the relevant time limit.[92] Similarly, your tax credits can be suspended if you do not provide information or evidence by the date requested.[93]

The complexity of the immigration status, residence, presence and European Union (EU) co-ordination rules, together with the additional information and evidence requirements these rules generate, means that the likelihood of your benefit being suspended on the above grounds is increased if they apply to you. For information on some of the practical issues involved in satisfying the information and evidence requirements, see Chapter 20.

If an appeal is pending

Your benefit or tax credit can be suspended if the DWP, HM Revenue and Customs (HMRC) or local authority is appealing (or considering an appeal) against:[94]

- a decision of the First-tier Tribunal, Upper Tribunal or court to award you benefit (or to reinstate benefit); *or*
- a decision of the Upper Tribunal or court about someone else's appeal if the issue could affect your claim – ie, a test case (see p468). For HB only, the other case must also be about an HB issue.

The DWP, HMRC or local authority must (although for tax credits this is only guidance[95]) give you written notice as soon as reasonably practicable if it intends to:[96]

- request the statement of reasons for the First-tier Tribunal's decision; *or*
- apply for leave to appeal; *or*
- appeal.

The decision maker must then take that action within the usual time limits for doing so (generally within one month in each case). If they do not, the suspended benefit must be paid to you.[97] The suspended benefit must also be paid to you if the decision maker withdraws an application for leave to appeal, withdraws the appeal or is refused leave to appeal and it is not possible for them to renew the application.

The decision maker still has discretion not to suspend your benefit or tax credits if they consider it would result in hardship, and they should keep their decision under review so that the suspension can be lifted if your circumstances, including the level of hardship experienced, change.[98] You should therefore write to the relevant benefit authority if the suspension will cause, or is causing, you or your family hardship.

Suspension on this ground is particularly common following appeals about the right to reside requirement. This is due to decision makers appealing to the Upper Tribunal against a First-tier Tribunal's decision, and the large number of ongoing cases about right to reside that are in the higher courts.

If your appeal concerns your rights under EU law (eg, your right to reside or the effect of the EU co-ordination rules), see below.

If your appeal concerns European law

If the issue in your appeal concerns EU law, and the rights you are exercising are still covered by EU law (see Chapters 12 and 16 for when EU law may still apply to you), you may be able to argue that your benefit or tax credit should not be suspended, or that you should receive some form of interim payment. European caselaw has established that national governments cannot automatically refuse requests for interim relief to people seeking to exercise their rights under European law, and that national courts must be able to grant interim relief to ensure EU rights are respected.[99]

This argument could be used, for example, if the issue in your appeal is whether you have a right to reside in EU law (see Chapter 12) or whether you are entitled to benefit because of the EU co-ordination rules (see Chapter 16).

It may be possible to make this argument in the following circumstances.

- If you are waiting for your appeal to be heard by the First-tier Tribunal, you may be able to argue that you should be paid an advance payment or that you should receive some form of interim payment while waiting. You must request a payment outside the benefit rules ('extra statutory') from the benefit authority, because its decision is that you are not entitled under the rules.
- If action on your appeal has been deferred (known as 'stayed' or, in Scotland, 'sisted') because there is a test case pending (see p473), you may be able to argue either that these rules deferring action should not be applied or that you should receive some form of interim payment until your appeal can be determined.
- If you have won your First-tier Tribunal appeal and the decision maker suspends payment of your benefit or tax credit because they have appealed, or intends to appeal, to the Upper Tribunal, you may be able to argue that your benefit should not be suspended, or that you should receive some form of interim payment pending the further appeal.

If there is a difference of views over which state is the 'competent state' under the EU co-ordination rules for paying your benefit or tax credit, you may be entitled to receive provisional payments (see p403).

Note: the benefit authorities can still lift the suspension of your benefit on grounds of hardship (see p476).

Notes

2. **Waiting for a decision on a claim**

1 *SSHD v R (S)* [2007] EWCA Civ 546, para 51
2 *R v Secretary of State for Social Services and Chief Adjudication Officer ex parte Child Poverty Action Group* [1990] 2 QB 540
3 See, for example, 'Definition/ Calculation' column for 'Customer service and support' under 'A journey through HMRC' in Analytical Annex to *HMRC Quarterly Performance Report,* available at gov.uk.
4 DWP, *Single Departmental Plan: 2018 to 2022 headline indicators technical detail,* updated 17 February 2020, now withdrawn and replaced by *Outcome Delivery Plan,* available at gov.uk
5 See DWP *Annual Report and Accounts 2021-22,* pp50-51, available at gov.uk
6 Art SSC5 UK-EUP; Art 4 EU Reg 883/04; Arts 18 and 45 TFEU; Art 24 EU Dir 2004/38; Art 7 EU Reg 492/2011
7 DWP guidance for UC advances can be found at rightsnet.org.uk/universal-credit-guidance and is summarised at gov.uk/guidance/universal-credit-advances
8 DWP guidance, *Short Term Benefit Advances: benefit centres,* paras 3, 5, 55 and 80, available at whatdotheyknow.com/request/operational_guidance_for_benefit
9 Regs 5 and 6 SS(PAB) Regs
10 Reg 17 UC(TP) Regs
11 Reg 4(2) SS(PAB) Regs
12 Reg 3 SS(PAB) Regs
13 Reg 7 SS(PAB) Regs
14 DWP guidance, *Short Term Benefit Advances: benefit centres,* paras 22-23, available at whatdotheyknow.com/request/operational_guidance_for_benefit
15 gov.uk/guidance/universal-credit-advances
16 Reg 7 SS(PAB) Regs; s137 SSCBA 1992
17 gov.uk/guidance/universal-credit-advances
18 DWP guidance, *Short Term Benefit Advances: benefit centres,* paras 3, 5, 55, 80 and 90, available at whatdotheyknow.com/request/operational_guidance_for_benefit
19 gov.uk/guidance/universal-credit-advances; DWP guidance, *Short Term Benefit Advances: benefit centres,* para 116, available at whatdotheyknow.com/request/operational_guidance_for_benefit
20 DWP guidance, *Short Term Benefit Advances: benefit centres,* paras 89-94, available at whatdotheyknow.com/request/operational_guidance_for_benefit
21 DWP guidance, *Short Term Benefit Advances: benefit centres,* para 93, available at whatdotheyknow.com/request/operational_guidance_for_benefit
22 gov.uk/guidance/universal-credit-advances
23 DWP guidance, *Short Term Benefit Advances: benefit centres,* para 35, available at whatdotheyknow.com/request/operational_guidance_for_benefit
24 Reg 8 SS(PAB) Regs

25 As announced in the March 2021 budget, the 24-month period applies from April 2021 for advances made from that date onwards. Prior to this the period was 12 months.
26 Reg 11 The Social Security (Overpayments and Recovery) Regulations 2013 No.384. This does not apply to UC 'benefit transfer' advance payments made under reg 17 UC(TP) Regs.
27 gov.uk/guidance/universal-credit-advances
28 DWP guidance, *Short Term Benefit Advances: benefit centres*, para 29, available at whatdotheyknow.com/request/operational_guidance_for_benefit
29 DWP guidance, *Short Term Benefit Advances: benefit centres*, paras 16 and 29-32, available at whatdotheyknow.com/request/operational_guidance_for_benefit
30 DWP guidance, *Short Term Benefit Advances: benefit centres*, paras 175-81, available at whatdotheyknow.com/request/operational_guidance_for_benefit
31 Sch 3 para 15 UC,PIP,JSA&ESA(DA) Regs; Sch 2 para 20 SS&CS(DA) Regs. This does not apply to UC 'benefit transfer' advance payments made under reg 17 UC(TP) Regs.
32 Sch 3 para 14 UC,PIP,JSA&ESA(DA) Regs and Sch 2 para 20A SS&CS(DA) Regs allow a right of appeal against decisions on deductions under reg 10 SS(PAB) Regs
33 Sch 3 para 14 UC,PIP,JSA&ESA(DA) Regs; Sch 2 para 20A SS&CS(DA) Regs; UC advances when transferring are made under reg 17 UC(TP) Regs and not the SS(PAB) Regs
34 gov.uk/short-term-benefit-advance; DWP guidance, *Short Term Benefit Advances: benefit centres*, paras 193-95, available at whatdotheyknow.com/request/operational_guidance_for_benefit
35 DWP guidance, *Short Term Benefit Advances: benefit centres*, paras 17 and 72, available at whatdotheyknow.com/request/operational_guidance_for_benefit
36 DWP guidance, *Short Term Benefit Advances: benefit centres*, paras 7-11, available at whatdotheyknow.com/request/operational_guidance_for_benefit
37 For UC advances, see DWP, *September 2019: Touchbase edition 137*
38 DWP guidance, *Short Term Benefit Advances: benefit centres*, paras 66-67, available at whatdotheyknow.com/request/operational_guidance_for_benefit
39 gov.uk/guidance/universal-credit-advances and *Short Term Benefit Advances: benefit centres*, paras 16, 29-32 and 175-181, available at whatdotheyknow.com/request/operational_guidance_for_benefit
40 Reg 22 CB&GA(Admin) Regs
41 Regs 22(3), 41 and 42 CB&GA(Admin) Regs
42 Reg 22(2) CB&GA(Admin) Regs
43 Reg 89 HB Regs; reg 70 HB(SPC) Regs
44 Urgent Bulletin U1/2018, p2
45 Email to CPAG, 8 May 2018 (and no update at time of writing)
46 Reg 93(1) HB Regs; reg 74(1) HB(SPC) Regs
47 Reg 93(2) and (3) HB Regs; reg 74(2) and (3) HB(SPC) Regs
48 Reg 93(2) HB Regs; reg 74(2) HB(SPC) Regs
49 *R v Haringey London Borough Council ex parte Azad Ayub* [1992] 25 HLR 566 (QBD)
50 See mygov.scot/browse/benefits
51 gov.uk/government/organisations/department-for-work-pensions/about/complaints-procedure
52 cpag.org.uk/sites/default/files/files/resource/CPAG-scot-factsheet-Tax-credits-complaints-May-2021_0.pdf
53 s61 SS(S)A 2018
54 Civil Procedure Rules, Part 54.5
55 s27A Court of Session Act 1988
56 See Annex A, www.justice.gov.uk/courts/procedure-rules/civil/protocol/prot_jrv
57 **HB** Sch 7 para 16 CSPSSA 2000
Other benefits s25 SSA 1998
58 **HB** Sch 7 para 18(2) CSPSSA 2000
Other benefits s27(2) SSA 1998

59 **HB** Sch 7 para 16(3) and (4) CSPSSA 2000; reg 15 HB&CTB(DA) Regs
CB/GA s25(3) and (4) SSA 1998; reg 22 CB&GA(DA) Regs
UC/PIP/JSA&ESAunder UC s25(3) and (4) SSA 1998; reg 53 UC,PIP,JSA&ESA(DA) Regs
Other benefits s25(3) and (4) SSA 1998; reg 21 SS&CS(DA) Regs

3. Delays when challenging a decision

60 For benefits administered by the DWP, you only have to ask for a revision before appealing if the decision you want to appeal says so. The Upper Tribunal confirmed this in relation to a claim for UC which the DWP 'closed'. See *PP v SSWP (UC)* [2020] UKUT 109 (AAC).
61 *MM v SSWP (PIP)* [2016] UKUT 36 (AAC)
62 For tax credits, see s21A(2) TCA 2002
63 r7(2)(a) TP(FT) Rules
64 r6 TP(FT) Rules
65 s43 SS(S)A 2018; para 2(1) Sch 1 EYA(BSG)(S) Regs; reg 9(2) CA(YCG)(S) Regs; reg 6(2) FEA(S) Regs; reg 9(2) WHCYP(S) Regs; para 16(2) Sch SCP Regs; reg 37(2) DACYP(S) Regs; reg 54(2) DAWAP(S) Regs
66 DWP, *Employment and Support Allowance: outcomes of work capability assessments*, available at gov.uk
67 HMRC, Outcome Delivery Plan and 'Customer service data' under Analytic Annex in *Quarterly Performance Reports*, available at gov.uk
68 r2(2)(e) TP(FT) Rules; r2(2)(e) FTT(S) Rules
69 r24(1)(c) TP(FT) Rules; r21(7) FTT(S) Rules
70 rr2, 5, 6, 7 and 8 TP(FT) Rules; rr2, 4-7 FTT(S) Rules
71 rr5(3)(a) and 6 TP(FT) Rules; rr4(3)(a) and 5 FTT(S) Rules
72 r6(5) TP(FT) Rules; r5(5) FTT(S) Rules
73 Art 6 European Convention on Human Rights; s6 HRA 1998; CH/3497/2005; *MB v Wychavon DC* [2013] UKUT 67 (AAC)
74 Complaint 01/C/13400 against Scarborough Borough Council
75 See *PP v SSWP (UC)* [2020] UKUT 109 (AAC)
76 *Connor v SSWP* [2020] EWHC 1999 (Admin) (24 July 2020)
77 R(H) 1/07; *FH v Manchester City Council(HB)* [2010] UKUT 43 (AAC)
78 R(H) 1/07; *FH v Manchester City Council (HB)* [2010] UKUT 43 (AAC)
79 cpag.org.uk/sites/default/files/CPAG-How-to-expedite-social-security-appeal-Aug-13.pdf
80 r2(3)(a) TP(FT) Rules
81 **HB** Sch 7 para 17 CSPSSA 2000
Other benefits s26 SSA 1998
Scottish benefits r4(3)(j) FTT(S) Rules

4. Delays getting paid

82 **UC/PIP/ESA&JSA under UC** Reg 45 UC,PIP,JSA&ESA(C&P) Regs
HB Reg 91 HB Regs; reg 72 HB(SPC) Regs
WTC/CTC Regs 8 and 9 TC(PC) Regs
Other benefits Reg 20 SS(C&P) Regs
Scottish benefits s24 SS(S)A 2018
83 gov.uk/payment-exception-service
84 *Murdoch v DWP* [2010] EWHC 1988 (QB), paras 75-79; for HB, see *Jones v Waveney DC* [1999] 33 HLR 3
85 DWP, *Suspension and Termination Guide,* paras 1350, 2050-52 and 2301-02, available at gov.uk
86 **UC/PIP/JSA&ESA under UC** Reg 38(2) UC,PIP,JSA&ESA(C&P) Regs; reg 45 UC,PIP,JSA&ESA(DA) Regs
HB Reg 86(1) HB Regs; reg 67(1) HB(SPC) Regs
CB/GA Reg 23 CB&GA(Admin) Regs
WTC/CTC s16(3) TCA 2002
Other benefits Reg 32(1) SS(C&P) Regs; reg 17 SS&CS(DA) Regs
87 **UC/PIP/JSA&ESA under UC** Reg 45(6) UC,PIP,JSA&ESA(DA) Regs
HB Reg 13 HB&CTB(DA) Regs
CB/GA Reg 19 CB&GA(DA) Regs
WTC/CTC Reg 11 TC(PC) Regs (the word 'postponement' is used, rather than 'suspension')
Other benefits Reg 17(2) SS&CS(DA) Regs
88 **UC/PIP/JSA&ESA under UC** Reg 44(2)(a)(i) UC,PIP,JSA&ESA(DA) Regs
HB Reg 11(2)(a)(i) HB&CTB(DA) Regs
CB/GA Reg 18(2)(a) CB&GA(DA) Regs
WTC/CTC Reg 11(3A) TC(PC) Regs
Other benefits Reg 16(3)(a) SS&CS(DA) Regs
89 **UC/PIP/JSA&ESA under UC** Reg 38(2) UC,PIP,JSA&ESA(C&P) Regs
HB Reg 86(1) HB Regs; reg 67(1) HB(SPC) Regs
CB/GA Reg 23 CB&GA(Admin) Regs
WTC/CTC Reg 11(3A) TC(PC) Regs
Other benefits Reg 32(1) SS(C&P) Regs

90 **UC/PIP/JSA&ESA under UC** Reg 45(4)(a) UC,PIP,JSA&ESA(DA) Regs
HB Reg 13(4)(a) HB&CTB(DA) Regs
CB/GA Reg 19(2) CB&GA(DA) Regs
WTC/CTC Reg 32 TC(CN) Regs
Other benefits Reg 17(4)(a) SS&CS(DA) Regs

91 **UC/PIP/JSA&ESA under UC** Reg 45(4)(b) UC,PIP,JSA&ESA(DA) Regs
HB Reg 13(4)(b) HB&CTB(DA) Regs
CB/GA Reg 19(2)(b) CB&GA(DA) Regs
WTC/CTC HMRC leaflet WTC/FS9, *Tax Credits: suspension of payments*, March 2019
Other benefits Reg 17(4)(b) SS&CS(DA) Regs

92 **UC/PIP/JSA&ESA under UC** Reg 45(6) UC,PIP,JSA&ESA(DA) Regs
HB Reg 13(4) HB&CTB(DA) Regs
CB/GA Reg 19(5) CB&GA(DA) Regs
Other benefits Reg 17(5) SS&CS(DA) Regs

93 Reg 11 TC(PC) Regs

94 **UC/PIP/JSA&ESA under UC** Reg 44(2)(b) and (c) UC,PIP,JSA&ESA(DA) Regs
HB Sch 7 para 13(2) CSPSSA 2000; reg 11(2)(b) HB&CTB(DA) Regs
CB/GA Reg 18(3) CB&GA(DA) Regs
WTC/CTC Reg 11 TC(PC) Regs
Other benefits s21(2)(c) and (d) SSA 1998; reg 16(3)(b) SS&CS(DA) Regs

95 TCM 0014360, Step 1

96 **UC/PIP/JSA&ESA under UC** Reg 44(5) UC,PIP,JSA&ESA(DA) Regs
HB Reg 11(3) HB&CTB(DA) Regs
CB/GA Reg 18(4) and (5) CB&GA(DA) Regs
Other benefits Reg 16(4) SS&CS(DA) Regs

97 **UC/PIP/JSA&ESA under UC** Reg 46(b) and (c) UC,PIP,JSA&ESA(DA) Regs
HB Reg 12(1)(b) HB&CTB(DA) Regs
CB/GA Reg 21 CB&GA(DA) Regs
Other benefits Reg 20(2) and (3) SS&CS(DA) Regs

98 DWP, *Suspension and Termination Guide*, paras 2050-52 and 2354

99 *The Queen v Secretary of State for Transport ex parte Factortame and Others*, C-213/89 [1990], para 23; *Unibet (London) Ltd and Unibet (International) Ltd v Justitiekanslern*, C-432/05 [2007], especially para 77; see also obiter (not binding) comments in *R (Sanneh) v SSWP and HMRC* [2013] EWHC 793 (Admin), paras 104-14

Chapter 19

National insurance numbers

This chapter covers:

This chapter covers the rules on the national insurance number requirement for benefits and tax credits and the issues that arise in satisfying them, particularly if you or a member of your family are not British.

1. The national insurance number requirement

In general, to be entitled to any social security benefit or tax credit (or, in England and Wales, council tax reduction – see p623), you must satisfy the national insurance (NI) number requirement.[1] You and any partner included in your claim must:

- provide an NI number, together with evidence to show that it is the one allocated to you; *or*
- provide evidence or information to enable your NI number to be traced; *or*
- make an application for an NI number, accompanied by sufficient information or evidence for one to be allocated. **Note:** there is no requirement for an NI number to have been allocated to you before you make a claim (see p488).

Certain groups of people are exempt from the requirement (see p483).

There are no specific NI number requirements when claiming any Scottish benefits.

Note: in addition to satisfying the NI number requirement, in most cases you must also make a valid claim and prove your identity. For general information on these requirements, see p494. For detailed information on the requirements for each benefit and tax credit, see CPAG's *Welfare Benefits and Tax Credits Handbook*.

When the requirement applies

You must satisfy the NI number requirement to be *entitled* to benefit. You should not be prevented from making a *claim* for benefit because you do not yet satisfy the NI number requirement (see p488), but you may need to apply for an NI number (see p485) or show you are exempt (see below) before you can be *entitled* to and *paid* the benefit. The NI number requirement also applies when someone who will be included in your *existing* award of benefit joins your family – eg, if your partner joins you from abroad. Your benefit award must be 'superseded' and, if your partner does not satisfy the NI number requirement, your award ceases.[2]

If you have been getting universal credit (UC) as a single person and you become part of a couple, your award as a single person should end and you must reclaim UC as a couple and both satisfy the NI number requirement. The requirement applies to you, and also to your partner if you are claiming means-tested benefits or tax credits as a couple. That is the case even if, for income support (IS), income-based jobseeker's allowance (JSA) or income-related employment and support allowance (ESA), you are not going to receive any extra benefit for them because they are a 'person subject to immigration control' for benefit purposes.[3]

However, if you are claiming UC and your partner either is defined as a person subject to immigration control (and not in an exempt group) or fails the habitual residence test (see p155), you are awarded UC as a single person and, consequently, your partner does not need to satisfy the NI number requirement.[4] (**Note:** your partner's presence may still affect your UC entitlement.)

If you are claiming pension credit (PC) and your partner is a person subject to immigration control, they are treated as not being part of your household and so do not need to satisfy the NI number requirement. If your partner fails the habitual residence test, they are still included in your claim, you are paid PC as a couple and they must satisfy the NI number requirement.

For the definition of 'person subject to immigration control', see p93, and for more information about your entitlement if your partner is a person subject to immigration control, see p119 for means-tested benefits and p123 for tax credits.

Who is exempt

You do not need to satisfy the NI number requirement:

- if you are under 16 and you are claiming disability living allowance;[5]
- for statutory sick pay, statutory maternity pay, statutory paternity pay, statutory shared parental pay, statutory adoption pay or a social fund payment;[6]
- for housing benefit (HB) if you live in a hostel;[7]
- for tax credits if you have a 'reasonable excuse' for failing to satisfy the requirement (see p484).[8]

If a child or qualifying young person is included in your claim for benefit, they do not need to satisfy the NI number requirement.[9]

If you are the benefit claimant and your partner is included in your claim, your partner does not have to satisfy the NI number requirement if:[10]

- they are a 'person subject to immigration control' because they require leave to enter or remain in the UK, but do not have that leave (see p98); *and*
- they have not previously been given an NI number; *and*
- you are claiming IS, income-based JSA, income-related ESA or PC and your partner is not entitled to that benefit themself, or you are claiming HB and your partner fails the habitual residence test (see p155). In practice, that will always be satisfied if your partner satisfies the first bullet point since they do not have a right to reside.

You may still be asked for information about an NI number application for your partner, even though they are exempt. An NI number will be refused, but that does not prevent you from being entitled to benefits or tax credits or council tax reduction.[11]

Note:

- The above exemption for partners does not apply to UC. If your partner is defined as a person subject to immigration control (and is not exempt), you are awarded UC as a single person and therefore your partner is not required to have an NI number.[12]
- The above exemptions for partners and for a child or qualifying young person included in your claim also apply to your application for council tax reduction in England or Wales (see p627).[13]
- The above exemptions for children, qualifying young people and partners do not apply to the claimant. For example, if you are a child claiming HB, you are not exempt from the NI number requirement, even though a child included in the claim is exempt.[14]
- There is no specific NI number requirement when claiming Scottish benefits.

Tax credits

The NI number requirement for tax credits is as described above, including the exemption for partners who require but do not have leave to enter or remain in the UK. If you live with your partner, you must make a joint claim for tax credits and both of you must satisfy the NI number requirement unless one of you is exempt because you require but do not have leave. **Note:** in nearly all circumstances, you cannot make a new claim for tax credits (including if you have to make a new claim because your partner either joins or leaves you), but must claim either UC or PC instead. See CPAG's *Welfare Benefits and Tax Credits Handbook* for more information.

The NI number requirement does not apply if the Tax Credit Office is satisfied that you (and/or your partner if it is a joint claim) have a 'reasonable excuse' for not complying with that requirement.[15] A reasonable excuse is not defined; whether or not the Tax Credit Office is satisfied that you have one is a matter of discretion. Guidance to decision makers stresses that their discretionary decision must be reasonable, which includes being fair and taking all relevant considerations, including available evidence, into account.[16] A reasonable excuse could include if you are unable to prove your identity because the Home Office has all your documents and you can show this – eg, with a letter from your solicitor.

If the decision maker decides that you have not made a valid claim because you have not satisfied the NI number requirement and you believe you had a reasonable excuse for not doing so, you can appeal against that decision.[17] You must request a mandatory reconsideration of the decision first (see p490).

2. Obtaining a national insurance number

The DWP allocates national insurance (NI) numbers.

NI numbers are allocated automatically to children shortly before their 16th birthday, provided child benefit is being claimed for them. If you are under 20, you were in the UK when you turned 16 and you did not receive an NI number, you can telephone HM Revenue and Customs (HMRC) on 0300 200 3500.

If you have been allocated an NI number but do not know it or if you want written confirmation of your NI number, contact HMRC (see gov.uk/lost-national-insurance-number). If you attend your Jobcentre Plus office with evidence of your identity, a member of staff may be able to tell you your NI number.

If you do not have an NI number, see below.

DWP guidance on tracing or allocating an NI number is available online. As the procedures are often misunderstood and/or not followed, it can be helpful to refer to this. The guidance is split into documents covering specific groups or circumstances, and stages of the procedures. All these are available at gov.uk/government/publications/national-insurance-number-allocations-staff-guide.

NI number applications may be completed as part of the process of applying for immigration leave and/or a biometric immigration document. **Note:** guidance for immigration officers covering the procedures for completing an NI number application during an asylum interview, forwarding the application to the DWP if leave is granted, and notifying you of the NI number if one is allocated was withdrawn on 10 August 2018.[18] DWP guidance covers the procedures for tracing or allocating an NI number at the request of the Home Office to enable it to be included in the biometric immigration document.[19] These procedures are not always followed and do not always result in an NI number being allocated.

If an NI number has been allocated before a biometric immigration document is issued, the NI number may be included on this document.[20] If you have not been allocated an NI number as part of the process of your immigration application, you should apply in the usual way (see below).

Guidance to claimants who have been granted leave following an asylum application confirms that if an NI number has been allocated to you, written notification should have been sent to you. It also confirms that if you do not have an NI number, you should not delay making your benefit claim as you do not need an NI number to *claim* benefits, and an NI number application will be made as part of your claim for benefits.[21]

Applying for a national insurance number

You do not need to have an NI number before you make your benefit or tax credit claim. If you have not yet been allocated an NI number, you can apply for one by telephoning the NI number application line on 0800 141 2079 or by contacting your local Jobcentre Plus office. If you need an NI number because you are starting work, you can apply online at gov.uk/apply-national-insurance-number/how-to-apply.

Problems applying for an NI number

Some claimants may experience problems when trying to apply for an NI number. If you are affected by these problems, especially if it means that you cannot be paid your benefit, get advice and also see CPAG's Judicial Review Project webpages (cpag.org.uk/welfare-rights/judicial-review/judicial-review-pre-action-letters/national-insurance-numbers) for template letters and guidance about getting paid your benefit while waiting for an NI number to be allocated.

There are a number of other reasons why you may need an NI number, including for a student loan and to open an individual savings account (ISA).[22]

If you claim a benefit or tax credit, or you apply for a supersession of an award of benefit (eg, to include your partner) and you (or they) do not have an NI number, the benefit authority should complete Form DCI1 at the same time and send it to the NI number centre.[23] This counts as your having made an application for an NI number. It is advisable to state clearly on the form or letter that you do not have an NI number and you wish to apply for one.

Note: if your partner is a 'person subject to immigration control' because they have leave which is subject to a 'no recourse to public funds' condition and they are included in your claim, they can be allocated an NI number even if you do not receive an increased amount of benefit for them.[24]

When the NI number centre receives Form DCI1, it carries out checks to ensure that you do not already have an NI number. It should then contact you to arrange an interview at your local DWP office if this is required (usually the case for European Economic Area (EEA) nationals). Otherwise, the application can be processed without the need for an interview (often the case for non-EEA nationals who have leave to enter or remain in the UK, or if you or your partner included in your claim are living outside the UK). DWP guidance states that whether or not you have a right to work in the UK is 'not a consideration' when this interview is carried out for the purpose of claiming benefit.[25]

The interview is sometimes referred to as an 'evidence of identity interview' and you should be told which documents to take with you. It is important to take as many as possible that establish your identity.

DWP guidance on applying for an NI number lists the following examples of documents that prove your identity, often referred to as 'primary evidence documents':[26]

- a current passport or identity card;
- a biometric residence permit;
- Home Office documents;
- a full UK or Irish birth or adoption certificate;
- a certificate of naturalisation;
- a registration certificate or residence card;
- a travel document issued by the Home Office.

If you have any of the above, take them to your interview. If not, take any documents you have that could help prove your identity (often referred to as 'secondary evidence documents'). These could include:[27]

- a Home Office 'cessation letter' confirming the end of your asylum support (NASS35);
- a current travel document issued by any national government;
- a residence document issued to EEA nationals (see p504);
- a standard acknowledgement letter (SAL) issued by the Home Office;
- an application registration card (ARC) issued by the Home Office to an asylum seeker;
- a police registration certificate;
- a full or provisional driving licence;
- a marriage certificate;
- a local authority rent book or card;
- council tax documents;
- letters from social services;
- mortgage repayment documents;
- utility bills in your name;
- NHS medical card;
- divorce or annulment papers;
- a wage slip from a recent employer;
- a letter from an employer or contract of employment;
- a student identity card.

If you have other documents that are not in the above list, these may also help. Photocopies of documents can be relied on to establish your identity, but you should take the originals if you have them. If not, explain why you do not have them. For example, if some of your documents are with the Home Office, explain and, if possible, provide proof in the form of a solicitor's letter or some other evidence. The DWP should not ask you to provide documents which you obviously do not have.[28]

If you are unable to provide any documentary evidence of your identity (eg, because you are homeless or fleeing domestic violence), a decision should be made on the information that you are able to provide.

At the interview, you are asked to complete Form CA5400. The DWP may also ask you to complete a form allowing it to contact third parties to establish your identity.

An NI number might be refused for various reasons – eg, if you:

- have been unable to prove your identity or the documents you provided are not considered genuine; *or*
- have failed to provide sufficient information; *or*
- failed to attend an evidence of identity interview (you should be given two opportunities to attend[29]) or respond to correspondence.

If your application for an NI number is refused, the reason should be recorded and notified to you.

You cannot appeal directly against a decision not to allocate you an NI number.[30] However, you can appeal against a decision to refuse you benefit because the NI number requirement is not met (see p490).

3. Common problems

Migrants often have problems with the national insurance (NI) number requirement because, unlike most British citizens, they are not issued with an NI number when they turn 16. The three most common problems are:

- being told you cannot apply for benefit unless you have an NI number (see below);
- delays in benefit payment because of the NI number requirement (see p489);
- being refused benefit on the grounds that the NI number requirement is not met (see p490).

Making a claim

If you (or your partner if they are included in your claim) do not have an NI number, you may be told by DWP, HM Revenue and Customs or the local authority that you cannot claim a benefit or tax credit. Similarly, except for universal credit (UC), you may find it impossible to claim online if you cannot provide an NI number.

You do not need to have an NI number in order to *claim* a benefit or tax credit. You should not be prevented from making a claim and your claim should be treated as the first stage in your NI number application (see p486).[31]

You are not required to provide an NI number as part of your online claim for UC. On receiving your claim, the DWP usually tells you to make an appointment at your local job centre to provide proof of your identity and other information to support your claim.

For all other benefits, if you are unable to make your claim online because you do not have an NI number, you should be able to claim by telephone or on a paper claim form.

Have you been told you cannot apply for benefit because you do not have a national insurance number?

If you were prevented from making a claim and lost benefit entitlement because you did not have an NI number, you may be able to get a new claim backdated. If the rules for the benefit or tax credit you are claiming do not allow backdating at all, or for the full period, or if the arrears do not cover the full amount lost, consider requesting compensation. For the rules on backdating and further information on obtaining compensation, see CPAG's *Welfare Benefits and Tax Credits Handbook*. For official guidance and template letters, see cpag.org.uk/welfare-rights/judicial-review/judicial-review-pre-action-letters/national-insurance-numbers.

Delays

Payment of benefit or tax credits can often be delayed because you (or your partner) need to satisfy the NI number requirement or you are waiting for an NI number to be allocated. You can satisfy the NI number requirement by applying for an NI number and providing sufficient information or evidence for one to be allocated (see p482).[32]

Is your benefit delayed?

1. Check whether you or your partner are exempt from the requirement to have an NI number (see p483).
2. If you or your partner have applied for an NI number, but there is a delay in one being allocated, ask that your claim be determined, as there is no requirement for an NI number to be allocated (see p482). It is likely that your claim will have to be processed clerically before the NI number has been allocated, but that should not prevent payment. At the time of writing, a CPAG test case regarding refusal to pay benefit before an NI number is allocated was unsuccessful at the Upper Tribunal and CPAG has applied for permission to appeal to the Court of Appeal. However, the decision did make clear that where a claimant

does not yet have an NI number, DWP policy is that an application should be taken at the same time as a new claim and that the NI number requirement is satisfied once any necessary information or evidence has been verified.[33] Check the current test cases page[34] on the CPAG website for more details, advice and updates.

3. If it is a new claim for benefit, or you are adding a partner to your claim that will result in your award increasing, you may be able to obtain an advance payment (see p459). That can be paid if you do not yet have an NI number, provided you meet the usual conditions, including that the decision maker considers it likely you will be entitled to the benefit.[35] The guidance on short-term advances states they should be considered if you do not have an NI number, provided you can prove your identity and are complying with other requests for evidence. This guidance also states that the DWP should ensure that all action needed to allocate an NI number is taken promptly.[36] While this guidance only applies to the benefits that UC is replacing, the same principles should apply to UC advances, so applying for an advance payment may be a way of getting your NI number allocated more quickly. However, see also the CPAG test case referred to above.

4. If you have made a new claim for child benefit and/or guardian's allowance, you may be able to obtain an interim payment (see p463).

5. If you have made a new claim for housing benefit (HB), you may be able to obtain a 'payment on account' (see p464).

6. If you are adding your partner to your existing award and they do not have an NI number, your benefit may be suspended (see p475). You may be able to argue that payment should not be suspended if it is clear that the NI number requirement is likely to be met and the only factor is a question of time.

For further information on your options if your benefit or tax credit payments are delayed, see Chapter 18.

Benefit is refused

You cannot appeal against a decision not to allocate you an NI number.[37] However, if you are refused benefit or tax credits (or are refused an increase when your partner joins your household) because you (or they) do not satisfy the NI number requirement, you can ask for a mandatory reconsideration of that decision and then appeal if the decision is not changed. For HB, you can appeal directly or ask for a revision and then appeal if the decision is not changed. In your mandatory reconsideration, revision or appeal, you can argue that the NI number requirement was met.[38] DWP guidance confirms that if an NI number is provided after a decision to disallow your benefit, a reconsideration may be appropriate.[39]

Usually, if benefit is refused because the benefit authority says the NI number requirement is not met, the issue in dispute is whether your application was accompanied by sufficient information or evidence to enable a number to be allocated, even if the benefit authority has not identified the issue as such.[40]

Even if you have been refused an NI number, it may be possible to argue successfully that you still satisfy the NI number requirement if your application was accompanied by sufficient information or evidence to enable a number to be allocated.

The decision maker should accept that you satisfy the NI number requirement for your benefit claim if you applied for an NI number because you are employed or self-employed in Great Britain and you provided:[41]

- a birth or adoption certificate issued in the common travel area (the UK, Ireland, Channel Islands and the Isle of Man); *or*
- an immigration status document or letter issued by the Home Office indicating that you are allowed to be in the UK without a time limit, or that you are allowed to do that employment or self-employment.

Note: it is only a requirement to provide one of these documents if you apply for an NI number because you are employed or self-employed (or you wish to pay class 3 contributions). If you are applying for an NI number to claim benefits, you can provide other documents that prove your identity and you do not need to show you have the right to work (see p486).

If you have been refused an NI number after failing to attend an interview, the reasons why you failed to attend are relevant, so refer to them in any challenge if you are refused benefit as a result.[42]

Have you been refused tax credits?

If the decision maker decides you have not made a valid claim for tax credits because you or your partner do not satisfy the NI number requirement, you can challenge this decision. The Upper Tribunal has held that you have a right of appeal if the basis of your appeal is that your partner is exempt from the NI number requirement because they require but do not have leave to enter or remain in the UK (see p483).[43] In a subsequent case, the Upper Tribunal went further and held that there is also a right of appeal if you or your partner had a reasonable excuse for not satisfying the NI number requirement (see p484).[44] You must request a mandatory reconsideration before you can appeal.

Other remedies

If you are refused an NI number, you can write to your MP and ask them to help. Your MP can also complain to the Parliamentary and Health Service Ombudsman on your behalf. See CPAG's *Welfare Benefits and Tax Credits Handbook* for more information.

Problems with NI numbers also raise issues about race discrimination since, in practice, the NI number requirement often prejudices Black, Asian and minority ethnic groups. You may therefore want to refer to the DWP's Equality and Diversity statement when you contact it.[45] The Equality Advisory and Support Service may be able to advise or, in certain cases, take up the issue (see Appendix 2).

Notes

1. **The national insurance number requirement**

1 **TC** Reg 5(4) TC(CN) Regs
CB/GA s13(1A) and (1B) SSAA 1992
Other benefits s1(1A) and (1B) SSAA 1992

2 s1(1A) and (1B) SSAA 1992; reg 5(4) TC(CN) Regs; *Leicester City Council v OA* [2009] UKUT 74 (AAC), paras 27 and 28; Vol 1 Ch 2 para 02182 DMG; para A2152 ADM

3 *SSWP v Wilson* [2006] EWCA Civ 882, reported as R(H) 7/06

4 Confirmed in para A2155 ADM

5 Reg 1A SS(DLA) Regs

6 s1(4) SSAA 1992 and s122 SSCBA 1992

7 Reg 4(a) HB Regs; reg 4(a) HB(SPC) Regs

8 Reg 5(6) TC(CN) Regs

9 **UC** Reg 5 UC,PIP,JSA&ESA(C&P) Regs
IS Reg 2A(a) IS Regs continues to apply in these cases due to the transitional protection in reg 1(3) SS(WTCCTC)(CA) Regs
JSA Reg 2A(a) JSA Regs continues to apply in these cases due to the transitional protection in reg 1(7) SS(WTCCTC)(CA) Regs
HB Reg 4(b) HB Regs; reg 4(b) HB(SPC) Regs

10 **IS** Reg 2A IS Regs
JSA Reg 2A JSA Regs
ESA Reg 2A ESA Regs
PC Reg 1A SPC Regs
HB Reg 4(c) HB Regs; reg 4(c) HB(SPC) Regs
TC Reg 5(8) TC(CN) Regs
Bereavement benefits and retirement pensions Reg 1A(c) SS(WB&RP) Regs

11 Vol 1 paras 02184-86 DMG; para A2154 ADM; TCTM para 06110

12 Confirmed in paras A2154-5 ADM

13 **E** Sch 8 para 7(3) CTRS(PR)E Regs
W Sch para 111(3) CTRS(DS)W Regs; Sch 13 para 5(3) CTRSPR(W) Regs

14 *Westminster City Council v AT & SSWP (HB)* [2013] UKUT 321 (AAC)

15 Reg 5(6) TC(CN) Regs

16 TCTM para 06110

17 *CI v HMRC(TC)* [2014] UKUT 158 (AAC)

2. **Obtaining a national insurance number**

18 Home Office guidance, *Procedures for Issuing a NINO to Asylum Claimants Granted Leave to Enter or Remain in the UK*, available at gov.uk

19 gov.uk/government/publications/national-insurance-number-allocations-staff-guide

20 Reg 15 The Immigration (Biometric Registration) Regulations 2008 No.3048, as amended by reg 13 The Immigration (Biometric Registration) (Amendment) Regulations 2015 No.433

21 gov.uk/government/publications/claiming-universal-credit-and-other-benefits-if-you-are-a-refugee and DWP, *LA Welfare Direct 3/2020*, available at gov.uk

22 gov.uk/national-insurance/your-national-insurance-number; DWP guidance, *National Insurance Number Instructions for Staff: introduction to national insurance number allocation*, para 13

23 CH/4085/2007; *R (Bui) v Secretary of State for Work and Pensions; R (Onakoya) v Secretary of State for Work and Pensions* [2022] UKUT 189 (AAC); HB/CTB Circular A13/2010, paras 14 and 15; TCM 0066140 and 0316020; DWP guidance, *National Insurance Number Instructions for Staff: benefit inspired evidence of identity (DCI1 process)*, *National Insurance Number Instructions for Staff: contact centre appointment booking process*, para 92, and *National Insurance Number Instructions for Staff: completing the eDCI1 form*, all available at gov.uk

24 DWP guidance, *National Insurance Number Instructions for Staff: completing the eDCI1 form*, para 43, scenario 1

25 DWP guidance, *National Insurance Number Instructions for Staff: benefit inspired evidence of identity (DCI1 process)*, para 23

26 DWP guidance, *National Insurance Number Instructions for Staff: documentary evidence and checks*, para 7

27 DWP guidance, *National Insurance Number Instructions for Staff:documentary evidence and checks*, para 12
28 DWP guidance, *National Insurance Number Instructions for Staff: documentary evidence and checks*, paras 101 and 102
29 DWP guidance, *National Insurance Number Instructions for Staff:benefit inspired evidence of identity (DCI1 process)*, para 19
30 CH/4085/2007, paras 19-22; *Leicester City Council v OA* [2009] UKUT 74 (AAC), para 33; *OM v HMRC* [2018] UKUT 50 (AAC), para 35; reg 9 and Sch 1 The Social Security (Crediting and Treatment of Contributions, and National Insurance Numbers) Regulations 2001 No.769

3. **Common problems**

31 CH/4085/2007; TCM 0066140 and 0316020; DWP guidance, *National Insurance Number Instructions for Staff: benefit inspired evidence of identity (DCI1 process),National Insurance Number Instructions for Staff: contact centre appointment booking process*, para 92, and *National Insurance Number Instructions for Staff: completing the eDCI1 form*; gov.uk/government/publications/claiming-universal-credit-and-other-benefits-if-you-are-a-refugee, para 8; DWP, LA Welfare Direct 3/2020, available at gov.uk
32 See for example, *OM v HMRC* [2018] UKUT 50 (AAC)
33 *R (Bui) v Secretary of State for Work and Pensions; R (Onakoya) v Secretary of State for Work and Pensions* [2022] UKUT 189 (AAC)
34 Available at cpag.org.uk/welfare-rights/test-cases/current
35 Reg 5 SS(PAB) Regs
36 DWP guidance, *Short Term Benefit Advances: benefit centres*, paras 66-67, available at whatdotheyknow.com/request/operational_guidance_for_benefit
37 CH/4085/2007, paras 19-22; *Leicester City Council v OA* [2009] UKUT 74 (AAC), para 33; *OM v HMRC* [2018] UKUT 50 (AAC), para 35
38 CH/1231/2004; CH/4085/2007; *Leicester City Council v OA* [2009] UKUT 74 (AAC)
39 para A2151 ADM
40 CH/1231/2004
41 *OM v HMRC* [2018] UKUT 50 (AAC); reg 9 and Sch 1 The Social Security (Crediting and Treatment of Contributions, and National Insurance Numbers) Regulations 2001 No.769
42 CH/4085/2007, in particular paras 30-36; but see also *Leicester CC v OA* [2009] UKUT 74 (AAC), para 35, which held that you must have attended the interview, and *OM v HMRC* [2018] UKUT 50 (AAC), paras 36-38 on changes in the regulations that mean the position is different if you required an NI number to work
43 *ZM and AB v HMRC(TC)* [2013] UKUT 547 (AAC)
44 *CI v HMRC(TC)* [2014] UKUT 158 (AAC)
45 gov.uk/government/organisations/department-for-work-pensions/about/equality-and-diversity; but see also *R (Bui) v Secretary of State for Work and Pensions* paras 64-70; *R (Onakoya) v Secretary of State for Work and Pensions* [2022] UKUT 189 (AAC)

Chapter 20

Providing evidence

This chapter covers:

This chapter covers some of the issues that arise when you are required to provide evidence to show that you satisfy the immigration conditions (see Part 3), the residence conditions (see Part 4) or that you are covered by the European Union co-ordination rules (see Chapter 16).

1. General points about evidence

Evidence required when you make your claim

To be entitled to a benefit or tax credit, you must normally:

- satisfy the national insurance (NI) number requirement (see Chapter 19); *and*
- provide proof of your identity, if required (see below); *and*
- ensure your claim is valid (see p495).

To decide your claim, the decision maker may also need evidence that you satisfy all the conditions of entitlement (see p496) and that you are not covered by any of the exceptions that mean you are not entitled (see p496). You are usually asked for evidence to show that you satisfy all the conditions of entitlement, including the immigration, residence or presence conditions, or that the European Union (EU) co-ordination rules apply to you (see p379).

Proving your identity

You may be asked to produce documents, or other evidence, that prove your identity. If your partner is included in your claim, even if you do not receive an amount for them (eg, because they are a 'person subject to immigration control' – see p119), you may also be asked to prove their identity. In addition, if your claim includes an amount for your child, you may be asked to prove their identity.

There are various documents that you can provide to the benefit authorities as proof of your identity. DWP guidance on applying for an NI number has a list of documents that prove your identity, and you should provide one of these if possible (see p487). You should not be asked to supply any document that is unreasonable for you to have or obtain, and you should not be refused a benefit or tax credit simply because you can not provide a particular document. Be prepared to ask for an explanation of what is required and why, and challenge any unreasonable requests as well as a decision refusing your benefit. It can be helpful to provide details of anyone who can confirm what you have stated – eg, your solicitor or other legal representative or official organisation.

Note: if you are claiming universal credit (UC), you may be asked to prove your identity online using the Verify system. This uses various private companies to check your identity. If you cannot prove your identity online, you must do so at the job centre. If possible, take one of the 'primary evidence documents' and two of the 'secondary evidence documents' on p487 with you. If you do not have sufficient documentary evidence, you are asked a series of security questions. If you fail to answer the security questions correctly, the DWP can approach a third party, with your consent, to validate your identity.[1]

Making a valid claim

To be entitled to a benefit or tax credit, you must make a valid claim. You must claim in the correct way and your claim must not be 'defective'. The relevant benefit authority should inform you if your claim is defective and must give you the opportunity to correct the defect.

What counts as a valid claim varies between individual benefits and tax credits. How to make a claim in the correct way is also affected by the method by which you can make your claim – ie, in writing, only on a certain form, online and/or by telephone. You may also have to attend an interview to complete your claim, or be sent a written statement to sign and return. The rules for each benefit and tax credit are covered in CPAG's *Welfare Benefits and Tax Credits Handbook*.

If your claim is refused because it is not valid, you can challenge that decision.

Note: your right to challenge a decision that your claim for tax credits is not valid is based on caselaw, rather than legislation.[2]

In all cases, if you challenge a decision that your claim is not valid, you should also make a fresh claim.

If your claim is accepted as valid, the decision maker must make a decision on your entitlement and you may still be required to provide additional documentation and evidence. If you fail to do so within the time allowed (this can be extended if it is reasonable), the decision maker may conclude that you are not entitled (but see below).

Evidence that you are entitled

When you claim a benefit or tax credit, you must generally show, on the balance of probabilities, that you meet the conditions of entitlement.[3] That is confirmed in DWP guidance as a general principle[4] and also in specific cases. For example, guidance (now withdrawn) on means-tested benefits for Commonwealth citizens who are long-term residents of the UK (sometimes referred to as the 'Windrush generation' – see p82), but who lack documentary evidence of their immigration status, confirms that their entitlement can be accepted if the evidence indicates on the balance of probabilities that they are likely to have legal and habitual residence.

If you do not meet the conditions of entitlement under the UK rules but you do under the EU co-ordination rules (see p379), you must provide evidence of this.

If a decision maker asks for information or evidence that, despite your best efforts, you fail to provide, they can assume that you do not meet that particular condition of entitlement. However, they cannot do that if they fail to ask the relevant questions and do not give you a reasonable opportunity to provide the necessary information and evidence.[5] The decision maker knows what information and evidence is needed to decide whether you satisfy the conditions of entitlement and must ask you for it. They should also take into account alternative likely explanations for why you have not provided the information or evidence before concluding that you are not entitled.[6]

You should always submit any documentary evidence you have showing that you meet the entitlement conditions. However, if you cannot do so, your own verbal or written evidence, whether given in the process of making your claim or subsequently, can be accepted without being corroborated.

Corroborative evidence is not necessary unless there are reasons to doubt your evidence – eg, if it is self-contradictory or inherently improbable.[7]

If you are asked for a particular document that you do not have, ask why it is needed so that you have the opportunity to provide alternatives. If you cannot provide any documentary proof of a particular fact, explain why not (eg, because all your documents are with the Home Office) and, if possible, provide proof of this – eg, a letter from your legal representative. If you consider any requests for information are unreasonable, you can complain. Get advice if you think you have experienced discrimination – eg, from the Equality Advisory and Support Service (see Appendix 2).

Evidence that you are not excluded

If there is an exception to entitlement that excludes you from a benefit or a tax credit to which you would otherwise be entitled (eg, because you are not habitually resident or because you are defined as a 'person subject to immigration control'), the burden of proving that this applies to you lies with the relevant benefit authority.[8] However, you should always submit any evidence you have that an exception does not apply to your situation.

If you do not provide evidence that you are not excluded from entitlement when you make your claim, the decision maker must ask you for the information and evidence required for them to make a decision. The decision maker knows what information is required to determine whether you are entitled to benefit or excluded, and they must therefore ask for that information.[9]

If some relevant facts are still unknown after all the enquiries have been made, the question of whether an exception applies that excludes you from entitlement should be decided in your favour.[10]

If the decision maker failed to ask all the relevant questions and you appeal, the First-tier Tribunal must ask you those questions.[11] If you have evidence that an exception does not apply to you, submit this in advance of the hearing if possible.

If you cannot provide the evidence required to determine whether or not you are excluded, but that evidence is available to the benefit authorities, see p499.

Decisions to end your entitlement

If you are receiving benefits or tax credits and your award is terminated on the basis that you no longer satisfy the immigration, residence or presence rules, the burden of proof is on the benefit authority to show the evidence on which this decision is based. If the decision maker has not shown this evidence and based their decision on the fact that you failed to provide evidence that nothing has changed, you should challenge the decision, pointing out that the burden of proof lies with the benefit authority. Set out clearly the reasons why you continue not to be excluded from entitlement.

The same burden of proof applies to the First-tier Tribunal.

There are a number of Upper Tribunal decisions concerning tax credits that confirm that the burden of proof is on HM Revenue and Customs (HMRC) to establish that there are grounds for revising a decision that you are entitled to tax credits, and that the same burden of proof applies to the First-tier Tribunal. That applies if HMRC wants to revise an entitlement decision for the current year[12] or previous year for which the award has already been finalised.[13] However, if HMRC decides that you have ceased to be entitled during the tax credit renewal period, the onus of proof is on you to show your continued entitlement.[14]

Example

Nardos is an Eritrean national with discretionary leave to remain in the UK for two and a half years and no restriction on receiving public funds. She claimed child benefit, provided proof of her leave and the benefit was awarded. Her leave was due to expire two months ago. Before the expiration date, Nardos applied for a further period of discretionary leave. She received an acknowledgement letter from the Home Office and forwarded a copy of this to the Child Benefit Office, but has not yet had a decision from the Home Office. Her leave to remain is extended while she waits for the decision on her application for further leave (see p502).

The Child Benefit Office wrote to Nardos asking her for evidence that she was entitled to receive public funds, both now and since the start of her claim. Nardos did not know how she could show this and so did not reply. She then received a decision letter, informing her that, as she has not shown she can receive public funds, HMRC has decided she is a 'person subject to immigration control' (see p93) and not entitled to child benefit. Her award was terminated and HMRC decided to recover the overpaid child benefit since the start of her claim.

Nardos can challenge this decision by requesting a mandatory reconsideration. HMRC has not provided any evidence to show that her entitlement has ended nor that the original decision awarding her child benefit was incorrect. The evidence that she had already given HMRC shows that she has leave to remain with no restriction on receiving public funds. She does not need to provide any further evidence that she is not excluded by her immigration status because it has not changed. She should explain this in her mandatory reconsideration request and remind HMRC that the Upper Tribunal has confirmed that the onus of proof is on the HMRC to show the evidence relied on in its decision.

For information on when a decision to award you benefits or tax credits can be revised or superseded, see CPAG's *Welfare Benefits and Tax Credits Handbook*.

If you make another benefit claim

If you make another benefit claim, either for a different benefit or for the same benefit at a later date, a previous decision about whether you satisfied the immigration status, residence or presence requirements, or whether the EU co-ordination rules applied to you, is not conclusive.[15] However, it is a factor that should be taken into account.

There are limited exceptions to this, including if you claim housing benefit (HB) and the DWP has made a decision to award you income support (IS), income-related employment and support allowance or pension credit. In this case, you are exempt from the habitual residence test for the purpose of HB (see p159).

In practice, if you have had a successful previous benefit claim, mandatory reconsideration or appeal, it is helpful to tell the benefit authority or First-tier Tribunal. If you have a written decision, provide a copy, even if you think the decision maker already has access to this. If some time has passed since the earlier decision, explain why it is still relevant to your current situation.

Example

Carmen is a Spanish national and in 2017 claimed HB. Her claim was initially refused on the grounds that she did not satisfy the habitual residence test since she had no right to reside. Carmen was subsequently awarded HB after she requested a revision. The decision maker found that she had a right to reside as the primary carer of a child in education because her daughter was in school and her father (Carmen's ex-partner) had been a European Economic Area (EEA) worker when they all lived together in the UK. When they move to a new local authority area, Carmen is no longer entitled to HB and so she makes a new claim for UC. To show that she can still have a free movement right to reside and has a right to reside as a primary carer, she submits a copy of the HB revision decision to the UC decision maker, together with evidence that she now has pre-settled status and her daughter is still in school. Carmen should also check whether she can now apply for settled status (see p57).

If a decision on a previous claim was not favourable to you and you make a separate claim, or challenge a refusal of a separate claim, it may be helpful to remind the decision maker (or tribunal) that the earlier decision does not prevent them from making a different decision. Explain why the earlier decision was wrong or incomplete, note any challenge that you have submitted or intend to submit, and be clear whether there have been any relevant changes in your circumstances.

Note: if the DWP has supplied information, including evidence, which was used in connection with a DWP benefit claim to a local authority, it should be accepted without its accuracy being verified for the purpose of the HB claim. This does not apply if the information was supplied more than 12 months after being used or if there are reasonable grounds for believing it has changed. This also applies in reverse – ie, if the local authority supplied information to the DWP.[16] However, this does not prevent the decision maker from requesting additional information – eg, if the information supplied is insufficient to determine your entitlement.

If evidence is not available to you

If your potential exclusion from benefit entitlement depends on evidence that is not available to you, but which is available to the benefit authority, the benefit authority must take the necessary steps to obtain it. If it fails to do so and so it is not known whether or not you are excluded from benefit, the matter must be decided in your favour – ie, that you are not excluded.[17]

This principle was established by the House of Lords in the case of *Kerr*[18] and is significant for migrants. For example, if the decision maker needs evidence of your immigration status which the Home Office has but you do not, they must use their channels of communication with the Home Office to obtain it.[19]

The principle is also significant if your entitlement depends on someone else's circumstances and the relevant information about these is not available to you, but it could be available to the benefit authority if the decision maker made enquiries or checked records. For example, the decision maker may need evidence of your right to reside which depends on the current or past economic activity of a family member (see p240), but you cannot contact them or they will not provide you with the information you need.

If this applies to you, you should provide as much information as possible to the benefit authority to enable it to trace the evidence you cannot provide, but which could be available to the decision maker if they made enquiries or checked records.

Example

Kristina is a 19-year-old Slovakian national who came to the UK in October 2020 and has pre-settled status. She is due to give birth next week and wants the support of her father, Pavol, who has been in the UK for three years. However, Pavol disapproves of Kristina's pregnancy and has said that he never wants to hear from her again. Kristina is sleeping on a friend's sofa and has claimed UC. If Pavol has 'worker' status, Kristina, as his family member, is exempt from the habitual residence test for UC.

Kristina has her own birth certificate, which names Pavol as her father and confirms his nationality. However, she cannot get evidence of Pavol's worker status or that he has pre-settled status from him. Kristina has heard that Pavol was made redundant two months ago and is now claiming UC. Therefore, if she can provide sufficient information to the DWP for it to trace Pavol's UC claim, the DWP can obtain details of whether he has pre-settled status and so whether his previous work gave him worker status and he has retained that status while claiming UC. The DWP holds this information and, therefore, must take the necessary steps to enable it to be traced. If the DWP does not do so, Kristina can argue that she cannot be excluded from UC on the basis of not being habitually resident, because that has not been proven by the DWP.

How do you get the benefit authority to check someone's residence rights?

If your right to reside depends on someone else's residence rights, but you cannot obtain proof of these, ask the benefit authority to carry out the necessary investigations.

1. Although there is a duty on the benefit authority to take the necessary steps to trace information that is available to the authority and not you, it is unlikely to do so unless you clearly ask it to. Explain why you are unable to obtain the necessary information and remind the benefit authority of its duty to trace the information, citing the principles established in the *Kerr* case.[20]

2. Explain your right to reside, how this results from your relationship with the other person (eg, as their family member or primary carer of their child) and what information needs to be obtained – eg, evidence of current or past employment.

3. Provide as much information as possible on the relevant person's:
- name;
- date of birth;
- NI number;
- last known address;

– last known place of work;
– nationality;
– previous benefit claims.

4. The benefit authority must then take the necessary steps to trace the information, by checking records of any benefit claims or NI contributions. **Note:** guidance confirms that decision makers should use additional records available to them (eg, NI contribution records) to confirm whether a claimant has permanent residence.[21]

5. If the benefit authority fails to make the necessary investigations, you cannot be excluded from benefit on the basis of not having a right to reside, as the burden of proof is on the benefit authority to show that you do not have a right to reside (see p496).

6. If the benefit authority tells you it is prohibited from carrying out the investigations under data protection legislation, it is arguable that this is incorrect as there are exemptions in the Data Protection Act.[22] However, in any event, you should appeal if the benefit authority refuses to carry out the investigations and ask the First-tier Tribunal for a direction requiring the decision maker to carry out the necessary investigations. It can make such a direction once you have appealed.[23] The Data Protection Act permits disclosure of personal data if it is required by an order of a court or tribunal.[24] Asking for a direction before your appeal hearing avoids the need for the hearing to be adjourned. It can also mean that, once the necessary information has been traced, the decision refusing your claim is revised, you are awarded benefit and your appeal lapses.

7. In urgent cases, you can use judicial review if the benefit authority is not carrying out the required investigations. See the judicial review project pages on CPAG's website at cpag.org.uk/welfare-rights/judicial-review for template letters that can be adapted.

2. **Evidence of immigration status**

If you are claiming any of the benefits or tax credits listed on p111, the decision maker needs evidence of your immigration status to determine whether you are a 'person subject to immigration control' (see p93). If you are a European Economic Area (EEA) national, you may need to provide evidence that you have pre-settled or settled status under UK immigration law (see p55) rather than rights under European Union law to claim benefits or tax credits.

If you are claiming means-tested benefits or tax credits and your partner lives with you, the decision maker also needs evidence of their immigration status to determine whether they are a 'person subject to immigration control' (see p119).

It is rare for a decision maker to need evidence of your child's immigration status, as this does not affect whether or not you can be paid for them. However, if your child is the claimant (eg, for disability living allowance), evidence of their immigration status is required to determine whether they are a person subject to immigration control.

Note: if your partner or child has leave which is subject to a 'no recourse to public funds' condition, this may be breached if they are included in your (or someone else's) claim and could put at risk their immigration status (see p101).

Further information on checking your immigration status is in Chapter 6. If you are unclear about the status of anyone who may be included in your benefits or tax credits claim, get immigration advice (see Appendix 2) before claiming.

Problems with evidence

Problems can arise if you do not have documentary evidence or if the documents you have are unclear. The general points about evidence all apply (see p494). You should not be refused benefit because you cannot provide a particular document, and you should ask why a document is being requested so you can provide the evidence in a different way. If you cannot provide a document (eg, because it is with the Home Office), it can help if you provide a letter confirming this from your legal representative. They may also be able to confirm your current immigration status and the significance of any applications you have pending.

If evidence of immigration status is not available to you, but is available to the decision maker (eg, by emailing the Home Office), they must take the necessary steps to obtain this (see p499).

DWP guidance (now withdrawn) on means-tested benefits for Commonwealth citizens who are long-term residents of the UK (sometimes referred to as the 'Windrush generation' – see p82) but who lack documentary evidence of their immigration status refers the *decision maker* to the Home Office 'task force'. However, the guidance to housing benefit decision makers suggests that *claimants* be referred to the task force and that decision makers should only contact the Home Office directly if a claimant is experiencing unacceptable delays in resolving their their status. The guidance for other means-tested benefits confirms that your entitlement should be assessed if the evidence held by the DWP and Home Office indicates, on the balance of probabilities, that you have legal and habitual residence.[25]

Note: if you are unsure of or you do not have documents to prove your immigration status, get independent immigration advice (see Appendix 2) before either contacting the Home Office or making a claim for benefits.

Changes in immigration status

If you have time-limited leave to enter or remain, you can apply to extend your leave or apply for further leave to remain on a different basis. Provided you apply before your existing leave expires, this leave is extended until your application is decided by the Home Office.[26] If your original leave was *not* subject to a 'no recourse to public funds' condition, you were not a 'person subject to immigration control' and were therefore entitled to all benefits and tax credits, subject to the usual rules of entitlement. So while your leave is extended, you continue *not* to be a person subject to immigration control and your benefit entitlement remains the same. It is important to notify the benefit authorities, as otherwise they may assume your leave has expired and that you are no longer entitled to benefit (because you are now a person subject to immigration control on the basis of being someone who requires but does not have leave – see p93).

The benefit authorities need evidence that you applied to vary your leave before your existing leave ended. If possible, you should submit documents showing when your leave was due to expire, which the benefit authorities may already have on your file, together with confirmation of the date when your application to vary that leave was submitted – eg, a letter from a legal representative who helped you with the application, proof of date of posting and any letter confirming the date your application was received. In practice, it also helps if you submit a covering letter explaining that your previous leave is extended because you applied to vary your leave before your previous leave expired, you therefore continue not to be a person subject to immigration control, and so your benefit or tax credit entitlement also continues. Include the relevant legal references in your letter.

Note: if your application to vary your leave is refused and your leave is extended while your appeal against that refusal is pending, you *may* count as a person subject to immigration control (see p106).

3. Evidence of residence rights

In many circumstances, providing evidence of your residence rights requires you to provide evidence of your nationality and, if you are not a British or Irish citizen, evidence of your immigration status.

If you need to provide evidence that you have settled or pre-settled status (indefinite or limited leave granted under the European Union Settlement Scheme – EUSS), or that you have applied for such leave and that application (or an appeal or administrative review of a refusal) is still pending, see p186.

If you are claiming a benefit that requires a right to reside and you have pre-settled status or a pending EUSS application for settled or pre-settled status, you also need to provide evidence of your European free movement residence rights (see p192). This process can be complex and can involve several steps, each requiring certain conditions to be met. It is advisable to set out to the decision maker the basis of your free movement residence rights, as clearly as you can and, wherever possible, provide evidence of every requirement. If you do not have documentary evidence of one requirement but you have provided evidence of others, it is more likely that the decision maker will accept your uncorroborated evidence on the remaining one (see p496).

If you have pre-settled status, but no free movement rights (or only one which is excluded for the benefit you want to claim – eg, as a jobseeker when you are claiming UC), and if refusal of benefit would mean you are left without sufficient resources, it may be possible to argue this refusal would be unlawful. For details of the potential arguments, other exemptions and the steps to work through if you have pre-settled status, see p170 for means-tested benefits and p176 for child benefit and child tax credit.

For details of the protected groups that can have a free movement right to reside, including the duration of the protection, see p188.

Residence documents issued under the European Economic Area Regulations

Since 30 June 2021, you can only have any free movement right to reside under the European Economic Area (EEA) Regulations, if you either have pre-settled status or you have a pending EUSS application for settled or pre-settled status (or a pending appeal or administrative review of a refusal). For details of these protected groups and others that applied during the period 31 December 2020 to 30 June 2021, see p188.

The only circumstance when you need a residence document issued under the EEA Regulations to have a free movement right to reside is if you are an 'extended family member' (see p243). In this case, you must have an EEA family permit, registration certificate or residence card, which remains in force (see below for periods since 1 July 2021), to be *treated as* a 'family member' of someone who can confer a free movement right of residence on you (see p243).

For any other free movement right to reside, although you could, until the end of the transition period, apply for the residence documents issued under the EEA Regulations listed below, they are not necessary because your right to reside depends on the facts of your situation. If you do hold a residence document issued under the EEA Regulations, that can only confirm your residence rights; it cannot *give* you a right to reside if, for example, it was issued in error or if it correctly confirmed your right to reside when it was issued, but your circumstances have now changed so that you no longer have that right to reside.[27]

The deadline to apply for the following residence documents was the end of the transition period (11pm on 31 December 2020),[28] unless the exception for an EEA family permit applied to you, in which case the deadline to apply was 30 June 2021:

- **a registration certificate**, if you are an EEA national with a right of residence under the EEA Regulations;[29]
- **a residence card**, if you are a non-EEA national and you have a right to reside as the family member of an EEA national who either has a right to reside as a 'qualified person' (see p193) or has a permanent right of residence;[30]
- **a derivative residence card**, if you have a derivative right to reside (see p253);[31]
- **a document certifying a permanent right of residence**, if you are an EEA national with a permanent right of residence, or a **permanent residence card** if you are a non-EEA national with permanent residency;[32]

- **a residence document** issued, or treated as issued, under previous EEA Regulations. These are treated as issued under the current EEA Regulations;[33]
- **an EEA family permit** issued for entry to the UK if you are a family member of an EEA national with a free movement right of residence in the UK and either:[34]
  - you applied before the end of the transition period; *or*
  - you applied by 30 June 2021 and you were in a protected group that could continue to have a free movement right to reside at the time (for details of these protections, see p188). After 31 December 2020, you could only be issued with an EEA family permit as an 'extended family member' if you were the EEA national's partner in a durable relationship.

Note: although you can no longer apply for these residence documents, if you applied before the deadlines above any residence document you were then issued remains in force, provided the basis on which it was issued continues to apply. See below and get specialist advice if your entitlement is not accepted.

EEA Regulations residence documents since 1 July 2021

If you are an 'extended family member', to be treated as a 'family member' of someone who can confer a qualifying right to reside on you, you need to have been issued with one of the residence documents under the EEA Regulations listed above, and that document must remain in force (seep243). It is no longer possible to apply for these documents. If you have already been issued with one, note that, at the time of writing, UK legislation and policy did not appear to provide for it to 'remain in force' in all circumstances.

If you have pre-settled status, the UK government's stated policy is that you can continue to use a residence document issued under the EEA Regulations until it expires, including to help prove entitlement to 'certain benefits'.[35] This should also apply if you have a pending EUSS application for settled or pre-settled status (or a pending appeal or administrative review of a refusal).

If your residence document issued under the EEA Regulations has expired, at the time of writing the Home Office policy was not to issue further residence documents under the EEA Regulations but instead, if you are a non-EEA national, to issue an EUSS biometric residence card when you are granted pre-settled (or settled) status.[36] However, although this document evidences your status under the EUSS, it does *not* enable you to be treated as a family member under the EEA Regulations, because those regulations specify that you must have one of the residence documents issued under the EEA Regulations listed above.

In these and other circumstances, it may be arguable that your rights as an 'extended family member' are protected directly under the Withdrawal Agreement. Consequently, it may be arguable that you should be *treated as* a family member for the purpose of accessing benefits, if, for example, your residence document issued under the EEA Regulations expired, but you cannot obtain a replacement because there is no longer an application process, or if you obtained an EUSS family permit when you would have been eligible for an EEA family permit. In support of the latter argument, note that the Upper Tribunal held in an immigration case that an application made for an EUSS family permit could be treated as an application for an EEA family permit.[37]

If you are an extended family member and are refused benefit, or your benefit award is terminated, because, for example, your residence document has expired and cannot be replaced, or your residence document has not expired but is not accepted as remaining in force, challenge the decision and get specialist advice.

4. Other types of evidence

Certain types of evidence are of particular significance for migrants and are discussed below. Depending on your circumstances and the benefit or tax credit being claimed, this evidence may be required by all claimants to satisfy the entitlement conditions or because it affects the amount to which you are entitled. You should not be required to submit *more* evidence because you are a migrant than would be required of a British person in the same circumstances. If you are asked for more evidence because you are not British, you may want to get advice from the Equality Advisory and Support Service (see Appendix 2).

It can be helpful to check the guidance issued to decision makers on acceptable evidence and refer to this when it supports your situation. Check the guidance on evidence in general,[38] on specific types of evidence (eg, of age, marriage and death[39]), and the guidance specific to migrants,[40] including on the right to reside and habitual residence tests.[41]

Evidence from other countries

If your documentary evidence is from another country and is not in English, it can be helpful to submit an authorised translation. If obtaining a translation will cause any delay, you should make sure you do not miss any deadlines for submitting evidence. For example, you could take the original document to a local benefit office to take an authorised copy and accompany this with a letter explaining that you are obtaining a translation.

The authenticity of a document issued outside the UK should not automatically be questioned. Decision makers are reminded in their guidance that certificates of birth, marriage, civil partnerships and deaths issued abroad can all be accepted as evidence of that event, unless there is a reason to doubt their authenticity.[42]

Even if a document is from a country in which it is relatively easy to obtain fraudulent documents, a decision maker (or First-tier Tribunal) cannot presume your document is not genuine. While the decision maker (or tribunal) may conclude on the balance of probabilities that a document is not genuine, they still need to decide the 'weight' given to that document by considering any evidence of the accuracy of record keeping by the issuing body, whether other evidence corroborates the document and your overall credibility.[43]

Evidence of nationality

The most common acceptable evidence of your nationality is a current passport, a current European Economic Area (EEA) identity card or, if you are a non-EEA national, a current travel document or biometric residence permit. However, if you cannot provide one of these, other official documents should be accepted (see p487). As with all evidence requirements, it helps if you can provide more than one form of evidence of your nationality.

If you are relying on someone else's nationality for your own rights (eg, to argue you have a right to reside as the family member of an EEA worker), you must provide evidence of their nationality – eg, to show they are an EEA national.

Evidence of a relationship

If your rights are based on being someone's family member or primary carer, you must provide evidence of this relationship. You must also provide evidence of the other factors that are relevant. For example, if you need to show you are the family member of an EEA worker, in addition to evidence that you are their family member, you must also provide evidence of their EEA nationality, pre-settled status and employment.

Non-European Economic Area nationals

If you entered the UK as the family member of an EEA national who is in the UK exercising their treaty rights (eg, as a worker), you usually have an entry clearance document that states this. You should provide this document to the benefit authority, as it is the most significant documentary evidence required. However, depending on your circumstances, the benefit authority may also want evidence that you are still their family member, or that you come within limited circumstances that enable you to retain residence rights as a former family member (see p249). To claim some benefits, you may also need to provide evidence of both the EEA national's and your status under the European Union Settlement Scheme (EUSS).

If you are the primary carer of someone who confers a derivative right to reside on you (see p253), the benefit authorities require evidence of each requirement that must be satisfied for you to have this right to reside. For example, if you are asserting that you are the primary carer of a worker's child in education, you must show:

- you are the primary carer of the child (see p260);
- they are currently in education (see p257);
- one of their parents (or step-parents) is an EEA national (see above);

- that parent (or step-parent) had worker status in the UK (see p258) while the child was in the UK; *and*
- you have pre-settled status under the EUSS so you can still have a European free movement residence right (see p192).

Note: if you are a non-EEA national and are the family member of an EEA national who confers residence rights on you, you may not be a 'person subject to immigration control' (see p89).

Evidence of marriage or civil partnership

If you have been given leave to enter or remain on the basis of being a spouse or civil partner of someone, evidence of that leave is generally accepted as sufficient evidence of your relationship for the purposes of proving your entitlement to a benefit or tax credit.

Spouses and civil partners have far greater rights under European Union (EU) law than partners who are not married or who are not civil partners. Consequently, it can be important to show that someone is your spouse or civil partner – eg, when they can confer residence rights on you. If you need to prove that you are someone's spouse or civil partner, you must show that you are still married or in a civil partnership. If you have separated and are no longer living together or in a relationship, you are still their spouse or civil partner until you are finally divorced or the civil partnership is finally dissolved.[44]

A marriage or civil partnership certificate is the best evidence. If the certificate was issued outside the UK by the appropriate registration authority, it should be accepted as valid evidence (see p506).[45]

If you do not have a marriage or civil partnership certificate, other evidence confirming your marriage or civil partnership can be accepted. Official documents that refer to your marriage or civil partnership, as well as official correspondence confirming you live together, can be be taken into account.

There is extensive guidance for decision makers on evidence of marriage and civil partnerships, including religious and national variations.[46]

If you are refused benefits or tax credits because your marriage or civil partnership is not recognised or is deemed to have been a marriage or civil partnership 'of convenience', get specialist immigration advice.

Evidence of parentage

If you have been given leave to enter or remain on the basis of being a parent or child of someone, evidence of that leave is generally accepted as sufficient evidence of your relationship for the purposes of proving your entitlement to benefits and tax credits.

If you are the child of someone who can confer residence rights on you under EU law, you must show that they are your parent and either you are aged under 21 or you are dependent on them. If you are the parent of someone who can confer residence rights on you, you must show that you are their parent and you are dependent on them.

A birth certificate, or official DNA test results, that names both child and parent should be sufficient evidence. If the document is from outside the UK, see p506.

If you do not have a birth certificate or official DNA test results, other documents can also be accepted. If you do not have anything decisive, submit the evidence you have to back up your own written or verbal evidence and ask for the decision maker to decide on the balance of probabilities (see p496).

Example

Nadifa is 18 and a Dutch national. She has health problems and wants to claim universal credit (UC). She came to the UK four years ago with her mother, who is also a Dutch national, having acquired Dutch citizenship after fleeing to the Netherlands as a refugee 15 years ago. Both Nadifa and her mother have pre-settled status. Nadifa's mother is a self-employed translator and has extensive evidence of this. However, Nadifa does not have any evidence that she is her mother's daughter. Her mother fled to the Netherlands without any documents. Nadifa therefore submits evidence of her mother's Dutch nationality and self-employment, together with a letter setting out the relevant details of her life history and documents showing that she was given leave to remain in the Netherlands as a dependant on her mother's asylum claim, evidence that she travelled with her mother to the UK four years ago and letters from her GP and dermatologist discussing Nadifa's eczema and the likelihood of its being linked to her mother's eczema.

Note: if you are trying to show that you are someone's father or that someone is your father, until officially declared otherwise, a man is deemed to be a child's father if he was married to the child's mother at the time of the child's birth or his name was registered on the birth certificate.[47]

Evidence of age

Your age (or someone else's age) can affect whether or not you meet the basic conditions of entitlement to a benefit, and the amount to which you are entitled. Age can also affect your residence rights, whether your immigration status excludes you from benefits and tax credits and/or whether you are covered by the EU co-ordination rules. In addition, age can affect whether you (or someone else) are defined as a 'family member' or as 'dependent'.

A birth certificate, passport or identity card is usually accepted as proof of your date of birth. Other evidence that can show your date of birth includes school, medical or army records. Guidance to decision makers states that the 'primary' or best evidence of age is a certified copy of an entry which must be made in a register by law, such as a birth certificate or adoption certificate.[48] If you were born abroad and have a certificate issued by the appropriate registration authority, that should be accepted unless there is reason to doubt its validity (see p506).[49] See also the other evidence that can be accepted as proof of your identity on p487, and guidance to decision makers on 'secondary' evidence of age.[50]

You may be able to show your date of birth by referring to the accepted birth dates of other relatives, such as siblings.[51] For example, if you are recorded as the eldest child and your sister has been accepted as born in 1995, you must have been born before then.

If you have no record of your date of birth, or there is conflicting evidence, it is possible for an age assessment to be carried out. However, there is no accurate scientific test that can establish a person's age and such an assessment can be disputed. See p557 for age assessments for unaccompanied asylum-seeking children. Guidance to decision makers covers the possibility of arranging a physical examination of an adult, but notes that this is generally only reliable five years either way.[52] However, getting your GP to state their opinion of your age, together with their reasons, can be helpful supporting evidence, particularly if it is clear that the GP has known you for some time and is familiar with your medical conditions.[53]

A common problem is conflicting evidence due to past errors. Your date of birth may have been wrongly recorded in your passport when it was issued – eg, because you gave the wrong date or because of an administrative error. The date in the passport may then have been used in many other official documents and it may be difficult to persuade the benefit authorities that all these dates are wrong. You should explain that all these dates come from one document and give a detailed account about how the wrong date came to be recorded. This explanation counts as evidence, but you should submit any other evidence you have (or can obtain) showing that date is not correct.[54]

While each piece of evidence must be considered, the oldest documents may be more reliable, since they were made nearer to the time of the events to which they refer.

Passports and other immigration documents commonly record '1 January' when your exact date of birth is unclear. However, if you obtain evidence of your exact date of birth later, this can be accepted.

The decision maker (or First-tier Tribunal) should weigh up all the available evidence and determine your age on the balance of probabilities.[55]

If there is no documentary evidence, the benefit authorities should accept your own statements, unless they are contradictory or improbable (see p496).

Evidence of work

Evidence of your (or someone else's) current or past employment or self-employment can be required to prove that you satisfy, or are exempt from, immigration or residence conditions, or that you are covered by the EU co-ordination rules (see p379). The exact evidence required depends on what you need to prove, so it is essential that you check the rules for the specific condition you need to satisfy or be exempt from.

Examples

Hassan is a Turkish national and is in the UK to study. He has a student visa, which gives him leave to be in the UK for the next two years, subject to the condition that he does not have recourse to public funds. Hassan is therefore a 'person subject to immigration control' (see p93). He works 15 hours a week, which is permitted under his student visa. Hassan wants to claim child benefit because his girlfriend's 14-year-old French son has come to live with him while she goes to Canada for a year. Hassan can claim child benefit if he can show that he is 'lawfully working' and 'lawfully present', because he is then exempt from the exclusion that would otherwise apply to him as a 'person subject to immigration control' (see p116). Hassan must provide HM Revenue and Customs (HMRC) with evidence of his employment (eg, a payslip or letter from his employer), together with confirmation that his work is allowed under the conditions of his immigration leave, and proof of his Turkish nationality and his student visa. **Note:** it is arguable that Hassan may also be entitled to UC (see p114).

Dimitra is a Greek national who wants to claim UC because she has had to temporarily stop her self-employed work as she is due to have a baby in three weeks. She came to the UK four and a half years ago and set up her business after being here a month. She has pre-settled status. If Dimitra can show that she had a right to reside as a 'self-employed person', she will retain that right if she intends to return to self-employment at the end of her maternity period (see p221), which satisfies the right to reside requirement for UC. Dimitra must provide evidence confirming that she was self-employed (see below) doing 'genuine and effective' work (see p215). Dimitra should also apply for maternity allowance.

There is no definitive list of what counts as acceptable evidence of work. Evidence is considered stronger if it has several ways of showing it relates to you – eg, if it shows your full name, your date of birth, your address and your national insurance (NI) number, rather than just one or two of these.

Evidence of employment includes:

- a contract of employment;
- payslips;
- correspondence from your employer to you – eg, offering you the job or confirming a change in hours;
- a letter from an employer confirming your employment;
- documents relating to your total pay and tax over a period – eg, P60/P45 forms;
- bank statements showing wages being paid in from the employer or, if you are paid 'cash in hand', showing you have deposited your wages on a regular basis.

If you are not actually working (eg, because you are on sick leave or maternity leave), you may not have ceased to have a right to reside as a 'worker' (see p217). You need to provide evidence that you are still under a contract of employment, such as a letter from your employer stating this. Alternatively, if you have ceased to be a worker, you may be able to retain your worker status and must provide evidence of the basis of this (see p222) in addition to the evidence of the worker status you had.

Evidence of self-employment includes:

- documents from HMRC confirming your registration as self-employed;
- evidence of paying class 2 NI contributions;
- bank statements showing payments from your customers;
- business accounts;
- samples of marketing;
- documents showing you have bought the required equipment needed.

If you want to demonstrate that you have a right to reside as a self-employed person, it should be enough to show that you have established yourself to undertake activity as a self-employed person (see p220). The Upper Tribunal has considered how self-employment should be evaluated for the purpose of working tax credit entitlement and, although this context differs from the context of having a right to reside as a self-employed person, these decisions give useful guidance.[56]

If you are not actually working, you may not have ceased to have a right to reside as a self-employed person. You must provide evidence of all the factors that are relevant in your circumstances (see p220).

You may be able to retain your self-employed status (see p222) and need to provide evidence of this in addition to the evidence of your self-employment.

If you need evidence of your past employment or self-employment, you can submit a 'subject access' request to HMRC, asking for a summary of your employment history for a specified period.[57]

If your right to reside depends on someone else being, or having been, a worker or self-employed, all the above points apply to evidence of their work. If you do not have any documentary evidence of this because you cannot contact the person or they will not provide you with the evidence, you can argue that the benefit authorities should obtain this evidence (see p499).

Croatian, A2 and A8 nationals

Restrictions, which could affect your residence rights based on employment, previously applied to Croatian, A2 nationals and A8 nationals (see p197). If these applied to you, you may have to supply additional evidence. If you need to show that you had a right to reside as a 'worker', or that you had retained 'worker' status, you must show that, at the time of working, you:

- were exempt from restrictions (see p199 for Croatian and A2 nationals, and p200 for A8 nationals); *or*
- (for Croatian and A2 nationals) worked in accordance with a valid authorisation document (see p198); *or*
- (for A8 nationals) worked for an 'authorised employer' (see p201).

If you are unable to provide your authorisation document or registration certificate because it has been lost or stolen, you should provide the benefit authority with as much information as you can about your employment and when it was authorised or registered, and ask the decision maker to confirm this through their contacts with the Home Office (see p499). You can also submit a 'subject access' request to the Home Office, asking for the details of your authorisation or registration(s). For details of how to do this, see gov.uk/government/publications/requests-for-personal-data-uk-visas-and-immigration.

Your employer at the relevant time may also be able to assist you with evidence confirming your authorisation or registration.

Do not delay making your claim while you gather evidence of your worker authorisation or registration(s).

Note: there were no additional restrictions, and therefore no additional evidence requirements, if you (or the person whose right to reside you are relying on) were self-employed.

Evidence of jobseeking

To retain your worker status while involuntarily unemployed (see p223),[58] you must provide evidence that you are seeking employment, but under the EEA Regulations, to have a right to reside as a jobseeker (see p203) you must also have a 'genuine chance of being engaged' (see below).

These requirements are similar to the requirements to be 'actively seeking' and 'available for' work for jobseeker's allowance (JSA) or NI credits, and to the work search and work availability requirements under the UC system. In most cases, if the decision maker accepts that you have provided evidence that satisfies these work-related requirements, this evidence should also be accepted as satisfying the requirements for you to have a right to reside as a jobseeker. For the circumstances when this might not apply and for more information on the type of work you must be seeking, see p208.

Note: you do not need to receive, or claim, benefit to have a right to reside as a jobseeker, as long as you provide evidence that you are seeking employment and, arguably only after a 'reasonable period', have a 'genuine chance of being engaged' (see p209 and p205).[59]

Under EU law, there is no time limit on how long you can have a right to reside as a jobseeker – it continues for as long as you provide evidence that you are looking for work and, arguably only after a 'reasonable period', have a genuine chance of being engaged.[60] There is also no time limit on how long you can retain your worker or self-employed status while involuntarily unemployed, provided you were employed for at least a year (see p226).[61]

However, under the EEA Regulations, in order to continue to have a right to reside as a jobseeker for longer than 91 days, the evidence that you are seeking employment and have a genuine chance of being engaged must be 'compelling'.[62] This requirement is referred to as the 'genuine prospects of work test' (see p206).

Examples of evidence

Evidence that you are seeking employment could include details of your:

- work search activities;
- enquiries made to potential employers;
- applications for employment, together with responses;
- requests to attend interviews, together with responses.

Evidence that you have a genuine chance of being engaged could include evidence of:

- your work history in the UK and elsewhere;
- your qualifications and other training undertaken;
- voluntary work (in the UK and abroad);
- your language skills;
- security checks you have satisfied;
- your proximity to potential employers;
- completion of a course on obtaining work as part of an employability programme;
- the broad range of types of work you are looking for and/or the hours of work you are able to do;
- your arrangements for adequate childcare to enable you to attend interviews and take up employment.

Whether you have a genuine chance of being engaged also depends on future events,[63] so you should provide evidence of any qualifications you hope to obtain and experience you will gain in the near future. If you appeal against a decision that you are not entitled to benefit because you did not have a genuine chance of being engaged, and by the date your appeal is heard you have obtained employment, the tribunal can take this into account as evidence of your *chance* of being engaged on the date of the decision.[64]

Although it is arguable that you should not be required to change the quality of your evidence after a particular length of time, in practice, the longer you have been a jobseeker without obtaining work, the more likely it is that the decision maker will argue that this shows you do not have a genuine chance of getting work. The Upper Tribunal has held that if you have been seeking employment without success for at least six months, this is relevant, but is only one factor that must be considered and can be outweighed by others.[65] You should therefore provide as much evidence as possible to demonstrate that, on the balance of probabilities, you have a genuine chance of being engaged, despite the long period of unemployment.

Notes

1. General points about evidence

1 DWP, *Identity Verification*, version 11, available at rightsnet.org.uk/universal-credit-guidance
2 *CI v HMRC (TC)* [2014] UKUT 158 (AAC); *HMRC v ED (TC)* [2021] UKUT 195 (AAC)
3 *LS v SSWP (SPC)* [2014] UKUT 249 (AAC); see also *KS v SSWP* [2016] UKUT 269 (AAC), paras 10-14 and *DH v SSWP* [2018] UKUT 185 (AAC), para 6
4 Vol 1 Ch 1 paras 01343-5 DMG; paras A1340-2 ADM
5 *Kerr v Department for Social Development (Northern Ireland)* [2004] UKHL 23, paras 15-17 and 61-63; *SS v HMRC(TC)* [2014] UKUT 383 (AAC), paras 28-30; *DD v HMRC and SSWP (CB)* [2020] UKUT 66 (AAC), para 28
6 *SSWP v HS (JSA)* [2016] UKUT 272 (AAC), reported as [2017] AACR 29
7 R(I) 2/51, paras 6 and 7; R(SB) 33/85, para 14; *EP v SSWP (JSA)* [2016] UKUT 445 (AAC), para 21
8 R(IS) 6/96, para 15; see also *Kerr v Department for Social Development (Northern Ireland)* [2004] UKHL 23, paras 16-17 and 61-69; CIS/1697/2004, paras 18-20; R(PC) 1/09, paras 16-18
9 *R v Medical Appeal Tribunal (North Midland Region) ex parte Hubble* [1958] 2 QB 228; *Kerr v Department for Social Development (Northern Ireland)* [2004] UKHL 23, paras 15-17 and 61-63; R(PC) 1/09, paras 16-20; *DD v HMRC and SSWP (CB)* [2020] UKUT 66 (AAC), para 28
10 *Kerr v Department for Social Development (Northern Ireland)* [2004] UKHL 23, paras 61-69; R(PC) 1/09, para 19
11 R(IS) 11/99; *AS v SSWP (UC)* [2018] UKUT 260 (AAC)
12 s16(1) TCA 2002; *NI v HMRC (TC)* [2015] UKUT 490 (AAC) – see also caselaw listed in para 4; *JR v HMRC (TC)* [2015] UKUT 192 (AAC)
13 s19 TCA 2002; *CS v HMRC (TC)* [2015] UKUT 407 (AAC), para 23; *TS v HMRC (TC)* [2015] UKUT 507 (AAC); *VO v HMRC (TC)* [2017] UKUT 343 (AAC), para 41
14 s14 TCA 2002; *SB v HMRC (TC)* [2014] UKUT 543 (AAC), para 12
15 See, for example, s17 SSA 1998; Sch 7 para 11 CSPSSA 2000
16 The Social Security (Claims and Information) Regulations 2007 No.2911
17 *Kerr v Department for Social Development (Northern Ireland)* [2004] UKHL 23, paras 61-69; R(PC) 1/09, paras 16-19
18 ADM Memo 30/20, para 42
19 R(PC) 1/09, paras 16-19
20 *Kerr v Department for Social Development (Northern Ireland)* [2004] UKHL 23, paras 61-69; *CP v SSWP (UC)* [2020] UKUT 309 (AAC), paras 10-11; ADM Memo 30/20, para 42
21 Vol 2 Ch 7 Part 3 para 073431 DMG; para C1810 ADM
22 Sch 2 para 5(3)(c) Data Protection Act 2018 (and s94(6) may also be relevant)
23 rr5, 6 and 15 TP(FT) Rules; *PM v SSWP (IS)* [2014] UKUT 474 (AAC) but see also the, albeit obiter, comment at para 8 of *FN v SSWP (UC)* [2022] UKUT 77 (AAC) that seeking such a direction should not be an adviser's first recourse

24 s35 Data Protection Act 1998 until 24 May 2018; Sch 2 para 5(2) Data Protection Act 2018 from 25 May 2018; *TM v HMRC (TC)* [2013] UKUT 444 (AAC), para 6

2. **Evidence of immigration status**

25 **HB** U1/2018, paras 6-10
26 s3C(2)(a) IA 1971

3. **Evidence of residence rights**

27 *SSWP v Dias*, C-325/09 [2011]; *EM and KN v SSWP* [2009] UKUT 44 (AAC); *MD v SSWP (SPC)* [2016] UKUT 319 (AAC); regs 17(8), 18(7), 19(4) and 20(5) I(EEA) Regs
28 See, for example, *Batool and others (other family members: EU exit)* [2022] UKUT 219 (IAC)
29 Reg 17 I(EEA) Regs; Sch 3 para 3(3) ISSC Regs
30 Reg 18 I(EEA) Regs; Sch 3 para 3(4) ISSC Regs
31 Reg 20 I(EEA) Regs; Sch 3 para 3(6) ISSC Regs
32 Reg 19 I(EEA) Regs; Sch 3 para 3(5) ISSC Regs
33 Reg 45 and Sch 6 para 2 I(EEA) Regs; Reg 10 CR(ADTP) Regs
34 Reg 12 I(EEA) Regs; regs 3(4)-(6), 4(2) and (5)-(8) and 6(b) CR(ADTP) Regs; Sch 3 para 3(1) and (2) ISSC Regs
35 See, for example, gov.uk/uk-residence-card
36 visas-immigration.service.gov.uk/product/biometric-residence-permit-replacement-service
37 Unreported linked cases EA/04026/2021 and EA/04027/2021

4. **Other types of evidence**

38 For example, Vol 1 Ch 1 DMG or Ch A1 ADM
39 For example, Vol 3 Ch 10 DMG or Ch B3 ADM
40 For example, Vol 2 DMG or Ch 20 CCM
41 For example, Vol 2 Ch 7 DMG
42 See, for example, Vol 3 Ch 10 DMG
43 *SW v SSWP (SPC)* [2016] UKUT 163 (AAC), in particular paras 28 and 41
44 *Diatta v Land Berlin*, C-267/83 [1985]
45 Vol 3 Ch 10 para 10155 DMG
46 For example, Vol 3 Ch 10 paras 10120-43 DMG
47 **EW** ss2 and 4 CA 1989
S s3 C(S)A 1995
48 Vol 3 Ch 10 paras 10030 and 10064-65 DMG; para B3016 ADM
49 Vol 3 Ch 10 para 10035 DMG; para B3021 ADM; *SW v SSWP (SPC)* [2016] UKUT 163 (AAC), in particular paras 28 and 41
50 Vol 3 Ch 10 paras 10036 and 10070-73 DMG; paras B3022 and B3051-58 ADM
51 Vol 3 Ch 10 para 10071 example 10 DMG; para B3051 example ADM
52 Vol 3 Ch 10 paras 10098-102 DMG; paras B3073-74 and B3086-89 ADM
53 For example, *SW v SSWP (SPC)* [2016] UKUT 163 (AAC)
54 For example, *SW v SSWP (SPC)* [2016] UKUT 163 (AAC)
55 *LS v SSWP(SPC)* [2014] UKUT 249 (AAC), para 5
56 *JF v HMRC (TC)* [2017] UKUT 334 (AAC), paras 30-31; *VO v HMRC (TC)* [2017] UKUT 343 (AAC)
57 For guidance on how HMRC records of national insurance records and contributions should be interpreted, see *SSWP v LM (ESA)* [2017] UKUT 485 (AAC), para 2 and Appendix 1
58 Reg 6(1), (2), (5) and (6) I(EEA) Regs; Art 7(3) EU Dir 2004/38; *KH v Bury MBC and SSWP (HB)* [2020] UKUT 50 (AAC); paras C1301-1304 ADM
59 *The Queen v Immigration Appeal Tribunal, ex parte Antonissen*, C-292/89 [1991], para 21; R(IS) 8/08, para 5; *GE v SSWP (ESA)* [2017] UKUT 145 (AAC), para 46; *GMA v État Belge*, C-710/19 [2020]
60 *The Queen v Immigration Appeal Tribunal, ex parte Antonissen*, C-292/89 [1991], para 21; *GMA v État Belge*, C-710/19 [2020]
61 Art 7(3)(b) EU Dir 2004/38; para C1302 ADM
62 Reg 6(1), (5), (6) and (7) I(EEA) Regs. Previously, DWP applied these requirements to those retaining worker and self-employed status while involuntarily unemployed, but see *KH v Bury MBC and SSWP (HB)* [2020] UKUT 50 (AAC); para C1403 ADM.
63 *SSWP v MB (JSA) (and linked cases)* [2016] UKUT 372 (AAC), reported as [2017] AACR 6, para 47
64 *OS v SSWP (JSA)* [2017] UKUT 107 (AAC), paras 5-7 and caselaw cited; see also *AMS v SSWP (PC) (final decision)* [2017] UKUT 381 (AAC), para 26
65 *SSWP v MB (JSA) (and linked cases)* [2016] UKUT 372 (AAC), reported as [2017] AACR 6, paras 49-60; *KH v Bury MBC and SSWP (HB)* [2020] UKUT 50 (AAC)

Part 8

Support for asylum seekers

Chapter 21

Asylum support overview

This chapter covers:

1. Introduction

Types of support for asylum seekers

Asylum seekers are excluded from claiming social security benefits on the basis of being 'persons subject to immigration control' (see p93).[1] Instead, there are three main types of government support for people who have applied for asylum in the UK.

- Support for an asylum seeker and their dependants for a period until a final decision on an asylum application is made, known as **section 95 support.** It consists of accommodation and cash (or the option of cash only) through a prepaid card known as an ASPEN card, which can be used both to withdraw cash and to pay for goods (see p522).[2]
- **Temporary support** (often called 'section 98 support', 'initial accommodation' or 'emergency support'), which is available to asylum seekers and their dependants waiting for a decision on their application for section 95 support. This support usually **comprises full-board accommodation** (see p535).[3]
- **Section 4 support**, which is for people whose asylum application has been rejected or declare inadmissable. It consists of accommodation and an ASPEN card, which can be used to pay for goods but not to withdraw cash (see p536).

In certain limited circumstances, people who have applied for asylum are eligible for:

- local authority support, for people who have claimed asylum (see p553); *or*
- discretionary support, for people on immigration bail, often called 'Schedule 10 support' (see p551).

Note: the Immigration Act 2016 made significant changes to the scheme for asylum support, especially the support of refused asylum seekers. The relevant provisions of the Act have not yet been brought into force, and are not referred to in this *Handbook*. However, this note is to draw attention to the possibility of change in what is, at the time of writing, a fast-moving and unpredictable legislative environment.

Home Office agencies

Since the Immigration and Asylum Act 1999 came into force, the responsibility for providing accommodation and support to asylum seekers has passed between several different Home Office agencies. Until April 2006, the support scheme for asylum seekers and refused asylum seekers was administered by the National Asylum Support Service (NASS). In April 2006, NASS ceased to exist and its role was taken over by the Border and Immigration Agency (BIA). On 7 April 2008, the UK Border Agency (UKBA) was formed, taking over the support role of the BIA, as well as the immigration and asylum functions of the Immigration and Nationality Directorate. The UKBA was abolished on 26 March 2013 and all its functions were returned to the Home Office. Asylum support applications are now dealt with by the UK Visas and Immigration (UKVI) department in the Home Office. For simplicity, we refer to the 'Home Office' in this *Handbook*.

You may find that some advisers and even officials still refer to asylum support as 'NASS' or 'UKBA' support, even though these agencies no longer exist.

Home Office guidance

The Home Office publishes internal guidance for its decision makers on deciding and processing applications for asylum support at gov.uk/government/collections/asylum-support-asylum-instructions. It is important to be familiar with the guidance in addition to the law. The guidance is regularly amended, so always check the website for the latest versions. The guidance published online by the Home Office at the time of writing included the following documents:

- *Allocation of asylum accommodation policy;*
- *Applications for additional support;*
- *Assessing destitution;*
- *Asylum seekers with care needs;*
- *Asylum support: policy bulletins instruction;*

- *Asylum support applications from European Union nationals or people with refugee status abroad;*
- *Asylum support, section 4(2): policy and process;*
- *Ceasing section 95 support instruction;*
- *Change of address;*
- *Conditions of support;*
- *Dependants on an asylum support application;*
- *Domestic abuse: responding to reports of domestic abuse from asylum seekers;*
- *Healthcare needs and pregnancy dispersal policy;*
- *Section 55 guidance;*
- *Support provided under section 4(1) of the Immigration and Asylum Act 1999: handling transitional cases; and*
- *Transition at age 18 instruction.*

In addition, simpler practical guides for asylum seekers are published by the Home Office, including:
- *Rights and expectations in the UK; and*
- *Living in asylum accommodation.*

Two of the guidance documents give an overview of the main types of asylum support, and are a useful starting point: one dealing with section 95 support (*Asylum support: policy bulletins instruction)* and the other with section 4 support (*Asylum support, section 4(2): policy and process*). The guidance is not law but gives a strong indication of how applications are likely to be processed by the Home Office. The law requires the Home Office to follow its own written policies unless there is good reason to depart from them. If in any particular case, however, there is a conflict between the law and Home Office guidance, the law must prevail.

Asylum Help

Asylum Help UK is a national confidential and impartial advice service for asylum seekers, funded by the Home Office and provided by the charity Migrant Help. The Asylum Help service can help you apply for support and give general advice about the asylum process and associated matters such as housing problems, dealing with agencies such as social services, finding English language classes, questions about asylum support, getting legal representation, finding schools and returning home. The level of advice provided is generally low. For contact details and a list of other organisations that provide advice services to asylum seekers, see Appendix 2.

2. **Support for asylum seekers**

You are entitled to asylum support under section 95 of the Immigration and Asylum Act 1999 (known as **section 95 support**) if:[4]
- you are an asylum seeker or a dependant of an asylum seeker; *and*
- you are destitute or likely to become destitute.

Note: while the Home Office considers your application for section 95 support, you may be able to get temporary support (see p535).

Who is excluded from support

You are excluded from section 95 support if:
- your immigration status does not bar you from getting social security benefits (see p113);[5]
- you are not being treated as an asylum seeker or the dependant of an asylum seeker for immigration purposes;[6] *or*
- you apply for support as part of a group and every person in the group is excluded under either of the above.[7]

Note: a child cannot be excluded from support, nor can someone if the provision of support is necessary to avoid a breach of human rights.[8]

Asylum claims not made as soon as reasonably practicable

If you do not have dependent children and you apply for cash-only support and not accommodation (see p587), you can also be excluded if you did not claim asylum 'as soon as reasonably practicable' on entering the UK.[9] However, even then, support should not be withheld if to do so would breach a person's human rights.[10]

There is no statutory definition of the term 'as soon as reasonably practicable'. When the rule was first introduced in 2003, it led to substantial numbers of in-country asylum seekers (ie, people who did not claim asylum at the port of entry but only after they had entered UK) being refused support, and subsequent judicial review cases in the High Court. The Home Office has since issued a policy stating that any claim made within three days of arrival is treated as having been made 'as soon as reasonably practicable'.[11]

Before support can be withheld on this basis, the Home Office should invite you to what is known as 'a section 55 interview', at which you will be asked about the timing of your asylum claim, and (if the Home Office concludes that you did not claim asylum as soon as reasonably practicable) whether you can access food and other basic living essentials from specific persons you may be living with or from charities. This information is relevant to whether withholding support would be a breach of your human rights. The Supreme Court has held that leaving destitute asylum seekers who have no right to work or claim benefits without food and shelter would be a breach of their human rights.[12]

Who is an asylum seeker for support purposes

For the purposes of asylum support, you are an asylum seeker if ***either***:[13]

- you are at least 18 years old; *and*
- you have made an application for asylum; *and*
- your application has been recorded by the Secretary of State (see below); *and*
- the application has not yet either been determined or declared inadmissable (see below);

or:

- you were (but are no longer) an asylum seeker; *and*
- at the time your asylum claim was finally determined you had a dependant child under 18 in your household; *and*
- the child remains under 18 (see p526).

Note: for asylum support purposes, an 'asylum application' is an application made either under the 1951 Refugee Convention (see p12) or under Article 3 of the European Convention on Human Rights (ECHR). If you have made a different type of application, such as under Article 8 of the ECHR or an application for indefinite leave to remain on non-asylum grounds (see p30), and you have not also made an asylum or Article 3 application, you cannot claim section 95 support. You may be eligible for support from the Home Office under Schedule 10 to the Immigration Act 2016 (see p551) or from your local authority (see p551). For further details on asylum applications, see p41.

Throughout this chapter and Chapters 22 to 24, references to an 'asylum claim' include either a claim that your return to your country of origin would be in breach of the Refugee Convention or that it would be in breach of Article 3 of the ECHR.

When an asylum application is recorded

Asylum applications made 'at port' (ie, on entry to the UK) are recorded immediately. If you are already in the UK and making an 'in-country' asylum application for the first time, you should normally telephone the Asylum Intake Unit (AIU) appointments line, to be given an appointment to attend the Home Office – eg, at the AIU in Croydon. If you have nowhere to live, you do not need to make an appointment to attend the AIU in advance; you can turn up at the AIU and apply on the same day. Your application is normally 'recorded' at your screening interview on the same day.

If your asylum application has been refused and your appeal rights are exhausted, you may be able to apply to make a fresh asylum application. Such an application is not recorded as a fresh asylum claim (which confers eligibility for section 95 support) until the Home Office accepts that it meets the relevant test – ie, it is 'significantly different' to the material considered but rejected in your first asylum application. It will be 'significantly different' if the new material taken together with the previously considered material creates a realistic prospect of success. Applications for a fresh asylum claim have to be made in person by appointment at the Home Office's Further Submissions Unit in Liverpool or Glasgow (or another specified Home Office Service and Support Centre), unless the Home Office agrees in advance to accept them by post or email.

While you are waiting for your further submissions to be considered, you may be eligible for section 4 support (see p536).

When an asylum application is declared inadmissible

Sections 15 and 16 of the Nationality and Borders Act 2022 amend the Nationality, Immigration and Asylum Act 2002 to provide that certain asylum claims may be treated as inadmissible.These are asylum claims by:

- European Union nationals;[14] *and*
- applicants with connection to a State that the Home Secretary considers to be safe.[15]

The Act defines a 'safe third State' as one which will, in the opinion of the Home Secretary, recognise and protect the applicant's rights under the Refugee Convention and under Article 3 of the ECHR.[16] An applicant has a connection to a safe third State if any of five conditions are met.[17]

- Condition 1: The applicant has been recognised as a refugee in the safe third State, and remains able to access protection there in accordance with the Refugee Convention and Article 3 of the ECHR.
- Condition 2: The applicant has otherwise been granted protection in a safe third State as a result of which they would not be sent from the safe third State to another State in breach of the Refugee Convention or Article 3 of the ECHR.
- Condition 3: The applicant has made a relevant claim to the safe third State and the claim has not yet been determined, or has been refused.
- Condition 4: (a) The applicant was previously present in, and eligible to make a relevant claim to, the safe third State; (b) It would have been reasonable to expect them to make such a claim; *and* (c) They failed to do so.
- Condition 5: In the applicant's particular circumstances, it would have been reasonable to expect them to have made a relevant claim to the safe third State (instead of making a claim in the UK).

If an asylum claim is declared inadmissible on the basis of connection to a safe third State:

- the claim is treated as if it were determined or rejected for asylum support purposes;[18] *and*

- the Home Secretary can nevertheless consider it under the Immigration Rules if the Home Secretary considers that there are exceptional circumstances for considering it, or if the Immigration Rules provide that it should be considered.[19]

If a claim that has been declared inadmissible is subsequently considered substantively by the Home Office under this provision, then it stops being treated as determined or rejected for asylum support purposes, and the applicant reverts to being an asylum seeker for the purposes of section 95 of the Immigration and Asylum Act 1999.[20]

When an asylum application is determined

For support purposes, until your asylum claim is determined, declared inadmissible or ceases to be considered by the Home Office (if it is withdrawn), you remain an asylum seeker and eligible for section 95 support from the time your asylum claim is recorded (see above), or any further submissions are accepted by the Home Office as constituting a 'fresh asylum claim' (see p541).

Once recorded, your asylum claim remains undetermined (and so you remain eligible for section 95 support):

- until you leave the UK (if you leave before it is decided); *or*
- until you withdraw your claim in writing; *or*
- until the Home Office treats your claim as having been impliedly withdrawn (see p548); *or*
- until your asylum claim is declared inadmissible; *or*
- if your asylum claim is refused, during the time allowed for any appeal to be brought, and during any appeal brought within that time to the First-tier Tribunal, or a further appeal to the Upper Tribunal or Court of Appeal.

If your asylum claim is refused and you bring any subsequent appeal after the time for appealing has expired, you cease to be an asylum seeker for asylum support purposes until the appeal is accepted by the relevant tribunal or court – ie, until permission to extend time for bringing the appeal is granted. Once permission to extend time for appealing has been granted, you are treated as an asylum seeker again, as above.

If your immigration application is successful, you continue to be treated as an asylum seeker for 28 days after:[21]

- your application for asylum is granted; *or*
- your application for asylum is refused but you are granted limited leave to enter or remain; *or*
- your asylum appeal is allowed.

If your immigration application is unsuccessful, you continue to be treated as an asylum seeker for asylum support purposes for 21 days after your asylum claim has been refused by the Home Office, or, if there is an appeal, for 21 days after the appeal is finally dismissed.

Similarly, as stated above, even if your asylum claim is declared inadmissible, the Home Office has the power in exceptional cases to consider and decide it as a normal asylum claim – ie, as though it had not been declared inadmissible. If your claim has been declared inadmissible, and the Home Office decides to exercise this power, you will be treated as asylum seeker once again, and will be eligible for section 95 support.

Note: if your asylum claim has been withdrawn, or has been treated by the Home Office as impliedly withdrawn, the Asylum Support Tribunal has held that your claim is neither determined nor undetermined for asylum support purposes. Instead, the tribunal has held that such claims are in abeyance, and no longer subject to consideration by the Home Office unless and until revived (see p548).[22]

Section 95 for families with children

If your household includes a dependent child when your application for asylum is determined, you continue to be treated as an asylum seeker for support purposes until the child's 18th birthday, while you and they remain in the UK.[23] Therefore, families with children aged under 18 continue to receive section 95 support, even after their asylum application has been refused. To remain eligible for section 95 support until your youngest child reaches 18, the Asylum Support Tribunal has held[24] that it does not matter whether you were receiving asylum support at the time your asylum application was determined, but you must have had a dependent child on this date.

This provision does not apply if your children are born after your asylum application was refused and you exhausted all your rights of appeal. In this case, you cease to be an asylum seeker for support purposes after your appeal rights are exhausted, and are no longer eligible for section 95 support. However, you and your children may be eligible for section 4 support as a refused asylum seeker (see p536) or for support under the Children Act 1989 (see p553).

It is open to the Home Office to withdraw section 95 support from failed asylum-seeker families who, in its opinion, have not taken steps to leave the UK voluntarily.[25] In such a case, you would be expected to demonstrate that you are taking steps to arrange your departure from the UK to return home. However, although this power was piloted across the UK in 2005, it has not been adopted as general practice. If the Home Office decides to withdraw your support because it says that you are not taking steps to leave the UK with your family, you can appeal against this decision to the Asylum Support Tribunal. For more information about appeals, see Chapter 24.

Who is a dependant for support purposes

Support is provided to asylum seekers and their dependants, provided they are destitute. You are a 'dependant' of an asylum seeker if you are:[26]

- their spouse or civil partner; *or*
- a child aged under 18 years of the asylum seeker or of their spouse/civil partner, and you are dependent on the asylum seeker; *or*
- a child aged under 18 years of the close family of the asylum seeker/spouse/civil partner (you do not have to be dependent on the asylum seeker); *or*
- a child aged under 18 years and you have lived in the asylum seeker's household for six out of the last 12 months, or since birth; *or*
- now more than 18 years old, but you were younger than 18 and came within one of the above categories when an asylum support application was made or when you entered the UK; *or*
- a close family member, or someone who has lived with the asylum seeker for six out of the last 12 months (or since birth), and you are disabled and in need of care and attention from a member of the household (regardless of your age); *or*
- the asylum seeker's partner and you were living with them as an unmarried (mixed or same-sex) couple for at least two of the three years before the application for support or before entering the UK.[27] If you are in an unmarried couple and want to be included as a dependant in your partner's existing asylum support, it can be difficult to comply with this condition. You may be caught in a 'catch-22' situation – eg, your relationship may have started at a time when either you or your partner were already on asylum support and you will not have been allowed to join their household. Therefore, you will have never been able to build up two years of having lived together before the application for support; *or*
- someone who has applied to the Home Office to remain in the UK as a dependant on another person's asylum claim.

Note: being a dependant for asylum support purposes does not necessarily mean you will be treated by the Home Office as a dependant on another person's asylum application for asylum purposes. Whether the Home Office allows you to be a dependant on someone else's asylum application (and whether that would be in your interests) and whether by that route you can be a dependant on their asylum support application, is not always a simple matter. You should obtain specialist advice if that affects you. See the Home Office's guidance on who is considered a dependant for asylum purposes[28] and for asylum support purposes.[29] Further information is in the Asylum Support Appeals Project Factsheet 11, *Asylum Support for Dependants*.[30]

The definition of destitute

You are considered **'destitute'** if:[31]

- you do not have adequate accommodation or any means of obtaining it (whether or not you can meet your other essential living needs); *or*

- you have adequate accommodation or the means of obtaining it but cannot meet your other essential living needs.

When you make an application for support, you are regarded as destitute if you appear to the Home Office to be destitute now or if there is a likelihood of destitution within 14 days.[32] If you already receive support, you continue to be regarded as destitute if there is a likelihood of destitution within 56 days.[33]

See p565 for what income and assets are taken into account when deciding whether or not you are destitute.

Applying for asylum support from prison or immigration detention

Some applications for asylum support (particularly section 4 support – see p536) are made by people in prison or in immigration detention. If you are applying for asylum support from prison or immigration detention, and you can prove that you do not have access to resources that would enable you to meet your accommodation and essential living needs, the approach of the Home Office and the Asylum Support Tribunal will be to consider whether your accommodation is 'adequate' (see p570). This will depend on whether bail in principle (pending a suitable address being obtained) has been granted. If you are in prison or immigration detention and have been granted bail in principle (or if, on appeal, the tribunal considers it is likely that bail in principle will be granted within 14 days), your accommodation will not be treated as 'adequate', which means you are liable to be treated as destitute (p571).

Permission to work

The general rule on which entitlement to asylum support is based is that asylum seekers are not allowed to work while their claim is being considered in the UK. However, the Immigration Rules provide that the Home Office may grant permission to work to asylum seekers whose claim has been outstanding for more than 12 months through no fault of their own.[34] If an application is made under this policy, and granted, the permission to work will generally be restricted to jobs on a shortage occupation list published by the Home Office. Any permission to work granted will come to an end if the asylum claim is refused and any appeals rights are exhausted. The position is the same for those refused asylum seekers who have made further submissions in support of their asylum claim, where the further submissions remain outstanding for more than 12 months.

If you have been granted permission to work, but nevertheless want to apply for asylum support, you need to explain in your application why you are unable to alleviate your destitution through finding employment in accordance with the permission to work that you have been granted.

Conditions on which section 95 and section 98 support is granted

Section 95 support is granted on certain conditions – eg, that you live at the address the Home Office has provided, and that you behave in accordance with the rules applying in your particular accommodation.[35] These conditions must be set out in writing[36] and given to the person who is being supported.[37]

Even if you have only applied for financial support and not accommodation (eg, because a friend has offered to let you stay with them), you must inform the Home Office of your address for support purposes, and that becomes your authorised address. You must tell the Home Office if you need to leave this address, and you are not allowed to leave the address for more than 14 days.

The Home Office may take into account any previous breach of conditions when deciding whether or not to provide you with support, whether to continue to provide support, and in deciding the level or kind of support to be provided.[38]

Note: the above provisions also apply to section 98 support (see p535).

Change of circumstances in relation to section 95 support

If you are provided with section 95 support, in addition to complying with the conditions on which support was granted (see above), you must notify the Home Office of certain relevant changes in your circumstances.[39] These are if you (or any of your dependants):[40]

- are joined in the UK by a dependant;
- receive or obtain access to any money or savings, investments, land, cars or other vehicles, or goods for the purposes of trade or other business, which you have not previously declared;
- become employed or unemployed;
- change your name;
- get married or divorced;
- begin living with another person as if you were married to them, or if you separate from a spouse or from a person with whom you have been living as if you were married;
- become pregnant or have a child;
- leave school;
- begin to share your accommodation with another person;
- move to a different address or otherwise leave your accommodation;
- go into hospital;
- go into to prison or some other form of custody;
- leave the UK; *and/or*
- die.

If there is a relevant change of circumstances, a decision may be made to change the nature or level of the existing support, to withdraw support or to provide support to different individual/s.

Note: it may be a criminal offence not to notify the Home Office of a change in circumstances (see p534).[41]

Termination of section 95 support

Section 95 support is terminated if:

- the Home Office decides that you cease to be entitled – ie, that you cease to be destitute and/or cease to be an asylum seeker; *or*
- your section 95 support is suspended or discontinued because the Home Office believes you have broken the rules.

The usual law on security of tenure does not apply to Home Office accommodation.[42] Tenancies or licences created when Home Office support is provided can come to an end when asylum support is terminated – ie, if:[43]

- you are no longer destitute; *or*
- your application for asylum has been determined; *or*
- you have moved to be supported in other accommodation; *or*
- your support has been suspended or discontinued (see below).

In any of the above circumstances, any tenancy or licence is terminated at the end of the period (minimum of seven days) specified in a 'notice to quit' given to you.[44]

When section 95 or section 98 support can be suspended or discontinued

If you have been granted section 95 support, the Home Office may discontinue or suspend it in certain circumstances. Support can be suspended or discontinued if:[45]

- the Home Office has reason to believe that you are accommodated in 'collective accommodation' (eg, a hostel or shared house) and you or your dependant have committed a serious breach of the accommodation's rules.[46] Each accommodation provider is likely to have a set of 'house rules', which everyone must follow – eg, to be respectful of other residents and not to make any noise late at night; *or*
- the Home Office has reason to believe that you or your dependant have committed an act of seriously violent behaviour;[47] *or*
- you or your dependant have committed a criminal offence under Part VI of the Immigration and Asylum Act 1999.[48] That includes making a false claim to get support and failing to report a change of circumstances to the Home Office – eg, a change in your financial resources; *or*
- you fail within a reasonable period (being no less than five working days) to provide the Home Office with information about an application for, or receipt of, support in response to a request by the Home Office;[49] *or*

- you fail to attend an interview relating to your or your dependant's support and do not have a reasonable excuse;[50] *or*
- you fail within a reasonable period (being no less than 10 working days) to provide information about your dependant's asylum application in response to a request by the Home Office;[51] *or*
- the Home Office has reason to believe that you or your dependant have concealed financial resources and unduly benefited from asylum support;[52] *or*
- you or your dependant fail to comply with reporting requirements;[53] *or*
- the Home Office has reason to believe that you or your dependant have made, or you attempted to make, a second application for asylum before the first application is determined;[54] *or*
- there are 'reasonable grounds' to suspect that you have abandoned your 'authorised address' (see p592) without first informing the Home Office or without its permission;[55] *or*
- your support is provided on condition that you reside at a specific place, and you or your dependant have failed without reasonable excuse to comply with that condition.[56]

Your support may be suspended (for a period up to 30 days)[57] if the Home Office requires time or more information to decide whether to discontinue (ie, terminate) your support. If the Home Office is satisfied that there has been a breach of conditions, it must take into account the extent of the breach when deciding whether or not to continue to provide support. In making this assessment, the Asylum Support Tribunal usually[58] applies the reasoning of the Court of Appeal in relation to the approach local authorities should take towards asylum seekers who breach the conditions of the support they receive from the local authority: that support should not be terminated unless the asylum seeker's breaches of conditions are 'persistent and unequivocal' and a warning letter has been sent.[59]

Note: even if the grounds to suspend or discontinue your support are established, you can still retain your entitlement to support if you can show that you are destitute and require support to avoid a breach of your human rights. However, if you were getting section 95 support because you were a refused asylum seeker with a dependant child younger than 18 (see p529), you will be in a vulnerable position. The Home Office may argue that there is nothing preventing you from avoiding a breach of your human rights by making a voluntary return to your country.

If you apply for support again after it has been discontinued, unless there are exceptional circumstances the Home Office may refuse to consider your application if there has been no 'material change in circumstances' since the original decision to suspend or discontinue the support.[60] A **'material change'** is any change in any of the circumstances that you need to notify the Home Office about if you were receiving section 95 support (see p561).[61] If the Home Office decides to consider your application for support in these circumstances, you may still be refused support.[62] **Note:** the above provisions also apply to section 98 support (see p535).

You can appeal a decision to refuse or discontinue support to the Asylum Support Tribunal (see Chapter 24). It is not possible to appeal either:

- a decision to suspend section 95 support; *or*
- a decision to refuse, suspend or discontinue section 98 support (see p535).

Such decisions can only be challenged by judicial review. **Note:** contrary to the position with section 4 appeals,[63] there is nothing to prevent you from being evicted from your accommodation, despite having lodged an appeal against a refusal or discontinuation of section 95 support. However, in practice most appellants are allowed to remain in initial accommodation until their appeal is heard, particularly if dependent minors are being accommodated.

Discontinuation of support to families with children

When considering whether to discontinue section 95 support for families with children younger than 18, the Home Office must discharge its duty under section 55 of the Borders, Citizenship and Immigration Act 2009 to ensure that the decision has regard to the need to safeguard and promote the welfare of children who are in the UK. Any decision to discontinue support must be proportionate. Accordingly, support should not be discontinued if a breach of conditions is minor – eg, a failure to report. If a breach of conditions is serious (eg, extreme violence or vandalism) and a decision to discontinue support is taken, the Home Office must nevertheless discharge its duty to safeguard and promote the welfare of the children. The Home Office guidance states:[64]

> Before any action is taken to begin the process to discontinue support, the case worker should liaise with the local authority, notifying them that the Home Office plans to discontinue support from the family, and request that the local authority provides alternative support. If the local authority makes an offer of support, the provision of support under Section 95 should be discontinued as soon as the family transfers in to local authority care.[65]

The purpose of the guidance is to help ensure that the local authority will be aware of the family's circumstances, and therefore able to intervene to safeguard the welfare of the children before any eviction actually takes place. See p555 and the Asylum Support Appeals Project's *Family support briefing*.[66]

Recovery of section 95 or section 98 support

There are four circumstances in which you may be required to repay your asylum support. The Home Office may require you to repay your section 95 or 98 support if:

- you had assets at the time of your application for support that you can now convert into money (see below); *or*

- you have been overpaid support as a result of an error (see below); *or*
- you have misrepresented or failed to disclose a 'material fact' (see below); *or*
- it transpires that you were not destitute.

In addition, the Home Office may try to recover any support provided to you from a person who has sponsored your stay in the UK (see p534). The Home Office can recover the support through deductions from your existing asylum support or through the civil courts.

Note: the above four scenarios apply to section 95 support. Some also apply to section 98 support. However, none apply to section 4 support, so there is no power for the Home Office to force you to repay any section 4 support you have received.

You have convertible assets

The Home Office can[67] require you to repay the value of asylum support you have received if, at the time of your application for support, you had assets (eg, savings, investments, property or shares) either in the UK or abroad that you could not then convert into money but which you can convert to money now (even if you have not done so).

The Home Office cannot require you to repay more than either:

- the total monetary value of all the support provided to you up to the date that it asks you to make a repayment; *or*
- if it is a lesser amount, the total monetary value of the assets that you had at the time of the application for support and that you have since been able to convert into money.

You were overpaid section 95 and/or 98 support

The Home Office may[68] require you to repay any section 95 and/or section 98 support that has been provided to you as a result of an 'error' by the Home Office. Unlike recovery of overpayments of most social security benefits, you do not need to have been responsible for the overpayment.

The Home Office may recover the support from you by deductions from support, if you are still being supported,[69] or as a debt, if you are no longer being supported.[70] The Home Office cannot recover more than the total monetary value of the support provided to you as a result of its mistake.

You have mispresented or failed to disclose

If the Home Office believes that you have received section 95 and/or section 98 support as a result of misrepresenting or failing disclose a material fact, the Home Office may apply to a county court (or, in Scotland, the sheriff court) for an order requiring you (or the person who made the misrepresentation, or who was responsible for the failure to disclose) to repay the support.[71] Recovery is possible from people other than yourself and your dependants. The total amount that the court can order to be repaid is the monetary value of the support paid as a result of the misrepresentation or failure to disclose, which would not have been provided had there not been that misrepresentation or failure to disclose.

Recovery of section 95 support from sponsor

Section 95 support may be recovered from a sponsor of someone who receives the support.[72] A **'sponsor'** is a person who has given a written undertaking under the Immigration Rules to be responsible for the maintenance and accommodation of someone seeking to enter or remain in the UK (see p34). This form of recovery is intended to deal with the situation in which someone obtains admission to the UK under a sponsorship agreement in a non-asylum capacity and then applies for asylum and becomes entitled to asylum support during the application process. The sponsor is only liable to repay payments for the period during which the undertaking was in effect. They should not, therefore, be liable for payments for any period of leave given subsequent to the original leave for which the undertaking was given, unless a further undertaking was also given. The sponsor is not liable for payments during any period of residence without leave.

To recover asylum support, the Home Office must apply for an order at a magistrates' court (in Scotland, the sheriff court). The court may order the sponsor to make weekly payments to the Home Office of an amount the court thinks is appropriate, taking into account all the circumstances of the case and, in particular, the sponsor's own income. The weekly sum must not be more than the weekly value of the support being provided to the asylum seeker. The court can order that payments be made to cover any period before the time the Home Office applied to the court. In such cases, the Home Office must take into account the sponsor's income during the period concerned, rather than their current income. The order can be enforced in the same way as a maintenance order.

Offences relating to sections 95 and section 98

It is a criminal offence[73] if, with a view to obtaining support under section 95 or section 98:

- you make a statement or representation (knowingly or otherwise) that is false; *or*
- you produce or cause to be produced any document or information that is false in a way that made a difference; *or*
- you fail to notify the Home Office of a change in circumstances when required to do so (see p529); *or*
- you cause another person to fail to notify a change in circumstances that the other person was required to notify the Home Office about.

Note: these offences do not apply to similar acts and omissions with a view to obtaining section 4 support. Prosecutions for these offences have been rare.

3. Temporary support

While considering your application for section 95 support, the Home Office can provide a temporary form of support to you or your dependant(s) under section 98 of the Immigration and Asylum Act 1999. This is known as **section 98 support** and is also commonly called 'emergency support' or 'initial accommodation'.

Temporary asylum support can be provided if it appears that you *may* be destitute at the time of the application – ie, even if there is some uncertainty.[74] The definition of 'destitution' is the same as for section 95 support (see p565),[75] except that temporary support can only be provided on the basis that you may be destitute now and not on the basis that you are likely to become destitute at any time within 14 days.[76] Temporary support can be provided at short notice. It can be authorised outside of office hours if you are considered to be particularly vulnerable – eg, you are a visibly pregnant woman or are able to prove you are pregnant, or you are part of a family with a dependent child younger than 18 or you are disabled.[77]

Temporary support may be provided subject to conditions, which must be given in writing. It can only be provided until the Home Office makes a decision on whether or not to give you section 95 support. If the Home Office refuses section 95 support, temporary support ends at the same time.

There is no right of appeal to the Asylum Support Tribunal (see p601) against a refusal or withdrawal of temporary support.[78] The only method of challenging such a decision is by way of judicial review.

Who is excluded from temporary support

You are excluded from temporary support if:[79]

- your immigration status does not bar you from getting social security benefits (see p113);
- you are not being treated as an asylum seeker or the dependant of an asylum seeker for immigration purposes; *and*
- you apply for support as part of a group and every person in the group is excluded under either of the above bullet points.

Termination of section 98 support

Your section 98 support is terminated:

- after the Home Office takes a decision on your application for section 95 support. If your section 95 application is refused, you have a right of appeal against that decision (see p600), and support might continue pending the appeal (especially if you have dependent children). If your section 95 application is granted, your section 98 support ends when you are sent to your section 95 accommodation (see p592). If you are granted asylum while in receipt of section 98 support, you are given 28 days' notice to quit the initial accommodation; *or*

- if the Home Office suspends or discontinues your section 98 support for breach of conditions (see p529) or for another reason specified in the regulations[80] (see p530).

Recovery of section 98 support and offences

See p532.

4. Support for refused asylum seekers

If your asylum application has been unsuccessful and you have exhausted all your appeal rights, or if your asylum claim has been declared by the Home Office to be inadmissible (in which case, you are referred to as a 'refused asylum seeker' in this *Handbook*), the general rule is that you are expected to return to your country of origin and are not entitled to support from the Home Office. However, if there is some legal or practical obstacle to you leaving, you may be able to claim support under section 4(2) of the Immigration and Asylum Act 1999. This is known as **section 4 support.**

Note: the legislative scheme for the support of refused asylum seekers is liable to change significantly if and when relevant parts of the Immigration Act 2016 come into force. This book does not include reference to the specific provisions of the 2016 Act that are not yet in force.

To get section 4 support you must:

- be a person who was but is no longer an asylum seeker and whose claim for asylum was rejected or declared inadmissible;[81] *and*
- be destitute (see below);[82] *and*
- meet one of the five criteria for support (see p537).[83]

Who is excluded from support

Certain people are excluded from section 4 support:

- refused asylum seekers who have not complied with removal directions and their dependants;[84] *and*
- refused asylum seekers with children who the Secretary of State says have failed, without reasonable excuse, to take reasonable steps to leave, or place themselves in a position to leave, the UK (although this exclusion is rarely used).[85]

However, people in these categories should not be excluded if section 4 support is necessary to avoid a breach of their human rights.[86]

In addition, those people who have never been asylum seekers and/or have never had their asylum claim rejected[87] are not eligible for support under section 4.

The definition of destitute

The definition of 'destitute' is the same as for section 95 support (see p527).[88]

In deciding whether you are destitute, the Home Office considers the time that has elapsed since you were in receipt of section 95 support and, if you have had any access to accommodation or financial support since then, evidence about whether that support is still available. If there has been no gap in your asylum support history, the Home Office is likely, in practice, to accept that you remain destitute once your eligibility for section 95 support comes to an end.[89] However, if you have not recently had support, the Home Office expects you to prove that you are now destitute, and requires detailed information on how you have survived and how your situation has now changed to leave you destitute. In these circumstances, the Home Office asks you to provide evidence, such as letters from friends, family and charities, explaining what support they have given you in the past and why that cannot continue. You may have survived from working (legally or illegally) in the past and so may need to explain this to the Home Office, so that it can fully understand your new situation. If you cannot obtain this evidence, you should explain to the Home Office (and the Asylum Support Tribunal in any appeal) why this is the case – eg, a friendship may have now deteriorated because you have overstayed your welcome.

Note: the test of destitution is set out in regulations (see p527).[90] If you have relied on friends and relatives, you may still have been destitute within the meaning of these regulations, even while receiving that help – eg, you may have spent nights sleeping on various friends' floors without a key to gain access, and walking the streets during the day, or have had no money and/or little food. In such situations, you have been destitute under the regulations throughout this period, because you have not had adequate accommodation and/or have been unable to meet your essential living needs. When applying for section 4 support in these circumstances, it is important to give full details about what support has been made available in the past. A 'self-statement' that fully explains your circumstances is recommended, with as much supporting evidence as possible (the Home Office frequently disbelieves uncorroborated statements by applicants).

Criteria for support

As well as being destitute, to qualify for section 4 support, you must also prove (see p578) that you are in one of the following situations.

- You are taking all reasonable steps to leave the UK (see below).
- You are unable to leave the UK because a medical condition prevents you from travelling (see p538).

- You are unable to leave the UK because there is no viable route of return (see p539).
- You have applied for judicial review of a decision in relation to your asylum claim (see p539).
- Section 4 support is necessary to avoid a breach of human rights (see p539).

You are taking all reasonable steps to leave the UK

To qualify for section 4 support on this ground, you must be taking all reasonable steps to leave the UK or place yourself in a position in which you are able to leave the UK, including, if relevant, applying for a travel document.[91]

The Home Office runs a 'voluntary returns service', through which refused asylum seekers and others without leave to remain in the UK can receive assistance and, in some cases, cash to return home. If you apply to the Home Office for assisted or voluntary return, that alone may not be sufficient to satisfy the requirement for section 4 support.

The Home Office will expect you to be proactive in arranging your return, for example, by making and keeping appointments with your embassy to attempt to get a travel document.

After granting support, the Home Office expects you to be able to leave the UK, as a general rule, within three months.[92] Therefore, if it is going to take you longer than that to leave, you should provide the Home Office with an explanation supported by evidence for the delay, otherwise your support will be discontinued. It is advisable to keep a diary of the steps you take. It is also important to keep copies of all letters and emails, and notes of telephone calls, emails and visits to, for example, the voluntary returns service and your embassy.

Support is often withdrawn on the grounds that someone has not taken *all* reasonable steps. It could be argued that the Home Office's view on this is often unrealistic, bearing in mind that applicants are destitute, desperate and may speak little English. However, on appeal, the Asylum Support Tribunal may take the view that if any reasonable step can be identified that you have not taken, even if you did not previously think of taking that step, you have not satisfied the requirement and should be refused support. Each case should be considered on its own merits.

Note: evidence required to prove you have taken all reasonable steps to leave the UK is explained on p578.

You are unable to leave the UK because a medical condition prevents you from travelling

To get section 4 support, you must be unable to travel (ie, to make a single journey from the UK, whether to your country of origin or to another country) because of 'a physical impediment' or other medical reason.[93] 'Unable' has been interpreted to mean more than 'unreasonable' or 'undesirable' but not 'impossible'.[94]

If you apply for support on this ground, you must submit a completed medical declaration ('Section 4(2) medical declaration'), available on gov.uk. If you cannot find the declaration form on this website and the Home Office does not send one to you, a copy can be obtained from local support agencies or the Asylum Support Appeals Project at asaproject.org/resources/library/section-4-support-pregnancy-and-health-issues. Arguably, a letter containing the same information on headed paper should be sufficient, but it is highly likely that the Home Office will insist on a completed medical declaration form (see p579).

Note: evidence required to prove that you are unable to leave the UK due to a medical condition is explained on p579.

You are unable to leave the UK because there is no viable route of return

To qualify for section 4 support on this ground, the Secretary of State must have made a declaration that, in their opinion, there is no viable route to a particular country.[95]

At the time of writing, there is no country to which that applies. Irrespective of your personal circumstances, therefore, you will not succeed in claiming support on this ground unless, by the time of your application, the Secretary of State has made a declaration that there is no viable route. The only time the Secretary of State has made such a declaration was in 2005 for a six-month period with regard to Iraq. If the Secretary of State refuses to make a declaration where there is evidence that there is no viable route of return to a country (eg, because there are no flights to that country from the UK), then it may be possible to challenge the Secretary of State's refusal by way of judicial review (see p617).

You have applied for a judicial review of a decision relating to your asylum claim

To get section 4 support on this ground, you must have lodged an application for judicial review to challenge a decision relating to your application for asylum and, in England and Wales, you must have been granted permission to proceed (or leave to proceed in Northern Ireland).[96] Simply lodging a judicial review application at court in Scotland is sufficient.

Note: If you have lodged an application and are waiting for the court to consider whether to grant permission, you are likely to be able to receive support to avoid a breach of your human rights (see below and p543).

Note: evidence required to prove that you have applied for judicial review is explained on p580.

Section 4 support is necessary to avoid a breach of human rights

You qualify for section 4 support if you can show that the provision of accommodation is necessary to avoid a breach of human rights.[97] The courts have said that denying support to asylum seekers whose claims are outstanding, in circumstances where they are not allowed to work or claim benefits, constitutes 'inhuman and degrading treatment'.[98] That is prohibited under Article 3 of the European Convention on Human Rights (ECHR).

If you are freely able to leave the UK to avoid destitution, however, your human rights are not breached if support is withheld. If you have an outstanding asylum claim, the Home Office will accept that there is a legal or practical obstacle to your making a voluntary departure from the UK to avoid destitution, since your fear of ill treatment may be well founded as far as the Home Office is concerned. However, the possibility of a voluntary return is always a central issue whenever an application for section 4 support is made by a refused asylum seeker (since the Home Office will proceed on the basis that a refused asylum seeker can return to their country of origin without problem). The law has developed some principles for deciding when a person whose asylum claim has been rejected should be granted support rather than asked to make a voluntary departure from the UK.

Multifactorial assessments and Home Office policy

The High Court has confirmed that in considering whether it would be a breach of human rights to withhold section 4 support, 'a multifactorial assessment [is] required in each individual case'.[99] Relevant facts include: 'age, gender, mental and physical health and condition, any facilities or sources of support available to the applicant, the weather and time of year and the period for which the applicant has already suffered or is likely to continue to suffer privation', as well as 'exposure to the elements [resulting] from rough-sleeping, [the associated] risks to health and safety...the effects of lack of access to toilet and washing facilities and the humiliation and sense of despair that attaches to those who suffer from deprivations of that kind'.[100]

The High Court made it clear that in considering whether to grant section 4 support, the Home Office should take into account these factors if relevant in every case *in addition to* the reasons why in individual claims they will not or cannot return to their country of origin.

Obstacles to return

The Home Office's current policy[101] provides for section 4 support to be granted in cases which there are 'legal or practical obstacles' to a voluntary return. The policy is unclear about what constitutes a practical obstacle. The policy states that whether there is a 'legal obstacle' should be considered on a case-by-case basis but accepts that two scenarios will usually meet the test:

- you have submitted further submissions against the refusal of your asylum claim, which remain outstanding; *and*
- you have appealed out of time against the refusal of your asylum claim and the First-tier Tribunal is considering whether to allow the appeal to proceed out of time.

However, the law also recognises additional scenarios that are not referred to in the Home Office's policy, and which are considered below.

Note: it can be argued that the test in the previous Home Office policy (ie, whether it was reasonable to expect you to make a voluntary departure from the UK) continues to apply in the sense that a legal or practical obstacle to voluntary return will be held to exist if you cannot be expected to make a voluntary departure from the UK because of that obstacle. The most common scenarios where this test is met are cases in which:

- you have made further submissions to the Home Office in support of your asylum or human rights claim, and the submissions are not hopeless or abusive (see note on p542); *or*
- you have issued or threatened judicial review proceedings in relation to your asylum claim (generally to challenge a refusal to treat your further submissions as a fresh asylum claim (see p543); *or*
- you have made an 'out-of-time' appeal against the refusal of your asylum claim to the First-tier Tribunal (Immigration and Asylum Chamber) (see p544); *or*
- you are a potential victim of modern slavery (see p544); *or*
- you have made an application for leave under Article 8 of the ECHR (see p545); *or*
- you have applied for leave to enter or remain as a stateless person (see p545); *or*
- you have an outstanding application to the European Court of Human Rights (ECtHR) (see p546).

Typical scenarios in which you can argue that support is necessary to avoid a breach of human rights

Each of the above scenarios is considered below. **Note:** for each scenario, the evidence you should provide in support of your application is explained on p578.

1. You have made further submissions to the Home Office

This is the most common situation in which a refused asylum seeker is given support to avoid a breach of their human rights.

Making further submissions

You must in most cases submit further submissions in person by prior appointment at the offices of the Further Submissions Unit (FSU) of the Home Office in Liverpool, Glasgow or another designated place. On telephoning the FSU to make an appointment, you may be permitted in some circumstances to send your further submissions by post or email.

Once the Home Office has considered your further submissions, it will confirm in writing whether, in light of your further submissions, your asylum claim has been granted or refused. If your asylum claim has been refused, the Home Office will confirm whether, despite the refusal of asylum, your further submissions have been accepted as a fresh asylum application. If they are accepted as a fresh claim, then:

– a fresh asylum application is formally recorded by the Home Office; *and*

– you are granted a right of appeal against the decision to refuse asylum.

At this point, you become an asylum seeker again and can reapply for section 95 support (see p522). If your submissions are not accepted (and recorded) as a fresh asylum application, your section 4 support will be discontinued unless you can prove that you meet one of the other criteria for section 4 support (see below).

As stated above, to show that it would be a breach of your human rights to withhold support, the Home Office's current policy requires you to show that there is a legal or practical obstacle to your making a voluntary departure (or, under the old policy, that it would be unreasonable to expect you to make a voluntary departure from the UK). To do that in this scenario, you must show that:

- you have made a further application to the Home Office to remain in the UK in support of your asylum claim, or in support of your claim that your removal from the UK would breach Article 3 of the ECHR (see p51). That is usually in the form of further submissions including any fresh evidence that you want the Home Office to accept as a fresh asylum claim, or a fresh claim made under Article 3 of the ECHR; *and*
- this application is still outstanding – eg, the Home Office has not yet decided whether it amounts to a fresh asylum application;[102] *and*
- your further submissions are not clearly hopeless and abusive (see below).

The High Court has indicated that in these circumstances, section 4 support should be provided.[103]

Note: the Home Office (and on appeal, the Asylum Support Tribunal) is liable to treat further submissions in support of a fresh asylum claim as 'hopeless and abusive' if, for example:

- the submissions contain no detail whatsoever – eg, if you are still fearful of returning to your country of origin but do not give any further information addressing the reasons why your asylum claim was previously rejected; *or*
- the evidence or arguments that you have submitted as part of your fresh claim have already been seen and rejected by the Home Office, or rejected on appeal, and do not disclose any change in the law or the factual circumstances of your claim since the previous refusal.

The more unsuccessful fresh claims you have made in the past, the more difficult it is likely to be to demonstrate to the Home Office (and on appeal to the Asylum Support Tribunal) that your present fresh claim is not hopeless and abusive.

2. You intend to make further submissions but have not yet submitted them to the Home Office

The Asylum Support Tribunal has often had to consider whether section 4 support should be granted when you intend to make further submissions to the Home

Office but have not yet done so, either because the further submissions have not yet been finalised or because you are waiting for an appointment at which you can submit them.

In such cases, the Home Office is likely to refuse support and to rely on a decision of the principal judge of the Asylum Support Tribunal[104] in which she stated that she 'could not conceive of a situation where the mere assertion that further submissions are in the process of being lodged will be sufficient to satisfy an asylum support judge' that section 4 support should be granted. However, the Asylum Support Tribunal judges will consider the facts of each case, including the steps the appellant has taken to progress the further submissions, and the extent to which any delay is outside the appellant's control – eg, delay in receiving an appointment from the Home Office to lodge the further submissions, or delay caused by a third party such as an expert instructed by the appellant's solicitor to prepare a report on which the further submissions will be based. While the judges differ in their approach, the Asylum Support Tribunal may allow an appeal where the appellant has prepared further submissions and has an appointment to attend the FSU to submit them on a future date and, less commonly, if further submissions are still being prepared.[105]

In practice, the judges will also take into account the apparent strength of your proposed further submissions. This will be a broad brush exercise, since the Asylum Support Tribunal should only be concerned with whether the further submissions are hopeless or abusive (see note on p542).

In practice, therefore, if you are applying for section 4 support but still have not submitted your further submissions, it is essential, if possible, to put evidence before the Home Office and the Asylum Support Tribunal showing:

- the reasons for the delay in submitting your further submissions (with a view to proving that the delay is not your fault); *and*
- that the fresh claim, when finalised, will not be hopeless or abusive.

To do this, you should, if you can, obtain a draft version of the further submissions from your immigration solicitor, or a note setting out the gist of the further submissions, and reasons why the solicitor considers that the further submissions contain new material and have a realistic prospect of success, with specific reference to the reasons why your asylum claim was previously rejected on appeal (or if you never appealed, the reasons why it was rejected by the Home Office).

Note: the evidence you should consider providing to prove you have made fresh submissions to the Home Office is considered on p581.

3. You have issued or threatened judicial review proceedings

If your further submissions are not treated as a fresh asylum claim by the Home Office, you can challenge the Home Office's decision by judicial review. While you are preparing to bring a claim for judicial review, you may be eligible for support to avoid a breach of your human rights.

A judicial review in the High Court on this issue in 2009 held that it would be a breach of human rights to withhold section 4 support in a variety of factual circumstances even if (in England, Wales and Northern Ireland) permission to apply for judicial review has not yet been granted. The judge did not define these circumstances, but the judgment implies that they include when your solicitor has sent the required 'pre-action' letter to the Home Office threatening judicial review proceedings or when you have already issued proceedings and are waiting for a decision on whether you can proceed.[106] You must show that your case is not 'entirely without merit'. If you have been granted legal aid to pursue your judicial review, that can be used as a persuasive, if not conclusive, argument that your case has some merit.

Note: the evidence you can provide to prove that you have issued or threatened judicial review proceedings is considered on p580.

4. You have made an 'out-of-time' appeal to the First-tier Tribunal

If you want to appeal against the refusal of your asylum application but the time for appealing has expired, you must ask the First-tier Tribunal (Immigration and Asylum Chamber) for permission for an 'out-of-time' appeal to proceed. If you have made such an application, the Home Office and the First-tier Tribunal (Asylum Support) usually grant section 4 support on the basis that it would be unreasonable to expect you to leave the UK in the meantime.

If the First-tier Tribunal (Immigration and Asylum Chamber) grants you permission to appeal out of time, you become an asylum seeker again and are eligible for section 95 support (and, at that stage, no longer eligible for section 4 support).

If you appeal within the prescribed time limits, you are still considered to be an asylum seeker and so you will still be eligible for section 95 support (see p561).

Note: the evidence you should provide to prove you have made an out-of-time appeal is given on p583.

5. You are a victim of modern slavery

Victims of modern slavery who are destitute have a separate route into support through the National Referral Mechanism (NRM). Detailed consideration of the NRM is beyond the scope of this *Handbook*. It is sufficient here to note the following.[107]

- A potential victim of modern slavery can be referred into the NRM by a first responder (organisations that are authorised for this purpose, including public bodies such as the police, the Home Office and local authorities, and voluntary sector organisations such as the Salvation Army).
- Identification of an individual as a victim of modern slavery by the decision makers (known as 'competent authorities') is a two-stage process. The first stage is known as the 'reasonable grounds decision'. It is a decision as to whether there are reasonable grounds to suspect that the individual has been

trafficked or is the victim of modern slavery. The second and final stage is known as the 'conclusive grounds' decision. It is a decision as to whether, on the balance of probabilities, there is sufficient information to conclude that the individual is a victim of modern slavery.

- Support may be available under the NRM following a reasonable grounds decision.
- There is some overlap between support under the NRM and asylum support for victims and potential victims of modern slavery. Both are intended to prevent destitution. The support available under the NRM is intended, in addition, to aid the applicant's recovery, and a cash sum is paid to this end. The premium payable under the NRM to aid recovery is disregarded by the Home Office as a matter of policy when assessing whether an applicant for asylum support is destitute.[108]
- An individual supported under the NRM should only be asked to apply for asylum support following a needs assessment.
- Individuals supported under the NRM who are refused asylum seekers may, following an appropriate needs assessment and depending on their individual circumstances, be directed to apply for section 4 support.

Home Office guidance recognises that an ongoing case in the NRM is a legal obstacle to a voluntary departure from the UK. The guidance states:[109]

> Whether there are legal obstacles to return or removal should be considered on a case by case basis on the information available, but examples of where it should usually be accepted that they exist are where:
> • they have been referred to the National Referral Mechanism (NRM) and are awaiting a Reasonable Grounds as a potential victim of modern slavery
> • they have received a positive Reasonable Grounds decision and are in the recovery and reflection period and are awaiting their Conclusive Grounds decision (where the Conclusive Grounds decision is negative, they will exit the NRM process)
> • where a Conclusive Grounds decision is positive and they are receiving support from the Modern Slavery Victim Care Contract, they are entitled to a minimum of 45 days of move-on support.

6. You have made an application for leave to remain in the UK under Article 8 of the European Convention on Human Rights

You may qualify for section 4 support if you have an outstanding application for leave under Article 8 of the ECHR (see p45), provided your application has some merit and is not obviously hopeless or abusive.[110]

7. You have applied for leave to remain as a stateless person

Refused asylum seekers who later apply to the Home Office for leave to remain because they are stateless are eligible for section 4 support on the basis that they have an outstanding application and it is not reasonable to leave the UK until that application has been decided.[111] There is a prescribed form on which to apply for leave to remain as a stateless person. If your application is refused, there is no right of appeal, so the only remedy is judicial review. If you apply for a judicial review of the refusal of your statelessness application, you can continue to receive section 4 support, provided your judicial review claim is not hopeless or abusive.

8. You have applied to the European Court of Human Rights

Refused asylum seekers who have exhausted their appeal rights in the UK but who claim that their removal would lead to a breach of their human rights can apply to the ECtHR in Strasbourg for an order preventing their imminent removal (called a Rule 39 order).

If that applies to you and you are waiting for a decision from the ECtHR and you are destitute, you may be eligible for section 4 support. In a decision in 2011, the Principal Judge of the Asylum Support Tribunal gave criteria for deciding when support should be granted.[112] You must show that:

- your application to the ECtHR 'has some merit'. This includes showing that it contains details and these are specific to your case. The level of detail required depends on the case; *and*
- you exhausted all remedies in the UK before applying to the ECtHR, including making a fresh application for asylum and challenging any refusal by judicial review. However, there is no need to have applied for a remedy if it was 'bound to fail'. So, for example, if you have been refused legal aid for a judicial review because of existing UK caselaw, you may still satisfy this ground. Alternatively, you should have evidence (eg, from your immigration solicitor) that any unexhausted domestic remedies were bound to fail and, therefore, were pointless to initiate before you applied to the ECtHR.

9. Other scenarios in which withholding section 4 support may breach human rights

Depending on the facts of your case and the available evidence, you may be able to argue that because of your personal circumstances (potentially including your medical condition, practical barriers to travel and legal commitments in the UK), it is unreasonable to expect you to return home voluntarily, so withholding support would breach your human rights. However, such arguments do not routinely succeed. Without powerful supporting evidence, the tribunal is liable to conclude that, even though you may be reluctant to leave the UK, there is no legal or practical obstacle to you doing so.

However, each case is considered on its own facts. By way of example, the Asylum Support Tribunal has granted section 4 support on human rights grounds when a medical condition makes travel risky or harmful but does not make someone 'unable to travel', including to a mentally ill person on the basis that he should remain on support while still in the UK, pending forced removal.[113]

Another example might be when a refused asylum seeker is on probation and subject to reporting requirements and medical tests because of drug offences. In such a scenario, it could be argued that leaving the UK would mean that the applicant could not comply with the probation order made by the court, and that section 4 support was therefore required to prevent destitution. In a similar case, a grant of bail requiring a section 4 applicant to attend a criminal trial in the magistrates' court on a date to be fixed was held by the Asylum Support Tribunal to be a legal obstacle to a voluntary return, conferring eligibility for section 4 support.

Termination of section 4 support

Your section 4 support may be terminated in one of two ways, namely:

- you have breached the conditions on which section 4 support was granted; *or*
- your entitlement to section 4 has been reviewed, and a decision taken that you are no longer entitled.

Conditions of section 4 support

Section 4 support is granted subject to conditions. The conditions must be given to you in writing and must involve:[114]

- specified standards of behaviour; *or*
- a reporting requirement; *or*
- a requirement:
  - to reside at an authorised address; *or*
  - if absent from an authorised address without the Home Office's permission, to ensure that the absence is for no more than seven consecutive days and nights or for no more than a total of 14 days and nights in any six-month period; *or*
- specified steps to facilitate your departure from the UK.

The Home Office usually writes to you about an alleged breach of conditions before terminating your support.

When support can be suspended or discontinued

In contrast to section 95 support, the Home Office has no power to suspend section 4 support. The Home Office can only review your entitlement and discontinue your support if it considers you are no longer entitled.

The Home Office may decide you are no longer destitute or no longer eligible – eg, because you are not taking all reasonable steps to leave the UK, your further submissions for asylum have been refused or your application for judicial review has failed.

The Home Office's policy is regularly to review section 4 support:[115]

- no later than three months after it was granted or last reviewed; *or*

- six weeks after the birth of a baby if you have received support on the basis of late pregnancy or birth of a baby (the Home Office accepts that a woman cannot travel six weeks before or six weeks after giving birth); *or*
- earlier:
  - when appropriate; *and*
  - specifically when a person is supported on the basis that they are taking all reasonable steps to leave the UK, to check that they are co-operating with Home Office efforts to arrange for their documentation or departure or that they have approached their national embassy for the purposes of obtaining a passport.

You can appeal against the decision to discontinue your support. See Chapter 24.

The best interests of children

The Home Office has a duty to ensure that all its decisions take into account the need to safeguard and promote the welfare of children.[116] In practice, it tends not to discontinue section 4 support for families who would otherwise be destitute. However, the wording in the policy guidance does not make this practice clear.[117]

If the breach of conditions is a minor one, it may not be appropriate to discontinue support. If the Home Office does decide to terminate your support, it should liaise with the local authority so that social services can carry out a child in need assessment, with a view to taking over the support. However, the relevant Home Office policy states (incorrectly, it would seem) that it is not necessary for the Home Office to liaise with the local authority if support has been discontinued because the Home Office believes you are no longer destitute. You can appeal if your support is terminated due to an alleged breach of conditions, and you should seriously consider doing so in this scenario, to buy time and minimise the risk of an unmanaged eviction.

Recovery of section 4 support and offences

In contrast to the position with section 95 and section 98 support (see p534), there are no specific offences in the Immigration and Asylum Act 1999 relating to obtaining section 4 support. The Home Office does not have any powers to recover the costs of section 4 support that has already been paid.

5. Support for those whose asylum claims have been expressly or impliedly withdrawn

Sometimes people claim asylum but then expressly or impliedly withdraw their claim. Typically, they may claim asylum on or soon after arrival in the UK but cease contact with the Home Office before their asylum claim is determined. They may re-establish contact with the Home Office years later in circumstances in which they need support. This section addresses the circumstances in which asylum support may be available to them.

Your asylum claim is treated as withdrawn if the conditions in Immigration Rule 333C are met – ie, if:

- you have expressly withdrawn your application (in writing on a prescribed form); *or*
- the Home Office decides that you have impliedly withdrawn your application:
  - by leaving the UK; *or*
  - by failing to complete an asylum questionnaire when requested to; *or*
  - by failing to attend your asylum interview, unless you can show that was due to circumstances beyond your control.

If you fall into any of these categories, then depending on your circumstances, it may not be possible for you to claim either section 95 or section 4 support because:

- your asylum claim is treated as no longer existing and so is not now recorded, which is a pre-condition for entitlement to section 95 support (see p523); *and*
- the Home Office and some judges of the Asylum Support Tribunal (different judges have taken different positions on this point) are liable to decide that your asylum claim was never rejected, which is a pre-condition for section 4 support (see p536).

Therefore, the general rule is that if your asylum claim has been withdrawn, then:

- you are very likely not to be treated by the Home Office as eligible for section 95 or section 4 support (although see below for exceptions); *but*
- in that event, you may be eligible for what is known as 'Schedule 10' support if you have been granted bail (see p551).

Exceptions to this general rule include the following.

- The Home Office was wrong to treat your asylum claim as impliedly withdrawn because the conditions enabling the Home Office to do so were not met – eg, the available evidence shows that you did not refuse to complete an asylum questionnaire; or that you never failed to attend your asylum interview; or that the Home Office did not follow its policy on withdrawn asylum claims, for example, to retain on file evidence that it warned you of the consequences of non-compliance. In such cases, you may be able to argue (depending on which judge hears your appeal) that the Home Office should not have treated your asylum claim as having been withdrawn, and that, since it was never refused, it remains outstanding. As a result, you can argue that you are entitled to section 95 support.[118]
- You succeed in reopening your asylum claim. The rules require you to do that by lodging further submissions with the Home Office's Further Submissions

Unit. The Home Office then makes a decision on whether your asylum claim has been reopened. If the Home Office decides to reopen your case (by recording a fresh asylum claim), you will be eligible for section 95 support if you are destitute.

- You have a child in your household younger than 18 *and* you were in receipt of section 95 support before your asylum claim was treated as withdrawn. You should remain entitled to section 95 support if you are destitute until the child reaches 18 years old. At the time of writing, the Asylum Support Tribunal has recently decided that you can never benefit from section 94(5) if your asylum claim has been expressly or impliedly withdrawn.[119] This decision appears likely to be challenged by way of judicial review. If you have one or more children under 18 when your asylum claim is expressly or impliedly withdrawn, you should take specialist advice as to whether you might subsequently claim the benefit of section 94(5).
- You applied for asylum before 7 April 2008, or between 7 April 2008 and 27 February 2015. The rules changed on those dates. If you applied before 7 April 2008, your claim is likely to have been refused rather than treated as withdrawn, so you may be entitled to section 4 support provided all other conditions of eligibility are met. If you applied between 7 April 2008 and 27 February 2015, your claim will only have been treated as impliedly withdrawn if you failed to attend your asylum interview.
- Some judges of the Asylum Support Tribunal have held that a decision by the Home Office to treat an asylum claim as withdrawn means that the claim has been rejected. That means that you may be entitled to section 4 support if you appeal, depending on which judge hears your appeal.[120] However, that is not the view of the Home Office or the Principal Judge.[121] 'At the time of writing, the Principal Judge's view that section 4 support is not available to those whose asylum claims were treated as impliedly withdrawn, but who seek to reopen their claims by making further submissions, has been upheld by another judge of the tribunal.[122] However, it is understood that the decision upholding the Principal Judge's analysis is likely to be challenged by way of judicial review. If your asylum claim has been treated as impliedly withdrawn, but you have sought to reopen it by making further submissions, you should take specialist advice about your potential eligibility for section 4 support.

There are other potential arguments in third-country cases in which the Home Office referred the asylum claim to another state for the claim to be considered there instead of in the UK, pursuant to the Dublin III Regulation (which ceased to apply in January 2021 following Brexit). In such cases, the Home Office was required to certify the asylum claim once the third country had accepted the referral. It is arguable that the Home Office certification should be treated as a rejection of the asylum claim, even if the asylum seeker subsequently absconded, making it possible to potentially claim section 4 support. There are also arguments about entitlement to section 95 being retained if the Home Office has failed to follow the correct procedures for treating the claim as withdrawn.

Overall, this is a complicated and fast-moving area, and you should seek expert advice. You can contact the Asylum Support Appeals Project either through an advice line, or by referring your case to them after you have appealed to the Asylum Support Tribunal (although representation is subject to the organisation's limited capacity, and is therefore not guaranteed).

If your claim has been treated as withdrawn and none of the above exceptions to the general rule apply (and if you appeal to the Asylum Support Tribunal but do not get one of the minority of judges willing to treat a decision by the Home Office to treat your asylum claim as withdrawn, as a 'rejection' of the claim), you will not be entitled to either section 95 or section 4 support. However, you may still be able to apply for what is known as 'Schedule 10' support or support from your local authority if you have accommodation-related care needs or minor children. These issues are addressed below.

6. Discretionary support for people on immigration bail

This section applies to anyone who has been granted immigration bail, not solely people who have claimed asylum. It may be relevant to people who have claimed asylum who are not eligible for either section 95 or section 4 support – eg:

- people who claimed asylum but whose asylum claims have been treated as withdrawn; *or*
- people who claimed asylum as children, became appeal-rights exhausted before reaching 18 years old, and who are seeking to pursue their asylum claims as adults.

Who is entitled to Schedule 10 support

You are entitled to Schedule 10 support if:

- you have been granted immigration bail; *and*
- you are required by your bail condition to live at a certain address (whether or not that address has yet been specified, bail can be granted in principle on condition that the applicant provides an acceptable address);[123] *and*
- you would not be able to support yourself at the address unless Schedule 10 support is granted;[124] *and*
- the Secretary of State accepts there are exceptional circumstances that justify the provision of support.

The Home Office's policy on granting support under Schedule 10 is contained in its policy on immigration bail.[125] Three types of cases are accepted as being generally exceptional, and therefore to be potentially appropriate for Schedule 10 support:[126]

- Special Immigration Appeals Commission cases, which involve national security; *or*
- harm cases, involving:
  - people, including foreign national offenders (FNOs), who are granted bail and who are assessed as being at a high or very high risk of causing serious harm to the public; *or*
  - FNOs at high risk of harmful reoffending against an individual (eg, offences of domestic burglary, robbery, sexual assaults and violence) who are assessed using the Offender Group Reconviction Scale (OGRS) with a minimum score of 70 per cent,

  if those FNOs have nowhere suitable to live in accordance with their probation licence and/or multi-agency public protection arrangements (for a limited period, or otherwise at the discretion of the Home Office in the interest of public protection); *or*
- cases in which failure to provide support is a breach of human rights.

Exceptional circumstances

For the circumstances in which a denial of support would lead to a breach of human rights, see p539. That section concerns the circumstances in which section 4 support is necessary to avoid a breach of human rights. Similar general considerations apply in Schedule 10 cases except that, unlike with section 4, the class of applicants for Schedule 10 support is not limited to refused asylum seekers. Nonetheless, the Home Office's policy[127] requires applicants for Schedule 10 support to also show that there is some legal or practical obstacle to returning to their home country. In the absence of such an obstacle, the Home Office is likely to conclude that it will not be a breach of your human rights to withhold support, because you could avoid that prospect by voluntarily returning to your country of origin.

Procedure for applying

If you are applying for Schedule 10 support under the human rights criteria, you should use form BAIL409. Note that an application for Schedule 10 support should be made in liaison with your immigration solicitor, if you have one.

Award

If support is granted, it is likely to be in the same form as section 4 support – ie, cash will not be provided, but instead the weekly allowance (£45.00 at the time of writing) will be put on an 'ASPEN' card to be used in designated shops.

Exclusions from Schedule 10 support

You will not be entitled to Schedule 10 support if you are eligible for another type of support. Asylum seekers and refused asylum seekers should in general apply for section 95 or section 4 support (unless their claims have been treated as withdrawn – see p548), and those with children or care needs should seek support from the local authority (see below). There is no provision for dependants to be supported under Schedule 10. Partners and other dependants need to apply for support in their own right (if necessary, to the local authority).

7. Support from your local authority

If you are an asylum seeker or refused asylum seeker, and you have care needs, or have a child or children, or you are a child, you may be entitled to support from your local authority.

Note: this is a complex area of law and detailed consideration is beyond the scope of this *Handbook*. What follows is an overview of the general forms of local authority support, followed by a summary of the ways in which asylum seekers and refused asylum seekers can access them.

If you believe that you may be entitled to support from your local authority, get expert advice from a children's law or community care adviser.

If you are an asylum seeker or a refused asylum seeker, the local authority may be under a duty to provide accommodation and financial support if you:

- have accommodation-related care needs; *or*
- have a child that the local authority has assessed as being a 'child in need' for the purposes of the Children Act 1989; *or*
- are an unaccompanied asylum-seeking child.

Asylum seekers with accommodation-related care needs

The legislation governing support for people with care needs changed in 2015, although it is generally considered that many of the previously established legal principles continue to apply. Different laws apply in the different regions of the United Kingdom.

- In England, local authorities' duties to assess any person who appears to need care and support, and provide appropriate care in accordance with their assessment, are set out in the Care Act 2014.
- In Wales, the equivalent legislation is the Social Services and Well-being (Wales) Act 2014.
- In Scotland, it is the Social Work (Scotland) Act 1968.
- In Northern Ireland, it is Article 15 of the Health and Personal Social Services (Northern Ireland) Order 1972.

All the legislation follows the same broad principle by which local authorities assess and then meet the needs of those in their area who appear to be in need of care and support. There is provision for urgent assessment when a person presents with apparently urgent needs.

Who is excluded from support

Local authorities are prevented by statute[128] from meeting the needs for care and support of an asylum seeker:

> ...whose needs for care and support have arisen solely because (a) the adult is destitute or (b) of the physical effects, or anticipated physical effects, of being destitute.

The meaning of the statutory language was considered in a series of cases in the early 2000s between the Home Office and local authorities to determine responsibility for funding the accommodation of asylum seekers with care needs. As Lord Justice Simon Brown famously observed in one of those cases:[129]

> The word 'solely' is a strong one and its purpose there seems to be evident. Assistance under the Act ... is, it hardly need be emphasised, the last resort for the destitute. If there are to be immigrant beggars on our streets, then let them at least not be old, ill or disabled.

In practice, therefore, the courts have held that there is a distinction between:

- asylum seekers who require care and attention solely because of the effects of destitution (and for no other reason); *and*
- asylum seekers whose need for care and attention arises independently of whether or not they may be destitute – eg, because of some disability.

The law prevents a local authority from supporting people in the first group but requires local authorities to meet the assessed needs of those in the second. The meaning of 'care and attention' (the previous statutory duty referred to 'care and attention' rather than 'care and support') was considered by the House of Lords in a subsequent case. Lady Hale held that:[130]

> ...the natural and ordinary meaning of the words 'care and attention' in this context is 'looking after'. Looking after means doing something for the person being cared for which he cannot or should not be expected to do for himself: it might be household tasks which an old person can no longer perform or can only perform with great difficulty; it might be protection from risks which a mentally disabled person cannot perceive; it might be personal care, such as feeding, washing or toileting. This is not an exhaustive list. The provision of medical care is expressly excluded.

In practice, this judgment has meant that to receive support from the local authority, an asylum seeker's need for care and support must be accommodation-related.

Refused asylum seekers with accommodation-related care needs

The duties owed by local authorities to refused asylum seekers with accommodation-related care needs are generally the same as are owed to asylum seekers (see above), with one further restriction. Schedule 3 of the Nationality, Immigration and Asylum Act 2002 prevents local authorities providing care and support to refused asylum seekers except in relation to children, or if support is necessary to prevent a breach of human rights.[131]

If you are a refused asylum seeker who has accommodation-related care needs, and you seek care and support from the local authority, the local authority may decline to help if you are able to make a voluntary return to your country. The local authority may argue that if you decide to remain and thereby face destitution, your destitution will be caused by your choice not to return to your country, not by its decision to withhold support. The court has ruled this approach to be generally lawful.[132] However, if you are a refused asylum seeker with accommodation-related needs for care and support, it may be a breach of your human rights to require you to leave the UK if there is a legal or practical obstacle to your making a voluntary departure from the UK. The most common such obstacle is when you have a pending immigration application that:

- can only be pursued from within the UK; *and*
- is not hopeless.[133]

The considerations that apply in these cases are similar to those considered in relation to section 4 (see p539). If you need care and support from the local authority, and (1) you have an outstanding application for leave to enter or remain (2) that cannot be pursued from outside the UK, you will need to satisfy the local authority of (1) and (2) and, in addition, that there is some merit in the outstanding application. To do that, you will likely need a letter from your immigration solicitor to support your request to the local authority.

If you rely on any a different legal or practical obstacle to a voluntary departure, you will also have to provide documentary evidence.

Asylum-seeking families with a child in need

Local authorities have a duty to safeguard and promote the welfare of children who are 'in need'. If you are destitute and have children, you may therefore be eligible for accommodation or support from your local authority under the Children Act 1989 (in Scotland, the Children (Scotland) Act 1995). A child who is destitute is generally considered to be 'in need', but a child can also be in need if they are disabled or if they are unlikely to achieve or maintain a reasonable standard of health or development without the provision of services by a local authority. The duty to support the child extends to supporting parents or other family members if that is in the child's best interests.

However, asylum seekers are eligible for support under section 95. This eligibility takes precedence over support under the Children Act: if a local authority has reasonable grounds for believing that a family is eligible for, and would be granted, section 95 support if applied for, the local authority is prevented by law[134] from providing support to a child of the family.

If an asylum seeker with a child younger than 18 receives a negative asylum decision (whether on first application or appeal), the asylum seeker is treated – for asylum support purposes – as though the asylum claim was not determined, and remains on section 95 support while the child is younger than 18 and the family remains in the UK.[135]

The majority of asylum seekers with children remain on section 95 support for some time after making a claim if their claims are unsuccessful. However, if a child is born to an asylum seeker after the asylum claim has been finally determined, the family is not entitled to section 95 support. In those circumstances, the asylum seeker may be able to apply for section 4 support if destitute and eligible under regulation 3(2)(a)–(e) of the Immigration and Asylum (Provision of Accommodation to Failed Asylum-Seekers) Regulations 2005. Once section 4 support is granted to a destitute family with children, the Home Office's unpublished policy[136] appears to be that it will not be discontinued unless the asylum seeker is no longer destitute or has breached other conditions of their support package or the children turn 18.

Note: before any decision can be taken to remove section 4 support from a family with a child, the Home Office should demonstrate, under section 55 of the Borders, Citizenship and Immigration Act 2009, how it has discharged its duties in relation to the safety and welfare of the child (see p532). The fact that you may be eligible for section 4 support (see p537) does *not* exclude you from claiming Children Act support if your child has particular welfare needs that would not otherwise be met. Unlike section 95 support, eligibility for which prevents local authorities from providing Children Act support (see above), section 4 is a 'fall-back power' and any duty to provide support under the Children Act should take priority. Despite that, some local authorities might still refuse support on the basis that you should apply for section 4 support before approaching the local authority. If that happens, you should get expert advice, because it may be possible to challenge the local authority's refusal by judicial review.[137]

If you are a refused asylum seeker with a child in need supported by the local authority, the local authority may attempt to discharge its duty to the child by offering to fund your and your child's journey to your home country. You should take expert advice if this happens to you: an attempt to terminate Children Act support for that reason has been held to be unlawful when the mother of a child in need had an outstanding immigration application that was not hopeless and that could not have been pursued if the family had left the UK.[138]

Unaccompanied asylum-seeking children

Local authorities are responsible for supporting children younger than 18 who arrive in the UK alone and claim asylum (who are often referred to as 'unaccompanied minors'). Unaccompanied asylum-seeker children are dispersed around the country. The local authority in the new area should then make arrangements for suitable accommodation, which can include foster care.

If you have already been supported by a local authority as an unaccompanied minor, the authority may continue to have a duty to provide you with support when you reach 18 under the Children (Leaving Care) Act 2000. That allows for a needs assessment and potential support up to the age of 21, or 24 if you continue in education.

There may be a dispute about your age. If you claim asylum as an unaccompanied minor, the Home Office should refer you to social services for support unless it strongly believes that you are older than 18. If the social services department (in Scotland, social work department) has any doubt about your age, it can carry out an age assessment. See p509 for more information on proving your age. You should seek specialist advice if your age has been disputed; refugee organisations, such as the Refugee Council, may be able to assist you (see Appendix 2).

Access to healthcare

Not all migrants are entitled to free NHS specialist medical treatment. Of the categories of supported asylum seekers and former asylum seekers considered in this chapter (ie, those supported under section 95 and section 4 of the Immigration and Asylum Act 1999, and Schedule 10 of the Immigration Act 2016, and those supported under (in England) the Care Act 2014 and the Children Act 1989), those supported under Schedule 10, and any adults supported as dependants of their children under the Children Act 1989, will only be entitled to very limited types of free NHS specialist medical treatment. Primary medical care and emergency care remain free of charge to all categories of supported person.

Further consideration of this issue is beyond the scope of this *Handbook*, but you should take specialist advice if you need special medical care and you are in receipt of Schedule 10 support, or you are an adult supported with your child or children by your local authority under the Children Act 1989.

Notes

1. **Introduction**

1 s115(1) and (3) IAA 1999 bar persons subject to immigration control from specified benefits. There are exceptions set out in regulations made under s115(4) but none of them apply to asylum seekers.
2 s95 IAA 1999
3 s98 IAA 1999

2. **Support for asylum seekers**

4 s95(1) IAA 1999
5 s95(2) IAA 1999 and regs 4(4)(b) and 4(6) AS Regs. See *R (AT(Guinea)) v SSHD and the FTT* [2019] EWHC 2709 (Admin) at paras 5 and 46-48 for an overview of the statutory framework.
6 s95(2) IAA 1999 and reg 4(3) AS Regs
7 Reg 4(3) AS Regs
8 Sch 3 paras 2 and 3 NIAA 2002
9 s55(1) NIAA 2002
10 s55(5)(a) NIAA 2002
11 Home Office guidance, *Asylum support: policy bulletins instruction* (version 9.0), Ch 5
12 *R v SSHD ex Limbuela and others* [2005] UKHL 66
13 ss94(1) and 95(1) IAA 1999
14 s80A NIAA 2002
15 s80B NIAA 2002
16 s80B(4) NIAA 2002
17 s80C(1)-(6) NIAA 2002
18 s94(4A) IAAA 1999
19 s80B(7) NIAA 2002
20 Home Office guidance, *Ceasing section 95 support instruction* (version 1.0), p10
21 s94(3) IAA 1999; regs 2 and 2A AS Regs
22 *AJ v SSHD* (Appeal ref: 43710)
23 s94(5) IAA 1999
24 Appeal refs: 44439 and 44739; see *R (VC) v Newcastle City Council* [2011] EWHC 2673 (Admin), paras 3-10 and 56
25 Sch 3 para 7A NIAA 2002
26 s94(1) IAA 1999; reg 2 (4) AS Regs; Home Office guidance, *Dependants on an asylum support application* (version 8.0)
27 Reg 2(4)(f) and (6)(a) and (b) AS Regs
28 Home Office, *Asylum Policy Instruction: dependants and former dependants* (version 2.0)
29 Home Office guidance, *Dependants on an asylum support application* (version 8.0)
30 Available at asaproject.org/resources/library/factsheets
31 s95(3) IAA 1999
32 Reg 7(a) AS Regs
33 Reg 7(b) AS Regs
34 See the Home Office guidance at gov.uk/government/publications/handling-applications-for-permission-to-take-employment-instruction
35 s95(9) IAA 1999; regs 19 and 20 AS Regs
36 s95(10) IAA 1999
37 s95(11) IAA 1999
38 Reg 19 AS Regs
39 Reg 15(1) AS Regs
40 Reg 15(2) AS Regs
41 ss105(1)(c) and 106(1)(c) IAA 1999
42 They are 'excluded tenancies' under s3A(7A) Protection from Eviction Act 1977
43 Reg 22(2) AS Regs
44 Reg 22(3) AS Regs
45 Reg 20(1) AS Regs
46 Reg 20(1)(a) AS Regs
47 Reg 20(1)(b) AS Regs
48 Reg 20(1)(c) AS Regs
49 Reg 20(1)(e) AS Regs
50 Reg 20(1)(f) AS Regs
51 Reg 20(1)(g) AS Regs
52 Reg 20(1)(h) AS Regs
53 Reg 20(1)(i) AS Regs
54 Reg 20(1)(j) AS Regs
55 Reg 20(1)(d) AS Regs
56 Reg 20(1)(k) AS Regs
57 Home Office guidance, *Ceasing section 95 support instruction* (version 1.0), p12
58 For example, *JKV v SSHD*, AS/12/03/28234
59 *R v Kensington and Chelsea RLBA ex parte Kujtim* [1999] All ER 161, para 35
60 Reg 21(1) AS Regs
61 Reg 21(1)(c) and (2) AS Regs, with reference to reg 15 AS Regs
62 Reg 21(3) AS Regs

63 Home Office guidance, *Asylum support: policy bulletins instruction* (version 9.0), para 6.6
64 Home Office guidance, *Asylum support: policy bulletins instruction* (version 9.0), para 25.2.1
65 *ZN v SSHD*, AS/17/09/37288
66 asaproject.org/resources/library/briefing-notes
67 Reg 17 AS Regs
68 s114 IAA 1999
69 Reg 18 AS Regs
70 s114(3) IAA 1999
71 s112 IAA 1999
72 s113 IAA 1999
73 ss105-106 IAA 1999; ss105-108 IAA 1999

3. **Temporary support**

74 s98(1) IAA 1999
75 s98(3) IAA 1999, applying s95(3)
76 See s98(3), which provides that the 'likely to become destitute' provision in s95(1) does not apply for the purposes of s98
77 Home Office guidance, *Asylum support: policy bulletins instruction* (version 9.0)
78 That is because s103 IAA 1999, which deals with appeals, does not refer to section 98 support
79 s95(1)-(2) and s98(3) IAA 1999; reg 4(3), (8) and (9) AS Regs
80 Reg 20A AS Regs

4. **Support for refused asylum seekers**

81 s4(2) IAA 1999
82 Reg 3(1)(a) IA(PAFAS) Regs
83 Reg 3(1)(b) and (2) IA(PAFAS) Regs
84 Sch 3 para 6 NIAA
85 Sch 3 para 7A NIAA
86 Sch 3 para 3 NIAA
87 s4(2) IAA 1999
88 Reg 2 IA(PAFAS) Regs
89 Home Office guidance, *Ceasing section 95 support instruction* (version 1.0)
90 Regs 6-9 AS Regs
91 Reg 3(2)(a) IA(PAFAS) Regs
92 Home Office guidance, *Asylum support, section 4(2): policy and process* (version 3.0)
93 Reg 3(2)(b) IA(PAFAS) Regs
94 *R (SSHD) v ASA and Osman, Yillah, Ahmad and Musemwa (interested parties)* [2006] EWHC 1248
95 Reg 3(2)(c) IA(PAFAS) Regs
96 Reg 3(2)(d) IA(PAFAS) Regs
97 Reg 3(2)(e) IA(PAFAS) Regs
98 *R v SSHD ex parte Limbuela* [2005] UKHL 66
99 *R (SSHD) v FTT* [2021] EWHC 1690 (Admin), at para 137
100 *R v SSHD ex parte Limbuela* [2005] UKHL 66, at paras 8-9 and 59
101 Home Office guidance, *Asylum support, section 4(2): policy and process* (version 3.0), pp12-13
102 The significance of whether the Home Office accepts that your submissions amount to a 'fresh' claim, is that if the submissions are refused but the Home Office accepts them as constituting a fresh claim, you will be granted a fresh right of appeal
103 *R (MK and another) v SSHD* [2012] EWHC 1896 (Admin), paras 166-169, and *R (Nigatu) v SSHD* [2004] EWHC 1806 (Admin), para 20
104 AS/14/11/32141, at para 31
105 For example, AS/19/07/40099, at paras 19-20
106 *R (NS) v First-tier Tribunal* [2009] EWHC 3819 (Admin)
107 For further information, see the resources provided by the Anti Trafficking and Labour Exploitation Unit at atleu.org.uk
108 Home Office guidance, *Assessing destitution* (version 4.0), p12
109 Home Office guidance, *Asylum support, section 4(2): policy and process* (version 3.0), p13
110 *R (Mulumba) v First-tier Tribunal (Asylum Support)*, unreported. The Home Office conceded in the 2015 judicial review that 'provision of s4 may in any particular case be necessary to avoid a breach of a person's Article 8 rights'. See also AS/14/11/32141. The basis of that decision was that if the applicant was required to leave the UK, the Article 8 claim would be treated by the Home Office as withdrawn (see *Birmingham City Council v Clue* [2010] EWCA Civ 460, para 65).
111 See appeal ref: 32141 at para 29, where the Principal Judge of the Asylum Support Tribunal held that any application for leave to remain in the UK could found a claim for section 4 support
112 AS/11/06/26857, 18 August 2011
113 AS/15/09/34157, 8 October 2015
114 Reg 6 IA(PAFAS) Regs

115 Home Office guidance, *Asylum support, section 4(2): policy and process* (version 3.0), pp15-16
116 s55 Borders, Citizenship and Immigration Act 2009
117 Home Office guidance, *Asylum support, section 4(2): policy and process* (version 3.0), pp16-17

5. **Support for those whose asylum claims have been expressly or impliedly withdrawn**
118 For example, AS/17/07/37027, although not all judges of the Asylum Support Tribunal are willing to follow this approach. See AS/21/11/43541 for an example of a different judicial approach. This highlights the need for specialist advice in this type of case.
119 Appeal refs: 44379 and 44439
120 AS/19/11/40826, at para 26; AS/19/11/40868, at para 21
121 For example, AS/21/03/42880
122 Appeal ref: 44492

6. **Discretionary support for people on immigration bail**
123 Sch 10 para 9(1)(a) IA 2016
124 Sch 10 para 9(1)(b) IA 2016
125 Home Office guidance, *Immigration bail, interim guidance* (version 15.0), pp86-92
126 Sch 10 para 9(3) IA 2016
127 Home Office guidance, *Immigration bail: interim guidance* (version 15.0), pp87-90

7. **Support from your local authority**
128 s21 Care Act 2014 (for England). Analogous provisions for Wales and Scotland are: Social Services and Well-being (Wales) Act 2014 and s13A Social Work (Scotland) Act 1968.
129 *R v Wandsworth LBC, Ex parte O, R v Leicester City Council, Ex parte Bhikha* [2000] 1 WLR 2539
130 *R (on the Application of M) (Fc) v Slough BC* [2008] UKHL 52
131 Sch 3 paras 1, 3 and 6 NIAA 2002
132 *Kimani v Lambeth BC* [2004] 1 WLR 272
133 *Birmingham City Council v Clue* [2010] EWCA Civ 460
134 s122(5) IAA 1999
135 s94(5) IAA 1999 and see the section, 'Discontinuation of support to families with children', in section 2 of this chapter
136 Disclosed following a High Court case (*MK and AH v SSHD* [2012] EWHC 1896 (Admin))
137 See *R (VC and others) v Newcastle City Council and SSHD* [2011] EWHC 2673 (Admin), paras 91-92
138 *Birmingham City Council v Clue* [2010] EWCA Civ 460

Chapter 22

Applying for asylum support

This chapter covers:

1. Section 95 support

If you are either an asylum seeker or a dependant of an asylum seeker for support purposes, you can apply for section 95 support from the Home Office.[1] The application can be for you alone, or for you and your dependants.[2] **Note:** the procedure for applying is essentially the same if you are a refused asylum seeker who is applying for section 4 support (see p576).

Under section 95, you can apply for accommodation and cash support or, if you have somewhere to live and can prove this to the Home Office, just for the cash support to meet your 'essential needs' (known as **'subsistence-only support'**). In rare circumstances, you may wish to apply for accommodation only.[3] Most people apply for both.

You must apply for support on Form ASF1, available from the Asylum Help service at Migrant Help (see p521) and from gov.uk/asylum-support/how-to-claim.[4] Even if the application is for both yourself and your dependants, you only need to complete one form. If you wish to apply for support as a dependant of a person who is already being supported by the Home Office, it is not technically necessary for you to complete the application form again – the Home Office considers providing the principal applicant with additional support for you if notified of your existence in writing.[5] However, in this situation, it is advisable for you to complete a separate application form, because that should ensure that any subsequent refusal is an appealable decision giving you a right of appeal to the Asylum Support Tribunal.[6] An asylum seeker is under a duty to notify the Home Office if they have been joined by a dependant – but without a formal application, the mere act of notifying the Home Office may be insufficient to generate a written decision on a dependant's claim.

Migrant Help can help you complete Form ASF1 and submit it to the Home Office. **Note:** in recent years the Home Office has shown an increased readiness to refuse applications for section 95 support on the basis that applicants have undisclosed resources or access to undisclosed resources, and so are 'not destitute'. You are, therefore, strongly advised to obtain specialist help with completing Form ASF1 from a local advice agency or, failing that, Migrant Help. If you fail to provide all the necessary supporting evidence with your initial application, it is likely to be refused. If that happens, you may need to appeal against the Home Office's decision (see Chapter 24).

You must complete the application form in full and in English.[7] There are detailed notes accompanying the form that give further information about the application procedure and guidance on how to complete the form.[8] The form asks for details of the stage your asylum application has reached, the kind of support you need, your current accommodation, any other kind of support you receive (including support from friends or relatives, details of cash, savings, investments or other property you own in the UK and abroad, any employment you have and state benefits you receive, both for yourself and your dependants), and details of any disabilities or special needs you have.

If you can, it is highly advisable to send documentary evidence to corroborate the information you give. **Note:** a false statement to obtain asylum support is a criminal offence (although it seems that prosecutions brought by the Home Office are rare).[9]

Form ASF1 can be downloaded, printed and filled in by hand, or completed and saved to a computer. The completed form must be emailed, faxed or posted to the Home Office. At the time of writing, all applications must be sent via Migrant Help. The address for this purpose is Asylum Support Casework Team, PO Box 471, Dover CT16 9FN or S95NewApplications@migranthelpuk.org if sending via email. The methods of, and addresses for, communicating with the Home Office frequently change, and if it is unclear from the website how to submit the form, contact a specialist agency for advice.

The Home Office may ask you for further information on any of the details contained in the application form.[10] It is important that you respond to any such questions because the Home Office has the power not to consider your application if it thinks that you have not completed the form properly or accurately, or if you have not co-operated with enquiries.[11] Such a refusal to consider an application is known as a 'section 57 decision'. There is no right of appeal against a section 57 decision, so it is therefore important to answer all further questions from the Home Office (known as 'further information requests') as best you can and within the time limit given to you.

If you have done your best but have been unable to provide all the information requested by the Home Office, and you have explained why you cannot provide the missing information, but the Home Office has nevertheless refused to entertain your application, you should seek urgent expert advice on whether to file a notice of appeal against the Home Office's decision. In some cases, the Asylum Support Tribunal has treated what the Home Office describes in correspondence as a 'section 57 decision' (ie, a refusal to entertain an application) as a substantive refusal, with the result that there is a right of appeal after all, which the tribunal can proceed to determine in an appellant's favour.[12] Alternatively, you may be able to bring a claim for judicial review. This is a potentially lengthy and uncertain procedure of last resort, which in practice will anyway require you to answer the Home Office's query in due course.

At the time of writing, the Home Office's use of the powers under section 57 has become much less common. Instead of refusing to entertain an application when an appellant is considered not to be co-operating in responding to the Home Office's questions, the Home Office tends simply to refuse the application on that basis. Such a refusal is better for applicants than refusing to entertain an application, because it gives applicants a right of appeal to the Asylum Support Tribunal. However, you should be aware that section 57 procedure remains a tool that the Home Office may legitimately use in some cases.

Proving you are entitled to section 95 support

To be entitled to section 95 support, you must prove:

- you are an asylum seeker (see below); *and*
- you are destitute.

Together, these provide entitlement (see p565).

Proving you are an asylum seeker

If you have applied for asylum and are awaiting a decision, the Home Office is able to determine that you are an asylum seeker from your Port and Home Office reference numbers, which you must include with your application for asylum support.

Similarly, it is straightforward for the Home Office to determine your status as an asylum seeker, if:

- your asylum claim has been refused; *and*
- you have appealed; *and*
- you have lodged your appeal within the time permitted.

In both these scenarios, there should be no need to provide additional evidence to prove that you are an asylum seeker. However, the Home Office does occasionally dispute whether an asylum appeal has been lodged. In such a case, you will need to provide a copy of your notice of appeal, proof that it was received by the First-tier or Upper Tribunal, and any correspondence with the tribunal concerned.

There are also other circumstances in which you may need additional evidence to prove that you are an asylum seeker for asylum support purposes (see p525) if your claim has been withdrawn, abandoned or rejected in the past, but you have successfully persuaded the Home Office to reopen your case. Typical scenarios when this might happen include the following.

- Your asylum claim was refused by the Home Office, and you did not appeal to the First-tier Tribunal (Immigration and Asylum Chamber) within the time permitted for appealing, but the First-tier Tribunal (Immigration and Asylum Chamber) granted you an extension of time for appealing (see p544). Following the grant of an extension of time for appealing, you are once again an asylum seeker for the purposes of section 95 until your appeal has been finally determined. To prove that, you may need to show the Home Office documentary evidence that the First-tier Tribunal (Immigration and Asylum Chamber) has granted you an extension of time for appealing, and that your appeal has not been finally determined.
- Your asylum claim was refused and your appeal against the refusal of asylum was dismissed, but you submitted further submissions (perhaps including fresh evidence) in support of your asylum claim. If the Home Office agrees that your further submissions meet the test for a fresh asylum claim (see p541), you are once again an asylum seeker until your fresh asylum claim and any appeal has been finally determined. To prove that, you have to show the Home Office documentary evidence that your further submissions have been accepted by the Home Office to be a fresh asylum claim, and that your claim has not been finally determined.
- You absconded and/or left the UK before a decision was taken on your asylum claim by the Home Office, but you subsequently lodged further submissions concerning your asylum claim with the Home Office's Further Submissions Unit. If the Home Office agrees to reopen your case, which it must do if it agrees that the threshold for a fresh claim has been met (see p548), you are once again an asylum seeker. To prove that, you have to show the Home Office documentary evidence that the Home Office accepts that your submissions meet the test for a fresh asylum claim, and that the fresh asylum claim has not been finally determined.

In the first two of the above three examples, you are likely to be treated as eligible for section 4 support on the basis that the outstanding applications in both cases are a legal or practical obstacle to departure from the UK (see p581).

In relation to the third example about absconders, the type of support you are eligible for while you wait for the Home Office to make a decision on your further submissions has been subject to conflicting decisions of the Asylum Support Tribunal. These cases can be complicated, and you should seek specialist advice (see p550).

The evidence you require may need to be obtained from your immigration solicitor. You should seek expert advice on your asylum support application if necessary.

Proving you are destitute

If you apply for section 95 support for yourself, you must prove to the Home Office that you are 'destitute'. If you apply for support for yourself and your dependants, you must prove that the group as a whole is destitute.[13] The same applies to applications for section 4 support (see p576).

To prove you are destitute for asylum support purposes, you will need to show either that you are destitute **now** or that you are **'likely to become destitute within** [for new applicants for asylum support] **14 days'**[14] - ie, you will need to prove that:

- you do not have 'adequate accommodation' (see p570), or any means of getting adequate accommodation; *or*
- you cannot meet your essential living needs (see p587), even if you have adequate accommodation.

It is an either/or test, so you are 'destitute' and therefore eligible for both accommodation and cash support, if you are without adequate accommodation *or* without the means to feed yourself or meet your other essential living needs.

The Home Office must follow regulations that set out what is and what is not relevant in deciding these questions. These apply from the time you make an application for support up until the Home Office decision (or the tribunal decision, if there is an appeal), and at any time thereafter if there is a question of whether support should continue. It is important to be aware of Home Office policy in addition to the regulations.[15]

When considering whether you are destitute, the Home Office must take into account those resources (known as 'assets') that are available to you, or likely to be available to you over the next 14 days (for a new application). If you are required to prove that you are destitute at a time when you are already being supported by the Home Office (ie, if the Home Office is considering whether to discontinue your support), the time within which you have to prove that you are likely to become destitute is 56, not 14, days.[16]

The **only** resources that the law permits the Home Office to take into account are:[17]

- cash;
- savings;
- investments;
- land;
- vehicles;
- goods for trade or business.

Any of the above assets held by a dependant on your asylum support claim must also be declared and will be taken into account. Your dependants include any children under the age of 18, any adult children who are disabled and in need of care or attention, your spouse/civil partner or your unmarried partner, provided you have been living together for at least two of the three preceding years[18] (see p526).

Land may include property, such as a house and other outbuildings. Investments include business investments, income bonds, life assurance policies, pension schemes, stocks and shares, and unit trusts. Your land, assets and investments could be in the UK or abroad and must all be disclosed on Form ASF1.

Note: resources 'likely to be available to you' might include support from friends and relatives in the UK (or abroad, depending on the facts) or from voluntary sector organisations.

When deciding whether you are destitute, the Home Office must ignore any:

- assets you or your dependants have that are not of a type listed above;[19] *and*
- asylum support that you are receiving.[20]

Home Office guidance sets out certain small cash receipts that can be disregarded – eg, small cash sums to help asylum seekers or their children meet needs related to coping with disability or a care need; occasional receipts from charities or other organisations to fund travel to attend classes or to buy course materials; additional payments by the Salvation Army or its contractors on behalf of the Home Office because the recipient is a potential or confirmed victim of modern slavery.[21]

Note: there is nothing in the regulations that requires you to sell your personal possessions such as your jewellery. However, if you choose to sell them when you are receiving section 95 support, you must declare the proceeds of the sale to the Home Office, which will review your eligibility for asylum support if it considers that you may no longer be destitute.[22]

Home Office guidance states that if assets (of a type listed above) held by a person in receipt of asylum support 'may be accessed, liquidated or realised at a later date the person may be provided with support but put on notice that they will be expected to take steps to access the asset and that their support may be discontinued if they fail to do so'.[23] The Asylum Support Tribunal has held in one case that: 'As a general rule, however, if an item of personal possession can be easily converted into cash (and vice versa) – eg, gold jewellery, or stocks and shares – it may be reasonable to treat such possessions as cash, savings or investments because they are easily converted into cash'.[24] Since most possessions can be 'easily converted into cash', the tribunal's general proposition and the Home Office guidance, if correct, would flout regulation 6 of the Asylum Support Regulations 2000, and so it would seem that both are likely to be incorrect.

Providing evidence of your resources

You should not assume that the Home Office will accept any information you include in your application form as credible without supporting evidence. As a general rule, the Home Office is likely to treat any significant gaps in your supporting evidence (particularly if the gaps are unexplained) and/or any inconsistencies in the evidence you do submit as providing grounds for doubting the credibility of your claim to be destitute. That said, the amount and quality of evidence you are able to include with your asylum support application to show that you are destitute will depend on your circumstances. If you are destitute and your application is urgent, then you may be able to provide further evidence later in the process in response to Home Office requests for further information or (if your application is refused) while you are preparing your appeal.

Bank and credit card accounts

You must disclose all bank and credit card accounts in the UK and abroad. **Note:** the Home Office regularly conducts Experian credit checks on applicants, which reveal all bank and credit card accounts held in the UK. If you do not disclose a bank account that is subsequently revealed through a Home Office Experian check, the Home Office is likely to conclude that you have concealed your resources and may be disinclined to believe that you are destitute.

Bank and credit card statements

The Home Office will want to see evidence of your income and savings, both in the UK and in your home country, to exclude the possibility that you have built up and retained savings from which you can now support yourself. You should, therefore, provide the Home Office with bank and credit card statements for the previous six months. You may want to include a summary explanation of all debits and credits of £50 or more (although sometimes the Asylum Support Tribunal judges may ask for an explanation of even smaller transactions – eg, all transactions of more than £30).

Evidence of bank accounts and savings abroad may be required to show that you do not have resources in your home country that could be used to fund your support in the UK. If you are unable to obtain statements in relation to accounts held abroad, you should explain why – eg, by providing evidence of unsuccessful attempts to obtain bank statements, such as email correspondence or screenshots of web chat with the bank. The Home Office will expect you to use online banking facilities if they are available, and you should carefully explain why you have been unable to access money held abroad (including by money transfer services such as Western Union) and what steps you have taken to try to access that money.

Earlier visa applications

If you claim asylum after entering the UK on a visa, the Home Office examines the information contained in your visa application and compares it with the information on Form ASF1. For example, you may have come to the UK on a student or visitor's visa and then claimed asylum. That process can lead to problems if you entered the UK on an illegally procured visa, which may typically have been granted on the basis of manufactured evidence that inflated your resources in your home country to increase the chances that a visa would be granted. In most cases, the Home Office will rely on the resources disclosed on your visa application, and dispute the credibility of your asylum support application if you disclose lesser resources in Form ASF1. This is a complicated issue that usually arises on appeal, and you should seek expert advice if this situation applies to you.

Evidence of employment

Evidence of any income you received in your home country from employment (or otherwise) may be required to show that that income stream is no longer available to you or would be insufficient to support you in the UK. If you have been working in the UK, you should explain how much you have earned and provide evidence of your income, such as a P60 or a wage slip. Working in the UK without permission to work is a criminal offence, and disclosing such work could expose you to criminal prosecution. That said, criminal prosecutions of asylum support applicants who have revealed details of illegal working in their applications seem to be rare. This is a sensitive issue and must be carefully presented, and if you have supported yourself by working illegally in the UK, you should seek expert advice.

Support from friends, family and charitable bodies

If you receive support from friends, family or charitable bodies, you should provide evidence (eg, a letter) from anyone supporting you, specifying what sort of support they provide and how much. If you are living with, or are partially supported by, close family members, you should consider providing evidence of their savings, income and outgoings to demonstrate why it is not reasonable for them to meet all your accommodation costs and/or essential living needs.

If your partner receives benefits

If your partner receives universal credit or another social security benefit, you must disclose their income in your application. The Home Office will refer to your household as a 'mixed household', and will apply its policy[25] on mixed households to determine the proportion of your partner's benefit that will be treated as reasonably available to you. These calculations can be complicated and are beyond the scope of this *Handbook*. See Asylum Support Appeal Project's briefing on mixed households[26] and seek specialist advice as necessary.

If you are a lone parent

If you are a lone parent, the Home Office may ask you for evidence that you have taken steps to seek maintenance from the other parent.

Support may be granted on condition you take steps to dispose of relevant assets

Even if you have declared relevant assets (eg, savings, investments, land, vehicles, goods for trade or business – see p565) to a substantial value, you may still qualify as destitute if you can show that you cannot realise the value of those assets within the relevant period (14 days for new applications). Proving that can be a contentious issue if you have property abroad that could be sold to pay for your support in the UK. The Home Office may provide you with support on a limited basis to allow you time to sell items of property – eg, six months to sell a house abroad. The Home Office would then treat the money received from the sale as cash or savings and would take it into account when deciding whether or not to continue to provide support. If you do not consider it reasonable that you should have to sell your property (eg, there are family members still living in the property who would be homeless if they had to leave), you should give your reasons and any supporting evidence when you send in your application form.

Evidence of essential living needs

Home Office policy lists those expenses that the Home Office generally considers make up an individual's essential living needs. The policy states:[27]

> The cash allowance [which is paid to asylum support claimants and is intended to cover essential living needs] should generally be sufficient to cover the following needs: food, clothing, toiletries, non-prescription medication, household cleaning items, communications, travel, and the ability to access social, cultural and religious life, which is covered by the funding provision for communications and travel. The level of the cash allowance takes into consideration that other essential living needs (eg, warmth, cooking, lighting) are covered by the provision of accommodation that is free of both rent and utility bills (fuel and water) and is also fully furnished and equipped with both household goods (eg, kitchenware, access to laundry services) and linens (eg, towels and sheets).

If you have adequate accommodation but claim that you are destitute because you cannot meet your essential living needs, it will therefore be relevant if you have to contribute to rent and utility bills, the cost of essential household goods and access to laundry services. You should provide evidence of the amount you are required to contribute to each such expense.

When the Home Office decides whether you can meet your essential living needs, the regulations state that certain items are treated as not essential[28] – eg, it is not relevant whether or not you can pay for the following items:

- the cost of sending or receiving faxes, photocopying, or buying or using computer facilities; *or*
- travelling expenses; *or*
- toys and other recreational items; *or*
- entertainment expenses.

When deciding whether you can meet your essential living needs in terms of clothing, the Home Office cannot take into account your personal preferences.[29] However, the Home Office can take into account your individual circumstances when deciding whether you can meet your clothing requirements. The level of support necessary to meet the essential living need for clothing was considered by the High Court in a case brought by Refugee Action.[30] The court held that essential living needs include the 'provision of suitable clothing to avoid any danger of illness'. Health-related clothing issues might include:

- whether you can afford to provide clothes for yourself that are suitable for the different weather conditions in the UK; *and*
- whether you have sufficient changes of clothes required for cleanliness and personal hygiene; *and*
- whether you have clothes that are suitable for any particular health needs that you have.

In relation to school uniforms, the court held that:[31] 'School uniform grants are often provided by local authorities but all other clothing for asylum seekers and their dependent children has to be paid for out of the s.96(1)(b) cash support. To the extent that school uniform is not provided in a particular case, this would fall for consideration as an exceptional case.'

If you are granted support, the cost of travelling to your new accommodation is paid for by the Home Office.

If, because of your specific circumstances, you have another need that is not referred to in the regulations, the Home Office must decide whether the need is essential,[32] taking into account your individual circumstances. Once you are in receipt of support, it is possible to apply for additional support if your needs are 'exceptional'.[33] Any such claim should be supported by objective evidence where possible.

Evidence of not having adequate accommodation

If you are applying for support but you have some form of accommodation, the Home Office must decide whether or not this is 'adequate'. The Home Office must take into account whether:[34]

- it is 'reasonable' for you to continue to occupy the accommodation (see p571); *and*
- you can afford to pay for the accommodation (see p572); *and*
- you can gain entry to the accommodation (see p572); *and*
- if the accommodation is a houseboat, a caravan or some other moveable structure that can be lived in, there is somewhere you can locate, and have permission to live in, the accommodation; *and*
- you can live in the accommodation with your dependants; *and*
- you or your dependants are likely to experience harassment, threats or violence if you continue to live in the accommodation (see p572).

Note: even if the accommodation is adequate, you are still destitute if you cannot meet your essential living needs. If you have told the Home Office that you want to stay in your current accommodation and only want financial assistance, the factors listed above are not taken into account when deciding whether you are destitute, except for the question of whether you can afford the accommodation.[35]

Note: in England, if you have sufficient savings to be able to rent accommodation for yourself, you must first obtain permission from the Home Office for the 'right to rent'.[36] Landlords can only legally grant tenancies or rent rooms to those with a right to rent. At the request of the landlord, the Home Office checks that you are still a current asylum seeker and may grant permission for you to rent a property. If you have been unable to rent a property because landlords will not apply for the right to rent on your behalf, you will need to provide evidence that you have been unable to obtain permission to rent. The Home Office policy states that 'permission to rent is normally granted to asylum seekers if their asylum claim, or appeal against refusal of the claim, is still outstanding'.[37]

Being accommodated in prison or immigration detention

If you are applying for asylum support from prison or immigration detention, you are likely to have to argue that your accommodation in detention is not adequate. A common scenario is that you require an address to which you can be bailed. The principal judge of the Asylum Support Tribunal has held that:[38]

> In the circumstances, I readily accept that accommodation in a prison cell does not amount to adequate accommodation and that it would not be reasonable to continue to occupy a prison cell where there is an alternative available. In the event that [the appellant is granted] bail, I am satisfied that the appellant will be destitute on the basis that he will no longer have access to adequate accommodation nor the means to meet his essential living needs.

Following this reasoning, the Asylum Support Tribunal judges will consider whether bail in principal (ie, to an address to be specified) has been granted, or, if bail in principle has not yet been granted, whether a grant of bail in principle is likely within the next 14 days. If, and only if, either of these questions is answered in the affirmative in your case, the Asylum Support Tribunal may accept that your accommodation in detention is not adequate.[39]

You will, in addition, still have to show evidence of your reasonably available resources, including the resources you can reasonably access from family and friends on the outside, but if you can show that the resources reasonably available to you are not sufficient to enable you to pay for bed and breakfast accommodation for 14 days, the Asylum Support Tribunal should accept that you are destitute.

Is it reasonable for you to continue to occupy the accommodation

The Home Office must consider whether it is 'reasonable' for you to continue to occupy the accommodation.[40] You will need to provide evidence of your personal circumstances, such as letters, medical reports and photos. For example, it may not be reasonable for you to continue to occupy accommodation if you are staying with a friend and sleeping on their floor, or if you cannot gain entry during the day, or if it is unsuitable for you because of your health needs or a physical disability, such that you are unable to safely negotiate the stairs in your current accommodation.

The Home Office may also take into account the general housing circumstances in the district of the local government housing authority in which the accommodation is situated.[41] To prove that it is not reasonable for you to continue to live there, you may have to provide evidence that your accommodation is worse or more overcrowded than other accommodation generally is within the area in which you live.

Can you afford to pay for the accommodation

The Home Office must consider whether you can afford to pay for your existing accommodation.[42] It must take into account:[43]

- any income or assets (other than from asylum support under section 95 (see p561), section 98 (see p575) or section 4 (see p576)) available to you or any of your dependants or which might be expected to be available; *and*
- the costs of living in the accommodation; *and*
- your other reasonable living expenses.

All your living expenses in relation to the accommodation (eg, your rent and any utility or other bills) should be evidenced (see p569).

Do you have access to the accommodation

You can be considered not to have access to your accommodation if you do not have access during the day. For example, a friend may allow you to sleep in their home but require you to leave during the day, or you may be staying in a hostel where occupants cannot remain during the day.

Have you or are you likely to experience domestic abuse

The Home Office must consider whether it is 'probable' that your continued occupation of the accommodation will lead to domestic abuse against you or any of your dependants.[44] The domestic abuse must be:

- from a person who is, or who has been, a 'close family member'; *and*
- in the form of either actual violence or threats of violence that are likely to be carried out.

There is no definition of 'close family member'. Depending on the circumstances, it may cover a married or unmarried partner and ex-partner, those to whom you have a blood relationship, in-laws, relatives of your partner and others who live (or have lived) in your household. **Note:** the family member does not have to live with you.[45] You may fear that because your address is known to them, your continued occupation of that accommodation is likely to lead to domestic violence.

Home Office guidance provides that 'all caseworkers, Home Office accommodation providers (including any sub-contractors) and Migrant Help UK' must take particular actions (and follow certain key principles) if a report of domestic abuse is disclosed to them 'from a person accommodated by the Home Office under the provisions of the Immigration and Asylum Act 1999'. These include that the person:

- (and their children) must immediately be offered safe alternative accommodation and if that offer is accepted, transferred without delay;
- should be supported to make a report to the police, should they wish to do so, and be reassured that doing so will have no adverse impact on their asylum claim; *and*
- must be referred to a specialist organisation for assessment and supported by a domestic violence specialist worker.[46]

In addition, if a person eligible for asylum support and not yet accommodated by the Home Office reports domestic abuse, 'priority should be given to finding safe alternative accommodation for the victim and any children, as a matter of urgency'. In such a case, the guidance states that 'it is usually unnecessary to make detailed enquiries to establish their destitution or require a full application for section 95 support at the initial stage'. The guidance further states that:

- the presumption is that the victim should be believed, at this stage corroborating evidence is not required;
- caseworkers must agree and adhere to a safe means of communicating with the victim; *and*
- some victims may wish to remain in their current accommodation and, in these cases, consideration must be given to relocating the perpetrator.

Although the asylum support rules only specifically refer to *domestic* violence, it is arguable that other forms of violence or threats you have received from anyone not normally associated with you are also relevant when deciding whether your current accommodation is adequate. For example, abuse may be in the form of racial harassment or attacks, sexual abuse or harassment, and harassment because of your religion.

If you are affected by domestic abuse or violence, contact Migrant Help or your accommodation provider. Alternatively, you can contact a Home Office safeguarding team directly.[47] If there is time and it is safe to do so, you should seek an expert adviser who has the relevant contact details and may be able to advocate on your behalf.[48]

What cannot be taken into account

Matters that cannot be taken into account when considering whether your accommodation is adequate are:[49]

- the fact that you have no enforceable right to occupy the accommodation;

- the fact that you share the accommodation or any part of it with one or more persons; *or*
- the location of the accommodation.

How the Home Office determines your section 95 application

To determine whether you are entitled to section 95 support, the Home Office uses the information and evidence contained in your completed Form ASF1 and supporting documents to decide whether:

- you are an asylum seeker; *and*
- you are able to:[50]
  - meet your essential living needs (if you have adequate accommodation and are only seeking financial support); *or*
  - secure adequate accommodation and also be able to meet your essential living needs (if you are seeking accommodation *and* financial support).

To determine whether you are an asylum seeker, the Home Office will generally just check its records. In some cases, that may be complicated (eg, if you made an out-of-time appeal or absconded before a decision was taken on your claim – see p584) and you may need to provide the Home Office with additional evidence.

To determine whether you are destitute, the steps the Home Office takes depend on the facts of your case and what you are applying for. If you have existing accommodation that you claim is not adequate, the Home Office considers the information and evidence in your application to determine whether the accommodation is adequate (see p570). If you do not have adequate accommodation, the Home Office determines whether you have the means to pay for your own accommodation.

To do that, the Home Office's policy states:

> As a general rule, the cost of obtaining adequate accommodation, which will vary by region, should be established by obtaining an average price for bed and breakfast in the local area. Bed and breakfast establishments offer simple and easily accessible accommodation and are relatively affordable compared to hotels. The majority of bed-and-breakfast establishments will have their own websites, containing price lists for varying types of room to suit singles, couples or families.[51]

From websites such as booking.com, it is relatively simple for the Home Office to determine the cost of a room for you and any dependants, for your asylum support claim, in a bed and breakfast near where you are currently staying for the next 14 days. Such research will give the Home Office a figure for the likely cost of your accommodation. Care must be taken to check what sort of accommodation is used in the Home Office research. Although the policy refers to bed and breakfast accommodation as a yardstick, the Home Office sometimes uses cheaper dormitory accommodation to bring down the amount it says you will need to avoid destitution, particularly if the cost of rented accommodation in the appellant's local area is high. This practice is contrary to the Home Office's policy and should be challenged when it occurs.

To calculate the cost of meeting your essential living needs, the Home Office calculates the amount of cash that you and any dependants would each receive in respect of essential living needs if your application for section 95 support was successful. This amount is set out in regulations as a weekly cash sum that the Home Office has calculated should meet essential living needs for a week.[52] The Home Office then multiplies the weekly amount by the number of people needing support (you and any dependants) to give the total weekly cost of meeting the essential living needs for your household. That figure is then multiplied by two to give the total cost over the next 14 days. If you are applying for accommodation and subsistence, the Home Office adds together (a) the likely cost of bed and breakfast accommodation in your local area and (b) the cost of meeting your essential living needs for you and any dependants over the next 14 days. That gives a figure that the Home Office refers to as the 'destitution threshold'. If you are applying for subsistence only, (a) is ignored. To determine whether you are to be treated as destitute, the Home Office simply compares your available resources over 14 days with the destitution threshold. If your available resources are less in value than the destitution threshold, you are treated as destitute, and will be entitled to section 95 support while your asylum application is determined.

The destitution threshold is a matter of Home Office policy, not law, and the Administrative Court has held that the Home Office has a discretion to recognise you as destitute even if your available resources exceed the destitution threshold – eg, if you have unusually high expenses because of an unusual long-standing essential living need.[53] If your available resources are just above the destitution threshold, you should therefore take specialist advice.

2. Section 98 support

While you are waiting for a decision on your application for section 95 support, you should be provided with temporary support under section 98 of the Immigration and Asylum Act 1999 (see p535) if it appears to the Home Office that 'you may be destitute'.[54] The accommodation that is provided as part of temporary support is often called 'initial accommodation'. It is temporary full board or self-catering accommodation intended for short-term use.

There is no application form for temporary support but there is an initial accommodation referral form that Migrant Help will complete on your behalf, if that charity is helping you.

Temporary support can be offered quickly, including out of normal office hours if you are particularly vulnerable. The Home Office will treat you as particularly vulnerable if:

- you are part of a family with a dependent child or children younger than 18 years old; *or*
- you are a visibly pregnant woman, or a woman able to prove that she is pregnant; *or*
- you are disabled (but are not considered to have clear and urgent care needs which might mean you are eligible to local authority support (see p553); *or*
- your individual needs appear to require special consideration.[55]

If you apply for asylum on arrival or shortly afterwards at the Asylum Intake Unit in Croydon and are street homeless, you should be given initial accommodation (usually, a full-board hostel). If you need to apply for support at a later stage and also need to apply for temporary support, you can apply via Migrant Help, although it is also possible to apply via other voluntary sector organisations.

Concerns have been expressed that the Home Office sometimes adopts an overly restrictive test of whether it appears that applicants 'may' be destitute.[56] If the Home Office refuses you temporary support, it will email its reasons to Migrant Help, which will communicate them to you. There is no right of appeal: the only method of challenging a decision to refuse temporary support is by judicial review. If temporary support is granted, initial accommodation continues until:

- (if your application for section 95 support is granted) the day on which you travel to your dispersal accommodation; *or*
- shortly (sometimes the next working day) after your application for section 95 is refused (although, in practice, many appellants are permitted to remain in initial accommodation until after their appeal, particularly if they have minor children dependants); *or*
- 28 days after your asylum claim is granted by the Home Office or on appeal; *or*
- 21 days after your application for asylum claim has been refused by the Home Office or on appeal.

3. Section 4 support

The procedure for applying for section 4 support is very similar to applying for section 95 support (see p561). You use the same Form ASF1, which can be obtained from Migrant Help or online from gov.uk/asylum-support/how-to-claim. There are additional sections at the end of Form ASF1 that you should complete to show the grounds on which you are eligible for section 4 support.

Most section 4 applications are dealt with by a centralised team in Leeds. As with section 95 applications, communication with the Home Office is via Migrant Help (see p521). If and when the Home Office decides that you should receive support and has made the necessary arrangements with an accommodation provider, you will be notified of the travel arrangements to the dispersal area (see p597). There is no interim or emergency support available. It is, therefore, crucial to submit all the necessary information and documentation with your application form, since if you supply insufficient or ambiguous information, your application will be rejected or the Home Office will write to you requesting more information, which will delay any support that may be provided.

Significant administrative delays are an unfortunate feature of section 4 decision making. Although the Home Office should provide support as soon as your eligibility is established, there are routine delays. Home Office policy has been to give accommodation providers up to 14 days in which to provide accommodation once entitlement has been established, but that often takes longer.

There are separate specific timescales for making decisions on applications for section 4 support based on further submissions (see p541). Home Office policy is to make such decisions within five working days and, for priority applicants, within two working days. Priority applicants include people who are street homeless, families with minors, disabled people, elderly people, pregnant women, persons who have been subjected to torture, rape or other serious forms of psychological, physical or sexual violence, and potential victims of trafficking.[57]

Proving you are entitled to section 4 support

To be entitled to section 4 support, you must prove:

- you are destitute – the evidence you need to submit to prove this is the same as for a section 95 application (see p565); *and*
- you are eligible – ie:
  - you have made a claim for asylum that was rejected; *and*
  - you fall into one of the categories set out in regulation 3(2)(a)–(e) of the Immigration and Asylum (Provision of Accommodation to Failed Asylum-Seekers) Regulations 2005 (see p537).

Proving you are eligible for section 4 support

You need to show that:

- you are a person who has made an asylum claim that has been rejected (see below); *and*
- you meet one of the section 4 criteria for support (see p578).

Proving you have made an asylum claim that has been rejected

This is generally straightforward because in the vast majority of cases, Home Office records show that your asylum claim was refused, and any appeal against the refusal has been dismissed. In general, therefore, no specific evidence of this fact is required in addition to your completed Form ASF1.

Occasionally, cases arise in which there is some uncertainty about whether an asylum claim has been 'rejected'.

- If you lodged an appeal against a negative asylum decision out of time, your asylum claim is treated as having been rejected (see p525) – that is, unless and until the First-tier Tribunal (Immigration and Asylum Chamber) grants an extension of time for appealing. If that happens, you are treated as an asylum seeker again and eligible for section 95, not section 4, support.
- If you expressly withdrew your asylum claim, but subsequently seek to renew it, the Home Office is likely to invite you to make further submissions as if your initial asylum claim had been refused rather than withdrawn. However, because the claim was withdrawn, the Home Office is likely to treat you as (a) not eligible for section 95 support as an asylum seeker (unless and until the Home Office decides to treat your further submissions as a fresh asylum claim), and (b) not eligible for section 4 support (because your original asylum claim was withdrawn and not 'rejected'). The Home Office's position is therefore likely to be that you need to apply for Schedule 10 support (see p551), unless you have a dependent child under 18, in which case you should apply for support to the local authority (see p555).
- If you claimed asylum and then absconded, your claim is likely, subsequently, to have been treated by the Home Office as impliedly withdrawn (see p548). If you later claim asylum support (possibly years later), your eligibility for section 4 support depends on whether your impliedly withdrawn asylum claim was 'rejected',[58] and that might not be clear from the papers in your possession. The Asylum Support Tribunal considered this scenario in two recent cases.[59]

In a minority of such cases, whether or not your asylum claim has been 'rejected' is a complicated question and you should seek expert advice.

Proving you meet one of the section 4 criteria for support

The section 4 criteria for support are set out in regulation 3(2)(a)–(e) of the Immigration and Asylum (Provision of Accommodation to Failed Asylum-Seekers) Regulations 2005 (see p537). The onus is on you to show that you meet the criteria, and a substantial amount of work may be necessary to do so. **Note:** for each of the scenarios considered from p537, the evidence you should consider providing in support of your application is considered below.

Proving you are taking all reasonable steps to leave the UK

You must show you are taking all reasonable steps to leave the UK or place yourself in a position in which you are able to leave the UK. This involves providing evidence that your approach has been proactive. If the Home Office can show that there is just one reasonable step that you could have taken but didn't, your claim is liable to be refused.

Reasonable steps might include:

- applying to the Home Office for voluntary departure;

- complying with the Home Office's re-documentation process – eg, providing bio-data or attending an interview;
- asking the Home Office for assistance in obtaining a travel document;
- contacting and/or attending your embassy to request a travel document;
- completing an application for a travel document; *and*
- contacting the authorities or family members in your home country for help in obtaining identity documents so a travel document can be issued to you.

It is important to carefully itemise the steps you have taken and to provide supporting evidence if possible – eg, copies of any letters or emails you sent and documents you signed in connection with a voluntary return, or an application for an identity or travel document. You should also keep a written record of all your dealings by telephone and in person with Home Office or UK Visas and Immigration officials, and officials of your home country in the UK and abroad.

Proving that you are unable to leave UK for medical reasons

If you apply for support on this ground, you must submit a completed medical declaration ('section 4(2) medical declaration'), available on gov.uk.[60] The medical declaration must be completed by your GP or a specialist medical practitioner. To support an application under this ground, the declaration must state that you are unable to leave the UK because of your medical condition. The Home Office pays a fee to doctors for completing this form.[61]

Some medical conditions do not enable a patient to undertake air travel safely. Eligibility for asylum support on this ground depends only on fitness to travel, not on what happens after you arrive in your destination (which is considered to be an immigration matter).

Accordingly, when asking your medical professional to complete the declaration, you should point out the method of travel (eg, by plane) and how many hours it will take to travel to and wait at the UK international airport as well as the number of hours to travel by air to your country of origin and home area. When deciding whether to grant support, the Home Office does not consider your doctor's opinion that you should be allowed to stay in the UK on compassionate grounds or to finish a course of treatment or to get medical treatment that may be unavailable in your own country. If your doctor says that, the Home Office might discount the report, believing that your doctor has applied the wrong test.

If your doctor certifies that, because of your medical condition, you are not fit to travel, the Home Office will refer your doctor's report to the relevant Home Office medical adviser. The Home Office generally consults one of two medical advisers: one for cases involving mental health concerns, and one for all other medical concerns. If the Home Office medical adviser agrees with your doctor that you are not fit to travel, your eligibility for section 4 support will be accepted. If the Home Office medical adviser disagrees (as is not uncommon), you can appeal to the Asylum Support Tribunal to ask an Asylum Support Tribunal judge to resolve the issue.

Mental health cases

There are particular considerations in mental health cases. In many cases, the prospect of return to an individual's country of origin will trigger suicidal ideation. If your mental health professional considers that you may act on any such suicidal ideation if you are required to leave the UK to avoid destitution, the Home Office will ask its medical adviser whether you can travel safely with, if necessary, trained medical escorts and appropriate medication for the duration of the journey. Any medical evidence you provide to the Home Office should consider whether these measure might alleviate the risk of suicide or harm to yourself or others. You and your doctor may find it helpful to refer to the relevant Civil Aviation Guidelines.[62]

Pregnancy

The Home Office accepts that a woman cannot travel during the period of 'around' six weeks before the expected date of giving birth and six weeks after the birth.[63] You must provide medical documentation (usually Form MAT B1 issued by your GP or midwife) to confirm the pregnancy and expected date of birth, or the birth certificate, with your application form. The Home Office recognises that a woman may be unable to travel for a longer period if there are particular medical problems with the pregnancy, so you may be eligible for section 4 support earlier in your pregnancy. You can also argue that, according to the NHS, pregnancy 'normally lasts from 37 weeks to 42 weeks from the first day of your last period', although the expected delivery date is 'calculated at 40 weeks from the first day of your last period'.[64] However, only 5 per cent of babies are born on their due date; a substantial number of babies are born up to three weeks before their expected due date. With appropriate evidence of complications in pregnancy, it is possible that the Asylum Support Tribunal may accept this argument as demonstrating the need to provide support earlier than six weeks before the expected date of delivery.

You should also consider providing evidence of how your social circumstances are affecting your pregnancy. So, for example, if you are experiencing any form of abuse or if you are unable to sleep and eat properly, include this information on the application form.

Proving that there is no viable route of return

At the time of writing, there is no country to which this provision applies (see p539).

Proving that you have applied for a judicial review

Although this is a free-standing ground in regulation 3(2)(d), in practice it is almost always simpler to rely on judicial review proceedings under regulation 3(2)(e) (see below). Unlike under regulation 3(2)(d), under regulation 3(2)(e), provided that a pre-action protocol letter has been sent and you are awaiting a reply (and provided that your prospective claim for judicial review is not clearly hopeless – p542), there is no express requirement that permission to apply for judicial review has been granted or even that proceedings have been issued. That applies in England, Wales and Northern Ireland; there is no such express requirement in Scotland (see p583).

Proving that section 4 support is necessary to prevent a breach of human rights

This category of cases covers a wide range of scenarios. In each case, the law recognises that it would be unreasonable to expect you to make a voluntary return (and, by so doing, avoid destitution). **Note:** the current Home Office policy requires a person claiming that withholding support would breach their human rights to prove that there is a 'legal or practical obstacle' to them making a voluntary return to their country. The concept of a legal or practical obstacle to a voluntary return can be difficult to apply in practice. It can be argued that the test in the previous Home Office policy (ie, whether it was reasonable to expect you to make a voluntary departure from the UK) continues to apply in the sense that a legal or practical obstacle to voluntary return should be held to exist if you cannot be expected to make a voluntary departure from the UK because of that obstacle.

Precisely what evidence you need depends on the facts of your case, but as a general rule, some objective evidence, including evidence from your medical practitioner and/or from your immigration solicitor, to support your claim will be necessary.

The type of proof required in a number of typical scenarios is considered below. The scenarios are:

- a fresh claim for asylum;
- a claim for judicial review;
- an out-of-time appeal;
- a claim to be a victim of modern slavery;
- a claim under Article 8 of the European Convention on Human Rights;
- a claim to be stateless; and
- an application to the European Court of Human Rights (ECtHR).

Proving a fresh claim for asylum

If you have made, or intend to make, fresh submissions to the Home Office with a request that they be considered as a fresh claim for asylum, the Home Office (or, if your application is refused and you appeal, the Asylum Support Tribunal) considers whether:

- you have already made further submissions or whether they are still being prepared; *and*

- whether those further or prospective further submissions, when considered with the material you previously submitted in support of your asylum claim, are clearly hopeless – ie, clearly bound to fail.

Although the Asylum Support Tribunal has indicated that it will not generally allow appeals on the basis of a mere intention to submit further submissions (ie, when the further submissions have not yet been submitted to the Home Office), there are frequent exceptions to this rule. If you are applying for section 4 support but still have not submitted your further submissions, it is crucial, if possible, to put evidence before the Home Office and the Asylum Support Tribunal to demonstrate that any delay in submitting your further submissions is not your fault. For example, delays that might justify a departure from the general rule that further submissions need already to have been submitted before you can rely on their existence to claim section 4 support might include:

- there was a delay in obtaining an appointment from the Home Office's Further Submissions Unit, particularly if the delay was lengthy and the further submissions were ready and clearly had merit; *or*
- a medical report could not be completed because the medical expert cancelled an appointment (through no fault of yours); *or*
- there was a delay due to your immigration solicitor's error (particularly if a date for submission of the fresh claim has been fixed and is imminent).

To demonstrate that your further submissions are not hopeless, it is important to seek a copy of the determination of the First-tier Tribunal (Immigration and Asylum Chamber) dismissing your appeal against the refusal of your asylum claim. This is important because the immigration judge's findings are the starting point in determining the merit of your further submissions – ie, both the Home Office and the Asylum Support Tribunal may seek to consider the immigration judge's previous findings to determine whether your further submissions are hopeless.

Further, you should obtain a letter from your immigration solicitor:

- enclosing a copy of the further submissions (in draft if not yet submitted), or at least the gist of the proposed submissions if they have not yet been drafted;
- identifying the fresh evidence or development you rely on, explaining in as much detail as possible what is new, and why, despite the immigration judge's findings, the new material means that your asylum claim has a realistic prospect of success;
- if the further submissions have not yet been finalised or submitted, estimating when those things will be done; *and*
- confirming, if relevant, that the solicitor's work is being funded by legal aid (which indicates that it has been subjected to merits testing by the solicitor).

Proving judicial review

If you have issued or threatened judicial review proceedings, you should obtain a letter from your judicial review solicitor, enclosing a copy of your judicial review claim form. If the claim has not yet been issued, enclose a copy of the solicitor's judicial review pre-action protocol letter and any response received. You must show that you are progressing a claim if one has not yet been issued (eg, by showing that your solicitor has applied for legal aid and is awaiting a decision), and that your judicial review claim has some merit. A letter addressing these issues from your immigration solicitor is likely to be helpful.

Proving an out-of-time appeal

Obtain a letter from your immigration solicitor explaining that an appeal was made out of time, and remains under consideration by the tribunal or court to which you are seeking to appeal. You should also enclose documentary evidence that your out-of-time application was received by the tribunal or court concerned and, if possible, that the appeal remains pending.

Proving you are a potential victim of modern slavery

See p544. The Home Office guidance on section 4[65] accepts that if you have been referred to the National Referral Mechanism (NRM), and are awaiting a reasonable grounds decision as a potential victim of trafficking, or if you have received a positive reasonable grounds decision and are awaiting a conclusive grounds decision, there is a legal obstacle to your departure from the UK.

Although the Home Office is a first responder through whom potential victims of modern slavery can be referred to the NRM, the asylum support part of the Home Office does not always provide joined up information about the existence, or progress, of a section 4 applicant's referral to the NRM. Those already supported under the NRM have access to a support worker who can be a useful source of information. Those who have been referred to the NRM, but who for some reason are not aware of the support that is available through that route (separate from asylum support), should be referred to specialist advice about their potential entitlement to support under the NRM.[66]

Proving you have applied for leave to enter or remain under Article 8 of the European Convention on Human Rights

You should obtain a letter from your immigration solicitor, as above, enclosing a copy of the application and explaining why it is not hopeless. You should check with your immigration solicitor whether there is any tension between your Article 8 application and your claimed destitution, before you apply for section 4 support.

Proving you have applied for leave as a stateless person

You should obtain a letter from your immigration solicitor enclosing a copy of your statelessness application, and confirming the stage it has reached. If the application has been refused and you have challenged the refusal by way of judicial review, you should provide evidence of the judicial review claim, as above.

Proving you have applied to the European Court of Human Rights
You should obtain a letter from your immigration solicitor enclosing a copy of your application to the ECtHR, explaining the stage at which your application has reached, its merits, and confirming that you exhausted all remedies in the UK before applying to the ECtHR.

4. Decisions on applications

If your application is granted

If the Home Office decides to provide you with support, it informs you in writing that your application has been accepted and about the package of support you will receive. Unless you applied for subsistence-only section 95 support (see p561), your package of support will consist of accommodation that is:

- generally provided outside London and south-east England (see p592);
- subject to conditions, the breach of which can in some cases lead to you being evicted, and/or in section 95 cases, to money being recovered from you, and/or prosecution (see p534) and/or being evicted (see p530).

See Chapter 23 for what support you will get.

If your application is refused

If your application is refused, you will receive a letter explaining why, and informing you of your right of appeal, together with an appeal form. See Chapter 24 for information about bringing an appeal (p601) and about further applications for support (p618).

Notes

1. Section 95 support

1 Reg 3(1) AS Regs
2 Reg 3(2) AS Regs
3 See *MYA v SSHD*, AS/19/02/39259, 5 March 2019, for an example of the Asylum Support Tribunal awarding accommodation only
4 Reg 3(3) AS Regs
5 Reg 3(6) AS Regs
6 s103(1) IAAA 1999
7 Reg 3(3) AS Regs
8 Form ASF1 and the accompanying guidance are available at gov.uk/government/publications/application-for-asylum-support-form-asf1
9 ss105-07 IAA 1999
10 Reg 3(5) AS Regs
11 s57 NIAA 2002; reg 3(5A)-(5B) AS Regs; see also Home Office guidance, *Asylum support: policy bulletins instruction* (version 9.0), Ch 10
12 For example, see Asylum Support Tribunal appeal ref: AS/17/03/36540. The wording of the Home Office s57 letter usually plays a crucial role in this type of appeal. Further information is available in Asylum Support Appeals Project, *Briefing note on when it is possible to appeal a decision under Section 57 of the Nationality and Immigration Act 2002*, September 2016, available at asaproject.org/resources/library/briefing-notes
13 s95(4) IAA 1999; reg 5(1) AS Regs
14 s95 IAA 1999; reg 7(a) AS Regs
15 Home Office guidance, *Assessing destitution* (version 4.0)
16 Reg 7(a) and (b) AS Regs
17 s95(7) IAA 1999 and reg 6(4)-(5) AS Regs
18 Regs 2(4) and 6(4) AS Regs
19 Reg 6(6) AS Regs
20 Reg 6(3) AS Regs
21 Home Office guidance, *Assessing destitution* (version 4.0), p12
22 While the duty to report a change of circumstances and the criminal consequences of failing to do so are clear if you are receiving s95 support, the extent of any such duty is not so clear if you are receiving s4 support. That said, obtaining s4 support to which you are not entitled (eg, if you cease to be destitute) may be a criminal offence, although this specific issue is beyond the scope of this book.
23 Home Office guidance, *Assessing destitution* (version 4.0), p12
24 *ZN v SSHD* (Appeal ref: 37288), at para 24
25 Home Office guidance, *Asylum support: policy bulletins instruction* (version 9.0), Ch 7.2
26 asaproject.org/uploads/January_2021_Mixed_Households_and_Asylum_Support.pdf
27 Home Office guidance, *Applications for additional support* (version 1.0), p4
28 s95(7)(b) IAA 1999 and reg 9 AS Regs
29 s95(7)(b) IAA 1999; reg 9(1) and (2) AS Regs
30 *R (Refugee Action) v SSHD* [2014] EWHC 1033, para 96
31 *R (Refugee Action) v SSHD* [2014] EWHC 1033, para 95
32 Reg 9(6) AS Regs
33 Home Office guidance, *Applications for additional support* (version 1.0)
34 s95(5)(a) IAA 1999; reg 8(1)(a)-(b) and (3) AS Regs
35 Reg 8(2) AS Regs
36 IA 2014
37 Home Office guidance, *Assessing destitution* (version 4.0), p14. In relation to eligibility for s4 support, the guidance states: 'Failed asylum seekers who can satisfy one of the conditions set out in the regulation 3(2) of the Immigration and Asylum (Provision of Accommodation to Failed Asylum-Seekers) Regulations 2005 will also normally be granted permission to rent.'
38 *MAS v SSHD* (Appeal ref: 9315), at para 33

39 Concerns have been expressed about the correctness of the tribunal's approach. This is because it could be said to be counter-intuitive (and potentially inconsistent with the regulations and the approach taken in other legal contexts, like homelessness) for the 'adequacy' of accommodation to depend on whether bail in principle has been granted, which is unrelated to the quality of the accommodation. However, at the time of writing the correctness of the tribunal's approach has not yet been tested in the higher courts.
40 Reg 8(3)(a) AS Regs
41 Reg 8(4) AS Regs. 'District', for these purposes, has the same meaning as in s217(3) Housing Act 1996 (reg 8(6)(b) AS Regs).
42 Reg 8(3)(b) AS Regs
43 Reg 8(5)(a)-(c) AS Regs
44 Reg 8(3)(g) and (6)(a) AS Regs; Home Office guidance, *Domestic abuse: responding to reports of domestic abuse from asylum seekers* (version 2.0)
45 Although Form ASF1 guidance notes ask for information if you are in fear of 'a person who normally stays with you as a member of your family'
46 Home Office guidance, *Domestic abuse: responding to reports of domestic abuse from asylum seekers* (version 2.0), p10
47 Information about how to contact the team can be found in the Home Office guidance, *Domestic abuse: responding to reports of domestic abuse from asylum seekers* (version 2.0), at Annex A
48 See Asylum Support Appeals Project, Factsheet 18, *Asylum support for survivors of domestic abuse*, available at asaproject.org/uploads/DA_factsheet.pdf
49 s95(5)(b) and (6) IAA 1999
50 Over the next 14 days (on a new application for support), or over the next 56 days (if the Home Office is minded to discontinue your existing support)
51 Home Office guidance, *Assessing destitution* (version 4.0), p13
52 At the time of writing, the weekly amount per person is £45.00. Additional sums may be claimed in certain circumstances (see Home Office guidance, *Applications for additional support*, version 1.0).
53 *R (SSHD) v Asylum Support Adjudicators* [2001] EWHC Admin 881, at paras 79-80

2. **Section 98 support**

54 You can also apply for temporary support before you have submitted an application for section 95 support in completed Form ASF1. If you apply for temporary support before you submit Form ASF1, the Home Office may grant support on condition that a completed Form ASF1 is submitted to the Home Office within two working days.
55 Home Office guidance, *Asylum support: policy bulletins instruction* (version 9.0), para 1.1.1
56 For example, see Refugee Action's July 2017 report, *Slipping Through the Cracks*, available at refugee-action.org.uk/resource/asylum-support-delays-report

3. **Section 4 support**

57 Home Office guidance, *Asylum support, section 4(2): policy and process* (version 3.0), p14
58 See Appeal ref: 43710 (although this decision is potentially flawed)
59 Appeal refs: 42880 and 43710
60 gov.uk/government/publications/section-42-medical-declaration
61 Home Office guidance, *Asylum support, section 4(2): policy and process* (version 3.0), p11
62 caa.co.uk/aeromedical-examiners/medical-standards/pilots/conditions/mental-health
63 Home Office guidance, *Asylum support, section 4(2): policy and process* (version 3.0), p11
64 See the NHS due date calculator at nhs.uk/pregnancy/finding-out/due-date-calculator
65 Home Office guidance, *Asylum support, section 4(2): policy and process* (version 3.0), p13
66 For example, the Salvation Army or the Anti Trafficking and Labour Exploitation Unit

Chapter 23

Asylum support: payment and accommodation

This chapter covers:

1. Section 95 support

Section 95 asylum support is provided in one of the following ways:[1]

- accommodation and 'subsistence' (cash, via an ASPEN card – see p588) to cover your and your dependants' essential living needs; *or*
- subsistence-only support for your essential living needs if you already have accommodation; *or*
- expenses (other than legal expenses) in connection with your asylum application; *or*
- if your circumstances are exceptional, any other form of support that the Home Office thinks is necessary.[2]

Note: the Home Office does not have to take into account any preference you or your dependants have as to how the support is provided or arranged.[3]

When deciding how much support to give you, the Home Office must take into account any income, support or assets (see p565) that you or your dependants have, or which might reasonably be available to you.[4]

Support to meet your essential living needs

If the Home Office decides you need support for your essential living needs, the general rule is that you are provided with cash on an ASPEN card (see p588) on a weekly basis.[5]

Amount of support

The Home Office reviews the amount of support annually. Since 10 August 2015, there has been a flat rate per person, regardless of age. The current rate is £45.00.[6] A previous allowance (of £39.63 a week) was broken down in a letter dated 27 October 2020 from then Home Office minister Chris Philp MP, as follows.

Categories of 'need'	Office for National Statistics expenditure data from 2018/19 (adjusted for single person) / 2020 market research	After Home Office adjustment and inflation
Food and non-alcoholic drinks	£25.23	£26.49
Adjusted for inflation since data collected – 1.5% CPI as at March 2020	2020 market research	£26.89
Toiletries	2020 market research	£ 0.69
Non-prescription medicines	2020 market research	£ 0.35
Laundry/toilet paper	2020 market research	£ 0.43
Clothing and footwear	2020 market research	£ 3.01
Travel	2020 market research	£ 4.70
Communications	2020 market research	£ 3.56
Subtotal		£12.74
Total		**£39.63**

Home Office guidance states that the weekly allowance 'should generally be sufficient to cover the following needs: food, clothing, toiletries, non-prescription medication, household cleaning items, communications, travel, and the ability to access social, cultural and religious life (covered by the funding provision for communications and travel).'

Furthermore, it states: 'the level of the cash allowance takes into consideration that other essential living needs (for example, warmth, cooking, lighting) are covered by the provision of accommodation that is free of both rent and utility bills (fuel and water) and is also fully furnished and equipped with both household goods (for example kitchenware, access to laundry services) and linens (towels and sheets, for example).'[7]

There are additional payments of:[8]

- £3 a week for pregnant women; *and*
- £5 a week for babies under one; *and*
- £3 a week for children between the ages of one and three.

The ASPEN card is a pre-paid Mastercard chip and pin that can be used in the same way as a debit card to pay for items in participating shops or to withdraw cash from most ATMs. The support is uploaded onto the card weekly. There is no limit on the amount that can be carried over from one week to the next, but the Home Office monitors spending. It can also monitor the location of where the ASPEN card has been used and is therefore alerted if you have spent time away from the place where you have been provided with accommodation.

Legal challenges to the rates of asylum support

Before August 2015, the rates of asylum support were based on the equivalent of 70 per cent of the applicable amount of income support (IS), without any premiums, to which an adult would otherwise be entitled if they qualified for IS and had no other income (see CPAG'S *Welfare Benefits and Tax Credits Handbook* for more details). Initially, the rates were increased in April every year, but from April 2011 the rates were frozen, meaning a cut in real terms over several years.

In 2013, the charity Refugee Action brought a judicial review challenge against the Home Secretary's decision to freeze the rate of asylum support. This was upheld by the High Court in April 2014,[9] which ruled that the Home Secretary had acted irrationally and failed to take all relevant factors into account, in accordance with her duties under the European Union Reception Directive and the Immigration and Asylum Act 1999 to provide for asylum seekers' essential living needs. Following the judgment, the Home Secretary reconsidered the level of support, but decided it should remain unchanged. In April 2015, the rate for single asylum seekers over 18 was increased by by 33 pence and then, from August 2015, the rates were cut to £36.95, representing a significant reduction in the rate previously paid for children in families (which had previously been £52.96 a week). In 2016, there was a further challenge to the level of support, but the Home Office's methodology for setting the rates was found to be lawful.[10]

Exceptional payments

The Home Office can provide additional support if the normal rate of support is not enough to meet your essential living needs and you can show that your particular circumstances are 'exceptional'.[11] The Home Office's ability to provide exceptional payments was a key part of its case in the Refugee Action judicial review (see above), and so you should not hesitate to apply for exceptional payments if you need them. For example, the High Court found that it was unreasonable to refuse a separated father help with the travel costs he incurred in visiting his young child because the Home Office was unable to provide him with accommodation closer than 130 miles away.[12] The court suggested that reasonable travel costs should enable him to visit his son at least fortnightly.

The Home Office has an application form (Form ASF2)[13] and guidance that allows asylum seekers to apply for exceptional payments for any 'exceptional needs'. You must give details on the form of your needs and circumstances, the support required and its likely duration, together with documentary evidence to support your application.

If your application is refused, the Home Office should provide the reasons in writing. However, if an application is refused, the only remedy is judicial review.

Health benefits

As part of your section 95 support package, the Home Office should issue you with a certificate (HC2) enabling you to get free NHS prescriptions, dental treatment, sight tests and wigs, and vouchers towards the cost of glasses and contact lenses. The HC2 certificate itself tells you how to use it and what you can use it for. If you have already paid for any of the above items or for travel to and from hospital for NHS treatment, you may be able to claim back the money.

Maternity payments

You may be eligible for a one-off maternity payment of £300.[14] You must apply in writing between eight weeks before the expected birth and six weeks after, enclosing evidence – eg, a birth certificate, Form MAT B1 from your GP or some other original formal evidence. A payment can also be made if you are a supported parent or a parent applying for support and you have a child under three months old who was born outside the UK. It is important to make this application in time. If it is made late, your application is likely to be refused. The Home Office policy on maternity payments appears to exclude the possibility of a late claim, but there is scope for payment in exceptional circumstances, so it may be worth applying if you can give good reasons for the delay.[15]

Expenses in connection with your asylum application

The Home Office may meet some of the expenses connected to your asylum application.[16] These do not include 'legal' expenses – eg, the costs of paying your lawyer to prepare your case and represent you.

Eligible expenses include the cost of preparing and copying documents and travelling to Home Office interviews,[17] and may include the cost of:

- sending letters and faxes to obtain further evidence; *and*
- your travel expenses (or those of your witnesses) to attend your appeal; *and*
- medical or other examinations in connection with your application.

Note: you may also be able to apply for exceptional payments (see p589).

Although not paid as asylum support, the cost of your fares incurred in travelling to comply with any immigration reporting requirements can be reclaimed from the Home Office if you live outside the three-mile radius of the reporting centre. You must claim these at the reporting centre. It is only possible to claim the travel costs for attending your next reporting date (ie, in advance), not costs already incurred. If you live within a three-mile radius of the reporting centre, you can claim travel costs if you can demonstrate an exceptional need – eg, medical grounds.[18]

Education and sports facilities

If you are receiving asylum support, the Home Office has the power to provide funding for the following services:[19]

- adult education, including English language lessons; *and*
- sporting or other developmental activities.

The Home Office is not under a duty to fund these services, which vary in each dispersal region.

Your children must attend school if they are aged five to 17. All state schools are free of charge and your children may be able to get free school meals and a clothing grant. You should check with your local authority.

Backdating support

There is often a delay between applying for support and getting paid. This delay can be serious if you are without support in the meantime. Unlike social security benefits, there are no rules in the legislation identifying the date from when support must be provided.

It is arguable that support should be payable from the date the Home Office receives a full and valid claim – ie, an application that shows that you are destitute and eligible for support. That should be the case no matter what delays are caused by the Home Office or the appeal procedure.

However, in practice, the Home Office does not backdate support to the date of the application. Support may sometimes be backdated to the date of the decision if there was then a further delay before payment started. If you have applied for subsistence-only support, you may be able to argue that a back payment should be made to your ASPEN card to the date your support should have started. If you have applied for accommodation and subsistence, you may, in any event, be in a full-board hostel until the date you are moved to your dispersal accommodation and your subsistence payments start. If you are not in full-board accommodation, the Home Office pays you a daily subsistence through your accommodation provider until you are dispersed.

Once you are getting support, the Home Office recognises in its policy guidance[20] that awards of asylum support can be backdated if payments have been missed through no fault of the applicant. The guidance gives examples of what the Home Office accepts are legitimate reasons why an applicant may not have collected their support that include, but are not limited to, the following:

- reporting event/asylum interview; *and*
- illness; *and*
- hospitalisation; *and*
- travel difficulties; *and*
- difficulties with your application registration card.

Note: this policy relates to missed payments of support *after* a favourable decision on eligibility has already been made, not to Home Office delays in processing an initial application for support *before* a favourable decision has been made.

Contributions to support

When deciding what level of support to give you as a destitute asylum seeker, the Home Office must take into account any income, support and assets that are available (or might reasonably be expected to be available) to you or any dependant (see p526).[21] If you have income and/or assets, it can decide that you should make a contribution to the cost of your support rather than reducing the level of support provided.[22] If that is the case, you are notified of the amount and you must make payments directly to the Home Office. If you are required to make a contribution, the Home Office may also make it a condition of your support that you pay your contributions promptly.[23] In practice, the Home Office tends to delay the start of the financial support or deduct the relevant amount from the initial support payment.

Note: if you have, in the past, litigated against the Home Office about something other than a protection claim or a nationality dispute, and have been ordered to pay the Home Office's costs, you may be required to contribute towards your litigation debt from your asylum support. See Home Office guidance, *Suitability: unpaid litigation costs.*

Section 95 accommodation and dispersal

The Home Office does not own and provide accommodation but makes arrangements with private contractors that provide the accommodation throughout the UK.[24]

When deciding the location and nature of the accommodation you are given, the Home Office must take into account that:[25]

- you are only being provided with accommodation on a temporary basis until your application for asylum has been dealt with (including any period during which you are appealing); *and*
- it is desirable to provide accommodation for asylum seekers in areas where there is a good supply of accommodation – eg, outside London, given that there is an acute shortage of affordable accommodation in the London area.

The Home Office does not take into account your preferences on:

- the area in which you would like the accommodation to be located;[26] *or*
- the nature of the accommodation to be provided;[27] *or*
- the nature and standard of the fixtures and fittings in the accommodation.[28]

However, the Home Office should take into account your individual circumstances if they relate to your accommodation needs.[29]

The majority of applications for asylum and asylum support are made in south-east England. The Home Office has a strict policy of 'dispersal', which makes it difficult to succeed in arguing against being moved away from London and the South East or against being moved away from the area in which you already live.

However, there are exceptions to the general rule, which are considered by reference to the Home Office's policy on dispersal.[30] Potentially relevant factors include:[31]

- disruption to existing medical treatment or disability assistance; *or*
- disruption to a child's final school or college year, leading up to GCSE, Scottish Highers, AS or A-level exams (or their equivalents), provided the child has been enrolled at that school for a significant part of the previous school year.

The above list is not exhaustive, so the Home Office may consider delaying dispersal in other circumstances. If you need to be accommodated in a particular location, you should carefully consider the Home Office's allocation of accommodation[32] and healthcare needs and pregnancy dispersal[33] policies, and seek specialist advice before submitting a location request to the Home Office.

Helen Bamber Foundation and Freedom from Torture

If you are awaiting assessment from the Helen Bamber Foundation or Freedom from Torture (both of which have London offices), the Home Office may delay dispersal pending a decision by those organisations about whether to offer you treatment. If you are receiving treatment from either organisation, the Home Office may provide you with accommodation in London travel zones 1–6 or within a one-hour travelling distance from one of Freedom from Torture's regional offices in Birmingham, Manchester, Newcastle or Glasgow.[34]

Healthcare needs and pregnancy

The Home Office may delay dispersal on medical grounds, if you can provide evidence either that the medical treatment you are receiving is not available elsewhere or that transferring your care to a dispersal area would be unreasonably disruptive.

Note: as a general rule, some disruption to your healthcare may be insufficient to delay dispersal because the guidance states: 'the degree of disruption [should be balanced] against the overriding principle of allocating accommodation on a "no choice basis" and outside London and the South East'.[35] However, there is detailed guidance about specific health scenarios that should be carefully considered (see below).

The following are some of the circumstances in which the Home Office may delay dispersal:

- HIV;[36] *or*
- active TB;[37] *or*
- severe mental health problems;[38] *or*

- pregnancy;[39] *or*
- if treatment is ongoing and available only in the area where the applicant is living;[40] *or*
- if replication of treatment is difficult to implement, particularly in cases where the treatment is broad in its nature – eg, in cases which an applicant has more than one ailment that requires more than one specialist to provide treatment, and the individual has an active support network in that area;[41] *or*
- if the applicant is in receipt of specialist treatment that may be hard to replicate at advanced stages of treatment, especially if invasive surgery or intensive treatment is required;[42] *or*
- if invasive surgery has been booked to take place within a month or a person is recovering from an operation. If the applicant is recovering from an operation, dispersal that requires long-distance travel should not take place until the individual has been medically assessed as fit to undertake the journey;[43] *or*
- if invasive surgery has been booked to take place in excess of a month's time but evidence has been supplied that there will be a delay in rebooking the surgery at an alternative hospital, and the delay would have an adverse impact on the health of the applicant, and travel from out of area dispersal accommodation to the treating hospital is not appropriate;[44] *or*
- if it is necessary to arrange continuity of care – eg, a person is undergoing kidney dialysis;[45] *or*
- if there is a presence, or suspicion, of infectious and notifiable diseases – see patient.info/doctor/notifiable-diseases;[46] *or*
- if referral or admission to secondary care services is necessary due to acute need.[47]

The above list is not exhaustive.

Family ties

It is possible to request that accommodation be provided near to family if dispersal away from the area would disrupt family relationships. The Home Office must have regard to the right to respect for family life protected by Article 8 of the European Convention on Human Rights. The right to respect family for life is a qualified right, which needs to be balanced against the public interest and does not prevail if the state's countervailing action (eg, to disperse you away from your family members) is necessary and proportionate in the public interest. The guidance observes that disruption to relationships with friends and family does not usually outweigh public interest in dispersal out of London and south-east England. If dispersal would interfere with the rights of a parent and a child to maintain regular contact, that may be taken into account in dispersal decisions, including in some cases by the payment of travel expenses to enable regular visits to be made.[48]

Children's education

Requests for accommodation in a particular area to maintain continuity in a child's education are not usually successful but may be considered favourably if:[49]

- the child has started their final school or college year leading up to their GCSE, Scottish Highers, AS or A-level exams (or their equivalents), provided they have been enrolled at that school for a significant part of the previous school year;
- a child with special educational needs has gained entry to an appropriate school, unless it is clear that accommodation can be arranged near to another location where there is an appropriate school to which the child can be transferred.

Other factors

The guidance lists other factors that might be the subject of a request to be accommodated in a particular area, including the wish to remain close to other members of your ethnic group, your place of worship or your current solicitors. It will be difficult to succeed with a request for accommodation in a particular area based on these factors alone because you are likely to be able to access members of your community, a suitable place of worship and new solicitors in most dispersal areas.

2. Section 98 support

Section 98, or 'temporary' support (see p535), is intended for asylum seekers who appear to the Home Office to be destitute and require short-term accommodation while a section 95 application is being processed. It is generally provided in a full-board Home Office hostel. However, in some locations, the accommodation is self-catering and cash is provided to buy food (see p575).

3. Section 4 support

Section 4 support is provided as a package of accommodation and financial support. There is no subsistence-only support. The Home Office issues section 4 support recipients with ASPEN cards (see p588). These can be used to make payments in participating shops. Unlike section 95 support, section 4 recipients cannot use their ASPEN card to withdraw cash from ATMs.

Unlike section 95 support, there are no specific provisions to reduce the value of any support provided under section 4, to require you to make contributions, or to recover the value of any support provided by the Home Office in error.

Financial element of section 4 support

The amount of the financial element of section 4 support is not fixed in the legislation but is decided by the Secretary of State for the Home Department. When the regulations were made in 2005, the value of the vouchers was set at £35 per individual – ie, for each adult and child. The amount is now the same as the section 95 allowance (£45 at the time of writing). See p588 for more information about how that figure is broken down.

It is possible to carry your balance over from one week to the next – eg, to save for more expensive items. However, if too large a balance is accrued, the Home Office may query whether you are destitute.

Applying for additional section 4 support

There has been criticism of the low level of financial support provided under section 4 and, to comply with a European Directive, the government introduced additional section 4 support in 2007.[50] This additional support can be claimed by refused asylum seekers (and/or their dependants) in certain prescribed circumstances.[51] **Note:** this additional support is not provided automatically. You must make an application to the Home Office, using the form *Application for Provision of Services or Facilities for Section 4 Service Users*. Guidance on what can be claimed and what evidence is required is contained in the guidance notes accompanying the application form[52] and in the Home Office's separate policy document on section 4.[53]

You can claim additional support:[54]

- for the costs of travel to receive healthcare treatment if a 'qualifying journey' is necessary. A **'qualifying journey'** is a single journey of at least three miles, or of any distance if:
  - you or your child are unable, or virtually unable, to walk up to three miles because of a physical impediment or for some other reason; *or*
  - you have at least one dependant aged under five years;
- for the costs of travel to register a birth;
- to obtain a child's full birth certificate;
- for telephone calls and letters (ie, stationery and postage) about medical treatment or care and to communicate with:
  - the Home Office;
  - a **'qualified person'** – ie, a solicitor, barrister or authorised immigration adviser;
  - a court or tribunal;
  - a voluntary sector partner;
  - a Citizens Advice office;
  - a local authority;
  - an immigration officer;
  - the Secretary of State;

- if you are pregnant (up to £3 a week);
- if you have a child under one year old (up to £5 a week);
- if you have a child between one and five years old (up to £3 a week);
- for clothing for a child under 16 years old (up to £5 a week);
- for exceptional specific needs. The Home Office must be satisfied that there is an exceptional need (which may not be met by the above) for travel, telephone calls, stationery and postage, or essential living needs. These specific needs could include travel to your embassy.

There is also a one-off additional payment for pregnant women and new mothers similar to the maternity payment that can be made with section 95 support (see p590). The amount is £250 (£500 for twins) provided as a credit on your payment card. You should apply on the application form, with a MAT B1 certificate or birth certificate. You must apply between eight weeks before the expected due date and six weeks after the birth.

Many refused asylum seekers and others in receipt of section 4 support are required to sign at an immigration reporting centre at regular intervals and may be able to reclaim their travel costs (see p14).

Section 4 accommodation and dispersal

Section 4 accommodation is in general provided on a no-choice basis. However, Home Office policy on section 4 states that:[55]

> ...the caseworker may exceptionally consider providing accommodation in a particular location if there are particular reasons to do so, for example medical reasons. The Asylum Support Medical Adviser is able to provide advice on: the general availability of medical treatment in a particular region of the UK that the person may need to access; the person's fitness to travel to the region; any specific type of accommodation the person may need to be provided with because of a medical reason.

The guidance also specifies: 'Further information may be found in the Healthcare needs and pregnancy dispersal guidance', which it says applies to section 95 only. The policy determining the scope for requests for a departure from the general rule requiring dispersal is therefore the same as for section 95 (see p592).

No subsistence-only support

Subsistence-only support is not available under section 4. If you have friends or family who can provide you with accommodation but who cannot support you, the Home Office cannot provide you with the financial element of section 4 support unless you occupy Home Office accommodation.[56] You must therefore take up the offer of Home Office accommodation to receive payment card credits.

This situation can cause severe hardship and can seem absurd. You may have friends who could provide you with accommodation, companionship and social, psychological and moral support that may be crucial to you, thus it would be substantially less expensive for the government simply to provide you with the payment card without accommodation. You may, therefore, have to choose between living with friends but remaining destitute (with the risk that your friends may then refuse to accommodate you) or possibly being relocated far from your friends to a place where you know no one and, if you are a single person, where you may have to share a room with strangers.

The Home Office has split adults (ie, older than 18 years) from their families in this way when they have had separate asylum applications. However, it is possible for non-dependants (eg, siblings with separate asylum claims) to ask to be accommodated together.[57] It is, therefore, important that you obtain advice from your immigration lawyer on whether to include a family member in your asylum claim as a dependant.

In one case, the High Court found that a refusal to provide support to a refused asylum seeker in a way that allowed him to continue to live with his British partner and child did not breach their right to family life under Article 8 of the European Convention on Human Rights, but the Home Office stated that it would make 'every effort' to house the applicant within a 'reasonable walking distance' of close family members.[58] If you are dispersed to accommodation that is a long distance from your family, you may still be able to claim travel expenses to visit close family members (see p596). If the familial relationship is strong and your dispersal very disruptive, you may be able to challenge the dispersal by judicial review.

Notes

1. **Section 95 support**

1 s96(1) IAA 1999
2 s96(2) IAA 1999
3 s97(7) IAA 1999
4 Reg 12(3) AS Regs
5 Reg (10)2 AS Regs
6 *R (CB) v SSHD* [2022] EWHC 3329 (Admin)
7 Home Office guidance, *Applications for additional support* (version 1.0), 16 March 2017, p4
8 Reg 10A AS Regs; see also Home Office guidance, *Asylum support: policy bulletins instruction* (version 9.0), updated 26 May 2021, paras 24.2-24.8
9 *R (Refugee Action) v SSHD* [2014] EWHC 1033 (Admin)
10 *R (Ghulam, K, YT and RG) v SSHD* [2016] EWHC 2639 (Admin)
11 s96(2) IAA 1999
12 *R (MG) v SSHD* [2015] EWHC 3142 (Admin)
13 Available at gov.uk/government/publications/application-for-additional-asylum-support-form-asf2
14 Home Office guidance, *Asylum support: policy bulletins instruction* (version 9.0), updated 26 May 2021, para 24.2
15 Home Office guidance, *Asylum support: policy bulletins instruction* (version 9.0), updated 26 May 2021, para 24.3
16 s96(1)(c) IAA 1999

17 Expressly included in IAA 1999, Explanatory Notes, para 300, available at legislation.gov.uk/ukpga/1999/33/notes/division/5/14/1
18 Home Office guidance, *Reporting and offender management* (version 6.0), pp37-38
19 Sch 8 para 4 IAA 1999; reg 14 AS Regs
20 Home Office guidance, *Conditions of support* (version 1.0), 14 May 2021, pp25-26
21 Reg 12(3) AS Regs
22 Reg 16(2) AS Regs
23 Reg 16(4) AS Regs. Conditions may generally be imposed under s95(9)-(12) IAA 1999.
24 ss99-100 IAA 1999
25 s97(1) IAA 1999
26 s97(2)(a) IAA 1999
27 Reg 13(2)(a) AS Regs
28 Reg 13(2)(b) AS Regs
29 Reg 13(2) AS Regs
30 Home Office guidance, *Allocation of asylum accommodation policy* (version 8.0), p5
31 Home Office guidance, *Allocation of asylum accommodation policy* (version 8.0), pp8-10
32 Home Office guidance, *Allocation of asylum accommodation policy* (version 8.0)
33 Home Office guidance, *Healthcare needs and pregnancy dispersal policy* (version 3.0), updated 28 January 2016
34 Home Office guidance, *Allocation of accommodation policy*(version 6.0), pp12-15
35 Home Office guidance, *Allocation of accommodation policy* (version 6.0), p9
36 Home Office guidance, *Healthcare needs and pregnancy dispersal policy* (version 3.0), updated 28 January 2016, pp19 and 31
37 Home Office guidance, *Healthcare needs and pregnancy dispersal policy* (version 3.0), updated 28 January 2016, pp19 and 34
38 Home Office guidance, *Healthcare needs and pregnancy dispersal policy* (version 3.0), updated 28 January 2016, pp19 and 35
39 Home Office guidance, *Healthcare needs and pregnancy dispersal policy* (version 3.0), updated 28 January 2016, pp19 and 37
40 Home Office guidance, *Healthcare needs and pregnancy dispersal policy* (version 3.0), updated 28 January 2016, p19
41 Home Office guidance, *Healthcare needs and pregnancy dispersal policy* (version 3.0), updated 28 January 2016, p19
42 Home Office guidance, *Healthcare needs and pregnancy dispersal policy* (version 3.0), updated 28 January 2016, p19
43 Home Office guidance, *Healthcare needs and pregnancy dispersal policy* (version 3.0), updated 28 January 2016, p19
44 Home Office guidance, *Healthcare needs and pregnancy dispersal policy* (version 3.0), updated 28 January 2016, p19
45 Home Office guidance, *Healthcare needs and pregnancy dispersal policy* (version 3.0), updated 28 January 2016, p20
46 Home Office guidance, *Healthcare needs and pregnancy dispersal policy* (version 3.0), updated 28 January 2016, p20
47 Home Office guidance, *Healthcare needs and pregnancy dispersal policy* (version 3.0), updated 28 January 2016, p20
48 Home Office guidance, *Allocation of asylum accommodation policy* (version 8.0), 23 December 2022, p9
49 Home Office guidance, *Allocation of asylum accommodation policy* (version 8.0), 23 December 2022, pp9-10

3. **Section 4 support**

50 The Immigration and Asylum (Provision of Services or Facilities) Regulations 2007 No.3627; Home Office guidance, *Asylum support, section 4(2): policy and process* (version 2.0), pp18-22
51 Prescribed by the Immigration and Asylum (Provision of Services or Facilities) Regulations 2007 No.3627
52 gov.uk/government/publications/application-for-section-4-extra-services-or-facilities
53 Home Office guidance, *Asylum support, section 4(2): policy and process* (version 2.0), pp18-22
54 Home Office guidance, *Asylum support, section 4(2): policy and process* (version 2.0), p18
55 Home Office guidance, *Asylum support, section 4(2): policy and process* (version 2.0), p6
56 *R (Kiana and Musgrove) v SSHD* [2010] EWHC 1002 (Admin); *MK v SSHD* [2011] EWCA Civ 671; s4(2), (10) and (11) IAA 1999
57 Home Office guidance, *Dependants on an asylum support application* (version 8.0), 18 July 2014, p8
58 *R (Kiana and Musgrove) v SSHD* [2010] EWHC 1002 (Admin), para 45

24

Chapter 24

Asylum support: appeals

This chapter covers:

1. Introduction

If your application for either section 95 support or section 4 support is refused by the Home Office or, in some circumstances, if your support is discontinued, you can appeal to the independent Asylum Support Tribunal, also known as the First-tier Tribunal (Asylum Support), which is based in east London.[1] The Asylum Support Tribunal is part of a group of tribunals collectively known as the Social Entitlement Chamber.

A decision of the Asylum Support Tribunal cannot be appealed to the Upper Tribunal and can only be challenged by judicial review, except in limited circumstances in which the Asylum Support Tribunal can 'set aside' its own decisions (see p616).

The Tribunal Procedure (First-tier Tribunal) (Social Entitlement Chamber) Rules 2008 (referred to as the 'tribunal rules' in this chapter) contain the rules for appeals in the Social Entitlement Chamber.[2] Most of these are common to all tribunals in the Social Entitlement Chamber, but a few[3] refer solely to the Asylum Support Tribunal.

In all asylum support appeals, a single judge considers the appeal and makes the decisions. Tribunal judges have no power to make an order relating to the parties' costs, so even if you lose your appeal, you cannot be ordered to pay any legal costs to the Home Office or to the tribunal.

2. The right to appeal

The circumstances in which you have the right to appeal to the Asylum Support Tribunal are limited. You can only appeal if you have been refused support by the Home Office or your support has been stopped – ie:[4]

- you have applied for section 95 or section 4 support and it has been refused; *or*
- your asylum support has been discontinued – ie, your section 95 support has been stopped prematurely while you are still an asylum seeker,[5] or your section 4 support has been stopped for any reason.

Further information is in Asylum Support Appeals Project Factsheet 3, *Appealing to the Asylum Support Tribunal*.[6]

There is no right of appeal against any other Home Office decision about your support (such as the level of support or the place of dispersal) or *any* decision about temporary support. In addition, it is not possible to appeal if:

- the Home Office decides not to consider your application, saying:
  - you failed to provide complete or accurate information in connection with your application; *or*
  - you failed to co-operate with enquiries made in respect of the support application.[7]
- the Home Office refuses your application by saying you did not make your application for asylum as soon as reasonably possible.[8] (Seek specialist advice since the Asylum Support Tribunal may nevertheless treat the Home Office's decision as appealable.)

A decision by the Home Office not to consider your application for asylum support can only be challenged by judicial review, although the Home Office may be willing to reconsider an application if missing information is later provided.

Note: if you are appealing against a discontinuation of your section 4 support and you appeal within the time limits (or a late appeal is accepted) while you are still living in the section 4 accommodation, your support should continue until the day of the appeal.[9] Although there is no equivalent written policy in respect of section 95, in practice many section 95 appellants remain on support until their appeal is heard, particularly if there are dependent minor children.

3. Bringing an appeal

If the Home Office refuses your application for support or terminates your support, it gives you a written decision with its reasons. It also informs you in the decision letter whether you have a right of appeal and, if so, provides an appeal form. You can also get an appeal form (Form EO9) from the tribunal website at gov.uk/government/publications/form-t200-notice-of-appeal-form-eo9. The Home Office does not always get this process right. If your application for support is unsuccessful or your support has been discontinued and you want to appeal, but the Home Office says you do not have the right to appeal, seek legal advice immediately.

The appeal timetable

The tribunal rules set out a timetable for appeals to the Asylum Support Tribunal, a summary of which is set out below.[10]

Day	*Event*
Day one	Notice of decision is received by you.
Day four (latest)	Notice of appeal must be received by the tribunal. Delivery of a notice of appeal at any time up to midnight on the relevant day is sufficient. If not lodged in time, you must apply for an extension of time (see p606).
Day four or day five	Tribunal sends notice of appeal to the Home Office.
Day seven (latest)	You and the tribunal receive the Home Office's response to the notice of appeal, contained in a bundle of relevant documents, often called 'the Home Office bundle'.
Day seven or thereafter 'with the minimum of delay'	Tribunal judge decides whether to hold an oral hearing or to direct a paper determination instead, and fixes the hearing date for the oral hearing or paper determination, giving both parties one to five days' notice. It is likely that, at the same time, directions are given (see p608). If the judge believes the appeal should be 'struck out' (eg, if the tribunal does not have jurisdiction – see p614), they must give you an opportunity to make representations.
Day nine or thereafter 'with the minimum of delay'	Oral hearing held. The tribunal judge notifies the decision to you and the Home Office at the end of the hearing or, if not present, sends a decision notice. If the appeal is determined on the papers, the decision made and a statement of reasons are sent.
Within three days after an oral hearing	Tribunal judge sends a statement of reasons for the decision to you and the Home Office.

As part of its overriding duty to deal with cases fairly and justly, the tribunal must process appeals to avoid delay so far as compatible with proper consideration of the issues.[11] In practice, the tribunal usually holds an oral hearing within approximately two weeks of receiving your notice of appeal, depending on the volume of cases at any particular time.

Notices or documents can be sent to the tribunal by post, fax or email or given by hand.[12]

If a time limit expires on a non-working day (Saturday, Sunday and bank holidays), it is treated as expiring on the next working day.[13]

Notice of appeal

You must use the prescribed form if you want to appeal.[14] It must be completed in English (or in Welsh).[15] This is known as the **'notice of appeal'**. See Asylum Support Appeals Project (ASAP) Factsheet 4, *Filling in the Notice of Appeal,*[16] for more information.

You must state the grounds for your appeal on the form (ie, why you disagree with the Home Office's decision) and attach a copy of the decision you are appealing against. If your notice of appeal does not include all the necessary information and/or is not accompanied by the written Home Office decision, the tribunal will write to you or your representative requesting that you complete the information or provide the relevant documents.[17]

If you have any further information or evidence relating to your application for support or your appeal, you should (if possible) send copies of the relevant documents to the tribunal with the notice of appeal. However, do not delay submitting your appeal to obtain any further evidence, which can be sent to the tribunal later. It is very important that you provide the tribunal with any evidence that proves you are entitled to support as soon as possible. For example, if the Home Office does not accept that you are destitute, you may want to provide letters from one or more people who have been providing you with support but who cannot continue to do so, or a letter from a voluntary agency or from anyone else who has direct knowledge of your circumstances and is willing to give evidence in support of your appeal. Any supporting letters or statements should:

- contain a means of identifying the writer – eg, name, address, telephone number, passport number; *and*
- be signed (unless sent by email); *and*
- be in English if possible.

Even if it is not possible for supporting evidence to be produced in English, you should submit the evidence if relevant. You should explain what the document is, why it is relevant to your appeal, and why it has not been possible for you to obtain a translation. The Home Office generally refuses to take any document not submitted in English into account. However, if you cannot pay for the document to be professionally translated, the tribunal may find a way of taking it into account, including by asking the court interpreter to provide a translation during the hearing.

You should be aware that any supporting evidence you submit is scrutinised carefully by the Home Office and the tribunal. If any aspect of the evidence is inconsistent with your claimed circumstances, the inconsistency is liable to be taken as a sign that you and/or your witness are not telling the truth. This can be a particular problem if the witness is not a native English speaker, because inconsistencies due to language difficulties are not necessarily accepted by the Home Office or the tribunal.

There is a database of the most significant Asylum Support Tribunal decisions at gov.uk/asylum-support-tribunal-decisions, which you may want to use to see how the tribunal has dealt with similar issues in the past. Although past tribunal decisions are not legally binding on the judge who decides your appeal, the decisions may be persuasive and help support your appeal.

Once you have completed the appeal form, you[18] (or your representative – see p607[19]) must sign the form. You can send it to the tribunal by email, fax or post.[20]

Deciding whether to request an oral hearing

The notice of appeal form asks whether you want to attend, or be represented at, an oral hearing or whether you are content for the appeal to be decided on the papers submitted to the tribunal. You must also state whether you will need an interpreter at the hearing and, if so, in what language and dialect. If you have any difficulties with the English language, you should ask for an interpreter. If required, an interpreter is paid for and supplied by HM Courts and Tribunals Service. Although it always depends on the particular circumstances of your case, it is usually advisable to request an oral hearing because the tribunal judge is better able to understand your case if you explain your situation in person. That is especially true if what you have claimed in your application has been disbelieved by the Home Office. Success rates are generally higher following an oral hearing than a paper determination.

In March 2020, face-to-face hearings of the Asylum Support Tribunal were suspended due to the coronavirus pandemic and were replaced by telephone hearings. At the same time, changes were made to the procedure rules to make it easier for the tribunal judges to dispense with oral hearings, even in cases which the parties agreed that there should be one, if the judges considered that a hearing could be justly decided on the papers.

In July 2021, however, the Asylum Support Tribunal reopened, and recommenced hearing face-to-face appeals. At the time of writing, the tribunal's caseload has reverted to mainly face-to-face hearings with some hearings by cloud video platform (CVP) and (infrequently) telephone hearings, plus appeals determined on the papers without a hearing.

The right to an oral hearing

The general rule is that although the tribunal has the power to decline to hold a hearing even if you request one on the notice of appeal, most appellants who request an oral hearing are granted one. You should be as clear as possible in the notice of appeal about any preference in type of hearing – eg, if oral, whether face-to-face, telephone or CVP.

Even if you ask for your appeal to be determined without an oral hearing, the tribunal can still hold an oral hearing if there are issues to be explored that are raised but not explained in the papers (see p611). If you choose to have an oral hearing, and a face-to-face hearing is listed, the Home Office will send you tickets to travel to the hearing centre in London for the hearing (see p612). If it is difficult to travel to the hearing (eg, because of medical problems, pregnancy or lack of childcare), you can request on the notice of appeal for the appeal to be heard by telephone or CVP. If the tribunal approves, you will be invited to attend a court in your local area, with a video line linking you to the tribunal in London, where the interpreter, Home Office representative and judge will attend.

As stated above, the tribunal procedure rules were changed in March 2020 to remove the right to an oral hearing in certain cases. This means that, even if you ask for an oral hearing in your notice of appeal, your appeal could be listed for determination on the papers. A paper determination presents obvious difficulties if you do not read or write in English, or do not have the facilities to prepare detailed written evidence – eg, if you are homeless.

There are three procedural rules that the tribunal can use to dispense with an oral hearing after it receives your notice of appeal and the Home Office bundle (see p608).

- **Rule 1**: under rule 5A,[21] an oral hearing can be dispensed with if three conditions are satisfied:
  - the matter is urgent; *and*
  - it is not reasonably practicable for there to be a hearing, including a hearing by videolink or telephone; *and*
  - it is in the interests of justice to dispense with an oral hearing.
- **Rule 2**: under rule 8(3),[22] the appellant's case can be struck out if:
  - the appellant has failed to comply with a direction or otherwise failed to co-operate with the tribunal to such an extent that the tribunal cannot deal with the appeal fairly and justly; *or*
  - the tribunal considers there is no reasonable prospect of the appellant's case succeeding.
- **Rule 3**: under rule 27(1),[23] the tribunal does not need to hold a hearing if:
  - each party has consented to, or has not objected to, the matter being decided without a hearing; *and*
  - the tribunal considers that it is able to decide the matter without a hearing.

When you receive the directions notice, you may find that your appeal will be decided on the papers without a hearing following one of the above three rules. If that happens, and you want an oral hearing, you should seek urgent advice if possible. In any event, you should consider urgently writing to the tribunal to object to your appeal being determined on the papers.

Depending on which one of the above three rules the judge has relied on to dispense with a hearing, your letter should address the relevant matters set out in the rule, as well as the reasons given by the judge for deciding that the appeal could be fairly decided without a hearing.

If you are not represented, cannot write in English, and/or have no access to word-processing facilities to prepare documents to send to the tribunal, these might be obvious reasons why it would not be fair to decide your appeal without an oral hearing in which you can make your case orally with the services of an interpreter provided by the tribunal.

Representation, including preparing submissions requesting an oral hearing, may be available from ASAP. However, ASAP's capacity to assist appellants is limited, so if you require representation before the tribunal (including if your appeal has been listed for paper determination but you would like an oral hearing), you should contact ASAP as soon as possible after you lodge your notice of appeal.

If, as in most cases, an oral hearing is granted (whether face-to-face or by telephone or CVP), you should ensure that your witnesses are aware of the hearing date and that they attend. Your witnesses may be able to give direct evidence about how you have been supported or about any aspect of your case that the Home Office disputes in the letter refusing your support claim.

Applications for an extension of time for appealing

Your notice of appeal must be received by the Asylum Support Tribunal within three working days of the day on which you received the notice of the decision on your asylum support application.[24] If you receive the Home Office's decision letter more than two days after the date it was written, it is advisable to state in your notice of appeal the date on which you received the letter to show that you are not (or not fully) responsible for any delay. You can submit the notice of appeal to the tribunal by email, fax or post – the details are on the appeal form.

If you do not appeal in time, you can ask the tribunal in the notice of appeal to extend the time limit for appealing.[25] You should explain why you could not appeal earlier – eg, if you were ill and incapable of dealing with your affairs at the time you received the notice, if you needed advice or if there was a delay before you received the Home Office refusal letter. The tribunal usually treats applications for an extension of time sympathetically, provided sufficient explanation is given for the delay. Judges recognise that the time limit to appeal is very short, and an extension of two or three days (or longer) is often granted, especially for destitute people who may not speak English and may be relying for advice on an advice agency that is only open at certain times. The judge must consider your application fairly and justly,[26] and must take into account why you (or your representative) could not comply with the time limit.

If the tribunal refuses to extend the time limit, your only alternative is to seek judicial review of the decision on your asylum application and/or of the decision of the Asylum Support Tribunal to refuse to give you more time (see p617). Alternatively, you may be able to reapply for support (see p618).

Confirming whether you have a representative

You may be represented throughout the appeal procedure by a representative of your choice. They do not have to be legally qualified.[27] If you are represented, the name and address of your representative must be given in writing to the Asylum Support Tribunal.[28] This can be done by including the details in the notice of appeal. If your representative is unable to attend the hearing with you, you should tick 'no' when asked this question on the notice of appeal.

It is generally understood that 'representation' implies an ongoing responsibility for the prompt conduct of all stages of the appeal, including:

- securing and preparing all available relevant evidence and submitting it to the tribunal; *and*
- dealing with all correspondence with the tribunal and the Home Office; *and*
- responding in writing to the directions given by the tribunal; *and*
- advising you on each of these steps and at every stage; *and*
- representing you or arranging for a legal adviser to represent you at your tribunal hearing; *and*
- advising you on the outcome of the appeal and on any steps to be taken – eg, to secure support if the appeal has been successful, or any further challenge (eg, by judicial review) if the appeal was unsuccessful.

An adviser should therefore *not* state that they are your representative if they are simply helping you to complete and submit the notice of appeal, and perhaps acting as a mailbox for you. In those circumstances, they should make it clear on the notice of appeal that this is the limit of their involvement.

If you state that you have a representative, the tribunal must give their details to the Home Office. Any documents that the Home Office is required to serve must be served on the representative (and need not be served on you).[29] Anyone else who accompanies you to the appeal hearing cannot assist in presenting your case without the tribunal's approval.[30]

Legal aid may be available in asylum support cases if you are at risk of homelessness, but (except in Scotland) only for advice to prepare your case, **not** to represent you at a hearing.[31]

ASAP provides free representation and advice before the Asylum Support Tribunal for as many people as possible (see Appendix 2). This service is provided by ASAP staff and volunteer solicitors and barristers. You can ask ASAP to represent you at any time before your hearing (although the later you refer your case, the less likely it is that ASAP will have capacity to represent you). Alternatively, and preferably, you can ask your representative (if you have one) to refer your case to ASAP in advance. If you do not have a representative, you can make the referral yourself. If your named representative on the notice of appeal is a firm of solicitors (and not an advice agency), the tribunal may not allow ASAP to represent you, unless you or your solicitor refer your case to ASAP in advance of the hearing.[32]

The Home Office bundle

On the same day as the tribunal receives your notice of appeal or, if this is not reasonably practicable, as soon as possible on the next day, the tribunal must send a copy to the Home Office, together with any supporting documents that you sent with the appeal.[33]

By the third day after your notice of appeal is received by the tribunal, the Home Office must send to the tribunal:[34]

- a statement saying whether or not it opposes the appeal; *and*
- a copy of the decision letter refusing or withdrawing support; *and*
- any other evidence that it took into account when refusing you support; *and*
- any other grounds and reasons for the decision that have not been included in the decision letter; *and*
- copies of all documents it has that are relevant to the case.

At the same time, the Home Office must provide you (or your representative) with a copy of all the above information and documents.[35]

This material is commonly referred to as the 'Home Office bundle'. It is important that you receive a copy of the bundle before the hearing so that you are aware of all the evidence in the appeal. If you or your representative have not received the bundle on time, you should alert the tribunal and/or contact the Home Office.

Tribunal directions and notification of the hearing date

If an oral hearing is listed, the tribunal must promptly inform the parties of the time and date. It is likely that the hearing will take place within two weeks or so of the tribunal receiving your notice of appeal.

When sending out the notice of a hearing date, the tribunal also sends a 'directions notice' to both you and the Home Office. The directions notice is prepared by a judge who has had an initial look at the case papers, and who then requests, by giving the directions set out in the directions notice, evidence and information from both sides on the issues that they consider to be relevant to the effective determination of the appeal. The directions notice will state what documents and/or information you should send to the tribunal and the Home Office, and by what date and time. For example, you may be asked to produce evidence relating to your destitution (eg, bank statements), medical evidence or copies of any missing documents that the tribunal considers may be relevant.

Typically, the tribunal requests evidence to be filed a week before the case is to be determined at a hearing (if there is one) or on the papers. However, these deadlines are not fixed and depend on the particular judge who has given directions, which may not be the same judge who eventually hears the appeal. Even if you cannot meet the deadline stated in the directions notice, you should still send the evidence and information requested when you can, and take your response to the directions notice with you to the hearing (if there is one). If you cannot get a full response to the tribunal before the deadline in the directions notice, you can email the tribunal to explain why you cannot meet the deadline, and to ask for additional time.

It is rare for documents sent to the tribunal after the deadline to be disregarded, but the tribunal will appreciate your efforts if you respond before the deadline set if you can, and request more time before the deadline expires if that is not possible. If an agency or solicitor has helped you to complete the appeal form, the directions notice may be sent to them, so it is important to keep in regular contact to check that the notice has been received and whether the agency or solicitor can help you respond.[36]

Responding to directions and submitting further evidence

The directions notice is an important document as it indicates how the tribunal is thinking about your appeal and what it considers to be the crucial issues. It is important to comply with any directions, because if you do not, the tribunal may not have all the evidence it considers necessary to make a decision on your appeal, and the judge may hold the lack of evidence against your case. However, if you cannot answer all the questions or provide all the evidence that has been requested, you should provide what information and evidence you can and provide an explanation for what is missing.

You should also note what further information the Home Office has been directed to provide and make sure you see the Home Office's response. Be aware that the Home Office does not always respond in time to the directions notice, and may only produce the information that the tribunal has requested at the hearing, if at all.

If you want to submit more evidence in support of your appeal that you did not send with your notice of appeal, you may still send it to the tribunal to be considered. In particular, you may wish to rely on evidence that shows a change in your circumstances after the date of the Home Office decision or which has only now come into your possession, or evidence that rebuts a new point that the Home Office has raised against you in the letter refusing your support, or in its response to directions. You should send this evidence to the tribunal judge before the date of the hearing, or the date on which you have been notified that they will proceed to determine the appeal. You should do this immediately and by email or fax if possible, especially if no oral hearing is to be held, because in those cases the tribunal may determine the appeal very quickly after the date specified in the directions notice.

You should also send a copy of any further evidence to the Home Office. Although the tribunal rules no longer require you to do so, the tribunal judge will want to ensure that the Home Office has seen any further evidence. If you explain the reasons for any delay, and copy in the Home Office when you submit further evidence, you will minimise the (very small) risk that the judge will refuse to allow evidence that is provided late and which has not been seen by the Home Office.[37]

During the appeal hearing, you should make sure that you have copies with you of all the appeal papers, including your evidence and the Home Office's documents and any new evidence, because you may need to refer to them. At the start of the hearing, you should also ensure that none of the papers have gone astray and that the judge has all your evidence.

The Home Office can also send further evidence to the tribunal before the appeal is determined. It is likely that the Home Office and/or the tribunal will send copies to you (or your representative) or, if there is not sufficient time, provide you with copies at the hearing. In any event, you must be provided with copies of any documents on which the Home Office intends to rely at the hearing and you must have time to consider them.

Withdrawing an appeal

If, at any stage before the hearing, you decide you do not wish to carry on with your appeal, you can give written notice of withdrawal.[38] If you give notice of the withdrawal orally 'at the hearing', the judge's consent is required.[39] The tribunal rules state that if either party withdraws from the case in writing before the hearing, the consent of a judge is not required and therefore no reasons need be given. However, if you give written notice of withdrawal on the day of the hearing, some judges may want you to attend the hearing to explain why you want to withdraw (although the lawful basis to require you to attend the hearing if you have given notice of withdrawal in writing beforehand is not clear).

If the Home Office withdraws, that can be unfair on you because, unless the Home Office immediately substitutes its negative decision with a positive one awarding you support, you still need your appeal to go ahead to get support.

If the Home Office withdraws from an appeal when you are not yet receiving support, you should refer it to its policy on withdrawals.[40] Under this policy, if the Home Office serves a notice of withdrawal before 12 noon on the day before the hearing, it should immediately make a fresh decision, which must be posted or faxed to you or your representative. If this decision is again negative (but for a different reason than the first), you need to appeal immediately again. This process will have caused a delay in your getting support (assuming you win your eventual appeal). You should make sure that you compare the two decisions and if there is no substantial difference, draw that to the tribunal's attention when you appeal.

Under the withdrawal policy, if the Home Office withdraws after 12 noon on the day before the hearing, it must apply to do so at the hearing itself. The judge only consents to the withdrawal if:

- the Home Office confirms in writing that the decision under appeal is being withdrawn and you are to be granted support immediately; *or*
- the Home Office serves you with a copy of a fresh refusal or discontinuation decision letter, and you or your representative agree that the hearing can proceed on the basis of this new decision; *or*
- you agree with the Home Office to adjourn the proceedings (for no longer than 14 days) and the Home Office confirms in writing that you will be provided with support in the meantime.

In practice, the tribunal allows the Home Office to withdraw from appeals at any time before the day of the hearing (as opposed to only up to midday) without providing reasons and it is difficult to prevent this. If you are not immediately provided with a new decision letter, whether positive or negative, refer the Home Office to its policy and consider taking advice on bringing a claim for judicial review (see p617) if there continues to be a significant delay.

Paper determinations

After it receives the Home Office's response, the tribunal judge must consider all the documents and decide whether it is necessary to hold an oral hearing, or whether the appeal can be determined simply by considering the papers. It is possible (albeit unlikely) that your appeal will be listed for paper determination even if you requested an oral hearing in the notice of appeal.

If your case is listed for a paper determination, you can write to the tribunal to object to your appeal being decided on the papers and to request an oral hearing. See p609 for the issues you should address in your submissions to the tribunal.

You may have stated on the notice of appeal form that you did not want an oral hearing, but you may not have been aware of all of the information or evidence relied on by the Home Office until afterwards – eg, new papers might subsequently be disclosed to you by the Home Office or the tribunal. If, having seen any new material, you change your mind and decide that you want an oral hearing at which to make direct representations to the tribunal, you should notify the tribunal as soon as possible by email, fax or telephone. The judge must then take this into account when deciding whether to grant an oral hearing. If you want to make written representations to the tribunal about this further evidence, you should do so as soon as possible.

Oral hearings

Travel to the hearing

You are sent tickets for your travel to and from a face-to-face hearing. If you live too far away from east London (where the tribunal is situated) to be able to travel on the day and arrive on time for your hearing, overnight accommodation is arranged and paid for by the Home Office. Unless you specifically request help with travel for a witness and the tribunal directs the Home Office to comply with your request, you are only sent travel tickets for yourself. That may affect you if you want to call detailed evidence from a witness whose evidence is important for your case – eg, you have a British national partner with leave to remain who is in receipt of social security benefits and it is important for them to attend the appeal to be able to give full details with documentary evidence of their benefits and to explain why they cannot support you.

What happens at the hearing

In principle, oral hearings before the Asylum Support Tribunal take place in public, although it is rare for members of the public to attend.[41] The tribunal judge can decide, if appropriate, that a hearing or part of it should be in private, and can exclude anyone who is likely to cause a disruption or defeat the purpose of the hearing. In practice, judges tend to check who is present in the hearing room to ensure that there is no one present who might intimidate the appellant or otherwise hinder a fair hearing. If, for any reason, an appellant believes that someone should be excluded, they can tell the tribunal either before or at the start of the hearing. When oral hearings are conducted by telephone, you or your representative, if you have one, must inform the tribunal before the start of the hearing of your telephone number, as well as the telephone numbers of your representative, anyone who you wish to give evidence in support of your appeal, and anyone who wishes to observe the proceedings. A court interpreter will also attend (in person, by video or by telephone) if requested in the notice of appeal.

Whether the hearing is face-to-face or by telephone or video, the procedure that must be adopted at the oral hearing is decided by the tribunal judge. They should explain the procedure to you at the outset. There are no strict rules on evidence, and so hearsay and letters from third parties can be considered. You can provide oral evidence and call any witnesses to give oral evidence in support of your case. The Home Office is usually represented by a 'presenting officer', who sets out its case and asks you questions. Sometimes the Home Office is unrepresented at the hearing. You or your representative must also have the opportunity of directly addressing the tribunal about the decision it should make and commenting on all of the evidence, documentary or oral. If witnesses are called, they may be required to give their evidence under oath or affirmation (although this is not the tribunal's usual practice).[42]

If either you or the Home Office attend the hearing with further evidence that has not previously been provided, the other party must be given the opportunity to look at and comment on this evidence before the hearing proceeds, although that can be difficult in practice if the hearing is a telephone hearing and you are unrepresented and do not have access to email facilities. The judge often checks at the beginning of the hearing whether any further documents need to be made available to either party.

If possible, take notes of what is said at the hearing. It is usual for the judge to make their own written record. If you later want to challenge the decision by judicial review, you can request a copy of this record. Although you are allowed to take notes, you must not make a video or audio recording since that is a criminal offence.

If you are not present at the time of the hearing, it may go ahead without you (or in the absence of a Home Office representative) if the judge:[43]

- is satisfied that you/the Home Office have been notified of the hearing or that reasonable steps have been taken to notify you/the Home Office of the hearing; *and*
- considers that it is in the interests of justice to proceed.

The judge usually waits 30 minutes from the listed start time before starting the appeal without you (although that is a matter of general practice rather than a rule that you can safely rely on).

Burden and standard of proof

The tribunal judges decide issues of fact on the balance of probabilities. This simply means deciding which facts in your case are more likely than not to be true. In appeals against a refusal of an application for support, it is up to you to prove, on the balance of probabilities, that you are entitled to support and meet the relevant criteria. If you are appealing a decision to discontinue support, it is up to the Home Office to establish, on the balance of probabilities, that your support should be terminated.

The tribunal can take into account any change of circumstances that took place between the date on which the decision of the Home Office was made and the date of the appeal.

The tribunal sometimes hears cases in which people are not sure of their immigration status, which may have changed since their appeal was lodged. If it is apparent at the hearing that you have applied for the wrong form of support (eg, you are eligible for section 95 support as an asylum seeker, but you applied for section 4 support as a refused asylum seeker or vice versa), most judges are willing to grant the right type of support (whether it is section 95 or section 4 support) if eligibility is established, even if you applied for the wrong type of support.[44]

Giving the decision

In all cases, the tribunal will reach a decision with the minimum of delay.

If there is an oral hearing, the judge may retire for a period to consider the decision. However, they must tell you and the Home Office representative the decision that has been reached at the end of the hearing and must provide notice of the decision the same day (unless the judge decides to adjourn the appeal or reserve their decision until another day).[45] The notice does not give any reasons for the decision, but simply states whether the appeal has been allowed, dismissed or remitted (see below). This notice is an important document if you win, because it is evidence of the outcome of your appeal that will be accepted by the Home Office and accommodation providers. The notice is also sent on the same day to any party (ie, you or the Home Office) who was not present at the hearing. Unless the appeal has been adjourned or a decision reserved by the judge to another day, the judge announces a final decision at the hearing and then prepares written reasons, which the judge must send to the parties within three days after the hearing.

If there is no oral hearing, the appeal is determined on the papers on or after the date notified in the directions notice (see p608), which will be a date following the time limit for complying with the directions. Unless the appeal has been adjourned, the tribunal must send a copy of the decision notice together with the judge's written statement of reasons for the decision to both parties on the same day as the appeal is decided.[46]

4. Decisions the Asylum Support Tribunal can make

When deciding an appeal, an Asylum Support Tribunal judge can:[47]

- substitute their own decision for the decision made by the Home Office and thus allow the appeal, so you are entitled to support; *or*
- dismiss your appeal, so that the decision of the Home Office stands; *or*
- require the Home Office to reconsider the matter. The Asylum Support Tribunal calls this 'remitting' the appeal (see below).

If your appeal is allowed

If your appeal is successful, the Home Office must provide support on that day. However, if you attend your appeal hearing, you may be left with a difficult choice. In practice, the Home Office is likely to offer 'emergency' accommodation situated in a hostel in south-east London while you wait to be allocated 'dispersal' accommodation elsewhere in the UK.[48] This emergency accommodation can be requested from the Home Office representative at the hearing or, if the Home

Office did not attend your hearing, you can ask the tribunal clerk to put you in contact with the representative on duty that day. The accommodation is offered on condition that you stay there on the night of your appeal. If you are then allocated accommodation in a different part of the UK to where you were previously living, the Home Office does not provide travel costs to allow you to return to collect any belongings.

Alternatively, after the hearing, you can return to the town in which you were living, using the return ticket provided by the Home Office. The Home Office should then contact you directly, or through your advice agency, to arrange your accommodation. This usually takes two to three days to arrange (and, in some cases, even longer) during which time you may be left homeless. You are given travel tickets to get to your new accommodation. This option is therefore more appropriate if you need to collect belongings and you have somewhere to stay and the ability to feed yourself in the short term.

This arrangement is particularly unsatisfactory if you are street homeless but have left belongings (eg, medication) in the town where you were sleeping.

Further information is in Asylum Support Appeals Project Factsheet 16, *Emergency Support following a successful section 4 appeal*.[49]

If there is any delay by the Home Office in providing support immediately after a successful appeal, the Home Office may be acting unlawfully, and you may be able to challenge the delay by bringing, or threatening to bring, a claim for judicial review (see p617).

If your appeal was heard by video, the Home Office can provide emergency accommodation at your nearest initial accommodation centre. You should request this at the end of the hearing; although the judge has no power to require the Home Office to provide emergency accommodation, it can nevertheless be useful for the judge to request that the Home Office lawyer make the necessary arrangements.

If your appeal is dismissed

If your appeal is dismissed and if you are currently receiving asylum support, your support will be terminated soon; if you are not receiving asylum support, you will remain without support.

If your appeal is remitted

The effect of remitting a decision is to set aside the decision of the Home Office. This requires the Home Office to reconsider and come to a new decision on whether you should be provided with support. This puts you back into the position you were in before the decision was made. If you had been receiving support and the Home Office's decision to withdraw your support is remitted by the tribunal, the Home Office must immediately reinstate the support until it comes to a new decision. If you were previously without support and are appealing the Home Office's decision to refuse your application, a tribunal decision to remit that refusal decision leaves you in your previous position of being without support, at least until the Home Office comes to a new decision.[50]

Other types of tribunal decisions

The tribunal can make other types of decision.

Adjourning the appeal, often at the same time giving directions for the future conduct of the case. Adjournments are relatively rare, as tribunal judges tend to treat asylum support cases as urgent.

Striking out the appeal, thereby determining in favour of the Home Office. A tribunal 'strikes out' your appeal by taking a decision that your appeal cannot continue to a final hearing, either following a hearing about whether or not to strike out your appeal or even before a hearing has taken place. The tribunal must strike out your appeal if it does not have jurisdiction to decide the matter – eg, the tribunal cannot consider an appeal about how much asylum support the Home Office should pay you each week. The tribunal may also strike out your appeal without a hearing if it considers your case has no reasonable prospect of success. Before striking out your appeal, the tribunal must give you the opportunity to make representations. It may direct you to make these in writing by a certain deadline, following which a decision is made by the judge 'on the papers'. Alternatively, the tribunal may fix a date for you and the Home Office to attend to make any representations about whether the appeal should be struck out. If, following such a hearing, the appeal is not struck out, the appeal then proceeds to a full hearing, usually on the same day. As a complimentary power to its power to strike out an appellant's appeal, the tribunal can also bar the Home Office from taking further part in an appeal.

5. After the decision

There is no right of appeal against the Asylum Support Tribunal's decision. If you are dissatisfied with the decision, in limited circumstances you can ask the tribunal to set it aside (see below). Otherwise, the only way of challenging the decision is by judicial review (see p617).

Setting aside a decision

The Asylum Support Tribunal can only set aside its own decision and make a new decision (or set aside and remake part of a decision) if:[51]

- it was a decision 'disposing of the proceedings' – ie, a final decision or a decision to strike out the appeal, *and*:
  - a document relating to the proceedings was not sent or was not received at an appropriate time by either party or their representative; *or*

  - a document relating to the proceedings was not sent to the tribunal at an appropriate time; *or*
  - a party or representative was not present at a hearing; *or*
  - there has been some other procedural irregularity in the proceedings; *and*
- the tribunal considers that it is in the interests of justice to do so.

You cannot, therefore, ask the Asylum Support Tribunal to set aside a decision because you do not agree with the decision. Bear in mind that, even if one of these conditions does apply, the tribunal may still decide that it is not in the interests of justice to set aside the decision. For example, even if you did not receive a relevant document at the appropriate time, the tribunal may still consider that this did not make any difference to the decision that was eventually made, and so it is not in the interests of justice to set the decision aside.

If you wish to apply to set aside a decision, your application must be in writing and received by the Asylum Support Tribunal no later than one month after the date on which it sent the decision to you.[52]

Challenging the tribunal's decision by judicial review

Judicial review is a type of procedure by which a High Court or Upper Tribunal judge considers the lawfulness of a decision of a public body, including a decision of the Asylum Support Tribunal. There must be an error in law for an application for judicial review to succeed; it is not enough that you do not agree with the decision the judge made. Whether there is an error of law in the judge's decision is a complicated matter beyond the scope of this book. To be successful in judicial review proceedings, you will need help from a public law solicitor.

An application for judicial review must be made promptly and, in any event, within three months of the decision you want to be reviewed. The application must be in writing, laying out the facts and legal arguments, and be accompanied by copies of all relevant documents.

Judicial review is a two-stage procedure. You must first get the permission of a High Court judge to proceed with the claim. At this stage, a judge gives preliminary consideration to the case to establish whether there is an arguable error of law. If the judge concludes the decision maker made an arguable error of law, they grant permission for the judicial review proceedings to proceed to a full hearing.

If the judge is not persuaded that there is an arguable error of law, they will refuse you permission to proceed. In any event, a judge has a discretion to refuse you permission (or to reject your case at the full hearing) if they do not think an order should be made. Judicial review proceedings can be expensive, and although the court can intervene quickly in an emergency, the proceedings can take months or even years to be determined. Unless legal aid is granted, an unsuccessful judicial review applicant is liable to pay the Home Office's legal costs if the judicial review claim is refused. In many cases, a further application for asylum support may be a more practical remedy than judicial review, and legal aid may be available to advise you on the application. If you think judicial review might be appropriate in your case, you should immediately get legal advice from a solicitor specialising in judicial review. If your case is strong, legal aid should be available to pay the solicitor's fees.

Making a new application for support

Following an unsuccessful appeal, the Home Office cannot consider any further application for support from you, unless the Home Office is satisfied that there has been a 'material change in the circumstances' between the time of the appeal and the new application.[53] If you are destitute, you should not, therefore, just submit an identical application to that which was dismissed on appeal. However, you should reapply if you have new evidence of destitution that could be a material change of circumstances – eg, street homelessness following your appeal. The Home Office and tribunal will want to see evidence that your situation has changed since the last decision. If you decide to reapply for support after a dismissed appeal, make sure your application deals with the points raised in the 'statement of reasons', including by providing information or evidence that the previous judge considered was missing, or otherwise found to be unsatisfactory, and by addressing the reasons why the previous judge dismissed your appeal.

Responding to a fresh Home Office decision following a tribunal decision to remit

If the Asylum Support Tribunal decides to remit the matter (see p614) and the Home Office then makes a new decision refusing you support, you may appeal again against the new decision.

Notes

1. **Introduction**
  1 2nd Floor, Import Building, 2 Clove Crescent, London E14 2BE
  2 TP(FT) Rules available at gov.uk/government/publications/social-entitlement-chamber-tribunal-procedure-rules
  3 For example, rr29(2)(a) and 33(3) TP(FT) Rules

2. **The right to appeal**
  4 s103(1)-(3) IAA 1999
  5 s103(2) IAA 1999. The legislation provides a right of appeal if a decision is made to stop providing support 'before that support would otherwise have come to an end'. The intention is to allow a right of appeal in any case where support is terminated before the asylum seeker has ceased to be an asylum seeker for support purposes. See IAA 1999, Explanatory Notes, para 317.
  6 Available at asaproject.org/uploads/Factsheet_3_-_Appealing_to_the_Support_Tribunal_28_july_2021_1.pdf
  7 s57 NIAA 2002
  8 s55 NIAA 2002
  9 Home Office guidance, *Asylum support: policy bulletins instruction* (version 9.0), updated 26 May 2022, para 6.6

3. **Bringing an appeal**
  10 rr22(2)(a) and (7)(a), 24(1)(a), 29, 33 and 34 TP(FT) Rules
  11 r2(2)(e) TP(FT) Rules
  12 r13(1) TP(FT) Rules
  13 r12(2) and (3) TP(FT) Rules
  14 Available at gov.uk/government/publications/form-t200-notice-of-appeal-form-eo9
  15 r22(3) TP(FT) Rules
  16 Available at asaproject.org/uploads/Factsheet_4_-_Filling_in_Appeal_Notice_November_2018.pdf
  17 The Asylum Support Tribunal has previously agreed to list appeals in which appellants only have an eviction notice but no Home Office decision letter
  18 r22(3) TP(FT) Rules
  19 r11(5) TP(FT) Rules
  20 r13(1) TP(FT) Rules
  21 r5A TP(FT) Rules
  22 r8(3) TP(FT) Rules
  23 r27(1) TP(FT) Rules
  24 rr12 and 22(2)(a) TP(FT) Rules
  25 rr5(3)(a) and 22(6) TP(FT) Rules
  26 r2 TP(FT) Rules
  27 r11(1) TP(FT) Rules. Note also that asylum support law is not immigration law, and so an asylum support adviser does not have to be registered with the Office of the Immigration Services Commissioner.
  28 r11(2) TP(FT) Rules
  29 r11(6a) TP(FT) Rules
  30 r11(7) TP(FT) Rules
  31 Sch 1 Part 1, para 31 Legal Aid, Sentencing and Punishment of Offenders Act 2012
  32 See ASAP's 'easy read' guide on ASAP and asylum support appeals at asaproject.org/guides
  33 r22(7)(a) TP(FT) Rules
  34 r24(1)(a), (2) and (4) TP(FT) Rules
  35 r24(5) TP(FT) Rules
  36 r15 TP(FT) Rules
  37 r15(2)(b) TP(FT) Rules
  38 r17(1) TP(FT) Rules
  39 r17(2) and (3)(c) TP(FT) Rules
  40 Home Office guidance, *Asylum support: policy bulletins instruction* (version 9.0), updated 26 May 2022, para 6.5
  41 r30(1) TP(FT) Rules
  42 r15(3) TP(FT) Rules
  43 r31 TP(FT) Rules
  44 See *Razai and Ors* [2010] EWHC 3151 (Admin), para 29
  45 rr33(3) and 34(1)(a) TP(FT) Rules
  46 rr33(3) and 34(1)(b) TP(FT) Rules

4. **Decisions the Asylum Support Tribunal can make**
  47 s103(3) IAA 1999
  48 Home Office guidance, *Asylum support, Section 4(2): policy and process* (version 3.0), 28 June 2022, p6
  49 Available at asaproject.org/uploads/Factsheet_16_-_Emergency_support_following_a_succsessful_s4_appeal.pdf

50 On an application for section 95 support you could, in theory, receive temporary support under s98 IAA 1999 until a new decision is made

5. **After the decision**

51 r37(1) TP(FT) Rules
52 r37(3) TP(FT) Rules
53 s103(6) IAA 1999

Part 9

Other sources of help

Chapter 25

Other sources of help

This chapter covers:

1. Council tax reduction

If you need help to pay your council tax, you may be able to get help under your local authority's council tax reduction scheme. **Note:** council tax reduction is not a social security benefit or a tax credit, and how the scheme operates depends on where you live.[1]

- In England and Wales, local authorities can devise their own local schemes, which must meet minimum requirements. In Wales, if a local authority does not set up its own scheme, a default scheme applies. Check with your local authority whether it has its own local scheme or whether the default scheme applies.
- In Scotland, there is a national scheme, administered by local authorities.

The regulations for all the schemes are in CPAG's *Housing Benefit and Council Tax Reduction Legislation,* and see CPAG's *Council Tax Handbook* for more information.

All the schemes have immigration and residence rules. To be entitled to council tax reduction, you must:

- not be defined as a 'person subject to immigration control' (see below); *and*
- be habitually resident in, including having a right to reside in, the common travel area (see p625), unless you are exempt.

You are not entitled to council tax reduction if you are absent from the property, although certain temporary absences are disregarded. These rules can be affected by whether your absence is in, or outside, Great Britain (see p627).

To be entitled to council tax reduction in England and Wales you, and anyone included in your application, must satisfy the national insurance (NI) number requirement (see p627).

Note: in Scotland, new council tax reduction regulations came into force in April 2022. While most of the residence and immigration conditions have remained the same, there are some notable differences. For the rules before April 2022, see the 13th edition of this *Handbook*.

People subject to immigration control

You are usually not entitled to council tax reduction if you are defined as a 'person subject to immigration control' (see p93).[2]

However, in Scotland, and until 1 April 2023 in England and Wales, you are not excluded from council tax reduction on the basis of being a person subject to immigration control if you are:[3]

- a national of a country that has ratified either the European Convention on Social and Medical Assistance or the European Social Charter (1961). The only non-European Economic Area (EEA) countries to which this applies are Turkey and North Macedonia; *and*
- 'lawfully present' in the UK. You satisfy this if you currently have leave to enter or remain in the UK. However, see below if your leave is subject to a condition that you do not have recourse to public funds.

Note:

- You must satisfy all the other conditions of entitlement for council tax reduction, including the requirement to have a right to reside (see p626).
- The courts have held that although asylum seekers with temporary admission are lawfully present in the UK, they do not have a right to reside. Temporary admission was replaced by immigration bail on 15 January 2018, but the same arguments are likely to apply.[4]

Public funds

Council tax reduction is defined as a public fund in the Immigration Rules (see p102).[5]

If your leave to enter or remain in the UK is subject to a condition that you do not have recourse to public funds, you are defined as a 'person subject to immigration control' (see p101) and (unless you are covered by the above exception) you are not entitled to council tax reduction.

If you are exempt, and are therefore entitled to council tax reduction, this may still be regarded as having recourse to public funds. Receiving council tax reduction breaches this condition of your leave and could affect your right to remain in the UK (see p103).[6]

If your leave is subject to a 'no recourse to public funds' condition, you should also avoid being included in someone else's claim because if they receive a larger council tax reduction because of your presence (eg, if they lose the single person discount and become liable for 100 per cent of the council tax), this may breach your no recourse to public funds condition and could affect your right to remain in the UK (see p29).[7]

Note: although council tax reduction is defined as a public fund, a discount in your council tax liability (eg, a single person discount because you live alone) or a discretionary reduction is not.[8]

See p101 for more information on public funds.

Asylum support

In England, local authorities can choose to treat asylum support as income for council tax reduction, unless you are a pensioner,[9] so check your local scheme. In Wales, asylum support you (but not your partner) receive counts as income for council tax reduction, unless you are defined as a 'pensioner'.[10] In Scotland, asylum support cannot count as income for council tax reduction.[11]

Residence requirements

To be entitled to council tax reduction, you must satisfy both parts of the habitual residence test: you must be 'habitually resident in fact' (see p163), and have a non-excluded right to reside (see p626), in the common travel area (ie, the UK, Ireland, Channel Islands and the Isle of Man), unless you are exempt from the habitual residence test.[12]

The same exemptions from the habitual residence test for housing benefit (see p159) apply to council tax reduction, except:[13]

- you are *not* exempt if:
  - you receive pension credit; *or*
  - other than for pension-age council tax reduction in Scotland, and from 1 April 2023 in Wales only, you have been granted leave outside of the Immigration Rules (see p48), other than discretionary leave, destitution domestic violence concession leave or leave granted under the Afghan Citizens Resettlement Scheme; *or*
  - until 31 March 2023 other than for pension-age council tax reduction in Scotland only, you were living in Ukraine immediately before 1 January 2022 and you left in connection with the Russian invasion of 24 February 2022, and you have leave, or a right of abode (see p16), in the UK (including if you are British); *or*
  - in Wales and for pension-age council tax reduction in Scotland only, you are a frontier worker (see p278), the family member of a frontier worker or family member of a relevant person of Northern Ireland (see p171);

- you are exempt if:
  - other than for pension-age council tax reduction in Scotland, you are a Crown servant or member of the armed forces posted overseas and immediately before your posting you were habitually resident in the UK; *or*
  - for pension-age council tax reduction in Scotland only, you:
    - are the 'extended family member' (see p243) of an EEA 'worker' (see p211) or 'self-employed person' (see p218), including someone who retains either status (see p222); *or*
    - receive income-based jobseeker's allowance (JSA).

If you are not exempt from, or do not satisfy, the habitual residence test, you are treated as not being in Great Britain and so are not entitled to council tax reduction.

Note: a local authority cannot require you to have resided in that local authority area for a set period of time before you can be entitled to council tax reduction.[14]

Right to reside

To satisfy the right to reside requirement for council tax reduction (other than pension-age council tax reduction in Scotland – see below), you must have a right to reside in the common travel area, *other than* as:[15]

- an EEA national with an initial right of residence during your first three months in the UK (see p203); *or*
- a family member of the above; *or*
- an EEA jobseeker (see p203); *or*
- a family member of an EEA jobseeker; *or*
- a person granted pre-settled status (see p55); *or*
- the primary carer of a British citizen who is dependent on you and would have to leave the European Union (EU) if you were required to leave (see p261); *or*
- (except Wales) a family member granted pre-settled status of a relevant person of Northern Ireland (see p171), if the relevant person's only rights to reside are under the first two or last bullet points above; *or*
- (except Wales) a person with limited leave to enter as a holder of an EU Settlement Scheme family permit or travel permit (see p68).

For pension-age council tax reduction in Scotland only, you can satisfy the right to reside requirement if you have any right to reside other than the first two listed above.[16]

The exclusions above prevent entitlement to council tax reduction if they are your *only* right to reside. If you also have another right to reside that is not excluded, including if you are in a protected group who can still use free movement residence rights (see p188), you are not excluded from council tax reduction provided you meet all the other entitlement conditions.

For information on who has a right to reside, see Chapter 12.

National insurance number requirement

If you apply for council tax reduction in England and Wales, you and anyone included in your application must satisfy an NI number requirement that is similar to that for benefits (see p482).[17] However, that does not apply to a child or young person, or if:[18]

- you are defined as a 'person subject to immigration control' because you require leave but do not have it (see p98); *and*
- you have not previously had an NI number; *and*
- you do not satisfy the habitual residence test. **Note:** this is always likely to apply if you satisfy the first point, as you do not have a right to reside (see p625).

Absences from home

Although you must be living in your property to qualify for council tax reduction, certain temporary absences are allowed. An overview of the rules is provided below, but you should also check the details of your local or national scheme.

In England if you are a 'pensioner' (ie, you have reached pension age and you are not receiving universal credit, income support, income-related employment and support allowance or income-based JSA), you continue to receive council tax reduction during an absence for up to:[19]

- **four weeks** if you are absent *from Great Britain*, provided the absence is unlikely to exceed four weeks. This can be extended by up to four weeks if the absence is in connection with the death of your partner, a child for whom you (or your partner) are responsible, or a close relative of you or your partner or child, and it is unreasonable for you to return within the first four weeks;
- **13 weeks** if you are absent *in Great Britain* and the absence is not intended to be longer or is due to your being in residential accommodation;
- **26 weeks** if you are absent *from Great Britain* and you are a member of the armed forces posted overseas, a mariner or a continental shelf worker, or you are resident in a hospital as a patient, or you (or your partner or dependent child) are undergoing medical treatment or medically approved convalescence, or have left the property through fear of violence, and the absence is unlikely to exceed 26 weeks;
- **52 weeks** if you are absent *in Great Britain* in limited circumstances. Those include if you, your partner or dependent child are a hospital inpatient, you are undergoing or recovering from medical treatment, or you are absent from home because of domestic violence.

If you are not a 'pensioner', there are no prescribed rules on absences, so check the details of your local scheme.

In Wales, you can continue to receive council tax reduction during an absence for up to:[20]

- **13 weeks** if your absence is not intended to be longer or is due to your being in residential accommodation;
- **52 weeks** in limited circumstances. Those include if you, your partner or dependent child are a hospital inpatient, you are undergoing or recovering from medical treatment, or you are absent from home because of domestic violence.

In Scotland, you can continue to receive council tax reduction during an absence for up to:[21]

- **one month** if you are absent *from Great Britain*, and for pension-age council tax reduction only provided you have not been absent on more than two occasions in the previous 52 weeks. This may be extended by a further month if the absence abroad is in connection with the death of your partner or a child for whom you (or your partner) are responsible;
- **13 weeks** if you are absent *in Great Britain*, provided your absence is not intended to be longer or is due to your being in residential accommodation;
- **six months** if you are absent *from Great Britain* and the absence is abroad solely in connection with your treatment, or recovery from treatment, for an illness or disability, or you are accompanying someone else for such treatment;
- **52 weeks** in limited circumstances. Those include if you, your partner or dependent child are a hospital inpatient, you are undergoing or recovering from medical treatment, or you are absent from home because of domestic violence;
- **indefinitely** if you are abroad in your capacity as (or accompanying your partner in their capacity as) an aircraft worker, mariner, continental shelf worker, Crown servant or member of the armed forces and you satisfy, or are exempt from, the habitual residence test (see p625).

2. Local welfare assistance schemes

Help may be available under local welfare assistance schemes set up by your local authority (in England) or by the Scottish and Welsh governments. The DWP may refer to this as 'local welfare provision'.

Depending on your circumstances and where you live, you may qualify if you need help – for example:

- with immediate short-term needs in a crisis – eg, if you do not have sufficient resources, or you need help with expenses in an emergency or as a result of a disaster, such as a fire or flood in your home;

- to establish yourself in the community following a stay in institutional or residential accommodation, or to help you remain in the community;
- to set up a home in the community as part of a planned resettlement programme;
- to ease exceptional pressure on your family;
- to enable you to care for a prisoner or young offender on temporary release;
- with certain travel expenses – eg, to visit someone in hospital, to attend a funeral, to ease a domestic crisis, to visit a child living with their other parent or to move to suitable accommodation.

In **Wales**, the Discretionary Assistance Fund offers non-repayable emergency assistance payments and individual assistance payments.

In **Scotland**, the Scottish Welfare Fund is administered in accordance with the Scottish government's national guidance, but local authorities have some discretion. You can apply to your local authority for community care grants and crisis grants, and can be entitled if you are (or are about to be) resident in the local authority's area, homeless or stranded in the area, or if there are other exceptional circumstances.[22] The guidance excludes you from the scheme if you are an asylum seeker, despite there being no such exclusion in legislation.[23] You can claim a family reunion crisis grant if you have been granted refugee leave or humanitarian protection and your family members have been granted permission to join you under the family reunion provisions (see p130). You can apply before they arrive for assistance with living costs and essential items to help your family settle into the community.[24]

In **England**, the local scheme is entirely at your local authority's discretion. Check with your local authority to find out what help is available, whether you qualify and how to apply. It is arguable that a local authority cannot require you to have resided in that local authority area for a set period of time before you can be entitled to assistance under the local scheme. This argument is based on a High Court case in which it was held to be unlawful for a local authority to require you to have resided in its area for a set period of time before you can be entitled to council tax reduction (see p626).

Public funds

Local welfare assistance scheme payments, other than from the Discretionary Assistance Fund in Wales, have been defined as 'public funds' under the Immigration Rules since 6 April 2016 (see p103).[25] If you have leave to enter or remain in the UK that is subject to a condition that you do not have recourse to public funds (see p32), you will breach this condition if you receive a payment from one of these schemes on or after this date. Get immigration advice before you make a claim. The guidance on the Scottish Welfare Fund specifically excludes 'expenses to meet the needs of people who have no recourse to public funds'.[26]

3. Early years food and vitamins

If you are pregnant or have a young child, in England and Wales, you can qualify for Healthy Start food and vitamins. In Scotland, you can qualify for Best Start foods and can also register with your midwife while pregnant to receive a free 'baby box' of essential items.

Healthy Start and Best Start food

If you qualify for Healthy Start food (see below), you:[27]

- get a payment card credited with £4.25 a week that can be used to pay for 'Healthy Start food' at any shop that accepts Mastercard; *or*
- are paid an amount of the same value, if you cannot use the card within a reasonable distance of your home.

If you qualify for Best Start foods (see below), you are issued with a payment card credited with £4.95 (£9.90 while a child is younger than one year old or within a year of the child's expected date of birth, whichever is later) a week to be spent on 'Best Start foods'.[28]

Healthy Start and Best Start food [29]

'Healthy Start food' and **'Best Start foods'** are liquid cow's milk and cow's (or goat's in Scotland) milk-based infant formula, fresh, frozen or canned fruit, vegetables and pulses including loose, pre-packed, whole, sliced, chopped or mixed (but not to which fat, salt, sugar, flavouring or any other ingredients have been added) and (in Scotland only) fresh eggs.

Who can qualify

In England and Wales, you qualify for a Healthy Start voucher in *each* of the following situations that apply to you (but also see the note on p631):

- you are at least 10 weeks' pregnant, and you are:
  - aged 18 or over and are entitled to, or you are a member of the family of someone who is entitled to, a 'qualifying benefit' (see p632); *or*
  - under 18, unless you are defined as a 'person subject to immigration control' (see p93); *or*
- you are a mother who has 'parental responsibility' (see below) for a child and:
  - you are aged 16 or over and entitled to, or you are a member of the family of someone who is entitled to, a qualifying benefit other than income-related employment and support allowance (ESA). If you are entitled to universal credit (UC), your child must be younger than one year old. For other qualifying benefits, your child must be younger than one or there must be less than a year since their expected date of birth. Therefore, you can

continue to qualify for credits on your payment card for a period after your child is one – ie, if born prematurely; *or*
  - it is less than four months since your baby's expected date of birth and you have not yet notified Healthy Start of the birth. You must have been getting a qualifying benefit before your baby was born. That allows your entitlement to continue until you notify Healthy Start of the birth. Once you do, you can then qualify under the rule above (if you are 16 or over). **Note:** as long as you provided the notification within the four-month period, you can also get extra credit on your card for your child from their date of birth.

  If you qualify for more than one child under this rule (eg, you have twins), you get a credit on your card for each. If you do not have parental responsibility but would otherwise qualify, your child qualifies instead of you.
- You get a voucher for a child younger than four years old who is a member of your family (see below) if you or a member of your family are entitled to a 'qualifying benefit' (see below) other than income-related ESA.

In Scotland, you qualify for a Best Start foods payment card in *each* of the following situations (but also see note below).
- If you are 'ordinarily resident' in Scotland (see p147), as soon as you are pregnant, and you are:
  - aged 18 or over and are entitled to (or the partner or dependant of someone who is entitled to) a 'qualifying benefit' (see below); *or*
  - younger than 18, including if you turned 18 while pregnant, and you are habitually resident (see p151). However, if you are, or your partner or someone you are the dependant of is, entitled to a 'qualifying benefit' (see p632), the habitual residence requirement does not apply.
- You are ordinarily resident in Scotland (see p147) and 'responsible' (see below) for a child who is:
  - younger than three years old and you are, or you are the partner or dependant of someone who is, entitled to a 'qualifying benefit' (see below); *or*
  - younger than the age of one or has not yet reached the first anniversary of their expected date of birth – eg, if born prematurely. *You* must also be younger than 18 or have turned 18 before the child's first birthday and be 'habitually resident' (see p155).

In practical terms, each week you could get one credit for each of your children aged between one and four (three in Scotland), two credits (or the higher credit in Scotland) for each child younger than one (or within one year of their expected date of birth), plus one credit if you are pregnant.

Note: following a legal challenge in England, the UK and Scottish governments have extended Healthy Start and Best Start foods entitlement to the parents of British children who would qualify if not excluded from claiming the qualifying benefits by their immigration status.[30] At the time of writing, the legislation has not yet been changed and payments are being made on an ex gratia basis. The parents must have a net monthly income of £408 or less in England and Wales, or £726 or less in Scotland.

Definitions

The following are **'qualifying benefits'**:[31]

- UC if, during the last complete assessment period (or the one before), you (and your partner if you have a joint claim) had earned income of £408 (£726 in Scotland) or less. If your earned income subsequently increases to more than £408/£726, you continue to qualify for a further eight weeks after the last complete assessment period;
- income support, income-based jobseeker's allowance and (in some cases) income-related ESA. In Scotland, also housing benefit, provided your income is not more than £358 a week, and pension credit (PC);
- child tax credit (CTC), provided your gross income for CTC purposes is not more than £16,190 (£18,725 in Scotland). In England and Wales, you must not be entitled to working tax credit (WTC) as well, other than during the four-week WTC 'run-on' period. In Scotland, you can be entitled to both CTC and WTC provided your income for tax credit purposes is less than £8,717.

The Scottish government has stated that it will remove the income limits for qualifying benefits in 2023/24.[32]

'Parental responsibility' is as defined in section 3(1) of the Children Act 1989 (in England or Wales).[33]

Being **'responsible'** for a child means:[34]

- the child is 'dependent' (see below) on you; *or*
- you are the child's parent, the child normally lives with you, and you are younger than 20 and are the 'dependant' (see below) of another person; *or*
- you are legally recognised as the child's adoptive parent or the child has been placed with you by an adoption agency; *or*
- you are the child's legal guardian; *or*
- you are the child's kinship carer.

'Family' means a person and their partner and any children or qualifying young people who are members of their household and for whom they or their partner counts as responsible.[35] So, for example, if you are not entitled to a qualifying benefit, but are included in your parent's claim for one of these, you can qualify for Healthy Start food vouchers.

Being the **'dependant'** of someone means they are:[36]

- your kinship carer; *or*
- awarded child benefit, CTC or PC for that week, or UC for the assessment period including that week or for the previous assessment period, and you are treated as a child or qualifying young person for that benefit, even if no benefit is actually paid for you.

Claims

You can apply for Healthy Start food online, by email or by telephone depending on your circumstances. Your application must provide specified information and evidence.[37] You can:

- complete the online form at healthystart.nhs.uk/how-to-apply if you are getting UC or CTC; *or*
- apply by telephoning 0300 330 7010 or emailing healthy.start@nhsbsa.nhs.uk.

You apply for Best Start foods in the same way that you apply for a Best Start grant (see mygov.scot/best-start-grant-best-start-foods). You do not need to make a separate application; one application is used to work out your entitlement to both. Remember to apply when you are first pregnant as you can qualify for Best Start foods immediately, even if you do not qualify for a Best Start grant until later.

If you are getting Healthy Start food or Best Start foods while you are pregnant and then inform Healthy Start or Social Security Scotland (SSS) of the birth while your baby is younger than four months old, you can get additional credits from their date of birth.[38] You may need to claim UC, PC, CTC or child benefit (or add your baby to your existing UC, PC or CTC claim) to ensure that you continue to get the credits.

If you do not get credits to which you think you are entitled, or have any other problems with these, contact the Healthy Start helpline on 0300 330 7010 or SSS on 0800 182 2222.

Vitamins

If you qualify for Healthy Start food, you also qualify for Healthy Start vitamins.[39]

In Scotland, with the introduction of Best Start foods, all pregnant women should still be entitled to free vitamins (see mygov.scot/free-vitamins-pregnant).

Mothers and pregnant women are entitled to 56 vitamin tablets, and children younger than four to 10 millilitres of vitamin drops, every eight weeks.

You need to show your Healthy Start payment card to collect the vitamins.[40]

The ways that vitamins are made available vary throughout the UK. For details, see healthystart.nhs.uk. Ask your health professional what the local arrangements are for getting your free vitamins.

4. Free milk for children

Children younger than five (in Scotland, pre-school aged) are entitled to 189–200 millilitres of free milk (or in Scotland, a milk alternative and, from six months old, a portion of fruit or vegetables) on each day they are looked after for two hours or more:[41]

- by a registered childminder or daycare provider (in Scotland, one who is registered with the Care Inspectorate[42]); *or*
- (except in Scotland) in a school, playcentre or workplace nursery which is exempt from registration; *or*
- (except in Scotland) in local authority daycare.

The milk can be any pasteurised cows' milk, including whole and semi-skimmed, and can be organic. Children younger than one are allowed fresh or dried milk.

In Wales, children in key stage one are entitled to free milk if the school has chosen to participate in the scheme.

In Scotland, free milk may be provided to school-age children by the local authority (see mygov.scot/school-meals).

5. **Education benefits**

Financial and other help is available from your local authority if you are in school or are a student, or if you have a child in school or college.

Free school lunches

School children are entitled to free school lunches if their families receive:[43]

- universal credit (UC). In Scotland, a parent on UC (whether single or in a couple) must not have earned income of more than £660 in the assessment period immediately before the date of claim. In England and Wales, your earnings (and those of your partner if you make a joint claim) must not exceed:
  - £616.67 in the UC assessment period immediately before the date you claim free school lunches; *or*
  - £1,233.34 in the two UC assessment periods immediately before the date you claim free school lunches; *or*
  - £1,850 in the three UC assessment periods immediately before the date you claim free school lunches; *or*
- income support (IS), income-based jobseeker's allowance or income-related employment and support allowance (ESA);[44] *or*
- child tax credit (CTC) and have annual taxable income of £16,190 in England and Wales, £18,725 in Scotland, or less. That does not apply if the family is entitled to working tax credit (WTC) unless:
  - this is during the four-week 'WTC run-on' period. See CPAG's *Welfare Benefits and Tax Credits Handbook* for when this applies; *or*
  - in Scotland only, the WTC award is based on annual taxable income of £7,920 or less; *or*
- in England and Wales, the guarantee credit of pension credit (PC). In Scotland, entitlement has not yet been extended to families who get PC including a child

addition but local authorities have the discretion to provide free school lunches in these circumstances.[45]

Also entitled are:

- 16–18 year olds receiving the above benefits or tax credits in their own right;[46]
- asylum seekers in receipt of asylum support (see p522);[47]
- in England, from 19 April 2022, children of some families excluded from receiving the qualifying benefits above due to having 'no recourse to public funds' (see p101) or being a 'person subject to immigration control' (see p93) or otherwise excluded due to their residence status (eg, Zambrano carers – see p169 and p176). In a family able to work, this only applies if the annual income of a family with one child is less than £22,700 (in London, £31,200) or with two or more children is £26,300 (in London, £34,800). This makes permanent a temporary policy that was introduced during the coronavirus pandemic;[48]
- in Scotland, children attending early learning and childcare who are entitled under any of the bullet points above or, at the local authority's discretion, if their family receives PC, incapacity benefit or severe disablement allowance, or if since the age of two they have been looked after by a local authority or are the subject of a kinship care or guardianship order.[49] Free meals are also provided to all children who are in 'funded early learning and childcare' settings in Scotland (see mygov.scot/school-meals).

Note:

- In England, free school lunches are provided to all children during the first three years, and in Scotland during the first five years, of primary school.
- In Wales, free school breakfasts are provided to all children in primary schools maintained by the local authority.[50] Universal free school lunches are being rolled out in Wales. By 2024, all primary school children in Wales will get free school lunches.[51]
- The Scottish government has pledged to expand free school meals to all Primary 6–7 pupils in receipt of Scottish child payment during 2023/24.[52]
- Pupils eligible for free school lunches in England on 31 March 2018 or in Wales on 31 March 2019, and those who became eligible after this date, remained so until 31 March 2022 in England or 31 December 2023 in Wales, whether or not they (or their parents) continue to be entitled to a qualifying benefit. Those entitled to free school lunches on 31 March 2022 in England or on 31 December 2023 in Wales, or who become entitled to free school lunches via UC after those dates, continue to be entitled until they finish the stage of education that they were in on 31 March 2022 (England) or 31 December 2023 (Wales) – eg, primary or secondary school, whether or not they continue to get UC.[53] In England, guidance states that any child gaining eligibility for free school meals after 1 March 2018 will be protected against losing free school meals until March 2025.[54]

School transport and school clothes

Local authorities must provide **free transport to school** for pupils aged five to 16 if it is considered necessary to enable that pupil to get to the 'nearest suitable school'. This applies if they live more than a set distance from that school. However, if there is no safe walking route, pupils must be given free transport irrespective of how far away they live from the nearest suitable school. Free school transport must also be be provided to pupils with special educational needs and to those whose parents are on a low income – ie, if they receive a benefit that would qualify them for free school lunches or the maximum rate of WTC.

Local authorities can give **grants for school uniforms and other school clothes.** Each authority determines its own eligibility rules. In Scotland, the minimum school clothing grant for 2022/23 is £120 for primary school children and £150 for secondary school children.

Some school governing bodies or parents' associations also provide help with school clothing.

Education maintenance allowance and 16 to 19 bursaries

Education maintenance allowance is a means-tested payment for young people who are aged 16 to 19, are resident in Wales or Scotland, and who stay on in further education. Payments are made directly to the young person and are conditional on regular course attendance. The young person receives a weekly allowance of £30 during term time. Entitlement depends on your being 'ordinarily resident' in Wales or Scotland. That is not solely determined by where you live but can also be affected by your nationality and immigration status. Entitlement also depends on the household income. For further details of each scheme, see studentfinancewales.co.uk/further-education-funding/education-maintenance-allowance or mygov.scot/ema.

16 to 19 bursaries are payments for young people aged 16 to 19 who stay on in further education or training in England, available through the school, college or training provider. Certain vulnerable young people (eg, young people in care, care leavers, young people who get UC or IS, or who get ESA and either disability living allowance or personal independence payment) can get the maximum bursary. Discretionary bursaries are available to those in financial difficulty. You should apply as close to the start of the academic year as possible, or as soon as you become in financial need if this is later. See gov.uk/1619-bursary-fund for further information.

Neither payment counts as income for any benefits or tax credits the parent may be getting. They are also not affected by any income the young person has from part-time work.

Note: if you are a student, to find out what help is available to finance your studies, contact your local authority or college or university, or see gov.uk/

student-finance. Also see CPAG's *Student Support and Benefits Handbook* and *Benefits for Students in Scotland Handbook.*

Free period products

Free period products are available in schools and colleges. In England, if you are in school or aged under 19 in non-advanced education, you should be able to access free period products when you need them. If you are aged 19 or older, you can access free period products if you are continuing on a course you began before age 19 or have an education, health and care plan.[55] In Wales, every school and college provides free period products.[56] In Scotland, education authorities are required to make period products available to all school pupils.[57]

6. Community care support from the local authority

If you have care needs, you may be able to get support, including accommodation, from your local authority or NHS primary care trust under community care legislation.

This is a complex area of law and beyond the scope of this *Handbook*, but see p553 for a brief description of the support available for asylum seekers and refused asylum seekers under the Care Act 2014 as some of the same provisions apply to other migrants.

There are restrictions and exclusions that affect all groups of migrants, but there are also exceptions to these rules that mean you may still be able to get support.

Note: community care support is not listed as a 'public fund' in the Immigration Rules. Therefore, if you have leave to enter or remain in the UK that is subject to a 'no recourse to public funds' condition, receiving community care support does not breach this condition. For more information on public funds, see p32.

Community care support is often misunderstood and poorly administered by local authorities and other providers. Get specialist advice before applying to your local authority for support or if you have been refused support.

Adults with care and support needs

Local authorities can provide support, including accommodation, to adults who have a need for care and support. However, if you are defined as a 'person subject to immigration control' (see p93), you are excluded if your need for care and support is solely as a result of being destitute or the physical effects, or anticipated physical effects, of being destitute.[58] Even if you are destitute, there must be another reason for your needing the care and support – eg, because of your age, disability, or physical or mental health problem. This test has become known as the 'destitution plus' test.

There are other exclusions that may also mean you cannot access support. For a summary of the exclusions that affect migrants, see p554.

For a summary of local authority support available to adults, see p553.

Other types of support

There are a number of other types of community care support that may be available from local authority social services departments or from NHS primary care trusts. The type of support available depends on your individual circumstances. The support may be services but could include accommodation – eg, if you have been detained, admitted or transferred to hospital under various sections of the Mental Health Act 1983, you are now no longer detained and you leave hospital, the clinical commissioning group, primary care trust or local health board and the local social services department have joint duties to provide you with aftercare services, which can include accommodation. A summary of the different community care provisions is in the *Disability Rights Handbook,* published annually by Disability Rights UK. The legislation under which these types of support can be provided is complex and frequently misunderstood. Get expert advice from a specialist community care adviser.

7. Support under the Children Acts

Local authorities have a duty to safeguard and promote the welfare of children who are 'in need' in their area.[59] If you are destitute and have children, you may be eligible for accommodation or support from your local authority under the Children Act 1989 or in Scotland, the Children (Scotland) Act 1995. Children who are destitute are generally considered to be 'in need', but a child can also be in need if they are disabled, or if they are unlikely to achieve or maintain a reasonable standard of health or development without the provision of services by a local authority.[60] Although the duty is to support the child, it extends to supporting parents or other family members if that is in the child's best interests.[61]

Some people are excluded from Children Act support, including some groups of adult migrants, but there are also exceptions. Children are always eligible for support under the Children Act regardless of immigration status.[62]

The provision of support can be complex, and is often misunderstood and poorly administered by local authorities. Get specialist advice before applying to your local authority for support, if you have been refused support or if the local authority tells you it can only accommodate your child but not you as well.

This *Handbook* does not cover support available under the Children Act. However, for limited further information about the rules affecting this support for asylum seekers and refused asylum seekers, see p555. For specialist advice on support available for destitute migrant families in England and Wales, contact Project 17 (see Appendix 2).

8. NHS healthcare

The UK's NHS is a residence-based healthcare system. Not all healthcare is provided free of charge to everyone, and the charges can be considerable. Since 23 October 2017, providers of chargeable NHS services must charge patients who are chargeable, *in advance* of providing the service, unless doing so would prevent or delay services that are urgent or immediately necessary. All maternity care is classed as immediately necessary.

The legislation setting out the rules for NHS charges is different in England, Wales and Scotland. The legislation and guidance on how it should be implemented is not always applied correctly by the relevant NHS bodies. Get advice if you have been told that you will be charged, if you want to challenge charges or you have been refused treatment due to charges. The following information gives a broad overview.

There is a charge for hospital healthcare service, unless:

- the specific service is exempt (see p640); *or*
- you are not chargeable (see p640).

NHS services are not listed in the definition of 'public funds' in the Immigration Rules (see p32). If you have leave to enter or remain in the UK on condition that you do not have recourse to public funds, you have not breached this condition if you receive NHS services. However, if the Home Office is notified that you have one or more NHS charges amounting to at least £500, that can be a reason for the Home Office to refuse an application for some types of immigration leave to remain.[63] NHS Trusts[64] and other providers of NHS hospital services have a duty to notify the Home Office of debts of more than £500 that have been outstanding for two months. However, the NHS providers should only notify the Home Office about the debt if certain criteria are met, including that there is no genuine outstanding challenge to the debt and no meaningful repayment plan is being adhered to.[65] If all the criteria cease to be met, the NHS Trust should update the Home Office immediately.

Services exempt from charges

Health services that are currently exempt from charges, regardless of immigration or residence status, are broadly:[66]

- accident and emergency services, but not any provided after you have been admitted as an inpatient or at a follow-up outpatient appointment;
- services not provided in a hospital and not provided by staff employed to work in, or under the direction of, a hospital;
- services for diagnosing and treating specified conditions, including food poisoning, HIV, measles, malaria, tuberculosis, viral hepatitis, whooping cough and coronavirus;[67]
- services for diagnosing and treating sexually transmitted infections;
- services for treating conditions caused by torture, female genital mutilation, domestic violence or sexual violence, provided you have not travelled to the UK for the purpose of seeking that treatment;
- in England only, family planning services (this does not include maternity services or services providing terminations of pregnancies).

Note: there are no residence-related charges for NHS primary healthcare, including NHS services delivered through GP practices, NHS walk-in centres, dentists, pharmacists and optometrists. However, some of these services have other charges (eg, for dental care or prescriptions), and these have different exemption criteria. For details of who is exempt from these charges, see CPAG's *Welfare Benefits and Tax Credits Handbook.*

Who is not chargeable

You are charged for NHS hospital services unless, at the time you receive the NHS care, you are 'ordinarily resident' in the UK or you are exempt from charges. The exempt groups and the interpretation of 'ordinarily resident' vary between England, Wales and Scotland. The rules are complex and can be affected by many factors.

Who can be ordinarily resident in the UK

If you are 'ordinarily resident' (see p147) in the UK, you are entitled to free NHS care.[68]

Whether you are 'ordinarily resident' in the UK for NHS charging depends on the purpose of your residence in the UK. You must be voluntarily and lawfully resident in the UK for 'settled purposes'.

If you are not a British or Irish citizen or do not have the right of abode (see p76), you cannot be ordinarily resident unless you have been granted indefinite leave to remain (see p30) or have either applied for, or been granted, pre-settled status or settled status under the European Union Settlement Scheme (see p57). It is possible to be ordinarily resident from the date of arrival in the UK, if you are in the UK for settled purposes. It is also possible to be ordinarily resident in more than one country at once.

In general, you will not be ordinarily resident if you are just visiting the UK. If you are not ordinarily resident you are termed an 'overseas visitor' in the charging regulations and you can be charged for NHS services unless either you are receiving a service exempt from charging (see p640) or you are in a group exempt from charging (see below).

Which groups are exempt from NHS charges

The groups that are exempt from NHS charges are numerous and the rules vary between England, Scotland and Wales, but the groups include those listed below. You will be exempt from NHS charges if at the time you receive your NHS care you:

- are covered by a reciprocal healthcare agreement;
- (except, in England, for assisted conception services) are within a period of leave to enter or remain in the UK, in respect of which you have paid the 'immigration health surcharge' (or it was waived) (see p20);
- are an asylum seeker;
- have been granted refugee leave or humanitarian protection;
- are a refused asylum seeker – in England only you must also be in receipt of section 4 asylum support (see p536) or Care Act support (see p637);
- are receiving local authority support as a looked after child;
- are in immigration detention;
- are a victim of trafficking with a positive conclusive grounds decision.

In England, people granted a positive trafficking decision are entitled to have the exemption backdated to cover the period before they were identified as a victim of trafficking. In England, people granted refugee status are entitled to have their exemption backdated to the date that they were in the UK for the purpose of claiming asylum but had not yet done so. Those who paid charges during those periods must have them refunded.

Further information

JCWI (Joint Council for the Welfare of Immigrants) has produced a short guide on NHS charging and also a detailed toolkit for advisers.[69]

Maternity Action has produced factsheets on the NHS charging rules and provides an email and telephone advice service on NHS maternity care and charging.[70]

Useful information on accessing healthcare in the UK, including if you are having difficulties in registering with a GP, is available online from Doctors of the World.[71]

9. Other financial help

Other financial help is available, especially if you are on a low income, have children, are an older person, or have an illness, disability or other special needs.

See the *Disability Rights Handbook*, published by Disability Rights UK, for other help if you have needs resulting from disability, health problems or caring responsibilities.

Food banks

If you are experiencing severe financial hardship (eg, caused by debt, or by having your benefits delayed or refused), you may be able to get vouchers for food that can be redeemed at a food bank. Vouchers are available from frontline care professionals, such as doctors, health visitors, social workers and advice workers. Jobcentre Plus staff may also provide vouchers. For more information and contact details for many food banks, see trusselltrust.org or foodaidnetwork.org.uk/our-members or contact your local authority.

You may be able to get help with food or meals through local community groups that are part of the FareShare network. Further information is available at fareshare.org.uk.

Repairs, home improvements and energy efficiency

Your local authority may be able to provide you with a grant to help with the cost of improving your home. The main types of grant available are:

- home improvement grants; *and*
- disabled facilities grants.

You may also be able to get:

- assistance from a home improvement agency (a local not-for-profit organisation) to repair, improve, maintain or adapt your home – sometimes called 'care and repair' or 'staying put' schemes – or with small repairs, safety checks and odd jobs from a handyperson service. For information see, in England, foundations.uk.com, in Wales, careandrepair.org.uk and in Scotland, careandrepairscotland.co.uk;
- a grant for help with insulation and other energy efficiency measures in your home. Help with fuel bills may also be available. Different schemes operate in England, Wales and Scotland. For further information, in England you can telephone 0800 444 202 (simpleenergyadvice.org.uk); in Wales, telephone 0808 808 2244 (nest.gov.wales); and in Scotland, telephone 0808 808 2282 (homeenergyscotland.org) or visit energysavingtrust.org.uk. For more details, see CPAG's *Fuel Rights Handbook*.

Special funds for sick or disabled people

A range of help is available for people with an illness or disability to assist with things like paying for care services in their own home, equipment, holidays, furniture and transport needs, and for people with haemophilia or HIV contracted via haemophilia treatment. Grants are also available for practical support to help people do their jobs – eg, to pay for specialist equipment and travel. For more information, see the *Disability Rights Handbook*, published by Disability Rights UK.

Payments for former members of the armed forces

If you are a former member of the UK armed forces, or your spouse or civil partner died while in service, you may be able to claim under the one of the various schemes administered by the Ministry of Defence. The benefits and lump-sum payments include pensions, disablement benefits and compensation payments. Your entitlement depends on your circumstances, including the dates of service and, if relevant, the degree and effect of any disablement or ill health and the final salary. Further details are available from Veterans UK (gov.uk/government/organisations/veterans-uk).

Charities

There are many charities that provide various types of help to people in need. Your local authority social services department or local advice centre may know of appropriate charities that could assist you, or in your local library you can consult publications, such as *The Guide to Grants for Individuals in Need* and *Charity Choice* (see charitychoice.co.uk/bookstore). The organisation Turn2us has a website (turn2us.org.uk) with an A–Z of charities that can provide financial help. In many cases, applications for support can be made directly from the website. Information on grants available for individuals can also be found at fundsonline.org.uk.

Notes

1. **Council tax reduction**

1 **E** CTRS(PR)E Regs
W CTRS(DS)W Regs; CTRSPR(W) Regs
S CTR(S) Regs; CTR(SPC)S Regs

2 **E** Reg 13 CTRS(PR)E Regs
W Reg 29 CTRSPR(W) Regs; Sch para 20 CTRS(DS)W Regs
S Reg 19 CTR(SPC)S Regs; reg 19 CTR(S) Regs

3 **E** Reg 13(1A) CTRS(PR)E Regs, omitted by reg 3 The Social Security and Council Tax Reduction Schemes (Amendment) Regulations 2022 No.449, from 1 April 2023
W Reg 29(2) CTRSPR(W) Regs; Sch para 20(2) CTRS(DS)W Regs, omitted for awards made from 1 April 2023 by regs 5 and 13 The Council Tax Reduction Schemes (Prescribed Requirements and Default Scheme) (Wales) (Amendment) Regulations 2023 No. 47
S Reg 19(2) CTR(SPC)S Regs; reg 19(2) CTR(S) Regs

4 *Szoma v SSWP* [2005] UKHL 64, reported as R(IS) 2/06; *Yesiloz v LB Camden* [2009] EWCA Civ 415

5 para 6.2(b) IR

6 para 6.2(b) notes under 'public funds' definition, IR. Council tax reduction is not included in the regulations that are referred to in the notes that disregard claims made as a result of exemptions.

7 para 6.2(b) IR

8 Confirmed in Valuation Tribunal for England appeal No.M0219600, 1 March 2018

9 Sch 1 para 16 CTRS(PR) E Regs

10 Sch 6 para 17(10) CTRSPR(W) Regs; Sch para 51(10) CTRS(DS)W Regs

11 Reg 57 CTR(S) Regs; Reg 27 CTR(SPC)S Regs

12 **E** Reg 12 CTRS(PR)E Regs
W Reg 28 CTRSPR(W) Regs; Sch para 19 CTRS(DS)W Regs
S Reg 16 CTR(SPC)S Regs; reg 16 CTR(S) Regs

13 **E** Reg 12 CTRS(PR)E Regs, as amended
W Reg 28 CTRSPR(W) Regs, as amended; Sch para 19 CTRS(DS)W Regs, as amended
S Reg 16 CTR(SPC)S Regs, as amended; reg 16 CTR(S) Regs, as amended

14 *R (Winder and Others) v Sandwell MBC* [2014] EWHC 2617 (Admin)

15 **E** Reg 12 CTRS(PR)E Regs
W Reg 28 CTRSPR(W) Regs; Sch para 19 CTRS(DS)W Regs
S Reg 16 CTR(S) Regs

16 Reg 16 CTR(SPC)S Regs

17 **E** Sch 8 para 7 CTRS(PR)E Regs
W Sch 13 para 5 CTRSPR(W) Regs; Sch para 111 CTRS(DS)W Regs

18 **E** Sch 8 para 7(3) CTRS(PR)E Regs
W Sch 13 para 5(3) CTRSPR(W) Regs; Sch para 111(3) CTRS(DS)W Regs

19 Sch 1 para 5 CTRS(PR)E Regs

20 Reg 26 CTRSPR(W) Regs; Sch para 17 CTRS(DS)W Regs

21 Regs 15, 17 and 18 CTR(SPC)S Regs; regs 15, 17 and 18 CTR(S) Regs

2. **Local welfare assistance schemes**

22 Welfare Funds (Scotland) Act 2015; reg 4 The Welfare Funds (Scotland) Regulations 2016 No.107; Scottish government, *Scottish Welfare Fund: statutory guidance*, March 2021, paras 4.3-4.11

23 Scottish government, *Scottish Welfare Fund: statutory guidance*, March 2021, para 6.11

24 Scottish government, *Scottish Welfare Fund: statutory guidance*, March 2021, section 10

25 para 6.2(b) IR

26 Scottish government, *Scottish Welfare Fund: statutory guidance*, March 2021, Annex A para 19; see also paras 6.8-10

3. **Early years food and vitamins**

27 Regs 5(2) and 8 HSS&WF(A) Regs. Note that reg 8 allows the value of each credit to be varied as long as it is not less than £3.10.

28 Regs 13 and 14 WF(BSF) Regs

29 Regs 2(1) and 5(1) and Sch 3 HSS&WF(A) Regs; HSS(DHSF)(W) Regs; reg 2 and Sch 1 WF(BSF) Regs
30 See matthewgold.co.uk/healthy-start-scheme; healthystart.nhs.uk/how-to-apply; mygov.scot/best-start-grant-best-start-foods/public-funds-access
31 **EW** Reg 3 HSS&WF(A) Regs
S Regs 6(3) and 10 WF(BSF) Regs
32 Scottish Budget 2023/24, Annex D: Detailed analysis of Equalities and Fairer Scotland Issues by Portfolio, p175
33 Reg 2(1) HSS&WF(A) Regs
34 Reg 4 WF(BSF) Regs
35 Reg 2(1) HSS&WF(A) Regs
36 Reg 5 WF(BSF) Regs
37 Reg 4 and Sch 2 HSS&WF(A) Regs
38 **EW** Reg 4(2) and (3A) HSS&WF(A) Regs
S Reg 11(2) WF(BSF) Regs
39 Reg 3 HSS&WF(A) Regs
40 Reg 8A HSS&WF(A) Regs

4. **Free milk for children**
41 Reg 18 WF Regs; The Milk and Healthy Snack Scheme (Scotland) Regulations 2021 No.82, as amended
42 In Scotland, childminders and daycare providers must register at gov.uk/registering-as-childminder-scotland

5. **Education benefits**
43 **E** s512ZB Education Act 1996; The Education (Free School Lunches) (Prescribed Tax Credits) (England) Order 2003 No.383; The Free School Lunches and Milk, and School and Early Years Finance (Amendments Relating to Universal Credit) (England) Regulations 2018 No.148
W s512ZB Education Act 1996; The Education (Free School Lunches) (Prescribed Tax Credits) (Wales) Order 2003 No.879 (W.110); The Free School Lunches and Milk (Universal Credit) (Wales) Order 2019 No.187 (W.47)
S s53(3) Education (Scotland) Act 1980; The Education (School Lunches) (Scotland) Regulations 2009 No.178
44 In England only, rules providing for this seem to have been removed from 31 March 2022: see the Welfare Reform Act 2012 (Commencement No.30 and Transitory Provisions) Order 2018 No.145. However, in practice free school lunches in this context have continued: see gov.uk/apply-free-school-meals
45 s53(3)-(5) Education (Scotland) Act 1980
46 For CTC, the legislation only provides for this in Scotland
47 Provided under Part VI of IAA 1999
48 gov.uk/government/publications/free-school-meals-guidance-for-schools-and-local-authorities/providing-free-school-meals-to-families-with-no-recourse-to-public-funds-nrpf
49 The Education (School Lunches) (Scotland) Regulations 2015 No.269
50 s88 School Standards and Organisation (Wales) Act 2013
51 gov.wales/universal-primary-free-school-meals-upfsm
52 Scottish Budget 2023/24
53 Art 3 Welfare Reform Act 2012 (Commencement No.30 and Transitory Provisions) Order 2018 No.145; Art 3 The Free School Lunches and Milk (Universal Credit) (Wales) Order 2019 No.187 (W.47)
54 gov.uk/government/publications/free-school-meals-guidance-for-schools-and-local-authorities, February 2023
55 Department for Education, *Period product scheme for schools and colleges in England*, 16 December 2020, gov.uk/government/publications/period-products-in-schools-and-colleges
56 Welsh government press release, 3 January 2020, gov.wales/its-just-ensuring-girls-period-isnt-barrier-her-succeeding-life
57 Period Products (Free Provision) (Scotland) Act 2021

6. **Community care support from the local authority**
58 **E** s21 CA 2014
W s46 Social Services and Well-being (Wales) Act 2014
S s12(2A) Social Work (Scotland) Act 1968

7. **Support under the Children Acts**
59 s17 CA 1989; s22 C(S)A 1995
60 s17(10) CA 1989
61 s17(3) CA 1989; s22(3) C(S)A 1995
62 Sch 3 para 2(1)(b) NIAA 2002

8. **NHS healthcare**

63 See, for example, paras S-EC.3.2, S-LTR.4.5, S-ILR.4.5 Appendix FM IR

64 An NHS trust is an organisational unit within the NHS in England and Wales, generally serving either a geographical area or a specialised function (such as an ambulance service). In any particular location, there may be several trusts involved in the different aspects of providing healthcare to the local population.

65 Department of Health and Social Care, *Overseas Chargeable Patients, NHS Debt and Immigration Rules: guidance on administration and data sharing*, 26 March 2019, s4

66 **E** Regs 8 and 9 NHS(COV) Regs 2015
W Reg 3 NHS(COV) Regs 1989
S Reg 3 NHS(COV)(S) Regs

67 **E** Sch 1 NHS(COV) Regs 2015
W Sch 1 NHS(COV) Regs 1989
S Sch 1 NHS(COV)(S) Regs 1989

68 s39 IA 2014
E Regs 2 and 7 NHS(COV) Regs 2015
W Regs 1 and 2 NHS(COV) Regs 1989
S Regs 1 and 2 NHS(COV)(S) Regs

69 jcwi.org.uk/nhs-charging-toolkits

70 maternityaction.org.uk

71 doctorsoftheworld.org.uk/useful-resources

Appendices

Appendix 1

Glossary of terms

A2 national. A national of one of the European Union member states Bulgaria and Romania.

A8 national. A national of one of the European Union member states Czech Republic, Estonia, Hungary, Latvia, Lithuania, Poland, Slovakia and Slovenia.

Absent. Not physically in an area such as Great Britain; the alternative to present.

Accession states. The newer members of the European Union: Croatia, the A2 states and the A8 states.

Administrative removal. A legal mechanism used to remove foreign nationals who have entered the UK illegally, including by deception, or to remove those who have breached the conditions of their leave, including overstaying.

Applicable amount. The maximum amount of benefit set by the government, taking account of certain factors such as age and whether someone is single or part of a couple.

Application registration card. The form of identification for those who have claimed asylum.

ASPEN card. A pre-paid visa chip and pin card, given to asylum seekers in receipt of asylum support. It is credited by the Home Office and can be used in a similar way to a debit card to pay for items in shops or (for those getting section 95 support) to withdraw cash from most ATMs.

Association agreement. A treaty signed between the European Union and a country outside the European Union, giving reciprocal rights and obligations.

Asylum. Leave to enter or remain in the UK as a refugee, given under the Refugee Convention or Article 3 of the European Convention on Human Rights (including protection under the Refugee Qualification Directive).

Asylum seeker. A person who has applied for asylum and whose application has yet to be decided, or whose appeal against a refusal of an asylum application remains outstanding.

Asylum support. Support provided by the Home Office to various categories of asylum seekers and failed asylum seekers. In the past, this was provided by a section of the Home Office called the National Asylum Support Service (NASS). This was abolished in 2007, but the term 'NASS support' is sometimes still used.

Certificate of entitlement. A certificate of entitlement to the right of abode demonstrates that a person has the right of abode – ie, the right to travel freely to and from the UK. British citizens have the right of abode and can demonstrate this by producing their passports. A few Commonwealth nationals also have the right of abode and can obtain a certificate of entitlement, endorsed in their own national passport, to demonstrate this.

Common travel area. The UK, Ireland, Channel Islands and the Isle of Man.

Commonwealth countries. Antigua and Barbuda, Australia, Bahamas, Bangladesh, Barbados, Belize, Botswana, Brunei Darussalam, Cameroon, Canada, Cyprus, Dominica, Eswatini (formerly Swaziland), Fiji, Gabon, The Gambia, Ghana, Grenada, Guyana, India, Jamaica, Kenya, Kiribati, Lesotho, Malawi, Malaysia, Maldives, Malta, Mauritius, Mozambique, Namibia, Nauru, New Zealand, Nigeria, Pakistan, Papua New Guinea, Rwanda, Saint Lucia, Samoa, Seychelles, Sierra Leone, Singapore, Solomon Islands, South Africa, Sri Lanka, St Kitts and Nevis, St Vincent and The Grenadines, Tanzania, Togo, Tonga, Trinidad and Tobago, Tuvalu, Uganda, United Kingdom, Vanuatu and Zambia.

Competent state. The European Economic Area country responsible under the European Union co-ordination rules for paying your benefit and to which you are liable to pay national insurance contributions.

Court of Justice of the European Union. The European Union institution that ensures that European Union law is observed by member states. It sits in Luxembourg. Previously known as the European Court of Justice.

Deportation. A legal mechanism used to remove a foreign national on the recommendation of a criminal court following their conviction for a criminal offence, or if the Home Secretary has decided that a person's presence in the UK is 'not conducive to the public good'. If an order has been signed to deport a foreign national, they may not return unless and until the order has been revoked.

Derivative right to reside. The term given to certain residence rights that are derived from someone else in specific ways.

Destitute. For asylum support purposes, someone who does not have access to adequate accommodation or who cannot meet their essential living needs.

Destitution domestic violence concession. A provision under which people who have immigration leave on the basis of a relationship that has subsequently broken down as a result of domestic violence can be granted three months' leave in which to apply for indefinite leave to remain.

Digital-only status. A digital/electronic record of immigration status and conditions that can be viewed by inputting data into a Home Office website.

Discretionary leave. Permission to enter or remain in the UK given to a person outside the Immigration Rules or to someone who is refused asylum but who cannot be removed under another Article of the European Convention on Human Rights or for other humanitarian reasons. Replaced by restricted leave.

eGate (also **Passport eGate**). An electronic immigration barrier at a UK port.

Enforcement. A term used to refer to any of the different ways in which a person can be forced to leave the UK for immigration reasons – ie, having been refused entry at a port, having been declared an illegal entrant, or having been notified that they are someone who is liable for administrative removal, or who is being deported.

Entry clearance officer. An official at a British post overseas who deals with immigration applications made to that post.

European Community. The European Union was previously known as the European Community and, before that, the European Economic Community. In this *Handbook*, the legislation of all three is referred to as European Union law.

European Convention on Human Rights. An international instrument agreed by the Council of Europe. The rights guaranteed by it have now largely been incorporated into UK law by the Human Rights Act 1998.

European Convention on Social and Medical Assistance. An agreement signed by all the European Economic Area states, plus Turkey, requiring the ratifying states to provide assistance in cash and kind to nationals of other ratifying states who are lawfully present in their territory and who are without sufficient resources on the same conditions as their own nationals.

European Economic Area. Covers all European Union states plus Iceland, Liechtenstein and Norway. European Economic Area nationals have free movement within these and all European Union member states. From 1 June 2002, the right to free movement also applies to Switzerland.

European Union. Austria, Belgium, Bulgaria, Croatia, Cyprus, Czech Republic, Denmark, Estonia, Finland, France, Germany, Greece, Hungary, Ireland, Italy, Latvia, Lithuania, Luxembourg, Malta, Netherlands, Poland, Portugal, Romania, Slovakia, Slovenia, Spain and Sweden.

European Union/European Economic Area national. The term used in this *Handbook* to describe citizens of European Union member states/European Economic Area countries.

European Union Settlement Scheme. The scheme administered by the Home Office under which European Economic Area nationals and their family members can apply for leave, enabling them to remain lawfully in the UK following the UK's departure from the European Union.

European Social Charter. The 1961 Council of Europe Social Charter, signed by all the European Economic Area countries, plus Macedonia and Turkey.

eVisa. A printed electronic visa.

Exceptional leave. A form of leave to remain granted outside the Immigration Rules that has now been replaced with humanitarian protection and discretionary leave for those seeking asylum.

First-tier Tribunal (Asylum Support). The tribunal that decides appeals against the refusal or termination of asylum support. It sits in east London, but hears appeals nationwide (by video link if necessary).

First-tier Tribunal (Immigration and Asylum Chamber). The tribunal that hears and determines appeals against decisions made by the Secretary of State for the Home Department about asylum, immigration and nationality.

First-tier Tribunal (Social Entitlement Chamber). The tribunal that hears and determines appeals against decisions made by the Department for Work and Pensions and local authorities about benefit entitlement.

Great Britain. Comprises England, Wales and Scotland.

Habitual residence. The type of residence someone must usually have to get universal credit, income support, income-based jobseeker's allowance, income-related employment and support allowance, housing benefit, pension credit, attendance allowance, disability living allowance, carer's allowance, personal independence payment, adult disability payment and child disability payment. The term 'habitually resident' is not defined in the benefit regulations and is determined by looking at all the person's circumstances.

Home Office. The government department responsible for asylum, immigration and nationality issues.

Humanitarian protection. Permission to enter or remain in the UK given to a person who needs to be protected from harm, but whose case does not fit the criteria for refugee status.

Illegal entrant. A person who immigration officials decide has entered the UK in breach of the immigration laws. This could be by deception or clandestinely.

Immigration bail. A form of lawful immigration status given as an alternative to detention and with certain restrictions on the person's liberty to work, and which sometimes requires them to live at a known address and/or report to an immigration enforcement office at specified times. Commonly given to people who have been refused asylum.

Immigration judge. A person who determines appeals in the First-tier Tribunal (Immigration and Asylum Chamber) or Upper Tribunal (Immigration and Asylum Chamber).

Immigration officer. An official, usually stationed at a British port of entry, who decides whether to grant or refuse leave to enter. Immigration officers also have responsibility for enforcing immigration control.

Immigration Rules. Rules made by the Home Secretary, setting out the requirements for granting or refusing entry clearance, leave to enter and leave to remain to people applying in the different categories.

Indefinite leave. Permission to enter or remain that has no time limit.

Integration loan. An interest-free loan made to assist people who have recently been given refugee status or humanitarian protection to integrate into UK society.

Lawfully working. Depending on the context, either working with the permission of the Home Office or, for accession state nationals, working in accordance with any employment restrictions that apply.

Limited leave. Permission to enter or remain that is given for a certain period of time only. Also referred to as 'time-limited leave'.

Maintenance undertaking. A written undertaking given by someone under the Immigration Rules to be responsible for the maintenance and accommodation of another person who is applying to come to or stay in the UK.

Ordinarily resident. A residence requirement for several benefits and tax credits. A person is ordinarily resident where they have their home that they have adopted for a settled purpose and where they live for the time being.

Passport eGate (also **eGate**). Automated self-service barriers, operated by the Home Office, that use facial recognition technology to verify a traveller's identity against the data stored in the chip in their biometric passport.

Past presence test. A requirement for some benefits to have been present in Great Britain for a period of time before the date of claim.

Person from abroad. A social security definition that refers to a person who has failed the habitual residence test for the purposes of income support, income-based jobseeker's allowance, income-related employment and support allowance or housing benefit.

Person subject to immigration control. A person in one of four specific groups of non-European Economic Area nationals who are excluded from entitlement to most social security benefits and whose entitlement to support under the Care Act 2014 is restricted.

Points-based system. The system of controlling migration to the UK from outside the European Union for economic purposes or studies.

Present. Physically in an area such as Great Britain; the alternative to absent.

Pre-settled status. Limited leave granted under the European Union Settlement Scheme to European Economic Area nationals, their family members and those with derivative residence rights who have lived in the UK for less than five years.

Public funds. These are defined in the Immigration Rules as: housing provided by local authorities, either for homeless people or allocated from the local authority's housing register; attendance allowance; carer's allowance; child benefit; child tax credit; council tax benefit (now abolished); council tax reduction; disability living allowance; housing benefit; income-based jobseeker's allowance; income-related employment and support allowance; income support; local welfare assistance (except the Discretionary Assistance Fund, in Wales); pension credit; personal independence payment; severe disablement allowance; social fund payments; universal credit; and working tax credit.

Reciprocal agreement. A bilateral agreement made between the UK and another country, with the purpose of protecting benefit entitlement for people moving between the two.

Refugee. A person who satisfies the definition of someone who needs international protection under Article 1A(2) of the 1951 Convention Relating to the Status of Refugees.

Refugee Convention. The 1951 United Nations Convention Relating to the Status of Refugees, a multilateral treaty defining who is a refugee and setting out the rights of people who are granted asylum.

Removal. The final procedure for sending a person refused entry, or who is being treated as an illegal entrant, or who is subject to the administrative removal or deportation process, away from the UK.

Resident. A requirement of a category D retirement pension and a necessary part of ordinary residence and habitual residence. Residence is more than presence and is usually where you have your home for the time being.

Restricted leave. Leave given outside the Immigration Rules to someone who is excluded from refugee or humanitarian protection leave but who cannot be removed from the UK for human rights reasons. Replaced discretionary leave.

Right of abode. The right to enter, remain, leave and return freely to the UK without needing to obtain leave from the immigration authorities. All British citizens, and some Commonwealth nationals, have the right of abode.

Right to reside. A residence requirement for entitlement to some benefits and tax credits. For child benefit and child tax credit, a person must have a right to reside in the UK, and, to satisfy the habitual residence test for means-tested benefits, they must have a right to reside in the common travel area. The right to reside depends on someone's nationality, immigration status and whether they have rights under European Union law.

Secretary of State for the Home Department (the Home Secretary). The government minister with primary responsibility for decisions made by the Home Office on immigration, asylum and nationality.

Section 4 support. A form of asylum support for destitute asylum seekers whose asylum application has been refused and who fit certain eligibility criteria.

Section 95 support. A form of support for people who have made an application for asylum in the UK.

Settlement/settled status. Defined in immigration law as being ordinarily resident in the UK without any restrictions on the time the person is able to remain here. Generally used to refer to those with indefinite leave, including when granted under the European Union Settlement Scheme.

Sponsor. The person (usually a relative) with whom someone is applying to join, or remain with, in the UK, and/or a person who is to be responsible for the applicant's maintenance and accommodation in the UK.

Stateless person. Someone who is not considered a national by any country.

Subject to immigration control. Often used to refer to those who need leave to enter or remain in the UK – and this is the definition given in the Asylum and Immigration Act 1996. However, the Immigration and Asylum Act 1999 gives a different, narrower, definition, which is used to exclude people from most benefits and tax credits and certain services provided by local authorities' social services departments. This *Handbook* uses the term as it is defined in the 1999 Act.

Temporary admission. A temporary licence given to people before 15 January 2018 to be in the UK while they are waiting for a decision to be made on their immigration status or while they are waiting to be removed from the UK. Now called immigration bail.

Third country. Usually used to refer to a country to which the Home Office wishes to send an asylum seeker for their application for asylum to be considered, other than the country of which they are a national, rather than in the UK.

UK Visas and Immigration. The Home Office department that deals with immigration control.

United Kingdom. Comprises England, Wales, Scotland and Northern Ireland. The Channel Islands of Jersey and Guernsey, and the Isle of Man, are Crown dependencies and not part of the UK.

Unmarried partners. A term used in the Immigration Rules to refer to couples (heterosexual or same-sex) who have been together for two or more years, who are in a relationship 'akin to marriage' and who cannot marry according to the law – eg, one of them is already married. The Immigration Rules give unmarried partners some rights to enter and remain in the UK if one partner is settled in the UK or has limited leave here.

Upper Tribunal (Immigration and Asylum Chamber). The tribunal that hears and determines appeals against determinations made by the First-tier Tribunal (Immigration and Asylum Chamber) and most immigration-related applications for judicial review.

Upper Tribunal (Social Entitlement Chamber). The tribunal that hears and determines appeals against decisions made by the First-tier Tribunal (Social Entitlement Chamber) about benefit entitlement.

Visa national. A person who must obtain entry clearance before travelling to the UK for most purposes, unless they are a person with indefinite leave returning within two years or returning within a period of earlier leave granted for more than six months. For a list of countries covered, see Appendix 1 to the Immigration Rules.

Work permit. A document issued by UK Visas and Immigration to employers, allowing them to employ a named individual in a particular job.

Appendix 2

Information and advice

Immigration and asylum

If you need help with an immigration problem, you can obtain advice from your local law centre, a solicitor specialising in immigration work or one of the agencies listed below.

Note: anyone who gives immigration advice must be professionally regulated. For further details, see p7.

AIRE Centre (Advice on Individual Rights in Europe)

Room 505
Charles Clore House
17 Russell Square
London WC1B 5DR
Tel: 020 7831 4276
info@airecentre.org
airecentre.org

Promotes awareness of European legal rights and assists people to assert these.

Asylum Aid (formerly Consonant)

Derry House
20 Penfold Street
London NW8 8HJ
Tel: 020 7354 9631
advice@asylumaid.org.uk
asylumaid.org.uk

Specialists in immigration law, offering advice and legal representation.

Asylum Support Appeals Project (ASAP)

Studio 11/12
Container City Building
48 Trinity Buoy Wharf
London E14 0FN
Tel: 020 3716 0284
Advice line (advisers only): 020 3716 0283 (Mon, Wed and Fri 2pm–4pm)
asaproject.org

Offers free legal representation and advice to asylum seekers on appeal at the Asylum Support Tribunal, and provides advice to frontline organisations and advisers.

British Red Cross

44 Moorfields
London EC2Y 9AL
Tel: 0344 871 1111
Support line: 0808 196 3651
contactus@redcross.org.uk
redcross.org.uk

Provides urgent support for refugees and vulnerable migrants in specific areas across the UK.

Civil Legal Advice

Tel: 0345 345 4345
Minicom: 0345 609 6677
(Mon–Fri 9am–8pm; Sat 9am–12.30pm)
gov.uk/civil-legal-advice
gov.uk/check-legal-aid

A legal aid eligibility checker: find-legal-advice.justice.gov.uk

A directory of legal aid suppliers in England and Wales.

Doctors of the World

The People's Place
80–92 High Street
Stratford
London E15 2NE
Tel: 020 7167 5789
Advice line for the public: 0808 164 7686 (Tues–Thurs 10am–12pm)
Advice line for organisations: 020 7078 9629
clinic@doctorsoftheworld.org.uk
doctorsoftheworld.org.uk

Runs clinics and advocacy programmes in London to groups such as destitute migrants.

EU Rights and Brexit Hub

York Law School
The University of York
Law and Management Building
Freboys Lane
York YO10 5GD
law-eurightshub@york.ac.uk
eurightshub.york.ac.uk

A legal action research hub that offers advice and support.

Greater Manchester Immigration Aid Unit

1 Delaunays Road
Crumpsall Green
Manchester M8 4QS
Tel: 0161 740 7722 (Mon and Fri 9.30am–1pm, Wed 12.30pm–4pm)
info@gmiau.org
gmiau.org

Provides free, confidential immigration and asylum legal advice and representation to people in the local community.

Immigration Law Practitioners' Association

Lindsey House
40–42 Charterhouse Street
London EC1M 6JN
info@ilpa.org.uk
ilpa.org.uk

A professional association aiming to promote and improve advice and representation in immigration, nationality and asylum law.

Joint Council for the Welfare of Immigrants

441 Caledonian Road
London N7 9BG
Tel: 020 7251 8708
Irregular migrants helpline: 020 7553 7470 (Mon, Tues and Thurs 10am–1pm)
info@jcwi.org.uk
legal@jcwi.org.uk (for assistance with an immigration application or legal case)
jcwi.org.uk

Supports individuals and families with legal advice and challenges unjust laws and practices.

Law Centres Network

1 Lady Hale Gate
Gray's Inn
London WC1X 8BS
Tel: 020 3637 1330
lawcentres.org.uk

Does not give advice but can provide details of your nearest law centre.

Maternity Action

Migrant Women's Rights Service
Second floor
3–4 Wells Terrace
London N4 3JU
Tel: 020 7251 6189 (Tues, Wed and Thurs 10am–12pm and 2–4pm)
migrantwomensrights@maternityaction.org.uk
maternityaction.org.uk/migrant-womens-rights

Advises supporters of migrant women who are pregnant or new mothers.

Migrant Help

Charlton House
Dour Street
Dover CT16 1AT
Tel: 01304 203 977
Free asylum helpline: 0808 801 0503
info@migranthelpuk.org
migranthelpuk.org

Delivers support and advice services to migrants in the UK.

Migrant Legal Action

53 Addington Square
London SE5 7LB
Tel: 020 7701 0141
Advice line: 020 3150 1470 (Mon–Fri 2–4pm)
info@migrantlegalaction.org.uk

Provides a specialist legal service, free of charge.

Project 17

St Joseph's Hospice
Mare St
London E8 4SA
Tel: 07963 509 044
Advice line (advisers only): 07701 330 016
info@project17.org.uk
project17.org.uk

Works to end destitution among migrant children. Helps families experiencing exceptional poverty to improve their access to local authority support.

Refugee Action

179 Royce Road
Manchester M15 5TJ
info@refugee-action.org.uk
refugee-action.org.uk

Refugee Action has projects in London, Birmingham, Coventry, Stoke-on-Trent, Manchester and Merseyside.

Refugee Council

PO Box 68614
London E15 1NS
Tel: 020 7346 6700
Infoline: 0808 196 7272
info@refugeecouncil.org.uk
refugeecouncil.org.uk

Provides asylum seekers and refugees in England with crisis advice and practical support.

Rights of Women

52–54 Featherstone Street
London EC1Y 8RT
Tel: 020 7251 6575
info@row.org.uk
Advice line for women: 020 7490 7689 (Mon and Thur 10am–12pm and 2pm–4pm)
EU Settlement Scheme advice line (for vulnerable women only): 020 7118 0267 (Tues and Wed 11am–1pm and 2–4pm)
Professionals' advice line: 020 8138 8028 (fortnightly on Friday 10am–12pm)
rightsofwomen.org.uk/get-advice/immigration-and-asylum-law

Advises on immigration and asylum law, with a focus on supporting survivors of domestic abuse.

Scottish Refugee Council

6th Floor, Portland House
17 Renfield Street
Glasgow G2 5AH
Tel: 0141 248 9799
Advice line: 0808 196 7274 (Mon–Fri 9am–5pm, closed Wed till 1pm)
scottishrefugeecouncil.org.uk

Provides direct support to people in need of refugee protection, as well as research, policy and campaigning for change.

Settled

R1.3 Riverside House
Newport Market
Upper Dock Street
Newport NP20 1DD
EUSS Multilingual advice line: 0330 223 5336
EUSS advice service: advice@settled.org.uk
EUSS Roma advice service: roma.advice@settled.org.uk
Ukraine advice service: ukraineadvice@settled.org.uk
settled.org.uk

Provides information, advice and support services for European Union citizens who have made a home in the UK.

The3Million

info@the3million.org.uk
the3million.org.uk

Campaigns to safeguard and guarantee the rights of European Union citizens in the UK and British citizens in Europe after Brexit.

Welsh Refugee Council

120–122 Broadway
Cardiff CF24 1NJ
Tel: 0808 196 7273 (Mon, Tues and Thurs 10am–1pm and 2pm–3pm, Fri 10am–1pm)
wrc.wales

Empowers asylum seekers and refugees to build a new life in Wales.

Work Rights Centre

379–381 High Road
London NW10 2JR
Tel: 0300 4000 100
contact@workrightscentre.org
workrightscentre.org

Helps migrants and disadvantaged Britons access employment justice and improve their social mobility.

Social security

Independent advice and representation

It is often difficult for unsupported individuals to get a positive response from the DWP, local authority or HM Revenue and Customs. It can help if you obtain advice about your entitlement and how you can demonstrate this. If you can get good-quality assistance from an adviser who will take on your case, this is even more helpful, particularly if you need to challenge a decision. The following may be able to assist.

- Advicelocal (advicelocal.uk) has details of advice organisations in your area.
- Citizens Advice. You can find out where your local office is from the Citizens Advice website at citizensadvice.org.uk (England and Wales) or cas.org.uk (Scotland).
- Law centres. You can find your nearest law centre at lawcentres.org.uk.
- LawWorks (lawworks.org.uk) has details of local legal advice centres that give free advice.
- Housing association welfare rights services for tenants.
- Local authority welfare rights services.
- Local and national organisations for particular groups of claimants may offer help. For instance, there are unemployed centres, pensioners' groups and organisations for people with disabilities.

Advice from CPAG

Unfortunately, CPAG is unable to deal with enquiries directly from members of the public, but if you are an adviser you can telephone or email for help with advising your client.

Advisers in England, Wales and Northern Ireland can telephone from 10am to 12pm and from 2pm to 4pm (Monday to Friday) on 020 7812 5231. Email advice is limited to enquiries that are specifically about universal credit, child benefit and tax credits. Our email address is advice@cpag.org.uk. For more information, see cpag.org.uk/advisers.

Advisers in Scotland can telephone from 10am to 4pm (Monday to Thursday) and from 10am to 12pm (Friday) on 0141 552 0552, or email advice@cpagscotland.org.uk.

CPAG's Upper Tribunal assistance project can provide support to advisers helping claimants challenge tribunal decisions. See cpag.org.uk/welfare-rights/upper-tribunal-assistance-project. We also provide training and advice to support advisers to pursue judicial review remedies: see cpag.org.uk/jr.

AskCPAG is an information and solutions platform for advisers, including a digital version of the *Welfare Benefits and Tax Credits Handbook*, fully searchable and updated throughout the year: see AskCPAG.org.uk.

CPAG takes on a small number of test cases each year. We focus on cases that have the potential to improve the lives of families with children in poverty. If you are an adviser and would like to refer a test case to us, see cpag.org.uk/legal.

Human rights

Equality Advisory and Support Service

FREEPOST EASS HELPLINE FPN6521
Tel: 0808 800 0082
Textphone: 0808 800 0084
equalityadvisoryservice.com

Information, advice and support on discrimination and human rights issues, and the relevant law.

Appendix 3

Useful addresses

Immigration and asylum

UK Visas and Immigration

Lunar House
40 Wellesley Road
Croydon CR9 2BY
gov.uk/government/organisations/uk-visas-and-immigration

UK Visas and Immigration Contact Centre

Tel: 0300 790 6268

Asylum support

Migrant Help
Helpline: 0808 801 0503
Webchat available at migranthelpuk.org/contact

Voluntary returns service

Tel: 0300 004 0202
gov.uk/return-home-voluntarily

Note: contacting the Home Office directly to discuss your assisted voluntary return may have an impact on any outstanding protection or human rights-based claim that you have made. You may therefore wish to obtain independent advice before doing so.

Enquiries from European citizens

Tel: 0300 790 6268

European Union Settlement Scheme

Tel: 0300 123 7379 (Mon–Fri 8am–8pm, Sat–Sun 9.30am–4.30pm)
Advisers tel: 0300 790 0566 (Mon–Fri 8am–8pm, Sat–Sun 9.30am–4.30pm)
Online applications: gov.uk/settled-status-eu-citizens-families

Employer and educational institution helpline

Tel: 0300 123 4699
businesshelpdesk@homeoffice.gov.uk
educatorshelpdesk@homeoffice.gov.uk

Citizenship and nationality

Tel: 0300 790 6268
nationalityenquiries@homeoffice.gov.uk

Passport Office

PO Box 767
Southport
PR8 9PW
Tel: 0300 222 0000
gov.uk/government/organisations/hm-passport-office

Independent Chief Inspector of Borders and Immigration

1st Floor Clive House
70 Petty France
London SW1H 9EX
Tel: 0300 072 0128
chiefinspector@icibi.gov.uk
gov.uk/government/organisations/independent-chief-inspector-of-borders-and-immigration

First-tier Tribunal (Immigration and Asylum Chamber)

PO Box 6987
Leicester LE1 6ZX
Tel: 0300 123 1711
customer.service@justice.gov.uk
gov.uk/immigration-asylum-tribunal

Note: urgent appeals must be addressed to:
Expedite Requests The First-tier Tribunal
Office of the Duty Judge
First-tier Tribunal (Immigration and Asylum Chamber)
PO Box 6987
Leicester LE1 6ZX
To check if your application has been received:
Fax: 0870 739 5895
customer.service@justice.gov.uk

Upper Tribunal (Immigration and Asylum Chamber)

1A Field House
15–25 Breams Buildings
London EC4A 1DZ
Tel: 0300 123 1711
Fax: 0870 324 0095
customer.service@justice.gov.uk
gov.uk/upper-tribunal-immigration-asylum

First-tier Tribunal (Asylum Support)

2nd Floor
Import Building
2 Clove Crescent
London E14 2BE
Freephone: 0800 681 6509
asylumsupporttribunals@justice.gov.uk
gov.uk/appeal-first-tier-asylum-support-tribunal
gov.uk/courts-tribunals/first-tier-tribunal-asylum-support

Office of the Immigration Services Commissioner

OISC
PO Box 567
Dartford
Kent DA1 9XW
Tel: 0345 000 0046
info@oisc.gov.uk
gov.uk/government/organisations/office-of-the-immigration-services-commissioner

Solicitors Regulation Authority

The Cube
199 Wharfside Street
Birmingham B1 1RN
Tel: 0370 606 2555
sra.org.uk

Legal Ombudsman

PO Box 6806
Wolverhampton WV1 9WJ
Tel: 0300 555 0333
enquiries@legalombudsman.org.uk
legalombudsman.org.uk

For complaints about lawyers.

European Delegation to the UK

Europe House
32 Smith Square
London SW1P 3EU
Tel: 020 7973 1992
Fax: 020 7973 1900
delegation-united-kingdom@eeas.europa.eu
eeas.europa.eu/delegations/united-kingdom_en

Independent Monitoring Authority for the Citizens' Rights Agreements

3rd Floor Civic Centre
Oystermouth Road
Swansea SA1 3SN
IMA@ima-citizensrights.org.uk
ima-citizensrights.org.uk

Social security

HM Courts and Tribunals Service

Appeal a benefit decision

England and Wales
HMCTS Benefit Appeals
PO Box 12626
Harlow CM20 9QF
Tel: 0300 123 1142
Welsh speakers: 0300 303 5170
contactsscs@justice.gov.uk

Scotland
HMCTS Benefit Appeals
PO Box 13150
Harlow CM20 9TT
Tel: 0300 790 6234
SSCSA-glasgow@justice.gov.uk
gov.uk/appeal-benefit-decision/submit-appeal

First-tier Tribunal (Tax Chamber)

PO Box 16972
Birmingham B16 6TZ
Tel: 0300 123 1024
taxappeals@justice.gov.uk
gov.uk/tax-tribunal

The Upper Tribunal (Administrative Appeals Chamber)

England and Wales

5th Floor
7 Rolls Buildings
Fetter Lane
London EC4A 1NL
Tel: 020 7071 5662
adminappeals@justice.gov.uk
gov.uk/administrative-appeals-tribunal

Scotland

George House
126 George Street
Edinburgh EH2 4HH
Tel: 0131 271 4310
UTAACMailbox@justice.gov.uk
gov.uk/administrative-appeals-tribunal

Northern Ireland

Tribunal Hearing Centre
2nd Floor
Royal Courts of Justice
Chichester Street
Belfast BT1 3JF
Tel: 028 9072 4848
tribunalsunit@courtsni.gov.uk
gov.uk/administrative-appeals-tribunal

The Upper Tribunal (Tax and Chancery Chamber)

England and Wales

5th Floor
7 Rolls Buildings
Fetter Lane
London EC4A 1NL
Tel: 020 7612 9730
uttc@justice.gov.uk
gov.uk/tax-upper-tribunal

Scotland

Upper Tribunal for Scotland
The Glasgow Tribunals Centre
20 York Street
Glasgow G2 8GT
Tel: 0141 302 5880
uppertribunalforscotland@scotcourtstribunals.gov.uk
scotcourts.gov.uk/the-courts/court-locations/the-upper-tribunal-for-scotland

Department for Work and Pensions

Caxton House
Tothill Street
London SW1H 9NA
gov.uk/government/organisations/department-for-work-pensions

Government Legal Department

102 Petty France
London SW1H 9GL
Tel: 020 7210 3000
Litigation enquiries: 020 7210 8500
thetreasurysolicitor@governmentlegal.gov.uk
gov.uk/government/organisations/government-legal-department

Department of Health and Social Care (Overseas Healthcare)

Overseas Healthcare Services
NHS Business Services Authority
Bridge House
152 Pilgrim Street
Newcastle upon Tyne NE1 6SN
Tel: 0191 218 1999

NHS healthcare information for visitors and residents from the European Economic Area (EEA) and Switzerland and for UK citizens living in the European Union, EEA and Switzerland.

Disability and Carers Service

Attendance Allowance Service Centre

Freepost DWP Attendance Allowance
Tel: 0800 731 0122
Textphone: 0800 731 0317
gov.uk/attendance-allowance

Disability Living Allowance Unit

Claimants born on or before 8 April 1948:
Freepost Disability Living Allowance 65
Tel: 0800 731 0122
Textphone: 0800 731 0317

gov.uk/dla-disability-living-allowance-benefit

Claimants born after 8 April 1948 who are over 16 years old:
Disability Living Allowance
Warbreck House
Warbreck Hill Road
Blackpool FY2 0YE
Tel: 0800 121 4600
Textphone: 0800 121 4523
gov.uk/dla-disability-living-allowance-benefit

Claimants aged under 16 years:
Freepost DWP DLA Child
Tel: 0800 121 4600
Textphone: 0800 121 4523
gov.uk/disability-living-allowance-children

Personal Independence Payment Unit
Personal Independence Payment New Claims
Post Handling Site B
Wolverhampton WV99 1AH
Claims: 0800 917 2222; textphone 0800 917 7777
Helpline: 0800 121 4433; textphone 0800 121 4493
gov.uk/pip

Carer's Allowance Unit
Mail Handling Site A
Wolverhampton
WV98 2AB
Tel: 0800 731 0297
Textphone: 0800 731 0317
gov.uk/carers-allowance

Exporting benefits overseas
Attendance Allowance Exportability Team
Mail Handling Site A
Wolverhampton WV98 2AD

Disability Living Allowance Exportability Team
Room C212 Pension, Disability and Carers Service
Warbreck House
Warbreck Hill Road
Blackpool FY2 0YE

Personal Independence Payment 7 Exportability Team
Mail Handling Site B
Wolverhampton WV99 1AE

Carers Allowance Exportability Team
Mail Handling Site A
Wolverhampton WV98 2AE
gov.uk/claim-benefits-abroad/disability-benefits

Jobcentre Plus

New benefit claims

New-style JSA
Tel: 0800 055 6688
Welsh language: 0800 012 1888
Textphone: 0800 023 4888
gov.uk/contact-jobcentre-plus/new-benefit-claims

Enquiries about ongoing claims – jobseeker's allowance, income support, incapacity benefit or employment and support allowance

Tel: 0800 169 0310
Welsh language: 0800 169 0207
Textphone: 0800 169 0314
gov.uk/contact-jobcentre-plus/existing-benefit-claims

Universal credit

Tel: 0800 328 5644
Textphone: 0800 328 1344
Welsh language: 0800 328 1744
gov.uk/universal-credit

Social fund

Tel: 0800 169 0140
Textphone: 0800 169 0286
Welsh language: 0800 169 0240

Maternity allowance

Tel: 0800 169 0283
Textphone: 0800 169 0286
Welsh language: 0800 169 0296
gov.uk/maternity-allowance

Bereavement benefits

Tel: 0800 151 2012
Textphone: 0800 169 0314
Welsh language: 0800 731 0453

The Pension Service

New claims tel: 0800 731 7898
Textphone: 0800 731 7339
Welsh language new claims: 0800 731 7936
Welsh language textphone: 0800 731 7013
Change of circumstances tel: 0800 731 0469
Textphone change of circumstances: 0800 731 0160
Welsh language change of circumstances: 0800 731 0453
Welsh language textphone: 0800 731 0456
gov.uk/contact-pension-service

Winter fuel payment

Winter Fuel Payment Centre
Mail Handling Site A
Wolverhampton WV98 1LR
Tel: 0800 731 0160
Textphone: contact Relay UK on 18001 then 0800 731 0176
gov.uk/winter-fuel-payment

International Pension Centre

The Pension Service 11
Mail Handling Site A
Wolverhampton WV98 1LW
State pension:
Tel: 0191 218 7777
Textphone: 0191 218 7280
Other benefits:
Tel: 0191 206 9390
gov.uk/international-pension-centre

HM Revenue and Customs (tax credits)

Tax Credit Office

HM Revenue and Customs
Tax Credit Office
BX9 1ER
gov.uk/child-tax-credit
gov.uk/working-tax-credit

Tax credit helpline

Tel: 0345 300 3900
Textphone: dial 18001 then 0345 300 3900
Intermediaries advice line for voluntary and charitable organisations: 0345 300 3943

HM Revenue and Customs (child benefit and guardian's allowance)

Child benefit

Child Benefit Office
PO Box 1
Newcastle upon Tyne NE88 1AA
Tel: 0300 200 3100
Textphone: 0300 200 3103
Welsh language: 0300 200 1900
gov.uk/child-benefit

Guardian's allowance

Guardian's Allowance Unit
PO Box 1
Newcastle upon Tyne NE88 1AA
Tel: 0300 322 9080
Textphone: 0300 200 3103
gov.uk/guardians-allowance

HM Revenue and Customs (national insurance)

PT Operations North East England
HM Revenue and Customs
BX9 1AN
Tel: 0300 200 3500
Textphone: 0300 200 3519
gov.uk/topic/personal-tax/national-insurance

HM Revenue and Customs (Statutory Payment Dispute Team)

PT Operations North East England
HM Revenue and Customs
BX9 1AN
Tel: 0300 322 9422
Textphone: 0300 200 3212
gov.uk/guidance/statutory-pay-entitlement-how-to-deal-with-disagreements

NHS Business Services Authority (Help with NHS Costs)

NHS Help with Health Costs
Bridge House
152 Pilgrim Street
Newcastle upon Tyne NE1 6SN
Low income scheme: 0300 330 1343
Medical and maternity exemption certificates: 0300 330 1341
NHS tax credit exemption certificates: 0300 330 1347
nhsbsa.nhs.uk/nhs-help-health-costs

Local Government and Social Care Ombudsman

England

PO Box 4771
Coventry CV4 0EH
Tel: 0300 061 0614
lgo.org.uk

Scottish Public Services Ombudsman

Bridgeside House
99 McDonald Road
Edinburgh EH7 4NS
Tel: 0800 377 7330
spso.org.uk

Public Services Ombudsman for Wales

1 Ffordd yr Hen Gae
Pencoed CF35 5LJ
Tel: 0300 790 0203
ask@ombudsman.wales
ombudsman.wales

Parliamentary and Health Service Ombudsman

Millbank Tower
30 Millbank
London SW1P 4QP
Tel: 0345 015 4033
ombudsman.org.uk

The Adjudicator

The Adjudicator's Office
PO Box 10280
Nottingham NG2 9PF
Tel: 0300 057 1111
gov.uk/government/organisations/the-adjudicator-s-office

Independent Case Examiner

The Independent Case Examiner
PO Box 209
Bootle L20 7WA
Tel: 0800 414 8529
Fax: 0151 221 6601
ice@dwp.gov.uk
gov.uk/government/organisations/independent-case-examiner

Judicial Conduct Investigations Office

81–82 Queens Building
Royal Courts of Justice
Strand
London WC2A 2LL
Tel: 020 7073 4719
general.enquiries@judicialconduct.gov.uk (no longer accepting complaints by email)
complaints.judicialconduct.gov.uk

Standards Commission for Scotland

Room T2.21
Scottish Parliament
Edinburgh EH99 1SP
Tel: 0131 348 6666
enquiries@standardscommission.org.uk
standardscommissionscotland.org.uk

Ethical Standards Commissioner

Thistle House
91 Haymarket Terrace
Edinburgh EH12 5HE
Tel: 0300 011 0550
info@ethicalstandards.org.uk
ethicalstandards.org.uk

Appendix 4

Useful publications

Many of the books listed here will be in your local public library. You can find Stationery Office books at Stationery Office bookshops or you can order them by telephone, email or online (tel: 0333 202 5070; email: customer.services@tso.co.uk; web: tsoshop.co.uk). To pay by cheque, select 'Pay by post' from the TSO Shop online checkout section, then print your order form and post it to TSO Customer Services, 18 Central Avenue, St Andrews Business Park, Norwich NR7 0HR. Many of the publications listed below are also available from CPAG; see below for order details, or order from cpag.org.uk/shop.

Immigration, nationality and asylum

Immigration Law Handbook (11th edition), F Allen, J Gasparro, J Swaney, M Phelan and J Gillespie, Oxford University Press, 2022

Best Practice Guide to Asylum and Human Rights Appeals, M Henderson, R Moffatt and A Pickup, Immigration Law Practitioners' Association, 2022 (available only from ein.org.uk)

Children

Children in Need: local authority support for children and families (2nd edition), I Wise QC and others, Legal Action Group, 2013

Caselaw and legislation

The Law Relating to Social Security

All the legislation but without any commentary. Known as the 'Blue Book'. Available at legislation.gov.uk/uksi/social%20security.

Sweet & Maxwell: Social Security Legislation series, with commentary

Volume I: Non-Means-Tested Benefits

Volume II: Universal Credit, State Pension Credit and the Social Fund

Volume III: Administration, Adjudication and the European Dimension

Volume IV: HMRC-administered Social Security Benefits and Scotland

CPAG's Housing Benefit and Council Tax Reduction Legislation, with commentary

CPAG's Child Support: the legislation, with commentary

Official guidance

Decision Makers' Guide: staff guide
Available at gov.uk/government/collections/decision-makers-guide-staff-guide.

Advice for Decision Making: staff guide
Available at gov.uk/government/publications/advice-for-decision-making-staff-guide.

Housing Benefit Guidance Manual
Available at gov.uk/government/collections/housing-benefit-claims-processing-and-good-practice-for-local-authority-staff.

Discretionary Housing Payments Guidance Manual
Available at gov.uk/government/publications/discretionary-housing-payments-guidance-manual.

Healthcare professionals: information from DWP
Available at gov.uk/government/collections/healthcare-practitioners-guidance-and-information-from-dwp.

Work Capability Assessment (WCA) Handbook
Available at gov.uk/government/publications/work-capability-assessment-handbook-for-healthcare-professionals.

Tax Credits Technical Manual
Available at hmrc.gov.uk/manuals/tctmanual.

Social Fund Budgeting Loan Guide
Available at gov.uk/government/publications/budgeting-loan-guide-for-decision-makers-reviewing-officers-and-further-reviewing-officers.

Personal Independence Payment (PIP) Assessment Guide for Assessment Providers
Available at gov.uk/government/publications/personal-independence-payment-assessment-guide-for-assessment-providers.

Leaflets

The DWP publishes many leaflets, available free from your local DWP or Jobcentre Plus office. To order DWP leaflets, or receive information about new leaflets, contact HH Global, 2nd Floor, 2 Navigation Walk, Wakefield WF1 5RH, email dwp@hhglobal.com or complete the order form at gov.uk/government/publications/dwp-leaflets-order-form. Leaflets on housing benefit are available from your local council.

Periodicals

Welfare Rights Bulletin (CPAG, bi-monthly)
Available in print or online, this covers developments in social security law. For more information, see cpag.org.uk/subscriptions.

Articles on social security can also be found on AdviserNet (Citizens Advice) and in *Legal Action* (Legal Action Group) and the *Journal of Social Security Law* (Sweet & Maxwell).

Other publications

AskCPAG

The full text of the *Welfare Benefits and Tax Credits Handbook* online and updated throughout the year. See cpag.org.uk/subscriptions for details.

AskCPAG+

CPAG's full digital package which includes the full text of the *Welfare Benefits and Tax Credits Handbook* and *Benefits for Migrants Handbook* updated throughout the year, the *Welfare Rights Bulletin*, *Poverty* journal and decision-making tools and appeal letter generators. See cpag.org.uk/subscriptions for details.

CPAG guides

Universal Credit: what you need to know
Financial Help for Families: what you need to know
Personal Independence Payment: what you need to know
Winning Your Benefit Appeal: what you need to know

Other CPAG handbooks

Welfare Benefits and Tax Credits Handbook
Child Support Handbook
Council Tax Handbook
Debt Advice Handbook (available free on AskCPAG)
Fuel Rights Handbook (available free on AskCPAG)
Mental Health and Benefits Handbook (available free on AskCPAG)
Student Support and Benefits Handbook (available free on AskCPAG)
Benefits for Students in Scotland Handbook (available free on AskCPAG)
Children's Handbook Scotland (available free on AskCPAG)

Books from other publishers

Big Book of Benefits and Mental Health, Tom Messere (subscription available on AskCPAG)
Disability Rights Handbook, Disability Rights UK (subscription available on AskCPAG)
Help with Housing Costs Vol 1: guide to universal credit and council tax rebates, Shelter
Help with Housing Costs Vol 2: guide to housing benefit, Shelter

For CPAG titles and most other publications contact:

CPAG, 30 Micawber St, London N1 7TB (tel: 020 7837 7979, email: bookorders@cpag.org.uk). Discounts on CPAG publications are available to CPAG members and Citizens Advice. Order forms are available at cpag.org.uk/shop. Postage and packing: free for online subscriptions and orders up to £10 in value; for order value £10.01–£100, add a flat rate charge of £3.99; for order value £100.01–£400, add £7.49; for order value over £400, add £11.49.

Appendix 5

Reciprocal agreements

Reciprocal agreements with European Economic Area states

State	*Retirement pension*	*Bereavement benefits*	*Guardian's allowance*	*'Sickness benefit'*	*Incapacity benefit*	*Contribution-based jobseeker's allowance*	*Maternity allowance*	*Disablement benefit*	*Industrial injuries benefits*	*Child benefit*	*Attendance allowance and disability living allowance*	*Carer's allowance*
Austria	✓	✓	✓	✓	✓	✓	✓	✓	✓	✓	–	–
Belgium	✓	✓	✓	✓	✓	✓	✓	✓	✓	✓	–	–
Croatia	✓	✓	–	✓	✓	✓	✓	✓	✓	✓	–	–
Cyprus	✓	✓	✓	✓	✓	✓	✓	✓	✓	–	–	–
Denmark	✓	✓	✓	✓	✓	✓	✓	✓	✓	✓	✓	–
Finland	✓	✓	–	✓	✓	✓	✓	✓	✓	✓	–	–
France	✓	✓	–	✓	✓	✓	✓	✓	✓	✓	–	–
Germany	✓	✓	✓	✓	✓	✓	✓	✓	✓	✓	✓	–
Iceland	✓	✓	✓	✓	✓	✓	–	✓	✓	–	–	–
Ireland*	✓	✓	✓	✓	✓	✓	✓	✓	✓	–	–	–
Italy	✓	✓	✓	✓	✓	✓	✓	✓	✓	–	–	–
Luxembourg	✓	✓	✓	✓	✓	–	✓	✓	✓	–	–	–
Malta	✓	✓	✓	✓	✓	✓	–		✓	–	–	–
Netherlands	✓	✓	✓	✓	✓	✓	✓	✓	✓	–	–	–
Norway**	✓	✓	(✓)	(✓)	(✓)	(✓)	(✓)	(✓)	(✓)	(✓)	(✓)	–
Portugal	✓	✓	✓	✓	✓	✓	✓	✓	✓	✓	–	–
Slovenia	✓	✓	–	✓	✓	✓	✓	✓	✓	✓	–	–
Spain	✓	✓	✓	✓	✓	✓	✓	✓	✓	✓	–	–
Sweden	✓	✓	✓	✓	✓	✓	✓	✓	✓	✓	–	–
Northern Ireland***	✓	✓	✓	✓	✓	✓	✓	✓	✓	✓	✓	✓

* In addition to the reciprocal agreement between the UK and Ireland, a new convention on social security came into effect on 1 January 2021, which co-ordinates the social security systems between these two countries. For further details, see p435 and Chapter 16.

** The reciprocal agreement with Norway has been significantly restricted for claims made since 1 January 2021. Since this date, most provisions now only apply to retirement pensions and bereavement benefits, except if you are moving between Norway and Jersey or the Isle of Man (see p437).

*** Although Northern Ireland is part of the UK, there are reciprocal agreements between Great Britain and Northern Ireland. That is because benefits in Northern Ireland and Great Britain are separate and administered under different social security legislation. For details of these agreements, see p435.

There is an agreement with Gibraltar, which treats the UK and Gibraltar as separate countries (except for child benefit) for the purposes of the European Union (EU) co-ordination rules. For further details, see p436.

For all European Economic Area states, first check if you, and the relevant benefit, are covered by the EU co-ordination rules – see Chapter 16.

Reciprocal agreements with non-European Economic Area states

State	*Retirement pension*	*Bereavement benefits*	*Guardian's allowance*	*'Sickness benefit'*	*Incapacity benefit*	*Contribution-based jobseeker's allowance*	*Maternity allowance*	*Disablement benefit*	*Industrial injuries benefits*	*Child benefit*	*Attendance allowance and disability living allowance*	*Carer's allowance*
Barbados	✓	✓	✓	✓	✓	–	✓	✓	✓	✓	–	–
Bermuda	✓	✓	–	–	–	–	–	✓	✓	–	–	–
Bosnia-Herzegovina	✓	✓	–	✓	✓	✓	✓	✓	✓	✓	–	–
Canada	✓	–	–	–	–	✓	–	–	–	✓	–	–
Chile	✓	✓	–	–	–	–	–	–	–	–	–	–
Israel	✓	✓	✓	✓	✓	–	✓	✓	✓	✓	–	–
Jamaica	✓	✓	✓	–	✓	–	–	✓	✓	–	–	–
Kosovo	✓	✓	–	✓	✓	✓	✓	✓	✓	✓	–	–
Mauritius	✓	✓	✓	–	–	–	–	✓	✓	✓	–	–
Montenegro	✓	✓	–	✓	✓	✓	✓	✓	✓	✓	–	–
New Zealand	✓	✓	✓	✓	–	✓	–	–	–	✓	–	–
North Macedonia	✓	✓	–	✓	✓	✓	✓	✓	✓	✓	–	–
Philippines	✓	✓	–	–	–	–	–	✓	✓	–	–	–
Serbia	✓	✓	–	✓	✓	✓	✓	✓	✓	✓	–	–
Switzerland*	✓	✓	(✓)	✓	✓	✓*	✓	✓	✓	(✓)	–	–
						*(new agreement only)					–	–
Turkey	✓	✓	✓	✓	✓	–	✓	✓	✓	–	–	–
USA	✓	✓	✓	✓	✓	–	–	–	–	–	–	–
Isle of Man	✓	✓	✓	✓	✓	✓	✓	✓	✓	✓	✓	✓
Guernsey	✓	✓	✓	✓	✓	✓	✓	✓	✓	✓	✓	–
Jersey	✓	✓	✓	✓	✓	–	✓	✓	✓	✓	✓	–

* The UK-Swiss Agreement, provisionally in force since 1 November 2021, does not cover family benefits. The previous agreement continues to apply to child benefit and guardian's allowance claims made before that date.

You can find the agreements at legislation.gov.uk, by searching for the relevant country.

The UK also has other types of agreements with other countries. For more information on all agreements, see Chapter 17.

The agreement with Chile has only been in force since 1 June 2015.

The agreements with Bosnia-Herzegovina, Croatia, Kosovo, North Macedonia, Montenegro and Serbia are in a single agreement with former Yugolsavia, but are treated as separate agreements.

Until 1 March 2001, there was an agreement with Australia. That was then revoked, subject to limited savings provisions in relation to retirement pensions and bereavement benefits.

There is an agreement with Japan but that only covers liability for contributions.

Appendix 6

Passport stamps and other endorsements

Figure 1: UK passport

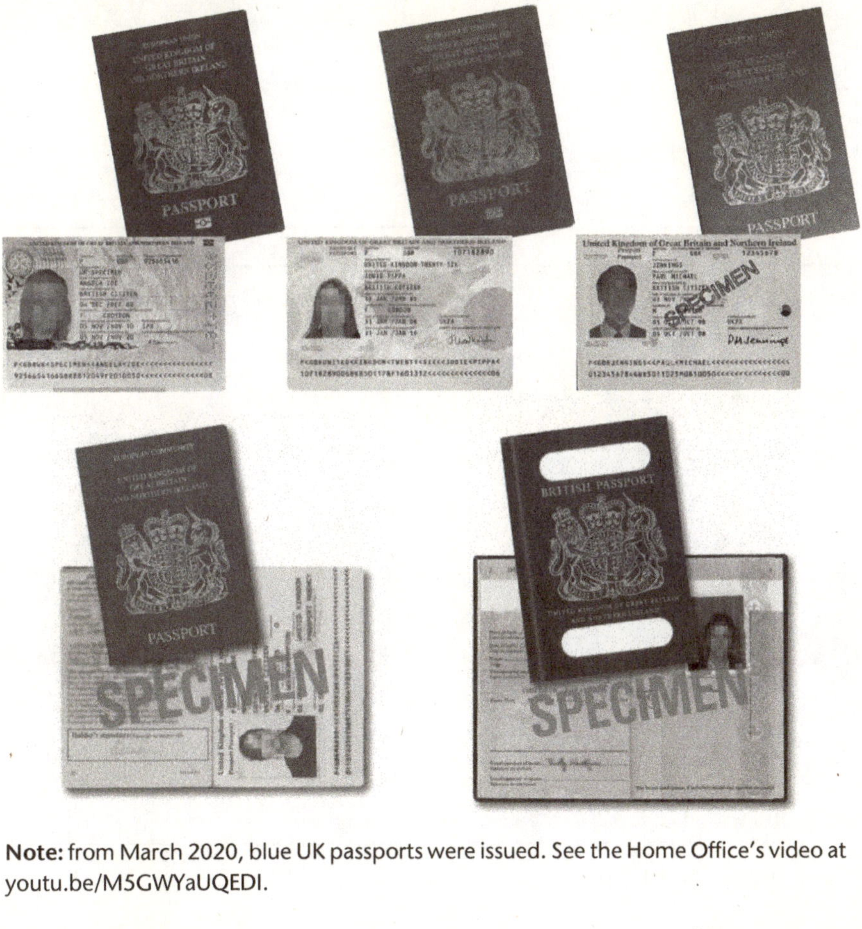

Note: from March 2020, blue UK passports were issued. See the Home Office's video at youtu.be/M5GWYaUQEDI.

Figure 2: Certificates certifying naturalisation and registration as a British citizen

Figure 3: Certificate of entitlement to the right of abode

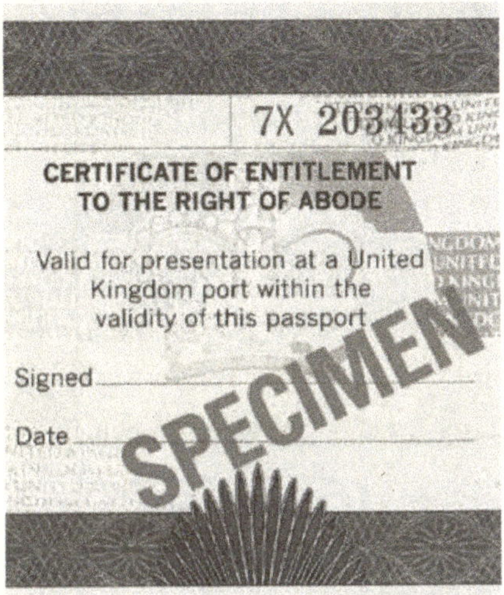

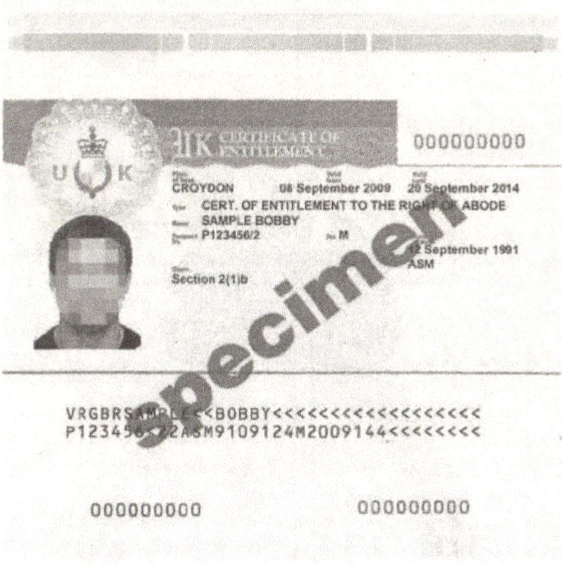

Figure 4: Immigration status document

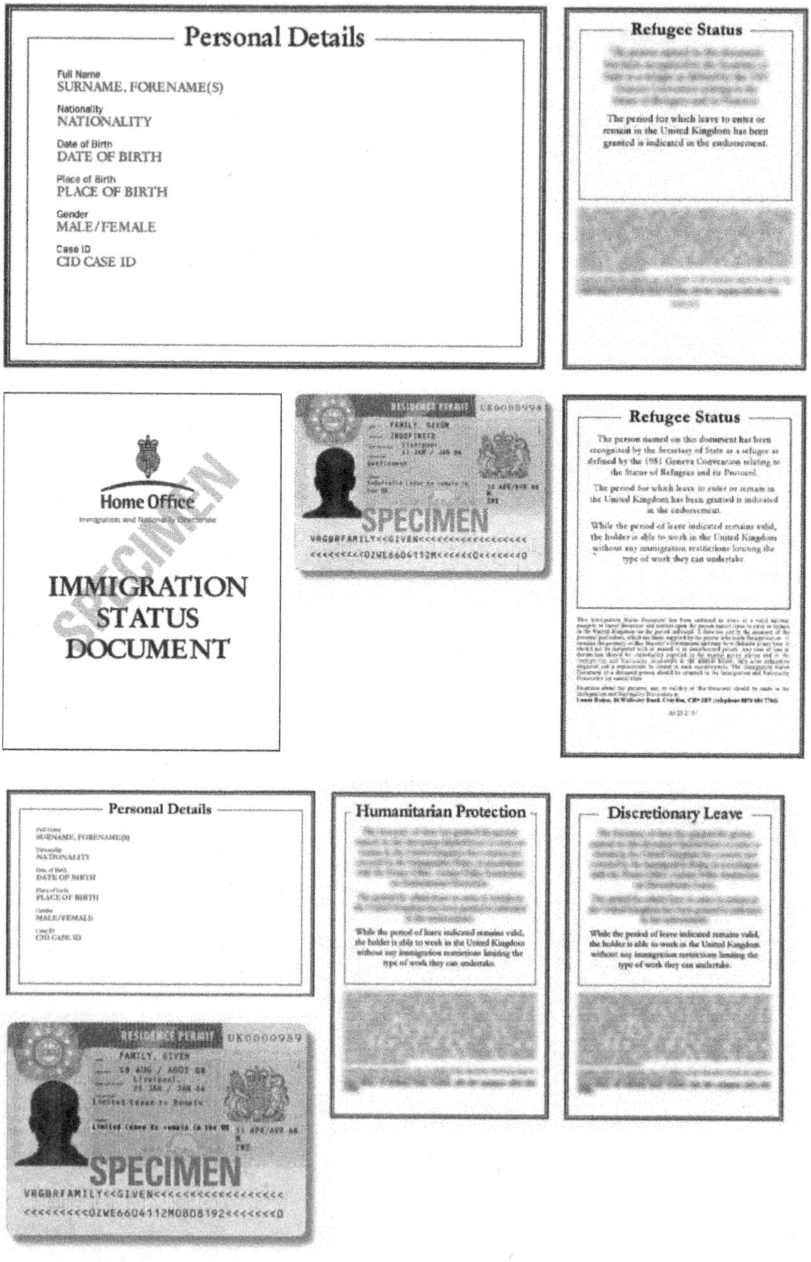

Figure 5: Biometric residence permit

The card's design is set by European Union (EU) regulation. It is a standard credit card size (86mm x 54mm) and will look similar to identity cards issued by other EU countries. The card is made from polycarbonate plastic and contains a chip to make it more secure against forgery and abuse.

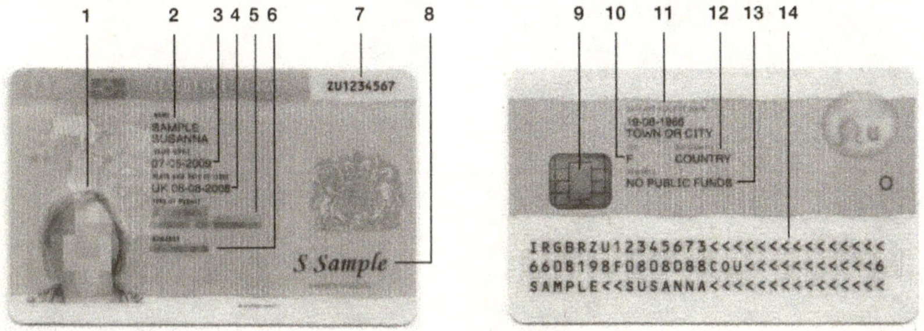

1. Holder's digital image
2. Holder's name
3. Valid until – the date the card expires. This date is at the end of the time the holder is allowed to stay; or five or 10 years if the holder has been given permission to settle in the United Kingdom (known as indefinite leave to remain)
4. Place and date of issue – this is the UK followed by the date the card was issued
5. Type of permit – this is the immigration category the holder is in (for example, STUDENT)
6. Remarks – these are the immigration entitlements for the length of the holder's stay, and may continue on the back of the card
7. ZU1234567 – unique card number
8. Holder's signature
9. Biometric chip
10. Holder's gender
11. Holder's date and place of birth
12. Holder's nationality
13. Remarks – this is a continuation of immigration entitlements for the length of time of the holder's stay (see 6 above)
14. Machine readable zone (MRZ) – this area allows information printed on the card to be read quickly by machine

Figure 6: Registration certificate or document certifying permanent residence

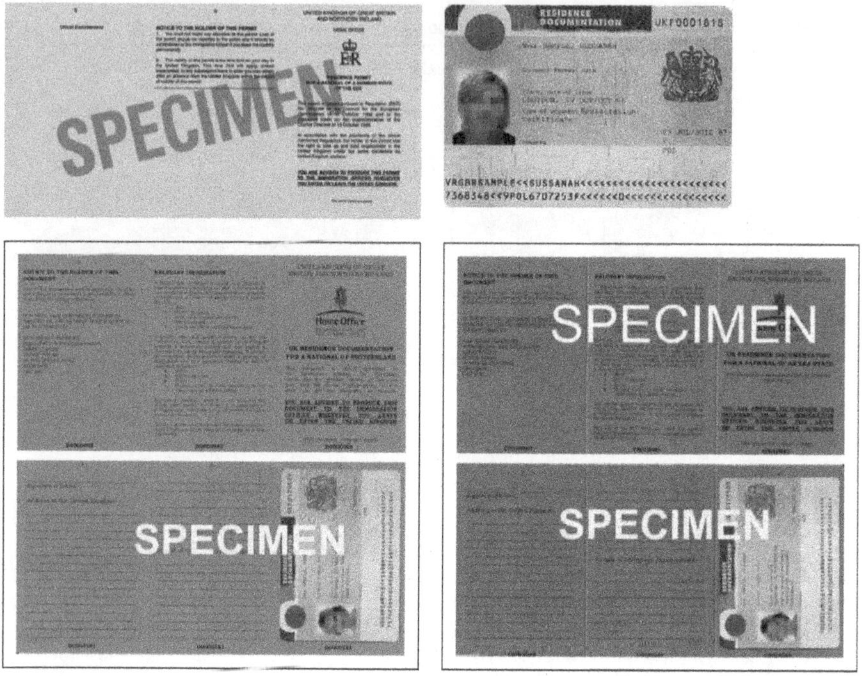

Figure 7: Residence card (including an accession residence card or a derivative residence card) issued by the Home Office to a non-European Economic Area national who is a family member of a national of a European Economic Area country or Switzerland or who has a derivative right of residence

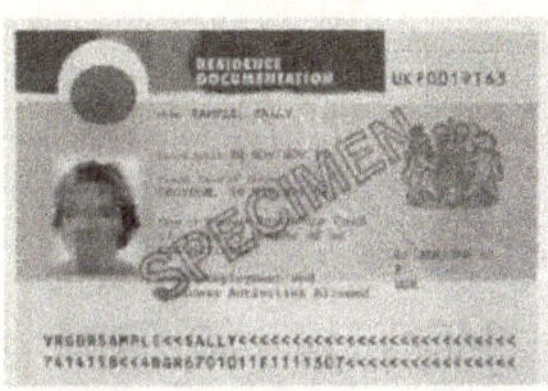

Figure 8: Historic ink stamp endorsements (top left, top middle and middle second from top), application registration card (top right and bottom right), visa vignettes (bottom middle and bottom left) and residence permit vignette

Figure 9: Entry clearance vignette

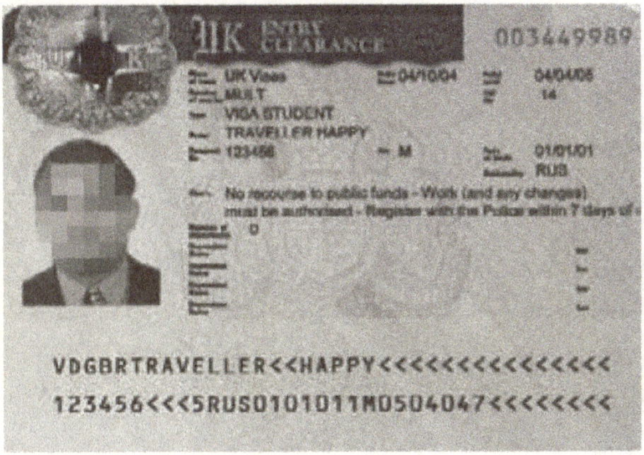

Figure 10: Date stamp on entry clearance vignette

Figure 11: Refugee Convention travel document

Figure 12: Notice of removal

Home Office

Home Office Reference: HO Ref/UAN

To:

Notice of liability to removal

What this means for you

You do not have a right of appeal or administrative review against the decision to remove you.

You do not have leave to enter/remain in the UK. You must now leave the country.

If you think there are other reasons why we should allow you to stay in the UK, you must tell us now. Instructions on how to do this are in the 'next steps' section.

Before removal, you may be detained or placed on immigration bail.

The reasons for this decision are set out in the next section.

Information about help and advice on returning home is in the next steps section.

Reasons for decision

You have stated that You are therefore considered to be an Illegal Entrant to the UK: Entry Without Leave, a breach of S3 (1) (a) and an offence of S24 (1) (a) of the Immigration Act 1971.

Next steps

You must now do one of the following:

- tell us any other reasons you think you should be allowed to remain in the UK
- seek help and advice on returning home
- leave the UK

If you think there are reasons why we should allow you to stay in the UK

If you think you have a reason to stay in the UK that you have not yet told us, you need to complete the attached form RED.0003 and send it to us:

RED.0001 1

Figure 13: Notice of immigration bail

BAIL 201

Home Office

Per ID: [redacted]
Port Ref:
HO Ref: [redacted]

Becket House
60-68 St Thomas Street
London
SE1 3QU
Tel: 0207 238 0084 Fax: 0207 238 1411

NOTIFICATION OF GRANT/VARIATION OF IMMIGRATION BAIL[1] TO A PERSON DETAINED[2] OR LIABLE TO BE DETAINED[3]

To: [redacted]

Date of Birth: [redacted]
Nationality: [redacted]

This notice is given to you because your immigration bail is being varied

The Secretary of State may grant immigration bail to a person who is detained, or who is liable to be detained, for the reasons listed below. The following reason applies to you:

Mark one box		
A	☐	You are liable to be detained pending examination because you are a person required to submit to examination / pending a decision to give, refuse, or cancel leave to enter.
B	☐	You are liable to be detained because you are a person who has been refused leave to enter the United Kingdom.
C	☒	You are liable to be detained because you are a person without leave who has been served with a notice of liability to removal, or are a dependant of such a person.
D	☐	You are liable to be detained because there is reasonable suspicion that you may be liable to removal from the United Kingdom.
E	☐	You are liable to be detained pending a decision to deport you / because a decision has been made to deport you.
F	☐	You are detained pending [a decision to issue directions for] your removal from the United Kingdom.
G	☐	You are the subject of a deportation order and are detained pending your deportation from the United Kingdom.
H	☐	You are detained / liable to be detained for the following reason:

[1] Schedule 10 to the Immigration Act 2016
[2] Paragraph 1 of Schedule 10 to the Immigration Act 2016
[3] Paragraph 2 of Schedule 10 to the Immigration Act 2016

BAIL 201

BAIL 201

☐ You have made a claim for asylum:

A ☐ I hereby grant you immigration bail subject to the following conditions or

B ☒ I hereby vary your conditions of immigration bail as follows

☒ You are <u>not</u> allowed to WORK

CONDITIONS

You will be subject to at least one bail condition. A marked box indicates the bail condition(s) applicable to you.

☒	You <u>**must**</u> REPORT to **an immigration official** at: Becket House 60-68 St Thomas Street London SE1 3QU On [redacted] Between 09:00 and 11:30 Hrs And then fortnightly on Tuesday until further notice

ANY CHANGE OF CONDITION

You must not change your conditions without the agreement of the Secretary of State. If these conditions are to be changed, you will be notified. This notice is correct at time of service and is recorded on Home Office systems.

- Although you may have been granted immigration bail, you remain liable to be detained
- This document must not be accepted by employers as evidence of a right to work or by landlords as evidence of a right to rent (this does not apply to EEA nationals, or the family member of an EEA national, exercising an EU treaty right).
- You have NOT been given leave to enter the United Kingdom within the meaning of the Immigration Act 1971

FAILURE TO COMPLY WITH CONDITIONS

Failure to comply with any of the above conditions may lead to arrest, your conditions being varied, the requirement to pay money under any financial condition, and/or your detention.

Failure to comply with any of the above conditions, without reasonable excuse, is also a criminal offence which may be punished by a fine or a prison sentence[1].

Any unresolved application which you may have made for leave to enter may be refused.

Your details may also be placed on the Police National Computer (PNC).

Should you have difficulty in being able to comply with any of your conditions, you must immediately contact [Becket House] and give your reason.

IMMIGRATION BAIL AUTOMATICALLY ENDS WHEN:

BAIL 201

BAIL 201

- You are no longer liable to be detained and the Secretary of State is not considering whether to make a deportation order against you,
- You are granted leave to enter or remain in the United Kingdom,
- You are detained, or
- You are removed or otherwise leave the United Kingdom.

HELP AND SUPPORT ON RETURNING HOME VOLUNTARILY

The Home Office Voluntary Returns Service can be contacted for help on returning home.

The team can discuss your return, help to obtain your travel document and send it to the port of departure, help with the cost of your tickets, and in some cases provided other financial and practical assistance to use once you have returned to your home country.

Please note that if your documents are held by the Home Office please contact the voluntary returns service before you book your flight if you are paying for your own return, this will help us ensure that your passport is available for your flight.

Contact the voluntary Returns Service

Telephone: 0300 004 0202 (Monday – Friday between 9:00 and 17:30)

Web: https://www.gov.uk/return-home-voluntarily/who-can-get-help

Date [redacted] [redacted] **On behalf of the Secretary of State**

[1] Section 24(1)(h) Immigration Act 1971

BAIL 201

Figure 14: Embarkation stamp

Figure 15 Digital status for European Union Settlement Status

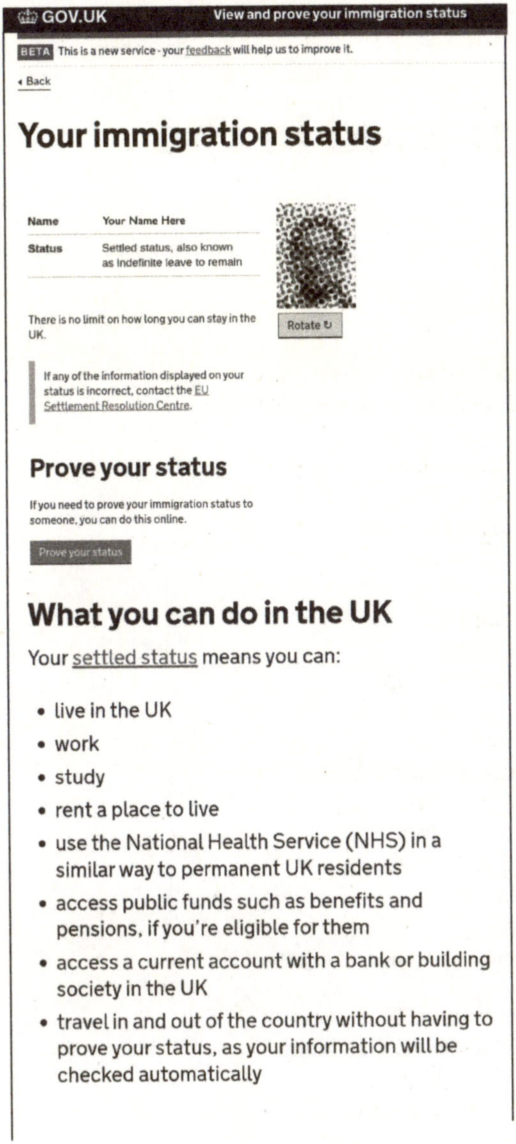

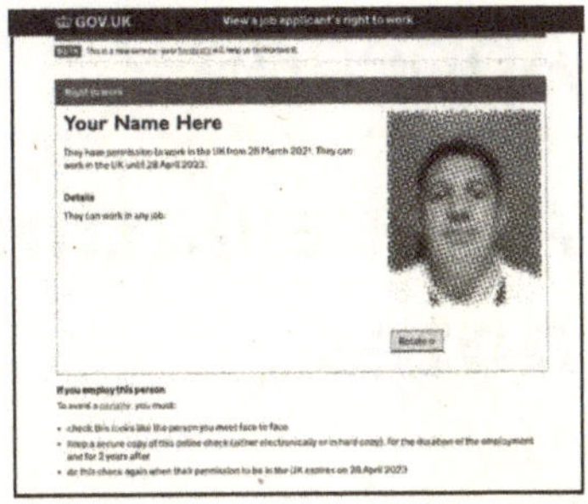

Appendix 7

Abbreviations used in the notes

AAC	Administrative Appeals Chamber
AACR	Administrative Appeals Chamber Reports
AC	Appeal Cases
Admin	Administrative Court
AG	Advocate General
All ER	All England Law Reports
All ER(D)	All England Law Reports (Digest)
Art(s)	Article(s)
BSG	Best Start grants
CA	Court of Appeal
CAS	carer's allowance supplement
Ch	chapter
Civ	Civil Division
CJEU	Court of Justice of the European Union
Crim App R	Criminal Appeal Reports
CSIH	Court of Session, Inner House
CSOH	Court of Session, Outer House
DC	District Council
Dir	Directive
DSDNI	Department for Social Development Northern Ireland
EC	European Community
ECHR	European Court of Human Rights
ECJ	European Court of Justice
EEA	European Economic Area
EFTACR	European Free Trade Association Court Reports
EU	European Union
EWCA	England and Wales Court of Appeal
EWHC	England and Wales High Court
FEP	funeral expenses payment

FLR	Family Law Reports
FSP	funeral support payment
HL	House of Lords
HLR	Housing Law Reports
IAC	Immigration and Asylum Chamber
Imm AR	Immigration Appeal Reports
IR	Immigration Rules
NICom	Northern Ireland Commissioner
NIQB	Northern Ireland Queen's Bench Division
OJ	Official Journal of the European Union
p(p)	page(s)
para(s)	paragraphs(s)
PTA	permission to appeal
QB	Queen's Bench Reports
QBD	Queen's Bench Division
r(r)	rule(s)
Reg(s)	regulation(s)
s(s)	section(s)
Sch(s)	Schedule(s)
SLT	Scots Law Times
SSAC	Social Security Advisory Committee
SSC	Social Security Protocol
SSH	Secretary of State for Health
SSHD	Secretary of State for the Home Department
SSWP	Secretary of State for Work and Pensions
TFEU	Treaty on the Functioning of the European Union
UKAIT	United Kingdom Asylum and Immigration Tribunal
UKHL	United Kingdom House of Lords
UKSC	United Kingdom Supreme Court
UKUT	United Kingdom Upper Tribunal
Vol	volume
WLR	Weekly Law Reports
YCG	young carer grants

Agreements and conventions

UK–EFTA	Agreement on arrangements between Iceland, the Principality of Liechtenstein, the Kingdom of Norway and the United Kingdom of Great Britain and Northern Ireland following the withdrawal of the United Kingdom from the European Union, the EEA Agreement and other agreements applicable between the United Kingdom and the EEA EFTA States by virtue of the United Kingdom's membership of the European Union, 20 December 2018
UK–EUP	Trade and Cooperation Agreement between The European Union and The European Atomic Energy Community, of the one part, and the United Kingdom of Great Britain and Northern Ireland, of the other part: Protocol on Social Security Coordination, 24 December 2020
UK–IC	Convention on Social Security Between the Government of the United Kingdom of Great Britain and Northern Ireland and the Government of Ireland, 1 February 2019 – reproduced in the Schedule of The Social Security (Ireland) Order 2019 No.622
UK–Norway Convention	Convention on Social Security between UK and Norway (19 June 1990), reproduced as Schedule to The Social Security (Norway) Order 1991 No.767, significantly amended by The Social Security (Norway) Order 2020 No.1597
UK–Swiss Agreement	Agreement between the United Kingdom of Great Britain and Northern Ireland and the Swiss Confederation on Citizens' Rights following the Withdrawal of the United Kingdom from the European Union and the Free Movement of Persons Agreement, 20 December 2018
UK–Switzerland Convention	Convention on Social Security Coordination between the United Kingdom of Great Britain and Northern Ireland and the Swiss Confederation, 9 September 2021 – reproduced in the Schedule of The Social Security (Switzerland) Order 2021 No.1088
WA 2019	Agreement on the Withdrawal of the United Kingdom of Great Britain and Northern Ireland from the European Union and the European Atomic Energy Community, 19 October 2019

Acts of Parliament

BNA 1981	British Nationality Act 1981
CA 1989	Children Act 1989
CA 2014	Care Act 2014
C(S)A 1995	Children (Scotland) Act 1995
CSPSSA 2000	Child Support, Pensions and Social Security Act 2000
EU(W)A 2018	European Union (Withdrawal) Act 2018
EU(W)A 2020	European Union (Withdrawal Agreement) Act 2020
HRA 1998	Human Rights Act 1998
IA 1971	Immigration Act 1971
IA 1978	Interpretation Act 1978
IA 1988	Immigration Act 1988
IA 2014	Immigration Act 2014
IA 2016	Immigration Act 2016
IAA 1999	Immigration and Asylum Act 1999
ISSCA 2020	Immigration and Social Security Co-ordination (EU Withdrawal) Act 2020
JSA 1995	Jobseekers Act 1995
NAA 1948	National Assistance Act 1948
NIAA 2002	Nationality, Immigration and Asylum Act 2002
PA 2014	Pensions Act 2014
SPCA 2002	State Pension Credit Act 2002
SSA 1975	Social Security Act 1975
SSA 1998	Social Security Act 1998
SSAA 1992	Social Security Administration Act 1992
SSCBA 1992	Social Security Contributions and Benefits Act 1992
SS(S)A 2018	Social Security (Scotland) Act 2018
TCA 2002	Tax Credits Act 2002
TCEA 2007	Tribunals, Courts and Enforcement Act 2007
WRA 2007	Welfare Reform Act 2007
WRA 2012	Welfare Reform Act 2012

Regulations and other statutory instruments

Each set of regulations has a statutory instrument (SI) number and date. You can find all regulations at legislation.gov.uk.

A(IWA) Regs	The Accession (Immigration and Worker Authorisation) Regulations 2006 No.3317
A(IWR) Regs	The Accession (Immigration and Worker Registration) Regulations 2004 No.1219
AC(IWA) Regs	The Accession of Croatia (Immigration and Worker Authorisation) Regulations 2013 No.1460
AS Regs	The Asylum Support Regulations 2000 No.704
ASPP(G) Regs	The Additional Statutory Paternity Pay (General) Regulations 2010 No.1056
CA(YCG)(S) Regs	The Carer's Assistance (Young Carer Grants) (Scotland) Regulations 2019 No.324
CB Regs	The Child Benefit (General) Regulations 2006 No.223
CB&GA(Admin) Regs	The Child Benefit and Guardian's Allowance (Administration) Regulations 2003 No.492
CB&GA(DA) Regs	The Child Benefit and Guardian's Allowance (Decisions and Appeals) Regulations 2003 No.916
CR(ADTP) Regs	The Citizens' Rights (Application Deadline and Temporary Protection) (EU Exit) Regulations 2020 No.1209
CR(FW) Regs	The Citizens' Rights (Frontier Workers) (EU Exit) Regulations 2020 No.1213
CTC Regs	The Child Tax Credit Regulations 2002 No.2007
CTR(S) Regs	The Council Tax Reduction (Scotland) Regulations 2021 No.249
CTR(SPC)S Regs	The Council Tax Reduction (State Pension Credit) (Scotland) Regulations 2012 No.319
CTRS(DS)E Regs	The Council Tax Reduction Schemes (Default Scheme) (England) Regulations 2012 No.2886
CTRS(DS)W Regs	The Council Tax Reduction Schemes (Default Scheme) (Wales) Regulations 2013 No.3035 (W.303)
CTRS(PR)E Regs	The Council Tax Reduction Schemes (Prescribed Requirements) (England) Regulations 2012 No.2885

CTRSPR(W) Regs	The Council Tax Reduction Schemes and Prescribed Requirements (Wales) Regulations 2013 No.3029 (W.301)
DACYP(S) Regs	The Disability Assistance for Children and Young People (Scotland) Regulations 2021 No.174
DAWAP(S) Regs	The Disability Assistance for Working Age People (Scotland) Regulations 2022 No.54
EYA(BSG)(S) Regs	The Early Years Assistance (Best Start Grants) (Scotland) Regulations 2018 No.370
ESA Regs	The Employment and Support Allowance Regulations 2008 No.794
ESA Regs 2013	The Employment and Support Allowance Regulations 2013 No.379
ESA(TP)(EA) Regs	The Employment and Support Allowance (Transitional Provisions, Housing Benefit and Council Tax Benefit) (Existing Awards) (No.2) Regulations 2010 No.1907
FANIII(Y)O	The Family Allowances, National Insurance and Industrial Injuries (Yugoslavia) Order 1958 No.1263
FEA(S) Regs	The Funeral Expense Assistance (Scotland) Regulations 2019 No.292
FTT(S) Rules	The First-tier Tribunal for Scotland Social Security Chamber (Procedure) Regulations 2018 No.273
GA(Gen) Regs	The Guardian's Allowance (General) Regulations 2003 No.495
HB Regs	The Housing Benefit Regulations 2006 No.213
HB(HR)A Regs	The Housing Benefit (Habitual Residence) Amendment Regulations 2014 No.539
HB(SPC) Regs	The Housing Benefit (Persons who have attained the qualifying age for state pension credit) Regulations 2006 No.214
HB&CTB(DA) Regs	The Housing Benefit and Council Tax Benefit (Decisions and Appeals) Regulations 2001 No.1002
HSS(DHSF)(W) Regs	The Healthy Start Scheme (Description of Healthy Start Food) (Wales) Regulations 2006 No.3108 (W.287)
HSS&WF(A) Regs	The Healthy Start Scheme and Welfare Food (Amendment) Regulations 2005 No.3262
I(EEA) Regs	The Immigration (European Economic Area) Regulations 2016 No.1052

I(EEA) Regs 2006	The Immigration (European Economic Area) Regulations 2006 No.1003
I(EEA)A Regs 2012	The Immigration (European Economic Area) (Amendment) Regulations 2012 No.1547
I(EEA)A Regs 2018	The Immigration (European Economic Area) (Amendment) Regulations 2018 No.801
I(EEA)A Regs 2019	The Immigration (European Economic Area) (Amendment) Regulations 2019 No.1155
IA(PAFAS) Regs	The Immigration and Asylum (Provision of Accommodation to Failed Asylum-Seekers) Regulations 2005 No.930
ILRFO Regs	The Integration Loans for Refugees and Others Regulations 2007 No.1598
IS Regs	The Income Support (General) Regulations 1987 No.1967
ISSC Regs	The Immigration and Social Security Co-ordination (EU Withdrawal) Act 2020 (Consequential, Saving, Transitional and Transitory Provisions) (EU Exit) Regulations 2020 No.1309
ISSCA(C) Regs	The Immigration and Social Security Co-ordination (EU Withdrawal) Act 2020 (Commencement) Regulations 2020 No.1279
JSA Regs	The Jobseeker's Allowance Regulations 1996 No.207
JSA Regs 2013	The Jobseeker's Allowance Regulations 2013 No.378
NHS(COV) Regs 1989	The National Health Service (Charges to Overseas Visitors) Regulations 1989 No.306
NHS(COV) Regs 2015	The National Health Service (Charges to Overseas Visitors) Regulations 2015 No.238
NHS(COV)(S) Regs	The National Health Service (Charges to Overseas Visitors) (Scotland) Regulations 1989 No.364
SCP Regs	The Scottish Child Payment Regulations 2020 No.351
SFM&FE Regs	The Social Fund Maternity and Funeral Expenses (General) Regulations 2005 No.3061
SFWFP Regs	The Social Fund Winter Fuel Payment Regulations 2000 No.729
SMP Regs	The Statutory Maternity Pay (General) Regulations 1986 No.1960
SMP(PAM) Regs	The Statutory Maternity Pay (Persons Abroad and Mariners) Regulations 1987 No.418

SPBP(PAM) Regs	The Statutory Parental Bereavement Pay (Persons Abroad and Mariners) Regulations 2020 No.252
SPC Regs	The State Pension Credit Regulations 2002 No.1792
SPPSAP(G) Regs	The Statutory Paternity Pay and Statutory Adoption Pay (General) Regulations 2002 No.2822
SPPSAP(PAM) Regs	The Statutory Paternity Pay and Statutory Adoption Pay (Persons Abroad and Mariners) Regulations 2002 No.2821
SS(AA) Regs	The Social Security (Attendance Allowance) Regulations 1991 No.2740
SS(C&P) Regs	The Social Security (Claims and Payments) Regulations 1987 No.1968
SS(DLA) Regs	The Social Security (Disability Living Allowance) Regulations 1991 No.2890
SS(GBRA)(A)NI Regs	The Social Security (Great Britain Reciprocal Arrangements) (Amendment) Regulations (Northern Ireland) 2016 No.393
SS(GBRA)(NI) Regs	The Social Security (Great Britain Reciprocal Arrangements) Regulations (Northern Ireland) 2016 No.149
SS(HR)A Regs	The Social Security (Habitual Residence) Amendment Regulations 2004 No.1232
SS(IA)CA Regs	The Social Security (Immigration and Asylum) Consequential Amendments Regulations 2000 No.636
SS(IB) Regs	The Social Security (Incapacity Benefit) Regulations 1994 No.2946
SS(IB-ID) Regs	The Social Security (Incapacity Benefit – Increases for Dependants) Regulations 1994 No.2945
SS(ICA) Regs	The Social Security (Invalid Care Allowance) Regulations 1976 No.409
SS(II)(AB) Regs	The Social Security (Industrial Injuries) (Airmen's Benefits) Regulations 1975 No.469
SS(II)(MB) Regs	The Social Security (Industrial Injuries) (Mariners' Benefits) Regulations 1975 No.470
SS(IIPD) Regs	The Social Security (Industrial Injuries) (Prescribed Diseases) Regulations 1985 No.967
SS(NIRA) Regs	The Social Security (Northern Ireland Reciprocal Arrangements) Regulations 2016 No. 287

SS(NIRA)(A) Regs	The Social Security (Northern Ireland Reciprocal Arrangements) (Amendment) Regulations 2016 No.1050
SS(PA) Regs	The Social Security Benefit (Persons Abroad) Regulations 1975 No.563
SS(PA)A Regs	The Social Security (Persons from Abroad) Amendment Regulations 2006 No.1026
SS(PAB) Regs	The Social Security (Payments on Account of Benefit) Regulations 2013 No.383
SS(PIP) Regs	The Social Security (Personal Independence Payment) Regulations 2013 No.377
SS(RA)O	The Social Security (Reciprocal Agreements) Order 2012 No.360
SS(SDA) Regs	The Social Security (Severe Disablement Allowance) Regulations 1984 No.1303
SS(WB&RP) Regs	The Social Security (Widow's Benefit and Retirement Pensions) Regulations 1979 No.642
SS(WTCCTC)(CA) Regs	The Social Security (Working Tax Credit and Child Tax Credit) (Consequential Amendments) Regulations 2003 No.455
SSB(Dep) Regs	The Social Security Benefit (Dependency) Regulations 1977 No.343
SSB(PA) Regs	The Social Security Benefit (Persons Abroad) Regulations 1975 No.563
SSB(PRT) Regs	The Social Security Benefit (Persons Residing Together) Regulations 1977 No.956
SSCBCTC(A) Regs	The Social Security, Child Benefit and Child Tax Credit (Amendment) (EU Exit) Regulations 2020 No.1505
SS&CS(DA) Regs	The Social Security and Child Support (Decisions and Appeals) Regulations 1999 No.991
SSP Regs	The Statutory Sick Pay (General) Regulations 1982 No.894
SSP(MAPA) Regs	The Statutory Sick Pay (Mariners, Airmen and Persons Abroad) Regulations 1982 No.1349
SSPP(G) Regs	The Statutory Shared Parental Pay (General) Regulations 2014 No.3051
SSPP(PAM) Regs	The Statutory Shared Parental Pay (Persons Abroad and Mariners) Regulations 2014 No.3134
TC(CN) Regs	The Tax Credits (Claims and Notifications) Regulations 2002 No.2014

TC(DCI) Regs	The Tax Credits (Definition and Calculation of Income) Regulations 2002 No.2006
TC(Imm) Regs	The Tax Credits (Immigration) Regulations 2003 No.653
TC(PC) Regs	The Tax Credits (Payments by the Commissioners) Regulations 2002 No.2173
TC(R) Regs	The Tax Credits (Residence) Regulations 2003 No.654
TP(FT) Rules	The Tribunal Procedure (First-tier Tribunal) (Social Entitlement Chamber) Rules 2008 No.2685
UC Regs	The Universal Credit Regulations 2013 No.376
UC(GBRA)Regs	The Universal Credit (Great Britain Reciprocal Arrangements) Regulations (Northern Ireland) 2020 No.129
UC(NIRA) Regs	The Universal Credit (Northern Ireland Reciprocal Arrangements) Regulations 2020 No.677
UC(TP) Regs	The Universal Credit (Transitional Provisions) Regulations 2014 No.1230
UC,PIP,JSA&ESA(C&P) Regs	The Universal Credit, Personal Independence Payment, Jobseeker's Allowance and Employment and Support Allowance (Claims and Payments) Regulations 2013 No.380
UC,PIP,JSA&ESA(DA) Regs	The Universal Credit, Personal Independence Payment, Jobseeker's Allowance and Employment and Support Allowance (Decisions and Appeals) Regulations 2013 No.381
WHA(LI)(S) Regs	The Winter Heating Assistance (Low Income) (Scotland) Regulations 2023 No.16
WHACYP(S) Regs	The Winter Heating Assistance for Children and Young People (Scotland) Regulations 2020 No.352
WRA(No.23)O	The Welfare Reform Act 2012 (Commencement No. 23 and Transitional and Transitory Provisions) Order 2015 No.740
WRA(No.31)O	The Welfare Reform Act 2012 (Commencement No.31 and Savings and Transitional Provisions and Commencement No.21 and 23 and Transitional and Transitory Provisions (Amendment)) Order 2019 No.37

WRA(No.32)O	The Welfare Reform Act 2012 (Commencement No. 32 and Savings and Transitional Provisions) Order 2019 No.167
WRA(No.34 etc)(A)O	The Welfare Reform Act 2012 (Commencement No. 34 and Commencement No. 9, 21, 23, 31 and 32 and Transitional and Transitory Provisions (Amendment)) Order 2022 No.302
WF Regs	The Welfare Food Regulations 1996 No.1434
WF(BSF) Regs	The Welfare Food (Best Start Foods) (Scotland) Regulations 2019 No.193
WTC(EMR) Regs	The Working Tax Credit (Entitlement and Maximum Rate) Regulations 2002 No.2005

Other information

ADM *Advice for Decision Making*
CBTM *Child Benefit Technical Manual*
CCM *Claimant Compliance Manual* (HMRC guidance on investigation of tax credit claims)
DMG *Decision Makers' Guide*
DWPWAG *DWP Guidance Relating to the UK's Operational Implementation of the Social Security Coordination Provisions of Part 2 of the EU Withdrawal Agreement: citizens' rights* (11 November 2020, updated 29 November 2021)
GM *Housing Benefit/Council Tax Benefit Guidance Manual*
HB *Housing Benefit Bulletin*
IDI Immigration Directorate Instructions
IR Immigration Rules
SSS DMG ADP(R and P) *Scotland Social Security Decision Making Guide – Adult Disability Payment: residence and presence* (27 July 2022)
SSS DMG CDP(R and P) *Scotland Social Security Decision Making Guide – Child Disability Payment: residence and presence* (24 August 2022)
TCM *Tax Credits Manual*
TCTM *Tax Credits Technical Manual*

References such as CIS/142/1990 and R(IS) 1/07 are references to commissioners' decisions.
References such as *TG v SSWP (PC)* [2015] UKUT 50 (AAC) are references to decisions of the Upper Tribunal.
References such as ASA/02/02/1877 are references to decisions of the First-tier (Asylum Support) Tribunal.

Index

How to use this Index

Entries against the bold headings direct you to the general information on the subject, or where the subject is covered most fully. Sub-entries are listed alphabetically and direct you to specific aspects of the subject. The following abbreviations are used in the index:

AA	attendance allowance
ADP	adult disability payment
CA	carer's allowance
CDP	child disability payment
C-ESA	contributory employment and support allowance
C-JSA	contribution-based jobseeker's allowance
CTC	child tax credit
DLA	disability living allowance
EC	European Community
EEA	European Economic Area
EU	European Union
HB	housing benefit
IB	incapacity benefit
IS	income support
I-ESA	income-related employment and support allowance
I-JSA	income-based jobseeker's allowance
MA	maternity allowance
NI	national insurance
PC	pension credit
PIP	personal independence payment
UC	universal credit
WTC	working tax credit